WITHDRAWN

THE TRANSIT OF LEARNING

The Transit of Learning
A Social and Cultural Interpretation
of
American Educational History

Edward J. Power
Boston College

Alfred Publishing Co., Inc.
Sherman Oaks, California 91403

Alfred Publishing Co., Inc.
15335 Morrison Street
Sherman Oaks, California 91403

Printed in the United States of America

Current printing last digit:
10 9 8 7 6 5 4 3 2 1

Library of Congress Cataloging in Publication Data
Power, Edward J.
    The transit of learning.

    Bibliography: p. 441
    Includes index.
    1. Education—United States—History. 2. United States—
Civilization. 3. United States—Social policy. I. Title.
LA212.P68   370'.973   78-24318
ISBN 0-88284-073-8

PREFACE

This book tries to reduce the enormously complex social and cultural dimensions of the American educational experience to a single volume. A melding of these various sides to life is seldom an easy exercise, even when a historical period is brief and compact; and in this case, with a period of about three and one-half centuries, brevity and compactness are inappropriate characterizations. Some periods in the history of Western civilization, as long as three centuries, could be handled with some confidence in a few paragraphs, for the character of the times and the disposition of the people refused to metamorphose. But even a superficial inspection of life in America, beginning with the first settlement, leads to an abandonment of any simple thesis. From rude and rough settlements in what amounted to wilderness, the current of American life flowed through a variety of tributaries, finally to follow a mainstream to the complexities and turbulences of the late twentieth century. To find these tributaries, estimate their cultural depth and direction, and assess their influence on learning is this book's purpose.

Beneath cultural shifts and altered social stances, with multiple and inevitable false starts, stood a fundamental philosophy of life, society, and education. Appurtenances to life—say, religion, politics, economics, and education—changed or tilted only when dominating principles affecting the substance of life in society were amended. Thus, as the story of learning in the American nation unfolds, it follows certain principal themes, and these themes form the paradigm of this book. First, life directed and dominated by a theological interpretation of man and the world; then, society and thought woven as lesser threads in the fabric of political purpose, survival, and expansion; then, a mentality of acquisition recommending the development and refinement of a great economic machine; and finally, a pricking of society's conscience relative to equality of opportunity and social justice. If these were the themes of an evolving American life, they were also the themes directing the course of formal and, to some extent, informal learning.

It is good to know the schools, how they functioned, who the teachers and students were, and what was taught. These, of course, are unavoidable preambles in the transit of learning, but being preambles they leave unmentioned sides to learning cultivated in social, political, religious, and cultural fields. Yet, one place where modern society has said learning should occur—not the only place, but important nevertheless—is the school. History does education no favor, and even engages in some distortion, by a studied indifference to schools. On the other hand, an early disposition of historians to write histories of schooling and call them histories of education has quite sensibly been criticized by a cadre of revisionists, and this criticism has had the effect of broadening educational history's scope and extending its depth. This is good so long as historians realize they should be able to say something about the record of educational progress without saying everything about life in society.

This book seeks to put the schools, learning, and education in perspective—well within the context of social and cultural life: neither slighting nor inflating them, but always perceiving them as instruments of basic social policy. And it tries its best to find basic social policy, as that policy evolved in the American temper of life, and elaborate it fairly and accurately vis-à-vis the various enterprises of education. In this attempt, comprehensiveness is an extravagant ambition; completeness is not.

Colleagues and students have over the years contributed in various ways to my historical hypotheses: sometimes to confirm, sometimes to amend or contradict them. These sources of inspiration and interpretation are too general to recite. But there are those who must be mentioned. A book of this kind necessarily owes a great deal to the scholarly work of others, and I have done my best in the notes to record the sources—books, articles and monographs—on which I depended. In addition, I am grateful to Professors Pierre D. Lambert and George M. Woytanowitz, and Dean Lester E. Przewlocki, who read the manuscript at various stages of its development. For their generosity in so time-consuming a labor, and for their gentle, perceptive criticism, I want to thank them publicly.

Edward J. Power
Boston, Massachusetts
January, 1979

CONTENTS

CHAPTER ONE

The
Colonial
Inheritance

The pioneers who sailed toward what was to become English America, carrying with them cultural traditions antedating the seventeenth century, were driven westward by winds of anticipation, by grand expectations for a society to be built by persons who were masters of their fate, and by cultural convictions that helped form a collective personality. Such cultural convictions had taken some time to shape. These brave colonial men and women have often been characterized as persons of humble, even immature values, with a single-minded purpose of creating a haven in the wilderness of America where God could be worshiped according to private plan.

No doubt keen religious motivation did generate power in the souls of many colonists, and more so among those sailing toward what was to become New England, but religious motives were not always dominant. Perhaps just as many colonists approached the New World seldom thinking about religion as others did who agonized under the burden of theological ferment and discord. In any case, whatever their reasons for leaving their land of birth and early nurture, it was plainly impossible for them to migrate and survive without taking along some of the usual appurtenances of economic life; but this was not all. Sensitive to the exigencies of living, they wanted also to live well and this implied something more than day-to-day provisions for the kitchen. It was easy to transport material possessions with confidence but it was essential, although more difficult, to transport cultural values as well.[1]

And when we examine their values we begin to lose interest in the tools and equipment they loaded on the ships, because in the final analysis it was a philosophy of life which shaped the character of the colonial mind

1

and milieu, and this philosophy, dispersed through different tributaries in various parts of the colonial world, eventually returned to a mainstream wherein the principal intellectual currents always flowed. But this is just part of the story. The philosophy of life represented in the value systems of these colonial men and women was bequeathed to them by their fore-fathers; whether our attention is on the Puritans of New England, the Catholics in Maryland, the Quakers in Pennsylvania, or the Anglicans in the South, the fact remains that all without exception fed on a common diet of European culture. These seventeenth-century men and women were products of a culture which had evolved over four preceding centuries. It is easy to point to the elements which at times so sharply divided them, and this simple exercise tempts us to forget what they had in common. The values which stood as bedrock to their philosophy of life were a com-mon possession of the European mind, sometimes only dimly perceived by the average man, but often fully articulated and competently under-stood by the scholar and clergyman.[2] What inheritance illuminated and stabilized colonial intellectual life?

EUROPEAN CULTURAL INFLUENCE

A complete reconstruction of colonial life and an analysis of the colonial mind would be too burdensome for these pages.[3] So one must be content with selection: a selection seeking to grasp the principal elements in colonial society and hold them up for review. Even here there is difficulty, for one is never certain that these elements had a uniform effect on a variegated colonial society. Theology, Humanism, Scholasticism, Puri-tanism, and individualism were staple fixtures in the intellectual bequest from the old world to the new.[4] Undoubtedly the relationship between these inheritances was close, so it is hard to keep them entirely discrete. Still, it is possible to consider their principal emphases without doing violence to a portrait of the colonial mind, while at the same time remem-bering that what stood as a persistent inheritance in one colony may have been barely apparent or rejected in another. Puritanism, for example, was taken to be foolishness by Anglicans in the South and theological in-temperance by Catholics and Quakers in the Middle Colonies, although in the end it was Puritanism that put an indelible stamp on the mentality of colonial America.[5]

Theology

The ordinary assumption that colonists were both preoccupied and men-tally crippled by theology needs revision. In some colonies the theological dimension to every condition of life had pride of place, but in other colonies it was easy for inhabitants to reserve their theology for Sundays and, while maintaining a nominal orthodoxy, to keep their religious feelings within bounds, not allowing them to intrude too much on the reality of daily life. Thus, depending on the level of inquiry, the colonial mind could have many sides. Yet, despite variations in zeal and orthodoxy, most colonists were fully aware of theology and were always capable of making it a topic of conversation even when refusing it a dominant place in their lives. The story about Cromwell's soldiers debating theology around their campfires may be pure fiction, yet it allows us to suppose that if common soldiers had sensitive theological temperaments, then people generally could have them too.

This interest in theology had evolved from origins in medieval life, where the overriding purpose of the philosophers and theologians had been to construct a world view consistent with the revealed word of God as it translated into religious dogma. The Scholastic effort had been extraordinarily successful and accomplished for the medieval world what apparently was most needed: a harmonizing of the classical legacy with scriptural direction from God, as that direction was codified in dogmatic theology.

Additionally, as it turned out, Scholastic theologians supplied a reasoned justification for the Church's infrangible right to interpret the revealed Word of God, so the arbitrament of scripture and doctrine vis à vis all of life was monopolized by the Church. But the great Scholastic monuments to harmony, and the intellectual tradition they stabilized, were no substitute for simple faith, and sometimes this simple faith, when lodged in the souls of fearless and frequently fanatic men, cultivated doubts sufficient to generate attacks on the precepts of dogmatic theology. During the Scholastic Age itself (1200–1300), doubt and veiled threat could be ignored so long as both remained beneath the public surface eventually to starve from neglect, and if opposition to official thought refused to disappear then instigators of opposition could be silenced or ostracized. History tells of men who overstressed zeal for reform and so magnified their rejections of ecclesiastical policy and dictum that they were branded heretics and removed from good standing in the Christian community.

Yet even before the Classic Renaissance (1350–1550) introduced somewhat more lenient ways of looking at the world, at man's relationship to God, and at priorities in ethics and religious doctrine, sensitive Christians were troubled by the institutional character of the Christian Church and spoke quietly about reform.[6] But these men were ahead of their time and the reforming winds they hoped to harness did not blow very hard. The spirit of the Renaissance, however, inspired and guided by the gigantic example and seminal advice of Francesco Petrarch (1304–1374), fanned the embers of Church reform to recommend an elaboration and application of less rigorous, less arbitrary and more humane theological doctrines.

But nothing of real significance happened until Martin Luther (1483–1546) took steps leading to a break with the Church of Rome, a break whose consequences were, as it turned out, incapable of repeal. Now for the first time the authority of the Church was put in jeopardy, and moreover men began to believe in the novel doctrine of salvation by faith. What need had they for Church ministers to pronounce the rules for salvation and to guide the faithful toward their eternal reward? And this rejection of the Church could be made all the more easily now, because the secular state was clearly more capable of establishing an order in society that men had looked to the Church to supply previously. What the reformers wanted to achieve, although their failure was frequent, was to strip away the ornamentation of ecclesiastical structure to return to a more primitive form of Christianity. Neither their own arguments or practice nor the realities of theological life and strife led directly to simplicity in religious worship. Yet, irrespective of the direction Protestantism took, the rupture between it and Rome was too great to be mended.

Overlaid by time and more recently by a spirit of ecumenism, it is not always easy for us to appreciate the zeal generated by denominational allegiance; and, it should be stressed, this ardent sectarianism was expressed more heavily on the levels of church organization and administration, along with a rejection of the pope's authority, than on dogma and doctrine. In time, of course, in order to purify their own religious outlook, Protestants inevitably constructed a theology of their own, but at the outset they felt compelled to deny the authority of Rome and during their formative years this single plank in their platform may well have been their sole theological distinction.[7]

Calvin   Broadly conceived Protestantism, however, was not the principal inheritance coming from the Old World to the New, although colonial Protestantism, stripped of distinctive sectarian features, was considered to be, with the exception of the Maryland colonists, a religious conviction worth defending. A strong spirit of sectarianism was introduced to the New World, despite the absence of explicitly stated theological difference to which nominal allegiance could be paid. And the denomination containing theological assumptions most nearly consistent with the general colonial mind was Congregationalism. In Congregationalism was lodged the hard theology of John Calvin (1509–1564), but it should be understood that while Calvin was responsible for setting the direction for a theology which men of fundamental Christian spirit could embrace, he had not sculptured the vessels of faith the people carried to colonial New England. Calvin, no doubt, was a principal inspirer and giver of truth, and all New England divines knew his writing, but Calvin spoke in broad terms and left much unsaid. He gave his flock a deposit of Christian belief; it was up to them to explicate it and to command allegiance to the multiple interpretations they could make from it.

Shortly after abandoning his studies for the Catholic priesthood and after a brief interlude of legal study, Calvin wrote his *Institutes of the Christian Religion* (the first edition was published in 1535), wherein he elaborated a profound and inflexible moral pessimism in a doctrine of human depravity. Although once a student of the classics, apparently captivated by their Humanistic spirit, his fundamental theology depressed the spirit of human hope so characteristic of Renaissance attitude and turned instead to an attack on the doctrine of transubstantiation, the sacraments, purgatory, the saints, and the function of an ordained clergy as mediators between God and man. Ceremony and liturgy were replaced by preaching, "godly preaching" it was called, which, barren of oratorical style, was expository, edifying, evangelical, and "so spiritual, and yet so plain, that poor simple people that never knew what Religion meant" could understand it.[8] In this emphasis on a systematic exposition of doctrine, Calvinism may well have established its perennial association with teaching and formal education. It was, Miller said, "the portal through which ran the highway of intellectual development."[9]

Calvinism put an emphasis on piety, so piety was the preoccupation of Puritan ministers who engaged in theological speculation. Their education in piety, following the dictates of John Calvin, may have contained some novelties but mainly repeated Christian convictions which, originating with St. Augustine (354–430), had been buried away and almost forgotten by theologians who populated the universities of the Middle Ages and the early Renaissance.[10] Yet enough of the Scholastic spirit was stamped on this brand of piety to recommend to Calvin's followers that they remain men of the world and find salvation by using worldly means. Had they embraced pure Augustinian piety, they would have fled to the desert or, at least, hidden away in monasteries to find salvation like medieval monks. Instead they fled to New England and, rejecting a monastic model, tried to lead good and satisfying lives while using the method of Scholasticism to anchor further their already substantial faith in piety.[11]

Among the one hundred and thirty university-trained men who were in New England by 1645, several were proficient in theology; and, it is fair to say, that all were profoundly interested in theological issues. Lacking such interest they could hardly have been true sons either of the English universities or seventeenth-century England.[12] Led by such men, an immigrant generation of religionists was not ready to despair of man and the world. Their view of piety betrayed some optimism; in any case it kept them from being gloomy and despondent: they were stalwart souls capable of enduring misfortune with resolution. They knew and understood Calvin's teaching on depravity, but they took it as a metaphysical and theological convenience offering a solution for a religious conundrum more than as a sense of personal weakness and sin;[13] and on the whole their divorce of belief from conduct was probably no greater than was common among the ordinary European Christians of the day. On current pragmatic questions they were not, despite appearances, hypocrites, who could for convenience abandon their character as Augustinian pietists, but men who could capitalize ordinary worldly wisdom. These were the true Puritans who impressed the next generation of native theologians with the essentials of their belief along with the rational Scholastic techniques for explicating them. And thus Puritanism remained throughout the seventeenth century in New England, changing in the next century, it is true, but only after a newer, less Scholastic and more extravagant evangelicalism succeeded in spreading denunciations on everything giving men comfort and pleasure.[14] These denunciations alone, however, would not have changed seventeenth-century theology had later generations of Puritans been able "to face reality as unflinchingly as their forefathers." The rather hopeful Puritanism of the seventeenth century, regularly evidenced in pulpit literature, was not, Miller remarks, deflated by superior forces of logic and theology. It simply capitulated to the austerities recommended in evangelicalism; it lost both its sense of fundamental superiority and its inner logic.[15] But this drift away from orthodox theology was temporary and repairable; and the work of theological repair was delegated to colonial institutions of higher learning.

This ardent denominational spirit infected public policy in New England first, but Virginia, too, had a religious climate allowing it to thrive. England's James I (1566–1625) instructed Virginia colonists to plant, practice and preach the Christian doctrines along lines "now professed and established within our realm of England."[16] The regulations of the Virginia colony (1619) gave ministers of the Anglican church a yearly allowance of two hundred pounds, directing them to conduct religious services, instruct children in the creed, administer the sacraments and keep vital records. The people, for their part, were obliged to attend religious service on Sunday.[17]

Religious appetite was too varied to be satisfied by an exclusively Anglican diet, and moreover left out of account the less politically powerful but more numerous Puritans who settled in New England and elsewhere in the New World. Massachusetts Bay formed strong Congregational churches in various towns, beginning with Salem in 1629, and demanded from every inhabitant contributions for church support.[18] Church membership had nothing to do with this obligation, nor did it, apparently, when laws were passed making church attendance mandatory.

Despite the determination of public policy to maintain what amounted to an establishment of religion, diversity in religious practice and belief invaded both the colonies of Massachusetts and Virginia.[19] And this led the ministers of established churches to intensify their efforts to hold their people to the "true faith" and to ban through preaching and teaching the doctrines of nonconforming sects. Both Congregational and Anglican ministers distinguished themselves in their general ministry, and for their devotion to the church and the ministry alike they stand out as representatives of an exceptional clerical generation. Inevitably this work of protecting congregations from the contagion of pernicious doctrine assumed an educational character. Especially in New England, preaching and teaching were inseparable duties of pastors of souls. As we move from Virginia and New England, sectarianism, while less zealous, was still in evidence and frequently, as in the Middle colonies, it retained fundamental Calvinistic theses. Yet, and here motives for colonization become critical, the colonists in New York, Pennsylvania, New Jersey, and Delaware were traders, merchants, and farmers before they were sectarians; they were converts to the doctrine of mercantilism more than to the doctrine of piety and they never gave any serious thought to creating a Bible commonwealth. While their theology was prominent, and sometimes inconvenient, it could be tempered to suit the conditions of life. Living in a world where toleration was recommended even if only by the exigencies of nature, they could and did take a stance allowing for latitude in specific religious belief. The absence of social and religious homogeneity, bespeaking some tolerance for sectarian variety, became, in the last analysis, a great human resource.[20]

New England declared dissenters and papists anathema and made them unwelcome, but the practical theology of the Middle colonies was capable of allowing diversity in religious practice without ever encouraging it. And the theologians who entered these colonies and serviced the churches were never so dominated by the certitude of their own convictions as their brethren to the North.[21] The Maryland assembly, for example, adopted an "Act for Church Liberties" in 1637, wherein ambiguity in expressed policy allowed various sects of Christians to coexist. In 1649 the Maryland Act of Toleration granted freedom to Protestants and Catholics who professed the doctrine of the Trinity. And in other Middle colonies, Baptists, Quakers, and German Lutherans were represented in sufficient number to discourage the adoption of highly restrictive policies relative to sectarian affiliation and belief. While complete religious toleration was absent from the colonial scene, religious rectitude and fervor could countenance sectarian diversity.

In the South, both Anglicans and aristocrats were favored. But Anglican fervor had long ago been spent in the multiple political associations and manipulations Henry VIII (1491–1547) had introduced out of necessity and then kept for convenience. Southern colonists, entirely capable of deep and serious thought about their way of life, were less inclined to direct their intellectual effort along theological channels. Doubtless many tributaries of religious fervor flowed among Southern Protestants, yet briefs for religious liberty were rare, and none of these tributaries turned out to be very deep; only a few followed unbroken channels to the mainstream of colonial intellectual life. The South began with its own interests and with an undoubted intention of perpetuating an English way of life; new brands of religious orthodoxy went unrelished by a majority of men, so a Southern gentleman could plant his crop and reap his harvest untroubled by the turmoil of theological dispute. Despite their philosophical and theological interest and ability, seventeenth-century Southern gentlemen had other preoccupations which, in the end, kept them from being influential shapers of the American colonial mind.[22]

Humanism

Exponents of the Classic Renaissance revelled in their conviction that they had made a great leap back over a thousand years; that through their own exertions they had dismissed the dismal intellectual pretensions of the Middle Ages; and that by an employment of personal brilliance they could lay a foundation for the good life by mining the almost inexhaustible treasuries of the classical age. Although the best Humanists always knew better, they, too, pretended to a cultural self-sufficiency and discounted the millenium preceding their own movement. Authentic intellectual history, however, always revealed that knowledge of the classics was valued by medieval scholars, who had a reasonably adequate command of their sources, although, it must be admitted, their interests centered on those parts of the classical legacy which could inform the great specialties of law, medicine, and theology, and were rarely comprehensive. As a matter of policy medieval scholars cultivated whatever of the classical heritage appeared useful in a construction of professional studies and neglected the rest.

Petrarch   Humanism represented a change in attitude and inevitably created new principles for prescribing categories of interest in the classics. The Humanism of the Classic Renaissance, reflected in cults of fame, cries of a return to antiquity, and a mystical striving for the good life was introduced, cultivated and brought to near-perfection by the high priest of Humanism, Francesco Petrarch (1304–1374). Petrarch's sonnets brought him his first public notice and gave him a glimpse of the general acclaim to be reaped from literary excellence. His own life demonstrated in hundreds of ways the relationship between Humanism and individualism; besides, he became the most illustrious example of a man of letters. He proved, as his followers also undertook to prove, that accomplished scholars and poets can achieve eminence in society and attain an influence equal to princes and merchants. Petrarch taught his generation an imperishable lesson: hard work and genuine talent are an unbeatable combination, and success is assured to the worthy. His models were based on what he knew best and loved most—the classics. In them he expected to find ideals for sustaining a full and satisfying life; and from them, moreover, he expected to attain a literary excellence ensuring personal stature, fame, and virtue. Undoubtedly Petrarch could have departed from the tradition identifying decency in learning with a knowledge of classical languages—Latin and Greek. It rested with him to choose and he could have chosen the vernacular as a means for literary expression. For highly personal reasons—he liked the rhythm, cadence, and sound of Latin and enjoyed using it—he stuck with Latin.[23] Although Greek's claim to classical standing was better, Petrarch's ability in Greek was slight, and for highly technical cultural reasons, he remained true to the convention that Latin was the only suitable language for an educated man. Rejecting the vernacular he also rejected Scholasticism, and thus was left to depend on his own cultural resources or to turn to the only other cultural tradition available: the classical tradition. Lacking sufficient cultural confidence to stand alone, he counseled a dependence on the classics. So in order to sustain the Humanism and individualism of the new age, and above all the quest for the good life, Petrarch recommended a return to the classics and therein "provided his generation with a design for living."[24]

Prosecuted relentlessly by Petrarch and his disciples, Humanism reached high points of scholarship, especially in those parts of the classical heritage left uncultivated by medieval scholars, and also in those classics where an accurate interpretation demanded a superior command of classical language. At its best, it developed enviable and exquisite human sensitivities; but as a human endeavor it could not always be at its best. Humanistic ambition always outran actual achievement.

Erasmus When, as often happened, Humanism retreated from high ideals, it became either a fanatical cult of literary and linguistic exactitude or, as in the case of *The Courtier,* by Baldassare Castiglione (1478-1529), a puerile digression into manners and morals for the court. Perhaps several strategically placed Erasmuses could have saved Humanism from pedantic influence, but there was but one Erasmus, and his eloquence and cogency were too often distilled by scholars sharing only part of his idealism. Desiderius Erasmus (1466-1536) had an inauspicious introduction to life, but from extraordinarily humble origins, a combination of talent, hard work, and good fortune led him to achieve almost universal recognition as the finest of European scholars, the Prince of Humanism. In his youth Erasmus followed a program of studies wherein parts of the new Humanism were grafted to the conventional medieval syllabus of the seven arts. After entering an Augustinian monastery, Erasmus, now a monk, enjoyed the luxury of time to pursue independent study. Exposure to medieval higher learning in the Parisian philosophy course, rather than exciting Erasmus over the possibility of philosophy, turned him away with a permanent disdain. And in rejecting philosophy as the custodian of knowledge enabling men to fathom the mystery of successful living, Erasmus adopted the classics. Crossing the threshold of Humanism Erasmus displayed none of the Petrarchan assumptions about the classics being the source of all human inspiration. The classics were good, he thought, and were filled with universal and ageless wisdom, but they were adumbrated by paganism, by their necessary neglect of Christian inspiration and wisdom. The classics containing all secular knowledge worth having were indispensable to a good education and an essential foundation to culture, but they had to be supplemented by the divine learning which only a profound knowledge of scripture could supply.

They should be studied not only for their wisdom, but because they were an essential intellectual foundation enabling men to master the mysteries of human life hidden in Christian sources. Erasmus downgraded the classics, but refused to abandon them. And finally, Erasmus never intended the good life to be interpreted along individualistic lines. True wisdom would prescribe social reform; he sought the betterment of mankind, the improvement of society, and was not driven by a passion for fame and fortune. All this, Erasmus was convinced, had its beginning with a broad education, one taking talented boys through the entire classical corpus.

This broad and difficult academic prescription was intended, of course, only for talented students, for the few whose natural brilliance and intense motivation could take them all the way through classical studies, studies contemplated to perfect the human abilities of thought and expression and open gateways to a higher divine knowledge. In his various educational writings, but most especially in *Copia Rerum et Verborum (Illustrations of Ideas and Words)*, Erasmus demonstrated a course of studies for producing scholars capable of using human ability for social purpose.

Melanchthon   Even with Erasmus' pedagogic advice before them, teachers of the imposing curriculum he recommended were regularly tempted to engage in some paring. And at this point Philip Melanchthon (1497–1560) entered the educational, cultural, and religious picture.

Melanchthon's scholarly credentials were exceptional by any standard, his theology progressive, and his commitment to Protestantism unshakeable. Early in his career he attracted Luther's notice and won his confidence; thereafter he was a spokesman for the cultural and educational philosophy of Lutheranism. At the outset of his crusade Luther tended to downgrade learning, so even modest scholarship was put in jeopardy. But Melanchthon supplied a reasoned justification for conducting schools and retaining a curriculum recommended by the Humanists. In his own background and experience Melanchthon found a formula for keeping most of the Humanistic curriculum. His early schooling exposed him to Scholastic thought and formal reasoning, his more advanced education familiarized him with the classics and convinced him of their value, and his association with Luther kindled an enthusiasm for religion which turned out to be permanent. His academic values represented a combination of these influences and his synthesis of them became the educational philosophy of early Protestantism. Scholasticism taught Melanchthon that organization of knowledge was essential and he set out to select from classical literature whatever conformed to his religious belief.[25] In Melanchthon's hands the curriculum recommended by Erasmus was narrowed and the classics studied were not used to inform the specialties, as had been common, but to build a foundation of learning enabling the good Christian to function effectively in political and religious society. He meant to use the classics to strengthen Christian resolve, and in his work we have the origin of Christian Humanism as an educational theory.

Work well begun by Melanchthon was continued by his pedagogic successors, and now the classical tradition resting in their hands was narrowed even more.[26] The principle Melanchthon employed and refined—selection —was applied with zeal and devotion by the most illustrious advocates of Christian Humanism: Johann Sturm (1507–1589), the Jesuits (founded in 1534), and Mathurin Cordier (1479–1564). What began as an effort to use the classics for broad cultural refinement ended up in a cautious policy of utilizing only those classical sources judged capable of shaping Christian character.

By the time this pedagogic tradition reached seventeenth-century New England it was overlaid by a Neo-Humanism wherein the form of its older and authentic counterpart was retained, but its content—if we judge from school studies in the colonies—was narrower than anything Erasmus proposed. In addition, classics selected for the curriculum were enjoined to augment religious belief, and any classic failing this standard was eliminated from the syllabus. So we should begin by recognizing that New England Puritanism was not authentically Humanistic, although it retained some of the usual appurtenances of Humanistic scholarship. Had New England been Humanistic rather than Puritan it would have been a far pleasanter place to live,[27] but considering that English Humanism had pretty well died with Thomas More (1478–1535), it is useless to speculate about what New England Puritanism might have been had its spirit been animated by the cult of the Renaissance rather than the cult of Calvin. The colonists had no real Humanism to transplant; for there was none at home, if, indeed, there was any in Europe at the time of colonization;[28] and had there been it is unlikely that anything so fragile as Humanism could have survived the severe colonial religious climate.[29]

Yet we must remember the noble auxiliaries of Humanism: grammar, literature, rhetoric, and logic. These studies the Puritans adopted (following established academic precedents) and brought their texts along. What Puritans did was done by others, for the colonists settling in the Middle and Southern colonies also packed their trunks with books on grammar and the classics. But where the Puritans had an emotional drive to maintain the human spirit, to protect it from materialism by preserving the Humanistic tradition, the colonists elsewhere were otherwise preoccupied and their apparent indifference to Humanism put it in jeopardy. New England Humanism was often diluted and subjugated, but its form was virile and vigorous. The paradox of Puritanism husbanding Humanism's formal elements while deterioration affected them in more liberal colonies is a strange accident of history.[30] To explain it one must recognize the character of the Humanism cultivated in Puritan schools. Logic, rhetoric, and Latin grammar and literature (the outward signs of Humanism) were always staples in the curricula of colonial schools and every schoolmaster paid them due heed, but this is only part of the story: they fairly dominated the syllabi of grammar schools and colleges.[31] In the chapters following we shall find the Puritan justification for these studies.

Scholasticism

Scholasticism, a method of organizing and interpreting knowledge devised by generations of medieval scholars, undertook to harmonize the classical conclusions in literature, law, medicine, and intellectual and natural philosophy with a Christian conception of the world God had made. Ultimate truth in human possession was a gift of faith, so the role of reason guided by Scholastic method was to handle all secular knowledge—mainly the classical legacy—in ways making it always correspond to articles of faith. Like boys working arithmetic problems, able to compare their answers with the ones in the back of the book, Scholastics could test their interpretations of the classics against a standard of truth. Anything at variance with the standard was bound to be wrong.

If this represents a harsh evaluation of Scholastic scholarship, it is tempered by the realization that in Scholastic hands methods of investigation and interpretation were perfected to a point never reached before. Accepting, as they did, the assumption that knowledge was hidden away in the classics, scholars justified every rational technique for excavating it. Thus they showed their contemporaries how to use grammar and literature for supremely rational ends, and most of all they demonstrated the extraordinary power of formal logic. The method of Scholasticism outlasted the detailed arguments and propositions it produced during the medieval years to become an indelible feature in the minds of educated Europeans. After the fourteenth century Scholasticism fell into disrepute and scholars with might and main tried to avoid being trapped in thickets of irrefutable Scholastic logic, but this revolt achieved only partial success and the logical tradition grafted itself solidly to the scholarly apparatus. On this level a Scholastic remnant remained alive.

If Humanists, pietists, and religious reformers were wrong in saying Scholastic method was useless and its result always dangerous, the Puritans in old and New England were wrong to believe they had jettisoned the whole of Scholastic philosophy. To be wrong was easy. Concentrating attention on philosophy's handmaiden relationship to theology, they saw Scholastics conclude their argument with a defense of the Church's authority and the Catholic faith. Their own argument led them to condemn Scholastic doctrines supporting the Catholic church, and it neglected other areas where the Scholastic tradition remained intact: Scholastic physics and astronomy, the Scholastic theory of four causes, the Scholastic distinction between potency and act, essence and existence, and Scholastic interpretations of psychology, ethics and motion. Besides these substantial illustrations of common philosophical traditions, we should note that Puritanism followed exactly the model of Scholasticism in organizing the academic curriculum, recognizing the same categories of knowledge and giving the same justification for the interdependence of disciplines.[32]

Scholasticism supported the authority of the Catholic church and the pope and this disqualified it in Puritan eyes; yet an outright rejection of the method was lacking, except when rejection served the end of religious polemic, and plans for its overthrow went unmentioned, except when specific issues of ecclesiastical order and theology were in dispute. After Puritans made corrections on these points to suit themselves, they embraced the general corpus of knowledge—organized largely by the Scholastic process—as being only what all intelligent men recognized to be true.[33]

Puritanism

External and systematic Puritanism favored by accidents of time and geography is frequently represented as a unique phenomenon of seventeenth-century New England, but such representations attach undue weight to appearance. Despite a variety of autochthonous colonial ideas eventually attaching themselves to Puritanism, giving it local and temporary emphases, the substance of Puritanism, animated by a spirit transcending the temper and conditions of the colonial epoch, existed as a peculiar human mood centuries before the New World was discovered by European adventurers. Its early form, unencumbered by modern theological dogmas, economic and political doctrines, and social philosophies, is accurately characterized as a mood whose source of inspiration was lodged in mankind's universal, but often inarticulated, capitulation to piety.[34]

St. Augustine This piety infected hundreds of years of religious history without ever belonging to any creed, yet affecting all denominations. Its origin, if indeed origin can be assigned, antedated Calvin, although Calvin's dogma was unquestionably deeply affected by its recurrent interrogations.

We are closer to its first consistent and deeply dedicated exponent in the person of St. Augustine (354–430), whose thought—and the thought of Calvinists, it must be said—lacked harmony on many essential points of theology, most especially the authority of the Church and the efficacy of the sacraments. Yet even when these monumental differences triggered theological tempests in the seventeenth and eighteenth centuries and provided Puritan preachers with ammunition for pulpit polemic, Augustinian and Puritan piety shared common ground, or better, a common "conviction that the universe conformed to a definite, ascertainable truth," and that the condition for praiseworthy life was to accept without flinching or failing the terms imposed by truth.[35]

Set in motion by St. Augustine, this doctrine of piety combined Platonic teaching, for the most part transmitted in the writing of Plotinus (205?–270 A.D.), and Neoplatonic elaboration, worked into a mosaic of Christian belief. Augustine's intellectual foundations were secured in a bedrock of classical learning, and his distinction as a savant preceded his Christian conversion. Yet his letters, tracts, books, but mostly his *Confessions* (an autobiography), recite the details of a conversion wherein he rejected the temporal world and embraced the eternal. This was more than an ordinary flight from the secular to the divine: Augustine ended up despising the world and doubting the integrity of human nature. His capitulation to the sacred included a dogmatic assumption that faith alone leads men to truth and wisdom. Sense and reason are both useless and dangerous.

Augustinian and Neoplatonic thought proceeded through the early Christian world largely unchallenged, for St. Augustine's reputation was enough to resolve, or quash, any doubt. But despite the nominal allegiance paid to Augustine's austere theology and mystical philosophy, both supporting the doctrine of piety, the mainstream of intelligence was flowing along another channel. Scholars could state the proposition that "faith is necessary to understanding" and believe fully in what they said, but they were not thus restrained from trying to uncover truth by the employment of rational methods, and once finding it, to trust it.

The invention of Scholastic dialectic, the method made famous by Pierre Abelard (1079–1142), called into question the ancient doctrine of piety as it affected man's ability to grasp truth, so as far as the Scholastic movement was concerned this doctrine was seldom more than a minor tributary of medieval thought. The work of Bernard of Chartres in the twelfth century temporarily revived both Augustinian piety and Neoplatonic thought and partially restored their respectability, but the Chartrain school represented an effort to propagandize rather than to teach, to gain acceptance to a point of view rather than to demonstrate its reasonableness and value. Under these circumstances the doctrine of piety survived, but among medieval scholars always as a minority culture. That it stayed alive is important to remember, and securely attached to ancient Christian tradition, sometimes almost as a subversive part, it reminded Christians of deposits of faith so far impervious to man's reason. These reminders had elements of truth sufficient to keep Augustinian formulations of piety from disappearing.

Long before the advent of the seventeenth century, determined effort was made to elaborate theological bases for this piety, for this mental condition which affected some persons so profoundly and left others completely unmoved. Piety was probably an intuition, one incapable of being taught or learned: once entering a man's conscience, it held fast. In the 1630s some twenty thousand souls, caught up most intensely by this mood of piety, settled in New England. Their fundamental conceptions of piety were expressed in traditional, always inherited formulations of God, sin, and regeneration.[36] These formulations when adopted by various sects, or even by different writers of the same sect, were subject to new and detailed definition paying no heed to agreement and sometimes not even to inner consistency, so under these circumstances we should expect to find New England theologians and preachers always exploiting opportunities to define and distinguish the bedrock of feeling and belief. Sometimes these distinctions assumed considerable significance as they were handled by the scholarly ministers in charge of New England churches, but for now we can ignore them. Our interest is greater in the survival of the tradition of piety than in the doctrinal development of Puritanism as a religious denomination.

Besides, despite a creedal exposition of piety, the fundamental meaning of God, sin, and regeneration could still be seen in simple inviolate terms. To the Puritan who now articulated his mood of piety, God is God. More need not be said. After taking this position, one understood well enough by Puritans, they nevertheless went on to attribute qualities to God, cautiously guided by the principle that God's reality should never be limited by the range of the human mind.[37] They railed against other sectarians and used the prodigious resources of their inkwells to produce sermons and handbooks which ended by repeating the mistake—explaining the mystery of God's being—others were indicted for. We must be careful about going too far, for our interest is in the inheritance of piety and not its explication by the scholar-ministers of New England; yet, it is probably worth adding that the Puritan vision of God was generated in habitually literal minds. Whatever could be known must come from scripture, for in their eyes and in their pietistic mood revelation counted more than reason, although in subordinating reason they did not mean to discredit it. Now we begin to see the threshold over which intellectual culture was allowed to pass.[38]

Preoccupations with God's majesty are evidenced not just in mood but in unequivocal pronouncement, and in these preoccupations we have the starting point for the piety animating Puritan mentality, but the Puritan would have left unfulfilled his code of life and could hardly have walked the path left blazed by Augustine had he stopped here. Sin was as obvious and deeply felt as intuition about an absolute God. Perhaps it is easy to understand human humility and even to find praiseworthy some tendencies for self-effacement, but anyone who regards the Puritan conception of man's corruption on these modest terms is bound to have the wrong impression of the Puritan mind. Man is corrupt, mired in depravity, with nothing to save him except when God's hand is sometimes extended to him. He is what he is partly through his own fault (a point which allowed Puritan debaters to make much of the theory of human responsibility), but also because of original sin. This sorry creature lives in a world largely of his own making, wallowing in transgressions he will not forego, and even refusing the help offered to escape his own corruption. Yet behind all this evil, for which man, not God, is responsible, lives a craving in man's soul which must be fed in part by the imperfection of self, an imperfection proclaimed by every tub-thumping preacher who imbibed the spirit of Calvinism, but a craving, too, which must be interpreted as an attraction to God's perfection. Here is man, a corrupt sinner, who seeks to find the perfection of God. He seeks because he must, for this is the mood of piety.

Man alone, hoping by his own strength to rise above his imperfection, is certainly lost, but regeneration is possible, although not by any power in man, when God chooses to make him the recipient of saving grace. The doctrine of sin left little room for optimism in the minds of Puritans, but it did not tell them all was lost. It permitted some hope that a stern God would decide to look kindly on some men some day.

Regeneration was a gift from God; nothing more and nothing less.[39] One could not be sure of finding God's favor and thus be better positioned to receive the gift of grace. Grace, too, was a gift, a point of doctrine no Puritan doubted or debated; it was moreover a mystery, and this, too, the ministers freely acknowledged. Nevertheless they tried to understand and explain it to their flocks. And here, as perhaps with the doctrine of original sin and human depravity, the doctrine of grace was not embraced because it had been rendered logically, for logic was never so powerful as to compel conversion, but because it was spread before hungry and anxious minds who had already assented and for whom demonstration was unnecessary. The driving force behind theologians laboring over their discourse was not to convince anyone not already in the fold, but to fulfill preconceptions both of sectarian belief and clerical industry. Sin could take different forms, and one was wasting time. No minister wanted to be found guilty.

The hard doctrine of sin and depravity was mitigated slightly by the possibility of a gift of grace from an omnipotent God to an impotent man. And why now, when hope was at last at hand, should pious men wonder why God would not grant his saving grace to all men? Was it not better for some to have this gift, to have the slate of past transgression wiped clean, to be regenerated, to be in communion with God, than that none should be blessed with divine generosity? Grace and faith, of course, went hand in hand, although certainly the latter was impossible without the former. This could be, and was, believed by all who surrendered to the mood of piety.

Still, with all their austerity, along with their capitulation to profound mystery, the Puritans were curious—a condition common to mankind, yet surprisingly common among Puritans—and what pricked their curiosity most were the signs distinguishing recipients of God's grace from un-regenerated humans who, in any case, made up the mass of mankind. Was it possible to be sure that natural morality, never counted sufficient for salvation or an adequate substitute for a supernatural infusion of grace, was not being confused with grace?[40]

A Puritan's religious experience could hardly be understood or explained outside the circle of believers.[41] Even so, how could the person to whom grace was given know what had happened, since experience could not tell him how to recognize conversion? This matter of recognizing conversion became a favorite topic for colonial theologians. With a fundamental piety, they could afford to examine the phenomenon of religious conversion and try to "explain specifically what happens in regeneration."[42]

Piety dominated the Puritan mind; with an excess of zeal it proscribed compromise; it substituted belief and feeling for logic and reason whenever logic and reason failed to suit its ends. But it never asked for reason's abject surrender to belief and it never doubted the worth of culture. Piety could catch men in thickets of inconsistency and breed intolerance, but it could also leave open a path to cultural respectability. Here, again, we find a narrow but satisfactory avenue leading to the culture and civilization of intellect. The paradox is worth noting: an attitude of anti-intellectualism which, in the end, had to be intellectualized. On this platform of human fallibility the precarious future of colonial intellectual life was made to stand,[43] and the "Humanistic tradition, one of the noblest inheritances of the English race, went hand in hand with conquering Puritanism into the clearings of the New England wilderness."[44]

Individualism

So far our attention to Puritanism has kept us from ranging more widely into general culture and religious activities in the colonial world. And, while we must be ready to admit, vast regions of English America held no brief for Puritanical predelictions, we must also be ready to concede that if any section of the colonies dominated the intellectual temperament of society it was New England.[45] In this light what might at first appear as an unnecessary preoccupation with Puritanism is really an important exercise. Now, however, in turning to another feature of inheritance—individualism —we are free to stray away from New England, although, again, Puritanism contained the most adequate justification for what turned out to be a cult of individualism, a cult capable of feeding a democratic appetite.[46]

Taking colonial men as a whole, one is struck by their character, one inbred or inherited from forefathers hardened by centuries of tumultuous experience. Its most remarkable feature was an indomitable spirit of self-reliance. No pioneer lacks an abundance of self-confidence, nor are colonists drawn from ranks of men with misgivings about their self-sufficiency. This spirit of self-reliance must have been subject to recurring anxieties, yet it persevered to distinguish itself as a special mode of the colonial personality, one especially evident among the Puritans of New England. Other colonists, self-reliant too, were confident of their ability to manage their own affairs and grasp plain truth, but the Puritan, almost more than any of his colonial companions, was encouraged to exercise his own wit by the precepts of an authoritarian creed. No Puritan doubted the status of the Bible as a revelation of divine will, nor did he question the obligation to read and interpret the Bible for himself. Inherent in Biblical literalism, a danger whose consequences were greater in later, more liberal eras, was an undisciplined ignorance and a vulgarization of truth, but at the same time it allowed for an exaltation of a person's mind.[47]

The ever-present danger of ignorance, coupled with a profound confidence in personal capacity to interpret and judge all matters, recommended a condition of intellectual enlightenment that only a program of education could supply. And on this point, although reached by somewhat different routes, the Puritans and the Jeffersonian Republicans (who appeared a century or more later) could agree wholeheartedly.

Similarly the inherited spirit approving material wealth and temporal bliss, which infected all colonists, and the Puritan conviction that divine favor might be disclosed in worldly reward, coalesced in a temper that could effortlessly justify private gain. A political philosophy promoting the doctrine of the common good was insufficiently strong in the colonies to dominate political policy, yet vigorous enough to affect political values in all the colonies. And this philosophy was augmented, especially in New England, by a painless piety which justified and advocated private gain. Private gain could end up being a condition for service to mankind; and, of course, it could simply be an unfolding of God's will.

Equally significant was the colonial assumption, distilled no doubt in a long European experience with religion and politics, of human dignity and equality. Whether based on purely natural evidence or on the mystery of God's providence, dignity and equality were deeply felt human phenomena, and both were reenforced by the realities of colonial life.

Finally, the colonists shared a sense of destiny, sometimes fed by fundamental religious convictions, sometimes simply by reason and conscience, that in this New World they could create a moral, mental, and spiritual climate wherein the best in men could be capitalized and mankind could be saved. They did not stop to debate the meaning of salvation.

THE NEW ENGLAND MIND

Puritanism had two sides and, although the two were unequal, both were considered important. An underlying commitment to piety was expected to shape every aspect of life; pronouncements on piety unstintingly recommended the revealed word of God as the most binding of all imperatives. We have wondered before how the Puritan mind, after paying allegiance to dogma as dogma was sensed by the natural process in a pious Puritan soul, could have any affection for philosophy, for the functioning of human reason. We have the feeling of being left with a brazen anti-intellectualism, wherein philosophy should be rejected as the work of unregenerate heathens and science should be condemned as tinkering in the devil's workshop. Taking the most extreme of Puritan statements seriously, we are left bewildered about the state of culture and education in a colony where both could be labeled superfluous if not actually dangerous.[48]

Puritanism's two sides were reason and revelation:[49] the former was expected to pay homage to the latter, and its subjugation was often so complete as to jeopardize its identity. Historians looking at Puritanism have concentrated on exploring the impress of piety as it was externalized in dogma and inculcated in the life and character of New England Puritans. There is justification for this preoccupation. Almost without exception, spokesmen for this pious creed echoed the sentiments of Augustine when he cried that men must believe in order to understand. The denial, moreover, that knowledge could contribute to Christian life was proclaimed time and again by preachers, who were convinced that liberal learning (knowledge for its own sake) would certainly be fatal. If men knew the answers to all questions without the benefit of reason, either from intuitions of piety or from hearing the undisguised word of God as found in scripture, of what use was reason? And it could mislead. A fallible mind incapable of fathoming mysteries of revealed truth could not expound these mysteries in the schools. With such attitudes, all deeply imbedded in Puritan mentality and spirituality, what convincing argument could be made for schools and colleges?

Yet this is only part of the story, although a part deserving of notice; the other part, where reason is rescued from a swamp of insignificance, is worth attention too. The Puritan mind, trained to put the things of God first, subordinated the arts and sciences to religion, but even when this was true it refused to surrender profane knowledge to the custody of unregenerate persons. Shaped first by the piety of Augustine, the Puritan mind was heir also to Scholasticism and Humanism.[50] But even when taking these influences into account, it is difficult to find priorities without the confusion of paradox, and for the Puritan it must have been doubly difficult, for he began by agreeing that one must believe in order to understand, and then after believing to try to understand as much as possible. He could idealize faith and assert that faith is an act both of will and intellect, never of will alone; he could maintain the impossibility of establishing principle by reason, but then use reason to stamp out corruptions of true faith or to lay the rational foundation for a functioning of faith; and, finally, he could pronounce that faith as an inner spiritual condition must be articulated.[51] In the end, with all the inconsistencies laid aside, divinity was a science to be mastered by industry and labor; and even for the ordinary Puritan this meant an ability to give reasons for belief. When the pronouncements of the Puritans are compared with the evangelical discourses of the period, it becomes clear that we are not dealing with simple men who missed the intellectual character of religion. It was the Puritan's duty to discover the true meaning in scripture and then to explain it with care and precision to all communicants; and after he had done this he could turn to controversy with doubting or antagonistic scholars and employ every device of reason and utilize any information to help make his case.

Committed to this attitude, the Puritan acknowledged piety as being only one side of his creed, but it was always the more important side. The other side, the intellectual, stood on less certain ground and its principal focus was always to be religious. Religion, of course, was revealed in the Bible; yet, Biblical meaning was seldom self-evident. Even plain meaning had to be proposed to true believers. Being enrolled in the ranks of true believers was due, no doubt, to supernatural grace; thus, the first step toward faith was never thought to be the consequence of human action, although it was eminently reasonable to believe fervently in the efficacy of this initial deposit of faith, and it was always understood that such belief—either assenting to belief or embracing faith itself—was not a function of human reason. Puritans, once believing, were compelled both by natural curiosity and spiritual necessity to judge the scriptures, to discover their meaning, and, finally, to affirm unequivocally the authority of God who made the revelation.

A Puritan's intellect was unquestionably subordinated to faith; reason, at best, was a mere adjunct to religious belief. But in seventeenth-century America the intellect was not thus rendered inconsequential. On the contrary, it lay within its province to expound a philosophy of knowledge which survived the purely religious side of Puritanism. The striking feature to the strictly religious dimension of Puritanism was the absolute authority of belief; and it would be easy to assume an authoritarianism of faith, blind to the possibilities of reason, ready to condemn reason whenever it threatened to impose its criteria on belief. There was something in Puritanism's dogmatic attitude toward religion and the social order to confirm and make this assumption appear stronger than it was. Yet the assumption errs on the side of claiming too much and misses this: unlike medieval Scholasticism, Puritanism was entirely capable of explaining something without at the same time trying to explain everything. However absolute its authoritarianism appeared to be, American Puritanism always left some room for an appeal to reason and experience. It was characteristic of Puritans to prove their "points first by authority and then by reason."[52] None was ever content to rest his argument solely on the force of authority. So to translate Puritanism as rationalism would be wrong, for simple belief played too great a part in moral and intellectual systems for this, and a Puritan did not have to be a rationalist to understand the worth of being reasonable. He felt duty bound to study hard to understand as much as possible—and always to be content with only a little—and even when he could not understand, to believe that what appeared to be a mystery was in the end reasonable. Allegiance to this moderate rationalism generated and directed Puritan intellectual energy, and it was this philosophy of knowledge that guided educational policy in New England and influenced school books and teaching methods in Puritan schools.[53]

Such an approach to the culture of mind is hardly compatible with the conventional Humanism of the Great Renaissance, for it never authorized a commitment to liberal learning, to knowledge for its own sake. We should think therefore, that Professor Morison is guilty of an exaggerated optimism when he attributed purely liberal motives to the educators who guided Harvard College and other New England schools along academic pathways.[54]

Faith and reason were never considered equal, as we have said, yet Puritan polemicists often gave them the appearance of equality. When a Puritan attacked Catholics or other Protestants for abandoning reason, or when defending his creed, he could use every tool of rational argument. But when positions were reversed and Puritans found themselves in combat with rationalizing theologians who ridiculed their simple confidence in faith, they could desert reason and subordinate everything to scripture, unvarnished and unelaborated by the rules of philosophy and theology.[55] Being men of extremes themselves, Puritans regularly deplored extreme positions in others and were capable of condemning such positions when they found them within their own ranks or among those they chose to call their enemies. Often on the fringe of contradiction, Puritanism was dogmatic and authoritarian, but never so dogmatic or authoritarian as to surrender demonstration or abandon rational comprehension. Reason and judgment were essential, although subordinate, to dogma and authority.[56]

With Catholics and Protestants more rationalistic than themselves, with evangelical sects more piety-ridden than their own, Puritan thinkers and writers were kept busy defending their bastions of belief, and they never lost sight of the fact that the schools could be of great help. If men fought about the meaning of scripture, was it not, Puritans thought, because hidden or plain, there was one true meaning? And they were willing to expend all their resources of faith and reason to discover what they confidently expected would be one stable and true meaning. Only on the broadest principles of religion was it possible to accept the word of God without interpretation; whenever scriptural investigation went beyond these broad principles, the interpretations of which a trained reason alone was capable were imperative. Puritan religion was conceived to be truly and nobly rational; reason was an essential, yet inferior, handmaiden to faith, so on the best of religious justifications Puritans could build their philosophy of education, a philosophy totally incapable of countenancing any tenet explicitly or implicitly recommending liberal learning.

Schools and colleges should be opened, the Puritan was certain of that, but he did not believe them equally important for all classes of students nor did he discount hierarchy of educational purpose. Faith needed persons capable of explicating it; the word of God needed trustworthy elaborators; and who could have more of a claim on the classrooms of schools and colleges than boys with a desire to be Puritan ministers, preachers, interpreters and defenders of the word of God? And what subjects could stand above all others requiring subordinate subjects to serve them? The answer came easily to the Puritan: everything in the curriculum of the colonial school and college was intended to promote the interests of religion.[57]

CHAPTER TWO

Colonial
Cultural
Life

American colonists, we have said, shared traditions common to European life, and these traditions accompanied them when, for a variety of reasons, they set sail for the New World. Landing on America's uncultivated, uncivilized, and often unfriendly shores, they tried to organize their lives along lines compatible with conventional taste. Yet this could seldom be done effortlessly, and sometimes not at all, for in this New World settlers had to spend energy and exhaust an abundance of ingenuity just to stay alive. The first decades were the most taxing and precarious; after they passed, life began to assume an orderly and sometimes a routine character. When this happened, although amendment to familiar habit and convention was frequent, cultural evolution was again subordinated to the principal social theses of European life.

Prominent features of early colonial life are illustrated in Louis Wright's *The Cultural Life of the American Colonies, 1607–1763,* and Lawrence Cremin's *American Education: The Colonial Experience, 1607–1783.* It is hard to follow a better trail than the one they blazed through those cultural, educational, and intellectual forests containing the timber used for building an orderly and coherent philosophy which, in the end, formed the foundation of colonial life. Declaring at the outset a special debt to these scholars, we adopt in general, because of its historical sense and balance, Wright's paradigm to elaborate the manifold sides of early cultural evolution.

SOCIETY AND LEADERSHIP

An environment full of natural hostilities urged on the first colonists a sense of community,[1] so whenever they could they gathered in settlements

23

to afford security and protection for their families and their homes. But frontier living foreclosed any temptation they may have had to stay huddled in village enclaves, since circumstance compelled them to make a living from the land. Throughout the colonial period, good authority tells us, "American life was profoundly influenced by the nearness of the people to the soil."[2]

So the view we have of these first two centuries is one wherein rural life distilled principal social values and was, in addition, the training ground for men who assumed positions of leadership in the colonial world. "Even the largest cities," and by 1740 Philadelphia was America's greatest urban center, "were never far removed from the back country that supported them, and town dwellers were in close contact with farmers."[3] The influence of farmers is deceptive. Their prominence was easily obscured and dramatic episodes seldom catapulted them to fame in colonial society; yet their influence should not be misjudged. As they went about their daily chores, as they met with neighbors in village, tavern, and church, as they taught their children and infused in them a yearning for social standing and a sense of work's dignity, they engendered the values that subsequently matured into hallmarks of a democratic society.

Farmers in Southern colonies were less likely than their New England counterparts to adopt a retiring social and political stance; above all the ownership of land unleashed their zeal to participate in public life. If they owned enough land to entitle them to vote, or if their social position recommended them to places in the colonial legislature, the assembly, or town meeting, they forgot their lessons in altruism and championed their own interest. Because this interest usually coincided with the interest of a majority of agrarian men in the colony or locality, patterns of social and economic value were registered, and in their registry social policy tended to follow a democratic furrow.

Still, to say that the rural voice was heard and frequently heeded, should not blind us to the fact that other voices competed for a hearing. But, single-minded and vigorous by nature, rural spokesmen stated their case with clarity, while the interest of other parties in this contest for influence in American society was blurred. And this blurring of interest is illustrated by Wright when he tells us that a Boston merchant of position and means "might graze his cows on Boston Common and drink milk" from them; a New York or Philadelphia businessman might use produce from his own garden or farm; and a Charleston shipper might own a plantation and live there during the year's cooler months.[4] So an aristocracy of wealth and position, while setting its face against a rising tide of rural influence, inevitably assimilated values generated in men and women who lived on plantations or on farms pushed to the back country.

The South Besides, turning our eyes away from wealthy and socially prominent city-dwellers to plantation life in the South, we see, not the same, but similar conditions conspiring to keep the integrity and dignity of a rural social order alive. If we are sometimes deceived by appearances relative to agrarian influence in early America, we must also advert to distortions in the picture of Southern life. There was a Southern aristocracy—one clearly influential in shaping the destiny of the American nation—but "even a cursory examination . . . dispels the old belief that [this was] the land of large plantations. . . . Thus vanishes the fabled picture of seventeenth-century Virginia"[5] and other Southern colonies.

A genuine understanding of the growth of Southern society must take into account the motives that led various groups and persons to come to America in the first place; it must notice the possibilities for social and economic advantage in the colonial enterprise; and it must pay heed to the geography of the region as well as to the fertility of the land for growing tobacco, which, almost by accident, became the principal crop of the South.[6]

Looking past these motives, and regional differences imposed by geography and climate, we see, too, a society with conflicting elements whose roots ran all the way to Europe. The New World did its best to resolve them. Some great men came to the Southern colonies and, utilizing their wealth and political influence, obtained huge land grants. Although relatively few in number, these estates turned out to be the ornamental plantations from which many portraits of Southern colonial life are drawn. And their owners, although some never bothered to come to America, were not idle aristocrats but hard-working persons who, according to Wright, lived and worked mostly in rough work clothes.[7] There were also those prominent merchants and traders who settled in the South to harvest profit from commerce. When trade in tobacco and rice made them prosperous, or added to their wealth, they sometimes invested in land and built up the kinds of estates which in England would have been beyond their means.

The picture is completed by sketching in those dependable farmers and skillful craftsmen who could afford their passage to the colonies, and who sought to own land in Virginia, Maryland, or the Carolinas. Obsessed with the idea of owning their own land—which in England could only have been a dream—they also had a fierce independence that, in addition to being a permanent bequest to later generations, was utilized to push back the borders of colonial society and extend its geographic frontier. "In their wake, they brought a rich cultural diversity that inevitably exerted profound and permanent influence on the character of American life."[8] But there were some, too, who came to the colonies as indentured servants without means to pay their passage, expecting to find a better life. They, with others (sometimes prisoners freed from English jails), formed the labor force to work the great estates; that is, until 1670, when slavery was introduced, and "wrought a revolution in the economic life" and the social order of great parts of the South.[9]

The cheapness of slave labor, along with the ever-present need to expand the acres under tobacco cultivation—for tobacco depleted the soil in less than a decade—fastened a plantation economy on the region near the coast. Once securely fastened, it had the effect of driving small farmers, and others unable to meet the competition these altered economic conditions introduced, to the back country. As these economic realities were exploited, the coast became a reservation for the gentry—for those most conscious of perpetuating an English way of life—and the German peasants, Scotch-Irish, and others who by this time had migrated to the South, were driven to the valleys and mountains of the back country. If their exodus from the coastal plains gave these poor and hardy souls greater opportunity, more land, and fuller independence, it deprived them also of a political and social influence which otherwise might have been theirs. As the years passed, an abiding distrust developed between the aristocrats on the tidewater and the peasants in the back country.[10] This distrust was sustained by such things as antagonism toward central government, fear of religious establishment, and the power of wealth; the tune played for its social recessional was slow and often disharmonious.

Turning quickly to another side of Southern life, we notice how the early hope of the promoters of colonization went largely unrealized. These entrepreneurs never meant to encourage the development of an agricultural economy based on the production of one staple crop. They expected Virginia, for example, to function as a tributary to the British economy and imagined that its people could invest time and talent making iron and glass, growing hemp, and producing silk, potash and wine.[11] Despite their intention, the economy and prosperity of Virginia especially (but other Southern colonies as well) became linked to the production of one crop—tobacco. And to succeed along these economic lines, it soon became apparent that nature had to be aided and abetted. Forests had to be cleared to make room for more tillable land, crops had to be planted, cultivated, and harvested. All this required a plentiful supply of workers, for an economy based on the production of tobacco could not prosper without them. So, in both North and South, although not for the same reasons, the importance of labor was emphasized and work itself was justified socially, economically, and theologically.

THE DOCTRINE OF WORK

For colonists work was a way of life, so they refused to waste time debating its utility. Moreover, life in Europe had taught them an unforgettable lesson: work alone might not guarantee economic advancement, but its neglect would almost certainly bring ruin. Even without what Louis Wright calls a "Gospel of Work,"[12] their solicitous attention to toil would probably have been the same: without alternative, they worked to live. So much is clear, but still an entirely satisfactory explanation of their ardent and zealous industry is lacking.

Much of the substantial conviction in New England was theological or inspired by theology, and what was true of New England was true, although to a lesser extent, in other colonies as well. This comes as no surprise, because the fundamental convictions of Europe were forged and tempered on a thousand-year affinity to religion. The world the colonists knew could be explained by an appeal to divine will or providence, and this appeal was answered for any man who could read and understand those scriptural injunctions and moral imperatives telling men, women, and children to employ God's gift of time usefully. Wasting time was a sin.

With a theology of work to guide them in their various exertions, the colonists, especially the New England Puritans, needed little help from anything else. Nevertheless, it was there. A long and substantial tradition respecting work and the dignity of labor had its origin in sixteenth-century European commercialism and this tradition was kept alive in America. Men who tried to transform a wilderness to a civil society, men who wanted to make their homes in this undeveloped continent, were almost certain to embrace the secular, prosaic, and pragmatic business of making a living and, if possible, to live well. However elevated their spiritual values may have been, American colonists were swept along in the direction of material wealth. They wanted wealth if they could have it; nothing in their religious creed or belief said they were wrong or called them to a halt.

If religious tracts were barren in condemnation of wealth and material success, there was no such silence in a little book whose colonial popularity was second only to the Bible. Our attention is called to Benjamin Franklin's *Poor Richard's Almanac*, published serially from 1732 to 1757. We are told that it came to be known as "The Way to Wealth."[13] Its litanies of good advice, however, were not entirely original. Taken largely from extant anthologies (forming what Cremin calls a "latter-day *Adagia*") and "rephrased in Franklin's terse and homely language, [they quickly became] proverbial in the English-speaking colonies."[14]

Franklin told his readers to be prudent, and they paid close attention to his advice; besides, religious counsel from Protestant spokesmen had an entirely orthodox sound when it reaffirmed prudence as a moral virtue. So when religion, good sense, and the common experience of mankind told colonists to avoid waste of all kind, they paid close heed; and they heeded no less those injunctions "that enjoined them to sobriety and thrift, and that urged them above everything else to avoid the waste of God's precious time lest idle hands find work for the devil."[15] Faithfully following this counsel of prudence in all material things in a country so full of opportunity came close to being a charter for prosperity.

Among the colonists North and South, none listened to this doctrine of work more carefully than the Puritans. Following it to the letter, they used it first to invigorate their economic lives, and then enlisted it to whet their appetite for education. One is not surprised, then, when the piety associated with a prudent and profitable employment of time was swept away and a materialistic conception of life crept in, that men like Cotton Mather, whose heads and hearts belonged to the old order, complained that the glory of the Lord might be leaving New England. While it is usually dangerous to take too seriously contemporary complaint about the insidious contamination of moral standards, Cotton Mather had a point, and when he inveighed against decadence he had more on his mind than the drinking in taverns, dancing, playing cards, and attending the theater.[16] He meant that evidence of secular rather than sacred motives could be detected among the people. The influence of the clergy, moreover, was declining, especially in matters of public policy, where heretofore it had been decisive and final; law and medicine were being regarded more favorably as professional careers and bright young men, neglecting their calling to the ministry, embraced them. His own books, along with those of his learned counterparts, were still being read, but other books, such as Thomas Prince's *History of New England,* which adopted the appurtenances of secular scholarship and concentrated on secular topics, had a larger following. Even Harvard College, appointing John Winthrop to a professorship, recognized the maturing credentials of science.[17] These things, Cotton Mather knew on the basis of intuition, were evil—heresies of a kind meant to be stamped out—but they were neither more significant nor more pernicious in their undermining of good order and religious disposition than an indifference to the gospel of work. As Mather looked around, he thought the gospel was being violated.

As it turned out, Mather was wrong. The Puritan virtue of incessant industry was still practiced, but in a different way, at least in a way unfamiliar and perhaps unacceptable to this Puritan divine. A man of many enterprises, the New England merchant sailed his ships searching for profitable trade; he sent vessels to catch fish off the bountiful coast and shipped the catches to places where prices were best; he exchanged commodities and imported products for sale in this country. When trading opportunities were offered with other colonies, he pursued them to his advantage; and when slave trade turned out to be profitable, he participated in that severely competitive commerce too. Cotton Mather was right to complain, we think, although he may have wasted ammunition aiming at the wrong targets.

As they husbanded the habits of their countrymen, neither Mather nor his Puritan confreres missed the relationship between industry and learning, and their almost boundless idealization of education had its basis in the conviction that "counted a day lost in which they did not spend ten or twelve hours in their studies."[18] These convictions on industry shaped social policies in the colonies. The natural tendency to fear and dislike strangers was stimulated by men who quaked at the threat of moral decadence from outsiders and by the fact that newcomers were not likely to be gainfully employed. Customs varied: some localities could welcome travelers cordially because they were windows to the world, but "in some New England towns," Farber says, "strangers were ordered to leave at once."[19]

Conditions for labor, and we must not forget those colonists who, without prosperity or social position, had to work the farms and operate the ships and shops, varied from one colony to another. Where the need for division of labor and technical skill was greater, usually in the Northern and Middle colonies, workmen had an excellent chance to become independent, and sometimes prosperous. Laborers practicing the work ethic were rewarded with good wages; should the god of luck smile they might win a home and a business of their own. Generally, however, the avenues to prosperity were open to men of trade and industry: lucky, enterprising, and occasionally ruthless, they found ways to travel them. When they did they were confident in their piety and they took their wealth and success as a sign of God's blessing on them.

COLONIAL POPULATION

British enthusiasm for colonizing North America paid huge dividends in wealth, influence, language, and culture, and a majority of early settlers were English; yet the colonization of the New World was neither totally a British enterprise nor was the population of the first colonies entirely English. Almost from the beginning the colonies attracted a variety of nationalities, who left the land of their birth for compelling reasons, and each had some influence on shaping what is called the American character. Not all early settlers were white; and native Indians had some influence on language (skunk, hickory, squash, caribou, pecan, pawpaw, chinquapin, persimmon, terrapin, menhaden, and catalpa are examples of American words borrowed from their dialects),[20] food, crops and herbal medical therapy. But the principal thrust for shaping American life came from Europe, represented by persons of various national backgrounds, and in this new land common issues and similar aspirations tended to maintain it. "If the melting pot fused them all into something new," a prominent cultural historian said, "nevertheless these new Americans could not help bearing evidence of their complex origins."[21]

New England

The men who planned and settled the Bible commonwealths of New England were products of England and the life and order they envisioned for their new state was remarkably similar to what they had experienced in the mother country. Besides, with one hundred and thirty university graduates joining the early Puritan migration,[22] many settlers were talented and educated, making it all the easier to introduce and maintain a social structure resembling the one left behind.

As they were transformed from Puritans to Yankees, they managed to keep intact most of the ideals that motivated them to cross the Atlantic. Although few were nobles, and fewer still titled, they embraced conservative, aristocratic attitudes and, with little sympathy for anything blighted by radicalism, steered clear of democracy and liberalism. Conditions of life and religious conviction afforded almost no time for leisure, and the region's geography made earning a living hard in the rocky and tree-covered settlements along the New England coast. Neither drudgery nor the threat of poverty, however, undermined their confidence in their own inner strength and superiority, or weakened their assumption that they were God's specially appointed agents to accomplish his purpose for the New World.[23] True to their vision of what a Bible state should be, and certain that God was their constant companion in the management of this pioneering venture, they put up with material hardship without murmuring, for when the accounts of life were finally balanced this vision would stand as tangible evidence of their constancy to Providence and their superiority. But if wealth and all it could buy was not the power plant firing their zeal, nothing in their code of life or religion told them to disdain it. Imposing homes (which eventually became a reality), fine clothes, good food, and a livery of domestic servants were outward signs—unmistakable and concrete—of their personal and social superiority.

With law, position, wealth, and religious prescript on their side, the prominent persons of New England, in Massachusetts especially, called the tune of the social dance; but despite all this some stubborn souls had other musical preferences. Farmers and artisans were essential to a maturing economy: having made the voyage to America because they wanted a better life for themselves and their children, they refused to acknowledge a social order telling them that social mobility was beyond their reach, and that they would have to submit to the status of their birth. It would be a mistake to think New England in these colonial years a democracy, or that much movement surfaced toward adopting democratic political and social sentiments, but the class structure imported from England and sustained by ministers, magistrates, and wealthy merchants eroded as years passed and as farmers, craftsmen, tenants, and laborers, asserting their independence, insisted on a fairer chance to obtain the better things in life.

As it turned out, this incipient movement toward democracy was aided and abetted by unexpected partisans: the Separatists of Plymouth, in adopting a congregational form of church polity, took an important step in the direction of religious democracy. If something like religion could be infected with democratic sentiment, why not politics and economics?[24] The trail the Separatists blazed was too clear to miss. In addition, other religious leaders, like Roger Williams in Rhode Island and Thomas Hooker in Connecticut, whose views sounded heretical in places like Massachusetts Bay, promoted theses conspiring to feed a democratic impulse. And with all this going on in the colonies, avenues of correspondence with Europe were good enough to carry casks of liberal political thought. As the colonial period drew to a close in New England, remnants of the aristocratic social paradigm were being shred by a cadre of social revolutionaries led by Samuel Adams. Adams' social doctrine called for a halt to the rule of an aristocracy. He, and those who shared his philosophy, were in the vanguard of a political system whose time was yet to come. The foundations of popular sovereignty, though, were being laid.

New Netherland

After the British, whose settlements in New England and Virginia bore permanent fruit, the first people to enjoy success in establishing the thirteen original colonies were the Dutch. But an arbitrary colonial government, poor colonial administration, and rigid commercial and land-allotment policies made emigration from Holland an unattractive prospect, so Dutchmen stayed home: "No sane mind could have expected the Dutch colonists to return without protest to a medieval system of government."[25] And the signs of medieval feudalism were all there in a system of land allocation allowing patroons (the colonial version of feudal lords) to own and govern immense tracts of land bordering the Hudson River.

In spite of this, New Netherland prospered enough to keep going, and its population increased slowly. From 1630, when the colony was mainly a few trading posts with a population of about 500, it doubled by 1640, tripled in the next decade, and by 1660 boasted almost 6,000 inhabitants.[26] However the majority of the population—at this time probably less than a quarter of the population of Massachusetts and a fifth of the population of Virginia—lived in and around New Amsterdam, on Long Island and along the lower Hudson. This concentration of persons lent some stability to the colonial venture. But many in New Netherland were scattered around the colony to outposts as far north as Albany and to others on the Delaware and Connecticut Rivers.

So sparseness of population was one factor slowing colonial progress; another was the great variety in nationality among the first settlers. The

Dutch themselves were reluctant to leave Europe, where they led comfortable and satisfying lives. The colony offered nothing in the way of religious, political, or economic advantage that was not already theirs. The first colonists to come to New Netherland were Walloons, French-speaking Protestants from Belgium who, for religious reasons, looked with hope to the New World.

The Walloons were followed by others: Germans, Danes, Norwegians, Swedes, Finns, Portuguese, Spaniards, Italians, Bohemians, Poles, and Jews. In all, we are told, eighteen different languages were spoken in the colony.[27] And religious sects may have been more numerous than nationalities. From the language of the first colonial charter, one gathers that a policy of religious tolerance was intended. The colony was to be a theological refuge for the persecuted in Europe. In consequence of this policy, Huguenots, Baptists, Quakers, Presbyterians, Lutherans, Mennonites, and other sects came to New Netherland and were accorded greater religious freedom than almost anywhere else, but it was never quite all they had been promised or exactly what the company charged with colonization wanted. Some colonial directors, or governors, interpreted religious rectitude according to their own standard and either prohibited religious freedom or interfered with it. Trying to suppress these tyrannies, the company reprimanded one director, Peter Stuyvesant, in gentle but clear language: "Let everyone remain free as long as he is modest, moderate, his political conduct irreproachable, and as long as he does not offend others or oppose the government. . . . Tread thus . . . and we doubt not you will be blessed."[28] Stuyvesant, however, read this admonition to suit himself and conducted his business of religious repression as before. But his attitude, for the most part, was atypical: if religious toleration in New Netherland was not actively promoted, it was, at least, permitted.

Despite the fact that the Dutch were a minority in New Netherland and an even smaller minority in the colonies as a whole, their influence on American life was impressive and took various forms. It was most obvious, however, in architecture, where town and country houses and outbuildings bore the mark of the Netherlands. The Dutch, moreover, managed to gain an almost permanent influence on American taste in household art and furniture.[29] In language and religion, though, their influence was weaker. The English language's power of predominance was demonstrated throughout the colonies, but Dutch made a valiant effort to hang on in New Netherland, where it was taught in the schools until 1664, and where it was the preferred language in the churches for a century afterward. Noah Webster said he heard "Dutch sermons at Albany so late as 1786." Although English's forward march could not be halted, Dutch made a linguistic contribution with such words as cruller, coleslaw, cookie, stoop, sleigh, waffle, and Santa Claus.[30]

New Jersey

Politically similar to New York, because after 1664 the Duke of York held what formerly had been New Netherland, New Jersey's colonial population consisted mainly of Quakers, Scotch, and Scotch-Irish. Some Dutch settlements remained, and to the south, along the Delaware River, a small settlement of Swedes flourished. But New Jersey, bordered on one side by a more vigorous New York and on the other by a thriving, industrious Pennsylvania, tended to be a follower rather than a leader on matters of American temper and taste.

Pennsylvania

When William Penn founded his colony, he introduced an extraordinarily liberal policy with respect to religious preference and sectarian practice; and this policy made Pennsylvania a haven for religiously oppressed people in Europe and other American colonies. When they flocked to the colony carved out for the benefit of mankind and for religious liberty, they found strange and unorthodox theological disposition and religious practice among the Quakers. Rejecting all sectarian and religious ceremony, Quakers counted on simplicity of belief and their own good conscience to keep them in harmony with God's rule. Deploring, moreover, social rank and distinction, they jettisoned many conventional social amenities, which some of their neighbors thought only decent manners, along with the taking of oaths and military service. As pacifists and as careful tillers of the "golden rule," they extended their remarkably progressive attitude especially to religious belief.

If Quaker liberalism was considered menacing to good order and religious regularity in some colonies—for example, in Puritan Massachusetts—and worthy only of being stamped out, it was nevertheless a beacon of liberty for persecuted Germans, Irish, Swiss, French, and other Europeans seeking American sanctuary for theological creed and economic opportunity. During Penn's lifetime, English, Swedes, Dutch, Welsh, and Germans settled in the colony by the thousands; later, with conditions in Europe worsening, with almost constant warfare, with depressions in industry and agriculture, and with religious intolerance becoming more zealous, motives for migration were stronger and the attractiveness of Pennsylvania became correspondingly greater.

LABOR SUPPLY

Despite a fairly solid financial backing for early colonial ventures, the capital requirements for colonial development eventually became greater than European investors wanted to risk. So money was in short supply for any great economic accomplishment during most of the first colonial century. A lack even more serious than capital, though, was labor. If the colonial adventure, both North and South, was to prosper, hands were needed to do those thousands of things which at that time could only have been done manually.

Indications are fairly clear in most of our sources that colonists married young and had large families. The size of colonial families amused some Europeans and prompted them, mainly Englishmen, to caustic comment. Still, it was no secret either here or abroad that a large family was a sound investment, for children could soon be put to work in shops and fields. So, we see the colonists tried to do their part to solve the labor problem, but it was not enough.

This labor shortage was redressed somewhat by the practice of importing indentured servants: contract laborers bound to work for a certain number of years in return for the cost of their voyage across the ocean.[31] For the most part, indentured servants came from England where their prospects for a good life were poor. Having nothing to lose by emigrating, they bound themselves voluntarily to a master, working and living with him until the contract was fulfilled. But for every indentured servant who came according to these conditions, another was shanghaied from London or Bristol streets and brought to this country against his will. Besides, there were others who, with their agreement to set sail for the colonies, were freed from English prisons. These unfortunate persons, though, were convicts only in a technical legal sense; the crime of the majority was most likely indebtedness. So we should correct any misconceptions we have about the number of our colonial ancestors who were hardened criminals, reprieved from the hangman's noose and sentenced instead to the wilderness of America.

After the first settlers in the colonies, mostly English, came others as a result of voluntary or forced emigration. And, as we have seen, they came from various parts of Europe. Sailing for the New World, they knew hardship awaited them on America's shores, but the ordeals of the voyage itself must have been unpleasant surprises. Ships were small, living conditions were cramped and unsanitary, food was bad, sickness was common, and the voyage was long and slow. Once in the colonies, the newcomers worked on farms and plantations, for generally they lacked skill for anything other than hard labor. Under these harsh circumstances many failed; for them the New World had not kept its promise. But for the hardy souls who survived the rigors of colonial life, America proved to be a land of opportunity. Once the contractual obligation of indenture was worked off, these persons were free to make a life for themselves. Land was available almost for the taking, especially in the back country, and land itself was a prize worth winning, but there were other ways to succeed, too, and success was not withheld by any stigma associated with a former condition of poverty or servitude.

If this picture is somewhat too bright, for all such colonists did not become prosperous, we should sketch into the picture those former servants and convicts who, even with freedom, were unable to improve their fortunes much. For whatever reason, thousands found it impossible to rise above their original and, in some cases, natural disabilities. Beginning at a low point on the social and economic ladder, they found positions of prosperity and respectability hard to achieve.

Negro slaves soon took the place of white indentured servants and formed the labor supply for many of the Southern colonies. Slavery, introduced to Virginia in 1619, became a vital element in this agrarian, plantation economy after 1700. Negroes, we know, were captured in Africa and brought to this country, mainly by British slave traders. Those surviving the rigors of a slave ship were sold in the colonies, held as chattels, and used for heavy manual labor. Unlike the indentured servants who had come before (and came still), Negro slaves were destined for a lifetime of bondage. Should some miracle free them, they continued to occupy a place below and apart from the white population. Because slavery contributed to economic gain, this competitive commerce increased rapidly in the eighteenth century.

Slavery was defended as an economic asset, but it was never a great enough asset to clinch the economic success of the colonies. More labor was needed, and it came in waves of immigration from Europe. Now Germans and Scotch-Irish outnumbered the English as immigrants seeking their fortune in America. The Germans were motivated to find a refuge from feudal economic and social conditions at home, from war that almost constantly plagued them, and from a brand of religious intolerance they could not abide. They were, moreover, industrious and ambitious and were confident of their ability to succeed in the colonies. Although some Germans settled in every colony, they were attracted to Pennsylvania, and flowed through the port of Philadelphia to build homes alongside the Quakers who had preceded them. Soon these Pennsylvania "Dutch" became America's most skillful farmers. They planted orchards, built huge two-story barns, and bred heavy draft horses. Sensitive to their own language, customs and religion, they did their best to remain apart from their fellow colonists. Benjamin Franklin is said to have worried about Pennsylvania becoming a German state.

Almost side by side with Germans came the Scotch-Irish; the attractions of Pennsylvania tempted them too. These Scotch-Irish came from Ulster, a district in northern Ireland. They had been transplanted to Ireland earlier by the British government, in the hope that their presence would somehow suppress the rebelliousness of the Catholic Irish. The Scotch-Irish, however, were too violent to be good emissaries. Finding the Irish inhospitable, they were compelled to live in a state of constant military readiness to protect themselves and to assault their Irish enemies. These conditions may have prompted them to emigrate to America; in any case, their sojourn in Ireland conditioned them for their later role as Indian fighters and American frontiersmen. Zealous Presbyterians, they husbanded their religion in Ireland and kept its doctrines pure and intact when they came to the colonies. They were restless, too, so after settling first in Pennsylvania, where they were reputed to have been quarrelsome, unruly, and contemptuous of authority, they moved farther inland. In later decades, they moved down the Appalachian valleys to the back country of Virginia, the Carolinas, and Georgia. Fond of primitive life and addicted to the open country, the Scotch-Irish were at the leading edge of Westward expansion. The hard frontier of wilderness America capitulated before their persistent assault.

Shortly before the Revolution the colonial population was about two and one-half million, compared to England's population of about seven million. Settlement in the colonies, for a long time close to the coast, was moving inland across the Alleghenies as far as the Ohio River valley. This expansion, although it may have had the effect of weakening the colonies in their struggle with Britain, was a good omen for the future of the country and for the promise of opportunity it contained.

RELIGIOUS DIVERSITY

The seventeenth century, especially in the American colonies, was an age of faith. Almost every Protestant sect was represented. Lutherans, German Calvinists, Anabaptists, Mennonites, Dunkers, Amish, New Born, Moravians, and others came from Germany; Huguenots from France and Acadia found refuge first in South Carolina and then moved to other colonies; Dutch Reformed communicants found homes in New Netherland; and Scotch-Irish Presbyterians migrated to the western sections of the South. Despite all this variety, however, the initial activity in colonizing the New World was inspired by British Protestants: Anglicans, Puritans, Separatists, and Quakers.

One should be clear and direct about colonial religion and the allegiance men paid to it. Toleration of dissenting creeds, despite what we have sometimes been taught about the religious disposition of our ancestors, was neither approved nor recognized. Most colonists wanted religious freedom for themselves; they refused to grant it to others. Coming to America to worship as they chose, they "used every means in their power—by fraud, trickery, and bloodshed, as well as by legitimate influence— . . . to uphold the power and authority of [their] Church."[32] Yet, Cremin reminds us, "both the Puritan and Anglican establishments in America were early challenged by diversity, both from within and from without."[33]

The embers of religious controversy in seventeenth-century England were fanned by Anglicans, Separatists, and Puritans. These were the denominations who, for one reason or another, set their course for the New World and, reaching it, did everything in their power, sometimes crossing the boundary of common sense, to impose their religious will on the colonies they opened. Anglicans embraced a political, economic, educational, and religious status quo; lacking a disposition to reform religion or remake the world they knew and loved, and always loyal to the aristocratic social tradition, they dominated the culture of the South and, in time, extended their influence to New York, Maryland, and Pennsylvania.

Driven from England where they were feared and despised, Separatists found an asylum in Plymouth Colony, where church "members administered church discipline. They also appointed the minister and could dismiss him. In the Separatist view, a minister became a minister only through election by a particular congregation."[34] This was congregational control.

Aggressive, domineering, and uncompromising, the Puritans settled in New England, and from this citadel of church and state spread their influence throughout the colonies. New England "was intended to be a holy and unique corner of the world, but it went into the eighteenth century well prepared to keep pace with the intellectual and emotional alterations of a new era,"[35] and in the end exerted a profound and lasting influence on American educational institutions, on trade and commerce, and on an emerging capitalistic social order.

We should take a closer look at Puritanism and the men who adopted its creed in order to build a new society for America. Puritan doctrine told men to obey God's will and enforce his law. Divine law covered every side of life. So persons God had selected were duty bound to see his law fulfilled to the letter. Massachusetts men enforcing this covenant had been nurtured by middle-class English society: their emblems were education, wealth, and social standing. Some had disposed of English estates to resettle in America; others, enterprising merchants, with shrewdness and good luck had managed to build a fortune; still others were the scholarly products of English universities. But being men of faith, and converts to the doctrine of piety, they sensitively and prudently heeded its constant urging. Even the majority of settlers in this colony, in this oligarchy of Christian grace, the small merchants, the craftsmen, the farmers—all persons of modest means and even more modest social standing —embraced the belief of their superiors and defended it with the same unflinching devotion.

Violations of good order were punished with a severity and an intensity not soon forgotten. Departure from sectarian orthodoxy was a more serious matter: it was heresy. And heretics were banished or worse. We may recall our early lessons of history and remember how Anne Hutchinson and Roger Williams were driven from the colony, but our recollection may not include, because such stories are not good for children to hear, tales of Quakers, half-stripped, tied to carts, being beaten as they were dragged along town streets; and the hangings of persons convicted of being witches. Religion, in this case Puritanism, validated and sustained government, law, and social relationship: unless everyone embraced the same faith and assented to a uniform set of fundamental principles, good order and tranquility would vanish from the community. So religious dissent was prosecuted as if it were treason. We are told, though, that only evidence admissable "in ordinary civil and criminal cases" was used in these prosecutions.[36]

Convinced that men could do nothing by themselves—that everything was ordained by God's will—it followed that personal success came as a gift from God and was a sign of His approval. These religious convictions on "calling" and "election" were easy for Puritans to understand and translate: never harboring any doubt whatever, they used them to justify their repressive social system, and they used them, too, to discourage any democratic sentiments arising among the people. If most men were naturally evil, as doctrine said, they would almost certainly choose evil whenever choice was allowed. It was more than folly—it was sin—to encourage political freedom and permit a majority to control government. John Cotton spoke for the Puritan leaders of New England when he asked: "If the people be governors, who shall be governed?"[37]

In the last analysis, this social and political experiment subordinated to God's holy purpose could not be maintained in the fragile climate of early America. If we look closely enough and are careful to interpret what we find, it is clear that the first century of the Massachusetts colony's history was one of erosion of the idea of a holy commonwealth. At first, the leaders tried to retain all political power for themselves, and divine resolve, which they alone were authorized to translate, was sufficient to silence any doubters.

Despite the apparent strength of its credentials, this society began to disappear. Of course, every weapon at the leaders' command was used to halt the groundswell of reform. They tried, for example, to preserve the religious requirement for voting, but it was replaced, in 1691, by a property qualification. And they tried to keep the affairs of state insulated from the unconverted by writing a legal code allowing only persons with church membership to hold public office.[38] But this turned out to be a mistake: church membership was too hazardous an ordeal for the younger generation. Choosing to forego it, the children of saints forfeited their chance to become leaders in society. Even in purely religious matters, discipline and regularity were difficult to maintain. Congregations, probably imitating their Separatist neighbors, began to choose their own ministers, and some appeared eager to lay down their own rule on church government and religious principle.

These liberal, heterodox sentiments respecting the conduct of religion and politics might have been sufficient to undermine the foundations of so severely disciplined a society, but liberalism, as it turned out, was coupled in this assault on "a rule of faith" by a dispersion of the population from colonial centers to the frontiers. Away from the fountain of true belief, the decline in piety accelerated and resolution for church discipline weakened.

Conservative opinion on matters of religion and politics refused to capitulate, but to no avail. The opportunities vested in a growing economy boosted material above spiritual value. In this contest, the tradition of piety was almost certain to lose. Besides, perhaps tiring of their pretentious exclusiveness, church members started to remove obstacles to God's house, so persons whose salvation was doubtful and whose claim to sainthood was flawed became church members. Ministers, now, were usually more liberal than their people: "never narrow bigots, [they] were the leaders in every field of intellectual advance in New England in these years."[39] By the early decades of the eighteenth century, though, although religion remained prominent, the idea of Massachusetts as a theocratic society was fast losing appeal.

Sometimes described as "the lower-class wing of Puritanism," Separatism was the sectarian preference of farmers and workingmen. Opinionated, zealous, even bigoted on matters of religious belief, Separatists had neither the means nor the will to impose their creed on others or to promote it as the official religion of society. Inventing the practice of congregational control, they thought they belonged to a voluntary sectarian association and never interpreted their religious conviction as a charter for requiring conformity. As a matter of fact, their view enabled them to promote the doctrine of separation of church and state.

One party of Separatists came to America and founded Plymouth Colony in 1620. Doing so, their belief was introduced to the New World, but Plymouth was soon absorbed by Massachusetts. The early colony, therefore, had little influence on the culture of the colonies.

Yet despite Plymouth's lack of extensive cultural influence, Separatism took its place in generating religious diversity in America. Pursuing this idea, we look toward Roger Williams (1603?–1683). Williams, a Separatist in England, was accorded a cordial reception by the leaders of Massachusetts Bay when he landed in America.[40] But these leaders soon found their cordiality wasted on a man whose intuitions told him that the colony's policy of dictating religious belief and enforcing uniformity on all people was wrong. They scheduled Williams for deportation but, eluding the sentence by fleeing with his followers, he organized a colony in Rhode Island. Freedom of conscience was established as a fixed policy and, in consequence, Quakers, Baptists, even Jews, and other minority and oppressed sects flocked to the colony. Courageous and eloquent, Roger Williams, carrying on an extended controversy with John Cotton, proclaimed and condemned the persecutions of Massachusetts. His eloquence was wasted on Cotton though, because Cotton knew, as did all respectable people of the colonies bordering Rhode Island, that the colony "was a sinkhole of religious and social radicalism."[41]

Pennsylvania, founded in 1682 by William Penn (1644–1718), demonstrated the liberal influence of Quaker belief. In England most Quakers were either poor farmers or workingmen and their religious attitudes were rejected as foolish or radical. Radicalism was dangerous, so Quakers in England were persecuted, jailed or boycotted. When the chance for emigration was presented. Quakers by the thousands sought a religious haven in the New World.

Once here, remembering the lessons learned at home, they abandoned official and state-supported religion in favor of a policy, which they meant to implement, of complete religious toleration. In this respect they had Penn's complete support—some say, his visionary leadership—for the colonial grant authorized him to conduct colonial affairs according to his own will. Instead, he instituted a constitution and thus diminished his own authority. Of all the American colonies, Pennsylvania grew most rapidly in the eighteenth century, not only because of her fertile lands, but also because the colony welcomed and freely tolerated people of different nationality, religion, and opinion.[42] Although this point could be overstressed, Pennsylvania became a model to be emulated by freedom-loving men and women. As colonists settled and matured in their new land, they began, slowly at first and then with an accelerated pace, to master the lesson Pennsylvania taught through precept and example.

For all its prominence and justification, religion played a secondary role in the colonial history of New Netherland. More often than not the Dutch were Calvinists and, faithful to the Dutch Reformed Church, tried to hold their churches to true doctrine and maintain its teaching in the schools. They failed at both. With the advent of English control, the Anglican Church should have been established. But Anglicanism waited until 1693 to be pronounced the official creed, and then only in four counties.[43] Even then, New York's attitude toward religious establishment lacked rigorous enforcement, and other religious sects were common. Quakers, Anabaptists, Presbyterians, and Jews settled there, and by all accounts were treated with civility and dignity.

The Southern colonies, except for Maryland, were meant for Protestants, and in all (even Maryland after 1692) the Anglican Church was established by law. Yet, since the governments of these colonies were interested in a thriving economy and a population adequate to support it, they moderated their prescripts on religious conformity enough to attract a diversity of religious sects. When these sects came—Presbyterians, Baptists, Methodists, Lutherans, and others—colonial leaders neither intimidated them nor tried to convert their adherents to Anglicanism.

By now we know the colonists, as representatives of European culture, were supremely conscious of religion and were used to reducing all life's issues to a fundamental theology. Seeing them in this light, it is easier to understand how differences in religious belief infected their ideas about politics, law, property and social stability. The struggle for religious toleration, waged more vigorously in some colonies than others, was preliminary to a larger struggle relative to basic human and social issues that were resolved in post-colonial periods. This conflict over social philosophy ranged far beyond the colonies, of course, but by attending closely to its colonial religious dimension we shall find that sectarian diversity stimulated man's appetite for a political system committed to promote the common good. Despite the ugly apparition of discord and hate too often accompanying sectarian dispute, the impact of religious dissent on American colonial development was considerable and, in the end, positive.

SCHOOLS AND EDUCATION

In familiar colonial venture over various parts of the world, European pioneers were in the habit of elevating their quest for profit and power above their thirst for culture and learning as they undertook to establish outposts of civilization. So we are right to be surprised, and pleased, when we find our colonial ancestors demonstrating a commendable zeal for schools and education and coordinating it with an assault on the wilderness they discovered on America's shores. We are prepared, of course, for regional variation both in zeal for learning and in securing means for schooling, but nowhere was education so consistently neglected that barbarism was imminent. Beginning, as most Protestants did, with the basic assumption that scriptural reading and pious books were good for the soul, the colonists found ways to teach their children to read.[44]

But reading alone was not enough. The tradition persisted that schools existed to serve the church, and it was endorsed, even as the first colonies were planted in America, by Catholics and Protestants alike, so elementary schools were encouraged by religious leaders everywhere in Europe with the primary purpose of inculcating denominational belief among the people. Enlisted to supply the perennial need for religious leadership, vested in either ordained clergymen or literate and learned men capable of pronouncing true doctrine, were secondary schools and universities. Secondary schools, we know, always ranged beyond sectarian dogma, but dogmatic rectitude had pride of place in their syllabi; and the universities, although never narrow theological schools, allowed theology to occupy the center of the scholastic stage.

Nowhere in Europe was this attitude wedding schooling to religion stronger than in England; in its transplantation to the New World, neither its vigor nor virility perished. For the entire colonial period, then, religion supplied education with dynamic motive, and it told American Englishmen to lay a foundation for learning among their children. If they had neither the time nor the talent to help their children and apprentices with their first lessons, they hired teachers when they could. Orphans and poor children were a constant source of worry, and how to educate them always generated a good deal of talk. In New England towns educational means were secured early and, it appears, the children of rich and poor alike used them. In other colonies, however, especially Southern ones, schooling suffered from the disadvantages of geography and distance, and always lagged somewhat behind New England.[45]

If the solid English tradition cementing education to religion were not enough to convince the men of New England, especially those in Massachusetts, that schooling required their solicitous support, other justifications were easy to find. In a society where law regulated almost every side of life, where civil government enforced sectarian conviction, where political authority drove out heretics and punished the exploitation of pleasure, where colonial policy intimidated the press, regulated wages and working conditions and set the conventions of dress and manners,[46] it could easily mount educational provision and see to it that the discipline of learning contributed to every element in the established social order.

We should not be seduced into believing that New England's prompt attention to schools and the means for education was dictated from liberal motive. Curti is almost certainly correct when, in *The Social Ideas of American Educators,* he argues that education in New England, and elsewhere in the colonies, was intended primarily to serve the ends of institutionalized religion and a class-structured society.[47] If leaders were aware of an infant democratic tendency in the world, as they may have been, to a man they declared it anathema. Yet we credit them for adopting the principle that education is essential to good government and the prosperity of mankind. Putting it to work they created a legacy from which later generations of Americans profited. And now the pernicious contagion of class status, which for so long infected the rules governing church membership, was sterilized from education: schools of the colony were open to all children without reference to social standing. This fortuitous policy may have put in place the first foundations for offering equality of educational opportunity to all the children of all the people; but ministers and magistrates of Massachusetts, wanting less, used it to discipline youth in the fundamentals of civics and religion. Principle and policy, we know, outlived the men who presided at their birth and were both extended and interpreted in ways that they would have repudiated. Without lavish praise, we must nevertheless point to their exceptional, although unintentional, educational vision.

In any case, Massachusetts Bay Colony enacted a law demanding some learning among all inhabitants, but even before taking this bold step it encouraged voluntary, private schools of all kinds. From this encouragement the Boston Latin School came into being, possibly as early as 1635, although dependable records justifying this date are lacking. The exact date of the Boston Latin School's founding is of slight importance; what counts is its excellence from colonial to contemporary times. The Latin School, moreover, was accompanied by others: by 1647, Jernegan says, eleven New England towns had "voluntarily established, managed, and supported town schools."[48] In some places, such as Boston and Dedham, town land was granted to schools and used for endowment; in others, philanthropists donated real property whose income helped support schools. Since most of these voluntary schools enrolled students who had graduated from the reading lesson, tuition was charged.

But to return to school laws: it is hard to be certain just what selectmen in New England towns meant by free schools—and we should be slow to assign a contemporary meaning. But clearly the authors of the Massachusetts law of 1642 intended instruction in reading for every child in the colony. Whether children learned to read at home, in school, or elsewhere mattered little, but Morison, using evidence from Essex County, is convinced the law was enforced.[49] Puritans may have had about as much difficulty with the law of 1642 as we do, so they recommended its clarification in the act of 1647. This act, more specific in its provision for schooling, told towns what was expected of them. The Old Deluder Satan Act—the popular name for the law of 1647[50]—required towns with fifty householders to hire a schoolmaster capable of teaching reading and writing. Towns with one hundred families were to have a master able to prepare youth "as far as they may be fitted for the university."[51]

The record of town compliance with the 1647 statute is scant, and various legends surround it. The educational policy of New England, we know, was shaped by an educated "elect" and these colonial leaders may have had some difficulty convincing others, for whom schooling was less than a burning issue, to comply faithfully with the law. Here historians disagree: some say "the laws requiring the maintenance of schools were more honored in the breach than in the observance, while others hold that they were reasonably well enforced."[52] Town records themselves are not much help, and the testimony from private schools—the various Latin grammar schools that sprouted spontaneously—is somewhat beside the point. Yet from "fragmentary town and court records, it is clear that many of the New England towns before 1700 undertook seriously to maintain schools," although some were negligent and "exhibited great cleverness in evading the law."[53] In any case, the law of 1647, amended frequently in subsequent years, remained in force for decades, and during these years schooling and means for education flourished.

Traveling south from New England we discover Dutch policies on education that at first blush appear enthusiastic in their support of learning and schooling. Kilpatrick and others tell us how both religious belief and political conviction supplied cogent justification for education in Holland; they imply that this justification was transplanted to Dutch America.[54] "In New Netherland, as definitely as in Massachusetts, the obligation to provide schools rested upon" the colonial government,[55] but it was an obligation easily neglected or artfully evaded. In 1657, a group of New Amsterdam's religious ministers prepared a report complaining of the colony's indifference to learning and, reciting the names of a half-dozen of the larger towns, stated "that so far as we know, not one of these places, Dutch or English, has a schoolmaster."[56] In general, then, despite some cultivation, schooling in New Netherland withered; English rule, so the record confirms, added little to its virility.

In Pennsylvania, where from the first William Penn introduced progressive policies of religion and government, the stature of education was less imposing than, say, in New England. Knowing learning good for persons and necessary to the prevalence of a sound social order, Penn stressed schooling for character, for the development of personal virtue, and neglected its role in perpetuating religious orthodoxy and promoting intellectual erudition. Speaking of the formation of children as future citizens of the colony, he wanted to "depress vice, and cherish virtue, that through good education, they may become good."[57] To this end, the "Great Law," enacted almost at once, and codifying Penn's intentions on the matter, spoke of erecting public schools and of encouraging and rewarding authors of useful sciences and laudable inventions.[58] Penn's investment in education paid only modest dividends, but had this original investment been capitalized the story of education in the Quaker colony would have been different: public schools would have flourished and private and pauper schools would have died from neglect. Penn, however, allowed his courageous policy to decay and his successors, without his intrepid conviction relative to the good of the colony, allowed it to deteriorate even more. In consequence, what we are tempted to call public education lacked intensive cultivation in Pennsylvania during the colonial years, although private schools were found, sometimes in plentiful supply in Philadelphia and elsewhere, and steps were taken by the practical Quakers to ensure a general respect for the fundamentals of learning. Enough was done to ensure that "an illiterate Quaker child was rare" in colonial Pennsylvania.[59]

In the Southern colonies interest in education was evident and considerable effort was spent to open schools wherein the rudiments could be taught, but too often this effort was hard to mount and difficult to sustain. Favoring and abetting it was an English confidence in the worth of knowledge for its own sake and for its efficacy in promoting religious and social stability. Besides, the prominent men who came to the colonies of the South were themselves graduates of ornamental British schools and, constant in their determination to avoid literary bankruptcy for their own children, they made learning a personal investment. Yet they refused to encourage the state to undertake school support on any broad basis, and their sense of religious duty absolved them from stripping away their own wealth in order to educate the children of others. Exceptions to this generalization abound, of course, for philanthropy in Southern education is too obvious to ignore, but the principle to which most colonists assented made education a private matter. They were fond of quoting what sounded like sagacious educational advice: "Every man according to his own ability instructing his children."[60] Governor William Berkeley of Virginia is credited with giving this principle colonial currency.

The general course of education in the Southern colonies is fairly clear: it lacked both a political and an emotional drive to repeal England's social code. Most colonists lacked any disposition to reconstruct society or religion. For the great and wealthy, but for the rank and file as well, Anglicanism commanded their allegiance and they meant to observe its tenets in their churches and in their lives. Yet their religious temperament was moderate rather than fervent: it allowed them to distrust Puritans and despise Catholics without ever becoming zealots. In addition, it discouraged indifference to education and learning in general, yet the church was never meant to form a great alliance with schools.

Anglicans were solicitous of means to train clergymen and their sensitivity to altruism, although often tainted, was keen enough to subscribe to means for training and teaching poor, neglected, and orphan children. History tells us that the church itself as well as societies allied to Anglicanism—for example, the Society for the Propagation of the Gospel in Foreign Parts—were active in promoting scholastic philanthropy, but even these good examples were incapable of disguising the fact that the general obligation for the education of children rested squarely on parents and the home. If certitude about the validity of this obligation atrophied, the geography of the Southern colonies and their scattered population, recommended most likely by a plantation economy, would have suppressed any incentive to follow in the educational footsteps of New England by instituting a colonial system of schools.

Working our way through the colonial educational scene, we see evidence of disorganization and confusion; pockets of progress existed in New England and elsewhere, but there were also vast areas where learning struggled against high odds. Still, despite testimony to frequent failure, we must certify some devotion to education almost everywhere: this devotion immunized the colonies from literary bankruptcy and provided a foundation whereupon later generations could build. One element in this foundation was the colonial college.

Planning for lower schools, and Latin schools to preserve a classical legacy they valued, our ancestors were often uncertain about educational issues we now take for granted: control and support. In turning their attention to higher learning—the college—they were absolved from wrestling with these issues, for the college was a religious institute. Its first charge, to prepare ministers, made moot any substantial question of control. Apart from grants, gifts, or land endowments to get a college started, support was a private matter. With these issues at rest, colonial enthusiasts could employ all their ingenuity and energy in the erection of a religious citadel. "The University of Cambridge as they knew it . . . was the standard . . . [they] attempted, however imperfectly, to attain."[61] Instead, they founded what we at once recognize as the American college.[62]

LITERARY TASTE AND
INTELLECTUAL CHARACTER

We should begin by jettisoning the myth that our colonial forebears restricted their reading to dull theological tracts and then, after digesting their directions on pious demeanor, used this information in theological and sectarian dueling. At the same time, an old misconception about reading tastes in the colonies varying sharply from region to region should be corrected: reading habits of college graduates in New England and Virginia, for example, were about the same, once we notice "that early New England ministers practised medicine as well as religion"[63] and kept a plentiful supply of books on both. They consulted them more often than their Southern counterparts. The reading lists of common men are more difficult to plumb.

Regardless of ownership, colonial books were read because they were useful. Colonists heeded the motto that knowledge is meant to be used, a sign of Francis Bacon's influence, so they and their children used and read a variety of textbooks intended to keep alive the cultural inheritance: grammar, rhetoric, and logic—the subjects of the ancient trivium—were represented in standard books: Aldus' *Latin Grammar,* Cicero's *Ethics,* John Clarke's *Formal Orations,* Comenius' *Gate of Tongues Unlocked,* Thomas Draxe's *Collections of Latin Words and Phrases,* Erasmus' *Colloquia,* Thomas Farnaby's *Rhetoric,* Charles Hoole's *The Common Rudiments of Latin Grammar,* Lily's *A Short Introduction to Grammar,* and Eilhard Lubin's *Greek Grammar* are reported in Morison.[64] Besides, needing books illustrative of general knowledge, they put a good deal of value on dictionaries, almanacs and "just plain books."

Men of education and culture, themselves beneficiaries of the humanistic tradition, wanted to spend some time with Latin and Greek authors. If their Latin and Greek were rusty, they read English translations of the classics. But refusing to be mesmerized by the past, they read contemporary historians too.[65]

It would have been impossible for men whose dedication to religion was so profound to have neglected spiritual subjects. Their bookshelves must have been lined with such volumes. And they read them. Time left over for lighter reading was used by turning to books on manners and morals. John Winthrop, who had the colonies' best private library, owned a copy of Castiglione's *Book of the Courtier.* Such books portrayed "the ideal character to be achieved through education and [suggested] the kind of education required for that achievement."[66]

Evidence is ample "of widespread possession of books by the colonists, though small [personal] libraries were the rule." Under these circumstances, it was common enough for books to be borrowed and read and then returned to the owner, but eventually the idea was heralded that something more might be done to allow persons greater satisfaction for their reading taste. Slowly and erratically, we see public and subscription circulating libraries coming into existence. The most notorious of the latter, although by no means alone, was the one started in Philadelphia by Benjamin Franklin in 1731.[67] Franklin's library company and other literary societies occupying themselves with opening libraries were successful enough to boast collections superior to those of the colleges. The early college library was hardly a literary oasis though: "it was open for an hour a week and a fee was charged for each book withdrawn."[68]

As libraries prospered around the country, booksellers found business getting better too. Boston, by 1700, had at least seven booksellers,[69] New York four or five, and Philadelphia six or seven.[70] Although these figures hardly make us think a literary renaissance was about to burst, they indicate, along with other evidence, a vital and genuine interest in books. American colonists learned early and quickly of internal satisfaction and material reward from reading: neither a pedant nor a dilettante, the pragmatic colonist perceived utility either for his body or his soul from the books he read.

The books imported from Europe were the staples of reading and education, but shortly they were supplemented by the literary fare of colonial writers. Though the writing in the colonies "is important for a full understanding of the later thought and expression in America, its value as pure literature is relatively slight."[71] Conditions of colonial life, on one hand, and on the other a lack of incentive to create a literature rivaling what they had, intimidated genuine literary aspiration. During the first half century or so, colonial Englishmen wrote narrative accounts of their trials and successes in the New World: Captain John Smith of Virginia, William Bradford of Plymouth, and John Winthrop were the most prominent.

Religion, everywhere a matter for serious consideration, had its heralds too, beginning with Rev. Alexander Whitaker's *Good News from Virginia,* in 1613, and going on to include the following: Thomas Morton's satire, *The New English Canaan;* "the spirited argument for toleration, *The Bloody Tenent of Persecution,* by Roger Williams; and the quaint and intolerant *Simple Cobler of Aggawam* by Nathaniel Ward."[72] Poetry of the period was religious, too. "The most popular poem that New England has ever known" was the grim and realistic *The Day of Doom* by Michael Wigglesworth.[73] Edward Taylor of Massachusetts, scholars say now, was the colonies' best poet. Frequently forgotten, but not totally ignored, a few women made their mark as colonial writers: Mrs. Anne Bradstreet was a much admired poet; Mrs. Mary Rowlandson was "the author of the best narrative of Indian captivity," and Mrs. Sarah Kemble Knight, a Boston teacher, entertained her readers with lively accounts of travel in America.

Running its course, the seventeenth century became more hospitable to a native literature and more writers appeared; still, they kept close to traditional topics and wrote theological tracts, chronicles, and journals. The most industrious and, perhaps, the most articulate were Increase Mather (1639-1723) and Cotton Mather (1663-1728), father and son ministers in Boston. Cotton Mather's masterpiece was *Magnalia Christi Americana (The Ecclesiastical History of New England),* an ambitious attempt to show how the achievements of New England were due to God's favors, merited through adherence to the true faith by the founders of the colonies.[74] History writers often dealt with the Indians and Indian warfare, and here, in addition to Mary Rowlandson, Daniel Gookin and Benjamin Tompson are thought best. The clearest picture of life in New England in the years around 1700 is in "the diary of Judge Samuel Sewall of Boston, rivaling that of Pepys in its fullness and frankness."[75]

After 1700 literary activity in Southern and Middle colonies accelerated, with contemporary accounts of life in Virginia by Hugh Jones and Robert Beverley. William Byrd wrote his *History of the Dividing Line;* John Woolman of New Jersey spent a good part of his mature years writing the *Journal,* described as a beautiful account "written with appealing simplicity and the directness of a life without guile but with a consuming sympathy for the lowly and distressed;"[76] and, although toward the very end of the colonial period, Michael Guillaume Jean de Crèvecoeur, a French colonist in New York, paraded minute and curious observations of country life and nature in *Letters from an American Farmer.* A friend of both Franklin and Jefferson, he was also "the earliest writer to stress the 'melting pot' conception of the American race."[77] Finally, among those writers who found a literary outlet dealing with topics in a lighter vein, Thomas Godfrey was America's first dramatist of note: his "imitative tragedy, *The Prince of Parthia,* was staged at Philadelphia in 1767."[78]

Cultural advance in the colonies was slow but sure: newspapers and magazines, although erratic in publication and distribution, evidenced a quickening of interest in contemporary political issues. Besides, they cultivated literary culture by providing some outlet for writers. Although a majority of the population around 1700 was literate, a general system of schools existed only in New England. In other places, we know, religious schools, private venture, and home instruction had to be trusted. Travel, although possible mainly by boat and horseback, was on the increase; in the eighteenth century road and bridge building increased rapidly, usually as private persons detected the profit to be made from turnpikes. And the colonial colleges stood ready to give culture, although habitually a religious one, a helping hand. Harvard (1636), as every schoolboy knows, was first; and then came William and Mary (1692), Yale (1701), Pennsylvania (1740), Princeton (1746), Columbia (1754), Brown (1764), Rutgers (1766), and Dartmouth (1769).

Among the various men of intelligence, learning, and wit, the ones with the best credentials for molding a colonial mental temperament and outlook were Jonathan Edwards (1703-1758) and Benjamin Franklin (1706-1790). Both merit our brief, additional, attention.

Edwards, a native of Connecticut, educated at Yale, became the scholarly pastor of Northampton, Massachusetts, in 1736. Somewhat retiring and reflective, rarely mingling with his parishioners, he spent, his biographers say, thirteen hours a day studying and writing. Famous for his eloquent preaching, he became increasingly evangelistic and is said to have stimulated a religious revival which added to his parish "three hundred members in six months."[79] The spirit of Edwards' evangelism had a hot spark—on this point testimony is ample—but it burned too fast to last. So when the Northampton congregation tired of their minister's picture of hell, he left for another pastorate in the town of Stockbridge. There, almost in seclusion, although ministering to Indians and preaching in the local church, he laid the foundation for his fame and influence. Tireless in scholarship, he produced four notable books: *The Nature of True Virtue, The End for Which God Created the World, The Great Christian Doctrine of Original Sin Defended,* and the masterpiece, *The Freedom of the Will.* Recognized for intellectual leadership, Edwards was appointed president of Princeton College in 1757, but death limited his service to a brief three months.

Born in Boston, apprenticed to his printer brother at the age of twelve, Franklin had little chance for schooling, so reading his inventories of advice about self-made men we are sure he is recalling personal experience. At seventeen he left Boston for Philadelphia and shortly thereafter traveled to London, where he remained for two instructive years. Returning to Philadelphia in 1726, his unassisted rise was so rapid that by 1730 he was the sole owner of the *Philadelphia Gazette.*[80]

A man of many parts, Franklin managed two enviable achievements: a large fortune and a flawless reputation. In company with men confident in their talent and eloquence, he occupied himself writing the *Busy-Body* essays, *Poor Richard's Almanac*—widely quoted for its homely and pungent wisdom—and the *General Magazine and Historical Chronicle*. There were other books, including his *Autobiography,* for Franklin was a man of exceptional industry. Besides, he mounted various civic and cultural enterprises: the Junto, the circulating library, the American Philosophical Society, a city hospital, and the Academy of Philadelphia (a distinctive school, of which we shall hear more later), which ripened into the University of Pennsylvania. Aspiring to public office, he was, in turn, an assemblyman, a deputy postmaster for the colonies, and a diplomat. Leisure hours were spent on scientific study and invention. By 1748 he retired from business to devote attention to experiments with electricity, "for which he was elected a Fellow of the Royal Society."[81] Soon, however, public affairs consumed his attention and for the rest of his life he looked after them. Franklin took some part in every intellectual and social movement of his time, and with his talent, wit, prudence, and industry left a permanent imprint on life in America.

THE PRESS

When the first colonists sailed for America, newspapers in England were only in their infancy, so we must be careful in assigning the press a major role in shaping the culture of the colonies. Yet the press played a part in keeping alive a cultural legacy and holding before the public a standard of educational decency: this confident assertion is untroubled by the somewhat tardy advent of the first successful newspaper, the *Boston News-Letter,* started by John Campbell, Boston's postmaster, in 1704.[82] By then the foundations of social philosophy and theological principle were securely anchored, and only a press gifted with the eloquence of genius could have moved them. But philosophy and principle need elaboration in order to thrive and spread and elicit zeal and devotion. This was the press' original commission.

Newspapers and magazines found many ways to prime the pump for school and college. If we search through the archives, we can find colonial newspaper accounts of school prospectuses, of institutional facilities, of subjects taught, of the academic pedigrees of teachers and professors, and of dates for the opening and closing of school terms. Interest in learning, moreover, may have been given lively stimulation in stories newspapers told of colonial college commencement exercises—there was an abundance of things to write about, because these exercises often lasted three days— and accounts of student success in school debate, examination, exhibition, and dramatic performance. Students themselves must have been the principal beneficiaries here, but the public was edified by what it read and a general appetite for learning must have been whetted.

This, however, is the easy side of the story that tells of colonial newspapers and their compact with a dissemination of learning; the other side, far more complicated, took a long time to mature. To be an effective medium, the press needed freedom. During the colonial era in places where a Puritan oligarchy governed and even in so temperate a political zone as Philadelphia, the press lacked freedom. And its freedom was deferred until later years, when Americans, after tiring of their flirtation with censorship and after agonizing through several celebrated court cases (the most dramatic and perhaps the most precedential involved John Peter Zenger's *The New-York Weekly Journal*),[83] tilted to the side of an unfettered press. This attitude toward a free press, tested time and again during the War of Revolution, was translated into a guarantee of journalistic liberty whose permanence is attested in the First Amendment to the United States Constitution.

Increasing in number from one in 1704 to about fifty by 1776,[84] newspapers up and down the Atlantic coast waded deeply in the swirling, treacherous waters of pre-Revolutionary political debate. One mistake made by the British government, says David Ramsay, in his *History of the American Revolution,* was to subject newspapers to a heavy stamp duty. This was fortunate for the cause of liberty, "for Printers, when uninfluenced by government, have generally arranged themselves on the side of liberty, nor are they less remarkable for attention to the profits of their profession. A stamp duty, which openly invaded the first, and threatened a great diminution of the last, provoked their united zealous opposition."[85] Imposing a stamp tax on newspapers and legal documents aroused opposition from two articulate and influential professions: journalists and lawyers. "Only a tax on sermons," Good says, "would have been more ill-advised."[86]

Despite their number, colonial newspapers were destined to back seats on the bandwagon of influence so long as their circulation was curtailed by an inefficient postal system. Such a system actually antedated the appearance of newspapers, for as early as 1692 the British government instituted weekly postal service between Boston and New York. Later, other routes were opened, but roads were bad and this condition contributed directly to a notoriously slow service. In addition, it may have prompted that early alliance between postmasters and newspaper publishers: with the post office situated in the newspaper office, editors could discourage competition from other papers by giving efficient distribution to their own.

In 1707 a colonial postal service was made part of the British postal system and "American postmasters general were thereafter appointed by the Crown."[87] But this experiment failed, as had the one of 1692, and improvement was without promise—that is, until 1753, when Benjamin Franklin and William Hunter were appointed deputy postmasters general.[88] Almost at once the efficiency of the postal system improved and newspapers benefited therefrom. Along with an increase in press activity, improvement was noticeable in communication and travel. And this improvement, in the delivery of newspapers and letters and in means for travel from place to place, had the effect of unifying and strengthening the colonies. By 1763 the colonists were able to engage in general social intercourse and, in touch with Europe as well, were in many respects less remote from culture and civilization than some isolated countries of the Old World.[89]

CHAPTER THREE

The
Colonial
Family

The culture and civilization of colonial America originated in Europe, and to some extent, colonial culture was European culture all over again. Yet this easy assertion, while accurate enough, conceals the enormous struggle our colonial ancestors waged to preserve a legacy whose worth they cherished. Transplanting culture was done, as we have seen, but keeping it alive, making it part of the living language of life was always harder. The schools, we know, were not the only places where culture was preserved and cultivated.

Until the past decade or so, histories of education were disposed to stay close to schools and colleges—to look at cultural and educational evolution through the eyes of specialists—and thus ran the risk of distorting the picture of education and its compact with life in society. With so much of social life educational, one must avoid being swamped in detail; yet in the American colonies family organization, church service and devotion, and general community economic and political activity had educational consequences frequently superior in scope and force to those nurtured in isolated schools and colleges, and this fact was true especially as it pertained to schools making their appearance in the first colonial century.[1]

For as long as most men could remember, formal education had occupied a position of relative importance in cultural transmission, and for almost as long schools had been defined as literary agencies capable of handling the work of instruction. So one is not wrong in paying historical heed to schools and colleges and excavating from them academic provision for instructing youth in the colonial era, or in conducting a close inspection of schools and colleges to discover how they were outfitted for their mission of preparing succeeding generations for life in society. Still, despite the part schools played in this general commission to transmit culture, colonists were unhampered by an inordinately high confidence in schooling so characteristic of their nineteenth-century humanitarian successors. Instead, they regarded the school as an important institution capable of conducting some necessary instruction for life, but there was no intention —indeed, it would have been unthinkable for them—to commission the school with broad and exclusive educational and cultural responsibilities.[2]

The natural place for learning to begin was the home, where the family was the custodian of educational function; this practical, convenient, and often unavoidable approach to learning persisted for a long time. Under the careful tutelage of parents, older brothers and sisters, and sometimes servants, children were taught what they needed to know to fulfill their obligations in life and to prepare for eternity. They learned to work and how to help provide for themselves and their family; they learned about their religious creed and had their faith cultivated and reinforced in the everyday duties and devotions practiced in the family; and they learned something besides in an oral tradition kept alive in the family and community.[3] Finally, they consulted the few books kept and treasured by almost every family. Boys, and girls too, could be reasonably well-instructed without ever spending a day in school.[4] We should try to see how this extraordinary accomplishment was managed by our colonial forefathers.

TRADITIONS OF FAMILY LIFE

Ancient educational theory persisted in the belief that the years between infancy and adulthood represented an interlude where children, doing the best they could, were obliged to assume the abilities and values of mature men. The standard of accomplishment was always the standard of the adult world. Considering the rigid adherence of early centuries to ancient dogma, we are unsurprised to learn how this hoary tradition was honored on the level of theory until the age of the Renaissance, when a new attitude toward the childhood years was adopted.

Yet, we should remember that ancient educational theory was always suspect in the eyes of early Christians. They could trust their children to the Roman schoolmasters when they wanted them to have a literary education, but they refused to believe that they were thus relinquishing a broad educational responsibility. What really counted—Christian learning—was handled by the family and whenever anyone spoke of Christian education in the early days of the Christian era, he meant those family activities centering on the formation of religious and moral virtue. Puritans, then, were doing nothing more than keeping faith with an old standard—one squaring with their definition of an undefiled Christian spirit—when they made the education of children in the family an article of religious belief.

Their conviction found lavish justification in humanist theory, and this apparently progressive theory tended to embellish the Puritan educational code with an aura of respectability and modernity.

The humanist attitude, one recognizing youth's legitimate interests, needs, and capacities, was popularized by Leo Battista Alberti, who in 1431 published his *Trattato della Cura della Famiglia (On the Care of the Family).*[5] He approached the education of children through the family, and made family life, family interests, the continuity of the family, and its quest for standing and recognition the object of educational decency. Without suppressing legitimate personal aspirations, family members were encouraged to set the family's good as their goal in life, but family good could be interpreted with enough latitude for individual talent to seek its full realization. The more ornamental a person's abilities, the more fame and distinction accrued to a family reputation, and the special excellence of a family was the contribution it could make to society. In this way the old-fashioned conformity expected both of persons within a family and families themselves was repudiated.

More important, however, than any repudiation of conformity was the affirmation that the cultivation of children's abilities is accomplished best and most fully in the custody of the family. Besides, following the convictions of the humanists, value and character were education's chief outcomes and where, so the theory ran, could this be done better than in the breast of the family? Traditional public-man education, conventionally fulfilled by putting a boy in the charge of some prominent person outside the family, cherished since the days of Cicero, was rejected in Alberti's document. Yet Alberti's tract, consequential as it turned out to be, was not entirely original, for there were evidences in it of his indebtedness to the book by Xenophon (434?–355? B.C.), *Control of the Household and the Estate.* But where Alberti's work could draw on Xenophon, it could easily move beyond the exceptional conservatism of that Greek master. After all, Alberti writing for an entirely new age, recognized what he was doing. Still, he speaks of the preparation for the head of a family in much the same terms as his ancient predecessor used when speaking of the citizen, and his contemporaries used when they spoke of the scholar. The book is divided into four parts: the first part contains a discussion of "the duty of the elders towards the children and of the children towards their elders, and the principles of the proper upbringing of the young."[6] Part two is concerned with marriage, the basis of true affection, of the cultivation of conditions for family loyalty, unity and welfare. Part three is a disquisition on the management of family affairs and is clearly preoccupied with property and finance; part four advances a theory of inter-family relationships and, finally, the relationship of families to civil society. How many of Alberti's ideas remained alive in New England or the other colonies is conjectural, and one would be safe in assuming that few colonial fathers had any direct knowledge of his discourse. But Alberti did not have to be read to be followed, because what he had to say was already part of European and English tradition. Families were the core of society and the future of children along with the good of society were in their hands.[7]

The doctrine of Alberti had earlier reshaped some English customs relative to family care and the custody of children. But Britain, nevertheless, wanted to be true to her own tradition, so the embracing of Alberti's theories on familial education was always conditioned by English preconceptions about family life.[8]

The custom in sixteenth-century England was to send children away from home and thus in the custody of relatives, friends, or masters have them learn both manners and a trade. The obvious obligation of masters to attend to the learning of their apprentices included some literary instruction, and to ease the master's burden here guild schools were founded and maintained. In any case, there remained a marked preference for educating children outside the friendly surroundings of the home. And it seemed to matter little whether the children were from poor, middling, or wealthy homes; their preparation for life was somehow judged more efficacious if managed outside the family circle.[9]

The theory elaborated by Alberti and adapted to the religious conditions in England tended to modify these common preferences. While the sons of gentry often left home to broaden their vision and prepare for their role in life, they were expected to get their basic education at home; and the children from less favored families followed pretty much the same pattern. Now parents trying to educate their children themselves sought the help of other families and of masters to prepare them for life only as a last resort. This preference for family education became so strong that law was needed to correct abuse creeping into the system. The laws deserving special notice were the Statute of Artificers (1563) and the Poor Law of 1601.[10]

In 1536 Henry VIII issued a royal proclamation directing families to teach children to read and understand the catechism of the Church of England. Narrow as Henry's motive was—a determination to denude England of all vestiges of the Roman Church—his decree put the clergy on notice that they should lend families a helping hand by giving sermons on the techniques of religious instruction. This provision, though, was phrased in language of assistance: ministers were to help parents, not replace them, in the religious tuition of children. Once religion was accounted for, vocational training needed attention. Here, too, the family was expected to bear the major weight of duty but, as with religion, it could have some help. Children were apprenticed to masters or, in exceptional cases, sent to workhouses where, in addition to being sheltered and fed, they learned a trade.[11]

This extra-family dimension to education, always considered at best only a substitute for what a family should do, justified the laws of 1563 and 1601. Yet even these laws could not eliminate the confusion surrounding apprenticeship practices in sixteenth-century England: neither masters nor apprentices knew their rights—and rights were important to Englishmen—so regional and local interpretation fragmented the national picture. A household economy, moreover, appeased this confusion, perhaps made it inevitable, for with thousands of masters, each working at home or in a shop adjacent to his dwelling, highly personal practice intruded on guild customs. Apprentices were held from three to ten years, or sometimes until they were twenty-one. For how long should a boy "live with his master, even if his own home stood next door?"[12] The Statute of Artificers set the term at seven years.[13]

The act, moreover, without being specific, alluded to a master's responsibility to apprentices including both instruction and practice in craftsmanship and literacy. By now it was clear, accredited members of craft guilds needed some literary skill to manage their trade, promote their business, and keep their accounts.

Expectation for the good the Statute of Artificers would do ran beyond its actual accomplishment, and as it turned out, new social issues arose, mainly in connection with the prevalence of poverty, recommending additional legislation. The Poor Law of 1601 stood solidly on the foundation of the earlier statute in affirming apprenticeship arrangements, but it went beyond and superseded the older law to prescribe vocational training: everyone should have a trade, for personal productivity and skill would reduce both poverty and indigence. Children from families incapable of handling vocational training could be removed from the family at the instigation of magistrates, church wardens, or persons of quality in the community and placed in situations where a trade could be learned. Children of the poor, the destitute, and the impoverished could be apprenticed to private masters or public workhouses.[14] The law's principal intent, to reduce poverty by ensuring a trade for every person, was reinforced by the feature enjoining masters to teach apprentices the bare elements of literacy.[15]

This was a background of legislation familiar to the colonists and they were prepared to perpetuate it. Whether or not English law was formally enacted in the colonies is relatively unimportant; the tradition of economic-educational legislation was established and the colonies were ready to adhere to it.

Looking at this legislation we see signs of affinity to family education, and when we look at colonial accretions—for example, the Massachusetts law of 1642, the Connecticut law of 1650, New York's law of 1665, and the Plymouth law of 1671—we see even more clearly the place the family was expected to occupy in the education of colonial children.

CARE OF THE FAMILY

None of these colonial laws could have asked for even modest literary accomplishment in the absence of traditional assumption wherein families were counted capable of handling the basics of literary instruction. Read through contemporary lenses these early laws asked too much, but what they asked then, they were confident the colonial family could deliver. The role of the family in shaping and invigorating social goals was justified by Renaissance writers, of whom Alberti was only the most prominent, by English public and religious policy, and by the admonitions of Puritan preachers. These colonial statutes, then, represented by the most illustrative and best-known Massachusetts Bay Act of 1642, imposed obligations on colonial families that English families had been accustomed to for generations. Embracing these obligations, Puritans went on to make them articles of religious faith.

Puritan doctrine spoke directly to parents about their children. Doing so, it was hardly engaging in theological novelty, for Christians had always known their parental duties. The Puritan parent was to care for the material needs of his children. And as if natural and divine law were not convincing, colonial law added its sanction. A father who wasted time and neglected his children was hauled into court and sentenced to jail or the workhouse, and definition of neglect ranged from failing to feed and clothe children to leaving them unattended.[16] Parental responsibility continued for a long time. In their hearts parents may never actually have abandoned responsibility for their children, but so far as social and legal convention was concerned, parents were told to look after their children until they could manage their own affairs.

From the first years of life, probably until about age seven, children spent their time playing, without objection from anyone.[17] Life would become hard enough as years passed, so to hurry little children to its obligations or to impose its restrictions too severely were rejected. And no one praised or even thought about the developmental possibilities of play. Without being indulgent, parents were careful about their youngsters, knowing how menacing colonial conditions were to life and health. The years of infancy were years of ordeal: with the benefit of primitive medical technique or none at all, only sturdy children survived. Taking this ominous fact into account, families in every colony were large, for infant mortality was high. A child surviving the first year of life was accounted to have a better than even chance to live a full life. So after baptism—and among this early generation of Puritans infant baptism was unacceptable —bearing a name usually plucked directly from the Bible, little boys and girls amused themselves with toys. The family toy-box had a store of dolls, tops, and balls intended for use by all the family's children, so toys were handled with care and affection. They were meant to last. When children moved from the cradle and the hospitable environment of the house, they began, as befits children, to engage in games, inventing some to suit their fancy, imitating the games older children played, or, on occasion, consulting a popular little colonial book for information and direction about childhood amusement: *The Pretty Little Pocket Book.* Dozens of games were described in rhyme and the descriptions contained moral lessons as well.[18]

In New Netherland, children took to skating and coasting in the winter, but in New England these pastimes were frowned on, especially if pursued on Sunday. In the South, where custom was less rigorous, common English games were popular: marbles, cricket, peg top, hunting, and fishing, to name only a few. Some Indian games were learned, played, and enjoyed by colonial children, but they never became popular. For girls, the doll, and for boys, the jackknife, were the most common toys and the principal instruments of childhood pastime.

As children grew older time for play was reduced and they began to follow a regimen of work and learning to immunize them from the contamination of idleness. Morgan, the authority on the Puritan family, tells us how seriously parents interpreted a theology of work and how they complied with laws that defined idleness as not just a fault, but a serious misdemeanor.[19] No one, adult or child, wasted time with impunity.

Without any doubt, Puritan parents loved their children, and were as capable as anyone of tenderness toward them. As a matter of fact, they had a reputation, and were afraid they deserved it, of being too tender; so resorting to ancient custom (which must, in any case, have been considered the lesser of evils), they farmed out their children to friends, relatives, masters or others who were capable of teaching them and of imposing a more severe character to discipline.[20] We know in general how this was done, and need not stop here to examine the details, but this decision to send children away from home was a hard one, and some parents refused to make it. In any event, in the home or elsewhere, parents listened to a divine injunction telling them to provide for their children and prepare them for a calling.[21] "Calling" sounds like a religious vocation —an easy misinterpretation—but it was meant to account for any honest occupation which seemed to fit a child's talent. Samuel Willard told his congregation that "God doth never call any to service but he fits them for it, hence we have a rule to judge our calling."[22] This may have been good advice. It could have been followed with some boldness, for it contains the implication that ultimate responsibility can, in the end, be shifted to God.

Duties of parents show one side of the picture; the other side was the responsibility children had to parents: they were to honor and obey them. Here Puritan doctrine merits no special credit, for this decree came directly from the Ten Commandments. In Puritan custody, though, the obligation lasted for a long time, at least until a son or daughter married and was entirely independent.[23] Even then family ties were strong. We would be wrong to think that children were abnormally impatient to cut cords of filial duty. Still, neither religious faith nor the hospitality of a loving family was capable of delivering parents and children from a friction inherent in the exercise of parental discipline when a son or daughter has reached a level of maturity where independence of action is jealously prized. Puritan parents perceived the advantage of having outsiders discipline their children in manners and morals, and this seemed to be a justification for allowing older children to be apprenticed and, sometimes, educated outside the family circle.[24]

That parents might delegate the education of children was never taken as a warrant either for parental indifference or a child's total freedom of action. Law discouraged children from doing what parents opposed. Save for engagement and marriage contracts the evidence here is modest, although what Morgan has accumulated is good enough to convince us that children were required to submit to the direction of their parents.[25] Again, while the evidence is slender, there is no reason to believe that these generations of youth were eager to abandon the kind of reverence children owe their parents.

No doubt parents found their children responding better to parental guidance in later years if early education had been efficacious. And in this respect a practical education for life in society was undoubtedly important. Still, we must realize, however much stock Puritan parents put in economic and political assets, they were obliged to infuse their children with higher motives. Edmund Morgan catches the spirit of this mission and sums it up in a phrase which he uses as a title for a chapter: "The Education of a Saint."

The law of nature and of God stripped this commission of sentiment, for parents knew their own spiritual reward as well as that of their children was at stake in this matter of education. "Every grace," Cotton Mather told his readers, "enters into the soul through the understanding" (a mental faculty), so grace without knowledge was extremely unlikely.[26] When such interpretations of doctrine were taken at face value, as generally they were, no parent could afford to neglect the instruction of children.

The ultimate educational goal was salvation;[27] an intermediate goal was cultivation of religious and moral virtue in preparation for church membership.[28] And in this case knowledge, while unable to guarantee an inculcation of virtue and eternal salvation, was an essential condition. So an important part of instruction was devoted to reading. A tradition of long and honorable standing, authenticated even by Francis Bacon, to whom the colonists paid close heed on educational issues, made reading the gateway to learning. What was read, though, Puritans knew, had to be good for the soul.

Reading had a cultural side, one known and prized by most Puritans, but they reserved their best recommendation for reading able to contribute directly to religious welfare. Eight laws of Massachusetts Bay passed between 1646 and 1769 called for education and five of them stressed "book education." Families, the laws said, were to teach or to get others to teach their children and apprentices "so much learning as may instruct them perfectly to read the English tongue, and knowledge of the capital laws."[29] Besides, these laws stipulated direct teaching of the catechism, usually without books, and provided for tests to see to it that children had mastered the elements of their faith.[30] We know almost nothing about the regularity or the severity of these tests, yet parents, masters, and selectmen were charged with giving them.

KNOWLEDGE AND DISCIPLINE

Can training, knowledge, and education correct the weaknesses of nature? Puritans may not have asked the question in exactly this way, but they were sensitive to the nature/nurture issue nevertheless and, as they pondered it, it took on a dimension which had never bothered the older educational theorists much. Turning back the calendar of educational history, at least as far as Quintilian, we know how much confidence was put in a student's natural ability. It was supposed, of course, that good care and excellent instruction could capitalize nature's assets and, possibly, repair its liabilities. Quintilian, for example, thought the faculties of imagination, memory, and sense perception could be improved by prudent cultivation at the hands of a good teacher.

There are faint but persistent signs that Quintilian's code on the education of a citizen remained alive in the European teaching tradition, and time after time those signs surfaced in the colonial world. But Quintilian looked only to natural virtue in the cultivation of talent and thought only of preparing a person to live well in this world. The Puritan's task was somewhat greater: he knew that human nature was wounded by original sin and he was disposed to believe that unless this wound were healed by the gift of grace it would be fatal. Grace, we have noticed, was shrouded in mystery, but just enough illumination came from parsons and pedagogues to make the rank and file believe that a proper cultivation of natural talent and disposition might attract grace and give it a fertile soil wherein to grow. If this were to happen, the person on whom grace was bestowed could aspire to an eternal reward. On his way to heaven he should try, of course, to be a good citizen.

Honoring the ancient watchword, "to make haste slowly," parents never swallowed the myth that either learning or discipline was easily mastered: they knew their work as teachers and their children's work as students would be slow, cumbersome, and frequently arduous. To complicate the matter even more, they knew that part of their task was to transmit the discipline of learning how to learn, learning how to be constant, and learning how to be a devout son or daughter of the Lord. It is easy for us to understand how they must have felt like shirking their assignment at times, because even in the best of homes the natural inadequacies of family education were too clear to miss. Besides, being for the most part simple folk, their knowledge of pedagogy was almost totally deficient. In the end, they depended on intuition and a general direction from their religious faith to pass on to youth necessary information and skill (primarily reading) and a personal piety generated in the bosom of a solid Christian home.

Almost inevitably they resorted to the simple and direct pedagogies associated with drill, repetition, and stimulation. Drill, they sensed, reinforced instruction. There is plenty of evidence of drill, both as parents quizzed their children on the catechism lesson and as they drummed into them the principal points of the preacher's sermon. On this last point, our sources tell us, it was a father's duty to spend most of Sunday evening reviewing the sermon with the full complement of his household.[31] Stimulation toward knowledge and virtue came more from example than from precept: eloquence here was vested in the way members of the Puritan family lived their lives. Being naturally imitative, children would follow in the virtuous footsteps of their parents.

It was good to be clever and Puritan parents could take as much pride in the accomplishments of their children as anyone else. An unblemished character, however, was better than erudition, so parents constantly had to watch for bad habits among their children. If a bad habit was detected, it should be corrected at once. The principle followed now was that a bad habit breaks easier than it bends, and the breaking should be done the sooner the better, "so strong is custom formed in early years." This shaping of character and the superintendence of habit recommended repeated admonition. Parents were told to speak of good things to their children, and we suppose they did. But they were told, too, that boys and girls, afflicted with the pride and wildness of original sin, sometimes needed more than kind words and good example. Parents were supposed to be stern and severe, and the literature is full of advice along these lines, but in actual fact they tried to be as temperate as possible in the administration of discipline. They had almost unlimited authority to govern their children and chastise them with intensity. But their good intuitions and their Christian faith told them that beating, pain, and fear breed shame, and shame unnerves and depresses the mind and turns the will away from the good to which it should be attracted.

A literature on child care, ranging from Wadsworth's *Well-Ordered Family*[32] to Cotton Mather's *Cares About the Nurseries*,[33] was extant in the colonies, but for most families it was out of reach. They had to depend on an inherited tradition to guide them. Yet this literature, when available, reminded them of their duties, gave them some direction on how to fulfill them, and in addition contained inventories of advice on how to discipline youth. If, at times, they felt forlorn and were ready to despair of the heavy obligation placed on their shoulders, they were reprieved slightly by the appearance of the colonial school.

These schools were commissioned to handle secular knowledge. Everyone knew the family was the place for Christian education, and few had confidence in the school's ability to meld the secular and the divine and thus help the family much. Yet, even with its secular standing fairly clear, the school cast its shadow over religious teaching. Its work centered on teaching the tools of learning, those noble auxiliaries enabling students to grasp spiritual meaning and find intellectual maturity. While this commission was clear enough to keep any schoolmaster from intruding too far into the educational work of the family, it was also true that the materials for school instruction—perhaps the best of all examples was *The New-England Primer*[34] —were thoroughly religious in tone and content. No instructional opportunity was overlooked to consolidate religious feeling and belief. It is hard for us today to distinguish these early schoolbooks from catechisms, and some New England Puritans may not have tried. In 1650, Richard Mather, better known for his polemical writing, published a book with the short title of *A Catechism* (the full title comes close to being a preface). In any case, Richard Mather is said to have boasted that this catechism was so well constructed that Luther would not have been ashamed to learn from it. Mather's *Catechism* found its way to the schools.

The New-England Primer   Despite some competition from other books, *The New-England Primer*—never, strictly speaking, a catechism—had an unquestioned influence on the lives of the people from the late seventeenth century on. The first edition appeared sometime between 1687 and 1690 and met with almost immediate success.

Beginning with the alphabet, it moved on to various arrangements of letters in order to distinguish clearly between consonants and vowels, double letters, italic and capital letters. Then followed the *syllabarium* with all kinds of combinations: ab, eb, ib, ob, ub, etc. Next came exercises in forming words, beginning with words of one syllable and working up to words of five or six. In some editions, we are told,[35] in order to save space the polysyllabic section was omitted. The section devoted to the formation of words was followed in most editions by what was called "An Alphabet of Lessons for Youth." This alphabet was hardly more than sets of moralisms taken from the Bible and arranged in an order that each new paragraph began with a successive letter of the alphabet. An example or two may help here: "*A* wise Son makes a glad Father, but a foolish

Son is the heaviness of his mother. *B*etter is a little with the fear of the Lord, than great treasure and trouble therewith." Apparently the editor felt compelled to make an exception in rendering the letter *X*. The paragraph reads: "e*X*hort one another daily while it is called today, lest any of you be hardened through the deceitfulness of sin."[36]

The best known feature of the *Primer,* though, was not the alphabet, the syllabaries, or the lessons for youth, or even "A Dialogue between Christ, Youth and the Devil" (appended in some editions), but the alphabetical rhymes with sketches that began in this way;

> "In Adam's fall
> We sinned all.
> Thy life to mend.
> This book attend."[37]

The Lord's Prayer and the Apostles' Creed were always part of the *Primer* and were variously placed in the book according to the edition (ordering the text may have been a matter of experiment). Finally, the *Primer* contained either the catechism of John Cotton—*Spiritual Milke for New England Babes*—or the Westminster *Short Catechism,* or both. This *Primer,* whether counted a schoolbook or a catechism, became highly popular in the colonies. Making what he calls a conservative estimate, Ford says that it averaged an annual sale of twenty thousand copies for a century and a half, or a total sale of about three million copies.[38] He goes on to assert that "it taught millions to read, and not one to sin."[39]

Most instruction of the type represented in the *Primer* took place on the elementary level, where a majority of students obtained all the formal instruction they would ever get. When more advanced learning was recommended, either because of a student's ability or the family's social station, a boy entered the grammar school, "in that day a school for beginners in Latin."[40] By careful and artful selection when teachers were good, or by crude rule-of-thumb methods in other instances, the books used were decontaminated of the dangers supposedly lurking in them. In any case, however important the classics were, they were always regarded as instruments for supplementing and bolstering denominational belief.

Lawrence Cremin tells us a great deal about the composition of colonial families and how they tried to imitate the family customs of England.[41] Poorer families had small homes, often only a room or two; in these homes they did everything associated with family life. The home was a place to live and work, there is no doubt about that; it was also a place to learn, and the universal principle of family pedagogy was the ancient one of learning by doing. In wealthy families, or in families trying to practice a specialized craft, cooperative effort could be added to learning by doing. The larger the family the more likely were the chances for exploiting special talent, so some division of labor could be arranged according to ability, age, and sex.

Despite differences in wealth and social position, or geographic region, the fundamentals of literary and religious education were handled in much the same way. English life was a model, of course, but English practices could not always be imitated in America. Prosperous families as well as their more humble neighbors were responsible for the education and upbringing of their children. "The Bible was treasured in nearly every home where, usually, no other book was found,"[42] and they used it, along with other books when they had them, to instruct their children in reading.[43]

Colonists were heir to a tradition wedding literacy, religion, and citizenship; besides, it had long been customary for skill in reading to precede attendance in school. Schoolmasters in England and in colonial town schools were used to assuming that their students could read the vernacular, and they based their syllabi on this assumption. Perhaps the English family had a broader array of reading materials on which to base its instruction; in any case, it could depend on a richer culture and an urban society for justifying reading and motivating boys and girls to master the skill. Whatever their advantages, English families could hardly have taken their teaching responsibilities more seriously than their colonial brothers. So, as we have said, using what was available the colonial family undertook to fulfill its pedagogic duty.

For decades schoolmasters in Europe had been repeating with undisguised approval the policy John of Salisbury lay down in his *Metalogicon:* "Little is concealed from the man who reads much." English kings and prelates had supported the same sentiment, so there is no doubt whatever that the common man of the seventeenth century took these assertions at face value. Yet reading to mine the treasures of secular knowledge was one thing; reading to understand God's word, and thus be better able to follow it, was quite another. So reading, in addition to being an important and useful secular skill, was a religious instrument as well. English and colonial religious sensitivities were keen enough to recommend reading without any reservation.

Under the circumstances, with so much religious motivation to spur them on, children turned first to the Bible and the simple catechism. Learning to read they used materials with which they were already familiar, for the books they used for their reading lessons were the books that contained the conventional religious wisdom of the day and formed the fiber of the colonial family's intellectual life. We must remember, too, the Protestant principle of personal interpretation of scripture and the doctrine that faith alone is necessary to salvation. All persons needed reading in order to cast scriptural meaning. If it is overstating the case for personal interpretation of the Bible to maintain that the operation of this principle vulgarized theology, it is not an exaggeration to say that reading had an absolutely unassailable justification. Colonists along with their European confreres generally put behind them the doubts and recriminations secular (classical) reading was surrounded by in earlier times. Worry may indeed have been superfluous, because the reading exercises of these simple pedagogies never proceeded far enough to endanger faith.

. England had several books for the elementary teaching of reading, but for the most part they stayed on their own side of the Atlantic. Edmund Coote's *The English Schoole-Maister* (1596) was an exception. This little book was written for family use and required no special skill in teaching.[44] Anyone who could read could use Coote's book for teaching others to read. It began with letters and, employing only recognition of literary elements, went on to syllables, words, and sentences. An estimate of this book's colonial popularity turns out to be nothing more than a guess. In any event, it seems never to have dominated the field. Hornbooks, primers, catechisms and other widely assorted materials were used more extensively. Of the native catechisms, the best known and possibly the most widely used was John Cotton's, the one with the extraordinary title: *Spiritual Milke for New England Babes.* However, Cotton's catechism had to wait for incorporation with *The New-England Primer* in 1690 before gaining notoriety.[45] Other books that found their way to the family's thin and primitive reading list, where they were regarded as "authoritative guides to Christian life" were: *The Book of Martyrs, The Practice of Pietie, The Whole Duty of Man, The Poor Man's Family Book,* and *The Pilgrim's Progress.*[46]

These, and other books whose titles are unrecorded or lost, were used in colonial households; readers read and reread them; children and nonreaders listened and learned; everyone memorized generous portions of this piety literature whose precepts, it seems, had a lasting effect.[47]

THE EARLY SCHOOL

We should pause for a moment to consider what would happen to instruction in the family unable to fulfill the most modest literary expectation. Our sources allow us to believe that wholly illiterate families were rare, but we know enough about the prevalence of literacy in colonial America to realize it lacked universality. When instruction in the most basic elements of literacy was unavailable in the home, help could be obtained elsewhere—in the dame school in New England, in the petty school in Virginia and other Southern colonies, or from a tutor whose services could be hired—but the family retained without delegation its obligation to piety and civility instruction. Reading was an important skill, the testimony is both ample and convincing on that, but it was a skill capable of being taught outside the home without destroying the integrity of household education. Manners and morals, however, were too important a part of education to be delegated to the woman who kept the dame school or, for that matter, to the master managing the episode of learning in the petty school.

While both dame and petty schools have had their influence inflated in many accounts of colonial education, because even in their best days these schools were always subordinated to the family, they were nevertheless important enough to the continuing current of colonial education to merit brief description now.

A dame school, sometimes called a kitchen school, was kept by a lady in her home, often teaching children from other families along with her own. In extending the boundaries of strict household education, she could make her teaching service available for a modest charge, or for nothing at all, to all the children of the neighborhood, or she could limit enrollment by taking only the children of her friends. Under any circumstance, it is hard to see the dame school as a regular and systematic form of colonial instruction. House dames capable of teaching reading used whatever materials of instruction they had and exercised any pedagogic ingenuity they possessed to do what other families, for any variety of reasons, could not do for themselves. These schools, modest as they were, were unquestionably useful, but their work was also sporadic and erratic and no one should claim that they had anything to do with a colonial revival of learning.

What has been said about dame schools applies to petty schools as well. The location of course is changed, for petty schools belonged in the Southern colonies, and the teacher of the petty school instead of being a housewife was usually a male servant. His teaching, in many respects similar to that of the dame, was usually restricted to reading. Although exceptions to the general objective of these schools were rare, they occurred often enough to allow us to say that some petty schools taught boys simple crafts and some dame schools taught girls sewing and cooking in addition to reading. Even at their best, however, these schools were never anticipatory of a system of elementary schools, and their teachers did not form the vanguard for a professional class of colonial schoolmasters.[48]

OTHER EDUCATIONAL RESOURCES

Part of home education was accounted for by reading instruction, but in spite of its undoubted importance, more than reading was needed if children were to be prepared for life. Piety and civility—complete codes of manners and morals—were part of the syllabus of learning as well. And there was more: boys and girls were expected to have practical art, so we should not miss the utilitarian and the vocational side of family education. Both law and tradition recommended the training of children "in some honest lawful calling, labor or employment," and where was this admonition to be honored if not in the household?[49]

We have a clear historical picture of boys being taught to manage the affairs of the home, the farm, and the shop. We see them learning trades too, either from their fathers or from masters, and we see girls being schooled in the household arts. Clever and intelligent boys who aspired to the higher professions left home to attend schools and colleges, and when they did it was assumed that parental authority followed them. Every colonial schoolmaster in the grammar schools and colleges accepted and understood the doctrine of *in loco parentis.*[50]

Except for the learned professions the economic education of colonial youth and the pedagogy accompanying it were practical and direct and almost never affected by a literary side. Boys learned a trade by observation and practice; theory was held to a minimum and we look in vain for a literature elaborating it.

Although books on the vocations were absent, we know colonial homes were not literary deserts. In addition to family resources for education and training, there were community resources, and here New England, because of its geography, enjoyed some advantage over the other colonies. Determined to use every means available to encourage culture and civility, parents prompted their children to attend to lessons friends and neighbors were willing to teach by informal contact and ordinary conversation. A consciousness of the value of community teaching was apparent in the colonies, although effort to capitalize it was curtailed in some places by geography, distance, and community organization itself.

Families, we have repeated, took their educational duty seriously, so seriously that one surely robs them of their true character if he is blind to their commitment to shape the religious, moral, and intellectual lives of their children. Yet, for all the attention families gave their members and the almost constant care visited on the manners and morals of children, there were other educational influences whose effects could neither be ignored nor rejected.

Some colonists, having made the long hard trip to America, preferred to remain in familiar surroundings, perfectly content in the settlements that slowly began to assume many features of civilized life. Others, however, were restless, always curious about the country lying beyond the borders of the first settlements; and still others, who found the means, returned to Europe to visit. These colonial travelers and adventurers proved to be reservoirs of information, and returning to more settled regions they shared their experiences with old and young alike. New ideas, different ways of thinking and acting entered the colonial community in a number of ways, but one way, we should not miss, was this intercourse between travelers and those who remained behind. It was a kind of education books could not supply. Then, too, the common portrait of colonial deportment, especially of Puritans, is too heavily drawn and is far too bleak, for they were quite ready to have fun, and in their fun a tempered zest for life was capable of broadening experience. "There was much opportunity for love and laughter in colonial New England, though not as much as there should have been;"[51] and in the colonies south of New England, where personal conduct was less carefully prescribed and scrutinized, leisure activity proved to be a fairly useful textbook.[52]

Companions for boys and girls were as evident in colonial days as they are now, perhaps more so, because relatives tended to live so much closer; so cousins, relatives of a lesser degree, neighbors, and from time to time the itinerant traveler, the wandering schoolmaster, and the single man brought novel ideals and manners to the community. These outsiders sometimes carried newspapers, magazines, and books. Their stories and the information they had of distant places and persons tended to fill out a colonial syllabus of informal education that from our distance in time and custom sometimes gives the impression of a precarious thinness. If elements of enrichment were masked, they were nevertheless there.

THE CHURCH AS TEACHER

The colonists generally, and Puritans especially, while they could see and appreciate informal educational prospects around them, were unwilling to leave too much to chance. If the family needed educational help, it could have it, and the church was both ready and able to lend a hand. Ministers, in fact, came to regard themselves as the appointed guardians of educational matters and the custodians of educational policy. They resented and sometimes actively opposed any intrusion on their self-proclaimed domain by magistrates or other laymen.

If families lost confidence in their ability to superintend education, it was natural for them to turn to the church. As we have said, ministers were quick to accommodate them. Now we must be prepared for anomaly because, despite the clarity of the doctrine that church membership was restricted to saints, with the services of the church and its ministers primarily for their benefit, ministers spent a great deal of time on the religious teaching of children. Children, we know, before formal conversion were outside the fold of church membership. Yet preachers gave sermons telling parents how to teach and discipline their children; doctrine spelled out in fine detail the duty of parents to them; "No one could be spared the exertion; the meanest believer must learn to give the grounds for his belief."[53]

We know that ministers undertook to measure the depth of religious knowledge among the children of the colony, but they did not restrict themselves to testing the grasp of true doctrine among the little ones: they used their sermons and their lectures to instruct them. Even here the minister's allegiance to the task of spreading doctrine did not cease, for conversion was a mysterious adventure which could always be helped along by some prompting—even when it was an accepted conviction that personal will had nothing whatever to do with a flowering of grace—and ministers were obliged to give whatever help they could. Indians, servants and all others outside the walls of religious faith were the objects of ministerial energy and Puritan literary talent. Far more than their European counterparts, New England Puritans became expert in phenomena of religious conversion.[54] Save for their extraordinary preoccupation with the experience of conversion, New England ministers displayed an interest in the religious education of children which makes us think that the informed mind was indeed a fertile place for faith to thrive. This interest, our sources tell us, was common among all colonial denominations. But in many places, especially in the colonies south of New England, this interest was not cultivated because ministers were few in number, churches were often poorly supported (despite the practice of giving them funds from the public treasury), and settlements and persons were scattered over areas so vast that ministers, assuming their zeal to do so, were simply unable to maintain the necessary contact with people who shared their faith.

Assuming that the policy of church support was fulfilled in practice (with every householder, irrespective of church membership, contributing his share) the Puritan churches of New England were far better off than their colonial counterparts and were able to afford a full complement of church officers. Such churches had two ministers—a preacher and a teacher. The former's principal responsibility was exhortation and inspiration; the latter's commission was to teach true doctrine.[55] It was the latter, then, the minister-teacher, who catechized children and generally supervised their religious upbringing.

The medium employed for elevating both intellect and will and bringing them into proper harmony with faith was the sermon. Hour upon hour were spent in preparing sermons, making them sound both in faith and learning, and putting them in a rhetorical form where their appeal to literary taste would be pleasant and their impact on the mind persuasive. Here, of course, theological scholarship and a command of liberal art were of immense worth. And when we recognize that the Puritan congregation was usually privileged to hear three sermons a week—two on Sunday (morning and afternoon) and one on Thursday evening—we can understand why ministers wanted to tend carefully to their preparation.[56] Sermons were neither extemporaneous discourses, helped along by an occasional note, nor written treatises read to congregations, but studied and intricate lectures, first cast, then revised, and finally delivered from memory. After delivery to a congregation, the sermons of more prominent ministers usually found their way to print and became part of the colonial religious legacy.[57]

These sermons, long by any contemporary standard, usually took about two hours, and save for the one given Sunday morning which was almost totally theological in content, ranged over a variety of topics and tried to touch the burning political, economic, social, and moral issues of the day. Their tone and perspective were moral and religious, of course, but they were in fact more lectures than sermons, so they belong as much to a colonial teaching tradition as they do to denominational doctrine and discipline. Religion was a vital social and political force in colonial America; as often as not the minister's learning and personality were critical factors in the direction society took; and religion must be seen as an active educational instrument in all of colonial America. Standing alongside the family, the church was always prepared to illuminate and supervise the instruction and discipline of children which reason, tradition, and faith told colonial families was their principal duty.

CHAPTER FOUR

The Growth
of
Colonial Schools

Transplanting social institutions from one part of the world to another may appear effortless in historical perspective, although in this case appearances are deceptive. Social traditions and institutions having met the test of persistence and use were carried to the colonies as a perishable human inheritance, and it was important, if these traditions and institutions were to survive in a new climate, to adapt them to the conditions of the colonial world. Knowing, as we do, the religious temperaments of colonial people, and sensing also their implicit faith in the worth of education for substantiating religious belief, we are prepared to find them searching for practical ways to satisfy their objectives concerning religious education.

We must recognize at the outset, even in colonies where social homogeneity was common (New England is the best illustration of all), the variety of theories elaborating the relationship between government and religion, religion and education, and government and education. There were, moreover, various ways of interpreting educational purpose and this variety was reflected in schools opened within a colony and, possibly more clearly, among schools established in different sections of the colonies. Regional experience coupled with regional religious convictions and predispositions inevitably intruded on this definition of educational purpose and practice.[1]

At this point in our study we should pay attention to educational justification, to the philosophies of education underlying the establishment or suppression of schools, or the encouragement of or indifference to learning. And if, indeed, schools were founded, we must pay attention to who their clientele was. Clearly, both religion and educational theory had important parts to play in determining the nature of the school's curriculum and the academic purpose it should honor.

In the colonies, organized religion often stood as government's partner, sometimes as a senior partner. So whether acting on its own authority or merely as an agent of the church, we want to see the direction government began to take with respect to education, and the action colonial governments generated either to encourage or require the creation of opportunities for schooling. Reciting motives for encouraging education in the colonies is easy enough, although explaining them takes some time. They were lodged in religious, educational, social, political, and economic theory.

RELIGIOUS INFLUENCE

The wedding of religion and education in the early Christian period was presided over by Cassiodorus (480-575). The prescription telling how education could best help religion was contained in Cassiodorus' *An Introduction to Divine and Human Readings*.[2] If we recall how the schools of Rome were dependent on the state, we understand the fundamental reasons for the decline of learning beginning in the early sixth century. For centuries Christians were content to use the Roman (pagan) schools, because they needed the knowledge and skill they taught, and eschewed organizing a system of authentic schools of their own. Now with the Roman schools all but gone, due to internal social decay and external military force, Christian educational leaders were disposed to fill the scholastic vacuum. Cassiodorus entered the picture, advancing the famous thesis wherein the seven arts (grammar, rhetoric, logic, arithmetic, geometry, music, and astronomy) were useful to Christians and should be studied as instruments for mastering divine knowledge. They were to be studied along ancient lines, generally according to the order recommended by the great Quintilian (A.D. 35-97), but the goal of study should be Christian utility rather than ornamental oratory. Within this limit, Cassiodorus assured his confreres, liberal art was uncontaminating. Used but unloved its value could be demonstrated on a purely practical level.

While the spirit of Cassiodorus' formula was followed until the Classic Renaissance, one must allow for both tumult and progress on all levels of schooling in the long years intervening between the sixth and the fourteenth centuries. Space is lacking here for a detailed analysis of the maturing traditions as education evolved in history, but medieval education—always highly intellectual—encouraged the development of a trained reason, while at the same time restraining reason to a handmaiden role: reason should explain the world represented in revelation. It was possible, according to medieval educational theory, to maintain a distinction between reason and revelation without destroying either. Practicing this formula medieval learning erected great scholastic monuments.[3]

The theory sustaining medieval education directed the mainstream of policy, but there were always tributaries of dissent. On one side, the classical purists remembered the educational heritage of Rome and retained brief glimpses of the philosophy of education Quintilian expounded in his unexcelled *Education of an Orator,*[4] and were ready to embrace reason unencumbered by any limits revelation might set. Yet at the opposite extreme stood the followers of the doctrine of piety, who regularly dismissed reason as unnecessary and dangerous for persons committed to the Christian life. They refused to submit God's word as found in scripture to the arbitrament of reason. The doubts of this camp were kindled by the audacious promises the great dialectician, Pierre Abélard (1079–1142), was prone to make for reason's powers. Abélard's work of glorifying reason without diminishing the significance of revelation—and Abélard was almost certainly a sincere Christian—forms a watershed separating the ages of discovery (the Carolingian period, 800–950) and assimilation of classical material (the pre-Scholastic period, 950–1200), from the age of organization and selection of the classical legacy (the Scholastic period, 1200–1350). Thus toward the close of the medieval period Scholasticism, essaying to make clear its allegiance to Christian education, undertook to organize all knowledge (including classical knowledge) compatible with a theological interpretation of the world, and to discard from the corpus of secular learning those parts incapable of being harmonized with a fundamental view of Christian life.[5]

At this point—the end of the medieval period (around 1450)—a new intellectual force appeared in Europe to alter greatly the face of learning: the Classic Renaissance. The Renaissance should be distinguished from the medieval period mainly by its use of classical materials, for highly uncertain ground is trod when one alleges that the principal reward from Humanism was lodged in a discovery of literary monuments previously unknown. Medievalists used the classics first to master the liberal disciplines and then returned to them with scholarly intention to embellish the great specialties of law, medicine, and theology; Humanists studied the classics searching for the finest illustrations of men capable of living full and satisfying lives. A medieval student read the classics looking for evidence to support faith; the Humanist studied the classics to form his style and shape his character. Humanism was capable of intellectual arrogance and anti-Christian disposition, although both were masked by the fundamental Christian temper of the age, so apart from lack of allegiance to personal altruism, betrayed even in the best Humanists, elements of hostility between Christians resenting Humanism and authentic classical Humanists were sublimated. Hundreds of Christians, and scores were high ecclesiastics, found spiritual solace and satisfaction by enlisting in Humanist ranks, sometimes actively engaging in classical study with abandon or lavishly supporting other scholars already captivated by the Humanistic cult.

Both medieval educational models and high Humanistic inspiration had lasting influence, but neither medieval nor Humanist paradigms were carried unaltered to colonial America. After the initial force of Humanism was spent shortly after the death of Erasmus (1536), both Catholic and Protestant educators took another look at Humanist learning and concluded that it could be tamed and used. The religious ferment of the sixteenth century conspired to produce an educational theory best described as Christian Humanism, and this Humanism was transplanted to America.

Christian Humanists selected parts of the classical legacy friendly to their denominational preconceptions. But along with an undisguised determination to build Christian character from classical sources, they wanted a school syllabus capable of contributing to practical learning. Students were to leave the schools with a sound Christian character, but they were also to be well instructed and ready to take places of leadership in civil and ecclesiastic society. It was apparent to Christian educators—the Jesuits (founded in 1534), Philip Melanchthon (1497–1560), John Sturm (1507–1589), and Mathurin Cordier (1479–1564)—that a knowledge of language was eminently useful both in the scholar's study and administrator's office. And a concentration on language, especially Latin, had the additional advantage of protecting students from the substance of the classics which could be troublesome because of its paganism.

Thus we see the character of colonial Humanism. It was the same in all colonies, although, it must be admitted, efforts to master what passed as a decent part of the classical syllabus varied enormously from place to place.

In New England, where a philosophy of intellect was keenly felt, custody of the syllabus of Christian Humanistic learning was in the hands of ministers and schoolmasters; both were teachers, although the former taught with the sermon while the latter resorted to more conventional pedagogies of tutorial study and schoolroom. The minister expounded and interpreted the Bible according to approved and accurate dogmas, but for this training along traditional lines of Humanist scholarship was essential. This meant he should be schooled in the trivium (in the subjects of grammar, rhetoric, and logic), for without them he could neither find nor express the true meaning of scripture. His was a superior role in society: in addition to knowing God's plan for men, his theological insight qualified him to pass judgment on what appeared to be the purely secular side of life. His subordinate was the teacher, a man who someday, if fate were fortuitous, might become a minister. His function was to prepare children to hear and understand and then act according to the unvarnished truth of the gospel; and what they learned was presumed to be useful to all of life. This was the work of teachers in lower schools, both necessary and important yet always inferior to higher studies where, as for example in the colonial college, boys continued their study of grammar, rhetoric, and logic along with Latin and Greek and sometimes Hebrew and where, in addition, they practiced interpreting scripture under the sharp eyes of their masters. All sides of Christian Humanism asserted education's subordination to religion, and enjoined school studies to center on the literary and linguistic. Colonial schools obeyed this established code. The subtle difference between classical and Christian Humanism existed in the purpose for classical studies: with the former, the classics were the gateways to a finer life; with the latter, the tools of classical scholarship were given pride of academic place but were always used to advance and defend sectarian positions. Stated so quickly this difference may seem inconsequential, but it reset the compass of education and almost doomed the spirit and genius of classical Humanism to obscurity. Yet, although elements of Humanistic spirit were sacrificed to sectarianism, an embrace of school subjects praised and refined by the best scholars of Humanism remained possible.[6] No wonder commentators on Christian Humanism in colonial school practice were bewildered. Looking at colonial schools they found an educational program rescued from the great schoolmasters of the Renaissance, but not looking far enough they missed the motive behind the prosecution of these studies.[7]

Religious justification in the Middle and Southern colonies was the same as in New England. Despite this, educational opportunity and practice in these regions departed from a strict New England model, and this departure is explained by something other than religion or educational theory, for if Christian Humanism as theory and the church as custodian of educational effort were paramount in New England they were honored elsewhere in colonial America as well. Departure had its base, not in intention, but in an intensity and a zeal keeping intention pure. And now, if we look at New Netherland (later New York), where we find intention good—education should serve the interest of denominational religion, and the usual appurtenances of learning should be cultivated—social conditions were far from propitious. Thus New York's record of educational accomplishment, despite the visible authority of the Established (Dutch Reformed) Church, was always inferior to New England's. And this unenviable disparity continued even after political control passed from Dutch to English hands, for thereafter the motivating religious force of the Dutch Reformed Church atrophied. As a British colony, New York began to take the measured but undramatic educational steps conventional in England and also in the colonies of the South.

In New Jersey and Pennsylvania the traditional identification of religion and education was countenanced as the best (perhaps the only) way schooling and learning should proceed. But the churches were never in quite the same position as in New England: they lacked the status of senior partners to government. Even when the state refused to follow faithfully the church's directions on education in, say, the New England colonies or New York, the force of law was nevertheless behind the church's educational pronouncements and made its position somewhat more imposing. Still, in New Jersey and Pennsylvania, with a freedom of action extraordinary in a Bible commonwealth, various denominations sponsored schools if they wanted to, and in some cases (for example, with Princeton) expressed their interest in education by founding colleges.[8] These colleges were founded with a clear commission: they were expected to educate young men for the ministry. The only exception was Pennsylvania, where the College of Philadelphia (later the University of Pennsylvania), capitalizing the tradition of a nonsectarian spirit in education originating with William Penn's notions of religious freedom, came into existence. This attitude toward religious self-determination, along with a fundamental Christian altruism, directed education in Pennsylvania toward a philanthropic mainstream and left public custody and support of schools to the minor tributaries of scholastic endeavor.

The portrait of religion's relationship to education, and, in theory, to government, is clear in the colonies, so in turning South we should expect nothing very different. The Southern colonies, except for Maryland in its early years, were vigorously Protestant, so government and education were in the hands of men accepting unquestioningly the theological supremacy of the Church of England. Dozens of sects appeared on the Southern scene and for the most part they flourished, but the reins of social and political control were held in the secure and uncompromising grasp of members of the Anglican Church. We know the equivocal stance these men adopted on theology, but on the surface at least they were true sons of their Church and allowed it to retain an exclusive position. Thus the disadvantages of establishment, on one hand, and of religious and governmental conspiracy on educational issues, on the other, put an extraordinary weight on the future of Southern education.[9] Both in the eyes of churchmen and politicians traditional precedents of personal responsibility for educational opportunity were good enough, so the urge for revision was discouraged.

The image of religion was stamped on one side of the coin of colonial education; the other side revealed an indelible scholastic conviction that the first purpose of schooling is to put men in closer communion with their Creator. Other subordinate purposes were noted, and for the majority of men they were elaborated best in Francis Bacon's *The Advancement of Learning,* so whenever the colonists wanted advice on the formulation of anything other than the unavoidable preamble to educational policy they opened his book.

EDUCATIONAL INFLUENCE

Born in London in 1561, Francis Bacon, educated at Trinity College, Cambridge, entered political life in 1584 to begin a slow climb up the ladder to high and responsible office in British government. Both a lawyer and a scientist—with credentials in philosophy—Bacon wrote his influential *Advancement of Learning* in 1605, a book designed on the one hand to move knowledge beyond its classical and traditional compilations, and on the other to counteract the creeping tendency to regard knowledge as an impediment to piety and civility. Out of religious conviction the most orthodox American colonists harbored suspicion about the ancient corpus of learning, for religious reformers had told them, at least since Luther, that wisdom from the past, especially if nurtured by medieval scholars, could not be trusted. And now Bacon, without actually endorsing this allegation, affirmed the distressing undependability of traditional science and philosophy. It was time, Bacon told his readers, to remove the shackles of past mistake and to support a new beginning, and the colonists, especially New England Puritans, turned out to be a remarkably attentive audience. Learning in direct competition with religious piety was certain to lose; and we know how hard colonial religious writers worked to prove that a commitment to faith was not a ratification of ignorance. Bacon demonstrated for his colonial readers how to correct past error and how to advance learning without undermining faith, piety, or civility. Little wonder, then, when colonial scholars wanted educational assurance, when they sought reasoned justification for educational policy, they turned to Lord Bacon. They preferred him over all others.

It is easy to understand why colonial intellectuals consulted Bacon, one of the day's prominent writers; besides, *The Advancement of Learning* had the reputation of a book no educated man left unread. It is harder to understand their almost uncritical willingness to follow him, for nothing in the book, or for that matter in Bacon's general philosophic and scientific theses, could be called an endorsement of Puritan religious policy. Either the Puritans in New England, who paid close attention to Bacon, were inclined to read with a tolerant eye or were so desperate for sound educational advice that they overlooked the sections giving them neither aid nor comfort. Not knowing their motivation or their temporary lapses into tolerance, we can only suppose that colonial educational and religious leaders were determined to take good advice wherever found and mollify a troubled conscience with the salve of good intention. In any case, reading Bacon, what did they find?

If they began with the general introduction to *The Great Instauration,* of which both *The Advancement of Learning* and *Novum Organum* were parts, and we suspect they did not, they found statements both pleasing and displeasing. Although the foundations of grammar and logic to which the colonists subscribed were Aristotelian, they had lingering doubts about the effect of Aristotle's philosophy on orthodoxy, so Bacon's attitude toward Greek philosophy was comforting: "And as to the point of usefulness, the philosophy we principally received from the Greeks must be acknowledged puerile, or rather talkative than generative—as being fruitful in controversies, but barren in effects."[10] But Bacon hesitated, despite his reservation about the worth of ancient philosophy, to discredit the intellectual inheritance—as did colonial readers—so he was at pains to pay allegiance to the best ancient authors, while downgrading commentaries and amendments on them: "The intellectual sciences . . . sometimes appear most perfect in the original author, and afterward degenerate." This assertion was the starting point for *The Advancement of Learning:* he deplored a degeneration of knowledge and a paralysis of learning never evidenced in ancient authors. He had a formula to remedy both. This stand caused colonial readers no trouble, for they too were friendly to progress so long as it did not intrude on fundamentals of faith, but as they read on they must have been deeply disturbed by Bacon's willingness to admit that among contemporary scholars engaged in redressing learning's sterility the best were Jesuits. This hated society of a despised church was counted an evil influence; if its genius could not be ignored, it should not, in any case, be praised. Bacon's comment, "And of late years the Jesuits, partly of themselves and partly provoked by example, have greatly enlivened and strengthened the state of learning, and contributed to establish the Roman See,"[11] elicited only grudging acknowledgement among Puritan scholars.

After this general introduction, colonial readers were exposed to a carefully reasoned and highly perceptive philosophy of education. Their own disposition toward learning, one always taking schools into account, ranged beyond what schools were capable of doing, so Bacon's philosophy of education, while paying heed to schooling without ever being curtailed by it, complemented their own point of view. The family, the church, and society generally were all counted teachers of youth; of this colonial leaders were confident, so Bacon's confirmation of what they themselves held true was further testimony to his wisdom. In the last analysis, confirmation rather than conversion helped keep Bacon's educational views alive in the colonies; for his readers, instead of seeking instruction on educational policy, may have looked for support for an educational standard already erected. But this is conjecture and does nothing to subvert Bacon's position as a colonial educational authority.

The Advancement of Learning has another side making its reception all the easier. While Bacon, we know, deplored any unreasonable dependence on ancient authority or on knowledge stored in venerable tomes, he displayed a conversance both with classical authors and the Bible. Hardly a page of his book neglects classical reference or scriptural allusion, and this was not missed by readers ready to pay allegiance to both; an author who knew his sources so well and used them effortlessly, and one who seemed to count so heavily on the authority of the Bible, was worth attention. They must, at the same time, have overlooked the principal point Bacon was trying to make, even while using the testimony of ancient authority, that old storehouses of knowledge and the authors responsible for filling them were of questionable dependability. The colonists may have had sufficient reason for refusing to subscribe to *The Advancement of Learning*, but they had better reason, they thought, for adhering to its prescription.

Writing *The Advancement of Learning*, Bacon curried no favor among Puritans nor was he thinking of any colonial enterprise; still, more by accident than design, he often told colonists what they wanted to hear. Most of all they wanted to believe that education was good for faith, so they could continue to improve their own and their children's minds without at the same time putting any element of faith or piety in jeopardy. Here Bacon was accommodating: philosophy and human learning, he said, were useful to faith and religion when used for illustration and ornamentation, but this service was really inconsequential, a point to which the Puritans readily assented; what counted more than mere rhetorical flourish or felicitous expression was philosophy, "effectually exciting to the exaltation of God's glory," and human learning, "affording a singular preservation against error and unbelief."[12] He found justification for this assertion in scripture and went on to assure his readers of more divine testimony concerning the merit and dignity of learning. Colonists of tender religious conscience, after reading Bacon, resolved any doubt about the injury alleged to faith from learning, and this was no small matter, for pietism, as we have seen, had created a dilemma for the literal mind, and in many a colonial settlement the status of learning hung by a precarious thread, one easily cut in the absence of prudent and sensible counsel. By almost any standard, Bacon was prudent and sensible.

Intellectually vigorous persons, of whom the colonies counted many, followed the distinction between divine and secular knowledge without effort, and while their religious creed said that inspiration and faith could carry them through the labyrinths of divine revelation, they were sometimes troubled about how to approach secular knowledge, how to invent methods of selection and analysis and how to organize the secular inheritance in the most useful way. On this point, of course, they had plenty of help, for the scholarship of the past five hundred years had invested in the same enterprise. But could they follow older plans, many produced by Scholastic philosophers and churchmen, when religious intuition warned that exposure might lead to sectarian contamination? It was better to be safe than sorry, so they eschewed traditional paradigms and looked for something either new or uninfected by medieval scholars. Bacon's formula was handy, erudite, analytical, and, best of all, displayed a sturdy independence of earlier scholarship: when he spoke of elaborating a new method, his readers took him at his word.

The best organization of secular learning, he said, is one derived from the nature of the soul, wherein there are three faculties, each corresponding to one branch of knowledge: thus, the faculty of memory is concerned with history, imagination with poetry, and reason with philosophy. History's appropriate province is individuals, circumscribed by time and place; poetry is like history except individuals are either feigned or from fable; but philosophy "forsaking individuals, fixes upon notions abstracted from them, and is employed in compounding and separating these notions according to the laws of nature and the evidence of things themselves."[13] All this was traditional enough; it could, indeed, have been summarized from almost any Scholastic book on the subject, but Bacon said this was a departure from the past and, again, a colonial audience took his word for it.

Bacon's recommendations concerning the organization of knowledge were followed in colonial schools and colleges; one reason, we suppose, why these institutions displayed a common, if not identical, public face. But Bacon's book had the prior effect of convincing the colonists that colleges were good for them, and here his advice must have been comforting because the colonists were proud of having founded colleges even before doing anything about lower schools. He encouraged commitment to the extension of letters—in schools, universities, books, and professors— and told his readers: this "excellent liquor of knowledge, whether it descend from Divine inspiration or spring from human sense, would soon hide in oblivion, unless collected in books, traditions, academies and schools."[14] He told them, too, that schools and colleges needed buildings, endowments, privileges, and charters, and that learning required an environment of quietness and seclusion where professors and students could study free from care and anxiety. Colleges with good libraries "are as the shrines where the bones of old saints full of virtue lie buried," and good libraries should have modern authors whose editions contain "correcter impressions, more faultless versions, more useful commentaries, and more learned annotations."[15] He called for a close association and a regular collaboration among colleges in the prosecution of art and science. Learning should march to a common drum, so, unsurprisingly, he deplored the isolation characteristic of European colleges. And he criticized them for concentrating on the professions and neglecting the arts and sciences. In the sciences, especially, he was confident of great progress, so he encouraged professorships in the sciences. Finally, and in persuasive language, he urged reward for scholarship: "Since the founders of colleges plant, and those who endow them water, we are naturally led to speak in this place of the mean salaries apportioned to public lectureships, whether in the sciences or the arts. For such offices being instituted not for any ephemeral purpose, but for the constant transmission and extension of learning, it is of the utmost importance that the men selected to fill them be learned and gifted. But it is idle to expect that the ablest scholars will employ their whole energy and time in such functions unless reward be answerable to that competency which may be expected from the practice of a profession."[16]

Colonial activity in founding colleges was extraordinary by any standard, yet Bacon's influence on this point is unclear; apart from anything Bacon said, colonists may simply have followed their own objectives. In any case, they refused to follow the advice in *The Advancement of Learning* to the letter: energetic in founding colleges and meticulous in securing charters, and rejecting the example of European ancestors in creating schools concentrating on the professions, they turned their schools to a cultivation of the arts, keeping firmly in mind the fact that the arts were useful complements to religion. After doing this they ignored Bacon's counsel. With libraries small and little used, with privileges either for students or professors virtually ignored, with professorships in science allowed to go uncultivated, and with endowments (apart from land grants) small and ineffective, the colleges, rather than being free from care and anxiety were constantly fighting to stay alive.

Our colonial ancestors put a high premium on useful knowledge, and their reading habits, even when they devoured the classics, were dominated by the conviction that whatever was read should be either useful or edifying. With such attitudes toward learning, the colonists promoted an education in useful knowledge, and on this point Bacon gave them plenty of support. The great appendix to natural philosophy, Bacon asserted, should be elaborated in practical mathematics and applied science, wherein he listed astrology, medicine, physiognomy, and the interpretation of dreams. All these, he said, have possibilities for the development of human life; still, he reserved his warmest praise for medicine and mechanics.[17] A hierarchy of knowledge is clear enough in Bacon's theory and, unready to abandon or discredit pure science, he nevertheless tried to rescue the entire field of application from its deplorable state of inactivity and unhesitatingly pronounced the power and utility of knowledge. Here Bacon was either teaching his colonial readers a new lesson or reviewing for them a syllabus of pragmatism which, although vague, had some reality in their minds, because they never lost sight of the possibility, while paying allegiance to the higher things in life, of directing their activities toward profitable and useful ends.

The chain of intellectual influence between Europe and the colonies was unbroken, and its strongest link, one keeping the intellectual life of the colonies closely joined to the wisdom of the past, enabling so many colonists to think and act like educated Europeans, was logic. In connection with logical studies, Bacon promised to blaze a new trail through the wilderness of science, to turn over fresh soil enabling men to live more intelligently and to meet the physical world confidently. The relationship between religion, theology, and natural philosophy (science) had for a long time been cool, due largely to the erratic course Aristotelian science took during the Hellenistic period and its centuries-long custody in Arabic philosophy. In a word, the natural philosophy of the medieval and early modern world needed a good deal of correction to be compatible with Christian faith. The hopeful assumption that logic, a subject cultivated by medieval scholars in a four-century development of the science of human reason, would straighten out the most difficult issues and, in the end, invest natural philosophy with a Christian perspective, proved premature.

Under different circumstances logic might have been equal to the task, but Scholastic logic ran into bad days, and put in the position of having to defend itself, was unable to use its resources to reinterpret natural philosophy. Extending knowledge by using logic as an indispensable instrument for discovery was the special genius claimed for Scholastic logic, but in rewriting Aristotle's *Logic,* Peter Ramus rejected discovery and emphasized logic's capacity for arrangement, for organizing bodies of knowledge already in man's possession. So a logic capable of making distinctions and organizing bodies of knowledge was the kind of logic the colonists, especially the Calvinists, knew and approved. They had heard, and to a great extent believed, the old tales about the dangers lurking in deductive logic as practiced by Scholastics and were horrified at the possiblity of treachery vested in the syllogism. Thus the colonial mind proved receptive to the doubt about logic expressed by Bacon: "This part of human philosophy which regards logic, is disagreeable to the taste of many, as appearing to them no other than a net, and a snare of thorny subtlety."[18] Both Bacon and the colonists knew that logic was an important and necessary instrument in philosophy and science; it could hardly be neglected. It could, however, be invested with greater clarity of purpose, and its power to mislead could be defused. Bacon told his readers that logic's principal fault was not its concentration on analysis: "We find no deficiency in analytics; for it is rather loaded with superfluities than deficient."[19] And here the majority of colonial scholars and ministers agreed wholeheartedly, for they wanted, and needed, a logic helping them to distinguish truth from error, especially in religion. But wanting to avoid any obvious indebtedness to medieval scholarship, they were quick to abandon the syllogism, and Bacon was their authority for doing so. Speaking of various kinds of demonstration, but thinking mainly of the syllogism, Bacon concluded that "each of these demonstrations (common consent, congruity, induction, and syllogistic) has its peculiar subjects, and parts of the sciences, wherein they are of force, and others again from which they are excluded; for insisting upon too strict proofs in some cases, and still more the facility and remissness in resting upon slight proofs in others, is what has greatly prejudiced and obstructed the sciences."[20] The syllogism, worn by the file of many a subtle genius, and rendered into fragments, was, according to Bacon, nothing more than reducing propositions to principles by means of middle terms, and the middle term, the minor premise, was undependable and too often trapped men in thickets of uncertainty and confusion.[21]

Reading through the books in *The Advancement of Learning* treating of logic tempts one to conclude that Bacon, despite his assertions with respect to a new method, induction, was cultivating an old field. Most of what he said on the subject belonged to traditional formal logic and most of it, too, had its origin in Aristotelian and Scholastic thought. Bacon added a new emphasis: empirical verification; and he carried his argument for empirical verification farther than any of his predecessors. Without actually breaking new ground for the colonists to cultivate in the field of logic, Bacon gave them some assurance that using the logical tools of Peter Ramus to sort out philosophical and religious truth they were on the right track and could discard Scholastic logic with impunity. Bacon's discourse on logic gave the colonists confidence and they found his analysis satisfying.

The Advancement of Learning convinced colonial educators they were right to put logic in the curriculum, but other subjects needed consideration, so they could not rest on their laurels of being right about logic. We know of their attraction to books and the use they made of them, but a book once read was not always available for rereading. Readers wanted to retain the novelties books contained, so they, as their ancestors had done, carried their bibliographies in their minds. What, then, was the place of memory in schooling and how should it be trained?

Faced with remembering the treasures of the classics, scholars of the Great Renaissance (Erasmus is the best example) had shown students useful aids to memory and following this advice clever pedagogues invented mnemonic technique. But colonial teachers wondered whether time spent mastering technique to aid memory might not be used better, so they were pleased when Bacon wrote that "all the things of this kind [were] no more than rope-dancing, antic postures, and feasts of activity."[22] Such things, he said, abused the body and when technique was artificially employed to enforce memory the mental powers were abused. The best help for memory "is writing; and we must observe, that the memory, without this assistance, is unequal to things of length and accuracy, and ought not otherwise to be trusted."[23] A good and accurate memory was a sign of solid learning, so when colonial schoolmasters sent boys to the books and demanded an exercise of memory, they were doing nothing more than fulfilling the expectation of conventional educational policy. And this policy had Bacon's full support.

Grammar and rhetoric, alongside logic, were staples in a colonial curriculum: grammar, traditionally a beginning subject, was an appropriate subject for secondary schools, but rhetoric, usually thought more de-manding, belonged to a college course. None of these subjects, including logic, needed much support from theory in order to maintain its position in the schools, for the colonists, themselves products of classical education, could hardly conceive a program of schooling ignoring any of them. Their appraisal of *The Advancement of Learning* was positive when they read Bacon's justification for studies they had already accepted. Touching only slightly the literary side of grammar—for as a school subject it included literary study along with linguistic structure—Bacon preferred to con-centrate on grammar's role in making language an effective medium for scientific communication. "Grammar holds the place of a conductor in respect of the other sciences; and though the office be not noble, it is extremely necessary, especially as the sciences in our times are chiefly derived from the learned languages. Nor should this art be thought of small dignity, since it acts as an antidote against the curse of Babel, the confusion of tongues."[24] Clearly on the side of grammar study for students engaged in scholarship, Bacon acknowledged its "little use in any maternal language," and thus relieved generations of students and schoolmasters from trying to unravel the mysteries of English grammar, a subject whose impoverishment led masters to conclude it had neither rules nor standards. Learned languages, especially Latin, were different, so schoolboys turned to Latin grammar when they wanted to master the rubrics of correct speech.

These Baconian emphases in connection with grammar were appealing to the colonists: literature, after all, was a subject to be careful of, for it contained all kinds of stories and lurid tales capable of warping faith. Adding the classics to the grammar school's syllabus required an imposi-tion of precise principles of selection. Nothing injurious to faith or morals was allowed. Dismissing English grammar, so it seemed to most colonists (excepting, of course, Benjamin Franklin), was a matter of sensible edu-cational economy: why waste precious time studying a subject of such little use?

Rhetoric was a lesser problem, for, as Bacon said, the "end of rhetoric is to fill the imagination with such observations and images as may assist reason, and not overthrow it."[25] Employing rhetorical technique to ornament speech and writing and to make clear and convincing argument was, of course, the hope of every writer and preacher in the colonies and elsewhere, so it was easy to support rhetoric if, at the same time, one was careful to keep its purpose pure. Eloquence could, and should, be used to adorn virtue; it could also be used to praise vice. Despite rhetoric's utility, a point never missed by any colonial preacher and one fully under-stood by professors in early colonial colleges, it could be an instrument for deceit: Bacon wanted to restore rhetoric and his analysis, it must be said, went a long way toward doing so. Plato, he wrote, was unjust to rhetoric, although he "proceeded from a just contempt of the rhetoricians of his time, to place rhetoric among the voluptuary arts, and resemble it to cookery, which corrupted wholesome meats, and, by variety of sauces, made unwholesome ones more palatable."[26] Bacon told his colonial readers to make rhetoric obedient to reason and, to some extent, his book showed them how this could be done. When they read him on rhetoric they were precocious students.

Almost the whole of *The Advancement of Learning* dwells on the science of knowledge and the art of learning on the level of policy and stays away from day-to-day school practice. In this respect Bacon followed accepted canons of educational discourse, but there was another reason: not a schoolmaster, he felt uncomfortable with pedagogic technique. Concerned with method and amply demonstrating its worth, he was silent on directions to schoolmasters. Still, he was aware that to neglect entirely the art of teaching would render his book, if not deficient, at least incomplete, so in chapter four of book six he touches it briefly and lightly. He knows the subject is important and realizes his readers want information. They must have been disappointed, for the little he does say could neither have helped nor edified colonial educators: "For the doctrine of school-learning, it were the shortest way to refer it to the Jesuits, who, in point of usefulness, have herein excelled . . . ."[27] Bacon, we know, was capable of a discernment allowing him to utilize good advice wherever found, and he could make the distinction between the Jesuits as exponents of Roman Catholicism and their technical achievement as schoolmasters. We wonder if colonists were similarly capable? In any case, if they overlooked praise of the Jesuits and the recommendation for teachers to peruse the *Ratio Studiorum* for pedagogic detail, and read on, they would see Bacon on the side of school learning, rather than private instruction in the home— a recommendation John Locke, later, was unable to accept—and that he approved a school discipline allowing students, especially the more able, to conclude their lessons and then "steal time for other things whereto [they are] more inclined."[28] From this point on his pedagogic preoccupation is with the care of genius and how best to provide for its full academic realization. The technique recommended is a combination of exercising the powers of the mind and obtaining knowledge quickly and effortlessly: for, he says, "it is one method to begin swimming with bladders, and another to begin dancing with loaded shoes."[29] In any case, studies should be suited to the capacity of the student, although teachers must remedy the indisposition of some students to learn the essentials for life in society. He found special virtue in the study of mathematics for students whose quick minds and ready wit allowed them to master their lessons and then, largely through inattention, waste their time: "inattention and a volatility of genius may be remedied by mathematics, wherein, if the mind wander ever so little, the whole demonstration must begin anew."[30] He ends his discourse on the art of teaching by calling attention to the need for discipline in learning, a discipline sturdy enough to weather the storms of life long after school is over, and again refers approvingly to Jesuit practice: "We mean the action of the theatre, which strengthens the memory, regulates the tone of the voice and the efficacy of pronunciation; gracefully composes the countenance and the gesture; procures a becoming degree of assurance; and lastly, accustoms youth to the eye of men."[31] History tells how colonial educators refused to follow Bacon's advice and Jesuit practice; drama was too much. Yet, despite amendment to Bacon's *Advancement of Learning,* colonists, nevertheless, counted it on the whole as sound educational policy, agreeing, as it did, with so many of their predispositions, and leading them, also, into new avenues of heretofore untravelled educational thought.

ECONOMIC INFLUENCE

Adopting European economic practice, with its implicit link to capitalism, the colonists began to think of themselves as merchants and managers at the expense of an earlier jealous preoccupation with religion and patriotism. European feudalism, an economic system with roots almost too deep to disturb, recognized the right of private property, but the exercise of this right was severely limited to an aristocracy. Serfs owning no land labored for property owners and contributed enormously to their power and wealth. The economic theory and practice of mercantilism changed this and in the end remade the structure of economics. Mercantilism put economic power in the hands of the monarch, allowing the civil ruler to exercise economic along with political power, thus advancing the status of a nation. Unfettered political power, perhaps fundamental to orthodox mercantilism, quickly ran its course, for in France and England especially, the middle class began to recognize not only the essential worth of its contribution to economic vitality but to political power as well. Eventually the almost limitless authority of the king was brought to heel and many heads instead of only one or a few took charge of public policy. Concurrently, the philosophers—for example, John Locke, Adam Smith, Turgot, and Quesnay—expounded a theory of natural law and applied it to economics: human beings, they argued, are motivated by the chance for profit. On this basis natural law was easily recruited to a capitalism unleashed from royal, ecclesiastic, or government control. The noble auxiliaries of capitalism, a free market, competition, and supply and demand, were buried among the theories of the philosophers and it took some time to excavate them.

When colonial leaders learned of these new theories, they began to exhibit some discontent with contemporary economic practice. The economic world suddenly appeared to have new horizons, and if they were to be reached something had to be done to train and educate men capable of exploiting economic opportunity.[32]

The convenient and conventional interpretation of educational purpose was now open to doubt and debate, and although change occurred slowly in the colonies, we see defenses being thrown up around traditional educational values. Early in the eighteenth century, colonial spokesmen extolled the virtues of a new ethic wherein middle-class morality was codified along economic lines and where, in place of traditional religious virtues, frugality, perseverance, hard work and, of course, the honest fulfillment of contracts are given pride of place. Perhaps these economic-laden virtues were consistent with biblical morality, but their justification was propaganda for a new education which would be practical, useful, and above all profitable.

The old learning always had stout and sturdy defenders whose eloquence and orthodoxy succeeded in preserving its place in the mainstream of educational practice throughout most of the eighteenth century. But civility and piety, the banner of pedagogic tradition, were on a collision course with educational utility, an innovation bred and nurtured in the incubator of capitalism.[33]

POLITICAL INFLUENCE

Political theory worked hand in glove with capitalism and, in the end, was the catalyst enabling capitalism to succeed. Yet, even with a climate of opinion favoring capitalistic enterprise, the implementation of political theory could not be achieved if the calendar stood still. In the seventeenth century, divine right was practiced with a vengeance, so only the very brave or the exceedingly rash challenged the authority of a king ordained by God. And the theory of divine right was assented to by religious leaders and theologians of disparate sects. At first this theory satisfied emerging capitalists too, but greedy monarchs, instinctively driven to inflate their person, possessions, and power, sensed a threat to their assumed prerogatives from the wealth accumulated by practitioners of the art of capitalism. Essaying to trim the sails of great and wealthy merchants produced by mercantilistic and capitalistic policy, and thus invading the field of economic endeavor where ingenuity and ruthlessness paid huge dividends, the monarchs turned out to be their own worst enemies. Dismayed by royal interference with business, the middle class, now reaping its harvest of profit and supremely self-confident, began to reconsider its allegiance to political absolutism.

Based on an emerging theory of natural law assigning sovereignty to people instead of rulers, representative government made an appearance on the modern political scene. And with government control in the hands of the middle class, often nominally exercised by a king, political policy was shaped to benefit economic progress.

This, however, was only one dimension to political change and alone hardly accounts for the tumultuous centuries to follow. Theology, too, had its part to play, and again we come face to face with the doctrine of Calvin. The human world, to follow this doctrine, was divided into saints and sinners. Because grace was theirs, saints were ordained to handle the affairs of government; so this austere theology at once rejected divine right and democracy.

New England was at first alone in its sensitivity to political philosophy, while the Middle colonies played a game of political indifference, believing they were immune to Europe's problems of political control, and the Southern colonies, confident and conservative, refused to contemplate democracy or think about life without a king. Among New England intellectuals we need call the roll of only a few to see where they stood. John Winthrop, John Cotton, and Nathaniel Ward spoke as one asserting that government arose from a compact of free men. Religious regenerates and unregenerates comprised the body of free men, so the former were the rulers and their badge of authority was found in scripture. Democracy, the rule of the people, was abhorrent to these wise New Englanders, for people were unequal both in capacity to judge God's scriptural direction and in religious grace and enlightenment. Such leaders supplied New England with a theoretical foundation for the Bible commonwealth. Yet a Bible commonwealth was always a place where enterprising men could reap profit from their ingenuity and labor. Despite the formal austerity of Puritan doctrine, Winthrop and Cotton and others justified a capitalistic economic system.[34]

Still, despite its arrogant self-sufficiency, the Bible state was always in some jeopardy. Society sensed that a political theory based on natural law could lead to self-government. Although this was as yet a declaration for the future, the colonies were exposed to primitive democratic political philosophy harmonized in the writings of John Locke, Montesquieu and Sidney in Europe, and James Otis, the two Adamses, Benjamin Franklin, Tom Paine, and Thomas Jefferson in America. Philosophies of human right and dignity, based on the simple proposition of humanity, were laid bare and government, it was asserted, should exist to serve the needs of men.

Ferment surrounded colonial life and near the storm's center were political and economic theories. We must revise our vision of the colonies being untroubled by and indifferent to human forces at work in the world. The colonies were a long way from the cultural centers of Europe and their experience in a quickening of political discord may have been neither so full nor so quick as that of their European cousins. However, they were still culturally part of Europe, and they felt shocks coming from generators of the new political wisdom. As these shocks jolted colonial life, the educational theories of the colonists were shaped and reshaped to accommodate them. It is easy to see how education, which in the nature of things must serve the goals and aspirations of society, could be enlisted for service in a world beginning to wear a new economic and political face.

SOCIAL INFLUENCE

For as long as most men could remember, a principal justification for schooling had been religious; in consequence curricula were religious in both content and purpose. But as we move into the seventeenth century, there are signs, whose erection we have noted, of new dimensions. Economic and political impulsions affect educational thought and practice; more broadly, impulses are generated in society itself, and now these impulses conspired to produce a humanitarian social theory.

The strongest impulse of all came from scientific knowledge. Scientific quickening had its origin around the middle of the sixteenth century, but its capacity for exerting day-to-day influence on the educational structure was made to mark time while men disputed religious difference and ended up with uneasy compromise. In 1543 Copernicus published his magnum opus, *On the Revolution of the Heavenly Orbs,* with the audacious hypothesis regarded by some churchmen to be enormously dangerous to faith and morals. The sun, he wrote, not the earth, was the center of the universe and the planets revolved around it. If this proposition was dangerous, at least it was not entirely novel, for earlier astronomers had pronounced it: since ancient times heliocentricity contested with the conventional Ptolemaic theory as the correct explanation of the movement of heavenly bodies.

Copernicus formed the vanguard for a different and more realistic method of seeking for knowledge about the physical world. In his wake were men of hardly less impressive stature: Vesalius, renowned for *On the Structure of the Human Body;* Cardan, the author of a seminal book on algebra, *The Great Art;* Kepler, Galileo, Newton, William Gilbert, and Descartes—all were engaged in unearthing a scientific knowledge whose consequences had revolutionary impact.

The conventional theory of knowledge, one with extraordinary currency among Humanists, maintained that all knowledge worth having was in the classics, so according to confirmed Humanists it was pointless to look elsewhere. Sincere Christians who were exponents of Humanism amended this strict version to read: all *secular* knowledge of worth was to be found in the classics. In either version, authentic knowledge was in literature, so scholars should stay with their books. Now, however, convention began to lose appeal, for obviously all knowledge was not stored in literature and, moreover, bodies of scientific knowledge capable of explaining the operations of nature in a way classical authors could not have imagined were being accumulated. Unquestionably, scholars now assumed, an abundance of empirical data was hidden in the universe; it behooved good scholarship to develop a scientific method equal to the task of unraveling the mysteries of nature. This was not an easy job, nor was it done in a day. But good beginnings were made with the result that scholars rejected Humanism, with its veneration of the classics, for Realism, where the objects of study were man himself and the physical world. Without any blazed trail, men were expected to depend on themselves and put their trust in method and reason.

Reason unleashed to unravel cosmological mystery sought for philosophic support—for even scientists lacked some self-confidence—and ended up with two distinct philosophies capable of standing as counterpoises to Idealism and its Humanistic ally. Idealism supported organized religion and formal theology, and stood as the guardian against both religious and philosophical heterodoxy. But Idealism was a hard doctrine; even its most eloquent interpreters contradicted what sensory experience said was true. Yet rejecting Idealism was not the same as replacing it with a satisfactory solution. In one form or another Realism was an intellectual alternative to Idealism, but a choice between the two kinds of Realism could be difficult too. Descartes proposed a dualistic theory wherein mind and matter, the spiritual and the physical, stood side by side. Both were real, of that there was no doubt, but they were different. Cartesian Dualism contained elements for compromise between theology and science; both mind and matter, these Dualists were careful to explain, were created by God. Human reason could reveal order and meaning in the universe, so it was unnecessary to deny the existence of either spiritual or material reality. This Dualism, however, could lead to deism, and deism made theology arbitrary, abstract, and almost meaningless.

The other kind of Realism, Materialism, explicitly antithetical to religion, gave science an unrestricted license to explain everything. Accordingly, only matter is real and its investigation is the only way to discover anything about the operation of the universe. Theology was stripped of all consequence, because in its barren field the tools of science would not work. So far as the American colonies were concerned, Materialistic Realism was unacceptable and thus the matter stood on this side of the Atlantic until the eighteenth century, but even then the philosophic face of America was set to remain aloof to any religiously subversive doctrine.

This quick, and unavoidably superficial, survey describes an intellectual ferment to which the American colonies were largely immune, yet it serves as background to judge the increased secularization of knowledge, itself a reality in the colonies, and also a byproduct of European social philosophy. First, of course, knowledge obtained by using the trained reason became more and more important. And sources for knowledge, traditionally restricted to the books, now became the whole world. Accompanying this broadening was a tendency to discount knowledge with ornamental and aristocratic credentials. In a word, to be authentic, knowledge had to be useful. Under these circumstances, only a miracle could save the liberal arts in a country where utility had no peer.

The liberal arts had an affinity to educational goals respecting a refinement of human taste and feeling. Now, however, men thought the arts needed better justification if they were to keep a place in the curriculum of the schools. At this point, a utilitarian characterization of liberal art could find approval among Puritan intellectuals, for they themselves wanted to know the arts because of their use for scriptural and doctrinal study and not for their alleged intrinsic worth. But when Puritans accepted the fact that theory was now drifting their way, they were discomforted by erosions of Humanistic scholarship promoted in utilitarianism, in arguments for greater emphasis on vernacular language and physical science. The most perceptive of seventeenth-century scholars probably saw a new curriculum over the horizon, one wherein both modern language and science had a prominent place, but this prospect must have made them uneasy.

The social value of studying English in this good land could be authenticated easily, and the credentials of English literature were attested in the accomplishments of Shakespeare, Pope, Swift, and Fielding; it was easy, also, to demonstrate the technical achievements of science: the thermometer, the compass, electricity, and the steam engine were the most obvious, but not the only, witnesses. On this side of the Atlantic scientists were working too: Thomas Brattle, Charles Morton, Isaac Greenwood, William Small, William Smith, Benjamin Rush, and Benjamin Franklin were engaged in pushing back the frontiers of scientific knowledge.

Scientists along with their linguistic confreres showed persons susceptible of conviction by rational argument and demonstration that knowledge of things and knowledge of words had a practical value of about equal standing. They could demonstrate, moreover, that knowledge properly used generated power and contributed to comfort. Why not prosecute knowledge toward these ends? More often than not this case for knowledge was convincing and this conviction eventually affected school learning and reshaped educational policy. But educational policy moves slowly even when the distance is only from the library to the schoolroom, so despite knowledge's admitted social value, the curriculum of seventeenth-century schools responded sluggishly to appeals for utility. But schools were never strong enough, nor was conventional practice, to stop the calendar from turning: eventually utilitarians had their way.

Buried away and hardly visible in the seventeenth century was a nascent humanitarianism, a way of looking at man in society, with one foot in the camp of modern philosophy and the other in the camp of Christian altruism. So long as Puritanism was dominant, humanitarianism proceeded as a substitute for charity, but away from a Puritan creed of life—among men like William Penn, among Anglican charitable societies, and among evangelical religious sects—conviction was deep that life could be better for everyone. But in seventeenth-century America, humanitarianism was a subtle, almost subversive, movement. Yet when it found voice it stressed the need for both social and educational reform. Every humanitarian forged education as a vital weapon for fighting poverty, ignorance, disease, and inequality. A social philosophy with so much trust in education was ahead of its time and its effect was slight. Yet, while few in number, these almost silent tributaries of humanitarianism were deep and permanent and a century later became the thundering mainstream of educational activity and thought.[35]

Economics, politics, and sociology began to take their place alongside religion as justification for educational effort, and although exerting uneven influence on seventeenth-century colonial teaching and learning, they served notice that custody of educational theory was not being left by default to religion.

COLONIAL GOVERNMENT AND EDUCATION

As early in educational history as Plato the place states should have in the direction of educational affairs was debated. We remember how Plato's plan gave the state an extraordinary commission of authority for educational supervision and control. But colonial America was unwilling to imitate Plato's utopian political plan and relinquish the care and education of children to government. Although Plato's plan was never tested in practice, it stimulated educational theorists and political philosophers over the centuries to assess the merits of state control. Given their addiction to ideas from the ancient world, Humanists, unsurprisingly, promoted the state's right in education and declared that states should become directly involved in the management of schools.[36] This is one side of the story.

The other side, one articulated clearly in the English American colonies, was the British principle where, with government standing aside, the education of children was purely a private affair: each man educating his children according to his own means.

From the outset, conflicting theories on public and private education had some currency in the colonies. Colonists were equipped to ask whether the education of children was a collective responsibility to be managed by government, or a personal matter to be handled according to the resources of each family. But when they answered they preferred to follow English custom, one adhered to more faithfully in some colonies than others. Fair to say, the history of American education is in great part a record of the erosion of this British principle, for slowly but surely the collective principle spread and gained popularity until by the late nineteenth century no one seriously doubted that provision for public education was among the most significant affairs of government.[37]

Still, in colonial days the phrase *public school* was used in various ways, so when we credit colonial spokesmen with supporting public education we want to be fairly precise. In the New England colonies generally, public education meant an elementary school established by government authority, with a teacher licensed and appointed by town or colonial officers, open to the children of the community almost without regard to their station in life. Such schools, however, usually had rates or tuition charges, and children in attendance were expected to pay for the cost of their instruction. According to contemporary standards, these fees were so modest as to amount to almost nothing, but we must remember money for schooling was scarce in the colonies and a charge equivalent to fifty cents a term might have been too much for some families. Clearly, despite their nomenclature, such schools were equivocally public; created by law they were, in addition, subject only to superficial government supervision. And while some localities appropriated public money for education, it was by no means universal policy to support schools from the public treasury.[38]

Outside New England, especially in the South, *public school* had a different meaning. Schools were authorized by law, say by charter, but their supervision and control were delegated to boards of governors or trustees, so a school's relationship to the colony disappeared almost with its founding. To use the phrase *public school* indicating a method of founding was consistent with English tradition almost two centuries old, but this tradition conspired to reduce the attractiveness of schools, because under private management and catering to an aristocratic clientele, schools were insulated from the influence of public policy.[39]

In every colony some schools flirted with public support. When a family was able to pay for instruction, fees were charged, but poor families could sometimes have their children taught gratuitously. Throughout most of the seventeenth century experiments with free instruction in schools were rare, but their rareness went mainly unnoticed and uncriticized. In the first place, schooling was unpopular among the poor who resisted sending children to school to waste time. Then, too, the number of poor and orphaned children attending schools at public expense was small, so schools escaped a character of pauperism later, in the eighteenth century, almost indelibly printed on free schools. Besides, public education implied the most elementary kind of instruction reserved for children with little need for the refinement of more advanced schooling. Free schools meant schools for the poor, and with such economic stigma weighing them down public schools were places best avoided by children of the upper classes.

If public schools form one side of the colonial educational picture, private schools compose the other. For most of the seventeenth century, private schools were conducted for profit by persons engaged in a business enterprise. Students were admitted as these pedagogic entrepreneurs saw fit, followed courses of study suitable to their academic taste, and paid tuition fees according to what the traffic would bear. For the most part, except for the license most private masters needed, such schools were outside the reach of public policy. Obviously some public purpose was served by private-venture education, yet the colonies evidenced no urgent desire to regulate, supervise, or otherwise control such schools. During the seventeenth century private and public schools competed for colonial allegiance, but neither was successful in capturing it.

EDUCATIONAL LEGISLATION

Now, after distinguishing public from private education, we should look to the public action responsible for forging the legal principle of state educational authority. Whether or not this principle was strong enough to form the foundation for modern public education is debatable. What is clear is this: even the substantial effort of the colonies to supervise and control schools did not construct a model for twentieth-century American public education to imitate.

Between 1642 and 1671, the New England colonies, excepting only Rhode Island, enacted laws designed to impose a minimum standard for educational accomplishment. Differing on minor points, with some more demanding than others, these laws proposed to strengthen the fabric of society by means of modest learning and to ensure for each child simple literary skill useful for earning a living. This purpose complied with Puritan temperament when it paid allegiance to necessary learning; convinced that the success of religion depended on the ability of the people to hear and understand the word of God, Puritans, sensibly and practically, tried to ensure minimum standards of literacy in the Bible state. If religious motive had pride of place in the minds of public men promoting compulsory education laws, they were never blind to economic goals. And economic motive had its origin in English law: in 1563 the Statute of Artificers and in 1601 the Poor Law were passed by the British Parliament to redress the public burden of caring for destitute children.

These laws required public officers to find poor children in their districts and see to it that they learned a trade. If law proved remedy for poverty, the poor would soon be able to care for themselves. But British law, concentrating on economics, paid scant heed to the literary instruction of poor children. If this was oversight, it was not repeated in the New England colonies, for the first colonial law on compulsory education, enacted in Massachusetts Bay in 1642, made literary instruction mandatory.[40]

In considering the legislation of 1642, the model for similar laws in other New England colonies, we remember the meaning of compulsory education. The law directed parents and masters to make educational provision enabling children and apprentices to understand the principles of religion and the capital laws of the colony. It is probably right to say this law demanded instruction in reading. Directing selectmen to enforce compliance, the act told towns to see to the instruction of children or be fined. Parents or masters, moreover, found in violation of the statute could have their children or apprentices taken from them. Masters, the law said, should see to reading and teach their apprentices a trade besides. This old law, the first illustration of educational legislation in English America, demanded instruction but nothing whatever toward the establishment of schools or the attendance of children. Instruction was essential and it was assumed, perhaps naively, that its standards could be met either in existing schools or tutorial settings. But this was expecting too much. Yet, whether the law was observed wholly or in part, and without arguing its educational merit, it was a precedential act, expressing a principle later fundamental to educational law in the United States: the state has authority over education.[41]

The act of 1642 remained in force until 1648, when clarifying amendments were added. And, it should be said, the amended act turned out to be the one most often copied by other New England colonies. While the purpose of the original act remained intact, the 1648 law told selectmen to teach children and apprentices to read English perfectly, to instruct them in the orthodox catechism and to prepare them for an honest, lawful calling, labor, and employment.[42] Should parents or masters fail, selectmen were empowered to enforce the law by removing children or apprentices from their custody.

Without doubting the significance of this early compulsory educational legislation or its influence on subsequent educational affairs, we can, nevertheless, inquire into the rigor of its enforcement. Early records attest the effort on the part of selectmen to enforce the law: in some cases children or apprentices were removed from the care of parents or masters by the intervention of the courts; in other cases, where selectmen appeared remiss, they were indicted for negligence. Still, there must have been hundreds of instances where selectmen were either unaware of violation or refused with honest effort to apply the law. Besides, in colonies being carved from wilderness meeting legal standard was often difficult or impossible. These factors made uneven the enforcement of the act of 1642 and all its amended versions, but for the quarter-century following enactment this legislation was taken seriously. Then, in the last quarter of the seventeenth century interest in compulsory education declined: in the first years of the eighteenth century, earlier colonial laws requiring instruction in reading were either ignored or rescinded. Public policy changed because religious commitment eroded and people were no longer certain that their educational future should be dictated by religious ministers.[43] In addition, the Indian wars brought considerable social and economic disruption and, as often happens with war, a decline in standards of behavior. The Indian wars were followed by a period of political upheaval, illustrated most prominently in the regime of Edmund Andros, and all colonial laws relating to compulsory education were repealed. Thus after a brave, bold beginning, zeal for learning evaporated and within a span of fifty years compulsory educational legislation disappeared from the lawbooks.[44]

What we have so far seen is only one, although possibly the most important, side of state action in education. By the end of the seventeenth century collective effort toward decent educational standard was all but abandoned, but while drift was in the direction of decay, the New England colonies tried to repair their old educational foundation. One shortcoming of the act of 1642 was the absence of any requirement for the founding of schools offering the kind of instruction legally required. The law left the provision of instruction in the unsteady and uncertain hands of parents and masters, an oversight in need of prompt redressing.

Naturally enough, compulsory features of the law of 1642 led some towns to open schools and nothing in the law or public policy discouraged them, although, it must be added, special encouragement was lacking also. By 1647, eleven New England towns had their own schools. Apparently this experience with voluntary town schools motivated colonial leaders to add another plank to the platform of public education by passing the law of 1647, the famous Old Deluder Satan Act.

This act, praised by some scholars for being the cornerstone of American free public education and blamed by others for having no deeper purpose than to perpetuate religious orthodoxy,[45] directed towns to establish schools. The colony had compulsory education; now it enjoined towns to open schools. According to the act, every town of fifty householders was to appoint a teacher for "all children as shall resort to him to write and read," and for his service the teacher was paid either by parents, masters, or the town itself. Teachers collecting tuition is nothing new; yet the act had a novel side: the people of the town could appropriate public money for the teacher's salary. This point leads some educational historians to the conclusion that the act of 1647 was incontrovertably the principal legal precedent for free public schools. Such judgments may be debated; in any event, the calendar had to be turned hundreds of times before a system of universal, free, and public education became a reality. Aside from the provision for public financing, the statute, it should be noticed, required the first foundations of learning in smaller towns, but larger towns were to do more. Towns with one hundred families or householders, the law said, should have a grammar school for children who, after elementary schooling, could be prepared for the university.

Remembering the pedagogic language of the day, we recognize the grammar school as a secondary school. The reference to university education was probably promotional literature for infant Harvard. Boys from wealthy families went to English universities; historical record tells us this was common, so the law's reference to higher education cannot be taken too seriously, nor can it be interpreted as colonial backing for public colleges and universities.

Towns willing to establish schools and comply with law were permitted, if large enough, to open one school with a master capable of handling elementary and secondary instruction. Very likely most towns followed this route, but some had two schools and two masters: one for reading and writing and the other to teach the prescribed curriculum of secondary education. Some towns, however, elected to do nothing and were fined five pounds for every year of non-compliance. Fines were paid to the nearest town with a school.

If towns had relatively little difficulty in accepting the law of 1642, the act of 1647 has a less favorable record.[46] This, perhaps, should be expected because it imposed a heavy burden on towns. Yet, burdensome or not, the law, like the earlier one, became a model for other New England colonies, and again, as with its predecessor, every colony save Rhode Island adopted similar compulsory school laws during the remaining years of the seventeenth century. Guided only by the public record, one could conclude that the law of 1647 was popular. Such a conclusion may be accurate. But the public record, it is alleged, was deceived by towns using clever ways to circumvent an unpopular statute.[47] Amendment to it evidences both satisfaction and dissatisfaction: in 1671 the fine imposed for non-compliance was increased to ten pounds and in 1683 to twenty pounds, providing the non-complying town had a population of two hundred families. In 1683, moreover, amendment more substantive than the amount of fine was added: towns with five hundred families were ordered to have two reading and writing schools and two grammar schools.

ISSUES OF CONTROL AND SUPPORT

Perhaps little can be gained by debating motives for colonial educational laws (whether primarily religious, economic, political, or literary) or the level of compliance achieved. Historians disagree sharply on both points. But on other sides to the matter agreement is easier: first, the principle was clearly established in the act of 1642 and reinforced in later laws that the state has authority to require a minimum of educational accomplishment among its citizens; second, the state is authorized to either establish schools wherein children may be instructed or impose on local communities the obligation to do so; third, the state may supervise and control the schools in order to ascertain levels of instructional quality; and finally, the state may direct local communities to use public funds for the support of instruction or appropriate public money for schools itself. These principles formed a legal legacy left to public education in the United States by New England.

In Southern and Middle colonies, although the principle of state authority was probably implicit in public policy, a zealous commitment to education was lacking, so illustrations of state action and direction in the affairs of learning are somewhat harder to find. The South tended to follow British precedent faithfully and was disposed to delegate scholastic management to the church. And the Southern church, adopting polity different from Congregationalism, was a centralized ecclesiastical body with final authority vested in the bishop. Thus, a delegation of educational authority from state to church could have assumed general and uniform school policies. Instead, the colonial Church of England permitted the various parishes to do as they pleased in education. Supervision was expected and perhaps some minimum of educational standard was erected, but its assessment was left to vestrymen and church wardens to determine. In theory, an appeal to the courts for an enforcement of standard implied in announced policy was possible, but in practice it was seldom done. Persons with legitimate complaint about the deficiencies of the system lacked standing for having their allegations heard by the court or anyone else. In consequence, the ordinary literary education of the Southern colonies was an ecclesiastical matter, although extraordinary educational issues, for example, those involving poor, orphaned, or illegitimate children, remained within the scope of civil authority. If a principle of state educational control evolved in the South, it stopped short of including the whole of education in its purview. Either by accident or design the state's responsibility extended to the orphaned and the poor (statutes of apprenticeship were always enforced), but operated without direction or enthusiasm on the level of regular literary instruction for a majority of youth.

In Virginia, in 1642, a law governing apprenticeship practice was enacted, and later during the colonial period Virginia had more than a dozen statutes pertaining to apprenticeship, a few of which required, as had the Massachusetts Bay law of 1642, that children be taught to read and write along with learning a trade.[48] In the parishes little initiative was demonstrated in opening schools, although here and there a parish arranged for a minister, or some qualified person, to conduct a parish school. In such schools, students able to pay for instruction did so; those unable to pay were taught without charge. But nowhere is practice as progressive as in Massachusetts, where, after 1647, towns were allowed to use public money for supporting instruction. Nor is there much evidence pointing to the construction of schools.

Virginia, in the South, was able to stay in the vanguard of educational activity, but even in Virginia only about one-tenth of the parishes made provision for anything faintly resembling public education. Emphasized instead was a system to care for the poor. In public poor schools, the record suggests without confirmation, girls as well as boys were taught.

Following Virginia's example, Maryland (in 1694) and South Carolina (in 1710) created educational corporations to conduct Latin grammar schools. These schools, secondary rather than elementary, were free schools for the poor. But corporate initiative was largely ineffective in creating permanent schools (save in Maryland where King William's School became St. John's College) on a colony-wide basis; and what is more, being secondary schools, their offer of free education to poor children meant little. Poor children were unable to obtain the prerequisite elementary instruction, and in any case, there was among them no great thirst for knowledge of the Latin language or the ancient classics.

Compared to New England the educational zeal of the South is hardly praiseworthy; yet we must remember the political, economic, geographic, social, and religious realities of the South argued against energetic government action. Despite a haphazard record on schooling and schools, the South recognized the principle, regularly gaining strength in New England and elsewhere, that government authority over education was both right and proper.[49] Thus, the four legal principles we have noticed existed without active support in the South, but their authenticity went undiminished by educational inactivity.

In the Middle colonies the educational traditions were remarkably like those of New England. But political instability in New York and religious burden in Pennsylvania conspired to undermine them. Colonial government was willing to assert educational prerogative and, on occasion, to demonstrate it by creating schools, legislating standards for teachers' licenses, or promoting education generally. But these intermittent outbursts were insufficient to produce a vital state system whose worth, given the cultural differences and distinctive religious temperaments of the people, was obvious enough to kindle popular allegiance to schooling. In the end, private rather than public education took the lead and almost alone stands out in the educational history of the Middle colonies. Private educational leadership was accomplished, however, without rejecting state authority, so government held its educational powers in reserve, to exercise them later, as illustrated by the constitutional provision covering education (the first of any of the states) in the constitution of the state of Pennsylvania in 1776: "A school or schools shall be established in every county by the legislature, for the convenient instruction of youth, with such salaries to the masters, paid by the public, as may enable them to instruct youth at low prices; and all useful learning shall be duly encouraged and promoted in one or more universities."

Although exercised variously, and sometimes not at all, the principal educational legacy of seventeenth-century colonial America was that the state possesses, and may exercise, legitimate authority over education within its borders.

CHAPTER FIVE

Colonial Schools and Schoolmasters

In various ways the colonies clarified and endorsed the principle that education was within their ambit of authority, and from time to time they exercised this authority. The section of the country where colonial government was most active in exercising educational authority was New England, so we should look there first to see how educational principle was reduced to the level of day-to-day instructional practice.[1] But we should realize that even in New England, colonial government, working through the agency of its legislature (the General Court), was under no obligation to exercise directly the educational authority it claimed. It could require a minimum standard of instruction, demand that schools be opened and maintained, set the length of the school term, the subjects to be studied, the means of supporting schools, and the qualifications for teachers. But all these were subject to delegation, and in the case of the New England colonies this is usually what happened.[2]

Conceding that education might be managed more effectively on a level closer to the people, the General Court directed towns to open schools and maintain standards set by law.[3] The town was a local jurisdiction and its relationship to the colony was similar to the county's in the South,[4] or later, the township's in the Northwest Territory. Towns were managed by officers selected in and responsible to the town meeting, a legislative body of the town's citizens. It was the business of the town meeting to set public policy; selectmen and other town officers were expected to administer policy. Thus, in matters pertaining to education, the town meeting decided the degree of compliance with colonial educational law and articulated local policy with respect to the level and quality of schooling offered. And allowing for the permissive character of the

Massachusetts act of 1647, towns decided whether or not to support schools from the public treasury.[5]

This historic delegation of state authority led to the fiction that educational management is a purely local matter, entirely outside the legal competence of either federal or state government. No doubt New England towns had considerable latitude in exercising delegated authority, but colonial law was always ready to remind them where real authority lay.[6] In the first decades of experience with local and state relationships in education, it became clear that a formulation of educational policy and the supervision of schools were difficult charges for the town meeting itself to fulfill. Thus special committees were constituted and charged with responsibility for managing schools, and in these committees we see the genesis of local school boards, school committees, or boards of education.

Local management of education could pose a problem: some towns were extensive in geographic area, with scattered population, so establishing one town school was hardly the way to offer instruction to all children. Necessity being the mother of invention, districts were carved out in towns and a school was authorized for each district; sometimes these districts were permitted to have their own school committees. From this practice of making the means of education available and the management of schools a responsibility of those who used them, the district system of school organization had its beginnings. The district system appears to have originated in New England, where it became popular, but it was used in other parts of the country too.

Enough attention has been given to legal foundation for state authority in education. Now we should see what this meant to schools, the curriculum they offered, and teachers instructing students. At the outset, it is safe to assume, all levels of colonial instruction tried to imitate similar levels in England.

COLONIAL ELEMENTARY EDUCATION

Dame Schools

Private venture usually played a part in disseminating learning, so it is hard to think of a time in Western educational history when private venture went unpracticed.[7] Given England's educational preferences, the assumption is almost certainly correct that private venture was more popular there than elsewhere in Europe. And among the schools for elementary teaching the first and most popular private-venture institution (if it deserves so formal a description) was the dame school. Private as they were, and often conducted in the home of the schoolmistress, without any obligation to keep records or make reports to town or colony, the American history of dame schools is exceedingly hard to write and, at best, is supported by few documents. Still, we know with certainty that they—along with petty schools in the South—were extant, and we know, moreover, that they were fairly numerous. Given the character of such schools and the scholarly accomplishment of persons conducting them, one may make certain assumptions: their curriculum was a simple fare, consisting of the alphabet, a little spelling, the basic skills of reading, some moral lessons, and religious instruction.[8]

If girls attended, and good reason for doubting their attendance is lacking, they learned some sewing and knitting in addition to their A B C and reading. For girls the dame school was terminal: the wisdom of the day said this was all the formal learning girls would find useful.[9] Boys passed from the dame to the town school where, under a master's direction, they continued their elementary schooling. Some town schools, it appears, helped keep dame schools in business, for they expected their students to read when they arrived, and at that time, when family instruction could be erratic, skill in reading could be obtained by attendance for a term or two at a dame school.[10] Indeed, some dame schools were encouraged and supported by towns, and there is fragile evidence that the dame-school teacher sometimes received part of her salary from the public treasury. But this was unusual.

Further details on the dame-school course are needless, since its dimension is easily perceived; nor is anything gained by declaiming against the quality of the persons who conducted these schools. We may be fairly certain that dame-school teachers were seldom well-educated, but considering what they were expected to teach, no one complained.

Reading accounts of dame schools, those kitchen academies kept by ambitious women in their homes, we wonder where whatever erudition their mistresses possessed came from. In an age when women were only infrequently educated, the appearance of a woman capable of conducting a school even as simple as the dame school must come as a surprise. Perhaps she herself was an extraordinary product of another dame school; more likely she was a person of rare talent (history is full of them), who despite the convention of the time was nevertheless decently educated. Edward Eggleston quotes a colonial spokesman: "Probably not one woman in a dozen could write," and adds that "Governor Winthrop was convinced that much learning was dangerous to a woman's wits."[11] The best bet, considering the religious temperament of the colonies, is that they learned to read at home under the careful eye of parents, whose literary skill was honed in about the same way.

Yet private teachers, it appears, were plentiful enough to have accommodated some girls, and in a few instances energetic enough to open boarding schools where, now and then, a girl might appear for a period of instruction arranged to suit her convenience. It is hard to believe that many boarding schools for girls were extant anywhere in the colonies, although Seybolt mentions a few and quotes from a newspaper advertisement for one which, judging from the studies recited, must have been meant for girls: "At the house of Mr. George Brownell in Wings-Lane, Boston, is taught Writing, Cyphering, Dancing, Treble Violin, Flute, Spinnet, etc. Also English and French Quilting, Imbroidery, Florishing, Plain Work, Marking in several sorts of Stiches and several other works, where Scholars may board."[12] Still, despite some attention to their educational needs, colonial girls were always outside the scholastic mainstream. Considering centuries of neglect for the tuition of half society's members, and remembering that all colonial leaders were authentic heirs to this tradition of neglect, we are tempted to find praiseworthy what little was done on behalf of women's education.

One final word should be added about dame schools: most numerous in New England, all colonies had them and thousands of children in colonial America received all their schooling in them.

Town Elementary Schools

Searching for permanent historical foundations among early colonial schools, distracts us from the dame school, for its course was run early, and when better schools opened the dame school disappeared. But while dame schools were still alive, town elementary schools made an appearance. With ancient and honorable roots extending all the way to medieval Europe, it would be wrong to represent town schools as colonial inventions. In transplanted form town elementary schools had two sides: one concentrated on writing and arithmetic, the other on instruction in reading. In England, possibly because of the currency of special skill and the availability of essential instructional materials for writing and arithmetic, it was common to teach these basic educational tools, but only when their utility was clear. Reading, a more ubiquitous and essential skill than writing, was considered the equivalent of a general elementary education and was taught in a separate school. In the colonies, however, this somewhat unorthodox and, from a contemporary point of view, indefensible separation was halted, and town elementary schools tried to maintain a curriculum consisting of reading, writing, arithmetic, and religion.

Some towns, failing to find a pressing need for instruction in calculation, dropped arithmetic from the syllabus, but such cases were rare. Probably more commonly, especially in commercial centers, the significance of ciphering was inflated, and in consequence less heed was paid other studies in elementary schools. In any case, early laws pertaining to town-school instruction prescribed the teaching of reading and writing, and we may be fairly certain, despite the names of the schools, that both subjects formed staple elements in the curriculum. In Boston, for example, two types of public schools were conducted: the writing school, always elementary, and the Latin school, always secondary, but we know careful and regular instruction both in reading and arithmetic was given in the writing school.[13]

In large towns with a scattered population, before district schools were introduced, instructional opportunity afforded by town elementary schools was ensured for all children by having schools move from one part of a town to another at different times of the year. The moving school, although of no special historical significance should be on the record. It survived as long, and no longer, than was necessary.[14]

In colonies outside New England town schools were in evidence too. In New Netherland such schools resulted from the mutual action of municipal and church leaders, and in most cases some part of the expense of maintaining schools was shared between town and church. And in this colony the cost of such schools must have been considerable, for the teacher, often a minor church officer, received as compensation a house along with a small salary. This arrangement of sharing the expense of schooling implied that the appointment of town-school teachers required the ratification of both parties. In the absence of sectarianism this arrangement could succeed, but when religious diversity became rampant the town schoolmaster capable of fulfilling the expectation of orthodoxy became rarer and rarer.[15] Sectarian difference, more than anything else, stood as an obstacle to the stability of town schools in the Middle colonies. The nature of Southern settlement and society seldom recommended town elementary schools as a means for instructing children, so to search the records of the South for illustrations of town schools is unrewarding.

Wherever found, town schools were unpretentious educational agencies; and nothing sophisticated about the materials and methods of instruction or ornamental about the credentials of their teachers should be expected. In dame and town schools alike, reading materials were selected for their orthodoxy, and at this time, especially in New England, nothing could have been more orthodox than the *New-England Primer*. This was a simple book from which students learned their alphabet, the bare elements of reading skill, and some religious and moral precepts.[16] Writing instruction required paper and pen or chalk and slate and was mainly a matter of learning to trace letters. Even elementary composition was too ambitious for these schools. Arithmetic, taught without benefit of textbook for most of the seventeenth century, depended for its quality almost entirely on what schoolmasters knew about the subject.[17] And who were these schoolmasters?

A general and universally satisfactory answer to the question is almost impossible: elementary teachers varied greatly in educational accomplishment, dedication to teaching, and pedagogic skill. Despite the practice of licensing town schoolmasters, many persons unfit for teaching found their way to the schoolhouse; yet evidence of scholarship and commitment to solid pedagogy appears often enough to convince us that some young men, possibly using teaching as a stepping stone to the pulpit, came to town schools with superior qualifications for directing elementary instruction. These teachers could be called upon to conduct the higher classes preparing boys for college too. In any case, some young men took a furlough from college for a term or two and earned money by teaching. Uncommitted to teaching as a lifelong career, the refugee from Harvard or Yale was nevertheless taking a useful and not altogether unprofitable interlude from collegiate regimen. Others, having finished college studies, and aspiring to the ministry, became town schoolmasters while waiting for a vacant pulpit. And teaching gave them some practice for the ministry, because in most New England communities teachers were considered church officers, subordinate only to ministers.[18]

Teachers filling these two categories were unquestionably the cream of the crop, but their appearance, infrequent and irregular, never met the needs of colonial schools. Educated men could hardly be expected to remain in town schools, hearing lessons, passing the horn book for reading, watching boys trace letters on a slate, and demanding accomplishment by encouragement first, and failing this, by fear and punishment. So, under the circumstances, the places left vacant by good teachers were filled by those willing, for whatever reason, to try their hand at keeping school for a term or two. Most schoolmasters in early town schools remained less than a full term, so children experienced a good deal of pedagogic interruption as they progressed toward modest instructional goals.[19]

With the exception of dogmatic pronouncements on child care made by John Cotton and Cotton Mather from the sheltered theological precincts in Massachusetts and, in the late eighteenth century, the *Schulordnung* of Christopher Dock of Pennsylvania, educational literature was slim, and almost totally silent on the theory and practice of elementary instruction. Children should be taught reading and writing; in addition they should be drilled in preparation for a public catechizing (interrogation on religious precept) by the minister before the entire congregation. With these objectives so clearly understood, what need had elementary teaching for theory?

Still, this oversight was partly redressed in the first years of the eighteenth century by the Society for the Propagation of the Gospel in Foreign Parts. After reciting the usual preamble making instruction a handmaiden to religion, the Society's tract on schooling praised teaching for understanding, especially when knowledge was to be memorized; it recommended, besides, schooling in good manners and morals, and a tempering of the whole discipline of the school with a spirit of kindness and gentility instead of harshness and brutality. This was a good omen for elementary schools, but it is hard to believe that many eighteenth-century teachers heeded this excellent advice if, by chance, it was called to their attention.[20]

Dock's methods, coincidentally amplifying the recommendations of the Society, followed the same lines to kindle a spirit of curiosity about learning among young scholars. Believing motivation came from desire for learning itself, Dock downgraded fear, conventionally befriended by teachers, as a spur to study. It appears he was also innovative, since he introduced his classes to newspapers, letters, and books for the reading lesson rather than relying, as most teachers did, on catechisms and selections carefully culled from scripture.[21]

Other Schools

In the Middle colonies and the South, in addition to dame and petty schools and occasional town schools, elementary education was offered in charity schools, supported by public spirited citizens and sometimes by the public treasury or churches and religious societies; private elementary schools, conducted by persons who made teaching and schoolkeeping their business; parochial schools, activated by various religious sects; and endowed schools, educational ventures maintained by land and money endowments from private persons who took this way to show an interest in the education of children and the welfare of the country. All these schools conducted elementary instruction along entirely conventional lines. Innovation in teaching practice was infrequent and irregular, and almost purely accidental. If from time to time or place to place it wrestled with convention, it made only a small mark on history, and in the end its influence was erased by the obliterating forces of time.

COLONIAL SECONDARY EDUCATION

Wherever colonial secondary schools were located and whatever their name, all belonged to the same scholastic genre and followed the same academic regimen; courses in their curricula were similar, the same classical authors were read, teachers needed credentials to teach Latin and Greek and the literature of the ancient world, and students were expected to finish their education in a college or university. There is no reason to suppose that colonial grammar schools were, or wanted to be, different from their European counterparts. They recognized and prized their aristocratic image: the course of study and the whole atmosphere of the schools were geared to young men with the leisure, money, and talent to enter college and follow a trail of intellectual cultivation leading to positions of influence in society. The best colonial secondary schools were private, but geographic location was largely irrelevant, so we find excellent ones scattered around the colonial world. Grammar masters belonged to a tribe of remarkable men, exhibiting combinations of scholarship and business acumen, but as a class they avoided educational innovation. They took traditional models of secondary education and did their best to imitate them in the colonies.[22]

Boys entering grammar schools (the seventeenth-century name for a secondary school) were already able to read and write English, so teachers introduced them to Latin. With modest proficiency in Latin, they read the easier authors; but when they had mastered Latin they spent almost all their time reading and interpreting the classics. Later in the course Greek was tackled and some scholars, we are told, learned enough of this difficult language to read the Greek classics. But this was unusual. Most secondary schools were satisfied with elementary instruction in Greek and this would not have allowed boys to sample much of the Greek classical heritage. Hebrew, too, mentioned in accounts of the time, was a subject where only modest achievement was expected. Latin had scholastic pride of place and its place was justified: to master the Latin language personal discipline was essential and this discipline, it was argued, was the main reward from formal education. After discipline, Latin's utility was promoted. Knowledge was stored in Latin literature; theological discourse and dogma had Latin rendering; and the Latin legacy, so much a part of education, stilled the voice of colonial preacher, magistrate, or schoolmaster rash enough to question it.

The grammar schools prescribed by the act of 1647 and its amended versions almost defy accurate description, because of their variety. All embraced the same educational goals, but whether or not these goals were realized depended almost entirely on the quality of teachers towns could employ. Some towns, we know, had one teacher and commissioned him to handle both elementary and secondary instruction. Dividing time between teaching reading and writing, on one hand, and Latin, Greek, and classical literature, on the other, even gifted teachers must have found it impossible to be always at their pedagogic best. In any case, a grammar school's character and reputation depended on the teacher's ability and learning. But considering the range of the school's curriculum, we can be confident that grammar-school masters had no choice but to be superior to teachers in elementary schools. All had some college study, either here or in Europe, and many, no doubt, were college graduates waiting for an empty pulpit and a congregation ready to ordain them as ministers, if Calvinists, or to adopt them as preachers, if they adhered to some other denomination. The industry so characteristic of New England preachers may have been planted in the fertile souls of young men marking time as schoolmasters.

Solid learning, evidenced by most schoolmasters, was one thing; pedagogic insight and skill were something else, and we lack assurance that prospective ministers, possibly recent graduates from Harvard College, were skillful in transmitting their own knowledge in a systematic way to their pupils. Some few heaped considerable fame on their schools, but the majority are not remembered even in the schools they helped found. One of the best colonial grammar schools was in Boston and one of the ornaments of colonial pedagogy, Ezekiel Cheever, was the school's master for almost a quarter century. Neither Cheever nor his school is typical, yet both are illustrative of colonial secondary education at its best.[23]

The course in the Boston secondary school lasted seven years. This was probably a concession to colonial educational conditions because the conventional Latin grammar school had a nine-year course. Boys (never girls) who attended had a background of three or four years in the elementary school or equivalent instruction from a tutor, so secondary teaching turned immediately to the mysteries of Latin grammar. After grasping the elements of grammar and vocabulary, students began reading phrase books and graded readers. This occupied them for three years or so. Then came more serious Latin books such as Cordier's *Latin Conversations* and Aesop's *Fables*. After four years of study they were reading Erasmus, Ovid, and Cicero, and from now to the end of the course the classics occupied most of their time. Yet a little room was left for history, poetry, and rhetoric. Rhetoric and poetry were important and should not be slighted: leaving the secondary school a boy was expected to be able to understand what he read, to write and speak clearly and persuasively, and to think cogently.[24] However, in spite of these ideals, no grammar-school master was commissioned to complete the rhetorical syllabus. Tradition reserved the best treasures of this subject for higher education.

With the end of the course in sight, boys were introduced to Greek, and in the Boston school (perhaps the finest illustration of colonial secondary education), they were expected to read Greek with a facility enabling them to handle Homer, Hesiod, and the New Testament. Special courses in religion are notoriously missing from curricular muster, although we must take for granted the school's commitment to denominational religion. Opportunities were plentiful for introducing religious creed and perspective; the classics themselves were inexhaustible mines for moral and religious lessons, and the straight and narrow path of orthodoxy was always blazed by the Bible and the Church Fathers. Religion may not have been obvious but it was everywhere prominent in the books the young scholars read as part of their regular school studies.[25]

Colonial secondary education followed a nearly inflexible pattern except on the level of support: town Latin grammar schools received modest support from the town treasury in most colonies; in private schools tuition usually bore the whole expense of instruction, although some private schools were founded and partly supported by philanthropy and religion.

A function common to all Latin grammar schools was stated in published prospectuses and repeated every time a headmaster spoke of his
school: to follow the classical curriculum in preparing young men for
responsible positions in church and state. Once this preparatory function
was accounted for fully in secondary schools, and some colonial masters
believed fervently in their ability to fulfill it, but time and the inexorable
force of scholastic change took their toll to make secondary education
preparatory to college study. In the colonies, the college was the pinnacle
of educational accomplishment and in it ambitious and able young men
finished their preparation to meet the world.

But even with the college occupying the last rung of the academic ladder,
the secondary-school course was carefully selected and organized; its principal thrust, always classical, was supplemented by the Bible. School days were
long, discipline was severe; masters took seriously the business of learning
and allowed no boy to remain ignorant without protest. If school life was
dull, filled with routine, and starved for recreation, we must remind ourselves
that most boys in these schools came from aristocratic families wherein they
were steeled for a scholastic regimen of rigor and hardship. No one promised
them an easy life. Teachers leading students over the hurdles of scholarship
varied enormously in learning and ability to teach; their commitment to
teaching varied too. Some were themselves hurdles for students to leap.

THE COLONIAL COLLEGE

Infant colonial colleges were small schools with enrollments of a dozen or
two students; during the long years before the revolutionary war, a school
with a hundred boys in attendance was considered large and prosperous.
Because colleges were small, one or two buildings, interchangeable as
dormitories, chapels, refectories, and classrooms, were enough. Without
exception these schools were poor and their only dependable source of
income was tuition from students. Remaining solvent was a constant
worry, often a veritable conundrum testing the ingenuity of college
presidents throughout the colonial period. Handicapped by depleted
treasuries, the colleges followed practices of academic frugality, seldom
providing much beyond the bare essentials for the education of boys
who came. The appurtenances to learning, taken for granted in a more
modern age, were either unknown or unwelcome: they did without
libraries, except for books the president husbanded in his study or the
ones collected by student library societies, but many other things were
absent, too, and, for the most part, higher learning in America began by
practicing how to put up with impoverishment.

Neglecting the poverty and austerity of the colonial college leads to an
imperfect view, yet there were other sides and these other sides reveal the

character of the schools better than their perennial subscription to poverty and dourness. First and foremost, they, in company with other colonial schools, were transplanted. Trying to be authentic representatives of European models of higher learning, they traced their inheritance to medieval universities, and while this was good enough in some respects, for the foundations of medieval higher learning were solid, neither their religious appetite nor their temperament allowed them to overlook the amendments to medieval educational practice introduced by Humanists and Protestants. So their proximate model was not the medieval university, but one distilled in the ferment of reformation centuries. The most direct influence of all came from Emmanuel, a college of Cambridge University. The seeds of British influence were planted in Harvard Yard and the colonial educational wind was just strong enough to broadcast them to all the infant colleges. Their quick cultivation in fertile colonial soil produced a harvest of ministers, and for most of the colonial years the colleges were determined to fly the banner of religious or theological institutes from their academic mast.[26]

Of twenty-six colleges founded before 1800, twenty-three had predominantly religious goals, and the three state colleges—Georgia, North Carolina, and Vermont—although without official affiliation with religious sects came under definite denominational influence.[27] Even the University of Pennsylvania, a school nurtured in Franklin's Academy, while doing its best to abstain from sectarian domination, bowed at various times in its early history to religious control. Almost without exception the early colleges were presided over by minister-presidents, and the colleges themselves, although they may never have been mere theological institutes, were interested primarily in preparing an educated or a learned clergy. Religious sects whose theology was dogmatic and devotion ritualistic needed clergymen with a grounding in classical learning, but this was only a place to start. They wanted ministers who were expert in elaborating and defending their creed and who also were trained in performing the liturgical functions of the sect. Evangelical sects, however, without need for ministers trained along such lines, were ashamed when their ministers were ignorant, illiterate, and barren of polite learning, so they opened colleges to train ministers in their own way. Understandably enough, preference for classical learning was standard in a literary world taking pride in academic decency, so one need not ask why the usual humanistic studies were staples in the college curriculum. And for those sects whose ministers needed special theological knowledge, adding the specialty of dogmatic theology seems reasonable enough.

We understand the motivation of Congregationalists and Presbyterians who created colleges for the education of ministers, but the evangelical sects, the Baptists and others, needed better justification, for their ministers found the source of truth in inspiration and intuition, not reason, and the doctrine of justification by faith contained, at the very least, the implication that learning could be repudiated with impunity. Why did evangelical denominations extend themselves to found higher schools?

It was unquestionably hard for unlettered laymen to see why ministers should be skilled in science, rhetoric, logic, and philosophy when their profession was to preach lessons from the Bible. The word of God, they thought, had a clear, simple and unmistakable meaning, and man's mind, they had been told, was incapable of adding anything to what God had said. Thus, they could take a stand in opposition to education both for laymen and clergymen, because learning, at best, was useless and, at worst, could be a dangerous impediment to the undisguised teachings of the Holy Ghost, the only teacher acknowledged to be trustworthy. Within this context of a naive but plausible rejection of learning, Protestant theologians were forced to defend the proposition of justification by faith without allowing it to become a justification for ignorance and illiteracy.[28]

The colleges established by evangelical sects were intended to prepare ministers in polite learning, a learning allowing them to take positions free from the stigma attached to rude and ignorant men. Clerically-minded students could be educated in the colleges of other denominations, so every denomination did not need its own colleges, but such exposure might contaminate them and erode their sectarian loyalty and zeal. In the friendly climate of a college run by their own sect they could avoid the persistent proselytism so characteristic of the colleges of the time. Besides, the colleges of evangelical sects regularly regarded their purpose as being, in addition to education, highly missionary, and they sent out cadres of missionaries dedicated to the conversion of all manner of persons in this pioneer land. Whether or not this religious circuit-riding could be balanced with academic objectives was a small issue and gave neither devout professors nor ardent students any cause to worry about the literary credentials of their schools. Yet, despite the activity of missionary colleges, the chronicle of colonial college development is mainly one of colleges founded by dogmatic sects, where, if missionary zeal was not especially prominent, it was not totally abandoned either. Only about fifteen percent of the permanent colleges founded before the Civil War were evangelical in sectarian affiliation.[29]

Apart from the great design to educate ministers in their own way, what was the personality of these colonial colleges? What were their prominent and, in some respects, distinctive seventeenth- and early eighteenth-century features?

The sons of ministers, well-to-do merchants and planters, and others with sufficient leisure and money appeared at the colonial colleges' gates. They were there because their parents wanted them to be leaders in ecclesiastic and civic society. Beyond common parental purpose for sending sons to college, the boys themselves were hardly a homogeneous group.

Some were very young—nothing more than little boys—and others were mature young men. Most had attended a Latin grammar school, but for a few, who had their own tutors, the college course was an introduction to school. But this was of no concern to the college president, who fulfilled the role of admissions officer. He simply tested the boys' ability to read and translate some elementary Latin and Greek passages. Thus, at the outset, the college entrance examination was a reading test, but toward the close of the colonial period the admission standard was stiffened and arithmetic was added to the list of subjects in which prospective college students would have to show accomplishment. However, we think few boys were refused admission to any college because of their inability to pass the entrance examination. The college could make arrangements to tutor boys whose preparation was deficient, or simply ignore the standard of achievement the tests implied and admit all the applicants.

If there was wide difference in age, ability, and interest among colonial college students, there was also considerable latitude in religious commitment. Religious tests were denied official standing in the early colleges, so a boy could attend a school whose religious affiliation was different from his. But these claims for religious toleration in college life, while having a nominal authenticity, may really have been beside the point: what religiously-sensitive parent would send a boy to a college whose denominationalism was repugnant to him? Institutional religious affinity was no mystery to anyone, nor did the colleges try to conceal their intention of making all students conform to good order in the school; and first on the list of a litany of good order was participation in religious service and prayer. Almost certainly, only a rare student would have ventured bravely into a college conducted by a sect whose creed he disbelieved or rejected. And it would have been extraordinary for denominations to use their resources establishing and maintaining colleges where they wanted to prepare ministers for their churches and then admit students whose religious posture was uncertain or unacceptable.

Few lawful amusements are mentioned in the codes governing student life. Puritan temperament displayed a special fondness for hard work and personal austerity and was disdainful of all idleness and frivolity; in other colonies, although theological justification for self-abnegation was less certain, time was a precious commodity, too fleeting to be wasted on sport and games. Physical recreation must have been thought a frivolous pastime, for we look in vain for collegiate schedules providing for periods of diversion and enjoyable alternatives to the school books. Colonial colleges had no time for sport, so the accounts of student life are silent with respect to inter-school competition on the playing fields. If competitive traits were to be honed, this could be done, college officers said, in scholastic settings. But without the blessing or encouragement of their mentors, boys engaged in sport and provided for their own recreation, although they heard their teachers tell them that such things were subversive of serious study. Turning their back on the lighter side of life, these colleges did their best to maintain a social regimen (supposedly compatible with serious study) too severe for most monasteries wherein asceticism was an article of faith. Students spent their leisure time talking and walking when they were disposed to follow the regulations on behavior; nothing else seemed quite proper for young men in schools whose official policy made a fetish of religious regularity.

Still, these students were boys and young men, an unalterable condition even in the climate of places like Yale, Harvard, and Princeton. They could have fun on their own time. Students bowed to rule and regulation, as befits normal student temperament, when violation was impossible. Sometimes they challenged the official definition of good order, upset the tranquil environment for learning, ignored their disciplinary taskmasters and the bonds of college restraint to become wanton and disorderly. They brawled, broke furniture and windows, played practical jokes on their tutors and fellow students, and had what they chose to regard as good fun. If they were caught and convicted, they were punished according to the seriousness of their crimes, and this meant they could be assigned special prayers or studies, confined to a special room without food or drink, or whipped by the college disciplinarian. Some violations of college rule were unpardonable: for these offending students were expelled.

The college curriculum offers us a more penetrating view of the personality of these schools. The curriculum of any school or college reveals the expectations society has for its educational institutions and the students who attend them. It contains an explicit endorsement of the values of character and mind judged at that time to be most essential to an educated community. By examining the curriculum of the colonial college we are able to ascertain the cultural pressures affecting, and to a very considerable extent directing, the work of the colleges.

The curriculum was an adaptation of the course of study common in medieval universities; it was, moreover, prescribed and inflexible. Students were required to spend three fourths of their time on Latin and Greek, both language and literature; the rest of the time was spent on mathematics, natural philosophy (the academic designation for chemistry and physics), and rhetoric. And these studies were set in a context totally dominated by religious value and belief. The course of study was expected to produce ministers, lawyers, physicians, educated gentlemen and, above all, God-fearing Christians. Besides, it was commissioned to activate all the powers of the mind through mental discipline and it was the single avenue to the degree of bachelor of arts. Most American colleges began with a four-year course and styled the respective classes freshman, sophomore, junior, and senior, although a few colleges departed from this practice and organized a seven-year program, combining secondary and college studies.

The principal, sometimes the only, teacher was the college president himself. Assuming the stance of a universal man, he conducted classes, presided over all religious functions, cared for the sick, administered the school, collected money, recruited and admitted students, and in many cases acted as the pastor of the local church. When conditions warranted, that is, when the president was too busy or classes became too large, a few teachers were added with the assignment either to assist the president in his instructional duties or to teach their own classes. Teaching a class meant teaching every subject in the syllabus.

Neither specialists nor specializing professors graced the faculties of these early schools. College presidents and professors were young men who only a few years before had finished college study. They, too, along with masters in Latin grammar schools were waiting for a pulpit to call, and when it did they left college teaching. Although mature, brilliant, and cultivated men sometimes came to the colleges as presidents or professors, many college teachers, temporarily situated, were otherwise preoccupied and allowed their scholarly interests and aptitudes to atrophy. The colleges were poorly equipped to promote serious scholarship and good pedagogy.

This being the case, we should not be surprised when students scorned the college course, indicting its irrelevance and sterility and condemning repressive and unimaginative modes of teaching. Students, we know, were required to translate lines of Latin and Greek, to work problems in mathematics, to master a certain number of pages in a textbook, and to write compositions on vague and vapid topics. Classroom method seldom departed from simple recitation and drill and this reminded students of the lower schools where most of them had fulfilled an apprenticeship. Perceptive students wondered when the college course would enliven their minds, but prudence recommended some caution in expression of complaint against an established system, so we read these caveats, if we read them at all, in memoirs. Run-of-the-mill students, always in a majority, accepted collegiate fare with docility, suppressing any distress they might have felt, and looked forward confidently to better days with college life behind them. With so bleak an environment for life and for learning, we are led, not to complain of or concentrate on the weakness of colonial higher education, but to stand in awe of a program capable of producing generations of versatile, imaginative, perceptive, and decently educated men.

The colonial college was a private school with control vested in an external, self-perpetuating board of trustees. This board was responsible for articulating basic educational policy; the president, appointed by the board, was charged with conducting the school in a way compatible with this policy. Since the colleges were intimately associated with religious sects, owing their origin to them, we understand why boards of control were dominated by clergymen. At this point, external control, the colleges of America ruptured their lifeline with European university models: universities of Europe were governed by their faculties; colleges of the colonies were controlled by men who lived their lives and practiced their professions outside college gates.[30]

CHAPTER SIX

Intellectual Ferment: Learning and Education in a New Nation

The era of American national consciousness had its birth with the adoption of the Constitution, but before the War of Revolution—an essential antecedent to the Constitution—the seams holding the colonies fast to the mother country were beginning to give. We have no need here to follow the political and military history leading to the founding of a new nation, but we should understand that revolutions simmer before they boil, so in preparation for the American Revolution some tilling of political and social discord took place. Tilling consisted, first, of a gradual weaning of the colonies to the mother country were in place. Next, it meant some self-reliance and confidence, even when the political stanchions holding the colonies to the mother country were in place. Next, it means some discounting of the worth of an inherited culture. Old cultural bonds were obvious and commanded respect; colonists did not want to become cultural orphans, but this did not prevent them from trying to adapt old cultural convictions to the novel conditions of American life.

Third, the organization of society itself perpetuated class distinctions Europe had learned to embrace. While the social structure could be excused by good theoretic justification, it was constantly tested in a frontier land largely deaf to the persuasion of social philosophy. The pedigree of a man, or a family, counted less than an ability to cope with the changing and unpredictable conditions of wilderness life. Social distinction was hard to maintain in day-to-day life, and with practical weaknesses disclosed in the crucible of pioneer experience, the old theories convention kept intact began to disintegrate. Finally, religion supplied a cohesive element in colonial society; divergent and competing sects paid it homage. But the conditions of life in a new country argued against theological

119

exclusiveness, and men began to doubt the lessons they had been taught by their European forebears on theological purity and sectarian autonomy.

This foundation of discontent, so briefly touched, was laid insidiously: it started slowly and gained momentum as the outbreak of hostilities between England and the colonies became imminent. With the advent of the new nation the spirit of transition was fed by the urgent requirements of national life. If we think mainly of education, this movement of transition was one of adapting inherited (transplanted) intellectual patterns and human institutions, first to the conditions of colonial men and then to realities imposed by an infant state. Signs of instructional reorganization were evident in Benjamin Franklin's "Proposals Relating to the Education of Youth in Pensilvania" of 1749. One quotation is enough to indicate the direction a new education was expected to take: "As to their Studies, it would be well if they could be taught *every Thing* that is useful, and *every Thing* that is ornamental: But Art is long, and their Time is short. It is therefore propos'd that they learn those Things that are likely to be *most useful* and *most ornamental.* Regard being had to the several Professions for which they are intended."[1]

Franklin knew both the content and the goals of colonial schools, and moreover, he knew they had a commitment to perpetuating tested social traditions in their ornamental and gentlemanly objectives. He could see how in imitating the conventional curriculum of European Humanistic schools they were insensitive to colonial social horizons. His advice to schools, forwarding his own as well as the recommendations of others, was to apply principles of selection to school studies, always giving pride of place to practical ones. If this trumpeting of useful knowledge was not new—for we know Bacon idealized utility and the colonists themselves had usually displayed a healthy practical attitude toward learning—at least it provided a contemporary charter for scholastic reform, and it served to promote, not create, conditions leading to the birth of a new nation.

Writing more somberly than Franklin, although with perhaps a smaller audience, Noah Webster recited the dangers of a foreign education.[2] In "Dissertations on the English Language," published in Boston in 1789, he elaborated his objection to a continued dependence both on European educational models—which had for too long dominated the schools of the colonies—and on the practice of sending boys to Europe for their education. In any case, the effect of foreign education, he argued, whether obtained by going directly to Europe or by attending American schools infected by European prototypes, was injurious both to national pride and native political institutions, but most of all to an American language. These grave reasons, Webster said, should motivate Americans to direct their best energy to the establishment of school systems with instructional programs geared to serving their own interests.

He proposed an American standard, independent of the English standard, and that it be inculcated in the schools of the country: "As an independent nation, our honor requires us to have a system of our own, in language as well as government. Great Britain, whose children we are, and whose language we speak, should no longer be *our* standard; for the taste of her writers is already corrupted, and her language on the decline. But if it were not so, she is at too great a distance to be our model, and to instruct us in the principles of our own tongue. . . . Several circumstances render a future separation of the American tongue from the English necessary and unavoidable. . . . We have therefore the fairest opportunity of establishing a national language and of giving it uniformity and perspicuity, in North America, that ever presented itself to mankind. Now is the time to begin the plan."[3]

We are moving through an age as yet unready for independence and somewhat afraid of it, but one wherein sentiments for independence were too strong for suppression, and where in any case independence, once realized, made its own urgent demands. Political and social adjustment was imperative, and on a large scale; it started with an intellectual awakening, continued toward reappraisals of social, political, and religious thought, included, especially among plain people, an emancipation of American English, and ended with an adoption—while leaving the schools mainly intact—of a new, at least different, educational theory. Ferment was irrepressible, although attitudes toward it were chilly among illuminati, and proceeded at a dizzy pace as it was nurtured by Revolution, by the philosophic and scientific friction of Enlightenment thought, and by the incurable rivalries of religious liberalism and orthodoxy.

Allowing for periods of remission and pockets of resistance, this period evidenced a concentration of human endeavor directed toward political success in the creation of a national state, and there was an alliance between society and politics, science, and literature unmatched anywhere on earth. This alliance was kept intact by a humble auxiliary: from the gathering of the Revolution to the turn of the century there was immense activity in the concoction and launching of Americanisms in language, and more of them came into American speech than at any time between the earliest colonial days and the rush to the West. Despite economic, social, and political problems of all kinds following the Revolution, the general feeling prevailed that the new Republic was a success, and that it was destined to rise in the world as England declined. There was a widespread contempt for everything English, and that contempt extended to the canons of the mother tongue. Where, one could ask, could the fortunes of an American language be advanced better than in the schools?

THE REVOLUTION

Revolution itself was the most obvious of the age's realities: it terminated a long era of unrest and overt discontent with the handmaiden role imposed on the colonies in their political relationship with England. However, contrary to romantic versions of the American Revolution and its aftermath, it brought into the political world an infant country with limited resources, disparate philosophies of government, and a population beset by the ugliness of war, with divided loyalties vis-à-vis national independence on one hand, and allegiance to Great Britain on the other. With so many decisions to be made and with so few dependable assumptions to bolster them, the time was ripe for ferment.[4]

A few quantitative details are important. The population of the new country was not quite four million persons and more than half were farmers. The urban population was scattered among relatively small cities; the largest was Philadelphia with a population of about forty thousand. Travel and communication were primitive by any standard and social isolation rather than social intercourse was an inevitable result of the inability of people in different parts of the country to exchange goods and ideas. Neither industry nor manufacturing made speedy inroads on the established agrarian economy, and this tardiness had the blessing of colonial economic philosophy. Moreover, the war itself had cost the colonies dearly both in life and treasure. Deeply in debt, with land and productive property badly wasted, with political disenchantment all too common and with an obviously weak central government, the prospect for political survival was exceptionally dim.

Any genre so beset with fundamental issues of daily life is seldom disposed to assign priority to the guiding hand of theory, to a philosophy of life or of government to steady and sustain the halting progress of a new political society. Still, theories of reform, or justification for an already established order, are less exhausting and are more easily afforded than the implementation of new programs or the extension of old ones. Perhaps this commitment to social economy, as much as anything else, explains why the period of transition gives so much evidence of social and educational theorizing and so little of actual accomplishment either in the social order itself or in the schools society was motivated to establish and support.

Yet, while taking fully into account the scourges of war—even a fairly civilized war, as the Revolution turned out to be—and its inevitable mixed blessings, conditions were created for a new beginning. For the first time in the colonies' experience they had the opportunity—or rather the need—to make an entirely fresh start. And on the level of theory, at least, they did so by recognizing that many of the old assumptions relative to human institutions were of questionable validity.

We should be cautious about believing that war introduced social and political equilibrium, but it had the effect of loosing the grip of convention; and we should not assume that old ways of thinking about fundamental issues of life were discarded easily or that for these new Americans old values were jettisoned in haste. The colonial mind penetrated the early years of nationalism with a characteristic stubbornness and, despite all the brave talk about intellectual and literary independence, perpetuated an intellectual legacy for which Americans would long remain indebted to the Old World. Despite a spirit of adventure, along with ample evidence of undoubted courage, Americans were not disposed to blaze any new intellectual trails. The ideals governing life were the tested and true ideals of the past, and few men were bold enough to indict their validity. The fundamental problem demanding attention at the advent of the national era was: what social organization is best for man? Even tentative answers given during this agitated period were not wholly native to the New World, but were prompted by a generation of European intellectuals who began by abandoning much of their intellectual heritage. The leaders of this radical cadre were men we have met before on the pages of our history books and the sum of their work was contained in what is called the Enlightenment.[5]

THE ENLIGHTENMENT

The effect of Enlightenment both in Europe and America was to instigate a reexamination of ancient belief, which for the most part stood as dogmatic assumption. But the Enlightenment code for reform was direct: its principal theme was rejection; its main target was authority. Underlying Enlightenment thought was the conviction, itself no more than an assumption, that authority is evil and the only justification for action is reason itself, unadulterated by convention, tradition, or authority.

Along with the elevation of reason, Enlightenment thought idealized the scientific method, whose persistent and prudent use led to an abundance of new knowledge which under no circumstance could have been obtained by a further exploration of classical literary mines. The research and writing of men like Newton (1642-1727),[6] Harvey (1578-1657),[7] Boyle (1627-1691),[8] Descartes (1596-1650),[9] and Francis Bacon (1561-1626)[10] gave reason and science respectability and told future scholarship that these men were giants on whose shoulders it would have to stand if the boundaries of knowledge were to be broadened. The next generation of scholars who adopted the scientific method of their predecessors and put it to good use was led by Rutherford (1749-1819), Cavendish (1731-1810), Bergman (1735-1784), Priestly (1733-1804), Lavoisier (1743-1794), Galvani (1737-1798), and Volta (1745-1827).[11] Two generations of high scientific achievement could not have been ignored under any circumstance; in an age restive and uncomfortable under the restraint both Humanism and religion imposed, the result was too often an exaggerated embrace of science along with unrealistic expectations about what a scientific method could do.

Still, despite good omens evident in scientific quickening, the inherited traditions were not ready to capitulate timidly. In the end tradition proved a worthy adversary to science; its surrender was slow and uneven and, in any case, always conditional and fragmentary. Bastions of conservatism, the universities refused to countenance either the new method or the scientific knowledge it produced. The medical faculty of the University of Paris, good authority said, refused to acknowledge Harvey's discovery of the circulation of the blood for a full fifty years after its incontestable demonstration.[12] Equally fantastic positions were held, sometimes in the colleges of the colonies where the Ptolemaic theory was ratified long after most knowledgeable people had dismissed it. A long litany of illustrations could be recited to show resistance to change, even when change was certified by almost impeccable credentials. And this resistance was about evenly encountered in Europe and America.

Although no colonial spokesman infected by the spirit of Enlightenment is on record calling the colleges nests of ignorance, American intellectuals must have been horrified at the colleges' determination to remain true to the past, fighting with might and main to hold back a flood of progressive thought threatening to inundate them. If colonial colleges attract our attention first, we can, after looking to see how they responded to the challenge of the new age, drop our eyes to the condition of lower schools to ascertain their reaction to science. They, too, rejected it, but lower schools had a better excuse for being indifferent to reality: what they were teaching was always below the point where Humanism and science conflicted.

If schools were not the place to harbor intellect, what was the place? In the colonies and in the early national period, the Enlightenment spirit ignited sparks of genius in such men as Franklin (1706–1790), Rittenhouse (1732–1796), Colden (1688–1776), and Catesby (1697–1749). And attention must be given, too, to the American Philosophical Society—founded in Philadelphia in 1769—which almost at once became active in disseminating the creed of intellect and scientific idealism.[13] Schools could have been helpful in laying a foundation for intellectual culture, but they resisted, so other ways had to be found. Here, again, the pen proved mightier than the sword: confronted by the sword of European political dominance the colonies fought and won; but the pen brought them back to the European intellectual fold.

By the middle of the eighteenth century, bookshops in America were stocked with the latest editions of the works of European scholars, and sometimes of American authors, promoting the scientific vision distilled from Enlightenment thought. Before another half-century passed Enlightenment values were strewn by newspapers, magazines, tracts, and books before anyone who could read.[14] Much was propaganda which, even if believed by the average man, did not much affect his daily life, although both science and Enlightenment values were infectious and must have altered the measure of his thought.

Groundwork was laid for a culture based on science, and the foundation so far described was consequential; yet without schools enlisted in new learning the likelihood of a renaissance was remote and the possibility that the new philosophy being promoted would have profound appeal, except to an initiated few, was poor. Support for modernization of intellectual value came suddenly from an unexpected source, and led to a variety of educational reforms which, in the end, allowed for a dissemination of Enlightenment philosophy. To find the genesis of Modernism, we look again to Europe and to the work of two prominent educational thinkers whose impact on American schools turned out to be immense: John Locke (1632-1704) and Jean Jacques Rousseau (1712-1778).

Before becoming engrossed with the theory European educators bequeathed to their American cousins, we should stop long enough to gain our bearings: American educational innovation, drawing its inspiration from the realism of Locke and the naturalism of Rousseau, materialized slowly and, in any case, was introduced through apparently indigenous educational policies promoted by such seminal American thinkers as Benjamin Franklin and Thomas Jefferson.

What we want to see by returning to Europe is, first, that neither cultural nor intellectual bonds with the Old World were completely severed by political separation and furthermore that whatever the hopes and aspirations for American nationalism and intellectual self-sufficiency during this period, it would have been impossible for anyone, even Ralph Waldo Emerson himself, to have composed the "American Scholar" address and have been completely serious about it. There was simply no possibility of achieving intellectual independence from Europe at this time, and what can be said about the life of the mind can be said with equal confidence about the schools and the instruction they offered to generations of American girls and boys.

Locke

We have seen enough of colonial schools to know they served two masters: an aristocratic social order and denominational religion. The new educational theory coming from Europe, always put in the context of Enlightenment aspirations for mankind, set in motion new ways of looking at educational purpose. The man most responsible for this was John Locke, and his credibility was good because he said so many things about politics that gave substance to preconceived American notions on political theory. If Locke's political thought was dependable, it was logical to invest his educational theory with the same confidence for, in the last analysis, it would contribute vigor and consistency to practical politics.[15]

Locke rested his educational theory on a bedrock of philosophy; and Locke's philosophy was both radical and audacious, for it shook the foundations of conventional theological opinion, on one hand, and conventional conceptions of man's nature on the other. Being neither an atheist nor a theist, but a deist or an agnostic, Locke argued that pietism, which for centuries had infected both philosophies of religion and man, lacked any foundation in human experience and was probably nothing but myth. Men, he said, were born without innate ideas; nor were they endowed from birth with self-evident propositions, and they lacked knowledge of God except from a speculation based on personal experience. What men knew, or thought they knew, and whatever principles of religion or philosophy governed their lives, was learned in the only way anything could be learned: by experience. The old codes, so long revered, should, he averred, be subjected to a searching scrutiny: religion, philosophy, politics, indeed, everything fundamental to human life, should submit to the arbitrament of reason; anything incapable of passing reason's test should be jettisoned forthwith.

As a corollary to his doctrine of doubt about innate ideas, Locke offered the enticing proposition, enticing especially to a generation of intellectuals anxious to inflate the importance of the scientific method, that the mind at birth is blank—*tabula rasa*.[16] This was easy to understand, although at the time of its pronouncement notoriously difficult to embrace, but acceptance or rejection is not the point of our interest. We want to see the implications of this doctrine of *tabula rasa* for an American education slowly coming of age.

In the first place, assuming the correctness of Locke's contention that prior to the imprint of experience the mind is blank, the environment wherein men live and perforce from which they learn was raised to a level of heretofore unimagined significance. What men became was, according to this doctrine, determined by their experience and not by divine interference or direction. God's plan for men, if there was a plan, could be found neither in scripture nor in any hoary religious tradition, but only in the act of creation itself. From this point on, men were independent, and what they became resulted not from predetermination, as in Calvinist theology, but from the force of life. Human progress, although never so certain to Locke as to humanitarians, was possible if men had enough foresight to shape and control the environment and thus create the conditions to produce better and more noble persons. After this, only a short step was needed to explain education's role in improving the environment which, in the last analysis, was responsible for making men.

Never before had theory given schools such an important part in the play of human destiny. Still, the educational consequences of this theory were not at once perceived. It took social philosophers a long time to recognize the role mapped out for education;[17] in the United States, for example, the educational implications of environmental determinism had almost no influence on schools or instruction until the time of Horace Mann.

The other dimension to *tabula rasa* is equally intriguing and important to education, especially in a national system. If men are born with minds as clean as blank slates, it would be hard to disbelieve in a fundamental equality among persons. Everyone, at least, begins at the same starting line. Buried away in Locke's *tabula rasa* is the principle of equality of opportunity, a principle capable of recommending universal education. And this principle was recognized by the most advanced of American social theorists, Thomas Jefferson, when he made universal education a condition for the realization of political democracy.[18]

Locke's thesis was not essential to equality of educational opportunity, and in the evolution of American education other justifications were found; but Locke's principle, expressed by Jefferson, gave equality of educational opportunity—an extraordinarily avant-garde notion—its initial chance for respectability.

Finally, we see the influence of Locke in furthering an idea whose time had come: knowledge is useful and, what is more, it makes men powerful. But Locke and his disciples meant knowledge that had passed the rigid test of empirical validity. Their boldness, however, outran their common sense, for it was plainly impossible to purify the corpus of knowledge by culling from it everything whose validity was untested. So if the loyal followers of Locke were unable to apply his formula in a general way and thus end up with universally dependable knowledge, they could do the next best thing and recommend only knowledge with clear and obvious utility for the school's curriculum.

The lessons Locke taught his generation were easy to learn, but hard to apply. Besides, Locke himself was a friend neither of public nor popular education. Despite his theory and the direction it said schools should take, Locke refused to budge from the tradition of schooling that wanted to educate gentlemen in schools whose doors were open only to a select few. Considering the ambiguities implicit in Locke's attitude toward schooling, it is surprising that he was heeded; yet history shows how he influenced generations of Americans who wanted their schools to reshape society.[19]

Rousseau

Perhaps Locke's educational ideas would have lacked attraction and influence if they had not been followed by an even more outspoken critic of the established intellectual and social order: Jean Jacques Rousseau. Rousseau first attracted attention in France, where his radical interpretation of man and society gave credence to the French Revolution, and where his classic statement on education, *Émile,* was published.[20] Linking Locke with Rousseau in the work of educational reform, especially to educational reform in America, must be done with caution, for Locke would have rejected Rousseau as a disciple. In any case Locke was a revisionist who sought to improve the quality of human life by utilizing reason; he was never an intellectual nihilist and he refused to counsel, as Rousseau did, the abandonment of social institutions. So, it may be argued, the extremities of Rousseau allowed the more moderate Locke to appeal to persons interested in the betterment of human society.

Generation after generation of European schoolboys had been taught that God created them with an imperfect nature: one theology said they were wounded and regeneration was possible; another told them the damage of original sin was irreparable. But in either case education should do its best to mend the deficiencies of nature. Rousseau began by declaring both these theologies invalid. Man, he said, as he comes from the hand of Nature is good, without perversity needing correction or elimination, but as he is exposed to human institutions and as he is taught the traditional culture, he assimilates the evils of the race. From this position of natural goodness, it was possible for Rousseau to reconstruct the whole of society and education.

Traditional political theory subscribed to the doctrine that government was ordained by God; Rousseau rejected the conventions of political theory and replaced them with the social contract. And social contract, enabling men to create a political society, was reinforced by the doctrine of natural right, right unbestowed by anyone but belonging to men nevertheless, simply because they are men. Although Rousseau did not invent the doctrine of natural right, his work popularized it and thus forwarded an essential part of Locke's political philosophy.

Among American intellectual leaders, neither Rousseau's theory of government nor education was adopted, so we look in vain for an American who, during this period of intellectual transition, wanted to drive a naturalistic bandwagon. Yet a bandwagon carrying such lofty ideas as natural right, natural goodness, inevitable human progress, and ideally reconstructed social institutions could make deep tracks in American soil without the help of a native driver. Among Rousseau's many pronouncements on education and society, just enough truth was mixed with error to make his audience take heed. Who could doubt that learning was natural or that pedagogic technique should take its cues from learning itself? What was wrong with indicting the distortions of old schoolbooks? Why reject the optimistic promise that fundamental social reform would create a society with possibilities for unlimited progress? Was it false to criticize the corruptness of social institutions? If only a little in Rousseau was right, could Americans afford to ignore him and refuse to repudiate the mistakes of Europe?

While Rousseau's distrust of book learning was seldom shared even by his strongest admirers, his strident disclaimer always reminded them of literature's inability, regardless of its excellence, to account for all reality. Besides, Rousseau meant to eliminate, not correct pedagogy; yet correction was his principal bequest to education. Rather than paying Rousseau full heed and thus removing books from schools, teachers listened to him with mixed feelings and discounted the influence of the classics in the curriculum. The battle to drive books from the schools, despite the appeal of *Émile* to non-literary educational programs, always lacked scholastic bridgeheads. To share Rousseau's romantic vision of a society founded on naturalism was one thing, and Rousseau had disciples, but to reject pedagogic formulas tradition prescribed for an educational program based on a child's unsupervised personal experience was too much for eighteenth-century teachers. They wanted social reform but refused to believe that reform was impossible unless society started all over again. Part of society could be corrupt without all of society being contaminated.

So pedagogy was not Rousseau's strong suit; in another area his recommendations produced better results. But before we go on we should admit to Rousseau's influence on educational theory. In France, particularly, a number of books on pedagogy appeared with some indebtedness to him; all were on the side of change but, as it turned out, their authors were unable to circle the same tree of reform.

Taking a page from Locke's *Essay on Human Understanding,* both Étienne Bonnot de Condillac (1715-1780) and Claude-Adrien Helvétius (1715-1771) tried to amplify the importance of the senses in learning and the formative value of experience in the making of men. In his *Treatise on the Sensations* Condillac deployed a strategy for improving schools by taking into account the role of the senses in learning and by centering attention on the education and training of the senses themselves. Condillac's thesis was made of the stuff from which pedagogic innovation springs, but he was too far ahead of his time. Even his book on the *Course of Instruction,* where the application of his theory on the senses and their import for school practice is clear enough, had to mark time waiting its turn for attention in a more sensitive educational age.

Moving forward along the same line, with an emphasis on the senses in learning and attention to the environment as the principal means for the formation of men, Helvétius wrote two books: *On the Soul* and *On Man,*

His Intellectual Faculties and His Education. Helvétius was ready to elaborate the pedagogic implications of Locke's *tabula rasa,* and when he was taken seriously the old illusions about the prescriptiveness of nature on nurture were abandoned. The road to the better life, Helvétius maintained, was paved not with an indelible and constant mental capacity with which the child was born, but with a rich and fruitful environment, always capable of taking a person over the threshold of perfection. This was a lofty idealism for an educational age so recently awakened to the role education could play in uplifting society, for making the world a better place.

As it turned out, hope again outran realization and the great expectations of Condillac and Helvétius were condemned by neglect. Along with Rousseau, Condillac and Helvétius gave schoolmasters enough educational theory to keep them busy for a generation; yet neither in Europe nor, for that matter, in America, was much change seen in the schools. Still, behind this curtain of inactivity and apparent indifference, the ground was cultivated for an educational reform in the next century.

And this cultivation, at first appearing to have little or nothing to do with pedagogic practice, takes us back to Rousseau and, proving again that history can find room for strange bedfellows, to Louis-René de La Chalotais (1701–1785). What was being cultivated? What was being prepared as a springboard for educational reform? National education. And now La Chalotais rather than Rousseau was the trail blazer.

In 1763, a year after Rousseau published *Émile,* La Chalotais' celebrated *Essay on National Education* appeared. A detailed excursus of the book is apart from our purpose, yet we should know that it contained the theoretic base and the practical justification for a system of education created, maintained, and controlled by the state. Now, despite all the earlier talk about the worth of education in the formation of character, even Christian character, and the intimate personal values to be generated by a superior education conceived along naturalistic lines, the wind of educational reform changed and began to blow hard from the direction of education's civic purpose. La Chalotais is precise and clear: schools should be established by the state; the curriculum should be set in a context ensuring the acceptance of national (state) purpose; teachers were to be agents of the state with a responsibility for inculcating approved civic values. He stripped the schools of their religious teachers and insisted on educational goals being set and supervised by the state. Almost as an afterthought, he added a strange recommendation for a century just awakening to the importance of schooling: fewer rather than more children should be allowed to attend school.

Obviously La Chalotais and Rousseau had incompatible philosophies of education: where La Chalotais curtailed educational opportunity, Rousseau in his *Émile* expanded it; where La Chalotais put education in the state's custody, Rousseau divorced teaching and learning from all social institutions; where the former forwarded the notion that the best education makes persons ready servants of the state, the latter pleaded for an educational program centering exclusive attention on making men. Yet, in spite of these vast differences on the level of theory, within a decade, it appears, Rousseau capitulated to La Chalotais's principal theses. In 1772, at the suggestion of a Polish count, Rousseau undertook a study of political conditions in Poland and in 1773 produced a book on *Considerations of the Government of Poland and on the Reformation of It Projected in April, 1772.*

Spending time with this book would take us into issues of political philosophy, but one thing is clear: Rousseau retreated from his stand, taken in *Émile,* where the person was supreme. Now on the side of a state educational system, he saw nothing wrong in using schools as civic instruments. So in the span of a decade, Rousseau changed his mind. And by changing he put himself in the mainstream of eighteenth-century educational thought, for the development of schools to serve national purpose not pedagogic reform was the theme of this century.

Europe's educational preoccupation affected America. Report followed report—the majority prepared in France—extolling the virtue of national school systems, and Enlightenment partisans, among them Diderot *(Plan for a University),* and De Condorcet *(Report on the General Organization of Public Instruction),* used their skill of publicity to promote national education. This promotion carried to America: before it was prudent or fashionable for Americans to talk about national education, the school's civic purposes were warmly endorsed. Time and again America demonstrated her inability or unwillingness to live in intellectual isolation: philosophical and educational pronouncements made in Europe echoed all the way to the New World.[21]

RELIGIOUS LIBERALISM

Colonial Americans had the habit of trusting religion and giving it an important place in their lives. It stimulated their souls, and in addition had positive social worth. In the absence of a strong political system, religion could institute social and political stability; so we should understand the determination of our ancestors to support religious belief not just as a matter of simple faith—however profound faith might be—but in recognition of social necessity. When government became stronger, especially with the creation of a national state, religion was diminished as a stabilizing social factor. In consequence, religious freedom was less a luxury, and in some parts of the country intimations of religious latitude had been harbored for a long time. The stage was set for religious liberalism, a new religious perspective bound to affect the schools.

Reason had been praised by Enlightenment philosophers as alone being capable of creating and maintaining a social world worthy of human life. Sold at discount with this emphasis was the traditional allegiance to organized religion as a means for maintaining social and spiritual order. Clearly organized religion had itself become enamored of reason and had employed it to build theological castles, but buried away in the archive of religious thought was an old dogma subordinating reason to faith: belief is essential to understanding. This dogma Enlightenment philosophers rejected. But what could not be expelled from the cultural heritage was the undoubted fact that organized religion had proved useful in giving society law and order throughout centuries when other agencies were incapable of doing so. Thus, old allegiances welded from the positive social good of religion were not easily severed.

European and American intellectuals, however, were often uneasy with prescriptive and restrictive religious dogma standing as an obstacle to progress. Yet, except as a minority view, the place and worth of religion was understood and acknowledged even among the faithless who recognized that the mass of mankind still wanted to pay homage to a personal God.

An alternative to orthodox theism was needed if liberalism was to succeed, but atheism—an outright rejection of God—was too severe. Breaking old religious ties is never easy and in America the era of religious liberalism was introduced in a combination of zealous effort and fortunate timing.

On the level of theory we come face to face with new conceptions of God and his relationship to men. Theism was still the religious way of life for most, but irrespective of the terrain nurturing their seeds of conviction, Americans could not have been blind to religious ferment going on around them.

Deism, represented in such works as Ethan Allen's *Reason the Only Oracle of Man,* Thomas Paine's *Age of Reason,* and Elihu Palmer's *Principles of Nature,* offered an alternative to traditional theism. God, deists said, was the Creator but after creation his work was finished. He blazed no divine trail and left no instructions for mankind. Man was left to master his own fate by using his reason. God would never interfere; men would have to rely on themselves and no incantation was strong enough to attract divine intervention. Called religion by its friends and adherents, deism was branded as the worst kind of theology, no better than atheism, by orthodox critics. Yet name calling was pure waste, for deism made an impact by prompting men to examine traditional theistic and sectarian assumptions.[22]

Standing alone, unwarmed by other winds of religious reform, deism might have spent its force quickly and died as just another radical notion in the history of religious thought. But now it was supported obliquely from an unexpected source: Unitarianism. This sect of theists, to whom deism was totally objectionable, abandoned the doctrine of the Trinity—

Father, Son, and Holy Spirit—and substituted a doctrine of God's unity. Even when Unitarianism was instrumental in abetting the liberalism of deism, doctrinal affinity was lacking: religious expectation could at times make strange bedfellows. In any case, Unitarians discounted doctrinal adherence and emphasized the humanity of religion rather than the rigor of creed: they replaced religious zeal with love and charity and preached a sermon of salvation wherein a warm and loving God, indifferent to sectarian creed, would never condemn men to eternal damnation.

Besides, Unitarianism strayed from the tradition that God's mystery relationship with man is unravelled by specially trained interpreters of scripture and doctrine. Going directly to scripture, and depending on their own intelligence, men can find all the knowledge and inspiration they need. Religion was promoted as a highly personal spiritual experience and more than anyone else in America, William Ellery Channing preached this optimistic Unitarianism wherein moral sensitivity was a substitute for sectarian dogma and the welfare of mankind took precedence over denominational zeal.[23]

Almost inevitably Unitarianism abandoned its nonsectarian character and, as decades passed, followed in the footsteps of older religious sects. When this happened toward the end of the eighteenth century, although by then liberal religion had made its mark, another brand of nonsectarian spiritualism took its place. This was New England Transcendentalism, a philosophic creed steeped in Idealism, which began by putting trust in the Almighty and then, with a method learned from Puritan divines, spared no effort to explain the justification for such trust by turning to nature to find evidence of God's providence. With roots lodged in German Idealism, Transcendentalism preached a gospel of freedom from the restraint of convention, authority, and religion. Freedom, once gained, was to be used in the realization of personal fulfillment and social progress.[24]

Seeds of doubt once sown affected all but the most orthodox religious spirit; and these seeds of doubt never meant to question God's place in the lives of men, but only to restrictive features of exclusive sectarianism. The straight path to religious orthodoxy was permanently bent by deism, Unitarianism, and Transcendentalism. At the same time, when religious battles were fought over the custody of the human spirit, the cause of liberalism was aided considerably by infusions of a now abundant scientific knowledge. It was fast becoming obvious that the lesson the Enlightenment taught about the inestimable worth of reason was true.[25]

Despite an indictment drawn against orthodoxy and ardent sectarianism, the late colonial and early national period was unready for religious anarchy and refused to countenance it. Liberalism was one thing, and could be accommodated, secularism was another. Believing they lived in a world God had made, the majority of men found secularism unconvincing. So, while much orthodoxy was swept away, fervent religious belief remained;

and men still sought God's friendship, although at times they appeared to be looking for the friendship of their fellow men first. This change of philosophic and religious tone had considerable influence on educational thought, for now the school could hardly be regarded as an agent of any religious sect. Unquestionably education should do its best to inculcate religious and moral virtue, but it need not have, perhaps should not have, any commitment to sectarianism to fulfill this commission.

A combination of influences, but especially the optimism of a new country coupled with social, religious, and political ferment, generated the power to run the great experiment with democracy. Late in the eighteenth century a broad new social theory was about ready to impose itself on American life.

HUMANITARIANISM

Bred and nurtured by philosophies of religious liberalism, humanitarianism grew to modest stature shortly before the Revolution. But, despite the enormous good will of persons who espoused this cause and their determined effort to improve the lives of the masses, humanitarianism had to mark time while the impediments of religious orthodoxy were cleared away. Paying allegiance to religious belief and endorsing the charitable objectives of orthodox creeds, early Americans found it difficult or impossible to embrace a social theory with little or no time for conventional religion: one whose social gospel needed neither an ordained minister nor an inspired scripture.[26]

Once liberalism diminished denominational exclusiveness, social theory began to catch up with Enlightenment philosophy wherein reason was recommended as the only human guide; and at almost the same time the naturalistic pronouncement of Rousseau sowed seeds of doubt about the deprived and depraved character of man's nature. Still, we should be careful about discounting the spirit of humanitarianism, for it must have had elements of Christian altruism. Without trying to find the exact source of humanitarian inspiration in America, we can begin by admitting that it displayed an extraordinary interest in the common good and the general welfare.

Its specific endorsement of the sentiment of humanity, always more a feeling than a philosophy, was usually expressed in zealous concern for the human condition rather than in closely reasoned theological and philosophical tracts. The answer proponents of humanitarianism looked for was intended to satisfy them on these questions: How can society best serve its members? How can all men be helped to lead full and satisfying lives? What are the conditions of social progress? And how can the family of humanity improve itself?

Most humanitarians were considerably better at defining the limits of the social problem than at inventing solutions, but they always had plenty of company on this score and should be absolved from special guilt. A perceptive Benjamin Franklin, whose association with humanitarianism was remote, expressed in allegory an authentic humanitarian sense of social frustration. Leaving unmentioned humanitarianism's eternal optimism that society would improve, Franklin stated the perennial issue for persons embracing the sentiment of humanity in a cleverly written letter to a friend:

In what light we are viewed by superior beings, may be gathered from a piece of late West India news, which possibly has not yet reached you. A young angel of distinction being sent down to this world on some business, for the first time, had an old courier-spirit assigned to him as a guide. They arrived over the seas of Martinico, in the middle of the long day of obstinate fighting between fleets of Rodney and De Grasse. When, through the clouds of smoke, they saw the fire of the guns, the decks covered with mangled limbs and bodies dead or dying; the ships sinking, burning, or blown into the air; and the quantity of pain, misery, and destruction the crews yet alive were thus with so much eagerness dealing round to one another, he turned angrily to his guide and said: "You blundering blockhead, you are ignorant of your business; you undertook to conduct me to earth, and you have brought me into hell!" "No, sir," says the guide, "I have made no mistake; it is really the earth, and these are men. Devils never treat one another in this cruel manner; they have more sense, and more of what men (vainly) call humanity."[27]

This sentiment of humanity, so difficult to define precisely, was sometimes mistaken for a revived religious pietism. But in American humanitarianism, denominational affiliation was absent, and few humanitarians aligned themselves with any religious creed. They were content to look for the keys to social reform and human progress in man and not in religion. They wanted social reform—education was first on the list—and along with it to replace hatred and suspicion with sympathy and love.

Humanitarians were determined to multiply the occasions for human relations by means of a more open and sensitive society and by strengthening and developing altruism as well. With all the zeal they could muster, American humanitarians adopted the goals of human betterment and social progress, but they could not hoist this banner to their mast without recognizing the significance of schools to the attainment of their high-minded social goals.[28]

SOCIAL EQUALITY

The impressive language of the Declaration of Independence—"All men are created equal"—was distilled from John Locke's philosophy, to which Thomas Jefferson, the author of the Declaration, was always indebted for political inspiration, and Jean Jacques Rousseau's radical social theory. We have seen how eighteenth-century thinkers could substantiate social and political reform with philosophy, and we have noticed how philosophy crossed the Atlantic Ocean to gain a foothold in America. What we have not yet seen, however, is the rapid and enthusiastic acceptance of philosophy on the level of practical life.

Life in America, particularly frontier life, inevitably promoted the ideal of social equality which for so long had its only reality on the pages of the philosopher's books. Philosophy should now be put to work.

Illustrating in detail how the ideal of social equality was first grasped and then practiced in America is unnecessary here. For a long time the social structure of Europe was duplicated in the colonies, but the obliterating forces of time, distance from European social paradigms, and the circumstances of American life recommended a leveling process among men. The sharp class distinctions most colonial Americans remembered simply proved unworkable or meant little in a new country. Social pedigree was useless for clearing forests, cultivating land, fighting Indians, fording rivers, and hunting game. It did nothing to alleviate the pain, suffering, and hunger pioneer families felt when, moving West, they left behind the more civilized ways of the Eastern seaboard. On the frontier and in the wilderness men had daily object lessons in survival, and aristocratic blood, they learned, made no matter.

Besides, many American families lived in near isolation away from cities and settlements; learning to depend on themselves, they learned, too, to recognize human worth in what it could do rather than the bloodline or the social position from which it sprang. In actual practice equality was realized as pioneers carved out a living for themselves. For the most part, pioneer Americans lived from the land, so when we look for signs of equality, we see them first in an agrarian economy. And in it the excess of poverty then a scourge on the larger European cities was unlikely, for the provision of nature enabled most families to live modestly but well, assuming they were unafraid of hard work.

American social consciousness matured in the generation after the war, and in the early nineteenth century debtors' prisons were abandoned. And, though some families could trace their heritage to the first colonial settlers and others could boast of noble blood, these pretensions made almost no difference in day-to-day life. These cadres salvaged a certain social exclusiveness, but their former perquisites of power and privilege were usually stripped away. Rigid class lines, so common to Europe, atrophied too: by dint of personal effort one could move up the social ladder and leave behind the disadvantage of lower-class origin.

Even on less important levels of behavior old signs of distinction were disappearing: for generations, both in Europe and America, dress was an obvious and outward sign of social condition; certain fabrics were reserved for the upper classes and shoes with buckles were proscribed for the low-born. Always artificial, these distinctions, nevertheless, had been put up with; now in a more open and prospectively democratic society they were scuttled. The foundations for social democracy were broader than humanitarian altruism and Christian charity; equality was confirmed less by affirmations concerning the nature of man than by social pragmatism. If men were willing through hard work to climb the ladder to success, what justification was possible for setting an artificial limit on accomplishment? And accomplishment included the possibility of moving to a higher rung on the social ladder. Life in early nineteenth-century America proved that social democracy could work; it testified also to the merit of modern social philosophy. Yet it also illustrated in a number of ways how little the democratic spirit had penetrated into politics and economics.[29]

SECULARIZATION

A metamorphosis in public policy, altering the practice where church and state were a team of government to one where they were independent, if not hostile, took some time. Bible commonwealths husbanded established religions and allowed them to penetrate the lives of ordinary men. The theory justifying this was clear enough, and for a long time no one challenged it: the foundation to citizenship is a morality illuminated by religion.

The long colonial experience with established churches bred misgivings among political leaders (James Madison is a good example) about the simple efficacy of such a practice. If an established church policy caused some difficulty in colonies steeped in orthodoxy, it was nothing compared to what could happen when religious liberalism became widespread. One church making religious policy, which all were obliged to observe, and being supported by the public treasury, was unacceptable to religious liberals. And equally abhorrent to them were schools teaching the creed of an established religion to all children. Where dissenters were few in number and weak in political influence, the old policy had its way, but where religious liberals were more numerous (or simply where more persons had different sectarian preferences), and when they could exert political influence, the path of establishment policy was bound to be strewn with impediments.

The time needed to change public policy vis-à-vis an official religion was always too long for men who saw a danger to the political fabric of the nation in a continuation of the old policy, and too short for men convinced that the moral foundation of the nation depended on the inspiration and strength of religious virtue, and that religious virtue was unavoidably dependent on denominational religion. This second assumption was challenged by American political leaders. Instead of an established church they offered freedom for various sects to conduct their affairs without intervention from the state; and they advocated the creation of a political state where public policy would be secular. Never being totally irreligious, the policy of secularism was intended to make the state not only independent of religious creed but neutral on all religious issues as well. Whatever moral enlightenment was needed for the management of public affairs could come either from a general religious influence or from a morality based on the natural law.

An expression of the principle of separation of church and state was made in the First Amendment to the federal Constitution: "Congress shall make no law respecting an establishment of religion or interfering with the free exercise thereof . . . ." What now appeared to be so clear on the federal level, a restraint on congressional authority, remained to be clarified in the several states. When the First Amendment was ratified, it should be noted, informed opinion was confident of state immunity to it, for some states retained either single or multiple establishments of religion. Yet, as it turned out, established churches shortly became anachronisms because they were out of step with the spirit of the time. But old habits are tenacious and the compact between education and religion was hard to repeal in the face of a general assumption that a religion of humanity, without guidance from creed and ritual, was helpless to inculcate moral foundations essential to the government of life. So while the weight of public opinion acknowledged the good sense in separation of church and state and ratified the validity of civil authority, it kept intact its conviction that education needed perspective from denominational religion.[30] Despite the persuasive prose of the early constitutionalists to the contrary, history tells us that religion and education were still closely linked. Franklin's Academy demonstrated how schools could ignore religion with impunity, or at least without harming practical and utilitarian objectives, but Franklin's famous school was more a model for the future than a reflection of contemporary educational attitude and practice.

During this period of great intellectual and social transition, the colonies and then the states were never very active in separating religion from education either on the level of teaching or school support. Schools promoted denominational religion and, for the most part, remained in the custody of religious ministers; and some schools, while wearing a denominational face, were supported either fully or partially from the public treasury. Arguments to abandon this policy, holding it inimical to the common good, were heard in the land, but their translation to public policy was slow. Translation, though, continued at a steady pace and eventually became public policy, but this work of translation took most of the nineteenth century.

NATIONALISM

In this era of budding nationalism (about the middle of the eighteenth century) we see the colonies in the British Empire and, although signs of political unrest along with some avant-garde talk about independence are evident, public policy guarded the status quo and political dissent was vigorously discouraged. The Revolution (successful, as it turned out) was almost certainly an accident of history, and was not generated in the power plant of nationalism. However, it did rupture British hegemony and allowed for the development of nationalistic sentiment in this country.

In the first years of confederation, political allegiance was ambiguous, divided about equally among the colonies as a whole, a colony or Great Britain. This is partially illustrated in the case of Thomas Jefferson, whose affection for Virginia went undiminished even when he was President of the United States, and John Adams, who never tried to conceal a fundamental loyalty to his native Massachusetts.

With the ratification of the Constitution, the way was open for an American patriotism hitherto unknown. But the development of national feeling, history demonstrates, proceeds slowly and needs a catalyst to generate nationalistic zeal. So for two decades after the ratification of the Constitution, while the United States had the outward appearance of a nation, the spirit of patriotism was fragmented and ineffectual. The catalyst speeding the process and, in the end, welding the country together in common nationalistic sentiment was the War of 1812. Now nationalism was on the march and as it marched it cultivated a taste for native Americanism. This nativism was not defined merely along lines of national origin, although national origin was important even in a country where everyone save the Indian was a foreigner, but took into account indigenous attitudes toward religion, politics, economics, and language itself. Besides, Americans, feeling for the first time a nationalistic mettle, began to have visions of a promised land and a political system without peer.

We know the zeal and untiring spirit of religious evangelicals; in the generation after the War of 1812, Americans became political evangelicals who could be as zealous about their political experiment and as intemperate with obstacles as their forefathers had been about true religion. Thus, as the sentiment of nationalism marched at a steady pace, strange but strong antipathies developed against foreign states, foreign influence (intellectual, religious, and linguistic), and—paradoxical because so many

Americans were themselves foreign-born or the issue of foreign-born parents—recent immigrants. This was useful for inflating national pride but it also cultivated a nationalistic mentality rivaling in narrowness, intensity, and zeal that of any European state.

This spirit of nationalism once generated was sustained and advanced by the conventional symbols of national pride: monuments, flags, songs, myths, and a national history. The usual tools for building national spirit, vernacular language and national literature, were hard to use here. English, although without a monopoly, was a common tongue, but its lexicon was kept in Britain and this always inhibited the development of American English. However, in time, due partly to design and partly to the accidents of usage, the American language distinguished itself from British English, especially in vocabulary, and gained the approval of convention. National literature was more difficult to obtain, due to literary immaturity and to almost inevitable feelings of cultural inferiority. Americans stood in the cultural shadow of Europe and no rewriting of history could alter this fact, but given their preoccupations with settlement and expansion our ancestors had little leisure or disposition to grieve over their lack of literary self-sufficiency.

None the less, without a native literature or an exclusive vernacular, pride in the homeland was still cultivated. The first stone in the foundation of nationalism was secure.

Religion, too, had its nationalistic turn. The colonies experienced an ecclesiastical subordination to the British Church; they knew all about established religion. Eventually, as a matter of fixed policy, America rejected religious establishment. But even in pronouncing a policy of religious freedom where all denominations were welcome and where none was given a position of privilege, they adopted unofficial but effective antagonisms to Roman Catholicism, whose foreign ties appeared to them to be unbreakable.

The realities of economic life served nationalism too. After the revolutionary war, as we have seen, the country was fragmented politically, separated geographically, and impoverished economically. True to past policy, so long enforced by Britain, the economy of the country was agrarian and so it remained for a long time. This was a blessing in disguise, for in this agricultural economy the first seeds of capitalism were planted. They showed only modest and relatively unimportant growth for decades, but as they matured they spread to more fertile ground where the growth was phenomenal.[31]

Independent at last and ready to savor the full flavor of political independence, the citizens of the new nation discovered their need for economic muscle if political dreams were to come true. Even in the face of British determination to retain industrial supremacy and keep former colonies in economic bondage, America began to industrialize. And with industrialization urbanization began. Trade, commerce, transportation, communication, and technology all made spectacular advances in a country so young; and eventually formed a commercial movement strong enough to change the face of America.[32] Further development to shape the American character occurred in social practice, and most prominent was an educational system capable of advancing American destiny.

EDUCATIONAL THEORY

As the United States settled in the modern world, American social and political theory needed clear articulation, not just because such a theory was nice to have, but because society's decisions depended on it. Although the focus of our attention is education, we should be ready to admit that its theory is lodged in and subordinated to social value. In a new country testing a novel political system, sharp value differences were bound to occur. What should education be? What should schools teach? What values should teachers try to inculcate in their students? In the last analysis, the answers to these questions depended on the fundamental social values of the American people. What were their social and political priorities?

Almost with the advent of national status two social theories competed for dominance: one, eloquently pronounced by Alexander Hamilton, was profoundly aristocratic; the other, with Thomas Jefferson its principal advocate, was basically democratic.[33]

Rejecting with derision a naturalism promising to elevate men to the pinnacle of perfection and goodness, Hamilton, in company with other elitists and aristocrats, acknowledged "avarice and ambition" as the strongest human motives; the strong dominating the weak maintain a sensible and dependable social and political order to ensure the success of their ambition.[34] Power and authority, according to this Hamiltonian version of social theory, must be vested in "landowners, merchants, and men of the learned professions . . . [who will] insure the interest of landed property."[35] This apparently arrogant social philosophy infected educational theory with its basic distrust of mankind. And lack of trust had two sides: given the chance men will choose evil over good; and the mass of mankind is incapable of self-government. If altruism had a place in this social philosophy, it must have been buried in an aristocracy's function of protecting the masses from themselves. Poor and undereducated people must be governed. Clearly this version of social philosophy distrusted democracy and recommended a program of education wherein "the turbulent, uncontrollable and imprudent" disposition of the people could be checked.[36] Self-interest could support enough schooling for the masses to ensure their docility in the established order.

Much contemporary opinion branded this social theory reprehensible and its expression unbridled arrogance, but it was acceptable, nevertheless, to many wealthy merchants, landowners, and bankers. Perhaps Hamilton's theory was too harshly stated and needed softening. John Adams used the language of compromise and was given a more sympathetic hearing, although he stood by Hamilton's fundamental assumptions. And these assumptions dominated American society for several decades: men are naturally corrupt, preferring evil to good; their actions are guided by interest rather than reason, and their capacity for achievement is sharply and naturally divided along class lines. Adams looked at society and saw rich, poor, elite, and common people; and he wanted rich aristocrats to have enough political power to protect themselves and their property from the always more numerous poor lower classes. Unless political power were vested in the upper classes, Adams said, the poor would march to the drum of anarchy and tyranny and the possibility of having an orderly society would be forever foreclosed; yet while the rich and powerful were authorized to exercise political control and protect their property, they should be conscious of an obligation to allow poor and weak people sufficient latitude to make a life for themselves.[37]

In the long run neither Hamilton's hard line nor Adams' more moderately expressed—although hardly milder—version of a capitalistic oligarchy was adopted in American life. Still, a plausible alternative took some time to formulate. If the stern theory had been adopted, the history of the United States and its education would be different. With the presidency of Thomas Jefferson these harsh social opinions retreated before a social and political system based on substantially different principles.

Jefferson's social philosophy was rooted in a positive interpretation of man's nature, and was more progressive than anything Hamilton or Adams said. According to him, rather than being deprived or depraved, man was fundamentally good and fully capable of organizing and administering a social order wherein justice and law, truth and reason always have precedence over force and authority. The bedrock of this social philosophy was man's equality and his inalienable human rights. Translated into a political system, this philosophy made men the masters of their political institutions; translated into a social system, it made all men equal before the law and promoted a classless society; translated into an economic system it discounted without abandoning the right of property; translated into education it meant that all citizens should be given an opportunity to develop their intelligence according to their capacity, and with enlightened minds be ready to exercise the rights of autonomous persons.[38]

Predictably enough, the principal appeal of Jefferson's social philosophy was to persons who had experienced equality and had, in agrarian regions and frontier lands, been following such a code. Predictable, too, was the source of violent opposition to this democratic dogma: people of talent, property, reputation, and influence. Once erosion began it was hard to stop. In a new country with abundant resources to exploit, the class system was always in some jeopardy, and with the rise of a middle class, with the advent of separation of church and state and with a greater distribution of political power to the common man, the dead hand of archaic political and social philosophy fought a losing battle. This clash of social philosophy produced a democratic creed, largely Jeffersonian in elaboration, to shape the future of America.

While battles were fought over social and political philosophy, educators were, for the most part, mining the treasuries of educational wisdom to find, first, an educational plan for sustaining the old social system, and when the old system failed, to produce another plan wherein education could cultivate democracy. Educational theory, however, was too slow for either social or political change; and when the country was ready for a new education, the schools were unable to be of much help. Despite the progressive pronouncements made by educational theorists from Comenius on, knowledge was still regarded as foreign to real life and immunized from the physical world. Theories derived from the Enlightenment and naturalism had redressed somewhat these old attitudes toward knowledge, but classical Humanism had a perennial character and so dominated the curricula of the schools that most men habitually followed the cultural doctrine which said the classics held truth in their custody. While too few teachers were infused with a scholarship capable of excavating rich classical mines, they did their best: education centered on language and the curriculum of most schools, except those clearly elementary, was filled with Latin.

To find a good excuse to justify a preoccupation with Latin studies was becoming harder, for doctrines of utility promoted by John Locke had wide currency, but blunting the argument for utility was still possible. Latin study would not prepare students for practical life, but it could help strengthen the mind. Thus, running almost directly counter to the ideas of social progress so often proclaimed, educational theory chose to discount the present and live in the past. If truth and good judgment were prizes worth having, what better way could they be obtained than by having an educational program concentrate on training the faculties of the mind? This standard was expressed in the famous *Report of the Yale Faculty* (1828), and it held school practice on a steady course for decades.[39]

Later in the national period, and especially after a democratic social philosophy was more widely adopted, it became necessary to modernize educational theory, for education was perceived as an important instrument for achieving and maintaining a democratic society. This evolution of educational theory is worth a quick look and we should go back in colonial educational history to the time when Francis Bacon's *Advancement of Learning* began to decline in influence. Almost at the threshold of the national era, we meet a spokesman for all manner of things: Benjamin Franklin (1706–1790).

Franklin's Educational Thought

The founder of the famous Academy, a school wherein a decent English education was preferred to the classics in Latin, should not be coupled with Jefferson as an exponent of democratic opportunity in education, for Franklin's vision, though broad, lacked prophetic anticipation. Imbibing the spirit of nationalism and hopefully anticipating the advent of an American social order affording men greater opportunity for self-improvement, he was, nevertheless, the product of an aristocratic system and certain aristocratic tendencies never left him. However much he may have deplored convention when it discomforted him, Franklin was neither temperamentally nor intellectually prepared to jettison it. He belonged to a school of educational theorists led by John Locke and John Milton, and he did his best to promote their educational advice. However, this association with European scholars should not blind us to the fact that in the colonies Franklin's voice was a voice of studied prudence and many of the educational changes he recommended laid the foundation for more progressive pedagogic practice in later years.

If we begin by admitting that Franklin did not drive a progressive bandwagon, we can nevertheless acknowledge his educational philosophy as one ready to repair conventional learning in the schools and colleges. In the first place, he said, to promote the common good, government should assume some responsibility for learning. His reason for stressing government interest in education may have been based on his antipathy to a religiously-dominated school system; yet whatever the reason, his support helped make the principle of state responsibility for education respectable at a time when its respectability was doubted.

Franklin encouraged public cooperation in the enterprise of learning, but all the while remained convinced that in the end, irrespective of the source of opportunity, success depended on diligent and constant personal effort. Education could only help produce the self-made man.

With the principle of cooperation secure in his educational philosophy, and he meant both public and private cooperation, Franklin moved on to consider the worth of knowledge and its source. Here, of course, he could depart sharply from the past: the value of knowledge is found in what it can do (thus Locke's doctrine of utility is embraced) and its source is not a reservoir of classical Humanism but the world. Here the sense realism of John Amos Comenius and the empiricism of Locke are endorsed.

Franklin's confidence in scientific knowledge for training reason was high, and schools were important, but his own career confirmed one truth: experience is the best teacher. Where Locke was restrained and reluctant to broaden educational opportunity, thinking only of the sons of gentlemen, Franklin was more progressive and liberal without being fully democratic. His plans and proposals make us believe that Franklin wanted opportunity for schooling extended considerably beyond the levels current in his day.

However the curriculum was deployed (and we can see something of it in the *Idea of the English School*),[40] and whoever was qualified to attend schools (handled more liberally by Franklin than by Locke), the great purpose of education was to form character. In Franklin's lexicon this was another way of saying the good citizen. Long before it was popular for educational purpose to be set in civic terms, Franklin talked about the commitment American schools should have to the preparation of good citizens; and at this point Franklin and Jefferson begin to sound alike. Yet another side to the issue of character formation should be noted: classical educators committed education to it and used the classics as a means to this end. Franklin was ready to do the same. So with his head in the present and his heart in the past, he used the classics, too, asking only that they be taught in English. Still, in his English curriculum utility was given attention first, and character, a far more elusive goal, was shaped by a personal determination to be always honorable, upright, and honest.

Franklin's bias toward personal effort and his praise of the self-made man were drawn no doubt from experience. Born in Boston in 1706, his family wanted him to become a minister and began by preparing him for clerical life. This preparation, brief and incomplete by any account, amounted to two years of schooling divided about equally between the Boston Latin School and a private master, George Brownell. Such was the extent of Franklin's formal schooling; subsequent intellectual accomplishment was the result of personal effort. So in common with conventional opinion of self-made men, Franklin assumed that what had worked so well for him was unquestionably good for everyone.[41] At the same time, sensitive to the advantage of help from others in the business of learning, he published admonitions relative to public activity and state responsibility; and now we see his proclivity for organizing private groups to promote a public cause. The Academy was a mutual venture; self-improvement societies seem to have attracted his attention and support in almost every part of his long and illustrious career; and the founding of philosophical and library associations attest further his confidence in mutual effort.

One may wander through the thicket of Franklin's accomplishments— beginning with his humble schooling and going all the way to the end of his life when he was accounted the most civilized man in America—

looking for evidences of his educational theory and not be disappointed, but it is best to stay close to the one pronouncement wherein he stated his educational convictions: *Proposals Relating to the Education of Youth in Pennsylvania*, a discourse started around 1743 and published in 1749.[42]

Franklin begins by acknowledging his indebtedness to John Milton's *Of Education*, John Locke's *Some Thoughts Concerning Education*, David Fordyce's *Dialogues Concerning Education*, Obadiah Walker's *Of Education*, Charles Rollin's *The Method of Teaching and Studying the Belles-Lettres*, and George Turnbull's *Observations Upon Liberal Education in All Its Branches*. His frank admission that these were the principal sources for his educational plan makes unnecessary Cremin's argument in *American Education: The Colonial Experience* for the originality of Franklin's educational position.[43] If Cremin is unconvincing, it is because Franklin's place in American educational history is not dependent on originality but on a capacity for taking old ideas and reinterpreting them for American society.

The immediate outcome of Franklin's *Proposals* was the Academy, a secondary school whose notoriety was greater than its influence, but to pay too much heed to the Academy may be misleading, for it was not always true to its founder's intention.

This academic charter for the Academy, the *Proposals*, was read for years by scholars whose preconceptions never allowed them to get past two striking assertions: the absolute need for English teaching, and the prudence of combining the "most useful and the most ornamental" studies rather than trying to teach everything that was useful and ornamental. Literally interpreted, although unfairly and incorrectly, these assertions made Franklin an enemy of the classics, on one hand, and a stark utilitarian, blind to the values of civility, on the other. The school plan sketched in the *Proposals* was more liberal and humane than this.

It began by endorsing a fairly conventional school model: a resident institution with a master whose reputation for Humanistic learning was sound and with a curriculum capable of introducing students to the broadest kind of Humanistic culture. Even so, the dogmatic assumption that all knowledge is in the classics was rejected. Franklin's school plan did not start with an attenuated syllabus, one embracing only, or even mainly, knowledge for use. What was emphasized was a freedom to design the curriculum in relation to students' educational and vocational needs. One need was common: and it was satisfied in English classes where students could master their vernacular language. Franklin recommends the ancient languages for students who want and need them, and he is able to welcome modern language to the curriculum as well, but what is clearly new is the attention paid English study. Boys leaving such a school would have been able to handle the English language in a way befitting educated persons.

The emphasis on useful learning and on the study of the English language is clear enough and merits historical attention. But this attention often obscures Franklin's educational intention: "the great aim and end of all learning" is to lay the foundation for good breeding and a spirit of service to one's family, community, and country. Beneath the crust of utility was an undisguised commitment to altruism, and beyond Franklin's reputation for crass materialism was his unequivocal support of "a Publick Religion" which would contribute to a public character and morality. He was ready, moreover, to attest the "Excellency of the Christian Religion above all others ancient or modern." Franklin himself was unaffected by doctrines of piety, and he could not have been called a conventional Christian, but he was never blind to the social worth of religion.

Franklin's *Proposals,* followed mainly by private schools, were silent about public support and control for secondary education, although his encouragement of greater educational opportunity for the country's youth was obvious. They never mention universal education, and elementary school studies go unnoticed. What is said is meant for secondary-school boys who are now released from a traditional classical curriculum and are allowed to pursue (except for English) studies with personal appeal and utility. Planning their studies under the watchful eye of masters, boys could sample a broad range of subjects: arithmetic, bookkeeping, handwriting, and drawing are there, as are geometry, astronomy, rhetoric, geography, moral philosophy, and history. Despite Franklin's affection for utility, history is clearly one of his favorite courses. But there is more: natural history, natural philosophy, mechanics, and gardening serve to satisfy his penchant for science, invention, and common sense. Boys who attended a school modeled after Franklin's plan were intended to be public men capable of meeting the issues of real life—and this is the chief character of Franklin's utilitarianism—but their bodies needed formation as well as their minds, so health, recreation, and sport were accounted for in the general syllabus.

When we come to the end of the *Proposals,* we are uncertain about signs of educational revolution; more likely we have read a plan essaying to adapt the conventional school course to the changing conditions of life in America. Such a reading does nothing to dim the luster of Franklin's place in American educational history, or the Academy's bold assault on scholastic habit.

The Advent of Democratic Education

We know, from what has been said about the social policy of Thomas Jefferson (1743-1826), of his unbounded confidence in men to construct a flawless political system. While Jefferson eschewed utopian plans, he envisioned, nevertheless, an American society jealously committed to preserving man's natural right to happiness. The author of the Declaration embraced equality as a living principle and not merely as a social theory, something to be paid lip service, and he was serious in his conviction that government should be its citizens' servant.[44]

A confirmed friend of separation of church and state, he had misgivings about the benefit of organized religion for the general welfare. With a high confidence in the ability of citizens for self-government, he realized that public policy should be shaped by literate, informed, and prudent people. This condition led him to support a broad and generous distribution of opportunity for schooling. Without schools where intelligence could be cultivated, Jefferson's aspirations for America were sterile.

We find a commitment to schools and learning in almost everything he did, but most explicitly in the "Bill for the More General Diffusion of Knowledge," a plan presented to the legislature in 1779, a few days after Jefferson became governor of Virginia.[45] Its most striking feature was in the provision for three years of publicly-supported schooling for all free children, and this put Jefferson in the vanguard of educational theorists and public men whose vision was clear enough to see landmarks of democratic education on the distant horizon. Noting at once the failure of Jefferson's bill in 1779 (and its rejection when it was resubmitted in 1817), we find his conception of public education familiar: it became the standard for American educational policy. And this should warn us to be cautious when revisionist historians tell us that plans for public education in the early years of our country never included provision for universal opportunity. The late eighteenth and the early nineteenth centuries did not know public education as we know it, nor was there any general endorsement of universal schooling, yet educational theory, in the hands of some men, had advanced far enough to accommodate both. Jefferson's plan is sufficient proof.

In connection with a determination to revise the legal code—to make it fit conditions of contemporary life in Virginia by stripping from it the features of British law inconsistent with republicanism—Jefferson advanced his school plan as an essential part of public policy. The plan had two goals: to lay a basis for active and intelligent citizenship, and to enlarge prospects for a full and satisfying life.

Because Jefferson's plan was the first of its kind and, also, because it contained elements later grafted to the American system, its details merit close attention. According to the plan, Virginia was separated into districts, or hundreds, five or six miles square and in each district "a school for teaching reading, writing, and arithmetic" was established. Teachers conducting these schools were paid by the district and children in attendance received the first three years of instruction at public expense. If they wanted more schooling, they could get it at their own expense.

Supervisors—Jefferson called them visitors—of district schools annually selected the "best genius in the school, of those whose parents are too poor to give them further education," and sent him on to one of twenty grammar schools. The curriculum of the grammar school was Greek, Latin, geography, and "the higher branches of numerical arithmetic." After one or two years in the grammar school, "the best genius of the whole selected" was awarded a full scholarship for the six-year course. By these means, Jefferson wrote, "twenty of the best geniuses will be raked from the rubbish annually, and be instructed, at the public expence, so far as the grammar schools go."[46]

When the grammar-school course was complete, ten boys with the public scholarships were selected annually for study in the College of William and Mary, where they were expected to concentrate on science. Students not entering college, Jefferson thought, could return to the grammar schools as teachers.

Jefferson's plan offered educational opportunity to everyone: to the poor whose talented children could climb the scholastic ladder supported by state scholarships, and to the wealthy with schools convenient for their use. These broad and, Jefferson believed, generous means would ensure the "objects of this law . . . and provide an education adapted to the years, to the capacity, and the condition of every one, and directed to their freedom and happiness." On the first level, where all free children were entitled to three years of public schooling, the principal foundations of a social order were laid. Knowledge of history combined with the first elements of morality would enable maturing students to form their own judgments on ethical and political issues; thus Jefferson hoped to abandon traditional moral indoctrination by means of Biblical and doctrinal teaching.

The grammar-school level was concerned mainly with establishing sound learning in language. This emphasis, Jefferson argued, was justified in two ways: first, during these years the student is ready for instruction where memory plays a large role; second, although he did "not pretend that language is science . . . it is an instrument for the attainment of science," and he refused to follow the European example where learning in Greek and Latin, he was told, "is going into disuse . . . I know not what their manner and occupations may call for: but it would be very ill-judged in us to follow their example in this instance."[47]

The university, still attended by the wealthy, was open, because of public scholarships, to talented youth from the poorer classes. And Jefferson expected the state to avail itself "of those talents which nature has sown as liberally among the poor as the rich, but which perish without use, if not sought for and cultivated."

The plan contemplated the cultivation of talent, so much is clear, but liberal learning was only part of the story: The main object of the law,

Jefferson said, was "that of rendering the people the safe, as they are the ultimate, guardians of their own liberty." Learning as a safeguard to liberty figured large in Jefferson's educational theory, and the elementary schools of the districts were critical to this purpose. Elementary learning should center attention on the rudiments, but this would leave ample time for history. With a developed sense of history, citizens would be qualified to "judge the actions and the designs of men." They could recognize ambition in any disguise and keep it from destroying their liberty. Ambition, if vested solely in the private aspirations of leaders, infects government; so to block inordinate ambition and thus preserve political health "the influence over government must be shared among all the people . . . because the corrupting the whole mass will exceed any private resources of wealth: and public ones cannot be provided but by levies on the people."[48]

The system of education Jefferson proposed, especially the free-school feature, would enable the people themselves to stand as the safe depositories of liberty. This alone demonstrates Jefferson's allegiance to education's civic purpose.

Schools were essential to the wide dissemination of learning Jefferson held necessary for a republic, but schools should have supplements. His bill, therefore, proposed the creation of public libraries and, evidently in an effort to elevate the people's taste, galleries of painting and statuary.

Implied in his famous plan is Jefferson's fundamental philosophy of education—universal education is essential to civic virtue and citizenship is the primary educational objective. This philosophy was translated into the political principle making elementary education the natural right of every citizen. As it turned out, Jefferson's educational theory was both liberal and premature; the Virginia assembly was unprepared for anything so ambitious. Yet universal education as a corollary of political democracy could not be invalidated by neglect. In any case, Jefferson's theory of democratic education was the most advanced of the time and it influenced the development of popular education in the later years of the nineteenth century.

Education for National Purpose

Among the many educational projections made during the late colonial and early national period, a few were both distinguished and influential. One with good qualifications was produced by Benjamin Rush (1745–1813). Hardly a disciple of either Jefferson or Franklin, Rush was progressive on educational theory and practice without being liberal. His thought appears as a mixture of means to produce well-educated citizens for the nation—aided by state-supported elementary schools—following a pedagogic regimen and curriculum reminding us of colonial Latin grammar schools. The business of education, Rush wrote, "has acquired a new complexion by the independence of our country. The form of government we have assumed, has created a new class of duties to every American. It becomes us, therefore, to examine our former habits upon this subject, and in laying the foundations for nurseries of wise and good men, to adapt our modes of teaching to the peculiar form of our government."

In a discourse entitled "Thoughts upon the Mode of Education Proper in a Republic,"[49] old allegiances to Great Britain are pared away. He wants good citizens and is convinced schools can be of some help, but there is more: he wants persons of character too, and now he shows his affinity to educational tradition. The best (Rush may have thought the only) way to develop character was to begin by recognizing that the "foundation for a useful education in a republic is to be laid in religion." Not a religion of humanity or some generalized religious sentiments, but allegiance to a Christian denomination. Jefferson was horrified when he read Rush's assertions recommending a wedding of religion and education in the interest of character formation, for his own arguments were mustered to permanently dissolve their engagement.

After Rush took care of the foundations to character, telling his readers that "a Christian cannot fail of being a republican," he turned to the schools' curriculum. The Bible, he said, must have a permanent place and it should be read and explained to students. But the Bible alone was not enough. He wanted the best Humanistic education: "I do not wish the learned or Dead languages, as they are commonly called, to be reduced below their present just rank in the universities of Europe, especially as I consider an acquaintance with them as the best foundation for a correct and extensive knowledge of the language of our country." Everyone would not be a linguist, as Rush was quick to recognize, yet knowing the classics and especially the classical languages could facilitate English usage. Too much pains, he said, "cannot be taken to teach our youth to read and write our American language with propriety and elegance."[50]

Finally, and now Rush begins to sound up to date, the principle is established that government should have a role in the distribution of educational opportunity. Without adopting universal education as a social philosophy—in other words, without being Jeffersonian—he is, nevertheless, on the side of government action for the creation and maintenance of school systems where the country's children could be prepared for the society of a new America.

What sounded like a manifesto in the "Thoughts upon the Mode of Education Proper in a Republic" was elaborated in considerable detail in "A Plan for the Establishment of Public Schools."[51] Before we look at Rush's plan, we should remind ourselves that the eighteenth century had some notion of public education and could anticipate, at least in theory, a model for the future. Rush's advocacy of the public school in 1786 should temper the enthusiasm of educational historians for the proposition that public schools were the invention of late nineteenth-century educational activists without any indebtedness to their forebears.

Rush began with a justification for widely distributed educational opportunity, an argument with a redundant sound today, but one which must have been necessary then. In the first place, being himself a man of religious perspective, he defended the notion that learning was useful to religion. And without any commitment to sectarian schools, he assumed that higher levels of learning among the people would advance the cause of religion generally by eliminating prejudice and superstition and enabling persons to grasp the full significance of their relationship to God.

He realized, moreover, that the structure of political democracy rested on a fragile compact, one needing intelligence and learning to sustain it. Without learning, Rush wrote (borrowing a phrase from Rousseau), "men become Savages or Barbarians, and where learning is confined to a *few* people, we will always find monarchy, aristocracy and slavery." Without learning, and without means to advance it, the prospect for a successful American democracy was indeed dim. Law and justice, too, stood on a foundation of learning, for without learning neither good government nor legal authority had much chance. Knowledge is essential to the creation of just and equitable government; it is equally essential to the effectiveness of government which, in the last analysis, must depend on the understanding and good will of the governed.

Religion, law, and justice are important, indeed imperative to a democratic society, but alone they do not account for civilization. Civilization, according to Rush, comprised manners, civility, and an ability to conduct interpersonal dialogue. Men might live in society and subsist without learning, but lacking civilization they would sacrifice the better qualities of human life.

Finally, Rush accounts for economic value, and he saw it principally in agriculture and manufacture. Both stood to benefit from learning, because both depended for their advancement on art and science.

Always somewhat prosaic, but clear and persuasive nevertheless, Rush justified the worth of learning to a people who sometimes lost sight of its virtue or were too busy with the affairs of life to spend time on what they counted to be ornament and erudition. This was his plan: in every township, or in districts with one hundred families, he proposed to establish a free elementary school where children would be taught to "read and write the English and German languages, and the use of figures."[52]

Each county should have an academy where parents could send children who wanted more than an elementary education. These academies were to be classical schools, concentrating on the learned languages (Latin and Greek) and literature, and capable of preparing youth for college. But Rush did not make these academies free schools.

Keeping in mind that Rush was planning for Pennsylvania, we understand the recommendation for four colleges, located in regions accessible to college-bound students. Capping the system, Rush proposed the establishment of a state university, a school offering lectures and studies to advanced students and one observing the traditional standard of university scholarship.

While only one school in this educational plan was free, the academies, the colleges, and the university were to receive public support from taxes and land allotments. With so much land available, Rush was generous in its allocation to the schools, although subsequently, when federal and state land grants became a reality, the abundance of land depressed its worth and schools reaped little financial help.

Still, despite Rush's conviction that schools were essential to liberty, religion, and social and economic progress, he refused to leave all learning in their custody. His plan called for the multiplication of libraries with useful and cultural books available for everyone, and his advocacy for a vigorous press reminds us that Rush knew something about the possibilities of informal education. The newspaper was a modest teacher but Rush praised it unstintingly as a useful and noble auxiliary to schools and libraries.

Prizing sound and decent learning, Rush popularized the value of schools on all levels, and recommended free schools when free schools were viewed with suspicion, and sometimes alarm. Alongside this broad outlook, he was ready to preserve ethnic and religious distinction and made room for it in his school plan. So far as possible, consistent no doubt with local resources, he recommended that children of the same religion be educated together. And he was willing to accommodate German-speaking youth in one of the state colleges. At this time, at least in Rush's mind, national origin and language and religious preference were reasonable grounds for voluntary educational segregation. Such differences as nationality and denominationalism represented were counted strengths rather than weaknesses, to be capitalized and cultivated rather than eliminated.

Rush was a vigorous spokesman for the worth of learning, and he perceived its political, economic, and social value along with its personal worth. But his projected educational reforms were undramatic and totally silent with respect to new pedagogic technique; despite this, he was always on the side of progress. He wanted more and better education—husbanding the conviction that the seeds of economic and social betterment germinated in the schools—and thus anticipated in a modest way the gospel made notorious by nineteenth-century humanitarians.

With the educational wisdom of Franklin, Jefferson, and Rush at their disposal, and ready to embark on a nationalistic voyage, Americans were troubled. They entertained reasonable doubt about the effectiveness of the old education, but were unready to jettison it altogether. Events, however, took command of purpose and until nearly the middle of the nineteenth century—all the foreign and domestic educational plans notwithstanding—American educational policy and practice reacted to political, economic, and social disposition. It followed but did not lead the country over the threshold of national character.

CHAPTER SEVEN

Education in the Age of the Common Man— 1800–1870

New as a nation and eager to put to a trial the political theory of natural right, America entered the nineteenth century supremely confident of her future. Old sectional rivalry and disagreement on social theory were forgotten long enough for compromise to ensure the republic's health, and now, remembering Benjamin Franklin's famous remark that Americans had a republic if they could keep it, public men sought for ways to broaden the base of political support by pronouncing a theory with enough appeal to allow republicanism to succeed. Expedients of survival may, in better and more stable days, become elements of distrust, so now discordant dispositions and conflicting interests among various groups needed to be harmonized. On one hand were persons of wealth, property, and position, familiar with power and authority, and fully capable of wielding both; on the other stood the masses of people with little political and economic strength or influence, authentic common men.

The Constitution, common men thought, was written for them and they were determined to see its provisions applied. Their assessment may have been wrong, but even so the trend in the Western world was toward securing right and enriching opportunity for persons suffering political indignity and economic neglect.

To change the settled course of history, to dislodge old loyalties and ways of thinking and acting, to withdraw power from the few and distribute it to the many was a hard and time-consuming task. With Andrew Jackson's election to the presidency in 1828, common men began to cast a longer shadow on American political life. Then, and for the next half-century, whether in political theory or act, in political assembly or factory, in urban areas or rural districts, in homes or schools, common men learned to call the political tune. Neither becoming wealthy nor educated and socially cultivated overnight, they quickly became politically significant. And this fact alone constituted the most effective argument for educating them to function as informed and responsible citizens. The class of property and wealth lived in constant fear of ignorant and violent people roaming the cities and the fields with appetites for self-indulgence uncurbed by the steadying hand of civility, knowledge, and reason. They should be inducted into the company of civilized men, with more to lose than to gain from radicalism. Without being arrogant, we suspect this fear had a basis, and was always something more than an ugly apparition conveniently conjured up for pragmatic gain.

If confidence in national destiny was sometimes shaken by social reality, and if some men despaired of ever seeing society conducted according to precepts of law and order, these feelings were regularly redressed by surges of optimism generated in the powerhouses of abundant land and rich natural resources, and in a national expansion of population and territory staggering to the imagination. The West was open to any man vigorous and brave enough to make the long, arduous journey across the mountains, and once there the frontier was limitless, or so it seemed. The conquerors of America's frontier were shaped by their experience almost as much as they reshaped the land they settled, and this rough and ready experience confirmed new convictions about social equality and opportunity. These same convictions infected political attitudes and eroded old notions that men of privilege and position should always have the right of precedence in the conduct of public affairs. Common men, now, not only wanted to vote for their leaders, and therefore became constant advocates for universal manhood suffrage, they wanted also a chance to be counted among them.

Land and labor were plentiful and relatively cheap, the former available almost for the asking after the generous homestead acts were passed releasing huge sections of the national domain for private ownership; raw materials were abundant and natural resources seemingly inexhaustible. While one part of the working population turned to the West to find its subsistence in agriculture, hunting, and mining, the other part, attracted by the tremendous industrial growth in the East, flocked to the cities. Almost nothing, not even the Civil War, checked these developments of economic expansion and growth, which were always aided and abetted by improvements in communication and transportation. In this economic expansion we find the rise of two classes of common men which, while in many respects competitors, shared some basic interests: farmers and workingmen.

Both rural people and urban labor had for a long time been neglected or exploited, and frequently they were their own worst enemies; but now they were ready, anxious, and determined to reap some of the promises of this new, good land. Driven forward by motives for betterment, for securing some of the finer things of life for themselves, and for ensuring to their children a better life than theirs, rural and urban common men were quick to support bands of humanitarians, political leaders, social philosophers, progressive business men, and others of good will who, by reason and sentiment, were committed to fight the battle for the improvement of mankind. With all the force they could muster, these nineteenth-century reformers, after the manner of religious zealots, led the crusade for the common man's cause and in an almost unmatched display of altruism undertook to accommodate public policy to his interests. High on the list of priorities but not alone among worthy causes soliciting reformers' support, was education, for learning, these social activists argued, was a necessary condition for securing natural right and ensuring the progress of mankind.

Neither public attitude nor policy was easy to alter in a century still so steeped in tradition and so hesitant, despite the audacity exhibited in the rupture with Great Britain, to cultivate social or political novelty. History reflects this reluctance to change, but change occurred nevertheless, and we should now, so far as public education is concerned, try to follow its course.

THE STATE AND EDUCATION

The colonial educational experience left an impression of ambiguity: was education an individual or a collective responsibility? When colonial law prescribed a minimum level of literacy, it reflected the public mind; and the public mind was solicitous of the common good with government encouraging wider and richer distribution of learning. Yet, we must remember, while such laws were enacted in some places, in others the entire matter of collective educational responsibility was allowed to lie fallow. And even when colonial laws were passed certifying the duty of government to involve itself in education, such laws were often so modest in their provision as to make almost no difference.

Law could demand literacy and say nothing about schools; or it could embrace the idea of town and district schools and remain silent about their maintenance and support. Buried away in the recesses of public policy was the assumption that government could exercise authority over education, but the same assumption was encrusted with layers of tradition seldom allowing it to break through to practice. Competing with this assumption, however, was the common conviction that education was outside the authority of any government level. To shape an educational policy capable of finding its way through the dense thicket of these contending positions was never easy and we understand why so many false starts and compromises were made before public policy was clarified and finalized.

In the early years of the national period few persons were prepared to assign much authority to a central government: personal experience plus the recollections of history warned against conceding too much power to the state, so in education and in almost everything else the commission public men were willing to write for a national government was both weak and limited. Thus, the United States, held together by the Articles of Confederation, was to a great extent hardly more than a geographic expression. Central government, under the circumstances, had neither the will nor the authority to take a persuasive stand on the educational issue. Not only was the central government unable to assert any authority over education, it was likewise unable to say anything about the educational policy which should operate in the states.

The Northwest Ordinance

Yet, despite the absence of direct action with respect to educational policy, the national government quite fortuitously inaugurated a land policy that affected education on the state and local levels. Land policy was stated in the Northwest Ordinance of 1785. Under the Articles of Confederation, states claiming title to vast regions west of the Alleghenies ceded title to the national government. Shortly thereafter settlers began to move west with the intention of making their homes in an almost virgin wilderness, but before settlement became too great and personal ownership of land decided by the fact of possession, Congress authorized a land survey of the Northwest Territory. According to the Northwest Ordinance of 1785, the territory was to be laid out in townships (each six miles square), and each township was divided into sections one mile square. Sections were numbered from one to thirty-six and section sixteen of every township was reserved for the support of education. Reserving a section meant that its title remained public and that income from its use or sale would be applied to education. As the Northwest Territory was settled, the school section—often the site for the township school—tended to remain in public custody and even now some school sections in Western states retain this reserved status.

Subsequent to the act of 1785, Congress sold two large tracts of land to settlement companies. The sale agreement included a grant to each company of one township for a college, section sixteen of every township for the support of schools, and section twenty-seven of every township for the encouragement of religion. In 1802 Ohio was admitted to the union, and Congress granted the state section sixteen of every township for schools; thereafter, as each new state was admitted (except Texas, Maine, and West Virginia), Congress assigned section sixteen as school land. After 1850, beginning with the admission of California, federal grants became more generous: California received two sections of every township, and Arizona, New Mexico, and Nevada were given four sections of every township for school land.

These grants in the second half of the nineteenth century, although, important, interest us less than the earlier ones, for they were made after the role of the federal government in education had some definition. The early grants, especially the Northwest Ordinances, helped form a policy of national interest and involvement in educational affairs. Clearly such a policy was in the first stages of evolution, and one should be diffident about arguing that national educational policy was completed with the Ordinances. What was done was a beginning. Land granted encouraged the states to create permanent school funds from which local schools could obtain financial assistance. And the language of the Ordinance of 1787, an act incorporating the Northwest Territory, was a vigorous expression favorable to educational growth. Despite its limited authority in education, the national government took the side of learning: "Religion, morality, and knowledge being necessary to good government and the happiness of mankind, schools and the means of education shall be forever encouraged."[1]

This progressive policy was possible because a few exceptional leaders were in the vanguard of public opinion. Besides, even though good reason to doubt its sincerity is lacking, this policy neither demanded implementation nor entailed cost. Once expressed, it could be applauded and acclaimed and then ignored or followed as the people in the states saw fit. But regardless of the climate of acceptance in the decades following its pronouncement, this policy of interest and encouragement stood as a prominent reminder to national aspirations.

Leaders and Education

Irrespective of romantic appeal in national history, we have learned that national aspirations are seldom spontaneous outbursts of community will; rather, they are articulated by visionary spokesmen whose language carries enough persuasive force to elicit zeal and devotion to them. Generation of a national interest in education in the early nineteenth century followed this familiar pattern: leaders began by saying wise things about the worth of education and illustrated its value. Beginning with George Washington, in his address to Congress in 1790 and again in the famous Farewell Address of 1796, knowledge was stressed as "the surest basis of public happiness," an essential condition in a free society where the people should know and value their political rights, recognize the application of lawful authority and unite in "a speedy but temperate vigilance against encroachments" on their political autonomy. In the Farewell Address, Washington admonished his countrymen to "promote, then, as an object of primary importance institutions for the general diffusion of knowledge." To recommend attention to schools and colleges because they promote knowledge and enlighten public opinion is a long way from asserting for the central government any active role in the support, control, and operation of schools, but it was an unequivocal acknowledgement of the consequential link between learning and political life. Washington's support generated sympathy for the cause of learning and education.[2]

In the wake of Washington's progressive assertions, we find similar statements supporting education. John Jay, the first chief justice of the United States Supreme Court, praised knowledge "as the soul of the republic," although his endorsement led only to a policy which would have made education available, according to a person's need, "at a cheap and easy rate." Francis Marion, a popular and dashing general of the Revolution, spoke favorably of the national value of schools, although it appears that his view of public education was only large enough to allow government support for schools attended by pauper children. The names of Thomas Jefferson and James Madison can be added to a list of prominent men who regarded the means of education as essential conditions to political liberty. The litany could continue, but it is unnecessary because the point is clear: national educational aspirations were articulated by men in whom the people had confidence.

The uses to which education could be put were becoming clearer: political development in the nineteenth century paved the way for a fuller realization of the commitments made in the Declaration of Independence and the Constitution, but it was left to the nation to prepare its citizens to fulfill the new responsibilities thrust on them; and economic life, constantly increasing in complexity and thus more closely wedded to political policy, suggested the abandonment of the old and honored principle wherein the means of literacy and education are best left in the custody of personal decision and resource. Convictions from the past were not eroded in one decade or in a single generation, but the temper of the time, coupled with a variety of examples from foreign states where education became a function of government, recommended consideration of a public policy on the education of citizens.

This thought was neither new nor an invention of eighteenth-century philosophers, although they sometimes said states were responsible educational agents; it was, instead, a revival of Plato's educational theory. Plato's ideal state was small, with only a few thousand citizens, so it was hard to find formulas in Plato's *Republic* and apply them to a country so vast and various as the infant United States; but if Plato could not be followed, he could, at least, supply inspiration to an American movement for national education. Late in the eighteenth century, and perhaps in the first decade of the nineteenth, dozens of plans were forwarded on national education, and they had a common theme: to allow old educational policies to continue—ones distilled in colonial life—would put in jeopardy the political integrity of this new country and encourage monarchy to replace democracy. National education had support from various sources, but the most effective support came from a society which had exerted so much influence on American philosophy and science: Franklin's American Philosophical Society. It announced a prize for the best essay on a plan for national education, and almost at once proposals began to arrive in Philadelphia. Reading these plans today leaves us unconvinced of the merit of national education.

Benjamin Rush, Robert Coram, Samuel Knox, Samuel Smith, James Sullivan, Noah Webster, and Nathaniel Chipman were among the writers whose essays sought to fulfill the specifications of the Society's contest: A system of instruction "adapted to the genius of the Government of the United States; comprehending also a plan for instituting and conducting public schools in this country, on principles of the most extensive utility."[3]

Robert Coram's essay, published in 1791, is illustrative of the features common to all the plans. He began by endorsing the civic value of education, and was ready to quarrel with the assumption that education was subordinate to religion. Possibly more than any other feature, this preoccupation with education for citizenship, in an age still fundamentally religious, stalled the implementation of national education. Next, Coram outlined a curriculum stripped of religion, culture, manners, and classical language. His determination was to begin anew, leaving untouched all European belief, custom, and form of expression. Such outright rejection of the past coupled with a stark appeal to utility was bound to generate opposition among the educated classes in America who prized their cultural heritage and were prepared to defend its value. Along with other essayists, Coram distrusted parental authority, for parents, he asserted, were either too preoccupied with their own interest or too selfish to superintend properly the education of their children. But this was not all: any education left dependent on the resources of parents, or even of local communities, was almost certain to be unequal in instructional opportunity. Clearly some parents and some localities were poorer than others, so if some effort were not made to equalize opportunity, the children treated unequally—and eventually the country as a whole—would suffer. To eliminate educational inequality, Coram argued, schools should be organized, supported, and controlled on the broadest possible political base.

The bold assertion was advanced that education was a state function, and the equally bold claim was made that property was a social trust. The schools, Coram said, were within the ambit of state authority and their support could be sought legitimately from taxation. Schools should be organized in districts—familiar units, for they had long been used in New England—about the size of a township, and the design of school buildings should conform to a uniform building code. Teachers' salaries would be paid from the public treasury and public policy would fix the course of instruction.[4]

Noble as these sentiments were, they were rejected, and their rejection was grounded on an emerging American character which found a centralized system of education, shaped by national policy, ingenuous and incompatible with fundamental principles of democracy. Strong arguments for national education can be advanced, and some may be convincing today, but the American memory and experience blunted their thrust and, in the end, discredited them. Left on the heap of historical discard, these plans for national education, all prepared with care and good will, did little more than keep the educational issue current in the public mind. If the central government were to involve itself in education, it would have to find some other way.

Precedents for state action in education were far from convincing at the outset of the national period. While colonial arrangements for education sometimes implied a collective social responsibility for education, these implications were too weak to counteract the weight of practice. And when liberal political doctrines championed the common man as an authentic citizen, the lines of social control were drawn more tightly by aristocrats, who seldom thought kindly of participatory citizenship.

The Tenth Amendment to the Constitution, now correctly interpreted as a commission to states to manage affairs (such as education) not reserved to the federal government, was not a springboard for state action. Few framers of the Constitution ever thought they had either implicitly or explicitly delegated educational authority to the states. They were content with the educational status quo: leaving schooling and learning in the uncertain custody of denominational and philanthropic hands.

An ambitious dissenter could be reminded of the outcome of Jefferson's Virginia bill and its projected diffusion of knowledge. Jefferson, we know, wrote a grammar of social progress, but it went unheeded. Education was conventionally a private matter, and so the writers of the Constitution, as well as those responsible for amendment, appeared willing to leave it.

Yet the national government took some action on education in the Northwest Ordinances of 1785 and 1787; public men spoke of expanding educational means and the cultivation of schooled citizens; and private persons leaped on the bandwagon of educational reform. Such sentiments began with only modest support, but support increased and finally the states found justification for direct involvement in schooling.

At first this involvement was temperate and equivocal: in 1800 only seven of sixteen states made any reference to education in their constitutions.

State systems of education with implications of universality and freedom existed on the level of theory, as ideals but not yet matters of political practice.

Even so, in their first constitutions Massachusetts, Vermont, and New Hampshire took a progressive stand: without legislating a public school movement, they put the good will of the state behind the cause of education. Praising wisdom and virtue and averring knowledge essential to the preservation of right and liberty, they encouraged. the distribution of education among the people. But there was more: they affirmed it the duty of their respective legislatures to promote schools of all kinds and learning in general.

As new states were admitted to the Union, their constitutions usually had clauses praising learning and recommending its advancement. The justification for these assertions was always that a diffusion of knowledge among the people would promote and preserve morality and liberty. Still, the constitutions were mainly non-directive and state legislatures were left to their own discretion to ensure a diffusion of knowledge. Among the new state constitutions adopted before 1820, Indiana's was the most progressive, for it directed the legislature "to provide by law for a general system of education, ascending in regular gradation from township schools to a State university, wherein tuition [shall be] gratis, and equally open to all." No doubt this provision was applauded by persons convinced of the people's need for learning in a republic and the states' obligation to take an active role in providing and controlling education within their jurisdiction. Still, the Indiana provision, with all its vision, added the practical but somewhat chilly proviso: "as soon as circumstances will permit."[5]

However, omens were good and optimistic persons continued to expect state constitutional provisions and early state laws to do more. Law seemed most promising to men who saw in New England practice the prototype of public education. But New England's record, in spite of its historical kudos, was equivocal. True, towns and districts had long been told to maintain schools and the New England states, save for Rhode Island, appeared to have public school systems. A plethora of laws aimed at establishing schools, supporting them, and prescribing their curricula had been enacted, beginning even in colonial years. But in the face of reasonable doubt that such laws, even when permissive rather than mandatory, were a proper exercise of state authority and not an invasion of parental prerogative, this legislation was too often ineffective. In any case, to credit them with having created state school systems would be going beyond the evidence. And outside New England, educational crusaders found little support from history. They centered attention on New England because New England alone was capable of giving their intentions some hope. The older states, deprived of the Puritan tradition of using learning reverently, were dominated by political attitudes fixing learning as a personal matter, to be handled by parents as they saw fit, and completely outside the power of the state.

Before state action could proceed, it had to have support from political theory authorizing its educational authority. Where constitutions affirmed such authority, educational legislation had its mandate, but with few exceptions state constitutions chose to be guarded in educational affirmation. At this point, the best model was New York.

Although New York's constitution of 1777 left education unmentioned, the state became active in the first years of the national period and by 1784 had created the Board of Regents of the University of the state of New York. Indicating that the state was unwilling to grapple with the broad issue of the education of the people, the regents were empowered to supervise only secondary and higher education. And the high-sounding title of the University of the state of New York, adopted from the French, never meant to imply a university in the conventional sense. Secondary and higher education, it was generally assumed, were always outside the realm of public schooling and the state's responsibility was to maintain standards in a private arena of learning. Elementary education did not figure at all in the regents' commission.

Evidence of the state's commitment to a separation of public and private education appears in 1811, when the governor appointed a commission to recommend a plan for common schools. In 1812, a common-school system recommended by the commission was adopted and, still respecting the separation of elementary from secondary and higher education, a superintendent of common schools, Gideon Hawley, was appointed. Hawley's friends praised his effort to organize elementary schools, but his enemies, members of the legislature for the most part, believing he was moving too quickly to promote public education, abolished his office in 1821.[6]

With political and legal issues confused, the states hesitated to do much more than tinker with educational organization and administration; hardly any state initiative gripped the issue of state educational authority. On the level of organization, however, the states were fairly active: Connecticut provided for a commissioner of school funds in 1810; in 1815 Virginia established a state board for the Literary Fund; and during these early years the states of Georgia, Louisiana, and Michigan undertook to follow New York's model of school administration.[7] Yet, despite this state action, the question of authority remained unresolved and in the absence of resolution the old tradition prescribing parental prerogative was relatively undisturbed. States might organize educational programs; they might even support schools and encourage attendance, but they were not entirely certain that an exercise of educational authority was legitimate.

History says states were most active along lines of educational support, for by the end of the second decade of the nineteenth century almost every state had a permanent school fund. These funds, financed in various ways, sometimes with and sometimes without assets, were intended to help localities with educational expenses. Although general patterns are hard to distill, first claim on state funds was had by schools organized for paupers and orphans. There was no novelty here, for long-standing practice both in Europe and America recommended helping persons unable to help themselves. And this tradition, deeply imbedded in American social thought, stood for a long time as a decisive obstacle to free schools. Parents with any ability at all to pay for the education of their children resented and avoided the stigma of allowing their children to attend free schools. Then, too, it should be added, few persons in the early years of this century were amenable to bearing the cost entailed by any system of free schooling.

In any case, schools benefiting from state funds were almost always elementary, for there was another solid tradition: free education deals with the rudiments, because higher learning (anything beyond the elementary) is a personal responsibility. Possibly this restrictive tradition was a blessing in disguise, for state funds were never sufficient to give much help even to elementary schools. Coming from a variety of sources—sale of public land, public-land use, fines, licenses, and lotteries—money for these funds was scarce. In spite of these obvious limitations, state funds were the threshold over which a fuller definition of state educational authority was to pass. But definition came later and for now the state foot was merely inside the schoolhouse door waiting for a clearer affirmation that state educational authority could follow the public dollar.

If, during the first forty years of the century, the states were indisposed to exercise authority over elementary schools, they were, nevertheless, restless and resentful of the apparent autonomy claimed by private colleges whose founding antedated the republic's. Uncomfortable with Yale's colonial charter, Connecticut forced the college to compromise its independence by allowing certain state officers to become members of the college corporation. The University of Pennsylvania and Columbia University, in 1791 and 1787 respectively, had modifications in their charters enabling state officers to exert some influence over their affairs. Harvard and William and Mary were threatened by similar encroachments on their independence, but both escaped with their autonomy relatively unscathed. In connection with Dartmouth College, the issue—the right of a state to alter or repudiate the charter of a private college—was legally joined, and in the Dartmouth College decision private colleges received judicial assurance that their charters could not be invalidated by unilateral state action.[8]

The 1819 Dartmouth College decision of the United States Supreme Court was clear, and its effect on Dartmouth was clear too: the college had a legal charter which, although issued in colonial days, was immune to any attempt by the state to alter it. What was not so clear, however, and the point has been debated for years, is the influence this decision had on the course of American higher education. Did the decision, because it gave private colleges confidence, inaugurate a movement for the founding of private institutions? Did the decision, because of its declaration of a charter's inviolability, lead the states to guard their chartering authority more carefully, thus throttling efforts to expand private higher learning? Or did the states, seeing the decision as an obstacle to an exercise of control over private colleges, undertake with a new enthusiasm the establishment of colleges and universities they could control?[9]

Wrestling with these questions historians have been preoccupied with finding a single, uncomplicated outcome, and attribute it to the Dartmouth College decision. Hence the conclusion that private colleges multiplied dramatically after 1819; or the claim that a private-college movement was retarded because states tended to withhold charters; or the assertion that the decision contained the principal motive for the state university movement. We are closer to the truth if we agree that all of these were outcomes of the decision, but the decision itself was only a catalyst, not a driving force.

What was of greater significance to states from the Dartmouth case was the court's recognition of the state's right to grant charters in the first place and to exercise control over the kind and character of education within its borders. State authority in education was limited, to be sure, especially in connection with colleges whose charters were sound, yet broad enough to enable states to manage a variety of educational affairs. Rather than looking for direct influence on higher education from the Dartmouth College decision, we should be content to find a certification by the country's highest court of the legal propriety of state authority over education. One way states began to employ this newly affirmed authority was to encourage the founding of state universities, although this limited and somewhat premature adventure into public higher education belongs to the last half of the nineteenth century, when there was a great surge of interest in state universities.

PRIVATE EFFORT TO CONDUCT SCHOOLS

Expressions of good will toward education—made almost from the first days of colonization—and modest public provision for schools in some parts of the country, kept the educational issue alive. Most Americans readily acknowledged literacy as a condition for good government, but even with few doubters agreement was lacking on how to achieve this modest objective within the limit of public resource. The cost of a comprehensive elementary school system, although a mystery, was assumed too great a burden for state and local governments to bear; and cautious policies on land grants and state school funds did little to alleviate natural reticence or financial fear of universal schooling. Thus, as the nineteenth century proceeded, public education marked time.

Private effort to compensate for a lack of forthright public action, while generally praiseworthy and effective, permitted public school policy to develop erratically and listlessly: here and there gaining ground and popular support but elsewhere losing momentum because private and denominational schools were doing what seemed necessary. Harsh criticism of private effort is undeserved, yet the enthusiasm displayed to provide education by private initiative and resource deferred the formulation of a consistent and coherent policy on public education.

Adopting a conservative political principle—that government should do only what people cannot do for themselves—the public applauded the educational effort of philanthropists, sectarians, and private masters to organize and conduct schools on all instructional levels. Only when it was patently obvious that private means were unequal to the monumental task of educating an entire nation, only when it was evident that the burden of preparing generations of boys and girls for citizenship could not be handled by private schools alone, only then did popular sentiment alter its dilatory course and ratify a crusade for common schools.

Sunday Schools

Before the crusaders for public education began their long march through nineteenth-century America though, private effort had what may have been its last chance to capture the educational allegiance of the American public. In looking at these last gasps of private effort, we are well advised to be careful about attributing to them inherent stimulants for public education. This is true especially in the case of Sunday schools. Their admirers were fond of saying that these schools, generally undenominational but having a good deal of backing from churches nevertheless, were responsible for laying the foundation for public schools. Sentiment aside, such assertions are mainly myth. Yet, Sunday schools were evident in the early years of the nineteenth century and, from all accounts, were responsible for the instruction of thousands of children who otherwise would have been denied the advantages of some schooling.

In their best days, even in those sections of the country where they were most popular—the Southern seaboard states—Sunday schools were temporary expedients. They always lacked the essential elements of public education. Old imports from England, where English educational historians say they achieved some stability, they were never more than garnishes to substantial learning in the United States. Without claim to public support, although from time to time, especially in South Carolina, their advocates petitioned for modest public aid, there was never any chance for them to have mounted and supported a movement to educate all the children of all the people. With a narrowly circumscribed curriculum and an even more narrowly circumscribed teaching schedule—they were open for only three or four hours a Sunday—they lacked both the time and the means to educate the nation's youth. Despite these defects, however, they form part of a picture which shows America moving slowly and cautiously toward public elementary education. Had they lasted past the 1840s, they would have encountered an insurmountable obstacle to public support (a feature absolutely essential to their success) in the doctrine that denominational religion should be separated from education under public auspices. Certainly these Sunday schools were never blatantly sectarian; yet they always wore a religious face, and this could have been enough to discredit them either as genuine public institutions or adjuncts to public education.

In addition to Sunday schools, other scholastic transplants merit at least a quick historical notice. The justification for this notice, it should be said again, is not so much that they broke ground for public education but rather that they whetted a public appetite for education. And experimenting with them revealed such glaring educational deficiencies that the public was reminded of a fact which, at this time, it would have preferred to forget: public education even on a modest scale needs considerable financial backing.

Infant Schools

In the early years of the century, infant schools were tried in Boston and elsewhere. It has always been hard to understand why infant schools—downward extensions of elementary education—would have captured the scholastic imagination of Americans at a time when there was almost nothing from which to extend schooling downward. Still, probably because these schools had some success in Great Britain, they were imported to America and were tested for their instructional versatility. Such schools took young children—sometimes as young as three or four—and tried to teach them reading and writing. We know almost nothing of their successes or failures here, although suspicion that failure was more common than success is tempting. In any case, these infant schools, wherever conducted, were short-lived ventures. Illustrative of private effort, this characteristic disappeared in one of two ways: some infant schools were absorbed as lower rungs on a public elementary school ladder; others were simply abandoned because they lacked money or clientele.

Monitorial Schools

The final import, as much a method as an institution—the famous, or in-famous, plan of mutual instruction—was invented by Andrew Bell and Joseph Lancaster.[10] This plan, of course, was developed without any affinity whatever to the United States. Practiced in Scotland and India, extravagant praise and persistent propaganda preceded its translation to other parts of the world. When Americans first heard of Joseph Lancaster, for it was Lancaster who came to this country to herald his novel plan, they were reminded that Columbus had discovered America and were promised now that Lancaster would educate her. The plan was simple enough; besides, it could be made to work in some settings. Everything depended upon the effectiveness of only one teacher, regardless of the size of the school, to instruct older, more mature students who, in turn, would instruct succeeding classes below them. Learning was made to conform to the law of gravity: in the end, it reached the lowest instructional level.

When a nineteenth-century American public was willing to make a generous, and optimistic, assumption about the worth of such instruction as the monitorial plan could supply, the feature of educational economy came naturally to the fore. Perhaps pedagogic efficiency was not so rare a commodity; maybe good teachers were unnecessary. Advocates of mutual instruction pretended this was so. And their pretensions were contagious; at least, for a while. Many towns and cities were infected by the enthusiasm Lancaster and his associates kindled for their plan. Monitorial schools multiplied. In the end, however, educational reality caught up with novelty and what had been trumpeted as a pedagogical revolution turned out to be only a minor skirmish, and a losing one at that. After a brief interlude, while monitorial schools flourished, the American public regained its educational equilibrium and discarded mutual instruction. Yet this innovation lingered long enough to retard rather than, as Adolphe Meyer says in his *An Educational History of the American People,* "to give a tremendous boost" to the development of a publicly supported school system.[11] Edgar Knight's surmise that monitorial schools were "forerunners of normal schools in the United States"[12] is equally hard to accept.

Subscription Societies

While various imported teaching plans were tested in this country, one of native birth was tried as well. Philanthropy had always played some part in American education, for even colonial records evidence bequests and grants of one kind or another for schools. Besides, we know, the history of early American colleges is one wherein philanthropy, although religious, had a decisive role. So philanthropy alone is hardly novel enough to attract our attention. But this philanthropy now catching our eye was something different. It aimed not at the erection of a single school, but at the operation and support of a school system for an entire town or city. Here and there around the country, but mainly in the Middle Atlantic states, subscription societies were organized for educational purposes and public-spirited citizens made voluntary financial contributions to them.

With whatever resources they had, these societies tried to mount educational programs. In many respects, save for the source of funds, they had the appearance of public schools. And some adopted this nomenclature as, for example, the Public School Society of New York. Michael Katz's *Class, Bureaucracy, and Schools* offers some interesting hypotheses relative to the New York Public School Society,[13] and they are worth pondering in other contexts, but here we are concerned with these societies as they illustrated private effort toward a more generous distribution of educational opportunity in nineteenth-century America and not for either the politics or the ideologies behind them. In the case of the New York Society, though, discounting political considerations is hard, for politics were responsible for the Society's demise. After almost a half-century of operation, with an enviable record of having instructed thousands of children in New York City, the Society, running precariously short of money, appealed to the city for some financial support. This appeal was granted. But this grant stimulated similar appeals for funds from other philanthropic and religious agencies in the city, and when the city council rejected them it was faced with the need to justify its grant to the Public School Society.[14] In the best political and social situation good justification would have been unconvincing. And at this time, with all the social, religious, and political ferment in the city—and with a weak argument to defend—the council's justification lacked the ring of plausibility. Without public funds to augment its own depleted budget, the Society turned briefly to charging modest instructional fees. But this had the effect of driving from the schools the very students the Society wanted most to help. Even modest tuition was too much for some students to bear.

In the aftermath of the Society's collapse, a school district was erected in New York City. From this point on—that is, from about 1850—the future of education was put in the then unsteady and uncertain hands of the public. Philanthropy and pedagogic novelty had had their day; public education was to grow, if it was to grow at all, out of the failure of private effort. This effort, we know, was resilient and permanent, for we see it around us still, but never again was it to occupy so important a place in America as it had in the educationally tempestuous years of the early nineteenth century. Besides, it is worth mentioning here, as we shall have occasion to notice again, that out of the experience with private education's appeals to the public for some support, the precedent was formed making it illegal to appropriate public resources for private schools. Year after year this precedent was strengthened in the educational policy of the several states until it became an impenetrable barrier between private schools and public treasuries. Once reaching the pinnacle of rigidity, however, the policy began to erode, until in the later years of the twentieth century it is sometimes hard to tell the difference, looking only at financial arrangements, between public and private schools.

Significant and consequential as philanthropic and denominational effort was in connection with Sunday schools, infant schools, school subscription societies, and monitorial schools, the first half of the nineteenth century should be remembered, not for these adventures, but for an extraordinary expansion of academies and colleges, and all, or almost all, were founded on denominational zeal and labor. Public school policies, cautiously stated and even more cautiously practiced, varied from one section of the country to another, and it was impossible to predict that a coherent policy would emerge to supply vigor and direction for public schools. Even where public education had a brave beginning, a loss of momentum was signaled. The great problem was money. The public mind's reverence for learning and the conviction that literate citizens were essential to good government went undiminished, but the public attitude toward supporting education was also unchanged. How wide should the public purse be opened for the education of youth? Not too wide, was the common response. And this attitude was countenanced, encouraged, and commended so long as schools were able to survive without public support.

Academies

One institution, with credentials to elicit support and reap acclaim, was the academy. The academy's origin antedated the nineteenth century, but its character recommended it to this energetic, progressive, and optimistic national period; a period that put a high premium on initiative, on building, and on harvesting the genius of American life. The academy appeared to be the right institution for the time. With control vested in a private or denominational board of trustees, it could function apart from state authority; and this was a good recommendation, for Americans still harbored some doubt about the degree of control government should exercise over learning. And with academies carefully heeding the public good, local communities were happy to welcome authentic private schools capable of yielding a valuable public service. Local communities thought academies veritable treasures, and often assisted them with land and money grants. This was done without assuming any general financial responsibility for them. The age of academies was between the Revolution and the Civil War; they vaulted to prominence and kept their high educational station because in their custody, it was thought, secondary schooling was safe.

Besides, unencumbered by public control, academies were able to blaze new educational trails or travel ones without much traffic. Franklin's "Proposals" recommended putting students in touch with the contemporary world and supported the bold plan by appealing to John Milton's *Of Education,* where idle vacancies in schools and universities were deplored and where practical studies useful to commerce were praised.[15] Without abandoning respected curricular tradition, American academies introduced practical courses—English, bookkeeping, surveying, and navigation—alongside the classics, and in this way demonstrated how education could count in practical life. The academies, moreover, capitalized a fleeting resentment to the old classical course which, some said, was useless, without ever jettisoning the fundamentals of classical education.

Tradition was tenacious: academies could not simply ignore it to introduce an untested syllabus, for their clientele was heir to a notion of educational decency. The solution was to blend the traditional with the practical and novel and, exploiting basic religious affiliation, appeal to religious propriety and orthodoxy. Although here and there an exceptional academy refused to stray from the classical course, balked at offering the classics at all, or discounted sectarianism, the most successful academies melded the old and the new, coupled optimism with traditional restraint, imposed conventional religious instruction and discipline and, in the end, came close to filling Franklin's famous pedagogic prescription of teaching useful and ornamental knowledge. Sizer is right: "The academy movement, then, is not easy to label, but the general pattern—the establishment of schools offering a wide variety of subjects beyond the rudiments and organized largely on a private basis—is clearly apparent, the several exceptions notwithstanding."[16]

A spirit of national progress commissioned the development of this new land, and the academy movement contained motives remarkably similar to those urging the construction of canals, the invention of machines, the erection of factories, the cultivation of farms, and the excavation of mines. Where these secular exploits could be promoted by appealing to national interest and hunger for profit, academies had another ally: religious welfare. Pride, zeal, and sincere persuasion literally drove denominations to found schools, so from East to West, in settled regions and on the frontier, Methodists, Presbyterians, Baptists, Congregationalists, Roman Catholics, and others labored to open schools where the educational needs of a community and the interests of a religious sect were served. With all this activity, little wonder that historians have trouble counting academies. Henry Barnard found 6,185 academies with a total enrollment of 263,096 in 1855;[17] Alexander Inglis[18] and Walter Gifford[19] report lower figures for about the same time, although they counted only state-chartered academies, while Barnard counted everything, even unincorporated academies.

The hundreds of unincorporated academies tell us something: it was easy to open a school. Sometimes founders of an academy wanted only students and a teacher, neglected a school building, and expected tuition to support their venture. Many schools, failing support, closed their doors and were never heard from again. Money was a universal problem and successful academies learned the lesson of staying solvent. They added new and more practical courses to attract students for whom the classics lacked appeal, searched for endowments or outright gifts, and sometimes turned to the state for money or land grants. States could rationalize support of private, sometimes religious, institutions by pointing, on one hand, to the public service they afforded or, on the other, to the public money saved when private academies assumed the role of educators of youth. Until late in the nineteenth century, we should notice, neither law nor public sentiment enjoined states from aiding religious schools; the wall of separation between church and state had not been built.[20] State aid, however, varied enormously from place to place and one generalization is possible: it was neither so common nor so generous as to make academies genuine public institutions.

Academies got a good deal of mileage from an advertised intention to "train students for life," and prospectuses fairly bristled with such phrases; but this was a language of pedagogic propaganda creating the illusion that academy curricula were as different as night from day from the classical course in the old Latin grammar schools. It was effective, if inaccurate, publicity, and we should not assume that academies introduced vocational education to the nineteenth century, for, if we except the teacher-training courses some offered, they were not vocational schools at all. Talking about training for life, they meant "book learning" with an application to daily life. So when we see various academies over the educational horizon—schools for girls (Mount Holyoke Seminary, Troy Seminary, and the Elmira Female Seminary are examples), military institutes, especially in the South, and collegiate preparatory schools— they were cast from the same curricular mold: courses, with the classics deemphasized, where academic, intellectual, and literary achievement was the standard. In single-sex and coeducational academies alike, studies were directed at mental formation with scant heed paid to saleable skill; and, surprisingly, frontier academies had academic allegiances identical to those in the settled and somewhat more sedate East.[21]

One may wonder, however, if academies were not pretentious; their teachers, with some exceptions, were seldom liberally educated or pedagogically skillful, and their students, again with exceptions, usually found the fairly conventional and generally conservative academic fare unappetizing.

Academies talked bravely of turning over new curricular leaves, and a few did, but for the most part this was wishful thinking; academies were more disposed to turn back the calendar to Latin grammar school models than to break ground for their successors, the high schools. Finally, one wonders, despite their popularity, how academies could have passed muster as democratic schools. Secondary education was not a public responsibility, so the fact that they were tuition schools unavailable to many deserving students was overlooked; besides, more often than not they were boarding schools, and this added to their cost and exclusiveness, but apparently this was forgiven too. Their best features were the secondary education they gave to thousands of students at slight cost to the public and their academic respectability and religious trustworthiness. Flying this banner academies nearly monopolized secondary education in nineteenth-century America; not until the last quarter of the century do we see public high schools coming to life, readying themselves to make a permanent mark on the school system.

Private Colleges

Alongside academies, although always fewer in number yet more visible, were private colleges, schools reflecting the profound religious convictions of their founders and essaying to superintend higher learning within the responsible boundaries of sectarian belief. The foundations for denominational colleges were set in the colonial era and we know something about them. Two centuries of life had left their character fundamentally unchanged. The colleges were larger and most, with signs of anxiety and regret, had dissolved their early allegiance to the training of ministers, but they were still dominated by a heavy orthodoxy and felt an obligation to religion as keenly as their responsibility to sound learning. And here, on the point of sound learning, they wanted to stand with their ancestors.

College presidents heard whispers about making learning responsive to life and they studied the prospectuses of avant-garde academies; they read the arguments for new learning and realized the classics were subjected to sniping and attack. The time had come, the presidents said, to protect the college curriculum from fragmentation and erosion, to proclaim a philosophy of higher learning with a strength to preserve solid academic standard. In 1828 the Yale faculty issued a *Report* stating its academic creed.[22] Read today it sounds regressive and unimaginative, but it was intended to keep colleges true to their past and close to the classics. The colleges, the *Report* averred, should guard against becoming practical institutes or vocational establishments and recommit themselves to cultivating, disciplining, and strengthening the powers of the mind so that their graduates would be ready to enter any profession or occupation in later life. No college course, it alleged, could do this better or more dependably than the traditional curriculum. The Yale *Report* was unprogressive, a refusal to pander to public opinion, but its clarity and dogmatism made it convincing and conclusive to generations of presidents and professors.

Buttressed by the Dartmouth College decision of 1819, the nineteenth-century private colleges shared the general optimism of the nation, so the old colleges dating their origin from colonial days began to assume a missionary posture. The Yale *Report* carried a definition of higher learning and, though inappropriate as it turned out, college leaders thought that issue closed; what remained was the need to extend the benefits of college study. Old colleges became motherhouses for new schools and in a sincere effort to spread learning and religion to the frontier they cultivated infant colleges all across the country. Discounting the fact that these new schools were small and often scholastically helpless and, in any event, taught few students, the higher learning, adverting only to the number of colleges established, was on a road to popularity. Without much competition from public colleges, private colleges dominated the field and enjoyed a relative prosperity; they harvested the allegiance of a public still convinced that higher education was a personal responsibility best fulfilled in private schools and they capitalized further on the conventional wisdom making higher study and religious devotion inseparable companions.[23]

CULTIVATION OF PUBLIC EDUCATION

Humanitarianism, idealism, and altruism undoubtedly cultivated allegiances to public education and we should admit their significance; yet alone, or even in combination, they lacked the strength to create a system of common or public schools. Sometimes we forget that some motives generating passion for public schools were not idealistic but, in the end, were more durable than their idealistic counterparts. The full story of the development of public education must perforce tell of the political and economic alliances being forged between the South and the new and expansive West, and the threat these alliances and convenient loyalties posed to the capitalistic and industrial East. The oligarchies of the South, without any substantial friendship for public education, turned to it as insurance against a degradation of law and order; the West, without a profound affection for polite learning and letters adopted policies cordial to public education when it was evident that learning would be useful in redressing the East's political and economic power; and the East, with so much to lose in disorder and social disharmony, reread and heeded Plato's warning: that men without education are the wildest and most dangerous of beings.

First modest and then, with the passing of decades, vigorous action in support of public education sprang from a mixture of motives, some noble and generous, others mean and pecuniary, but all aimed at a perception of the common good. Yet there was a public idealism, either authentic or feigned, and it is hard for us to see why the inadequacy of a definition of public education almost totally ignoring both the Negroes in the South and the Indians in the great American West went unnoticed. Perhaps the definition was an accident of conditions prevalent in the Northeast, where the structure of common schools was first conceived and from whence it spread all across the land. There, coupled with a variety of idealistic justifications, the common school plan was revived, and there, too, it was stripped of its intimate association with religion: the old school was commissioned to serve religion; the nineteenth-century common school aimed at citizenship.[24]

Public education could guarantee good citizenship and promise prosperity, its most articulate spokesmen said, but they added other expectations. Property rights were jeopardized by undisciplined and revolutionary masses who, without anything, had nothing to lose by excess and, in addition, the ominous signs of Jacksonian democracy's connivances with universal suffrage, if left unchecked, could depose the propertied interests. In the last analysis, urged to conserve their own interests, persons of property and wealth heeded appeals for tax-supported schools. If hostile legislatures were to be converted, if mob violence attacking property was to be curbed, if vindictive and dangerous workingmen and crude and violent frontiersmen were to be tamed, it could be achieved only by inducting them into the established order; so persons of wealth and position lent their support to the movement for public schools.

Schools as a training ground for citizenship were praised, but what really counted was their ability to discipline and teach persons, who otherwise would prey on security and property, to embrace a social system where social unrest was deplored, where revolutionary tendencies were denounced, and where the right of property was respected. A mounting interest in public education, then, received solicitous cultivation from conservative factions.

The conviction, moreover, that education could be made to pay was by no means exceptional and, as Merle Curti so wisely said: "the movement for the education of the masses was not merely a democratic movement peculiarly at home in republican America. It was in part a product of the industrial capitalism rapidly becoming dominant throughout the western world. We tend to think of our American system of public schools as having been founded out of a great zeal for the welfare of the plain people. But actually this zeal was tempered by zeal for the welfare of the employers of labor, by zeal for maintaining the political and social *status quo*. These economic motives were frankly recognized in the days of the founding. Now, however, looking back, we tend to rationalize, and to recognize only the more idealistic motives, which were of course also operative."[25]

Activation of sentiments favoring public education rested largely with the motives we have mentioned, but we should not ignore the faint outlines of a policy defining education as an instrument for socialization. Still too awkward to adopt the melting pot thesis, education, except in the West, was expected to preserve the social system; whatever crusading elements were associated with the common school movement, schooling assigned priority to social stability rather than reform. In the West, however, where democracy was more genuine than in the East or South, and where it was practiced largely free from impediment, public education was promoted as a means for discouraging the development of a class society, and it was expected to ensure social mobility. Although the Western educational ideal failed of realization as often as it succeeded, we should be slow to disregard its significance as a code for the fundamentally democratic West.

Despite the urgency of motive, free public education came slowly and haphazardly. Once favorable sentiment was cultivated, it needed translation to a cohesive movement and this required ingenious and skillful leadership. So, circling the same tree we find public men, educational organizations, journalists and, most especially, persons of vision and determination. Common to crusading causes, the one for public schools was surrounded by its share of propaganda, exaggeration, and manipulation, but signs of vision, statesmanship, conviction, and common sense were evident too.

We may speculate whether political leaders generate public opinion or wait for it to form and then take the first seat on the passing bandwagon; in any case, following the example of presidents, generals, and justices who endorsed education in the early years of the republic, now state officers by the dozens converted to the common-school cause.[26] At the same time, various educational organizations only recently formed for the purpose of popularizing and improving schooling—the Western Literary Institute and the American Lyceum are good examples—engaged in free-school proselytizing and were remarkably effective in mustering support from teachers, parents, and others whose scholastic appetites could be whetted. But this was only one side of the story: these organizations were often energetic in creating training schools for teachers, in studying pedagogic technique and applying it to various types of instruction, in promoting state control of education, and in general trying their best to formulate a philosophy to guide public education. This effort paid a huge dividend by making the educational question current and pressing, in shaping public opinion to the point where education became a burning issue of the day.[27]

The public press, too, was an interested observer and kept the people informed on educational events. But newspapers were not disposed, or equipped, to lead an educational crusade. And this gave a new brand of journalism a chance to devote its columns to upgrading schools and generating educational progress: the educational periodical. Intended mainly for teachers and persons intimately associated with schools, these journals informed their readers on professional and technical developments in pedagogy and sometimes ventured on broader questions of educational theory as well. But most of all these journals enlisted support for a state controlled and supported public school system. In another way they substituted for today's professor of education—the colleges had no such professorships then—and told their readers about European scholastic development and pedagogic innovation. American educators knew their problem was novel, but they kept their eyes open for anything helpful along the lines of popular elementary education.

Students today who take time to peruse the long list of periodicals in *The Education Index* (a source always worth consulting) are probably amused at the paucity, to say nothing of the tardiness, of an educational literature in these early years. Slender though this literature was, it had influence. Among the periodical entries listed here, most were temporary, depending as they did on the interest and labor of a founder-editor to keep them going. Yet this alone is no reason to discredit the *Academician*, the *Teacher's Guide and Parent's Assistant*, the *Journal of Education*, the *American Annals of Education*, the *American Quarterly Register and the Journal of the American Educational Society*, the *Common School Assistant*, the *Common School Journal*, the *North Carolina Journal of Education*, the *Connecticut Common School Journal*, the *Illinois Common School Advocate*, the *Educator*, the *Academical Herald and Journal of Education*, the *Western Academician and Journal of Education and Science*, the *District School Journal*, the *Common School Journal of the State of Pennsylvania*, the *Journal of the Rhode Island Institute of Instruction*, and the *Ohio School Journal*. This is a partial recitation of early nineteenth-century educational periodicals, yet it illustrates the attention being paid to schools.

While the pronouncements of public men, the exertions of educational organizations, and printer's ink were important to the rise of nineteenth-century public education, they were also somewhat peripheral. Day-to-day leadership was needed and it came from a cadre of educational statesmen. Zealous in their cause, uninhibited by opposition, undeterred by criticism, these men refused to wait for an evolving public opinion to forward public education; they themselves would shape public opinion. Without exception they exhibited qualities of genuine leadership: Horace Mann, James Carter, Henry Barnard, Calvin Wiley, Caleb Mills, Calvin Stowe, and a dozen others must be given credit for leading a social movement to ennoble men through the medium of universal schooling.[28]

In 1828, after the election of Andrew Jackson to the presidency, the principal stanchions of republican government were in place; universal manhood suffrage was either fully or partially honored in every state. Now the political significance of an educated electorate could be described in practical language, and the time was ripe for a revived commitment to universal schooling which, in any case, could no longer be left in the sincere but often unsteady hands of private, religious, and philanthropic agencies. Public education, so its most effective advocates said, required stable public control and support from public resources. Educational statesmen affirmed this principle and employed their consequential talent in various ways to promote its adoption.

Scholarship has reported the accomplishments of the most prominent educational statesmen. It has told of the work of Horace Mann (1796–1859) in Massachusetts, where the common school was revived and where, through speech, article, and public act Mann rekindled a demand for schools where all the children of the commonwealth could be instructed.[29] It has led through a thicket of controversy over the place sectarian religion should have in the schools, and has related the struggle Mann faced when, as Commissioner of Education and Secretary to the State Board of Education, he sought to impose state control on local school districts.

Less prominent, but hardly less effective, was James Carter (1795–1849), also in Massachusetts, whose *Essays upon Popular Education* (1826) were enormously influential and mustered public support for the improvement of schools and a more generous distribution of elementary instruction.[30] Besides, Carter touched a too-often neglected point: the qualifications of teachers. Recognizing teachers' lack of pedagogic technique, Carter proposed—first in the legislature and, when his bill was narrowly defeated, by private means—the creation of state normal schools where they could be professionally educated.

With a more varied career than any of his counterparts, Henry Barnard (1811–1900) was also a scholar. As an educational publicist and administrator he made his mark; later, in 1867, he became the first United States Commissioner of Education. But among educational leaders of this generation his scholarship stands out. The thirty-two volume *American Journal of Education* (1855–1882) is a monument to his industry and ability.[31]

In North Carolina, Calvin Wiley (1819–1887),[32] and in Indiana, Caleb Mills (1806–1879),[33] followed in the crusading footsteps of their New England colleagues and their unfailing industry advanced the prospect for the common school.

This prospect always depended on the realization of state control and public support. The states, we know, had for some time assumed educational authority, but had left it unused. Now educational leaders like Mann and Barnard wanted state authority put to work in boards of education to set state policy, commissioners of education to superintend schools, codes stating qualifications for teachers, and, finally, a definition of curricula.

In the best circumstances this was a large order. Advocating public control, Mann in Massachusetts and other leaders elsewhere, met opposition from religious sects in the habit of having, and determined to maintain, some authority over education. Educational tradition was clear: schools had been extensions of churches and religious doctrine had been part of the syllabus. Religiously homogeneous communities husbanded this, but as sectarian unity dissolved before social mobility and religious liberalism, the problem of religious instruction in the schools became extremely difficult to handle.

Neither Horace Mann nor any of his counterparts was fundamentally antagonistic to organized religion and none, the records attest, was either a secularist or an atheist. Mann's theological stance is sometimes overstated and distorted: biographers tell of his full embrace of Calvinism at the tender age of ten and then a total abandonment of it only two years later. They make a pilgrimage of faith out of a drift from rigorous Calvinism to a more hospitable Unitarianism; neither his theological sense nor sectarian conviction was deep. Education was his religion and he wanted schools to give moral formation solicitous attention, but he knew public schools could never succeed if they were prizes in a constant tug-of-war among religious sects. Mann's solution, perhaps the only one possible, was to remove sectarian instruction from the common schools and establish them, not as secular, but as nonsectarian agencies. Both while he was active, and later, Mann was abused for leading an anti-religious crusade, but the record absolves him. In 1827, ten years before he became a state-school officer, the Massachusetts legislature passed a law prohibiting sectarian instruction in common schools. Mann, then, rather than being an anti-religious conspirator, tried to see the law faithfully enforced.[34]

Public control, however rigid and exacting, was unable to create a system of schools in the absence of public support. Here, too educational statesmen showed their talent for leadership. Rate bills, even in so-called public schools, defrayed part of the cost of instruction and sometimes paid for firewood. Pauper schools always retarded the development of authentic public schools, especially in the Middle Atlantic states, because the public was unable to disassociate free schools from pauper schools. So long as pauper schools remained, legitimate public schools marked time. Finally, it was asked, why should one man be taxed to support the education of another man's child? Tax support alone was capable of maintaining schools adequate to the needs of nineteenth-century America, but it became a reality only when an enlightened public admitted that education was worth its cost.

In the absence of a general precedent making public education a responsibility of property owners, educational leaders were faced with a monumental task of convincing taxpayers that revenue collected from them would redound to the common good and general welfare. Educational statesmen were not alone on the ramparts fighting the battle for tax support: help came from various sources, but they were in the vanguard. Without their bold leadership the battle for public education would have stood at impasse in the middle years of the century.

PROGRESS IN THE SCHOOLS

As public education gained ground, traditional antipathies toward free schools relaxed with a grudging acceptance of tax support; permissive legislation was printed in statute books, often allowing local communities to do as they pleased with respect to school support; pauper schools declined but their supporters refused to surrender; and rate bills lost favor, although rates were charged, in New York for example, as late as 1867. Gaining ground meant, moreover, a general endorsement of public control; and we have seen how states, one by one, with state superintendencies, with state boards of education, with regulatory legislation curtailing the independence of local school districts and repudiating their tendency toward autonomy, with limitations on sectarianism in the schools, began to use the authority vested with them.

Despite these evident gains, we should curb our enthusiasm to remember that these new policies were tardily translated to practice. The common school revival began in the 1830s and progressive policies were forged within a decade. By the close of this period of common school resurgence (about 1860), practically all the states had created public school systems; yet in none was the percentage of youth in common schools much higher than thirty years earlier, and few schools had a sound reputation for instruction. The upward extension of schooling, moreover, was nearly halted. Academies, largely by default, handled secondary education and the high school, a unique American institution making its appearance around 1821, was withering on the scholastic vine. These disappointments were distributed about evenly nationally and the differences in educational commitment from North to South, East to West, sometimes alleged, were not very evident. They were drawn along rural and urban more than geographic lines. If the percentage of children in school relative to the total population is used as an index of school attendance, all parts of the country scored about the same.[35] Almost everywhere some school-age children, for whatever reason, were not in school, and even when attendance was respectable, school terms were short and instruction primitive and, some say, unrewarding. Throughout most of the period, although schools may have been available, compulsory attendance legislation was lacking, so school attendance was erratic. In 1852 Massachusetts enacted the first law to require school attendance of children between the ages of nine and fourteen.

Still the picture was not entirely bleak. The colonial town school, the prototype for the common school, had an abbreviated curriculum—almost nothing beyond the rudiments of reading, writing, arithmetic, and religion—a shortage of materials for instruction, a poverty of suitable textbooks, a group of scholars unclassified in grade or age, and a teacher whose credentials were, to put it delicately, unimpressive. Perceptive educators were quick to see the model's defects. But even men like James Carter were unable to do everything and everything was not done at once. Beginning at the right place, appropriate textbooks were introduced, and then, to change chaos to order, pupils were graded according to accomplishment and age. All pupils were no longer taught the same lesson. To recite all the plans for classifying and grading students—and there was a bewildering array—is unnecessary, but eventually, in 1848, the first graded eight-year elementary school was opened in Quincy, Massachusetts. This pattern of graded instruction was adopted in the North; in the South the nine-year elementary school, and in the West the seven-year school, became conventional.

Textbooks

The grading of instruction, which up to now went unpracticed in elementary schools, and the classification of pupils according to their academic accomplishments, to which pedagogues heretofore had been largely indifferent, had salutary effects on learning. But these innovations had an unexpected side too. In the past, with the exception of *The New-England Primer,* and a few other books and catechisms, the task of preparing instructional material for the schools had been the work of British authors. Now, however, such books were regarded as inappropriate, and clever Americans capable of writing books for use in elementary schools entered an uncultivated domestic field. It is hard to be certain how many textbooks were published or how extensively they were used in the schools, for such records, if kept, are not easy to find. Various estimates, however, point to the fact that every elementary school subject, from spelling to arithmetic, geography, reading, and grammar had from ten to a hundred books to serve it. Some were outstanding; others were hardly more than pedestrian.

Almost every account of this period in our educational history reminds us of the prominent position Noah Webster's *American Spelling Book* occupied in the elementary schoolroom. As it ran through succeeding editions, its title was changed, perhaps to reflect more accurately its contents, but it never lost the popular name that somehow was attached when it first appeared: the "Old Blue Back." First published in 1783, and marketed for decades, it kept spelling at the forefront of polite accomplishment. Throughout the country, in small village and large town, in and out of school, spelling bees were organized; almost everywhere the authority upon whom teachers and spelling judges depended was Webster's book. As late as 1842, Knight asserts, "a million copies of the book were being distributed annually."[36] Although no other speller succeeded in replacing "Old Blue Back" during these years, some tried to capture a share of the market by representing themselves as self-teachers— one could learn orthography without the aid of a schoolmaster.

Next to reading, spelling was given more attention than other subjects and we are tempted to wonder why. There appear to have been three reasons: in the first place, Americans were gripped in a spirit of nationalism and wanted in every possible way to establish their autonomy. This prompted them to pay attention to spelling and to introduce authorized American spelling to replace British orthographic practices. Looking backward, this seems to us to have been a weak motive, but nineteenth-century Americans were in the habit of taking support where they found it. Then, too, it was becoming customary to associate correct spelling with culture. Whatever the source of this custom, and despite signs of artificiality and cultural deceit, it inspired Americans to use their language correctly. Grammar might have been too much of a mystery for the ordinary person to unravel, but correct spelling seemed to be within the realm of possibility. Finally, looking more closely at the language itself—either British or American English—we notice thousands of English words are spelled phonetically, but other thousands are not. In many respects different from other languages, where (for example, with Latin) words are spelled exactly the way they sound, English spelling recommended instruction. In a nation where self-reliance was fast becoming a discipline of educational life and where cultural self-confidence was clearly a national aspiration, it was not, Americans thought, asking too much for spelling to have a prominent position as an elementary school subject.

Reading and spelling occupied the first and second perches on the elementary school syllabus, but arithmetic, now, was not far behind. We remember how in former days arithmetic had been studied selectively; not everyone was expected to master the secrets of computation. Still, arithmetic was spared neglect. At least, it appeared with enough frequency in the earlier schools for British arithmetic texts to do a fairly good business. Among these, the historians of schoolbooks tell us, Nicholas Pike's five-hundred-page textbook on arithmetic was regularly used and praised. As we scan its contents today, however, we wonder how schoolboys managed to carry it to school, to say nothing of mastering its problems, which were almost always phrased as riddles or puzzles, and of following its comprehensive treatment of mathematics all the way from simple computation to plane geometry. Schoolboy slates, used more often than paper tablets for working problems, must have buckled at the weight of calculations for the date of Easter, of figuring the total tonnage of Noah's ark, and of counting the number of seconds that had expired since the beginning of the Revolution.

Such a book may have suited the diet of schoolchildren of earlier times, but in an era now becoming conscious of the worth of nearly universal elementary schooling something less severe was needed for the common school. Besides, educators were beginning to forget what their mentors had told them about the disciplinary value of arithmetic and were promoting the interesting notion that arithmetic's justification was principally practical application. Computing the number of days since the beginning of the Christian era may have invigorated the mind, but it was hard to convince anyone of the importance of the answer. Making change, figuring the area of a field, estimating the cost of taxes, and hundreds of other practical considerations needed attention. Warren Colburn's *First Lessons in Intellectual Arithmetic* appeared in response to the demand for arithmetic relevance. And relevance appeared all the more promising when it was noticed that Colburn incorporated Pestalozzian principles in his book. Adopting the object-lesson thesis, this book combined good pedagogy with carefully selected practical problems. Before publishing his text, Colburn tried it out and was thus able to adapt both content and technique to the ability and interest of boys and girls in the common schools. Colburn's book, published in 1821, was used for forty years. Unquestionably a good schoolbook, it has, nevertheless, been given somewhat more praise than it merits for having established arithmetic as a staple elementary school subject. If we stop to consider the pragmatic worth of computation in a growing and thriving country, we see that arithmetic's place in the schools was secured by the needs of practical life rather than by the appearance, however excellent, of any one book.

Reading, writing, and arithmetic established themselves in the schools and schoolbooks came along to help teachers illuminate the students' minds. But these were the bare bones of education and Americans seemed to want more from their elementary schools. So history, grammar, and geography were added, and in their wake came the textbooks to serve them. These subjects, of course, were not new, although they may not have been found very often in earlier elementary schools, and the literature on them was far from deficient. Yet such books as were extant were too demanding for the elementary schools. Children barely able to handle the rudiments could hardly have profited from reading them. Remembering again the flowering of American nationalism, we are unsurprised to discover a rich crop of histories of the United States. Two, however, seemed to dominate the field. Clifton Johnson's *Old-Time Schools and Schoolbooks* assigns Goodrich's *History of the United States* and Noah

Webster's book of the same title pride of place in the schools. For some reason now obscure, Goodrich employed the pseudonym Peter Parley for all the schoolbooks he wrote.

Geography, heretofore a subject for secondary education—and rendered along classical lines, with abundant attention to the ancient world but hardly a sentence on America—seeped down to the elementary school curriculum. It was important, Americans were convinced, for citizens to know about their own land and this knowledge could generate patriot zeal. Once again, as educational historians see, necessity was the mother of invention: books for elementary school geography were printed and used. Their preoccupation was always with the geography of the United States.

Earlier we recalled the complaint that English spelling, by its very nature, recommended instruction; English grammar belongs in the same category, and for many of the same reasons. If spelling was erratic, grammar was confusing, and so it remained to generations of teachers and pupils. But this confusion could be redressed somewhat by sound instruction, so again the scholars and textbook writers took their turn. Despite the urgent necessity of grammatical instruction, the subject never achieved popularity in the schools, although good books, such as Lindley Murray and Kirkman's English grammars, were available. As a class, though, these books shared a common deficiency, at least, a perceived deficiency: they were based too much on British grammatical models (Murray's book was a British publication) and lacked pedagogic advice and direction. Either shortcoming would have been enough to throttle enthusiasm for teaching and studying grammar.

All this scholastic planting bore good fruit: the curriculum of the elementary school was enriched, and textbook writers should be given some share of the credit. But nothing could undermine the primacy of reading instruction. We recall the old cultural doctrine, to which authentic humanists always subscribed, that books are mines with treasures of knowledge. Reading is the means of excavation. So for a long time in this country, and especially in colonial days, reading was cultivated in home and school. Sometimes it was the only subject taught. Primers and readers had two goals: to develop reading skill and to give sound instruction in religion. These goals were stamped on the character of early education and remained there until the principle of nonsectarianism erased religion.

With the rejection of sectarianism in schools, the old reading books had to be abandoned. Although scores of churchmen and hundreds of religiously sensitive people mourned their passing, the old books disappeared. Dozens of new readers flocked to fill the vacuum, and combining method with useful information tried to capitalize on the advances in scientific pedagogy. It may not be extravagant to claim, even in the face of books on arithmetic, history, and geography and the schoolmasters who set the pace for students through them, that the real teachers of this generation of American youth were the primers and readers they had on their desks. A teacher's inexpertness could be largely immunized when a student had a good reader on his lap.

Dozens of readers found their way into print and all of them, in one way or another, had some impact on instruction. However, none was more prominent, more popular, or more educationally and ethically sound than the graded readers produced by the Rev. William Holmes McGuffey. His *First* and *Second Readers* were published in 1836. Later, enlarged and graded further, they became a series of six and were titled *The McGuffey Eclectic Readers*. Either in their original or revised form, these readers became the standard fare for reading instruction in the schools, and for something more besides. As reservoirs of essential information, as a foundation for general education, and as a standard source of moral information, they essayed to produce sound, morally sensitive citizens. A brief quotation from *The Third Eclectic Reader: consisting of Progressive Lessons in Reading and Spelling* is instructive on this point of morality, although more extensive illustrations along the same line are conveniently quoted in David Tyack's *Turning Points in American Educational History:*[37] "This story of George Jones, which is a true one, shows how sinful and ruinous it is to be idle. Every child, who would be a Christian, and have a home in heaven, must guard against this sin. But as I have given you one story, which shows the sad effects of indolence, I will now present you with another, more pleasing, which shows the reward of industry."[38] Religious—though undenominational—and moral in tone, the *McGuffey Readers* took a place at the head of the school reading list for the rest of the nineteenth century, and for many a schoolboy were the foundation for the decency of his education. Whatever contemporary appraisal is made of their technique or content, they must, in the end, be credited with having been the principal schoolmasters of nineteenth-century America.[39]

Secondary Education

Free public education, cultivated with vigor by educational leaders for three decades before the Civil War, had support from educational theory too; enlightened citizens were essential to democratic government and, so theorists said, the right to be educated was natural. This justified basic, elementary instruction, but was silent about secondary and higher education. So when we read a history filled with talk about elementary education and the responsibility of public policy toward it, we know most students who wanted more than rudimentary instruction looked to private academies and colleges. Despite preoccupation with the common school and confidence in the definition of public education, the calendar turned: if some learning was good, more was better, and men began to argue that schooling extending no farther than the eighth grade was insufficient.

In 1821, almost by accident, the Boston English Classical School, sometimes called the first high school, came into existence.[40] It was meant for boys who needed, not the classics—which in any case were handled in the Latin School—but mercantile and mechanical training, something entirely outside the scope of elementary schools. Shortly other cities opened similar schools and when they did few of them, we think, had the Boston experiment in mind. They were simply reacting to their own vocational needs when they planned schools to substitute for or supplant the common schools. These needs, however, seldom took the educational aspirations of girls seriously. It took almost another half-century for the idea to mature that vocational education for girls was worthwhile, and then it was not the regular schools but the Women's Educational and Industrial Union who initiated the effort, in 1877. Beginning modestly, with a membership of thirteen and a fund of $185, this Boston-based Union undertook to demonstrate by research, study, and publication the urgency of guiding women toward productive work outside the home.[41] Although its goals included the preparation of women for a number of professional positions, including teaching and nursing, the Union's first school was a Training School for Dressmakers and its second a School of Housekeeping. Although these early investments in vocational education for women always lagged considerably behind similar ones for boys, and at first paid small dividends, they appear to have stimulated some support for high schools and for a more comprehensive curriculum in them. At the outset of this period, the schools generated by this vocational trend were secondary only in the most general sense, and were never intended as a substitute for the classical education husbanded by academies and Latin schools. Perhaps the historical significance of the Boston Classical School and its successors has been exaggerated, for these schools were hardly prototypes for the high schools of later years.

Yet, while discounting myths about high school origins, we should see the efforts made, first in Massachusetts in 1827 and later in other states, to incorporate secondary education as a legitimate part of the public school enterprise. Boston chose to exclude conventional classical study from the English High School, but this was a temporary condition, justified by the existence of the Latin School for boys who needed college preparatory studies; elsewhere in the state opportunity for schooling beyond the rudiments was less certain. Seeking to redress this, Massachusetts adopted the law of 1827, the High School Act, wherein towns with 500 families were told to employ teachers to teach the common branches: history, bookkeeping, geometry, surveying, and algebra. Towns with 4,000 or more inhabitants were enjoined to have teachers capable of giving instruction in Latin, Greek, history, rhetoric, and logic. The author of this act and its principal sponsor was James Carter.

The law of 1827 was rewritten in 1859 and broadened to ensure the growth of high schools. Massachusetts, undoubtedly a leader in creating high schools, soon had company: in 1853 New York permitted union school districts to maintain high schools, and in 1859 Michigan authorized school districts to establish schools with traditional secondary subjects.

These new high schools, neither fully accredited as public institutions nor generally accepted as a public responsibility, exhibited a slow but steady growth. Wherever found, in the energetic and educationally progressive East, in the conservative South, or in the virgin West, they tried to offer vocational study alongside the usual classical course. Some schools, well ahead of the times, either admitted girls to coeducational secondary programs or catered to girls alone. All across the country high schools made their appearance and, to a great extent, satisfied the educational, social, and political expectations of most progressive Americans, but even so, hardly anyone, say in 1860, was optimistic enough to predict that they would become the standard for secondary education, supplanting academies and Latin schools, and be free public institutions.[42]

Higher Education

If secondary education was the boundary between public and private support, we should expect to find American higher education following faithfully its old private way. And, for the most part, so it did. Yet state colleges and universities, with small faculties, low budgets, and few students, and always displaying proper deference to private schools began to stake out their modest claims.

The state college movement was abetted by the Dartmouth College decision, but public attitudes were comfortable with familiar ways, so public college expansion was undramatic until after the Civil War. The battles for public education were fought on other fronts; it was hard to convince anyone that higher learning was essential to good government and effective citizenship. Collegiate growth needed other justification. College purpose and curriculum were, in the last analysis, an accurate reflection of what a college clientele expected; when these expectations changed, the colleges changed too. The common tendency to idealize nineteenth-century colleges as academic trail-blazers needs revision.

In an era ready to put confidence in the utility of knowledge—and this undercurrent of belief persisted from the adoption of Lord Bacon's *Advancement of Learning* as an educational beacon—the colleges almost inevitably discounted their preoccupation with the training of ministers and the instruction of gentlemen in polite learning and turned a sympathetic, if reluctant, ear to the requirements of professional, scientific, and technical education. These studies neither needed nor wanted the traditional classical course; their heralds readily abandoned cultural in favor of useful subjects.

Utility was tempting but so was freedom: the single route convention marked out leading to the bachelor's degree was redrawn allowing college students to select from a variety of subjects the ones they wanted. At Harvard, in 1841, electivism appeared, and with it a fragmentation of the curriculum.[43] This course, gaining momentum as the century wore on, was irreversible. But this was one side of the picture and, in any case, affected only the traditional curriculum leading to the degree of bachelor of arts. The other side showed how professional schools, departments of law and medicine, were grafted to the old colleges.[44]

The paradox of college leaders reading, and publicly endorsing, the Yale *Report* and at the same time allowing the higher learning to take a different direction is clear. Whether this was deception, diplomacy, or simple concession to social reality is hard to say, but it laid the groundwork for the generation of science and technology in such institutes, schools, and departments as the Rensselaer Polytechnic Institute in 1824, the Sheffield Scientific School in connection with Yale in 1846, the Lawrence Scientific School at Harvard in 1847, the Chandler Scientific School, with Dartmouth, in 1851, and shortly thereafter the establishment of agricultural, industrial, mining, and engineering schools and colleges. The higher learning in America, evidenced by its action in the fourth and fifth decades of the century and the modest but persistent effort of public colleges (the opening of the University of Virginia in 1825, for example), wanted to be in the mainstream of American economic and industrial life. The safe, calm tributaries of academic solitude were no longer open.

Apart from the determined effort of colleges to engage in studies the public wanted, supported, and valued, hardly illustrative of academic boldness, a few colleges were truly daring: they admitted and conferred degrees on women. This experiment, a long time in coming, began at Oberlin College in 1833.[45] Always precarious and slow to mature, coeducation signaled a new age for higher learning. State universities—places like Michigan and Indiana and almost all state colleges founded after 1850—opened their doors to women on an equal basis with men.

Slightly earlier, but part of the same story nevertheless, older schools for girls abandoned their character as polite but inconsequential finishing schools, upgraded their courses of study, augmented their faculties, and introduced academic degrees to comport themselves henceforth as authentic colleges. These new institutions hoped to become colleges capable of speaking directly to the educational needs of women, and some made a valiant effort to be faithful to this purpose, but in the end they succumbed to the pressures of society and followed in the footsteps of colleges for men and coeducational schools. Doing so they subjected themselves to the evolutionary forces reshaping American higher learning.

THE EDUCATION OF TEACHERS

It would be a pleasant exercise to write an account of nineteenth-century higher education with fulsome praise of its role in the education of teachers for the common schools. Such an account, however, would be almost pure fiction. The colleges should have been more sensitive to conditions in common schools. Common-school teachers were seldom capable of shaping the country's youth and tutoring its future citizens. Almost without exception their own formal schooling was slight and their pedagogic skill, except in the rare person gifted by nature with a talent for teaching, was weak.

The colleges, however, remained aloof, proving their awareness to social need could be selective; but if they had had a consuming interest in American educational life they would have instituted programs for the education of teachers. Still, harsh criticism of the colleges may be undeserved: had their students wanted preparation for teaching, the colleges almost certainly would have done their best to satisfy them. But nineteenth-century college students, whatever their social vision, represented a class whose vocational aspirations never included teaching in common schools.

It has been common enough to maintain that the American college, with its commitment to liberal learning, rejected the prosaic business of teacher education as a matter of principle. We should be closer to the truth admitting that the colleges were perfectly capable of bending principle and, in any case, allegations relative to their fanatic allegiance to liberal learning are mainly myth. Exception here proves no rule; they abandoned liberal learning whenever it seemed prudent or profitable to do so. Still, while giving absolution is tempting and in some instances warranted, collegiate spokesmen were strangely silent when they should have been loud. Colleges can be forgiven for neglecting teacher education at a time when their students deplored such humble study, but it is hard to understand how educational leaders—as college presidents liked to characterize themselves—could have been blind, deaf, and mute for so long on a burning social and educational issue. College presidents of this period talked of many things, but common-school teaching was not among them.

Ignored, if not actually despised, by the colleges, teacher-education had to mark time until other things were done. Well aware of the pressing need for qualified teachers, educational statesmen (Mann, Carter, and Barnard), sought for public support to redress instructional deficiencies capable of swamping common schools. Occasional lectures on "school keeping" were delivered, talks on pedagogic technique were given, regional meetings (the early counterpart of contemporary workshops) on school management were conducted, and educational literature dealt with instructional issues, but these improvisations, while accomplishing some good results, left untouched the majority of teachers.[46]

A good omen for the professional education of teachers was evident in Samuel Hall's pioneering normal school in Vermont in the first years of the 1820s. Private in control and support, Hall's school demonstrated how teachers could be fitted for their role as educators of the nation's youth without a huge commitment of either public or private funds. With this sign so clear, Hall's model was imitated hundreds of times over throughout the country in the next seventy years. Although it is hard to be certain about many of the details of this first normal school, one can be fairly confident that it did not contain the full pedagogic charter for its successors. It was a beginning, but only a beginning. Because of its attachment to religion and, generally, a religious perspective to its instruction, Hall's school needed some reshaping before its model could be adopted for public normal schools. In any case, one looks in vain for any indication that this first private normal school was indebted, as is sometimes claimed,[47] to Lancaster's plan for mutual instruction. Private normal schools, despite their prophetic vision, were unable to carry the weight of American teacher education, so taking a cue from private initiative again, public normal schools began to flourish. The first of this type came into existence in Lexington, Massachusetts in 1839, due mainly to the promotional work, in and out of the legislature, of James Carter. And this school was permanent, although its location was changed in later years. We find it now as Framingham (Massachusetts) State College. After public normal schools were opened in every section of the country by the end of the century, common-school teachers were expected to have some instruction in them as a condition to getting a teaching position.[48]

Academies, we know, sometimes organized courses in school keeping, but this was extraordinary, for the academy was first and foremost a secondary school with a decent respect for traditional learning, and it refused to invest time and attention in the science of pedagogy. And pedagogy, crude though it may have been then, was where normal schools excelled. Almost without exception, normal schools admitted students, indifferent to their academic background, and taught them how to teach. Normal schools were committed to training more than to scholarship and throughout the nineteenth century gave no thought whatever to becoming authentic colleges.

Single-minded and zealous, for most of their directors thought them-selves social evangelists, normal schools participated in the crusade to extend and improve public education; unpretentious and fundamental in their approach to learning, they were content to train teachers for the common schools, leaving to others the education of teachers for academies and high schools; practical, precocious, and industrious, they remembered Europe and learned lessons on teacher education from Prussia and other countries. As a universal practice they adopted the ancient principle of learning by doing and gave it currency in their own training programs. They ended up monopolizing the preparation of com-mon-school teachers and, despite their deficiencies as institutions of higher learning, in them the foundations were laid for an approach to teacher education which was ratified in the half-century following the Civil War.

CHAPTER EIGHT

Public Policy and Popular Education: 1870–1910

For a long time one of the country's most popular books was Benjamin Franklin's *Poor Richard's Almanac;* its readers were told how to succeed and the formulas were neither hard to understand nor to follow: hard work and thrift mixed with prudence and ingenuity were an unbeatable combination. Franklin's advice was both good and believable; time and again put to the pragmatic test its results were praised and admired. But Franklin did not invent these directions. He appropriated them from an oral tradition at least two centuries old, so this kind of wisdom and optimism was in the air and it was easy to convince nineteenth-century Americans that if they followed this advice they would be rewarded.[1] Similar success doctrines, peddled in popular novels of the period telling of Horatio Alger's achievements, were found in schoolbooks too. William McGuffey's popular *Readers* idealized conventional virtue and to a great extent helped make exuberant optimism an American creed.[2]

Yet, even if none of these popular books had found its way to print, the outlook of most Americans would still have been optimistic. The country was large, almost boundless in territory, and size alone carried the infection of prosperity. Opportunity was apparently matchless when guided by the magnetism of inevitable progress. Under the circumstances how could the American people have lacked self-confidence? There was no time for uncertainty or for pondering the ancient issues of life's meaning, and no need to leaf through pages of past wisdom, for the future tranquility and prosperity of the country seemed guaranteed.

Yet outside this ring of optimism which, in any case, was too fragile to contain a society, despite the almost endless evidences of material progress, one could find, by looking past the periphery, a great deal of inequality in political right and economic chance. The country's forgotten men were there: in the days after Reconstruction, the Negro, the remote farmer, the urban laborer, and, later, the recent immigrant. These were the people, perhaps a majority of the population in the 1870s, whom the earlier reformers and humanitarians meant when they talked about the needs of common men; these were the people Andrew Jackson's democracy intended to rescue; these were the people the common school was supposed to raise to a higher level of cultural performance, political effectiveness, and economic security. Undoubtedly the reforms of the early nineteenth century influenced American life and expanded opportunity, especially in education, but the work of reformation was, at best, incomplete. Neither in politics, economics, nor education had the great expectations of reform come to full realization; much more remained to be done and it was left to the later years of the nineteenth century and the first years of the twentieth to complete work so well begun.

To translate the reforming mood and spirit of the thirties and forties into a social doctrine was a large undertaking, although necessary if this mood and spirit were to have direct and permanent force. The earlier successes, remarkable in their own way, were not taken seriously as social philosophy because, for the most part, they were regarded as the outward signs of altruism, a social sentimentalism too inconsistent to support the foundation of social philosophy. It could be practiced when useful and discarded when expensive or inconvenient.

So the threads of social reform were only basted on rather than woven into the fabric of American life. And American life, however this was concealed, was molded by old, deep convictions and sustained by the steady hand of philosophy that, while never especially visible and sometimes unknown to the rank and file, dominated attitudes toward the meaning of life and especially its important auxiliaries: politics, economics, and education. We should look at this philosophy and appraise its influence on the rule of American social life.

FOUNDATIONS OF POLICY IN PHILOSOPHY

The religious convictions of colonial Americans made it easy for them to assent to a system of philosophy wherein man's spirit was primary and where a divine being was at the center of the universe. But these early Americans were usually too busy keeping their theological doctrines intact and their daily lives in order—and those of their neighbors who might from time to time stray from orthodoxy—to invest time and talent in pure philosophy. They treated philosophy as a handmaiden to religion, as it had been for a long time, and were doubtful about the value of philosophical scholarship and erudition. With full awareness of society's need for substantial theoretic convictions on the fundamental questions of life, they were prepared to find the bedrock of principle in faith rather than in reason and speculation.[3]

So it is fair to say that the foundations of American life were set largely on theology rather than philosophy and that neither our Puritan ancestors nor other God-fearing men who settled this New World had authentic political, economic, or educational philosophies at all. They were guided more by belief than reason, although reason was neither rejected nor despised, and when it came time to settle policy with respect to problems besetting them they turned to a theology of politics, of economics, and of education. This intellectual condition persisted throughout most of the colonial period; its dogmatic presumptions kept men in their place and prescribed the boundaries of an orderly social life.

Still, however effective this was in the early days, it was, nevertheless, a rigid orthodoxy and concessions to it demanded a kind of allegiance to faith that succeeding generations sometimes refused to pay. Toward the end of the colonial period, although signs of deterioration appeared earlier, this austere and formal theology was subjected to doubt and fragmentation, and in place of the strict theology characterizing earlier generations of colonists, we find Americans moderating and liberalizing their religious convictions, being softened by what they heard and read about science, and adjusting their fundamentalist interpretation of the Bible. Religion still played an important part in their lives and even theologically liberated men and women wanted to be faithful to canons of belief, but they were no longer so certain or so rigid and uncompromising, no longer so confident of what they had been taught about the relationship between man and his Creator.[4]

If theology were not the only dependable code of life, if it lacked safe and certain directions to guide society through the turbulence of burning national issues, or even if it did, but these directions were hard to follow, then it might be better, so intellectuals began to think, to turn to another more promising and possibly more dependable guide: philosophy.

Our ancestors thought themselves prudent and wise, and so they were, but they were not philosophers and they chose to disregard philosophy, except when, as in the case of logic, it could be a useful instrument; and they could afford to be unphilosophical because they had, they thought, an impregnable reservoir of truth in theology. In later years, however, this theological citadel was weakened by dispute and defection, so almost as an accident of intellect, philosophy was invested with dignity and trust and accorded a new and cordial reception. Philosophical quickening began in the early years of the nineteenth century and responsibility for its first cultivation was assumed by a cadre of American philosophers calling themselves Transcendentalists.[5]

Transcendentalism

Drawing inspiration from the philosophical idealism of German scholars—Kant, Schelling, Fichte, and Schleirmacher—and the romanticism of British poets (Coleridge, for example), American Transcendentalists undertook to lead a new intellectual movement, one especially compatible with this country's taste and temper, which would halt, on one hand, recruitment to rationalism and naturalism, both philosophical products of Enlightenment, and, on the other, soften the rigidities of sectarian doctrine.

They hoped to replace the emphasis systematic philosophy attached to reason, scientific method, and positive laws of nature with a doctrine giving principal attention to human nature as the source of motive and act. Their vision of human nature was essentially spiritual and always in harmony with the universal spirit, sometimes called God. Man's spiritual nature, they maintained, transcends his body and all material reality: hence the name, Transcendentalism.

This definition contained elements of paradox: Transcendental philosophers were disposed to ignore nature, and nature's laws, as objects of study; indifferent to the scientific method, they nevertheless idealized nature as testimony to God's providence and, moreover, displayed an obsession with nature as the custodian of human spirit. Their cordiality to God and their outright rejection of naturalistic Materialism made their views congenial to those of orthodox sectarians, but this good will was lost in their assertion that God was an oversoul, a divine immanence, not the personal God men of traditional religious faith were ready to worship. And to make matters worse, they abandoned revelation and the authority of the Bible.

Some critics called Transcendentalism a strange concoction, more a liberal religion than a new philosophy, and in some respects they were right; yet its proponents were philosophical enough to steer clear of absolute Idealism and set a course toward individualism, self-reliance, and personal responsibility. Transforming individualism into a cult, they ascribed goodness and perfection to all men: many sounded as if they had just finished reading Rousseau. The doctrine of original sin, taken seriously and explicitly by orthodox theologies, was jettisoned: freedom from the restraint of creeds, institutions, and conventions was the Transcendental recipe for human and social progress.

Sincere in their convictions about freedom, Transcendentalists saw plenty of limitations; devoted to the thesis of human goodness, they were frequently bruised by evil they could identify: materialism, industrialism, commercialism, and all exploitation for profit. Assuming the posture of social protest, this philosophy could make common cause with reforming humanitarians, the ground-breakers of the preceding generation, who found the key to social progress in a more equitable management and distribution of economic resources. But this fellowship was blighted from the start, for Transcendentalism found progress in a revitalization of the human spirit and in opportunities for self-realization and not in material reward and creature comfort.

The cities, the factories, even the farms, were hardly the places to culti-vate an inner spiritual strength leading to self-realization. It was better to forsake civilization and return to a more pristine society where persons left to themselves could contemplate the mystery of existence. The cry "back to nature" was heard more often than heeded, but enough brave and dedicated souls repaired to the hinterlands or, at least, far enough from the cities to make their adventure appear authentic, searching for a suitable environment wherein to contemplate the condition of man. This flight from social reality, from the real issues in American society, to establish such places as the famous Brook Farm, did little to ornament the credentials of Transcendental philosophy, and it made its principal spokesmen appear incongruous in trying to solve society's problems while in full retreat from them.[6]

The other side of Transcendentalism, however, only partly obscured by isolation in the country, was disclosed in its confidence in man's ability to employ reason. Human reason, essential to social amelioration, had to be enlightened by spiritual intuitions and these intuitions could come, so Transcendentalists promised, either from religious piety or from moral sensitivity generated in the experience of daily life. Men could grasp the true and the good, this no Transcendentalist doubted, but to do so they would have to go beyond sense experience and find the true and the good in spiritual reality; and this reality, superimposed on useful sensory data, was unknown to the methods of science, for it disclosed itself only in an intuitive relationship between man's spirit and the divine spirit of God.[7]

Looking back, we can be fairly sure that Transcendentalism's chance for being either a prominent or a dominant American philosophy was slim. Its leaders, good and capable men—Theodore Parker, James Marsh, Caleb Sprague Henry, and, of course, Ralph Waldo Emerson—had admirable and praiseworthy instincts and aspirations; its theories were tolerantly non-sectarian without being anti-religious and it could appeal to the American intellect without, on one hand, being a completely secular philosophy or, on the other, a kind of theological rationalism. But if these were the strengths Transcendentalism could capitalize, they were never quite suf-ficient to outweigh a stubborn neglect of scientific method and knowledge and a tendency to let philosophy speak for itself. Failure to promote the doctrine, while clearly a serious flaw to greater visibility and currency, kept Transcendentalism as a cult among an initiated few; but more im-portantly, commitment to Transcendentalism demanded the kind of spiritual fervor and zeal so characteristic of evangelical religious sects.

In an age where the trend was away from sentimental spirituality and vague inner conviction, converts to Transcendentalism were hard to find.[8]

If this movement must, in the end, be counted a failure, it did nevertheless cultivate ground for other philosophies to grow on. In the wake of Transcendentalism's decline, we see signs that America was disposed toward things of the mind and in this maturing climate philosophy was welcomed. Now the ancient philosophy Idealism made its American debut. It had advantages Transcendentalism lacked, although the two had obvious similarities.

Idealism

Idealism could date its origin from the most popular of Greek philosophers, Plato, and point to its close association with Christian theology during those long centuries when theology was seeking support from the science of reason.[9] It could, moreover, at a time when religious fundamentalism was far from dead and when liberal sects were trying to generate a renaissance of faith, appeal to anyone who distrusted the doctrines of naturalism or doubted the promises of philosophic positivism. There was nothing newfangled about Idealism, a point noticed by persons used to putting trust in critically-tested traditions; and finally, Idealism was lucky enough to find a platform for its principles and doctrines: the colleges and universities, after shedding their rigorous sectarianism (except for the Catholic colleges growing by leaps and bounds in the nineteenth century) found Idealism appealing and began, one after another, to follow in meticulous detail the works of Fichte, Schelling, and Hegel. Even the Catholic colleges were not entirely immune to the influence of Idealism and, while it would be wrong to suppose they preferred it to Thomistic philosophy, it approximated their philosophic convictions and received their unintentional support. More exactly, except to skillful philosophers, Catholic philosophy appeared to be a kind of Idealism, so with the dramatic growth of the Roman Catholic Church in this century, the philosophy of Idealism gained additional strength and prominence.[10]

The world's libraries contain thousands of volumes covering every aspect of Idealism and every variation of its philosophic theme, so only a witless person would pretend to summarize this ancient philosophy, even if the summary were intended only to tell of Idealism's history in the United States, yet something of the fundamental stance of this philosophy is necessary if we are to see how American attitudes on social life were affected by it.

Conventional Idealism begins with the proposition that man's nature is essentially spiritual and that his principal human relationships occur in a world of ideas. Physical nature, whether the human body or the world around it, may be nothing more than an illusion. If it is more than an illusion, the possibility of correspondence between it and the mind is difficult, unimportant, and, very likely, impossible. Man, then, is substantially mind and the fulfillment of his personality depends on the extent to which his mind is capable of coming in contact with, and sharing in, the operations of the Absolute Mind. Introducing the Absolute Mind, the supreme spiritual essence of the universe, makes us think of God, a term with which Idealists are comfortable, although they feel no compulsion to practice a traditional theological reverence to him or to pay any special allegiance to Him as their creator. This absolute, entirely impersonal spirit is content to leave to men the responsibility for setting the directions for working out human destiny.

Taking Idealism at face value, which in the ordinary course of daily life is not easy to do, the world of sticks and stones becomes shadowy and unreal. No one should depend upon the content of an experience based on a relationship with an incomprehensible reality, for the source of knowledge and truth is not found in experience but in intuitive transactions. These transactions may be entirely personal or they may involve interpersonal relations. What is transacted, though, either by introspection or by personal exchange, is securely lodged in the spirituality of ideas. By definition, empiricism is abandoned, so knowledge, or truth, is never distilled or tested by the canons of science but by the friction of mind on mind in an authentic dialectical process.

Because man's nature, according to Idealism, is spiritual, and because the only way the dignity and worth of human life can be advanced is by providing a social environment wherein the genius of personality can be reaped, certain imperatives bear heavily on the discipline and order of political and social life. Men are responsible for their actions, and they should be rewarded or punished for what they do, but they must be given a decent chance for personal spiritual development. Besides, being expressions of the Absolute Mind or God, they are due a dignity and respect that even their own human nature by itself does not authorize. The world is the place where they are given the only chance they will ever have of realizing their full potential as human beings. Idealism as a philosophy was filled with implications for social uplift and for the development of an American social order wherein the best capacities of human beings could be brought to realization.

Expressed this way, Idealism was hastily adopted as the guiding philosophy for American education and so it remained throughout the nineteenth century, although the implementation of Idealism's principles often left much to be desired on the level of educational practice. Stressing the spiritual side of man, it was easy to neglect his body, and almost no one, either teacher or philosopher, gave any thought whatever to physiological bases of learning. This serious oversight goes a long way toward explaining the character of nineteenth-century schools and their insensitivity to teaching methods. But American Idealism's connection with education was new and, understandably, some important things were left undone; in any case, the defect was never serious enough for the educators to look elsewhere for their theory's support or to think about forsaking their allegiance to Idealism.

William T. Harris was educational Idealism's leading spokesman,[11] but others too, always in sufficient number and with enough talent, promoted a cause they thought good; and educational philosophers were regularly abetted, as was Idealism, by academic philosophers in some of the nation's leading colleges and universities. The *Journal of Speculative Philosophy* was founded as the official organ for Idealist philosophical communication, and cultural and philosophic clubs, catering to Idealism, sprang up across the country to promote and popularize speculation, virtue, the fine and liberal arts, and the better things of life. In various ways Idealism was promoted as the intellectual guidepost for American life and this promotion bore good results: human personality was stressed as an end in itself and, so it was said, should have a chance to grow and unfold according to inner will rather than outside pressure; and the idea of the common good, where persons are intimately associated in social and community life, was given the support of dependable doctrine rather than resting, as before, mainly on a pragmatic foundation of convenience.

Idealism contributed greatly to the further development of democracy in politics, economics, and education and, to a great extent, this philosophy was responsible for the stimulation of nineteenth-century national growth and the cultivation of a progressive spirit, but when the sums are added it is hard to believe that the full possibility for human development predicted in Idealist literature was recognized by Idealists themselves.[12]

Realism

While Transcendentalists and Idealists pondered the mysteries of human spirit and their relationship with a divine essence, another philosophic system with credentials as respectable as Idealism's began to assert itself: Realism. Never entirely unknown to American thinkers and often adopted as a common sense approach to the world, Realism, nevertheless, had an affinity to Scholasticism making it unpalatable to colonial intellectuals, who always tested their philosophy for compatibility with religious belief.[13] Yet even these tests for orthodoxy were insufficient to halt the introduction of Locke's empiricism or nullify his doctrine of natural law and right in American political theory. We have seen something of John Locke's influence on the American intellect and we know that without ever becoming a popular philosophy, it was, nevertheless, an effective force in political and economic life. Too much in Locke's doctrine ran counter to Christian suppositions about man, the world, and its operations, so the Realism promoted in Locke's books had to wait for another time to get its reception in this country.

Realism, however, had many recommendations and not the least was its affirmation that reality is both material and spiritual. The world and man are real; everything within the orbit of sense experience is real; neither nature nor nature's laws are forever hidden from man, and while it may not be easy to grasp the true functioning of nature, including man, with the right methods of investigation it is possible. With dependable methods men can submit nature to the arbitrament of reason and arrive at certifiable and accurate knowledge. Mystery abounds but it is never unfathomable; and to depend on intuition for understanding nature, man, and society is unreasonable.

Realist philosophy could subscribe to a dualistic interpretation of man's nature, thus leaving intact fundamental religious belief on human spiritual and material composition, but it could, as in the case of evolutionary hypotheses, turn to Materialistic monism and define man as a product of the evolutionary process, more complicated than other forms of matter, but not essentially different from them. Idealism, we have seen, could make provision for a kind of evolution wherein, given first the spiritual nature of man as defined by his Creator, men could achieve more fully the potentialities of their spirit, but this was not the evolutionary hypothesis that made its appearance with the publication, in 1859, of Charles Darwin's *Origin of Species* and, in 1871, his *The Descent of Man.*

In the absence of Darwin's seminal work, Realism gained ground as a respectable theory: natural law, whether ascribed to the moral condition of man, to the preservation of an orderly society, or as a way to expand man's knowledge of the physical world, was at the end of the scientific trail and this trail could be followed, Realist philosophers were prone to say, by adopting the method of science. Inspiration from the Enlightenment still infected nineteenth-century Realism and, with a fundamental appeal to common sense, it could easily be the general, although somewhat unsystematic, philosophical persuasion of a generation assuming the independent reality of the world, and this, in the last analysis, was the central thesis of Realist philosophy. It was, moreover, sympathetic to science, and in an age just becoming aware of science and technology, this advantage was hard to discount. Finally, it was convenient to believe that social and economic progress ultimately depended on man's ability to understand social and economic law. Had it not been for the theory of evolution, introduced now in a systematic and scientific way, Realism might have become the dominant American philosophy, because it conformed so nicely to what most educated Americans already assumed to be true.[14]

The theory of evolution was a philosophic distraction. Centering attention first on the origin of man—always a critical issue and a controversial one too, as it turned out—little time was left for attending to other, probably more vital issues. Evolutionary hypotheses were current in the nineteenth century, so Darwin was not their inventor, but the prior claims for evolution, based on scientific evidence, had left man alone. They depicted the evolutionary progress of various animals and plants and demonstrated convincingly that higher plant and animal forms had started at lower levels. These novelties were easily accommodated to the conventional scientific and religious wisdom, and even orthodox theologians found ways of making scientific facts amenable to deposits of faith. After all, God had a reason to create the world, and if he wanted some forms of life to evolve, it was hardly man's place to question the order of creation. Darwin's theory, however, went outside the boundaries scientists and theologians had up to now considered respectable and decent.[15]

Darwin posed an issue too consequential to neglect. His hypothesis with respect to man's origin put man on the same level with all other forms of life and made him a descendant of a common stock of nature all the way back to the simple cell. No person to whom religious belief meant anything could abide this crass degradation of the human being, for it mocked the biblical account of creation and severed man's special— and personal—relationship with God. Even for the freethinker, the deist, or the atheist this view of man's nature lacked appeal, for theological issue aside, it made man an accident of nature, extracted his power and spirit, and denied him the conviction that he alone among God's creatures transcended the ordinary operations of nature.

Besides, to contemplate the doctrine of natural selection and the thesis of survival of the fittest was to envision life as being dominated by a cruel, wasteful, and indifferent nature. One could wonder how human society succeeded in escaping the law of the jungle. Slow of acceptance, the theory of evolution nevertheless gained widespread attention, particularly in its application to man's origin, and it affected profoundly both the general public and the philosophers and scientists whose business it was to study the assumptions on which an orderly society is based. In any case, once making its appearance, and aided and abetted by its leading exponents, who seem to have found a base in the universities, evolution proved a most radical, disturbing, and persistent conception of life. It was thrust on an intellectual world in the habit of assuming fixed species, the creation of a Divine Being, and men different in kind from animals by virtue of intellect and will. Holding the human abilities of thought and expression to be materially based, evolution activated a ferment affecting all of society, and in education, although in some states schools were forbidden by law to teach the theory,[16] its influence was insidious.

FOUNDATIONS OF POLICY IN SOCIETY

Coming out of the Civil War and pausing, during Reconstruction, to regain national equilibrium, the United States registered an amazing industrial surge. To some extent, this remarkable industrial development was inevitable in a country so rich and large and patiently awaiting an honorable and responsible exploitation of its reservoirs of wealth, but motivation for expansion can be found in social theory too.

In 1776 Adam Smith's *Wealth of Nations* elaborated the doctrine of economic laissez-faire. American readers paid close attention to its advice on economic motive and growth. Industrialists and politicians were cordial to any theory conspiring to unleash the expanding resources of capitalism; the federal department of Agriculture, for example, went so far as to encourage farmers to read Smith and to apply his theories to their agrarian enterprises. After the Civil War, it was probably unnecessary to read the *Wealth of Nations* at all, for what it had to say was already imprinted on the minds of men who were to lead the nation in its quest for industrial supremacy.

So the central theme in the last forty years of the nineteenth century was industrial development. And this theme was honored with enough frequency to guarantee huge national reward. Between 1850 and 1910 the value of American manufactured goods increased thirty-nine times, and the number of wage earners grew seven times. Such increases were sustained, and by the end of the century the United States was the foremost industrial nation in the world.

Although the whole of the country was affected by all this, the whole of the country was not responsible for the achievement of so monumental an economic goal. The northeast section of the country, from Chicago in the west to Baltimore in the east and then north to New England, was the industrial center. This center was helped somewhat by the rest of the country, but as we look back we wonder if the rest of the country was needed. Within the industrial core were almost all the resources needed to spur on industrial development: coal, iron, timber, and rich agricultural lands were all within this region's boundaries. Geography and terrain posed no special transportation problems and the ports of New York, Philadelphia, and Baltimore provided easy and ready access to markets abroad.

All this was enough to spell success, especially when impediments from any kind of government regulation were absent. But, as it turned out, favorable government attitude proved to be a boon to all manner of entrepreneurs. Policies of the federal government—high tariffs, liberal administration of the Homestead Act, unrestrained immigration—provided a hospitable environment for industrial growth and expansion. In this period, despite the high-sounding pronouncements of converts to the doctrine of economic laissez-faire, government influence on economic life was pervasive and almost always on the side of capital and industry. Favorable immigration laws, or none at all, supplied an abundance of cheap labor, so much is clear; but these same laws had a salutary effect on markets for goods too: more persons needed to buy the products ready for sale. The generous, almost unrestrained, distribution of parts of the national domain under the terms of the Homestead Act encouraged the settlement and development of the West, and the West turned out to be another source of cheap raw materials and good markets. Federal and state governments subsidized the railroads in a way we now find impossible to believe and, moreover, conducted the public business in a way always friendly to industry and business. The courts, too, lent a hand by finding in statute and constitutional provision legal doctrines and precedents for protecting the right of property against the claim of the common good.

The Railroads

This policy of government munificence to private enterprise could be illustrated in various ways, but the railroads are, perhaps, the most striking illustration of all. Beginning with the principle that the national good required adequate means of transportation and communication, federal and state governments had for a long time sought for ways to bind the country together. Such binding could only help capitalistic and commercial interests. Easy waterways, we know, had invited settlement and business to the Ohio and Mississippi Valleys, but no such water highways connected the East and West. Stages and overland freighters, the former drawn by horses and the latter by oxen, were tried, but the journeys were long, slow, and immensely expensive. At this time in our history we meet the famous freighter, Wells, Fargo & Company. Then, looking for something more expeditious, the "pony express" was given a trial. Carrying mail on horseback, good riders with fleet horses could make the trip from Missouri to California in nine or ten days, but such speed was impossible with freight. The "pony express" was a courageous enterprise, and we can still read the exploits of brave riders in our literature, but it gave way to technological progress: a telegraph line connected the East to the Pacific coast in 1861. Only a year later the Pacific Railway Act became law, and this law exhibited an open-handed generosity to railroads.

The argument was, of course, that the possibility of profit for the railroads was slim, if forced to use their own resources they undertook to construct a line across the country. So the law provided that for each mile of track laid the railroad company was to be given twenty sections of land (a section is 640 acres) arranged alternately on both sides of the track. This grant was in addition to the right of way itself. Besides, the federal government made loans to the railroads to help finance the cost of construction, for land grants, though huge and eventually profitable, could not be liquidated quickly: depending on the ground to be covered, these loans ranged from sixteen to forty-eight thousand dollars per mile of track. Graft and corruption too often accompanied these land and railroad transactions; prominent Eastern financiers became wealthy and powerful in the wake of their assignation with capitalists and politicians; and natural resources, which otherwise might have been used for general social purpose, were put at the disposal of arrogant men, the robber barons made notorious in journalism and literature. In the end, however, the 158 million acres of the national domain awarded to railroad interests contributed directly to the construction of a nationwide, integrated railway system. When the last spike in the Union Pacific track was driven on May 10, 1869, the country was laced together by bands of steel. Old impediments to progress lodged in poor transportation and communication were removed. Yet national interest took second place to private good in this giant industry until the enactment of the Interstate Commerce Act in 1887. But the language of the law left large loopholes through which clever railroad lawyers crawled, so for the next fifteen years the companies were unencumbered by the law's enforcement. In any case, with government on the side of industry, the will to enforce even a sound law was lacking.

When Andrew Carnegie wrote his *Triumphant Democracy* in 1886 to express his profound interest in the development of democratic institutions in his adopted land—a view that set him apart from his fellow capitalists—he displayed some indifference to the West. He may have been right. The new West, now no longer an unbroken frontier, enticed settlers to till its rich and productive soil and harvest its natural resources. What could have been done only in hardship and inconvenience a few decades earlier was now made easier by the railroad system linking the West to Eastern markets. Casual observation of the burgeoning West might have led him to predict that national prosperity had its base there, but a more careful appraisal of economic reality put the seat of economic power elsewhere: Western expansion and productivity were inescapably dependent on the financial resources of the East. And while Western development was dramatic and often romantic, if we choose to believe the Western novel and the country ballad, the fundamental thrust in American economic life came from industrialization. And whatever else industrialization meant, one important consequence was urbanization. From now on the American character was tempered more in the city than in the fields and forests. Town and country in earlier days had been close; towns and cities knew country ways. Now, however, the city became a dominant social force and its pattern of life, its problems and values superseded the conventions and convictions of rural America.

The nineteenth century records a retreat from rural culture before the vigorous, although not necessarily superior, culture of cities. In any case, and value judgments aside, the culture of cities put an indelible stamp on American life; only the most remote areas of the land were immune to this social development, and while the rusticity of country living never vanished entirely, its remnants lingered precariously and vicariously, mainly in literature and folklore. Its nostalgic rendering therein mourned its passing, but rural culture was a thing of the past. This past, honest and respectable, was reflected in an attitude about life and social institutions; something in it was worth rescuing.

With boys and girls flocking to cities because opportunity in rural areas seemed slight, industry benefited from an abundance of cheap labor. In earlier days, labor, dignified by a theology of work, was expensive; men and women could look forward to an improved social and economic status through expenditures of effort, but these things changed, especially in cities, and now a majority of workers employed in factories and mills were satisfied with a wage sufficient to maintain themselves and their families. This was just one side of the story of nineteenth-century workingmen, and probably the better one, for native American workers suffered fewer disadvantages than the recent immigrants who now began an assault on America's shores.

The Immigrants

The principal impediment to American industrialization during these years of growth was a shortage of cheap factory labor; this impediment was removed by a flood of immigrants. Once here, they worked for long hours in mills and factories: their reward was a low wage, little credit for accomplishment, and no thanks for the part they played in providing sinew for industry. We remember that for about a century after 1740 immigration had been slight; and we think this century (1740–1840) was the one wherein the American character matured. This may be so. In any case, in the late 1830s and 1840s, Irish and Germans came to this country in such numbers that, for the first time, America was faced with a problem of assimilation. People who had been here longer thought themselves native Americans and were afraid of the newcomers—many of them Catholic— who, it was argued, would distort the quality of Protestant, democratic institutions. Total allegiance was a requirement for true Americanism: persons embracing a religious creed whose directives came from abroad were considered disqualified.

Between 1820 and 1860, the United States counted six million immigrants, but this was only a beginning: from 1860 to 1900, fourteen million more entered the country. Mainly Irish, there were also among these immigrants English, Scotch, and Germans. After 1890, Irish and other northern European immigration declined, but a steady flow of persons emigrated from Italy and eastern Europe. Between the Civil War and World War I, we are told, about thirty-one million persons immigrated: about five million British, two million Scandinavians, five million each of Irish, Germans, and Italians, and about seven million Hungarians, Russians, Poles, and Slavs. In addition, some came from every other European country, from China and Japan and from all other parts of the world.

In many cases European immigrants—Irish, Italians, and east Europeans—had their passage subsidized by agents of industry. So, in a sense, they were indentured until they worked off the money advanced for their fare to this country. These "indenture" contracts were authorized by law in 1864 and continued to have legal standing until 1885, when they were outlawed. Their illegality, however, was frequently ignored. English, Scotch, Germans, and Scandinavians usually arrived under more favorable conditions. With some money to pay for the voyage to America and with something left over to sink their roots in the New World, they were in a better position to reap economic advantage on farms, in factories, or in businesses of their own. Others, however, arriving in destitution, were in no position to bargain for the only thing they had to sell: their labor. Clever and ruthless employers were willing to take advantage of them. Such immigrants took the lowest rung on the social ladder. Crowded in the urban industrial centers, they lived in slums and competed—sometimes unfairly—with native American workmen.[17] So to the antagonisms visited on these unfortunate foreigners by other laboring men were added those of race and culture. They became, it seems, a common mass of persons to be despised; without facility in English, ignorant of the customs of their new land, and often unable to communicate with one another, they lived lives hardly better than the ones they left in Europe.

Even labor organizations—just now appearing over the horizon to strengthen labor's hand in its relationship with capital and management—demonstrated their hostility to foreign-born workers. And, in the long run, this division within labor's ranks weakened the movement which, from the first, had to contend with huge obstacles to success. On one hand stood the interests of industry itself, and these interests could not be advanced by a strong and vigorous labor movement. On the other, equally convincing, stood the American tradition that individual initiative—a kind of rugged individualism even for common men—was the answer to everything. Hard work and perseverance were an unbeatable combination for elevating anyone a notch or two on the social and economic ladder. The idea that unionism was un-American and could lead only to class conflict infected the American temper too. After all, America was a land of limitless opportunity; the most humble person, regardless of background, could, if he tried, raise himself by his own bootstraps. If this was mainly myth, it was a myth realized just often enough to make it believable: millions of workers graduated to a better economic and social condition. Now and then, say in the case of Andrew Carnegie, some immigrants even became capitalists. Faced with such a heady idealism, organized labor fought a losing battle for several decades to come. Neither law nor public attitude showed labor much sympathy or understanding.

Fortified by a public attitude which had been schooled to think social and economic reform was the counsel of softness and sentimentalism, American industry set its face against any interference with laws of supply and demand or, generally, with the natural competitive order by unionization or government regulation. It displayed little of this opposition to government action in law, regulation, or court interpretation when it could profit from it. So a formidable array of moral, legal, economic, and philosophical justification had an easy time persuading the already converted industrialist that such things as economic reform, government regulation, and labor unions were subversions of civilization and destructive of all social order.

The most striking illustration of the effectiveness of this ideology can be found in the courts themselves. Even the United States Supreme Court felt compelled to protect capital and the right of property from any interference or erosion. The Court, in decision after decision, voided the regulation of business, invalidated laws meant to curtail the power of industry, declared the income tax null and void, overturned antitrust laws, and interpreted the Fourteenth Amendment in a way enabling it to block the states from enacting and enforcing laws regulating commerce and industry. Taking the side of big business, ignoring the legitimate interests of the common man, the Court took a consistent stand of unfriendliness to labor and even proved hostile to laws meant to protect the health and working conditions of laboring persons.

This official, judicially sanctioned ideology kept the theory of Adam Smith in place: private industry can be trusted to produce and distribute wealth when it is free from any kind of restraint and control. But this official ideology cultivated an urge for reform among those who suffered from it. Slow to mature, a reforming spirit was kindled in the first years of the twentieth century. It reached its full maturity in the optimistic years of the Progressive period.

Taking into account such phenomena as urbanization, industrialization, and immigration, we can see the monumental task facing American schools. It would take a great deal of educational wisdom for America to accommodate to its new social face; it would take even more wisdom if education were to have any share in reconstructing the social order and bringing to heel the flagrant application of laissez-faire and rugged individualism in social and economic life. But for now, at least, the attention of educational leaders was centered on issues of expansion and systemization of schools, of making an educational program, acknowledged generally to be satisfactory, available to more and more of the nation's youth.[18]

Retrospectively it is easy to catalogue the abuses of educational theory: its indifference and docility before social theory were probably its greatest; yet one should remember that men are to a great extent the products of their society and the tendency is nearly unavoidable to ratify its principal conventions.[19] Society accepted, even idealized, the doctrine of laissez-faire; political leaders, if they had any social theory at all, were prepared to endorse the dogmas maintaining industrial capitalism; the economic system, most men thought, could be trusted if economic law were allowed to operate unimpeded by government regulation. Difficult issues would have to be met as they appeared on the social scene, as in the case of immigrants who should be introduced to American ways in the schools and otherwise be taught to accept the usual mores of American life. It was here, and not only in connection with what schools should do, but society generally, that the great melting-pot thesis was advanced as the best, possibly the only, way to maintain an orderly society and ensure the perpetuation of what most men thought was the American way of life.[20]

The definition of the American way of life was conservative: it pronounced and gave unswerving loyalty to democratic dogma; it supported the extension of educational opportunity to all youth and called for an improvement of educational facilities and methods of teaching; it wanted the schools to prepare each succeeding generation for a society whose principal foundations were already in place; and it deplored and sought to suppress all manner of social conflict.[21]

Social conflict was not just deplored, it was also ignored. The struggle, for example, between rural and industrial interests was brushed aside when possible or settled in favor of the latter when decision could not be delayed; labor's efforts to improve the condition of workingmen and to get fairer treatment in the distribution of industrial wealth were opposed for decades by restrictive laws and unfavorable court decisions; and educational leaders the country over were silent on the critical issue of capitalistic exploitation of persons, of land, and of natural resources.

William T. Harris, the principal educational spokesman in the last years of the nineteenth century and an educational philosopher with good instincts for educational progress and efficiency, turned out to be a faithful friend of the established order. His Idealist philosophy defended social doctrines supporting capitalistic enterprise and undertook to demonstrate how schools could help sustain them by inculcating habits in youth of docility, regularity, and industry, and of teaching students from their first days in school that the rights of property and business enterprise should be respected. Harris' educational philosophy was both plausible and acceptable as the educational creed for nineteenth-century America, because it repeated for at least two generations of Americans what they already knew to be true; it discouraged experiment with the social and economic order and, in the end, it succeeded in preserving the doctrine of individualism and laissez-faire.[22]

THE AMERICAN EDUCATIONAL LADDER

Philosophical dispute over the nature of man and doctrinal differences relative to political and economic policy were always consequential for education, but in the early years of the nineteenth century American education was in its infancy and too awkward to play with theory. For the most part, the investment in schools was on an elementary level, and such schools, husbanding the rudiments of literary learning, turned a deaf ear to theory. But now social policy awarded schools greater attention because they were beginning to cast a long shadow on American life. High schools added to the system had yet to become genuinely public, although here and there they demonstrated a capacity for competing with common schools in educating citizens. The growth of American education on all levels recommended consistent and coherent policies and to this end a philosophy of education was imperative. Unavoidable questions were: who is to be educated, for what purposes, and by what means? The time had come for educational theory to lead the march for popular education.

William Harris

Foremost among the expositors of philosophy for American education was William T. Harris (1835-1909). He took Idealism, a philosophy that even in colonial days had appealed to American intellectuals and for so long had occupied the attention of academicians, and applied it to education. His task had elements of novelty: Idealists had shown an interest in schooling and they thought their philosophy had a bearing on learning, but interest stopped short of the point where theory speaks directly to pedagogy, and moreover left untouched the issue of education's relationship to social democracy. Harris' translation of Idealism to education was attenuated, but it had a profound effect on the country's schools all the same.[23]

In Harris' college days at Yale, two currents were evident in American philosophical thought: one was orthodox, but unsystematic, Idealism allied with Calvinism; the other was a sophisticated, but often superficial, Transcendentalism cultivated by a New England elite. Neither affected Harris until, quite by accident, the link between philosophy and life was demonstrated by Bronson Alcott in a lecture at Yale. Irrepressible, progressive, sometimes inconsistent, but always a pedagogic innovator bent on making schooling more effective, Alcott infected Harris with an enthusiasm for social causes and impressed on him the commanding role of philosophy.[24] The lesson once learned was unforgettable. With his college course unfinished, Harris left Yale, settled in St. Louis, became a teacher and, from 1868 to 1880, Superintendent of Schools in St. Louis. In 1889 he was appointed United States Commissioner of Education.[25]

Harris' career as a teacher and school administrator sharpened his interest in basic educational issues and, remembering Alcott's theses, he returned with a renewed vigor to the philosophy that had whetted his intellect at Yale. By preference and training Harris was an Idealist, so, as it turned out, he chose to follow the philosophic trail of German Idealism rather than New England Transcendentalism. In company with German Idealists, especially Hegel, Harris identified mind and matter and (although they differ in appearance) thinking and the object of thought. To accept this thesis meant that the educational process was mainly a matter of clarification, and that truth was the outcome of an intense appraisal involving rational distinction, dialectical investigation of alternatives, and, of course, energetic self-activity. The notion that truth comes from revelation, by intuition or some kind of spiritual disclosure, was discarded and, similarly, the belief that the mind need only wait for enlightenment was rejected.

The road to learning, and eventually to truth, is paved, Harris was convinced, with vigorous and precise attention to the subjects of logic, grammar, and language. Despite a slight drift in both elementary and secondary schools to make curricula utilitarian, Harris put confidence in school subjects whose cultivation of the mind would prepare it to pursue and grasp truth. Conventional academicians applauded Harris' scholastic rigor.[26]

If Harris had his way public schools open to all would set as their educational goal intellectual and moral autonomy. This proposition, with schooling for a person beginning on the elementary level and extending as far as his talent allowed, was consistent with Harris' view of education's place in society and the integrity of persons as well. Up to now the idea of popular education had the support of various groups, some stressing the economic benefit from learning, others promoting citizenship, some talking about its relationship to nationalism, and others just thinking about all the good it would do, but Harris' elaboration of Idealism included philosophy's unequivocal endorsement of popular education. Now the inevitable question: what kind of education? Should it be vocational, thus ensuring economic security? Or should it be cultural, aimed at society's good and the intellectual and moral refinement of persons?

Here Harris' language was traditional. He endorsed the liberal arts because they kept culture alive, and he downgraded, without dismissing, Herbert Spencer's bold assertion that learning, in concentrating on scientifically dependable and useful knowledge, could contribute to man's material and bodily welfare. On the elementary and secondary levels the principal business of education, Harris and his Idealist confreres said, is culture, and cultural education aims at personal self-realization, not vocational training. And by promoting traditional culture the school was a friend to social stability and an enemy of radical reform and revolution, for, Harris was convinced, social institutions in various stages of evolution were expressions of a divine plan for an orderly society. Individual and social progress depended on following this plan.[27]

Industrialization and urbanization introduced alarming complexities to life in the United States and Harris believed the formula for resolving them rested on more and better schooling. Children could hardly be expected to learn the critical art of social adaptation along with the elements of reading and writing, so high schools, his theory said, should be official and regular parts of public education. High schools so bravely begun in the early years of the century and so crippled by competition from Latin schools and academies and by resistance from a public unwilling to support them became, in Harris' prospectus for American education, an essential rung on the educational ladder. With its place secure in theory, further development of the high school as an official part of public education was left to legal definition; its popularization awaited a clarification of basic instructional function.

Harris' interest in educational issues was comprehensive, as befits an authentic educational philosopher, so he went beyond his recommendations for expanding the system of education to include elementary, secondary, and higher levels to lay down certain theses on psychology and its nexus with pedagogy and the place of religion in public schools.[28] In *Psychologic Foundations of Education* he looked for a middle ground between faculty psychology, a popular doctrine of the day, and physiological psychology, a theory emerging from evolutionary hypotheses; and in various lectures and articles endorsed nonsectarianism. Harris' nonsectarianism was public, not personal. Devoutly religious personally, he was completely convinced of religion's vital contribution to Western culture and civilization.[29]

At a time when the nation was undergoing a rapid transition from a rural, agricultural economy to an urban, industrialized society; when rugged individualism was considered a valid way to ensure one's claim to the rich resources of the national domain; when new hostilities were growing between capital and labor; when corporations were monopolizing production and distribution; when the nation was becoming more and more conscious of poverty and disease; when a variety of pressing social issues could hardly be ignored by any sensitive society; at this time Harris fashioned an educational philosophy intended to superintend the country's educational policy and lead the nation's youth through troubled social waters by educating them for activity, responsibility and freedom. His formula left social institutions intact, and put a high premium on culture and a person's ability to adjust to social reality. Without a reformer's motive or zeal, Harris, nevertheless, was effective in stimulating a significant educational accomplishment: a unitary system of education leading all the way from the first grade through the college. He was the architect for the American educational ladder.

Compulsory Attendance Laws

In 1852, although the idea of the common school had been current for decades, another step was taken to make educational opportunity universal: a Massachusetts law required school attendance for twelve weeks of the year for children between the ages of nine and fourteen. From this time on compulsory attendance was controversial. Its proponents stressed the importance of rudimentary learning for social solidarity and expressed the fear that if school attendance were entirely voluntary many Americans would be illiterate; its opponents usually began by acknowledging the worth of universal schooling and general literacy, yet asserted the right parents had to control the education of children, and it authorized them to ignore common schools. Intrusion here, even by state compulsory attendance laws making children the beneficiaries of public policy, was a violation of and a trespass on parental right.

Some thundering against compulsory attendance legislation was motivated by sincere belief that parental right was put in jeopardy, but some of it, too, arose in a studied rejection of the principle that public money, raised by tax levies, could be used to maintain public schools. If arguing the position of parental right appeared stronger than the issue of school support, then opponents of compulsory attendance were ready to use their best weapon. In the end, however, despite the relentless battle waged by enemies of public education, in and out of state courts, the policy had social, political, and legal sanction, and was incapable of repeal.

From 1865 to 1920 forty-six states enacted compulsory attendance laws. The tardiness of state action after Massachusetts, in 1852, and New York, in 1853, passed compulsory attendance statutes must be charged to social and political unrest preceding and accompanying the Civil War rather than to any basic indifference to universal schooling.

Compulsory attendance laws were written to suit the states, so stipulations varied on such things as term of attendance, method of enforcement, and compulsory age range. For most states, however, the term of attendance was brief, methods of enforcement were neglected or erratic, and the age range was narrow.

When school attendance was purely voluntary, or a response to social pressure, schools were frequented by children whose good will toward learning was evident. Now, however, elementary schools had all the children of all the people, the bright and the dull, those who wanted to learn along with those who resented "book learning." Undoubtedly universal elementary education, enforced by compulsory attendance legislation, had plenty of justification, but unquestionably, too, it altered the character of elementary schools. Now they had to satisfy the educational appetite of a clientele as vast as it was various.

Compulsory attendance laws, moreover, were by no means easy to enforce. In both rural and urban areas the employment of children was often a matter of economic necessity, and under such circumstances parents and guardians could find artful ways to circumvent the strictest laws. Eventually, in order to correct the abuses of child labor, legislation was enacted either to regulate (and thus restrict) or abolish it. As the practice of employing children declined, attendance in schools increased and the enforcement of compulsory attendance statutes subsided as a problem.[30]

Perhaps the issue of enforcement is overstressed, for the record on school attendance was good, especially among Negro, Indian, and immigrant children. The census of 1920, for example, reported a regular school attendance of these children between the ages of seven and fifteen at higher than seventy percent. At the same time a marked increase in attendance was reported for those children who because of some handicap—the blind, the deaf, and the mentally retarded—had formerly not attended school at all. Special public schools by the hundreds were opened for them.

Elementary Education

Secured by public policy, nineteenth-century elementary education shortly began to extend its horizon: first, its regular course was lengthened to eight grades, and then the kindergarten was grafted on. German in origin, the kindergarten all too often had been thought a waste of time, unrelated to genuine learning, and a costly impediment to the freedom a growing child should enjoy before beginning the serious business of schooling. Time corrected these impressions. In 1860, Elizabeth Peabody opened an English-speaking kindergarten in Boston and soon had thirty pupils (earlier, in 1855, a German-speaking kindergarten had been founded in Watertown, Wisconsin), but Miss Peabody's venture was premature and, although not counted a failure, its influence modest.[31] A more promising beginning, and the authentic foundation for the kindergarten movement in the United States, was Susan Blow's kindergarten in St. Louis. There, with the support of William T. Harris, the kindergarten was adopted by elementary schools, and shortly its attachment to school systems became common the country over, although city schools embraced it more quickly than rural schools.[32] By 1918 the kindergarten was generally acknowledged as the first rung on the American educational ladder, although its legal incorporation into the school system was several years away.

While elementary schools in every part of the country were broadening their curricula to meet the various needs of children, and while many of the nation's school systems adopted the kindergarten, private elementary education received a renewed and somewhat unexpected emphasis from religious denominations. American traditions for private education were solid, but during the years when attention was riveted on the expansion of public education and the stabilization of common schools, private elementary schools declined. This decline turned out to be permanent. Yet various classes of Americans, convinced by their experience with public schools stripped of religion, were determined to have schools wherein religious perspective was cultivated along with a nurture of denominational allegiance. Following years of debate the Roman Catholic hierarchy, in 1884, decreed the establishment in every parish of elementary schools where children of Catholic faith could have religious along with secular education. Catholic parochial education, experimented with in earlier years but underdeveloped, now attained maturity and became the largest private school system in the United States.[33] But other denominations—the Lutherans especially—established schools too. Although private religious schools never jeopardized public education, they offered an alternative to it for children who wanted an education along lines closed to public schools. By 1910 more than a million children in parochial elementary schools attested to the value American parents put on them.

Critics of private and parochial schools were quick to indict them for inculcating separatism in American education; a dual system—one public, the other private—contributed, they said, to educational and social divisiveness. But the historical evidence bolstering these assertions is weak. The schools, we know, were places for academic learning; they were not, and were never intended to be, obstacles to social intercourse. And money should be noticed too: private schools, usually legally excluded from public funds, educated millions of children without cost to the public treasury. This, unavoidably, contributed to the fiscal stability of public schools.

Finally, with the advent of comprehensive state supervision, public schools were restricted by law or regulation to certain scholastic avenues; private schools, of course were expected to follow the law, but were free to engage in educational experiment, novelty, and innovation. Private education, capitalizing on this freedom, unquestionably contributed to scholastic progress in the United States; many innovations in method and curriculum had their origin in private schools. Not yet mesmerized by educational standardization, nineteenth-century Americans recognized the salutary influence of private schools.

High Schools and Colleges

By 1870 public elementary education had gained nearly universal acceptance; a maturing society, however, wanted more. The high school now appeared more and more frequently as part of public schooling and over the next twenty years became a regular rung on the American ladder. Colleges, moreover, weaned from their religious orthodoxy, broadened their studies to include technological, scientific, and professional education and became attractive to students who had heretofore ignored them. The Dartmouth College decision, we know, stimulated public higher learning, and in the thirty years after the Civil War considerable progress was made in founding state universities and colleges. The great stimulant to public higher education, however, was the Land-Grant College Act, passed by Congress in 1862.[34]

The rungs of the American educational ladder were now in place; during the last years of the nineteenth century their proper and permanent alignment created an educational system beginning with kindergarten and ending in the state university.

THE NEW AMERICAN HIGH SCHOOL

American secondary education had a solid beginning in colonial Latin schools and these schools, as well as later academies, were always clear illustrations of private, religious, educational effort. Almost without exception private secondary schools set their curricular sights on college preparation and were thoroughly committed to standards of decent classical scholarship. The schools were simply following an educational tradition developed over the past several hundred years.

A slight but impermanent rupture of this tradition occurred after Franklin established the Academy in Philadelphia in 1749 and, again, in some high schools modeled on the 1821 Boston Classical School. As high schools appeared more frequently in towns and cities across the country, they turned back the curricular calendar and reversed the practical and terminal prospects evident in Franklin's bold experiment. Instead of following in the footsteps of the common school to become institutions friendly to common men, high schools adhered faithfully to the tested policies of secondary education and attended to the preparation of students for college. Wedded to the colleges, they refused to flirt with curricular modification or liberalization. Although nomenclature was new—the place was called a high school—its character was shaped by the Latin school. Under the circumstances, the high school's chance for popularity was remote; too small a proportion of students of high-school age had collegiate aspirations.[35]

Still, it was becoming evident, the regimen of learning in common schools was insufficient to prepare citizens for an active role in a dynamic American political and economic society. If some education was good, more would be better, so the reasoning went; and the success of the common school prompted a new generation of public-spirited citizens to promote the extension of public education through secondary schools. This exercise of social altruism met stiff opposition from citizens unsympathetic to any further burden from public education. And now, support for public high schools came from an unexpected source: in early constitutional provision most states had used language obliging state legislatures to establish and maintain systems of public education. For a long time the phrase "a system of public education" was interpreted by legislative bodies to mean the common schools, but now some state legislatures gave the phrase a more generous translation and enacted permissive laws authorizing school districts to establish high schools and support them from the public treasury. So the future progress of high schools depended on interpretations of state constitutions and, in the end, definitive definition was left to the courts. Tradition, of course, clearly supported a policy of moderation in the extension of public education, and could illustrate the conventional position of secondary education: it was a private matter; any schooling beyond the rudiments, tradition said, was a personal responsibility.

On the fringe of this opposition to public high-school expansion were private schools, academies, and Latin schools, all manner of private educational activities, who sensed a threat to their survival in any broadening of public education. Yet, while this opposition was real and persistent, it lacked effectiveness. The authentic battle over the legal status of the high school as a legitimate part of public education was fought on other ground by other contestants: people sincerely convinced of the social worth of public education's upward extension all the way through the university, and citizens who, on principle, restricted public educational duty to the elementary school and argued, moreover, that any extension of public support beyond the common school would lead to national bankruptcy. When legislatures neglected or refused to enact permissive legislation allowing school districts to support high schools, the issue was forfeit and temporary victory belonged to the conservatives; but when legislatures, especially in Middle Western states—Michigan, Illinois, Wisconsin, and Minnesota—where a progressive spirit was fashionable, passed enabling legislation, the legal foundation was laid for educational expansion and it was left to the courts to define the meaning of public education.

The principal litigation over the legal status of the high school was the Kalamazoo case. The Michigan High School Act of 1859 permitted school districts of certain types to establish high schools, so shortly thereafter the school district in Kalamazoo opened a high school as a genuine public institution. Some citizens of the district, professing friendship for the high school, were determined to test the constitutionality of the legislation that allowed the district to support a high school. Maintaining they were trying to prevent public waste by clarifying the legal status of the high school at the outset, the litigants, in 1872, challenged the high school as a legitimate part of public education, and the courts of Michigan were asked to decide the meaning of the constitution's phrase: a system of public education. The plaintiffs were careful not to contest the right of the state to support public education and expressed allegiance to common schools. But, they contended, secondary education, organized with a heavy emphasis on foreign languages and the classics, was without public purpose and, catering to the accomplishment of personal culture, lacked justification as a publicly-supported venture. If the high school were illegal, they argued, a prompt declaration would save a huge investment of public resources.

The 1874 decision, written by Justice Thomas M. Cooley of the Michigan Supreme Court, said public education should extend from the first years of schooling through the most advanced instruction. Elementary education had clear constitutional support and so did secondary schools and universities. No limitation was placed on the curriculum of high schools to offer practical, useful, cultural, and preparatory studies. This Michigan decision authorized the legislature to pass laws allowing school districts to establish and support high schools.[36] In 1878 the Illinois Supreme Court upheld an Illinois law permitting the founding of high schools. Neither decision, of course, was binding outside the respective state, but both decisions created favorable sentiment and strong judicial precedent for public high schools.

Within a decade precedent stood on precedent, and the legal status of high schools was assured. Legislatures passed laws permitting local school boards to establish high schools and offered state aid to those that did. Eventually, legislation graduated from its permissive character and certain types of school districts were required to have high schools. But, for the most part, the legislatures waited until the demand for high schools was evident before enacting mandatory laws. And demand for secondary education continued low until after 1890, because most high schools still followed traditional curricular patterns and prepared students for college entrance. The classical syllabus satisfied some students, although it was generally unattractive to a majority of youth who, without college aspiration, wanted a high-school course to prepare them for life. Unquestionably the legal foundation for high schools was securely laid by the favorable court decisions, but the character of secondary education needed overhaul before high schools could become popular.[37]

As early as 1875, although high schools were then only infrequently incorporated into public school systems, the narrow classical and preparatory character of secondary education was criticized. Private secondary schools did their best to remain true to tradition and allowed few novelties to invade the curriculum, but public high schools were fairer game; they were expected to give the common man a course of studies augmenting his elementary school experience and were always more susceptible to public pressure than private academies or grammar schools. Public elementary schools had been dubbed "universities of the common man" and now high schools were called the "people's colleges." Since few common men looked forward to an interlude of college study, the incongruity of high schools persisting in offering college preparatory courses stood out and progressive critics talked about the need for a secondary school course with commercial, industrial, and manual studies.

The commercial and industrial significance of high schools geared to an expanding American economy was missed neither by industrialists, who could profit from a contingent of trained workers, nor by the people themselves, who could benefit from a secondary school course infused with utility. Both industry and labor expressed support for a secondary education capable of responding to stern reality and absolute practical necessity. Doubtless the high school would be a terminal school for most students, so it was only natural to expect the high school to do its best to prepare students for the serious business of practical life.

Industry and labor were quick to endorse any steps high schools took in the direction of practical education, but business, commercial, and agricultural interests were not far behind: they, too, became vocal proponents of a secondary education committed to offering lasting benefits to the American public, and the most lasting benefits, they thought, were always vocational.

Prompted by these sentiments, critics of secondary education found persuasive arguments for decreasing the high school's traditional emphasis on classical study. Despite the urging from various groups who wanted to change the high-school course, to make it prepare students for the labor of life, high schools resisted anything conspiring to alter their character. And here they were subsidized by clever men capable of defending conventional secondary-school studies as being at once eminently practical and cultural. The standard secondary-school course, these men averred, had time and again proven its utility, and while obviously it was not in the business of preparing students directly for farms and factories, it gave them cultural insight, enabled them to communicate with clarity and precision, and trained their minds to meet almost any situation in later life.

Still, while the fundamental character of secondary education remained intact, it was simply impossible for any nineteenth-century school to ignore reality or the needs of students. Although not yet a popular institution, the high school attracted students whose interests and abilities were unsuited to classical study and whose aspirations were for success along practical avenues of life. The net result of the high school's determination to be socially significant was a variety of new courses in the curriculum. So high schools kept their old classical courses, always giving them curricular pride of place, and offered new ones in science, social science, industrial and manual art, homemaking, and occupational guidance.

Almost unconsciously high schools began to wear a new scholastic face and, sometimes, a confusing one. In actual fact, high schools tried to have something for everyone and, though their social responsiveness is due praise, the record demonstrates how chaotic their curricula became. In earlier days a high school had one course, now it had many: classical, business, commercial, preparatory, short commercial, English, science, and general. Either high schools were without models or old models were unsatisfactory for the new academic conditions. School districts trying to find their way through a confusing thicket of curricula experimented with two-, three- and four-year high-school courses.

For a while, at least, argument over the function of high schools ranged from narrow skill and vocational efficiency, on one hand, to breadth of culture, on the other; and for a while the public appeared to accept the proposition that high schools should not invest in studies of narrow utility or be preoccupied with preparing students for jobs, but should be broad and generous in their teaching and immerse their students in culture. Perhaps this position would, in the end, have come to dominate their character had high schools been able to disengage themselves from the rigorous demands of college entrance requirements. By attending too closely to what colleges wanted, high schools too often turned out to be preparatory schools rather than schools for culture and they missed a good opportunity to allow their new character to evolve directly from the educational needs of society.

Under these circumstances the prospect for high schools to become people's colleges seemed dim; they satisfied neither those who wanted schools with vocational objectives nor those who asked for cultural institutes. After twenty years of bewilderment the high school's purpose was in desperate need of clarification if it were to become a successful public institution, and moreover its strict program of classical study needed relaxation, if it were to attract American youth in large numbers. In 1890 the time for decision was at hand: what should high schools be? Nothing so far really qualified them for the second rung on the American educational ladder.

In 1893, with the appearance of the Report of the Committee of Ten, the drift ceased, for this report defined the high school and gave it the character of a popular educational institution.[38] Popularity came with extraordinary speed. The high school, the Report said, is a terminal school for most students and should concentrate on preparation for life rather than for college. The language was mild but effective: it transplanted high schools to the contemporary educational world.

Appointed by the National Education Association to consider the relationship between high schools and colleges, particularly on the matter of entrance requirements, the Committee almost by accident broadened its commission to examine the fundamental character of high schools. Members of the Committee knew high schools were in trouble and hoped to give them useful guidance. Read today, the Report of the Committee of Ten sounds conservative in educational philosophy, and so it is, but it was progressive enough to invigorate high schools. Tied to the apron strings of college preparation, high schools were unable to break the spell that secondary education was inappropriate and unnecessary for a majority of youth; yet the members of the Committee were loathe to jettison what they sincerely believed to be the genius of secondary-school study.

In carefully phrased language the Committee recommended that subjects with college preparatory (or classical) standing be taught to everyone, although these studies were assigned general instead of preparatory objectives. Besides, new programs were encouraged and new subjects recommended for an orderly broadening of the curriculum; and students were allowed to select, or elect, the most useful and attractive ones.[39]

Finally, the Committee defined a unit of high-school study. Searching for a criterion for judging the quality of a subject, the Committee settled for the amount of time spent in its study. In the end, following the recommendation of the Committee, a student could pursue any subject for full scholastic credit so long as the subject was taught well, studied hard, and a standard investment of time was made. This standard—time spent in study—was later adopted and refined by a commission of the Carnegie Foundation for the Advancement of Teaching and was awarded almost universal recognition as the Carnegie unit, a quantitative measure of the worth of high-school work.

Despite contemporary criticism of its heavy conservative tone, the Report of the Committee of Ten infused high schools with a liberal spirit, allowed them academic self-respect and public support, and at the same time enabled them to construct programs of study to meet the divergent needs of students. So long as the high school remained classical, its prospect for popularity was poor, but with a new definition of purpose and with the conservative counsel of the Committee of Ten to ensure its academic integrity, it became, after 1890, an extraordinarily popular school. Growth was striking: during each decade between 1890 and 1930 except one (1900–1910), the enrollment of public high schools increased by at least 100 percent. During this same period the high school was recognized as the school for all adolescents, as elementary schools were expected to be the schools for all young children.[40]

With its legal status clarified, with its definition of purpose settled, and with its place on the American educational ladder assured, the high school was unique and distinctively American. Yet, conditions in life and education scuttled any chance it had for academic solitude. Even while educators struggled to clarify high-school purpose, questions were raised relative to the high-school course and its relationship to the elementary school. Whether or not Charles W. Eliot, Harvard's president from 1869 to 1909, was the first to call attention to the crowded syllabus of secondary schools and the long and frequently redundant instruction in elementary schools, he must be credited with having publicized the issue. As early as 1888, Eliot asked, in an address before the National Education Association, incisive questions about the length of school programs. He wondered if they could be shortened and enriched? Even the Committee of Ten adverted to this when it conceded that the four-year high school was unable, because of time limitations, to offer a fully satisfactory secondary education. The solution proposed by the Committee, one implemented in the twentieth century, was to abbreviate the elementary school by two years and add two years to the high school.[41]

Although the Committee's solution was eventually adopted by many school systems, change came slowly. It had taken decades to create a unified system with an eight-grade elementary school and a four-year high school, and the public was understandably chary of further reform. As a matter of fact, reorganization plans were regularly labeled as nothing more than frivolous tinkering with an already sound system. Still, the validity of the pedagogic issue was evident and the argument that elementary schools wasted time teaching the rudiments became more persuasive.

A division between elementary and secondary study after six years was represented, moreover, as paralleling mental and physical development in youth more closely than after the eighth grade. Besides, two years more for secondary education would allow abundant opportunity for vocational training, for liberal learning, and for a schooling calculated to meet the challenges of life.

By 1910, persuaded by reams of reports and studies documenting the superiority of an educational program devoting six years to elementary and six years to secondary education, American schools began the serious business of reorganization. So within a brief period of two decades, secondary education was subjected to fundamental change: first, it was redefined as being primarily terminal rather than preparatory and, then, it was separated into junior and senior schools. Almost before the eight-year elementary and the four-year high school had time to prove itself, or even to be opened throughout the country, a new plan was trumpeted.[42] Still, with all its support—some scientifically based and some nothing more than propaganda—the reorganized school, as the six-three-three arrangement of studies came to be called, never dominated school organization in the United States. Followed faithfully in some school districts, the reorganized school was consistently shunned in others, a situation persisting in school organization even to the present day.

THE AGE OF THE UNIVERSITY

From the founding of the colonies to the end of the Civil War, the American public trusted private colleges to manage the affairs of higher learning. For the most part, the colleges were conducted in close association with religious denominations and, while it may never be entirely accurate to label them religious institutes or appendages to churches, they benefited from a common appraisal that collegiate objectives should concentrate on cultural refinement and contribute to religious stability rather than engage in vocational and professional training.

From time to time colleges seemed ready to accede to social temptation to alter their course and modify their objectives to accommodate life's practical needs; they entered the modern world with a tardy addition of scientific subjects to their curricula, but they tried to be true to a tradition of liberal learning even as they listed away from it. Evolutionary doctrine infected the temperament of American life and proved a highly disturbing element in the conventional pattern of learning the colleges wanted to follow; yet, however seriously the expositors of evolution took themselves and their theory, society was loathe to abandon a spiritual interpretation of man's origin. In the last analysis, the college curriculum, the curricula of all schools, is shaped by intellectual values adopted in society. So the American college entered the nineteenth century, aware of ferment surrounding it, but determined nevertheless to spend its best effort perpetuating the cultural legacy and maintaining decent standards in college education.[43]

American higher learning during the long years preceding the nineteenth century was predominantly private, and so it remained until the twentieth century was well advanced, although there were signs, especially after the Dartmouth College decision in 1819, that states wanted more direct involvement. But whatever the state effort, whether illustrated early, as in the case of the University of Georgia, or later, in the Universities of Virginia and Michigan, it was no match for the private colleges cultivated since the founding of Harvard in 1636. Besides, the states themselves could only reflect a public sentiment as yet unready to endorse any full development of public higher learning.

Then, too, money was a consideration. Private colleges, supported mostly by tuition, left the public purse alone; this muted the appeals of the most zealous champions of public colleges. When common schools were in the process of development and needed public support, when high schools were going through a tumultuous first half-century of life, few resources were left for public colleges which, most people thought, would make little difference to society anyway and, even under the best circumstances, could not compete with old, established private colleges. If high schools foundered on the allegation that they were outside the scope of public responsibility, state colleges were bound to have trouble demonstrating their legitimate place in a system of publicly controlled and supported education.

The great impetus for state colleges depended neither on a new theory of higher learning nor, for that matter, on concerted state action, but on the federal government. It was the Land-Grant College Act of 1862. Any state opening a school of agriculture and mechanical art, including, if it chose, the liberal arts and sciences, could qualify for a land grant equal to the representation the state had in the federal Congress: twenty thousand acres for each senator and representative. With proceeds from the sale or other use of the land, state legislatures erected colleges or assigned the revenue from the land grant to existing colleges. No doubt federal stimulation was a great boon to the state college movement, but at the same time it concentrated attention on practical college study which so far had been allowed to lie fallow: technical, scientific, vocational, and professional curricula reaped direct and indirect vitalization from this federal grant. In looking for the source of inspiration for the development of public higher education, historians should abandon their liaison with the Dartmouth College decision and turn their attention to the Land-Grant College Act.[44]

While states cautiously entered a sanctuary of private effort, old colleges reviewed their customary policies. Obviously social and economic conditions had changed after the colleges took their first reading of the academic compass; the traditional college course was out of step with the pragmatic forward march of a capitalistic economy. Learning, moreover, had advanced considerably by the deployment of scientific methodology, and an upgrading of requirements for the established professions of law and medicine prompted college leaders to reconsider their dogmatic assumptions about the character of a college. These reconsiderations broke ground for the university, a different approach to higher learning, one American educators knew little about.

Presidents of the great colleges—Charles W. Eliot of Harvard, Andrew D. White of Cornell, and Frederick A. P. Barnard of Columbia—formed a vanguard to forge a sharp distinction between college and university functions. The old college with its commitment to liberal culture was to stand relatively undisturbed, for its value was apparent, but the higher learning nurtured in the university would till new fields. The age of the college, they said, was over; society wanted and needed more than colleges could deliver. The age of the university, characterized by a dedication to research and a devotion to scholarship, should commence.[45]

Although the college community—presidents and professors alike—was well represented in this crusade to create genuine universities, the leader was Daniel Coit Gilman who helped the Johns Hopkins University to achieve academic distinction and drove a bandwagon loaded with new allegiances for American higher learning.

Founded in 1876, and taking as its prototype the universities of Germany, the Johns Hopkins set its academic sights on the training of scholars rather than the instruction of schoolboys and committed its resources to the discovery of knowledge rather than to its transmission. Opened as a graduate school, without undergraduate students, the Johns Hopkins, according to Gilman, was to engage in the liberal promotion of all useful knowledge, the encouragement of research by students and professors, the prosecution of scholarship, and the advancement of science. Following the example of the Johns Hopkins, many American colleges tried to shed their old academic coats to become universities too. This change in academic character suited some schools, but in others affinity to the traditional definition of college life and purpose was so solid that even the Johns Hopkins' good example left it unshaken.[46]

As it turned out, the bold plan for a graduate university was too ambitious even for Hopkins. Still, its example and the exceptional effort of other good colleges to become universities altered the character of the higher learning so much that even the best of the old colleges found it impossible to adhere strictly to traditional objectives. State universities, appearing more and more frequently now, adopted the policies of university education and essayed to promote scientific, professional, and scholarly study along with conventional collegiate objectives. They tried to accommodate, as did their private counterparts, the purposes of a graduate university to those of an undergraduate college. History is filled with illustrations of the difficulties they encountered.[47]

With a broadening of purpose, curricula were expanded. All knowledge, not just liberal learning, was welcomed in a university; and all knowledge was the proper object of study and research. Charles W. Eliot of Harvard led the march for curricular liberation and expansion, but the tune was unfamiliar: electivism.

The old college had one avenue leading to the bachelor's degree and every student followed it; in a real university, Eliot liked to say, many roads led to a college or university degree and students themselves could decide which one to follow. Freedom to learn was the keystone in Eliot's foundation for higher education, and freedom implied curricular choice. Without preconception relative to the worth of any subject, all were equal.[48] Adopting a policy of electivism, as all colleges did even while loudly denying complicity, allowed for a scholastic specialization consistent with university perspective. But, conservative college spokesmen argued, electivism and specialization were too dear a price, for in the end they would inevitably tempt students to premature specialization before first obtaining a foundation in liberal learning and intellectual training, and furthermore students would flock to the easier subjects, thus putting in jeopardy the discipline derived from studying hard subjects.[49]

Giving American higher education a new image and introducing electivism are important parts of the story. The introduction of a curriculum capable of speaking clearly and precisely the language of social and economic need is another. Pure science had progressed far enough, thanks to the indefatigable work of foreign scholars, to provide a firm foundation for exceptional technological development, and many spokesmen maintained this was the side to learning colleges and universities should heed. In the end it would affect life in society a good deal more than all the attention paid to ancient classics, dead languages, and polite and cultural learning. Yet, any concentration on science and technology, and even on professional education, called into question the validity of the elective principle: in the preparation of scientists were all subjects of equal worth and could prospective physicians be allowed to follow a course of their own choosing?

It was hard to be confident that by following personal academic interests and instincts a sound education could be obtained in the demanding scientific, technological, and professional fields. If a commitment to these studies raised doubts about the credibility of electivism, it also generated new arguments for advocates of the classics and the liberal arts. After all, it was alleged, culture and mental discipline were highly significant outcomes from the old curriculum and neither could be sacrificed with impunity, for to do so would mean the virtual obliteration of liberal culture in America. Becoming a cultural wasteland was too high a price to pay for the benefit of technology and the reward of professional skill.

The age of the university, we see, was ushered in with a good deal of optimism about the social benefit to be derived from higher learning and the dividend a college education declared to the good life, but before the age was far advanced new problems arose, principally on the level of college management. The graduate school, superimposed on the traditional college, with distinct academic objectives, was destined to have a great deal of difficulty maintaining scholastic equilibrium. Only a few American colleges, or as they were now titled, universities, found their way unscathed through this confusing thicket.

One side of this development of higher learning was to discount the old college and make an act of faith in graduate study and scholarship; the other side was to extend higher education downward and make it available on attractive academic terms to more and more students. This latter side was accounted for in the junior college.

Junior colleges were two-year schools, conveniently located, designed to offer a liberal educational foundation for students whose formal schooling would terminate in the junior college or for students who would go on to the university. Although junior colleges made their first appearance in the last years of the century, due largely to encouragement from William Rainey Harper, president of the University of Chicago, their progress was slow and uncertain for decades and, in the end, even in the twentieth century, they never quite fulfilled the expectations of the educators presiding at their birth.[50]

Whatever colleges and universities did to extend their programs, to improve their quality, and to prove themselves socially useful, they overlooked one chance to do an immense amount of good. This oversight was so consistent that it must be interpreted as a conscious policy of indifference: almost no attention was paid the professional education of teachers. Left uncultivated by regular colleges and universities, teacher education became the special mission of a new college, one with a specific professional purpose: the teachers college.[51]

In the earlier years of the century, when the common school was gaining in popularity, normal schools had filled this vacuum in professional preparation caused by college inactivity. And while the normal school must be given credit for its work, it was clearly unable to educate a new class of teachers to guide and direct the learning of high-school youth. So, toward the end of the century, teachers colleges made their appearance and set down their objectives along the following lines: to offer advanced instruction in academic subjects, thus, in some respects, duplicating the work of regular colleges; and to instruct students in historical and philosophical issues of education, to apprise them of patterns of school organization and administration, to familiarize them with child development and principles of learning, and to train them in methods of teaching. Accepting this commission, teachers colleges became the principal suppliers of teachers for American elementary and secondary schools. And in their work the discipline of professional education advanced in academic maturity.

CHAPTER NINE

Goals and
Methods of
Popular Education

The nineteenth century turned out to be a time for sweeping change in American educational theory and organization. When the century began, schooling played a minor part in American life and the majority of youth did not pursue their studies very far. Abandoning their schooling usually as quickly as they could, they turned to the school of experience in factories, farms, and shops. Only a handful stayed with the books to continue studies through college. We know something of the assumptions underlying early nineteenth-century education and have seen some of their pedagogic consequences. Yet, as the century proceeded, as we have also seen, many ideals of popular education were realized: schools were established and children were legally persuaded to attend them; the humble educational opportunity of the first decades was upgraded in an extraordinary display of enthusiasm for learning; high schools and public colleges were grafted to the common school. So before American youth lay an open road to the better things of life; education, it was confidently assumed, was a warrant for success.

This enthusiasm for learning, which was usually genuine even when it slighted culture and erudition, has been explained as an inheritance from the prophetic policies of such early American leaders as Thomas Jefferson, Benjamin Franklin, Horace Mann, and Henry Barnard, and from the philosophic persuasiveness of William T. Harris, a nearer contemporary. There is truth in this explanation. The initial mood of expectation for the American nation, honed on the rustic wisdom of its early leaders and drawn largely from their own experience, made learning essential for persons and beneficial for society. The doctrine of universal education, then, became part of the political creed: it was easy to discourse on the significance of learning when citizenship was the thesis. Yet, if good citizenship was all America wanted from an investment in schooling, it is unlikely that the system would have been extended all the way through the public college. Something more than instruction in civics was desired.

We have read, for example, how Americans, bitten by the bug of Enlightenment, thereafter invested time and talent to rebuild a social order based on objective knowledge. But if the inspiration for American schooling is hidden away in the archives of European Enlightenment thought it would take a herculean effort to excavate it. American educational partisans were not restating Enlightenment convictions or reciting lessons learned from the books of European savants when they canonized universal learning. The foundation for distinctively American convictions relative to the uses of learning was native, and for the most part matured from economic, political, and social theory, which also had an indigenous character. While it would be arrogant to deny any indebtedness to wise men from the past, the surge of American interest in popular education was not merely imitation, not simply a matter of standing on the shoulders of the giants of earlier generations, but a conscious decision to direct American society along the path of progress and find the most dependable and efficacious way. One natural means was the school.[1]

Some of this enthusiasm for progress was consistent with the native optimism of nineteenth-century humanitarians of whom in educational circles, Horace Mann was probably the most prominent exponent. He, along with his colleagues, expected schooling to balance the social machinery of the nation, and in Mann's day this superficial humanitarian social philosophy was probably good enough to be convincing. But the later nineteenth century was socially more complex and the issues the people faced were considerably more acute than ones which, in less fretful times, could be settled by building a schoolhouse and tearing down a jail, and then enacting legislation putting children in school where, humanitarians said, they ought to be for their own good.

A special solicitude for personal formation was characteristic of humanitarian dogma and for a long time the justification for more and better schooling rested on the premise that it was, after all, the citizen's natural right. But when stretched too far the doctrine of natural right injected laissez-faire into various areas of life. Could America continue to leave things alone? Was it possible for schools to educate a nation if they concentrated wholly on personal development and neglected the advancement of society? Insidiously the dogma shifted its emphasis from the good of persons to the good of society; and complementing this shift the proposition was advanced that societies just don't happen; to succeed, they must be planned.

SCHOOL AND SOCIETY

A social theory embellished with precision and structure became a reality long before it found a way into textbooks on social philosophy or socio-logical manuals. In Lester Frank Ward's *Dynamic Sociology*[2] we are not reading a manifesto identifying new points on the social compass, but are seeing a view of society already firmly entrenched in American life being ratified in print. This appraisal of the course of American social theory dims some luster from Ward's accomplishments as a leader in American social thought, but it does not make him inconsequential as a spokesman for social planning and the preeminent social purpose of learning. Yet one can hardly miss the incongruity Ward's admirers have been unable to explain: they address him as a principal shaper of American social thought but, with almost the sole exception of *Dynamic Sociology,* have to use unpublished and little-known manuscripts to make their case for him. What is left for clarification is how a man whose theories were mainly private could be a trail-blazer in American social and educational life.[3]

Still, one may follow Ward as one follows a journalist, recognizing that he is rendering a faithful account of American social theory without being its creator. Education, he said, should be universal, compulsory, and entirely public. The long and honorable tradition of private education was discounted with a single stroke of Ward's pen: "The secret of the superiority of state over private education lies in the fact that in the former the teacher is responsible solely to society."[4] The weakness of this argument is obvious, but what stands out is Ward's conviction that education's object is social improvement. And education aimed at social improvement must be authenticated by a dependable corpus of knowledge. Sound knowledge widely distributed is the ultimate source of social power; it is, in the end, the only fuel capable of firing the plant of social reform.

A progressive reform of society should be husbanded by a valid con-ception of the good society, and this would be dignified when means of learning were generously distributed to cultivate the heretofore hidden genius among the country's youth. Ward worried about talent forever lost when schooling was insufficient to cultivate solid and dependable knowledge.[5] His praiseworthy thesis was almost adopted, but another critical issue had to be handled before schools turned too fully to exploit the natural mental talent among the nation's youth. The economy of the country needed help to maintain its record of growth and expansion and once again the leaders of industry turned to schools for assistance. By now, we know, various educational leaders had defined the schools, especially the high schools, as places for preparing students for life. And it was easy to show how economic skill was important. So schools were asked to adopt vocational education, and social theorists and educators were quick to justify industrial education, manual training, or anything qualifying as economic education.

Although vocational education had its American advent before 1876, the Philadelphia Centennial Exposition of that year focused attention on education and training for work in one of its exhibits, the Moscow Imperial Technical School.[6]

The idea that labor was important and dignified was authenticated by the country's experience dating from colonial days and was grounded on the hypothesis of God's intention for man. If nineteenth-century ideals were less firmly rooted in a theology of work, work was obviously necessary to success in life and it was tempting to contemplate the part schools might play in training a work force for the nation.

Industrialists were quick to perceive the advantage lodged in programs of manual training, and while labor leaders, and labor organizations generally, were aware of the decline of old apprenticeship arrangements, they were never entirely certain whether to be for or against school programs designed to train workers for industry. Agriculture, too, stood to benefit from a kind of training capable of equipping rural youth with skills of farming and husbandry, but farm leaders were seldom able to speak for agriculture, so it was hard to tell where rural support would finally come to rest in a contest over the school's involvement in vocational training.

In any case, Washington University of St. Louis, in 1879, initiated a vocational education experiment by developing a three-year secondary school wherein mental and manual training were combined. This bold step was meant to blend liberal learning with training for a productive role in industry.[7] As the Washington University model was adopted elsewhere, the balance between mental culture and vocational skill often became uneven. Proponents of vocational training, those assigning pride of place to a kind of education enabling students to leave school with saleable skills, were prepared to downgrade, or eliminate, the cultural side of the curriculum. More traditional educational spokesmen wondered if all the talk about vocational training was sham. Could schools keep up to date with the training various industries needed? And if they could, would this create a cultural vacuum severe enough to deprive the nation of cultivated human talent? There was, they said, more to life than keeping factories running.[8]

Whether or not the vocational education movement was ever in real danger is hard to say, for it had the enthusiastic support of industry, the mild support of labor, and the equivocal support of agriculture. Still, whatever the level of pragmatic support, vocational education lacked the backing of a respected and prominent educational leader, and to this extent educators were somewhat unwilling to give it their blessing. They redressed their natural timidity, however, when they read Nicholas

Murray Butler (a prominent philosopher, president of Barnard College and Teachers College of Columbia University, and later president of Columbia University) in *The Argument for Manual Training,* telling them to dismiss their uneasiness about vocational education. He relieved the apprehension of his attentive audience by defining the problem as semantic: the phrases industrial and manual training were ambiguous. Neither, he said, was technical training in the narrow sense, for neither was concerned with teaching particular skills. Either was meant to imply an education broad enough to develop mental and moral culture and, at the same time, lay a foundation for effective vocational skill. And this vocational skill could be employed with equal success on farm or factory. A curriculum, he concluded, "which includes manual training, in addition to meeting the demands of our present knowledge of the pupil's mind and its proper training, is better suited to prepare the child for life than that curriculum which does not include it."[9] After Butler gave vocational schooling an unsolicited endorsement, isolated pockets of doubt persisted, but, for the most part, the educational fraternity was ready to acknowledge the role vocational training could play in a decent educational program. For a time at least, the cause of vocational education in the schools, especially in high schools, made rapid progress.

Part of this progress was due to the interest the federal government began to show in education. We know, of course, of the limited ambit of federal authority and the constitutional circumscription surrounding federal educational action, yet the Morrill Act of 1862 (the Land-Grant College Act) broke ground for federal activity in education, and the generally good reports received from this kind of federal involvement stimulated federal authorities to think of other ways education might be helped. In 1867, largely at the instigation of Henry Barnard, Congress created a federal Department of Education.

Even a cursory reading of the act tells us the Department was intended as little more than a clearinghouse for educational information; yet, as a clearinghouse it provided an important service to the schools the country over. Between 1870 and 1890 Congress considered a number of bills for extending federal aid to education, but none, for a variety of reasons, was passed. In 1887, however, Congress voted the Hatch Experimental Station Act for research in agriculture; in 1890 the Second Morrill Act was passed with provision for continuing federal support for agricultural colleges; and in 1914 Congress authorized a study of the problems of vocational education by the Commission on National Aid to Vocational Education. The report of this commission led to the enactment of legislation designed to help various vocational programs: in 1914 the Smith-Lever Act made federal grants available for diffusing information on practical and useful subjects relating to agriculture and home economics; and in 1917 the Smith-Hughes Act directed the federal government to cooperate with the states "in paying the salaries of teachers, supervisors, and directors of agricultural subjects, and of teachers of industrial subjects, and in the preparation of teachers of agriculture, trade and industrial, and home economics subjects." In the support this and other federal legislation gave to vocational education, it was becoming clearer that the federal government wanted to broaden its role in the education of the people.

With social theory telling the schools of their responsibility for developing and maintaining an orderly society, with philosophers claiming the right to draw the blueprint of an ideal social organization, with labor and industry looking to the schools for help in the training of workers, with farmers suspecting that finally they were the beneficiaries of wise educational policy, and with the federal government lending its moral and financial support to various educational projects, it seemed important for the country's educators to look more closely at the means used to educate the youth of the country. To reap the full benefit of universal education and to honor their enlarged commission, the time had come for schools to take scientific pedagogy seriously. With parts of society paying homage to science, could the schools afford to follow a policy of indifference?

Invested with the appurtenances of a social medium, education was prepared to till new pedagogic soil; and faced with another crusade the native, intuitive pedagogy of older eras recoiled to safety in schools where claims for learning were more modest. But what most schools wanted, to keep pace with rapidly rising scholastic expectations, was a system of instruction, direct, substantial, and solidly grounded on a foundation of scientific knowledge. For a while at least, educators neglected the cultivation of social and philosophical theory to harvest the field of pedagogic technique.

THE SCIENCE OF EDUCATION

Wise men were in the habit of saying that teaching was an art, so the legend grew that teachers are born, not made. In any case, the record was long and clear—and the relatively few great teachers known to education's history could be called as witnesses: all the exertions of study and skill were wasted to remedy nature. Yet this tale, so often told and so confidently believed, was repeated with less assurance as the dawn broke on modern education. Sincere and dedicated teachers, inspired by the example of the great Comenius (1592–1670), continued his awkward investigation into the mysteries of natural learning. By the time American education began to mature, European educators had already made good progress turning pedagogic chaos into order, and generations of scholars were intrigued by the possibility of imposing a scientific character on teaching and learning. Pedagogy—an array of techniques for managing learning—was not their invention, but invention aside, it was now hoisted to a level of high urgency, and in many of Europe's universities, especially in those of the inquisitive Germans, considerable professorial time was spent searching for a solid foundation of dependable psychological principle whereupon pedagogic practice could rest.

This enthusiasm may indeed have had its origin in Comenius' work for the *Great Didactic* was a manifesto of fundamental purpose for human learning and for valid, natural, and universal teaching methods.[10] Comenius ended his book with the sensible conclusion that learning, a natural process, leaves signs to be read by any man careful enough to perceive them. These signs, he said, are rooted in the physiological and psychological composition of man. If Comenius was responsible for driving a bandwagon of scientific education, his optimism, despite sound instinct, outran his evidence. The trail of natural learning was too cold to be read with underdeveloped tools of physiology and psychology. Whatever his or his disciples' hopes, this always retarded them, and in the end they too had to depend too much on progressive intuition about the natural method of teaching. Still, first steps were taken and the clue implicit in Comenius' bold assertion—learning is a natural process—was remembered. It was the business of science to discover what it was.

Despite an abundance of good intention, Comenius' thesis remained underdeveloped so long as psychology was tied to the apron strings of philosophy, for a philosophical psychology was incapable of saying much more about the nature of learning than Aristotle had said. What was needed—insight into physical and psychological processes of learning—was slow in coming. And in the United States it came no faster than in Europe.

In the first place, nineteenth-century American education was anchored in Idealism, and Idealism's instructional assumption allowed teachers to act as if students left their bodies at home when they came to school. So it is easy to understand why a science of education, taking into account a physiology and psychology of learning based on observation of behavior, was neglected. Furthermore the colleges, where in the natural course of events the frontiers of knowledge could be enlarged, were preoccupied with an intellectual ideal fortified by its own convictions of nobility and sufficiency: a transmission of the cultural legacy. Without support from men with training and intelligence, with the scholarly leisure and zeal to carry on the necessary investigation, scientific education was left without native promoters and lacked a solid platform.

Normal schools, of course, had been affected by the pedagogic recommendations of Pestalozzi (1746-1827), the famous inventor of object-lesson methods; and almost without exception these methods were endorsed as effective instructional tools for common schools. Yet Pestalozzi's good work was indebted more to intuition than science and, critics said, it sometimes violated accepted principles of psychology. But had American Pestalozzianism been an unqualified success, fulfilling all the canons of psychology, it was still geared to the work of common schools, to elementary teaching: its most enthusiastic adherents admitted its unsuitability to secondary-school instruction.[11]

Conceding a traditional reverence for learning, the American people were disposed to invest confidence in schools and teachers. In their turn teachers were uneasy and fretted about the absence of positive, dependable methods to carry out their commission to fit youth for the business of life. Ready and anxious to follow anyone who could tell them how to do their work better, they had illustrations of science speaking directly to problems of social life. Could science have beneficial consequences for education too?

Herbartianism

Considering this disposition, unsurprisingly enterprising schoolmasters became excited about a new book, *The Science of Education.* Once understanding its directions on conducting classrooms and laboratories, they followed them. The author, a German scholar, was Johann Herbart (1776–1841).[12]

By the time American educators were ready for Herbart he was dead, but his theories were rescued and, in pure or diluted form, were transplanted to America by disciples who, following nineteenth-century fashion, had studied for advanced academic degrees in Europe. Herbart's doctrines of scientific education were spread over the country by Charles DeGarmo and Frank and Charles McMurry. These men, so the authority on the Herbartian movement says, departed from the educational and psychological principles of their teacher so often, and sometimes so sharply, that their recommendations about educational practice were more theirs than his.[13] This observation, almost surely valid, admits that DeGarmo and the McMurrys found the source and inspiration for pedagogic invention in Herbart's work even when invention was at variance with authentic Herbartian psychology.

In any case, whether American education's indebtedness to Herbart was authentic and direct or counterfeit and indirect, teaching and learning were henceforth submitted to the arbitrament of science. A new creed, a new confidence in the relationship between pedagogy and science can be traced to the undaunted optimism of Herbart himself. Reviewing with competent scholarly demeanor the commission tradition had over the centuries accorded education, and always confirming rather than rejecting it, Herbart, nevertheless, tried to take learning—for too long subject to hunches and unclear thinking—and illuminate it with moral science (ethics) and the science of man (psychology). On these foundations, Herbart confidently asserted, education could stand and the science of education could prosper.[14]

Yet both his philosophic instinct and scholarship revealed how moral philosophy, whose function was to elaborate principles of behavior, was beset by substantial differences of opinion: the likelihood of obtaining quick and universal agreement on fundamental ethical principles was remote. While his conviction about the possibility of arriving at an unassailable posture in moral philosophy was unshaken, he was enough of a realist to admit how much time this intellectual exercise would take, and when the philosophers debated the orthodoxy of moral principle the important matter of educating youth correctly and scientifically would have to mark time. Despite an unyielding confidence in ethics as a dependable guide for education, but understanding the ineptitude of current moral philosophy, he turned to another source of illumination, from whence, he thought, the bright light of unanimity could shine: psychology. Without abandoning moral philosophy or retracting a single word of his commitment to education's ubiquitous moral function, he expected that with a strict scientific mining of psychology's treasures methods of pedagogy would be revealed enabling teachers to direct learning effectively and efficaciously.[15]

After intensive psychological study, Herbart concluded that man's will—a blind faculty, but capable of choosing from among alternatives—is unable, without the help of an informed mind, to distinguish good from bad, desirable from undesirable alternatives. Besides, in its original state, man's mind is blank: a tablet, following the proposition Locke made credible, without any scratch or mark. So men with a blind will and a blank mind are dependent on instruction to become responsible human beings. The fundamental issue in formation, Herbart asserted, is knowledge; it is the bedrock of human action. And knowledge depends on instruction. Without doubt, even taking into account Herbart's solid affirmation of education's primary moral purpose, the school's principal work is to teach students what they do not know, but need to know if they are to lead responsible and productive lives. Instruction, then, always the principal business of any school, must never be allowed to drift away from accuracy and efficiency. For teachers nothing was more important than a grasp of right methods of instruction grounded on valid psychological principle.

How far could superior learning, or learning of any kind, proceed without the good will of students? This question, always uppermost in Herbart's mind, urged him to invest a good deal of attention in the complicated, but vital, issue of motivation. Learning, Herbart said, is prompted by interest, but interests are multiple and various and are lodged in diverse sources. Some interests, nurtured in personal experience, should be channeled by instruction toward praiseworthy purposes. So Herbart heeds out-of-school experience, without conceding that its motives are either innate or intuitive. These pre- and out-of-school interests are outside the school's immediate control; so much was readily acknowledged; what was not conceded, however, was that these interests were either unmanageable or extraneous to the school's commission to modify or exploit them. Yet, despite the attention Herbartians gave to spontaneous interest, leaving learning a quality of personal distinction, the main source of interest was learning itself; the content of learning kindled interest and the process, the learning experience, was expected to keep it fresh and vigorous.

The function of instruction was to cultivate the mind, give direction to the will, and to stimulate a variety of personal interests. Thus the curriculum became the beneficiary, or victim, of intense examination. In American education especially, this appraisal incited controversy over what should be taught. The old disciplinary theory promoting a curriculum intended to strengthen mental power, with little or no attention to content so long as it contributed to intellectual vigor, was put to a severe test by a new doctrine whose articles of faith refused to compromise the usefulness of knowledge. And this appraisal affected principles of curricular organization lodged in the bold theory of electivism so arrogantly advanced by Charles W. Eliot,[16] and, in somewhat more compromising language, by the authors of the Report of the Committee of Ten. Asserting, in effect, the equal worth of all studies and, though the Committee's recommendations sometimes made it appear that the Committee could not follow its own advice, introducing the novel notion that what counts is the amount of time and effort spent on the study of a subject, the Committee tended to make the school's syllabus redundant.[17]

Herbartianism, then, as it appeared in America and as it made its mark on instruction, led educators to rethink old assumptions about method and curriculum. Fair to add, the curricular issue, intensively debated in connection with secondary schools, usually left the content of elementary schools unmentioned, for, it was generally admitted, the purpose of elementary education was to lay a respectable foundation in the tools of learning: reading, writing, and arithmetic. These subjects needed neither special recommendation nor defense. They were spared assault.

Besides centering attention on curriculum and method, Herbartian pedagogy paid heed to the highly consequential role teachers play in the educational process. The point needed emphasis. Rather than make teachers the sole actors in the drama of education, the dividend of attention was to assure their leading role and fend off subversive allegations that in directing learning they should relinquish center stage. Neither Herbart nor his American followers ever seriously contemplated downgrading the school's instructional character or, for that matter, amending the teacher's charter to create a learning environment. What was done, a revision of overriding significance, was to change teachers from hearers of lessons to directors of the learning process. This subtle revision of function turned out to have an immense influence on the professional status of American teachers. Up till now, as hearers of lessons, they had had little need for schooling or skill in the complexities of the learning process; now, as architects of learning, they needed credentials of decent scholarship and professional skill to fulfill their broad obligation to the educational enterprise.[18]

A whole generation of American teachers, despite the expanding capacity of normal schools and the growing resources of the more recently founded teachers colleges, could hardly be reeducated overnight. Yet something could be done and the Herbartians, with characteristic zeal, took their place in the vanguard of a movement offering American teachers pedagogic methods they could follow with confidence. This method now deployed, and called the Herbartian steps (whether it was actually Herbart's invention can be debated), quickly became an almost universal pedagogy in American schools.

Interpreting Herbart's various pronouncements on the way the mind is formed or the instructional technique complementing its formation is seldom an easy exercise. With a reputation for being an energetic, stimulating professor, Herbart's lectures were attended by crowds of admiring students, who left the lecture hall in awe of his erudition and clarity. The German university has had few scholars superseding him in popularity or excelling him in the art of teaching. But it was the misfortune of educators to depend for knowledge of Herbart's psychology of learning and methods of teaching, not on lecture-hall performance, but on books. And they were troublesome. After more than twenty years of Herbartian scholarship, Dunkel still finds the text cumbersome and confusing. Once ready to attribute the obscurity in Herbart's books to poor translation, he found the German no better.[19] Herbart encumbered complex ideas with an equally complex literary style and left his readers wondering whether they were following his or their own interpretation.

To a great extent, then, the version of Herbartianism adopted was the one Americans brought home from their study in German universities. Clearly Herbart had stressed morality, but this was a broad educational commission; the school's purpose was instruction. And if instruction were to be superior it should follow nature. Herbart, apparently, and his American disciples, certainly, thought a method paralleling learning had been found. But American teachers, for the most part weak on psychology, dispensed with following step by difficult step the psychological foundation of Herbart's method. It was in his books, of course, but method could be crafted without plumbing theory. Teachers were given a formula and were assured that its employment would result in effective instruction. The formula, by happy circumstance, was simple and easily understood; any classroom teacher could master it.

Beginning with the conviction that mental operations prescribe the course of instruction, the first step in this widely heralded new method was *preparation*. On the psychological side it meant a cultivation of students' minds. Later, the nomenclature was changed, and to some extent clarified, so in Herbartian textbooks introduction and orientation are used. The point, according to elaborators of Herbartian methodology, was to link a student's current level of experience with the lesson. Hardly a novel idea, since many illustrations of its use surfaced in the pedagogy of ancient teachers, it was formalized and paraded before teachers whose intuitions of good teaching technique were underdeveloped. The other side of preparation, too obvious to display, critics said, was simply a matter of teachers being prepared to teach fully, flawlessly, and un-hesitatingly. The emphasis is clear: to teach effectively teachers must command their subject. Herbartians told teachers to prepare, leaving nothing to chance, and sometimes, they said, this could mean memorizing the lesson to be taught. Preparation was first, next came *presentation*. Occupying instructional center stage, teachers, using appropriate means, communicated the lesson's content. The range of acceptable technique was wide: lectures, textbooks, demonstrations, experiments—all were authorized.

When a subject was taught fully and completely, it should be welded to the student's background of experience, to bodies of knowledge already in his possession. This involved finding instructional and con-textual relationships between the old and the new, and here, at this step, a stability of knowledge was sought. According to almost any version of Herbartian psychology, new information had to be anchored to a fund of knowledge in the student's custody. This was *assimilation*. Now the formula was imprecise and the techniques obscure. In any case, responsi-bility for retention weighed heavily on the teacher, so by questioning, illus-tration, demonstration, and discussion students were helped to apprehend the relationship between fresh and old knowledge. Block on succeeding block a structure of knowledge was built, and teaching was expected to supply the mortar.

Having laid a foundation and erected a structure, the next step was to organize knowledge into categories. This process put knowledge in logical segments, and of course the teacher's scholarship played a vital role. The teacher's erudition and pedagogic skill imposed order on learning and students were directed to master its details. This was hard work, for which Herbartian methodologists never apologized. It required a good deal of intellectual discipline too: neither Herbart nor his American followers ever countenanced soft pedagogy. And it demanded good order in the classroom. If schools were not happy places, they were at least workshops for decent instruction, and the reward was sound and dependable knowledge. This phase of instruction was *systemization.* After leading students so far through the complexities of learning the time came for *application.* Application could be achieved by various techniques, and the more imaginative the teacher the better the possibility for interesting and artful means. In actual practice, however, teachers, busy and overworked, were unimaginative: they settled for oral and written recitations.

This method was designed to manage the daily lesson, and each day's lesson was planned to follow yesterday's instruction and ready students for tomorrow's. The Herbartian teaching formula, one undoubtedly implicit in Herbart's psychology, was neat and precise; little was left to the teacher's ingenuity and nothing at all to chance. In addition, it was easy to understand and follow. Good teachers used it to produce excellent results; but too often the Herbartian method was applied mechanically and such rigidity eroded spontaneity and novelty.

Once introduced, Herbartian methodology swept the country and was heralded as another panacea. Understandably enough, in an age when the method of science produced impressive consequences, teachers wanted an arsenal of techniques whose dependability was certified. Herbartian methodology stood on a solid foundation of psychological evidence and, moreover, the evidence was mustered by scholars with scientific credentials. Yet, despite the undoubted good in Herbartianism and its extensive and friendly reception in schools, method continued to evolve. Shortly, the Herbartian formula was a stepping stone to other techniques and, its critics said, to better ones. The Morrison Plan, a method whose affinity to Herbartianism was unconcealed, superseded its progenitor and, in its turn, swept through the classrooms. Concentrating attention on the unit and, with an undisguised allegiance to the communication of dependable knowledge, the Morrison Plan is still current.[20]

Whatever appraisal is made of the effectiveness of Herbartian technique, it must finally be acknowledged, Herbart's chief influence was on teachers' professional status. On this point, historians should praise him. The method, however, while in theory geared to capitalizing student interest, individual differences, and a careful and exact application of principles of learning, was subject to misuse and abuse. Instead of cultivating school learning in novel and imaginative ways, always a real possibility, it too often turned out to be dull and mechanical. Neglecting individual differences, it too frequently became a justification for educational paralysis, the academic lock step. Ignoring variety in learning and life and largely indifferent to the gulf separating the academic from the real world, it became a catalogue of facts and skills to be taught and mastered at almost any price. And all this was done in the name of instructional good order. Based on a psychology of learning never pretending to having drained the well of psychological wisdom, it adhered with surprising tenacity to the status quo. From a brave beginning, exhibiting a remarkable sensitivity to excellence, the method deteriorated in the hands of practitioners to the point where critics could rightly characterize it as a prescription for routine. What was left of Herbartianism after it reached the pinnacle and then, almost by accident, slipped into rigidity, was the idealization of teachers as professional persons, in possession of some art, but forged mainly on the anvil of science whereon the rules of natural learning could be hammered out to produce skillful technicians.

Starting as science's contribution to pedagogy, Herbartian educational policy was soon under assault for not being scientific enough. Its psychology, a new breed of American psychologists said, lacked credentials of authentic science: it neither plumbed the nature of man nor revealed the basic elements in the learning process. The leading spokesman for this cadre of American psychologists and the principal architect designing an infant educational psychology separated from philosophy and wedded to experimentation was Edward L. Thorndike (1874–1949). Following in the wake of Herbartian psychology was Connectionism; and this psychology downgraded further the old notion that teaching is an art.

Connectionism

Connectionism, praised by its justifiers as objective psychology, had a stance incompatible on its main points with Idealism and with the traditional disposition of educators to be guided by philosophy or common sense. Whereas Herbartian psychology found some common ground with Idealism, especially in the assumption that association of experience is mental rather than physical, Connectionism, with convictions buried in theories of biological evolution, tolerated no compromise with a mythical view of man. In early writings, based on his doctoral dissertation, *Animal Intelligence,* Thorndike nailed this banner to Connectionism's mast: "Nowhere more truly than in his mental capacities is man part of nature. Amongst the minds of animals that of man leads, not as a demigod from another planet, but as a king from the same race."[21] Here was scientific psychology taking at full face value the doctrine that men are highly complex organisms and that mental processes, thought so long by Idealists to have spiritual character, are only functions of a highly developed nervous system.

It would be a mistake, however, to attribute originality either to Thorndike or his associates in the elaboration of experimental psychology, for the roots of mechanical psychology ran in one direction to the philosophies of Thomas Hobbes and John Locke, and in another, to the psychological speculations of Alexander Bain, a prominent British associationist, and Herbert Spencer, the philosopher who tried so hard to convert everyone to the religion of science.[22] Theories of association were old, so what in Connectionism, as developed by Thorndike, was capable of creating such convulsions among philosophers and psychologists? Throughout its long history, associationism seemed harmless, hardly more than common sense, but once wedded to Connectionism it tried to explain human behavior mechanically: associations were physical connections in the nervous system and could be demonstrated in the laboratory. The premise was broadcast that psychology could be an exact science and that behavior could be explained with the same precision and validity as the facts of physical science.

Psychological experimentation antedated Thorndike, yet, to acknowledge undoubted accomplishment, he took experimental psychology down roads heretofore untraveled and expounded laws of learning whose impact on schools was exceptional by any standard. Blazing a trail for scientific psychology, Wilhelm Wundt opened a laboratory at the University of Leipzig in 1879 where he analyzed sense perception by studying how the five senses respond to various stimuli. But the story of scientific psychology's evolution includes Francis Galton's study of heredity in genetics, Ivan Pavlov's experiments with dogs and a theory of conditioned reflex, and Alfred Binet's testing of memory, skill, attention, and intelligence.[23]

From this earlier work, irrespective of its application, the experimental trend in psychology had an irreversible start, and a whole generation of American psychologists, led by the enormously productive scholarship of Thorndike, endeavored to make psychology, and especially educational psychology, an objective science. Other scholars engaged in cultivating the same field were: G. Stanley Hall, Joseph Jastrow, James McKeen Cattell, and Lewis Terman.

In 1890 William James published *Principles of Psychology,* sometimes extravagantly described as the American psychological declaration of independence, wherein with clarity, wit, and good literate scholarship he commissioned psychology to deal with consciousness. If it were too much to say that American psychologists could now disdain European scholarship, it was probably true that James' work stimulated a scholarly energy which for decades had been subservient to theories from abroad. But the real issue was never the freedom of American psychology to be scientific: it was whether the essential purpose of its study was with consciousness or behavior.

At this fork of the intellectual road James and Thorndike parted. Although a faithful reporter of psychological experiment, James disdained its practice. As a friend and student of James at Harvard, Thorndike admired this masterful thinker and writer but, as it turned out, could not embrace his psychological creed. Instead Thorndike went to the laboratory. Assuming behavior the principal business of psychology, and with all the resources he could muster—a forty-year professorship at Columbia University made them considerable—Thorndike built a system of psychology by experimenting with animal behavior. Experiments with animals—some even while he was at Harvard, for there is the amusing story of his having kept chickens in the basement of James' Cambridge home—supplied valuable information about their learning; and then, taking a step characterized by some critics as fatal, foolish, and unscientific, he translated these data to human learning. Always staying close to laboratory evidence, Thorndike cultivated ground for the measurement of intelligence and performance; he debated the important educational issue of transfer of learning—not whether transfer occurs, but the nature of transfer—and his theory of identical elements conspired to affect both the curriculum and method of schools.[24] He published studies on intelligence, individual differences, and the nature of skill and growth. All this was important and affected American schools, but the balance sheet of accomplishment shows Thorndike's laws of learning as the capital from which pedagogy was to draw.

Thorndike's three-volume *Educational Psychology*, published in 1914, elaborated the laws of learning with all the confidence positive science could muster. And for more popular academic consumption and a better guide to teachers wanting these revelations, he published *Educational Psychology, Briefer Course* in 1917. In *Educational Psychology* Thorndike attempted to demolish the prevailing assumptions about consciousness, faculty psychology, mental discipline, and transfer of training. The intellectual faculties, he argued, are not inherited, although intelligence, formed in experience, is limited by the biological condition of the nervous system. The nervous system is a dense network of broken routes over which stimuli pass, erratically, slowly, and precariously to muscles and glands where a response is elicited. The condition of this network affects the flow of stimuli, for weak bridges and unmarked trails cannot carry the same load as finished highways, so, assuming the ability of the system to carry stimuli in the first place, sure and certain routes over which they can travel without detours or impediments must be built. Learning, therefore, according to Thorndike, is not training faculties or searching for some imprecise mental discipline, but is a process of forming a series of bonds or connections, coordinating situations disposing the organism to act with the responses they generate. The process is entirely physical, Thorndike maintained, and follows the laws of effect, exercise, and readiness.

Literature on the laws of learning is abundant, some of it technical and confusing. In addition, Thorndike, as befits a good experimentalist, was prompt to revise the laws when evidence warranted; and since experimentation with learning continued for a long time, the evidence piled up. Still, the general thrust of the laws is clear and their substance can be grasped without following every detail of their codification and articulation. Thorndike valued most the law of effect and in rendering the nature of learning always gave it pride of place: "When a modifiable connection between a situation and a response is made and is accompanied or followed by a satisfying state of affairs, that connection's strength is increased; when made and accompanied or followed by an annoying state of affairs, its strength is decreased."[25]

Educational maxims as old as man himself heeded the principle that learning—all human action, in fact—is spurred by pleasure and braked by pain, so Thorndike's law of effect hardly qualified as a revelation; yet the old and the new differed. And the difference lay in Thorndike having experimental evidence to support his law.

The law of exercise stipulated a bond between a stimulus and a response, one strengthened by use and weakened by disuse: the more frequent and recent the connection the stronger the bond. At first given a good deal of attention, the law of exercise promoted a pedagogy of drill, so Connectionists repudiated the notion that repetition alone could strengthen a bond. This tended to downgrade the law of exercise and left the law of effect as the standard bearer for Connectionism. But the law of readiness, although never essential to explain learning, had its part to play. When an organism is ready, the law said, acting will be satisfying and will strengthen connections; inaction will annoy and weaken them. Readiness implied also a maturity to the nervous system enabling it to handle stimuli. Some learning, therefore, could begin early, other would have to await greater maturity.

Fortified with a scientific explanation of learning, Thorndike and his followers hastened to apply this new psychology to education. With a confidence in psychology to illuminate pedagogic technique, they dogmatically assumed that psychology could identify educational purpose too. The implications of Connectionism were clear: they aimed directly at the curriculum where certain subjects were vested as staples because of disciplinary value or because their content was alleged to have inherent worth, and they affected the technique of teaching where heretofore, and especially in the case of the Herbartian steps, ideas were enlisted for cultivation. Connectionists told teachers to replace ideas with information, skill, interests, habit, attitudes, and ideals and teach them according to the laws of learning.

Educational objectives were turned away from literary refinement, from discipline, and from the artifacts of culture traditionally characteristic of educated men, to performance on the job of life. What was needed, Connectionists said with scientific confidence (illustrated in the report of the Committee on Economy of Time), were clear and specific outcomes—sometimes called minimum essentials—to which the study of any subject should lead, and these outcomes could be discovered by making a scientific analysis of the habits, skills, ideals, and attitudes people need to function in society. This new theory on the selection and organization of curricula took time to develop and more time to implement. It was endorsed in the 1918 Report of the National Commission on the Reorganization of Secondary Education. This report represented the Seven Cardinal Principles as objectives for secondary education, and for decades secondary schools tried to comply. The philosophy of education on which these principles rested was stated thus: "In order to determine the main objectives that should guide education in a democracy, it is necessary to analyze the activities of the individual."[26] From this analysis the curriculum would get its direction. Now Thorndike's doctrine of transfer of identical elements and a pedagogy based on the laws of learning became important factors in setting the dimensions of instruction.

Competing for attention and allegiance, Herbartianism and Connectionism affected schools more directly than psychological theory had before. For a while, it appeared, one or the other would dominate the schools. But Herbartianism, despite its foundation in respectable scholarship, proved less durable than Connectionism; the precision of the formal steps was unable to match the easy pedagogic lesson of Connectionism. But the bright light of Connectionism's hope was dimmed by a cloud just becoming visible on the psychological horizon. Gestalt psychology, a novel theory introduced by Max Wertheimer in Germany, challenged the assumptions of Connectionism with the proposition that learning is unmechanical and proceeds according to patterns grasped by the mind rather than bonds between nerve cells. Gestalt psychology, appearing in 1912 in Germany, was retarded in public notice by World War I and reached America slowly. After the war, Wolfgang Kohler, who spent years observing the behavior of chimpanzees, published *The Mentality of Apes.*[27]

Evidencing skepticism about Thorndike's thesis making animal learning primarily, if not entirely, an exercise in trial and error, Kohler attributed to animals an ability to grasp patterns in a situation. Their learning, he held, however primitive it may be compared to man's, is generated in a mental process. Gestalt, or pattern, implied a basic mental attitude which, according to the theory, is a vital element in all learning; parts making up a situation are important but without some vision of the whole, learning, Gestalt psychologists said, does not occur very effectively. Without crippling Connectionism, Gestalt psychology (which was later called Field Theory) carried just enough weight among educators and psychologists to again call a halt when a theory of learning and a method of teaching were about to monopolize instruction.[28]

After decades of debate over the possibility of a science of education and then over the significance of scientific data collected, even the most traditional critic could hardly be indifferent. Progress unquestionably had been made in upgrading learning, and some of it could be credited to educational scientists. Still, an impartial observer of nineteenth- and early twentieth-century education would have admitted that the bold claims for scientific teaching and learning made in 1870 had not been realized. Grand expectation, for the most part, had gone unfulfilled; certitude and scientific exactitude once again slipped from the grasp of educators. The most controversial of human issues, wrestled since the classical age—the proper education of children—was unabated by data produced in the scientific laboratory.

EXPANDING THE SCIENCE OF EDUCATION

History shows educational science exceeding its reach, but the same record evidences accomplishment. Despite elusiveness in learning's nature, educational psychologists and methodologists succeeded in translating their discoveries to the classroom. We need only recall the impression the Herbartian steps and the laws of learning made on schools. Scientific method applied to psychology, which for so long resisted rupturing its intimate association with philosophy, and to vexing issues in pedagogy, which for decades obstructed instructional efficiency, bore good results. If the resolution of psychological and educational dilemma were incomplete, there was evidence that science could illuminate and make it amenable to further study. The age was optimistic and confident; if scientific psychology and pedagogy had unfinished business, they gave unsolicited assurance of consummating their work successfully. This took time, of course, and as the work along psychological and pedagogical lines continued other avenues susceptible of exploitation became apparent. One avenue led to measurement and testing, and its utilization had seminal consequences for schooling. One measurement inquiry ended with the mental test, an ingenious way of discovering basic talent; another aimed at ascertaining accomplishment in school studies.

Measurement was implicit in the early experiments of Wilhelm Wundt, but Wundt was otherwise preoccupied and left this field fallow. His followers, however, perceiving the possibilities of measurement, were disposed to cultivate them. On this side of the Atlantic, James McKeen Cattell, a student from Wundt's Leipzig laboratory, became professor of psychology at Columbia University where, over a long career, he carried on studies and experiments inspired by his mentor. He introduced novelty, however, by using the language of statistics to report his findings with mathematical clarity and precision. In 1890, Cattell published *Mental Tests and Measurements,* a book credited with igniting the spark to explode the mental measurement movement in the United States. Meanwhile, in France, Alfred Binet was pioneering in intelligence testing. Beginning his study in 1895, Binet formulated a scale describing general intelligence by 1905 and then with help from his co-worker, Thomas Simon, improved the scale in 1908 and again in 1911. Binet's achievement in testing intelligence was brought quickly to the notice of American psychologists, who began almost at once to add refinements and revisions.

At about this time, when Binet and Simon were working on intelligence tests, Joseph Rice tried testing achievement. He assumed it would reveal something about the educational process. Although he had greater ambitions, Rice began with a spelling test. In 1897 this test was administered to 30,000 schoolchildren, half of whom were given daily fifteen-minute intervals of spelling instruction, and half were given intensive forty-five minute sessions in spelling. Rice discovered, and the record stands mute on his reaction to the result, that time for instruction made no substantial difference in the performance of the two groups.[29] What could, and perhaps should, have been considered anomalous was ignored; Rice concentrated instead on the precision in reporting his data statistically. The significance of Rice's labor, then, lay in a fact so far either little noticed or obscured by other issues: school achievement could be reported objectively and quantitatively. It was, the heralds of objectivity said, no longer necessary to rely on subjective evaluation of student performance. It is easy to exaggerate Rice's stature in the testing movement, and his admirers have succumbed to temptation, yet, it is also clear, Rice's work publicized statistics, henceforth put at the disposal of psychologists and educators. At this point, Thorndike, fully aware of precision and accuracy in reporting data, elaborated a fundamental philosophy for testing, one he reaffirmed countless times over the next half-century. In a book published in 1904, Thorndike articulated his philosophy of testing, intending it to have equal validity in psychology and education: "Whatever exists, exists in some amount. To measure is simply to know its varying amounts."[30] Here in the *Theory of Mental and Social Measurements,* and in two sentences, Thorndike pronounced a creed for measurement; and despite the controversy erupting from this mechanical appraisal of human nature and its implied dogmatism, and apart from whether Thorndike was right or wrong, this creed sustained mental and educational measurement. To be measured something must exist. With quantity ratified and respectable, Thorndike and his disciples allowed their enthusiasm full play and produced hundreds of tests to measure many kinds of achievement and reported results statistically.

With Thorndike's tremendous prestige behind testing, the schools quickly became places where objectivity and performance were equated, with the risk that teachers, captivated by discovering what students knew, spent less time instructing them. But achievement testing, could not monopolize measurement and, in any case, testing achievement was different from assessing intelligence and less hazardous.

The substantial achievement of Alfred Binet was confirmed and advanced by Lewis Terman, a professor at Stanford University and author of the Stanford Revision of the Binet Scale. Using the Stanford test, it was possible to arrive at a person's mental age and intelligence quotient (I.Q.). But before Terman's Revision was ready the United States entered World War I, and as it turned out, the war (or conditions connected with it) proved a great stimulus to measurement. Nearly two million men entering military service needed classification, and for this the Alpha and Beta group intelligence tests were designed.[31] After the war, the testing movement shifted back to classrooms and university laboratories, but it appeared promising enough to attract the attention of intelligent outsiders who, without professional axes to grind, complained about the uncritical use of mental measurement and most of all about the assumption basic to the testing of intelligence.

Demurrals elicited rejoinders, and together they illustrate the spirit and sometimes the acrimony of the debate. The main contestants, Lewis Terman, the leading spokesman for mental measurement and a prominent psychologist, and Walter Lippmann, a respected journalist and insightful social philosopher, fought their battle in public print, and for several months in 1922 and 1923 the strengths and weaknesses, the claims and counterclaims, the merits and defects of intelligence testing were paraded in public view. A quick review of this controversy may be instructive for understanding the assumptions psychologists made and the dangers seen in such tests by reasonable men, uneasy about the consequences of an uninhibited testing movement.[32]

Allegedly Terman and Lippmann agreed that intelligence is hereditary and, although environment can influence it, the native endowment is unalterable. While the allegation may be correct for Terman, Lippmann was hardly a confirmed hereditarian. Searching for common ground for the disputants is irrelevant; they acknowledged intelligence, its nature and significance, but parted company on whether or not, with the psychological instruments available, it could be measured and reported precisely and validly. Terman said it could; Lippmann called this a monstrously unscientific assertion.

Lippman, it should be said, readily admitted the worth of testing, saw it as useful for classifying students about to engage in various academic activities, but was at pains to reject the larger claims resting on the assumption that intelligence could be isolated, identified, and measured. This, he thought, was a leap unsupported by evidence: without a clear idea of intelligence, testers guess at abstract mental abilities comprising it and then invent puzzles and problems to see how children of different ages handle them.[33] Thereafter, they set standards of accomplishment and end up classifying children. In administering tests, Lippmann agreed, psychologists made every effort to be fair and confused fairness with reliability.[34]

Allowing for good intention and even the possibility of sometime finding a way to appraise intelligence, Lippmann found fault with the interpretation of tests. He called it arrogant, unfounded, and "glittering towers of generality." He abhorred especially talk about the average mental age of Americans, estimated by some psychologists to be fourteen, and said it was nonsense to use statistics to demonstrate that the average adult intelligence of a representative sample of the nation is the same as the average intelligence of an immature child. Such a statement, Lippmann wrote, is as silly as saying the average mile is three-quarters of a mile.[35]

Calling for modesty and balance in connection with the use and interpretation of tests, Lippmann hoped that in classifying schoolchildren the tests would be administered with skepticism and sympathy. But this was unlikely unless the testing movement were purged of the dangerous assumption that intelligence tests measure intelligence, one fixed by heredity. To seek tests capable of probing native intelligence based on this assumption, would, he thought, be an interesting theoretical experiment; but to assert the existence of such tests, or even their imminent discovery, was unscientific and could lead to social injustice as well as to grave injury to persons arbitrarily classified as superior or inferior.

Instead of acting as if they had tests of intelligence, psychologists should, Lippmann maintained, try to develop a variety of tests classifying persons for certain kinds of work. In this way, he said, testers could contribute to civilization and save themselves from the reproach of quackery in "a field where quacks breed like rabbits, and they will save themselves from the humiliation of having furnished doped evidence to the exponents of the New Snobbery." Various demands of modern life, he concluded, are much too complex to be measured by a single and universal test. "One series of tests for intelligence is as meaningless as would be the attempt to measure time, space, weight, speed, color, shape, beauty, justice, faith, hope and charity, with a footrule, a pound scale and a speedometer."[36]

Terman began the debate with this ominous and unilluminating assertion: "After Mr. Bryan had confounded the evolutionists, and Voliva the astronomers, it was only fitting that some equally fearless knight should stride forth in righteous wrath and annihilate that other group of pseudoscientists known as 'intelligence testers.' "[37] Indicting the testing movement for advancing beyond the evidence hardly made Lippmann a fearless knight infused with righteous wrath, and his reasonable reservations about psychological testing deserved better. Terman used his considerable skill of invective to charge Lippmann with ignorance, and in any case, he averred, psychological testers could be trusted. They were as much interested in the welfare of a democratic society as Lippmann.

Terman's response to criticism of testing is not altogether satisfying. The tone of his rejoinder is one of pique; page after page is used to discharge clever thunderbolts of rhetoric at his tormentor. What was needed was a clear and careful representation of the bases for testing and a justification for interpretations of test data. There was ample ground for sound argument. He parried questions rather than answering them, and moreover heaped ridicule on Lippmann who, if we read the record right, was registering a legitimate complaint.

It would be wrong, of course, to invest this debate, or diatribe, with too great a significance. Lippmann did not call a halt to testing. He asked for a cautious interpretation of test results, and to a great extent was heeded. While Terman refused to acknowledge any validity to Lippmann's interrogations, testing henceforth was handled more prudently. This, naturally enough, accompanied the greater maturity of testing. But Lippmann exposed a common currency of extravagant claim and made respectable an attitude of wariness in connection with psychological measurement. Still, the movement for achievement and psychological testing marched on to alter and improve the character of schools. This controversy, however, was only a prelude to later commotion over test results and hereditary endowment.

As the nation's schools grew, another use of measurement was discovered, so neither achievement nor psychological testing monopolized statistical technique. At the outset, the school survey—a study of district and state school systems—was intended to assess scholastic performance.[38] Something along these lines had been done by Henry Barnard, in 1845, in Rhode Island. Yet when, in 1911, Calvin Kendall, chief administrator of the Indianapolis schools, was commissioned by Boise, Idaho, and Professor Paul H. Hanus of Harvard was engaged by Montclair, New Jersey, to conduct surveys of the respective school systems, survey techniques were crude and underdeveloped. Kendall and Hanus, in fact, observed the schools, formed some personal judgments about them, and submitted reports. They did this without comparative data, without teams of experts, and without testing students. It was still too early for the employment of statistical technique in field work and, moreover, with critical issues facing psychological and achievement measurement, the attention of statisticians was riveted elsewhere. Yet, for all its lack of sophistication, the school survey began with the Idaho venture. From this beginning, school surveys swept the country. Baltimore, Cleveland, St. Louis, Salt Lake City, and Portland, Oregon, engaged teams of experts to make scholastic inquiries. And at about the same time a few universities organized survey crews, called them field service centers, and put them at the disposal of the country's schools. The first of these centers was in Teachers College, Columbia University; George Peabody College for Teachers followed suit quickly.

In the hands of specialists school survey technique was expanded and refined. New York State, in 1935, mounted an ambitious survey: the

Regents Inquiry into the Cost and Character of Public Education. Borrowing instruments from measurement and assuming technical sophistication, school surveys were useful for identifying parts of the educational apparatus and judging their contribution to learning. At the same time, surveys allowed for judgment about the efficiency of schools and the cost of operating them. In the early years of the twentieth century, the survey was one way of coordinating purposes schools set for themselves and practices employed. The significance of school surveys may have been exaggerated; it was hinted that some educators thought them another panacea. Yet they gave citizens, who in the last analysis were responsible for their schools, a more complete picture of them than ever before. And measurement always played a part, another application of science to American education.

Science turned also to the study of children. Initiated as a scientific undertaking and calling on data from research for support, this movement, under early cultivation by G. Stanley Hall, illuminated child psychology and shed some light on pedagogy for children. Hall's *The Contents of Children's Minds,* a pioneer study published in 1883, was bound to suffer from defects common in plowing new fields of knowledge, yet it set a course for later scholars to follow and it "catapulted its author to leadership in a movement whose elements were as diverse as those of his own personality."[39]

With Hall's backing, Clark University became a center for the study of genetics and child psychology, and this trend, once begun, enriched the science of education long after Hall's early theories were either superseded or discredited by later research. A Department of Child Study organized in the National Education Association in 1893 was a result of his dedicated effort, and at leading universities across the country this long-neglected subject began to receive attention. In concentrating on the study of children's motivation and learning, a good deal of information was added to the syllabus of educational psychology and pedagogic technique.[40]

The education of exceptional children—gifted, retarded, handicapped—benefited from science too. Beginning with Thomas Gallaudet's school for the deaf, founded in Philadelphia in 1817, education for exceptional children made slow progress. In the late nineteenth and early twentieth century interest was revived. Due largely to the work of psychological and achievement testers, and somewhat to revelations from child study, programs were started for the special education of gifted, slow-learning, and physically handicapped children. Educational science gave educators a new perspective in connection with exceptional children and, eventually, it paid dividends.

THE EDUCATION AND STATUS OF TEACHERS

Before normal schools were established around 1840, little attention was paid the preparation of teachers. Town by town, city by city, district by district, standards for teachers were set and enforced and, we are led to believe, these local standards maintained praiseworthy levels of instruction. Too often, however, despite the work of academies with occasional courses in schoolkeeping, and college graduates who sometimes became teachers, schools were conducted by persons ill-prepared either in general scholarship or pedagogic technique. Much was improved when normal schools appeared; we have seen how quickly they covered the country and their contribution to instructional efficiency made in the face of acknowledged academic weaknesses. Eventually both private colleges and public universities, tardy in their heed to scientific education, engaged in the preparation of teachers, but during the part of the nineteenth century when popular education was advancing phenomenally, the colleges, for reasons they no doubt supposed sufficient, were largely indifferent to teacher education. Other functions were prized and, in any case, their students were disinclined to become elementary or secondary school teachers.

The normal school, at first erratic and nonacademic, became, by the century's end, a two-year venture into pedagogy, and its curriculum combined (or tried to) technical instruction with a review of elementary school subjects. In 1898, 167 public normal schools were functioning and, besides, private normal schools by the dozen engaged in preparing teachers. Even so, fewer than forty percent of the country's public-school teachers had attended a normal school, and fewer still had graduated from one. Some teachers, whose pedigree neglected normal schools, were college graduates, but the number in this category was always too small to be cheering. Most public-school teachers finished their education in elementary or high schools. No one was bold enough to claim professional status or much more than bare adequacy for the typical American teacher toward the end of the nineteenth century.

But conditions changed rapidly and for the better. High schools posed instructional problems incapable of solution in normal schools and, though colleges were somewhat better suppliers of teachers for high schools, they were mainly interested bystanders. On one hand, normal schools were upgraded: in 1890, state normal schools in Albany, New York, and Ypsilanti, Michigan, were raised to a college level. This upgrading of normal schools was contagious and those affected by a strategic reorganization made important contributions to teacher education, but for the most part qualified teachers came from teachers colleges. These were schools sometimes, as in the case of the teachers college affiliated with Columbia University, in liaison with colleges, but more often they were independent, organizing a curriculum along lines common in professional schools with liberal studies and courses in pedagogic theory and practice grafted to them. And the teachers college, unlike its earlier counterpart, set entrance requirements comparable to those of conventional colleges. For a long time after their appearance, teacher education was virtually monopolized by teachers colleges.[41]

While teachers colleges demonstrated how they could be professional, the colleges, especially state colleges and universities, encouraged by the urgency of public demand and by an internal desire to be relevant, reversed the characteristic attitude of collegiate indifference to teacher education. In 1873 the University of Iowa tried to organize a normal school department, but succeeded only in establishing a chair of pedagogy —a single professorship in the subject—and then, in 1907, added a school of education. The University of Michigan followed suit in 1879 to establish a chair in the Science and Art of Teaching. By the end of the century, perhaps as many as two hundred colleges had modest provision for the education of teachers. Yet the study of education as an accredited course in higher learning fought what must often have seemed a losing battle against firmly-lodged convictions by a majority of academicians to gain a precarious foothold. In the first place, the study of pedagogy or anything associated with the art of teaching was assumed to belong to secondary schools, entirely inappropriate for higher study; and, in the second place, scholars, at this time striving with might and main to make pedagogy scientific, had yet to demonstrate the subject's credentials as an academic discipline. Lacking disciplinary status, its detractors said, education could hardly pass muster in a university curriculum nor could degrees be awarded for its study.[42]

To take up scholastic slack, which needed to be done if lower schools were to find teachers, teachers' institutes were revived. But this was retrogressive, inconsistent with the ideals of American educators and a public optimism. These institutes, usually little more than short courses in classroom management, were inadequate substitutes for a professional syllabus. Perhaps recognizing their shortcomings, on one hand, and the exceptional need for good teachers, on the other, colleges at last tried to help by resorting to educational novelty—a nineteenth-century version of innovation: extension courses and summer schools. Neither was entirely satisfactory, but either was better than nothing. Faced with an extraordinary demand for educated teachers, academic fastidiousness retreated before the assault of necessity.

Higher institutions, however, while they could be indicted for indifference, were not alone to blame for the lack of professional teaching standards. The science of pedagogy was young and immature; the discipline of education had advanced only far enough to convince the converted of scholastic orthodoxy. But this was a nugatory victory. It had yet to demonstrate its pedigree to scholars endemically suspicious of youthful science. Normal schools and teachers colleges had a long way to go to certify their status as respectable academic institutions. Meanwhile, it was apodictically clear, the teaching profession was so underdeveloped, insecure, and unremunerative that talented people were repelled from rather than attracted to it. Another recitation of the American teacher's unenviable status in the waning years of the century is unnecessary: teaching lacked appeal. Redressing conditions relative to status took time; the pace was slow but signs of progress were detected.

Although over the centuries education commanded the attention of good minds, its essentials were subordinated to other disciplines, so lacking its own disciplinary paradigm, education played second fiddle to philosophy, politics, and psychology. In any case, early American schools were seldom disposed to engage scholars of these subjects as teachers: it was more important to find someone to hear lessons. And so long as education lacked credentials as an authentic academic discipline, an independent scholastic record was difficult or impossible. Thus the first step on the long road to respectability lay in its development as an academic discipline worthy of collaboration with other recognized studies in the syllabus of higher learning.

Something along this line had been accomplished by Herbart and his followers, who planted seeds for the science of education. But neither psychological wisdom nor precise methodology was enough to convert teaching from knack to discipline; something more was needed, and was finally supplied in the scholarship of Paul Monroe, Ellwood Cubberley, John Dewey, William Bagley, Nicholas Murray Butler, Edward L. Thorndike, and James McKeen Cattell. There were others, of course, some remembered, some forgotten, who through diligent and dedicated effort, and against considerable resistance from established college disciplines, cultivated this new field and husbanded it to maturity.[43]

The universities most active in promoting this infant study, not from conscious commitment or keen sensitivity, but the accident of having certain scholars on their faculties, were Teachers College, Columbia, the University of Chicago, and Stanford University. From these oases of scholarship pedagogic wisdom flowed, and with what amounted to missionary zeal the scholars broadcast their enthusiasm, their learning, and the results of their research to other colleges and universities now jumping on the bandwagon of teacher education. Although never among its drivers, they proved in the long run to be alert and responsible riders.

Yet decades before the discipline of education was established in the curriculum of higher schools, licensing teachers was common. The practice originated in the colonies, where church officers and town officials weighed the qualifications of an applicant and, if satisfied, granted a license authorizing him to teach. This, though, was only the American side of an ancient practice: for centuries teachers were expected to have authorization, and in university teaching the master's degree, since the days of the medieval university, was a license to teach. So states followed solid precedent when they regulated conditions for teaching.

At first, aspiring candidates were examined, sometimes by state authorities themselves, and successful candidates, after attesting their moral character, obtained a license. But this system was erratic and undependable: after the first decade of the twentieth century, about fifteen states had teacher certification codes; and high-school graduation was commonly a minimum educational requirement. These early certification codes, moreover, were often indifferent to pedagogic competence. As the discipline of education matured this deficiency was remedied and basic courses in professional education became standard requirements. The evolution of teacher certification is a story of states setting educational and professional standards.

State authority to certify teachers went largely unchallenged, and regular progress along this line is clear and convincing, but when a variety of nonpublic schools opened their doors, especially Catholic parochial schools after the Church legislation of 1884, something new was added. Should private-school teachers have state certification? Here the historical record is complex and confusing: some states carefully prescribed certification for teachers in public and private schools; other states, however, allowing private schools surprising freedom, applied teacher certification statutes only to public schools.

Setting standards and enacting certification codes regularized conditions in the teaching profession, and the overall result of this action was good. But there was always another side to teaching untouched by requirements. If teachers were to be capable and responsible, it was imperative to enlist talented and imaginative people. But teaching had long stood on a low rung of the professional ladder and its emoluments, even in colleges and universities, were insufficient to attract ornamental talent.

With the popularization of common schools and with generally low salaries, few men could be expected to compete for the ever-increasing number of positions in public schools. They neglected teaching for more rewarding occupations, thus leaving forfeit a career henceforth pursued by women. Conditions in the schools, lack of financial promise, along with an almost total absence of professional status altered the portrait of the American teacher from schoolmaster to schoolmistress. Under these circumstances, teachers' salaries improved slowly: from 1865 to 1918 their salaries compared unfavorably with those of artisans; moreover, sharp differences existed between men and women and urban and rural teachers. In 1895, for example, a male teacher in a rural school earned an average weekly salary of $11.70; a woman in a rural school was paid $8.91. In urban districts the weekly average was $31.63 for men and $13.40 for women. In 1915, although the standard and cost of living had increased, men in rural districts earned an average weekly salary of $18.61 and in urban districts $37.15; women in respective situations received $13.63 and $21.06.[44]

Coupled with poor and inadequate salaries, teachers were further disadvantaged by the absence of perquisites, such as retirement and tenure, which have become commonplace. Early tradition had accorded teachers property rights in their positions but this tradition was the victim of desuetude. Throughout the nineteen century, with the exception of a few school systems where death benefits were granted deceased teachers whose estates were too meager to cover burial expenses, neither tenure, retirement, nor any other provision was made to improve the economic side of a teacher's life.

Early in the twentieth century, however, retirement plans, probably following precedents set in industry and government, appeared: between 1905 and 1914, sixty-five cities established public retirement plans, and by 1910, four states had inaugurated state-wide retirement systems for teachers. Tenure arrangements lagged however, and this situation was not materially altered until 1920. Tenure, wherewith a teacher had a legal claim on his position, was generally opposed as an unusual and indefensible infringement of the right of school boards to hire and fire as they pleased. A policy of open competition among teachers, it was argued, would enable schools to employ the best.

In spite of a determined resistance to permanence of appointment, professional organizations for teachers on national and state levels—the most influential, the National Education Association (founded as the National Teachers Association in 1857 and reorganized and renamed in 1870)—exerted enough political influence to obtain the enactment of tenure laws in seven states and the District of Columbia by 1918. These laws, although laying a foundation for later legislation, were largely ineffective and gave teachers only tenuous security.

Still, the American teacher, despite a generally unenviable status, had by all accounts come a long way and so had the quality of instruction. Without explicit public support other than a general desire for good learning, and left largely to fight their own battles, schools and teachers made considerable progress. Encouraged by professional organizations on local, state, and national levels, teachers labored to establish teaching as a legitimate profession. To this end both the National Education Association and the American Federation of Teachers (the latter organized in 1916 and affiliated with the American Federation of Labor) were of immense help.

Apart from economic issues, always capable of motivating teachers to circle the same tree of reform, another side to the picture of American education affected teachers greatly and, over the years, proved to be an almost constant source of irritation: academic freedom. Strictly construed, academic freedom affected all teachers and all had a stake in its affirmation and application; yet, in the nature of academic affairs the issue was more sensitive in higher than lower schools, so college professors were called upon to define their freedom to follow truth, and when they did they met formidable obstacles.[45]

Throughout most of its history in America, higher education had been absolved from controversy about what could and could not be taught, and the degree of freedom professors had to purvey their scholarship. Conventional college instruction steered clear of controversy, not out of timidity, but because the usual curriculum contained what most educated people believed to be true, so in the nature of things professors seldom trod a dangerous path. Staying within the strict limits of academic and religious orthodoxy, both scholarly and public utterance was aimed less at the dispersion of novelty than at amplification and elucidation of undisputed religious and intellectual stances. As the calendar's pages turned, however, the face of American higher education changed; in place of, or alongside, the old college stood the university, an institution whose nature and purpose had definitions unfamiliar in the American experience. Academic freedom, never a critical issue before, became with the founding of the Johns Hopkins University a matter of vital educational significance.

With its new image, the American university was disposed to engage in studies, at least to put them at the forefront of academic effort, which would make an economic and social difference. This was what the architects of the new universities wanted, and moreover what the philanthropists responsible for the founding of many said they should do. Under the circumstances, it was difficult for universities to avoid the public arena, and in entering it they were constantly exposed to the vagaries of public opinion and popular will. At the same time, the tradition of the college was too clear to ignore and too valuable to jettison: colleges had been commissioned, among other things, to safeguard the morals of youth and ensure that they were uncontaminated by the college experience. Besides protecting morals, the colleges were regularly directed by their constituents, and unquestionably by their own convictions, to cultivate character.

The conventional commission of higher learning might have been managed, even in universities, except for curricular novelty. The old curriculum, composed largely of the classics, was there to be mastered; neither invention nor metamorphosis was countenanced. The social sciences, however, introduced shortly before the advent of the twentieth century, were vitalized by the action of society and could not have matured without immersion in the froth and foam of life itself. If the colleges of the country had been ivory towers, they could not now, at least in the social sciences, afford a life of solitude. And when scholars representing social science ventured into public with their theories, their research findings, and their sometimes unpopular opinions relative to social and economic reform, the trouble started.

As it turned out, the public—at least that part of the public wherein power was vested by law and tradition—cared a great deal about what colleges were doing and what professors were saying on matters affecting public policy. The influence of scholars was inflated by their exploitation of public platforms. Could the American public (or more exactly those threatened by these academic pronouncements) afford to allow professors to preach, teach, and publish without restraint? Could schools dependent for their stability on huge financial interests, or in public universities the votes of legislators, support and defend a scholarly enterprise and initiative bringing them into conflict with their benefactors? And could colleges and universities be vital, useful, and honest institutions if they were reined in by extramural force?

Harnessing the freedom of universities to go their own scholarly way, the way of responsibility and truth, was hardly a matter of malicious restraint imposed by elements in society apprehensive about the social ferment created by new and sometimes radical academic hypotheses. Determination to control colleges and impose trustworthiness, and thus to limit academic freedom, was nurtured by the best intentions and always by a desire to protect vested interests which, by extension, were alleged to be the public interest as well. Truth could stand unhampered unless it led to an erosion of public confidence in existing institutions or to a diminution of political and economic power. Control, not truth was the issue. Unfortunately, in colleges, the two were inseparable.

However important academic freedom was in connection with the advancement of knowledge, it must not, of course, be assumed that every professor who chose to teach and publish was standing on sacred ground. Professorial opinion, usually responsible and praiseworthy, could also be erratic and subversive. Truth sometimes eluded the grasp of scholars and even when possessed its meaning was hard to fathom. Still, and this point needs emphasis, in these frantic years the colleges were free from interminable dispute and the threat of external control was seldom at their door: research remained largely unhampered, and the more theoretical its character the less likely interference; teaching was generally acknowledged to be the business of schools, so classrooms were usually free. But when professors took theories from the laboratory, the study and the classroom to the public platform, when they expressed social, economic, and political views in public and tried to be consequential, then, and only then, did the issue of academic freedom become critical.

A notorious litigation, although not definitive in developing a policy on academic freedom, testing the scholastic exercise of scientific hypotheses in conflict with traditional belief, was the 1925 Scopes trial in Tennessee.

There at issue, skirting vested interest and social theory, was state law proscribing the teaching of evolution. Despite unfavorable light cast on the law by the famous attorney, Clarence Darrow, it survived the assault and Scopes, who had flaunted it, was found guilty. In some respects touching academic freedom, this litigation meant to preserve religious fundamentalism rather than defend academic right.

Returning to the more troublesome side of academic freedom, and one yet eluding clear resolution, we find the American Association of University Professors, organized in 1915, laying down guiding principles with respect to professorial use of public forums. Beginning with a clear acknowledgement that professors had all the rights of citizens, either to seek public office or appraise public issues, the American Association of University Professors' statement, nevertheless, imposed some sensible restrictions on their public activity. These restraints, the Association said, should be self-imposed or enforced by the profession itself, and any judgment rendered in particular cases at issue should come from faculty committees designated to hear them rather than from outsiders. Professors' freedom to make public utterances or to enlist in questionable causes was limited but, the Association asserted, their freedom to pursue science unimpeded by limitations external to scholarship was absolute.[46] This eminently sensible principle appealed to good scholars everywhere and added an element of equilibrium in universities where prerogatives of scholarship were shaky; yet for all its appeal, the principle was hard to administer with equity and prudence.

American universities found it difficult to choose between competing loyalties to donors and scholars, and because these pragmatic and academic loyalties were deeply lodged in university life, the issue of academic freedom never really disappeared. Neither reasonable men nor respectable scholars claimed immunity from control for professors; academic freedom demurred from endorsing irresponsibility or licentiousness. But this issue, so complex and emotional, even with sound principles for guidance, eluded precise standards for administration. Controversy was its almost constant companion.

EDUCATION AND PUBLIC POLICY

When Thomas Jefferson advanced his theory of natural aristocracy and later coupled it with a plan for a more general diffusion of knowledge throughout Virginia, this avant-garde social philosophy was unacceptable. The common opinion of the day assumed a social aristocracy established by wealth and pedigree and was amused at the suggestion of talent buried away among the people to be excavated by artful social and educational programs. Even Jefferson had only modest hope for upgrading the masses and, while he was confident about rescuing some from ignorance and forming them as leaders, his expectation about the universality or abundance of intelligence among his countrymen was modest. A few talented persons rescued from poverty and ignorance would hardly flood society with leaders. It was important, nevertheless, to find those who, with proper nurture, could make significant contributions to society; yet it was probably pointless and, in Jefferson's view, unproductive to venture beyond the already radical recommendation traced by his versatile pen. Still, if deficiencies existed in Jefferson's social theory, they were small compared to its prospective remedies.

The Jeffersonian thesis on democracy and an aristocracy of ability was adopted by humanitarian social and educational reformers in the early nineteenth century, but for a variety of reasons they missed translating it to an acceptable social doctrine. An unexpected source, however, forwarded an only partly exploited social theory: Darwin's evolutionary theory and its implications for society and social betterment were reflected in an attitude called Social Darwinism. Coupled with science it led a cadre of social reformers to conclude that at last the road to utopia was open.

Old literary utopias—dozens had been published over the centuries—filled with prophetic social illustrations, depended for realization on the rule of reason and the law of science applied to human affairs. In the late nineteenth century, utopians were convinced that means for leading society into a promised land of human contentment were lodged in science. And the complex apparatus of science could be applied to education. But to believe so sincerely and profoundly in the power of education to effect change meant first a jettisoning of old notions about an intellectual elite; talent, the argument ran, was distributed throughout society and sometimes, buried deeply, excavation was enormously difficult. Still, mining was rewarding.

In the embrace of Social Darwinism, education converted to social science and schools became workshops for social progress. A long line of social scientists, including Edward Bellamy, August Comte, and Herbert Spencer, fueled the fire of social thought. Shortly, and almost unanimously, educators capitulated to the doctrine that men are made not born and that the environment's effect on human development is more important than hereditary endowment. If this were so, and it was not, we know, an entirely novel thought, education held nurture in its hands. At this point Lester Frank Ward's social philosophy was appealing and Ward, it should be said, was in the enviable position of expressing in clear and sometimes emotional language what a majority of social reformers already believed. They had supreme confidence in the power of education. The thesis most simply stated was that education, used the right way, could create talented people.

Despite some crudeness in expression, Ward's philosophy of man—
"Every child born into the world should be looked upon by society as
so much raw material to be manufactured"[47]—infected the philosophy
of education destined to dominate the schools for the next century.
The school, where nature's raw material was processed, readied boys
and girls for society. And it was never a matter of just working on raw
material and repairing nature, but of reworking the material and adding
definition and quality or, as Edward Ross said, of collecting "little plastic
lumps of human dough from private households and [shaping] them on
the social kneadingboard."[48] Although the language used lacked finesse
and dignity, it conveyed the message: talent should be sorted and refined
or, in its absence, manufactured. And a complementary system of testing
should be used. In this blunt way Ward nailed testing to social philosophy's
mast: "The process of universal education is that of first assaying the
whole and rejecting only so much as shall, after thorough testing, prove
worthless."[49] Measurement was embraced as an essential component
in an educational program designed to produce a social utopia but, as
it turned out, the men who had custody of science and technical skill
in measurement were unready to invest in Social Darwinism or to adopt
without reservation the theories of their precocious colleagues. Still, in
the late years of the nineteenth century, despite the cautious attitude
of educational scientists, proclamations of educational expectation were
extravagant.

This progressive social philosophy applied to the whole of American
society without separatist tendencies. But as it invaded schools and in
a general way affected popular social thought, it changed. Hardly a generation away from slavery, American Negroes were in desperate need of
social and educational upgrading, and some valiant effort was made.
But there was resistance. As the coach of social reform clattered down
the road leading to educational and social equality, riders descended at
almost every stop. Social expectation, always involving educational
opportunity, marked time when hostility was registered to educational
opportunity and social amelioration for Negroes. Law, generally favoring
limitations on educational opportunity and social freedom, embraced
the doctrine of separate but equal social and educational facilities. It
would be inaccurate to say America was socially blind, for some progressive action was taken, although too often in isolation, too modest in
dimension and too late in application to do much good.

Another side of the picture portrays social classes who, along with
Negroes, had every right to a place of notice in a movement of social
reform: American Indians, women, and recent immigrants. Here the focus
is blurred by confusing priorities. American Indians were almost totally
ignored on the scale of social justice, and women, although suffragette
activity was an irritating nuisance, were admitted to schools and some-

times to colleges, but traditional obstacles blocked them from the mainstream of political, economic, and social life. Women, the conventional wisdom revealed, were a special class, with little to gain from this new vision of society. Yet, neglect was redressed when women became the nation's schoolteachers. Then, and only then, were halls of women's colleges and coeducational universities opened to them. Meanwhile, recent immigrants, although no surge of interest for their elevation on the social ladder was evident, were treated to a variety of educational inventions intended to Americanize them. Especially in parts of the country to which immigrants flocked, schools applied the melting-pot hypothesis with diligence and dispatch.[50]

Capable of forgetting certain classes in the population and looking at society from the vantage point of convenience rather than universality, Social Darwinism nevertheless attached supreme significance to education, but under the circumstances education could not work its miracle unless everyone ingested the same intellectual and social diet. Within the protective custody of social theory, the argument for a single school system attended by all was compelling. Yet, various religious groups, especially Catholics in their effort to immunize what amounted to Protestant bias in public schools, resolved to organize their own schools. Moving with surprising speed subsequent to the Church legislation of 1884, Catholics soon had an extensive parochial school system. In general, Catholics wanted an alternative to public education which, they were convinced, was doctrinally objectionable and a danger to faith—but there were also pockets of belief among Catholics going beyond this moderate position. The state lacked authority to conduct schools, for education was a province reserved exclusively to the family and church. Despite often bitter controversy among co-religionists on this matter of state authority, and a definite Catholic antipathy to any state educational monolith, the Catholic Church never officially rejected the legitimacy of state educational authority.[51]

What might have happened in this tug of war between public and private schools had world conditions remained normal is hard to say, but again, as in the case of the measurement movement, the Great War and its aftermath had a part to play. Among the hundreds of thousands of men drafted for military service, many were unable to use the English language with common efficiency and, moreover basic knowledge of American institutions was lacking. Following the war, with a zeal ignited in pseudopatriotism, well-intentioned but often fanatical people promoted legislation requiring all children of compulsory attendance age to go to public schools and, additionally, demanded the use of English in all elementary schools. Foreign language, wherever such legislation was enacted, was outlawed.

The traditional structure of American education, with public and private schools working in concert, was put in jeopardy as state after state restricted studies in language, on one hand, and tried to monopolize schooling, on the other. First in Nebraska, and then in nine other states, laws prohibiting the teaching of any language other than English in elementary schools were passed. The constitutionality of the Nebraska act of 1919, challenged by Meyer, a teacher in a Lutheran parochial school, was tested before the United States Supreme Court (*Meyer* v. *Nebraska*) in 1923. The court declared the Nebraska law, defended as a legitimate exercise of state police power, an unreasonable infringement of a citizen's liberty to puruse a lawful occupation. So a denial of the state's power to infringe arbitrarily the liberty of a teacher, even to improve English-language communication in the interest of the common good, had the legal effect of protecting parents' right to direct the instruction of their children. Clearly, state authority was curtailed.[52]

More voracious, the Oregon law, enacted by initiative process in 1922, required all children of compulsory attendance age to attend public schools. A community of Catholic Sisters, conducting schools in Oregon, and the Hill Military Academy challenged the law and raised the constitutional question of property under the Fourteenth Amendment: asserting deprivation of property without due process of law, the appellees maintained the law arbitrary and confiscatory. In 1925 the United States Supreme Court (*Pierce* v. *Society of Sisters*) declared the Oregon law an unconstitutional infringement of the property protection of the Fourteenth Amendment and by judicial interpretation protected the right of parents to choose schools for their children.[53] In limiting the power of the state to control both the curriculum and the kind of school children could attend, a permanent obstacle stalled the social doctrine that the common nurture of public education would produce an ideal society.

Another side of social philosophy was expressed in early proposals for federal aid to education. We have seen how the federal government exhibited interest in the progress of education and how, on occasion, it appropriated money for special programs. But nothing much was done until Representative George F. Hoar of Massachusetts sponsored a bill in 1870 to "compel by national authority the establishment of a thorough and efficient system of public instruction throughout the whole country." National authority, vested, as the bill specified, in the secretary of the interior, was intended not to "supersede, but to stimulate, compel, and supplement action by the State."[54] Supporters of the bill were ready to use federal authority to compel states to do what they refused or were unable to do themselves. Neither the Hoar bill nor several others introduced in the following decades was enacted, although groups in society, such as organized labor, favored federal aid to education. Aligned in opposition to what was considered an intrusion by the federal government in a field reserved to the states, were state and national teachers' organizations, political parties, and religious denominations. In the vanguard of denominational opposition to federal aid, which was predicted to lead to federal control, were spokesmen for the Catholic Church. And to the extent that official policy on such a matter could be distilled, the Church, too, took a stand in rigid opposition.

In this period encompassing the end of the nineteenth and the beginning of the twentieth century, educational accomplishments, unquestionably great, probably overshadowed those of any similar historical period. Various internal and external reforms were made: instruction on all levels was improved and moreover a heightened public confidence was invested in education. New social theory put in the school's custody a huge responsibility for creating a better society; for the most part, elaboration of theory was complete, but developing school programs to reap the kind of standardization and performance required by the ideals of social theory remained unfinished.

In standardization we see the beginning of regional accrediting associations. In 1885 the New England Association of Colleges and Preparatory Schools was formed for "the advancement of the cause of liberal education by the promotion of interests common to colleges and preparatory schools." By 1918 every section of the country had an accrediting association. These associations defined standards of instructional quality both for colleges and high schools and are generally acknowledged to have had a salutary effect, but at the same time they adopted the current social hypothesis that uniformity in school studies was an unmitigated good. Yet, whatever the social philosophy animating the standardization movement, accrediting associations were compelled by circumstances to stay on the less ambitious level of maintaining educational quality and, in fact, demurred from leading schools into the arena of social reform. The educational creed preaching social reform achieved a full flowering in the twentieth century, mainly under the auspices of Progressive education, and its justification was outlined clearly in a notorious, perceptive little book published in 1932: *Dare the School Build a New Social Order?*, by George S. Counts. Although Counts refused to adopt fully the thesis of nineteenth-century social philosophers who envisioned the schools as progenitors of a utopia, he forthrightly commissioned schools to remake the social order.[55]

With the development of new philosophies, psychologies, and methods for schools, and with the addition of a broad social philosophy exacting from schools a commitment to construct an ideal social order, we see, leaving this period in the evolution of American education, a maturing of social ambitions for schools and learning.

CHAPTER TEN

A Record of
Scholastic Accomplishment
and Progressivism

The optimism of the late nineteenth century, reflected in many avenues of life, was nowhere more apparent than in the schools. New and promising methods of teaching had been grafted to an expanding elementary school curriculum. Once thought the university of the common man, and for him the final rung on the educational ladder, the common school was revitalized as the first step toward an educational program leading all the way to the university. While most young men and women were disinclined to set their academic sights so high, they nevertheless could look forward to attendance in high schools everywhere becoming familiar. And schools, on whatever level, were ready to honor their commission to Americanize their students, to make them effective and decent citizens in a country where dream could easily be confused with reality.

Unquestionably the road of educational progress had been straight, and when obstacles appeared along the way they were removed by zealous effort cultivated in an unbounded enthusiasm for education. The old allegiances of earlier years were slowly abandoned in favor of a new one: education. History told stories of people who in ancient times were ready to invest confidence in schools because they were capable of transmitting culture; now, however, culture was downgraded or in some cases totally forgotten, so in place of cultural transmission schools were delegated as agents of social change and were asked to produce an ideal society, one wherein every citizen would find a place and have the good things of life bestowed on him.

Before, no one imagined the schools to be custodians of human happiness: now this was their mission. And educators, infected by this new spirit, when they allowed their imagination full play, considered themselves social missionaries and educational evangelists with a commission to create a perfect society. If these expectations for education sometimes outran the canons of common sense, there was nevertheless some basis for believing in education as a social catalyst. The record of educational accomplishment over the past several decades always made good reading; it held out the prospect of an even better future. Was there reason to despair? Could the accomplishments already on the record be capitalized for larger profit?

Almost from the settlement of the colonies and the erection of the first schools, American social and religious leaders had been conscious of variety in educational purpose. Even when their perceptions were dimmed by dogmatic assumption about the direction instruction should take, they knew of alternatives. When alternatives were rejected it was not because they were unknown. Despite a discord that from time to time was generated concerning how young persons in society should be educated, it almost never became a tempest, and what under other circumstances could have been a burning issue of the day was treated with equanimity, and comfortable scholastic convention inherited from the past was enforced on each succeeding generation as if dissenting voices were entirely mute.

What was neither heard nor heeded on the level of practice, where theory could be kept in the library, always a safe distance from the schoolhouse, was debated in halls of schools and colleges where men of learning had time to engage in civil discourse about theoretical issues, never really expecting them to find a way into the public arena. Few who participated in these intellectual exchanges ever gave much thought to the possibility that they were engaging in what was a prelude to fundamental change. In these mild and gentlemanly discussions over educational purpose in the early years of the nineteenth century, the fuel to generate the power plant of educational upheaval was mined. Men who stood with Humanism, sometimes aided and abetted by philosophic Idealism, argued for a continuation of an educational program directed toward intellectual decency and civility and a perpetuation of human culture.[1] Ranged against the Humanists, not always as antagonists, but only cogent dissenters, were proponents of mental discipline. Unprepared to jettison culture, they could forget it long enough to defend the citadels of their own belief with weapons forged on the anvil of hard and substantial study. Without total confidence in the power or authenticity of knowledge, they trusted the character and sturdiness of the disciplined mind. And they already knew the kinds of schools, curricula, and methods to produce disciplined minds.[2]

Still, these protectors of tradition had from time to time to fight a running battle with men fully immersed in the real world, whose approach to knowledge—and all the benefits of school instruction—was practical rather than theoretical and utilitarian rather than cultural. The final test of education, they said, was what a person would do in the battle of life. It made no matter what schoolmasters said about a boy's aptitude for study, decency and civility of learning, dignity of manner, or soundness of mind if on the demanding road of life he was unable to make his way. While old tradition died hard, because there was always something more than myth to the educational value in Humanism and mental discipline, the country was daily becoming more pragmatic and more demanding, not for the trained and erudite scholar and gentleman but for the practical man of affairs. There was work to be done building American society and the chances were not good that scholars could do it with expedition. Industry and agriculture ignored assertions for the primacy of the trained intellect when it was the work of skilled craftsmen and manual laborers they wanted most.[3]

Expressions of the doctrine of utility had been heard before and, as a matter of fact, without adopting the doctrine to superintend the education of the young, the conviction that children should be prepared to fulfill the obligations life imposed had always been part of the American outlook and implicit in her temper. For wilderness America to have followed educational practices ignoring the reality of life would have been foolishness and whatever else our early ancestors were, they were certainly not foolish or impractical. Yet it was possible to acknowledge a practical side to the upbringing of youth without at the same time swamping pedagogy with pragmatism; and it was also possible to respect civility and culture, because they were the practical means for keeping in touch with civilization, without endorsing the notion that good schooling makes young people indolent. So educational programs which up to this point have attracted our attention tried their best to maintain a healthy balance between the urgent demands of life and the fundamental requirements of culture. No deeply religious people could afford to condone ignorance, for a trained intelligence was always essential for explaining the elements of religious obligation, and throughout most of America's early history the call of the spirit rang in the ears of most men. They heeded the call and turned to schools for some means to respond to its constant urging.

But what was happening toward the end of the nineteenth century, when social reformers, authentic descendants of an earlier but less complex form of humanitarianism, bared another face to practical and realistic learning. Education's social purpose was idealized and its ability to produce a new and better society was trumpeted. Even persons who saw little good in the reforms projected were compelled to recognize the practical implications of an educational program disposed to remake society.

Undoubtedly the force of collective effort was considerable; the schools lingered under the spell of social theorists who preached a new sociology, one grounded in the assumption that human beings are shaped by their environment and are thus products of it. If environment were uncontrolled, without social restriction or restraint, then the formation of human personality and eventually social institutions themselves would be left to chance. Determinism was taken seriously and it was not the tired determinism lodged in a theology of predestination; the new determinism, invigorated by the research of social scientists, had its source in society itself and the call went out for an exercise of strict social control. Under the circumstances the schools could not have been expected to escape the imposition of social pressure, and all this was justified by the best excuse: the creation of a perfect society.[4]

The treadmill of time took its toll on this new social doctrine; not to stop the social reconstructionist entirely but only to slow him down. We have seen how new life was breathed into psychology by dedicated scholars and ardent practitioners, and now psychology began to assume a social dimension and exerted an influence which in the end proved to be a counterpoise to the doctrines of conventional sociology. Where sociologists liked to say that men were formed by utilizing the social forces around them and that they could be molded to fit the collective idea of what a good education and a good society were, the psychologists countered with the assertion that personality has a genius of its own. Its cultivation was personal and private. The business of society, however well-intentioned society might be, was not to shape the destiny of men. This was a personal matter and in the last analysis the fate of the person should be left to the person himself. What he wanted and chose to become were matters foreign to the influence of teachers and school curricula. Society as a whole and its schools should make available formative means for the personal use of children, but the extent of their use, or indeed their use at all, was in the end a matter for the student himself to decide. Personal growth was the final goal of social education and schools, according to this theory, were agents commissioned to perform whatever service their clientele required. The American public was unused to such advanced notions and it took time for the cult of personality to make its mark on education.[5]

Thus at the advent of the twentieth century, four theories were current with respect to educational purpose. Each had its own following and to some extent each spoke in tones loud enough to be heard in the schools. While the two older conceptions of educational purpose were losing ground,[6] it would have been hard to predict in 1900 whether educational purpose was tilting toward personality development or social betterment. Although these purposes were compatible, they differed enough in emphases and attachment to learning to affect the future character of schools. As it turned out, and especially in an age with sufficient self-confidence to experiment, social reconstruction was made to mark time while educators indulged themselves by idealizing the cult of personality development. For the greater part of the first half of the century, Progressive education paid the drummer and called the tune to which American education danced.

This dominance, though temporary, was nevertheless effective on education, many institutions, and much of American life. Still, the accomplishments of earlier times, accomplishments whereon Progressive education built, should be debited, for they were real and important and had they gone unrealized, had education in the first years of the twentieth century been less confident and effective than it was, had the schools been fewer in number and remote from children, and had social progress been less comprehensive, the cult of personal growth popularized in Progressive education would have been unable to attract the attention of a public with sufficient self-confidence to break bond with the past and blaze a new trail, to take an educational direction heretofore judged too impractical to countenance.[7] Progressive education stood on a record of past accomplishment, used it as a foundation, and scored educational gains and notoriety because the bedrock of American education was solid.

THE RECORD OF ACCOMPLISHMENT

It is instructive to survey American schools and ponder the extent of their accomplishment as we enter the twentieth century. And while it would be mainly accurate to think of education as America's new faith, one could easily exaggerate the place formal schooling occupied in the American mind, for there were large pockets of resistance, on one hand, to schooling itself and to the forward march of compulsory attendance laws and, on the other, to the insatiable appetite of public education and its campaign to monopolize schooling.

Religious conviction and philosophic persuasion were capable of generating cautious policy with respect to public education, and in the hands of articulate and eloquent spokesmen this policy was equipped to slow, but never to halt, the regimented advance of public schools. Yet, however influential arguments grounded on theory could be on men and women who, in the last analysis, were responsible for public policy, another even more compelling reason was mustered to check the inflation of public education. Almost from the first experiment with publicly-supported schools, their cost had been measured carefully against the public's willingness and ability to finance them; and now as public education showed every sign of becoming more comprehensive and expensive, the economic issue was revived and used to brake enthusiasm of converts to America's new faith. Despite the rich resources of a frontier land, the latent might of gigantic industrial enterprise, and the steady productivity of American agriculture, it was always sobering to contemplate the cost of learning and the economic burden of universal schooling. As one surveys the evolution of public education in the United States, it is hard to ignore the reality of economics and the moderating force it exerted on a theory of manifest educational destiny.[8]

Elementary Schools

At the outset, we know, elementary education—for so long the responsibility of common schools—repealed its traditional allegiance to religion and adopted a civic purpose. Now it was commissioned to teach the essentials of citizenship, and citizenship could be promoted best, it was said, by teaching the fundamentals of English and basic composition, and by inculcating sound principles of morality. The latter, ostensibly, was to be done without the aid of sectarian teaching—which, some said, was impossible—so when we rethink the historical function of common schools we see signs that the person who wanted only "reading, figgers, and the Bible" for his child was up to date after all. The definition of the common school was fairly constant even as we pass over the threshold of the century.[9] Perhaps all this would have lasted had it not been for a new theory advanced for elementary education by Johann Heinrich Pestalozzi.

His advocacy of natural methodology had affected instruction in the country's normal schools, and this lesson, at first so hard to learn, turned out to make an indelible impression on all pedagogy. But Pestalozzianism had another side, one affecting the content of instruction. Pestalozzi refused to minimize the significance of tools of learning (reading, writing, computing) or to alter their traditional place in the curriculum, but he wanted them taught with greater attention to understanding, exploiting sense perception, and less to formalism and memorization. All this had the ring of pedagogic truth and its effect on school practice was salutary.[10]

But Pestalozzi's school plan also acknowledged philosophic Naturalism and Realism wherefrom subjects usually neglected were invited to take a place in the classroom. The idea that children should know the world around them and have precise and accurate information about their community—a home geography capable of maturing from the immediate vicinity to its environs and then to the wide world—was implicit in Pestalozzi's theory of education. Yet, when introduced to America and harbored in the early normal schools, Pestalozzianism was preoccupied with method and technique and had little time to experiment with an expansion of the school curriculum. Time and improved teaching conditions changed this, so now when we meet the elementary curriculum in 1900, it boasts subjects unmentioned a generation before. These subjects—especially elementary science and geography—made abundant use of object-lesson technique, for it was obviously easier to achieve reality in demonstration and make a more direct appeal to the senses examining flowers, animals, and metals than teaching grammar or spelling. And it was easier to capitalize on student interest and natural motivation when teaching geographic details of a local community, following the sound learning principle of proceeding from the known to the unknown, than it was to stimulate interest in selections from a basic reader.[11]

The science taught in elementary schools seldom went much beyond classification and observation of flora and fauna (later called nature study), but in addition to catering to the practical side of learning it also dismantled a formalism associated with books. Geography was a slightly different matter. By no means new as a school subject, geography had a position in the classical syllabus and boys read of ancient travel and distant places as they were depicted in the literature of the best Latin and Greek authors. But for all the good writing in these classical tomes, geography itself was unsystematic, often fictional and fanciful, so under the circumstances it was natural for schoolmasters to wonder why such mixtures of fact and fiction should be taught in common schools.[12]

Pestalozzian recommendation put students first in intimate touch with their own surroundings, and by observation, mapping, models, and whatever else the teacher's ingenuity could supply, the most elemental character of the local environment was studied. Then, due largely to an advance made in the field of academic geography itself, the physical characteristics of the great world were revealed in a scientific and systematic way. In the years shortly after 1850, Arnold Guyot came to the United States from Switzerland and popularized the new geography, first in Massachusetts, where he lectured to teachers' institutes, and then as a professor of geology at Princeton University. With a manageable and dependable content, geography's admission to schools awaited only the development of technique for its teaching, and the first and foremost contributor here was Francis W. Parker (1837–1902), whose book, *How to Teach Geography,* published in 1889, was good enough to secure geography's place in the curriculum.

The shape of elementary education was changing: it was enriched further by history and literature. Neither, of course, was new to schooling, although both must at first have felt degraded being posted to common schools. History had long been justified, not so much as a record of past events, but as the custodian of general ideas and, in the last analysis, as a branch of literature enabling students to stock their minds with worthwhile information about the general condition of mankind. This estimate of history was conventional and we know how it was valued by men of ability and position, and by an educated public generally, because history kept its readers in contact with civilization. History, its admirers said, was a highly practical subject either for school study or general reading. Now, however, it was given a more mundane assignment. For generations the best educational theorists had promoted education's unique moral purpose and more recently—accompanying the popular Herbartian methodology sweeping the country—character education was reasserted. What school subject was ready to carry the weight of this heavy responsibility?[13]

One could hardly expect to find moral lessons in spelling books or grammar texts, although generations of American schoolboys had their character braced by the moral lessons and ethical maxims scripted in *McGuffey's Readers.* History appeared to have natural advantages, and their utilization could help the school realize its moral mission. Still, the theory making history a moral teacher was hard to implement, especially with schoolchildren too young and immature to do more than skim its surface. History's moral secrets were not so painlessly revealed. But civic purpose, allegiance to country, and a knowledge of the way the United States succeeded to an important place in the company of nations could be handled more expeditiously in a history syllabus. So retreating some-what from a larger goal of forming character, elementary-school history was assigned a more prosaic task: to teach students how the United States had become a nation to be envied. In this way the history of the United States, with the goal of inculcating civic virtue, good citizenship, and patriotism, came to maturity in the elementary-school curriculum. Pro-moting the case for history and justifying its curricular standing were such prominent advocates as the Committee of Ten, the Committee of Fifteen, and the Committee of Eight of the American Historical Asso-ciation.[14] Yet, as Adolphe Meyer says, the case for history did not rest here. In the first years of the twentieth century, history was redefined as a social study with a principal mission of preaching "the gospel of social change."[15]

Introducing literature to elementary schools was somewhat harder to explain to a public habituated to oral expression. Elementary schools, of course, had long been charged with teaching reading, and for the most part they fulfilled this charge. Educated persons, moreover, knew reading was a gateway to comprehensive and decent learning. The printed word had an authority perilous to ignore. Despite the schoolmasters' proud boast that their pupils mastered reading, troublesome questions remained: *did* they read? And *what* did they read?

Charles W. Eliot, whom we have met often enough before, a man whose interests ranged all the way from the integrity of the American university to the quality of elementary-school instruction, observed the reading habits of children and appraised their reading assignments. To his dismay, in a six-year curriculum elementary schools devoted only forty-six hours to reading instruction.[16]

Now, as it happened, the forming of character was still taken serious-ly as an obligation of elementary schools. If history were somehow unequal to this monumental task, then literature should be employed. Eliot, along with others, formed a vanguard to lead literature into the schools. The call went out for good literature; selections from the classics were preferred over the material of the ordinary school reader. Litera-ture's first obligation was to develop reading skill, but something more was added: cultivation of moral sensitivity. Under these auspices literature made its mark. It was too early for the rise of children's literature, as we know it now, but selections from the classics and other stories with literary and moral merit were put in elementary schools and remained as staples.

Once expansion affected and infected the elementary-school curriculum curtailment was hard. History, literature, science, and geography were unquestionably important in forming informed and responsible citizens, yet even with the usual tools of learning added, the curriculum gave the appearance of incompleteness. It did not account for all of life. So with an urge for comprehensive rather than intensive instruction, the architects of elementary education began to design expression subjects. Thinking, mistakenly perhaps, of elementary instruction as a total rather than a partial, introductory educational experience, there was anxiety about leaving anything out. Without ever being entirely certain how these new subjects should be taught or what they would accomplish, but thinking them good nevertheless, music, fine art, manual, and domestic art began to appear in elementary schools throughout the country. Later educa-tional specialists wondered whether this overburdening of the curriculum had academic justification and pondered its consequences; in any event, these curricular elaborations were premature and, despite their appearance in hundreds of schools, found a permanent position in a majority of schools only some decades later.

With so many children in elementary schools, the attention given their course of study is unsurprising. And recognizing the common opinion about the efficacy of early teaching, along with significant developments in the new fields of child psychology and child development, it is tempting to believe that this was a propitious time for restructuring early child-hood education.

This field, so long uncultivated because it was conveniently supposed that children just grew older and attained maturity naturally, provided special opportunity for practicing pedagogic innovation and imagination, and there was just enough dependable knowledge about the learning process to catapult it to the peak of educational priority. And now we meet the kindergarten.

Kindergartens

Kindergartens made their American debut shortly after the middle of the nineteenth century, and thereafter experienced halting progress because they were thought incompatible with public education. After commendable performance outside the public circle, kindergartens became part of public education. Yet their spread was hardly as rapid as Meyer suggests.[17] Due in part to the great influence of William T. Harris, a constant friend of the kindergarten, public school kindergartens were established in 189 cities by 1880.[18] By happy circumstance the Idealist philosophy of Friedrich Froebel (1782–1852), the kindergarten's German inventor, broke ground for Progressive education and, in the end, made its educational practices more palatable to an American public temperamentally unused to hasty scholastic innovation.

The plan for the kindergarten, one introducing children to school at a younger than normal age—sometimes as early as four—was based on a conception of human nature wherein capacities need uninhibited growth for complete maturation. This philosophy of the person, often staying close to precepts of orthodox Idealism, asserted that instinct and intuition rather than experience are critical in forming persons, and then translated this doctrine to educational practice. The seeds of inner growth, if prevented from germinating in freedom, would die; but if by some miracle they lived, any curtailment in their early years would stunt and distort their growth.

Committed to these propositions, exponents of the kindergarten repeated what Froebel himself had explained: education must begin early, before any of the child's capacities are allowed to atrophy; and these capacities grow best when they are unhampered and uninhibited by forces external to the child. Self-activity is generated in a personal power plant, and because the child is naturally social, the cultivation of personal talent is possible only in a social setting utilizing means of social participation.

Time and experience stripped kindergarten theory—especially as it came directly from Froebel—of most of its philosophic Idealism and left it as a downward extension of the elementary school where children would have opportunity for social development outside the confining environment of the home and where, too, they could adjust to the atmosphere of the school. Yet, whatever the departure from authentic Froebelian theory in the actual conduct of kindergartens in the United States, the theory retained enough currency and resiliency to inspire and invigorate Progressive educators, who now made their first appearance on the American educational scene. Self-activity (universally acknowledged as a sound principle of learning) and socialization became fundamental to the creed of Progressive education.[19]

Secondary Schools

Along with additions to the curriculum and the downward extension of elementary education, other evidences of pedagogic maturity were apparent, and now one must broaden his vision to include secondary schools as well. For long ignored, or employed with too little skill or knowledge, the grading of school subjects and the classification of students according to academic accomplishment became conventional. The old textbooks, written always with an abundance of good scholarship but lacking in pedagogic technique, were abandoned in favor of materials of instruction taking into account progress in teaching method and insight obtained from studies of the nature of learning.

If the Herbartian movement failed to achieve everything its disciples claimed in teaching method, it nevertheless made method significant and, as we have seen, teachers now appearing in classrooms were better equipped to conduct the serious business of directing learning than heretofore. Besides, both studies in psychology and research in educational measurement were convincing in their testimony on individual differences and both could inform the teaching fraternity of artful means for accommodating them.

While elementary education had a record of enviable progress and had altered its earlier character of being hardly more than reading and writing, elementary schools were by no means alone in evidencing scholastic improvement: both secondary schools and colleges were affected by the energetic spirit of the age.

An expansion of the curriculum noticed in elementary schools made its way to high schools, and high schools, heretofore so heavily dependent on local predisposition and personal definition of secondary education, were encouraged to abandon their individuality and subscribe to standardization. Expansion and standardization, however, were not always welcome on an educational level where for centuries the classics had been dominant. Precedents for secondary education were so entrenched in the United States and elsewhere, and the nature of secondary education was so narrowly defined, that sheer accident of history explained the appearance of the American high school; and even in the high school, in many ways an indigenous American school, the old conventions of secondary schooling continued unabated. The Latin grammar school, we know, had transplanted the usual classical course to this country and its attachment to classical language and literature had only slight and temporary modification in Franklin's Academy and its successors. With an abundance of good sense, Franklin recommended more attention to an English curriculum, on one hand, and to practical schooling, on the other. For a while he was heeded and for a while the school he started stood as a model for other secondary schools to imitate; but the weight of tradition was too heavy and the noble sentiments promoting school programs accommodated to the nature and needs of the country were allowed to evaporate.[20]

The high school was itself a new beginning with intentions of preserving the best from the past: a classical course taught in English. This redefinition of secondary education was barely tolerated, so the evolution of the high school from its birth in the 1820s to almost the end of the century was slow and sometimes painful. Its freedom of educational response to obvious instructional need was frequently curtailed by the grip the colleges had on all secondary education and, moreover, its ability to sustain innovation—when innovation was introduced—was restricted by constitutional voices saying high schools were outside public education and were, therefore, ineligible for support from public treasuries. A good omen for future high-school growth appeared in the famous Kalamazoo decision of 1874; henceforth, although the road ahead was seldom free from impediment, high schools made exceptionally rapid progress and perceptive observers had bases for predicting that high schools would soon replace elementary schools as terminal academic institutions for a majority of American youth.[21]

As the high school wedded itself to the educational program and as its population multiplied, a variety of social, political, and educational forces combined to make it at once a more respectable and useful school. Until now many high schools had operated as two-, three- or four-year schools and every time they made curricular departures from the classical course their academic respectability—whose definition was a college prerogative—was put in jeopardy. But curricular change, which in the nature of things had always to be made at some expense to the classics, if ignored, effectively closed the doors of high schools to thousands of students without any appetite for a classical diet. Still, the calendar of educational change turned: whatever assertions defended the nobility of the classical course, its place of supremacy began to decline sharply. The classics remained and attracted some students, but their day had passed.[22]

In their place, or as plausible alternatives, courses in science, working their way slowly down the ladder from the college curriculum, made an entrance and, although never achieving popularity, remained as permanent elements in high-school courses of study. Social science, after a hectic and precarious infancy in the scholar's study and the college lecture hall, was introduced to high schools too, and while the stature of the subjects constituting social science was at first disputed, an urge to understand the complexities of social, economic, and political life infected the curiosity of high-school students.

These evidences of expansion testify to the willingness of high schools to be contemporary, to keep pace with an evolving corpus of knowledge; and while it would be hard to deny the general social worth of the subjects now making their way into conventional high-school courses, there was, at the same time, some uncertainty about their practical utility. Claims for educational decency would always be honored in the high school, its most serious and articulate spokesmen said, but these claims were adjusted in an institution whose affinity to an industrial society was still an important educational consideration. Industrial and manual art had a justification from utility that the most practical of academic studies lacked, and industrial leaders wanted high schools to produce skillful persons to occupy positions in the factories. Only slightly less persuasive were agricultural interests whose demand was for persons schooled in ways of the soil.[23] Besides these conflicting positions, which led to a clouding of high-school purpose, the time had come when women, too, entered high schools. Although always fewer in number than men and with lesser opportunity in the world of work, prevailing opinion favored high-school courses wherein girls could be educated in domestic art and all those skills capable of making them more effective wives, mothers, and managers of households. With so many directions for the high-school course to take, their students were put in a quandary. To help them make curricular and career decisions, high schools introduced occupational guidance.[24]

New learning affected high schools and introduced subjects for study which in earlier days had never been thought of; and a high-school population, larger and more diverse than could possibly have been imagined in 1825 or even in 1875, made its demands as well. To handle these new fields of knowledge and organize subjects distilled from them, high schools were urged by necessity to depart from the convenient practice of simply offering subjects for study and to organize their various subjects into coherent curricular categories. Thus, in the twentieth century we see high schools with curricular variety: classical, business and commercial, college preparatory, English, science, and general are but illustrative of ways high-school curricula were organized. Students, guided now by vocational opportunity and by an appraisal of their own talent, chose one or another curriculum. The high school, in fact, became several schools in one.

With so many high schools and with so many offering a multiplicity of subjects and a variety of curricula, it was often hard to know much of anything about a standard of achievement consistent with secondary-school study. While this may not have been an urgent issue in the country generally, or even on farms or in factories, it was a pressing problem for the colleges. For a time they persisted in setting their own institutional standard for admission, but in the end this led to greater confusion. Besides, state universities, just now beginning to make a mark on higher education, were usually inhibited by law from setting admission standards detrimental to public high-school graduates. Clearly, something needed to be done to assure everyone depending on high schools of the worth of their instruction.

With their varied clientele high schools waited and listened for advice about how to present a single face of uniformity and academic quality and, surprisingly enough, the best suggestions came from the colleges, who by this time might have been expected to disdain the high school since it had departed in academic perspective so far from what colleges conventionally thought secondary education was. Actually, the agent selected to speak for the colleges was the Committee of Ten, formed in 1892 by the National Education Association to inquire into ways to improve and standardize secondary education. Although the Committee's commission was broad enough to cover all the problems of secondary schooling, the Committee narrowed its focus to concentrate on college entrance requirements. Keeping one eye on college expectations, the Committee defined the function of high schools as preparing youth for life but always left enough room for the development of high-school curricula capable of satisfying the most scrupulous college admissions officer.

Besides speaking directly to the issue of high-school function, the Committee told high schools to continue distinguishing fields of study in various curricula, such as, classical, English, and scientific, to liberalize their policies of course selection by introducing the elective system, and to define the value of a unit of study for purposes of high-school graduation or college entrance according to the amount of time given to instruction in a subject.[25]

Defining a unit of instruction was, at best, a complicated business, but to have such a definition accepted across the country by high schools was nothing short of miraculous. This took time; even the best arguments excavated from the Report of the Committee of Ten often fell on deaf ears. Still, progress toward standardizing units of instruction was steady. When the Report of the Committee on College Entrance Requirements, in 1899, added an affirmative voice, the issue was settled on the level of policy.[26] What remained was to find agreement on the constitution of a standard unit. Here the Carnegie Foundation for the Advancement of Teaching proved to be of considerable help.

This foundation, in its effort to classify colleges and universities for the purpose of instituting retirement programs for professors, decided to recognize colleges and universities accepting fifteen units of high-school study as eligible for participation.[27] A unit of study, according to the Foundation's definition, was a course of instruction meeting five days a week for an academic year.[28] This unit was eventually widely employed as a national norm around which high-school courses of study were built. So the Report of the Committee of Ten and the later definitions of units of study, employing the quantitative measure of time spent in instruction, marked a turning point in the history of the high schools of the United States. Henceforth, it took only time for high schools to become popular and to have custody, having inherited it from the elementary school, of an American birthright.

Colleges

Among the various schools of the country, colleges gave the appearance and had the reputation for stability; if the integrity of culture and sound learning was to have the protection of a citadel and thus pass through the tumult of life unmolested by clatterings of reality, that citadel was surely the old college. Serene and remote, college life could be lived without distraction imposed by urgent problems in society, and college students, mostly boys, could live like monks and learn like sages: their one last chance to make a disinterested assault on learning before entering the world of work. This, undoubtedly, was the picture the average American had of higher learning as he walked over the threshold of the twentieth century; but it was a picture slightly out of focus, for it distorted a reality wherein colleges were now immersed.

Rather than being comfortable and content, higher learning was in a state of urgent unrest. Only a couple of decades before, the university, almost unheralded, made a quick voyage across the Atlantic and before this, with remarkable stealth or an extraordinary persuasiveness, professional schools—law, medicine, and engineering—either attached themselves to existing colleges or, striking out on their own, organized new institutions for a prosecution of their studies. The old college, still confident of the rectitude of its scholastic way and the legitimacy of its classical curriculum (the *Report* of the Yale Faculty defending mental discipline was still a solid article of academic faith),[29] made a momentous decision. Allowing its curriculum to enter scholastic avenues represented by some of the new fields of knowledge, it began to accommodate students whose collegiate interests were neither liberal nor cultural but practical and utilitarian. Besides the traditional collegiate affinity to religion began a recessional to the disharmonious tune of secular thought and interest. Over the years the lower schools of the country had metamorphosed, and now American higher learning began to wear a new face.[30]

The details of collegiate revolution need not detain us, for the result of what occurred can be read in their catalogues three-quarters of a century later. Laboratory science, almost totally unknown in an earlier syllabus, now obtained a secure place in the course of study; social science, cultivated avidly in the first great and influential universities, percolated down to the colleges and found curricular exponents. And all manner of courses of instruction containing practical knowledge, intended to prepare students to do useful things in society, introduced to fulfill an alleged temporary need, turned out to be permanent. To manage this broad curriculum, which the colleges felt compelled to promote, an old cadre of classical professors had to be augmented by teachers and scholars of different caliber. So without any clear advice from a tradition to test the scholarly metal of these academicians, the colleges had specializing professorships virtually thrust on them.

Amid the complexities of the college way of life, always affecting private colleges first, came another novelty: the state university. Legally and temperamentally associated with a popular and practical view of higher learning, these state schools quickly assumed positions of scholastic significance and during this period the foundations were laid for some of the great state universities. But state schools had problems too. Along with their academic brethren in private institutions, the scholars who commanded the destiny of state universities pledged their faith to a conventional philosophy of higher learning, and this philosophy was sorely tested by the demands made on the universities to become schools for public service. One part, but only one part, of this pressure for public service was evidenced in the growth and influence of land-grant colleges either as separate schools or in affiliation with already existing state universities. At last rural America had its own institution of higher learning and the agricultural interests of the country were determined to make the most of their good fortune.[31]

If one side of the college problem was to slow the tendency for higher learning to drift in the direction of practical study, the other side was a matter of managing in a college curriculum all the studies with credentials to claim a place in the college course. Scholars, prosecuting their fields of knowledge, fashioned new disciplines of unquestioned stature and respectability. They, too, wanted to purvey their wisdom to inquiring minds. How could everything be represented in the curriculum? And if everything could not be represented, what should be left out? Again we meet the man who may have been the most influential figure on the university scene: Charles W. Eliot, for forty years president of Harvard. Competition among college studies, he said, should be encouraged, allowing students to pursue appealing subjects. Disputing the conventional opinion attributing inherent worth to some knowledge, Eliot maintained an equal value for all studies. What remained was for the student to make his choice. The solution, in the end, to the problem of overburdening students with a broad and demanding curriculum, yet still allowing any legitimate subject a place in the curriculum, was electivism.[32]

Eliot's pronouncement, scantly heeded at first, turned out to be the normal way to manage courses of study. But electivism was hardly more than a handy expedient and left questions of college purpose and curriculum more confused than before. Specialization, undoubtedly the natural consequence of an elective policy, raced through college campuses one after another, but intellectual refinement and cultural authenticity were arrested. Boys, and in some colleges girls, could satisfy their practical motives for higher education and follow courses appealing to them; but the legitimate claims of liberal learning, those Humanistic studies which for centuries had attended to the development of thought and expression, were sold at discount. Whether the halls of higher learning were to be intellectual centers for common culture or the workshops of society became a central question. This critical question the twentieth century was left to wrestle with.

APPRAISING THE RECORD OF ACCOMPLISHMENT

The record of educational accomplishment we have looked at so far is indisputable. Even the most eloquent revisionist historians do not question it. What they do dispute, however, is the purity of motive inspiring these accomplishments and the consequences of the accomplishments themselves. While there is no tendency to charge the educational activists of the late nineteenth century with evil, there is a conviction that however much their motives were mixed, they added up to an idealization of education as a method of social control. In effect, as schooling became more and more common and as it adopted a character of uniformity the country over, it subverted fundamental democratic ideals. So, they say, we must revise our appraisal of these accomplishments—they may have been more impediments than accomplishments—and withhold our praise for the dedication and good sense of the educational architects responsible for them.

This argument has the ominous ring of conspiracy. It would be easy to conclude after reading David Tyack's *The One Best System* and Michael Katz's *Class, Bureaucracy, and Schools*[33] that the late nineteenth century was overrun by a group of arrogant men who undertook consciously to impose their own preconceptions of life and education on the people of the United States. When this group of self-styled elite was unable to control the course of educational events directly, it employed lackeys to do its bidding. These lackeys were members of school boards, teachers in schools, superintendents of city and consolidated school systems, professors of education (those new experts in the science of pedagogy), and presidents of some of the great universities. The pawns in this great game of academic chess were the people of the country and their unsuspecting children who attended the schools. Indictment for conspiracy is hasty and inaccurate, for these spokesmen for revision are scholars of ability and integrity, and they do not intend their brush to blacken the whole of the educational establishment for these years. They admit to progress and they acknowledge accomplishment; yet they insist that the direction taken by the schools under the domination of this establishment too often repealed the best interests of children and the long-range unity of the nation.

Katz believes the great enemy was an idealization of standardization and its adoption as a principal plank in the philosophy of American education.[34] Tyack lists his demurrals under the heading of misconceptions: a notion that a uniform system of schooling would cater to social pluralism; a faith in an educational bureaucracy accurately to interpret the finest educational objectives and the best interests of the pupils; a confidence that effective systems of school administration ensure equality of educational opportunity; an obscuring of the melding of politics and school control by pretending the two were incompatible; and a tendency to find reasons for academic failure or retardation in the children themselves, rather than in the schools responsible for teaching them.[35]

These misconceptions, Tyack argues, whatever their source—even if it were in the best of intentions—created problems for the schools of the nineteenth century. Infection was most apparent in the common schools becoming more and more popular across the land. Once established, these schools were kept intact by compulsory attendance legislation. America trusted education to help make her dream come true; but education—or rather, the men controlling it—Tyack seems to conclude, violated this trust.

It all began with the conviction, expressed time and again by influential public men, that schooling was the bulwark of democracy, the one best chance most people would ever have for getting into the mainstream of American life. But where the aspirations of the people led toward social, economic, and cultural betterment, educational leaders thought along other lines. The schooling the so-called lower classes would get, whether these lower classes were recent immigrants, the children of factory workers and day laborers, the marginally stable farmers, the Negroes recently freed from bondage and now flocking to cities in the North, or denominationally distinctive citizens (such as Roman Catholics), was intended to keep them in their social and economic places. Rather than being the route to a better life, schooling habituated them to the tested values and mores of American society. They were to become accredited members of that society by conforming to the ideals and values which, it was assumed, had already been certified by social philosophy.

William T. Harris' record as a school superintendent in St. Louis would seem to qualify him best as the leader of an educational establishment willing to make common cause with this social doctrine for American education. We know, of course, how Harris shared the common aspirations of American industry and commerce; he believed deeply in social stability and was convinced that one of schooling's principal objectives was to instill discipline. All this idealism (for this is what it should be called) needed implementation. For this a system of education was essential and it should be a system with common purpose and, if possible, uniform methodology.

So the educational crusade mounted in the 1830s was, according to this thesis, resurrected toward the end of the century. But this time, instead of campaigning for common schools, those humble cradles of book learning where citizenship would be fostered, the campaign was waged for a centralized system of education. To some extent, history tells us, this campaign was successful. The federal government reacted early and favorably by installing a Bureau of Education in the Department of the Interior; state governments, after toying for a long time with their legal authority to establish state school systems, now responded with alacrity. State school systems became a reality, and as the state became more and more a factor in defining the nature of educational adequacy, local communities were deprived of scholastic autonomy. They were curtailed from saying what the schools of their districts should do and teach. The time had come for state educational officers to define a scholastic instrumentality that heretofore had been in the custody of local control. Local control of education, we have said before, though often practiced, lacked a solid legal base. This fact now became a matter of almost daily demonstration.

By the last years of the nineteenth century, we have also said, the face of America had changed from a country dominated by rural values to those current in an urbanized culture. Although this contention may be disputed, our thesis is that one place where rural values were told to retreat was in the schools themselves. As states assumed greater control over education in local communities, they sought for an organizational model which could be followed easily and effectively. That model was city systems. These systems had already succumbed to centralization; and now rural community schools were marked for consolidation. And with consolidation came a uniform method of administration and a common curriculum. Since most school managers were nurtured on urban rather than rural values, the farms and the fields were expurgated from the children who attended consolidated schools. Consolidation moved cautiously and slowly, we know; systemization never occurred overnight. But Tyack and Katz argue, considering the preconceptions current among social and economic leaders, that consolidation and systemization were inevitable. The best model to follow was the thriving corporation.[36]

Rural values capitulated to the weight of an educational program refusing to heed them. Yet rural America was not the only victim of this rage for organization and uniformity. Immigrants whose loyalty was transferred to their new land wanted their children to become part of life in America. In some places this loyalty argued for an abandonment of the mother tongue in the household. Schools were commissioned to do the rest, for Americanization, if it meant nothing else, put a heavy emphasis on the English language as a social bond. There were pockets of resistance, of course; in some parts of the country immigrant populations persisted in their old ways, refused to forsake their native tongue, and even tried to perpetuate their traditional culture. Before the irresistible assault of school learning though, and the irrepressible convictions of the educational establishment, these pockets of resistance were bound to surrender.

Black Americans and Irish Catholics proved to be a greater problem for the educators. The word went out that blacks might be mixed in white schools when it was clear that black children were capable of mastering the curriculum. If this were uncertain, or unclear, then it was better to keep them in separate schools where education could shape them in ways suitable to their station in life. Irish Catholics were more troublesome. When they resisted conversion to religious belief other than their own and complained of instruction engaging in denominational propaganda, school leaders, boards of education, and others tried for compromise. They offered Catholics some financial assistance for schools of their own. These experiments were tried in such places as Lowell, Massachusetts, Poughkeepsie, New York, and Faribault, Minnesota. For a while Catholics took the bait. In the end, however, neither Catholics nor public-school leaders could support these compromises. Still, the picture is clear: if Catholics were intransigent about accommodating to the culture of America as that culture was purveyed in public schools, they could go their own educational way. Doing so, they traveled at their own expense.

There was no escape for rural people, for immigrants, for blacks, and for Catholics. The law told them in clear and unmistakeable language that children must attend school; the educational establishment was ready to tell them what was best for their children. Tyack's thesis, unless we misread it, is that this diet of American schooling was almost certain to produce a socially controlled person. And control was always tempered by those values capable of subserving the interests of the great and powerful. The age of the "common man" is often characterized by its exuberant optimism. This reconstruction makes us think it ended on an extremely sour note. That is, unless "common men" were always to be "native American" stock.

Educational activity toward the end of the nineteenth century produced an educational establishment, one with enough intelligence, learning, and experience to direct the business of public learning. The practitioners of this establishment were most likely honest and capable persons, but they set their sights, so their critics say, on educational goals conspiring to bring most of their countrymen to heel. The watchword of the educational establishment was uniformity, a uniformity directed toward producing what David Tyack calls "the one best system." He says they failed. They would have disagreed.

In any case, pretending that politics and education were naturally separate, educational leaders marched to the beat of a common drum. School boards (in some parts of the country they are styled school committees) were elected to manage the affairs of the schools. Following the model of corporations, these boards functioned as boards of directors. The managers were the superintendents and their subordinates. The people were the stockholders; the teachers were labor; the products were the children being instructed.

These school boards, Tyack claims,[37] were praised for their selfless dedication to the public good. Accounted to be altruists of the first order, their public notice pictured them as disinterested, successful men. Without any educational axe to grind they could be counted on to speak for the decency of school learning and, ultimately the good of the country. Too often, though, they were neither independent thinkers nor sensitive and selfless educational spokesmen and policy-makers. They followed the line that schools should adopt practices confirming the social status quo.

School boards were commissioned to make policy, and this they did. But it was a policy too far removed from day-to-day practice in the schoolroom to be effective. So, in actual fact, this policy slack was taken up by the new educational professional, the school superintendent, who, it was widely proclaimed by scholastic insiders, held an office next in significance to that of the president of the United States.[38]

Tyack's assertion has a ring of truth, and it makes us wonder how thoroughly the American public at this time, or at any time thereafter, understood the meaning and function of school administration: to create conditions favorable to learning.

The alternative to this centralization and idealization of school administration, the critics say, was community control of schools. Their view is persuasive without, at the same time, being conclusive. The structure of school administration may have been overbuilt and school superintendents may have been invested with an excess of authority as American education searched for means to conduct schools with greater efficiency. An educational theory catapulting administration to the pinnacle of educational effort is exceptionally vulnerable; yet as this cult of administration matured it was authenticated by the models of industrial organization all around it. Schools were neither factories nor mercantile centers, and this point was neglected as school administration forged its domination over the whole of American education. It has always been hard to understand how, in an institution committed to instruction, the organizational structure and its managers can become more important than the work the institution is commissioned to do. This, Tyack complains, was a major deficiency in American education as it readied itself to step over the threshold of the twentieth century. An abundance of evidence suggests he is right.

With school superintendents or their subordinates in an educational bureaucracy calling the tune, everyone was expected to dance. Teachers were most vulnerable. Theirs was largely a subservient role. Conventional policy with respect to teachers neglected professional status and, although teachers were much in demand, few boards of education were solicitous of their qualifications. The teacher unable to, or refusing to, follow directives from educational bureaucrats was subject to summary dismissal. Besides, the record of history suggests, teachers at this time were expected to follow an official syllabus in meticulous detail. One superintendent made the proud boast that he knew exactly what was being taught at any hour in any of the schools under his jurisdiction. While this may have been hyperbole, it is illustrative of a general attitude toward and an inordinate confidence in instructional uniformity. This attitude carried forward from classrooms to school systems. The hope was obvious: eventually the schools of the country would embrace an academic lock step. And to this end, the school survey, to which we have already referred, was pressed further into service.

School survey teams began with their own convictions about a proper educational model, and this model extended all the way from administration, through curriculum, to classroom instruction itself. While the school survey, we must admit, gave citizens of a community a good deal of information about the effectiveness of their schools, its measuring rod of adequacy was seldom molded in the community itself. The instruments of mensuration were imported along with the model. To get a high mark, a school system had but one alternative: to conform. With professional careers, not to mention emoluments, depending on the record a school system was able to demonstrate to these survey teams, it is easy to understand why school systems wanted to present a common face.

One can go too far, of course, in decrying uniformity, for at several points in educational philosophy uniformity of standard and expectation can be recommended and justified. But the uniformity characteristic of these years, critics say, destroyed an enviable individuality and distinctiveness in the educational process from one to another community. Both preceding and following school surveys, and adding the same element of uniformity to education in the country, were accrediting agencies operating on a regional basis. If blame is to be assigned for the uniformity of American education, they must share some of it.

Both ability and achievement testing had a part to play too. The testing movement, for all the good things one can say in its defense as an instrument for better school learning, inevitably cast a mold curtailing the flexibility of schools and school systems to develop educational programs especially suited to their clientele. A prescribed curriculum with stated objectives, a student body whose abilities were assessed scientifically, put school officers, including teachers, in a position where accountability could be demanded and, it was claimed, assessed. What was expected was clear; it was clear, also, which students could meet the stated instructional goals. Failure to do so meant, of course, that either educational bureaucrats or teachers were deficient. When deficiencies were discovered, penalties could be meted out.

With education organized into a huge "establishment," some colleges and universities redressed their old indifference to the study of education as a professional subject. Here, it appears, the presidents of some great universities took the lead: Eliot of Harvard, Harper of Chicago, and Jordan of Stanford. They sympathized with the idea of constructing "the one best system," and at the same time realized that the scientific side to instruction and conducting schools would have to be improved. In a word, if the colleges were to allow the study of education an official place in their curricula, it would have to have respectable academic credentials. The story is told how the president of Stanford University commissioned Ellwood P. Cubberley to organize a Department of Education with the warning that if the department were not academically sound and scientific within three years, it would be abolished.[39] Captivated by the notion that they could contribute to the evolution of an ideal system of education for the United States, the colleges, one after another, promoted their professors of education to the forefront of the academic scene and, although somewhat tardily, leaped on the bandwagon of educational centralization. Colleges, professors, superintendents, and boards of education were the captains of the educational establishment. With a reservation to preserve, all together they popularized, promoted, and justified the uniform system of education then being forged.

All this, revisionist historians say, is a valid and accurate appraisal of educational events in the late years of the nineteenth and the early years of the twentieth century. They are not at all sure that Progressive education had either the intention or the vigor to alter the course of history.

PROGRESSIVE IMPULSES IN SOCIETY

The enormous educational change outlined in the first part of this chapter could not have occurred apart from a social ferment promoting and justifying it. From the founding of the Republic to the end of the Civil War, educational change was halting and irregular and gain had a tendency to be balanced by loss. A soldier from the Revolution would have understood, and been comfortable with, the appurtenances of life common in the decade of the Civil War. He would have been a foreigner in his own country had he wandered through the land forty years later. And following in the footsteps of social practice, education had made a great leap forward.

Throughout the whole of its antebellum history, the United States had been mainly a rural nation; and while clearly shopkeepers and city inhabitants affected the course of American life, their impact was imprecise and unimpressive because the bedrock of cultural life was rural. The shocking national experience in a war fought among its own people drove the country into a new era or, at least, supplied the conditions whereupon new direction could be based. Rural life and economy retreated before the advance of industrial capitalism, an advance consciously promoted by national policy and fortuitously abetted by the generosity of nature. Forest, mine, oil well, and waterway were abundant almost beyond the range of human imagination; tariff policy, banking practice, immigrant labor, and public land grant spurred on the race of industry toward a theoretic affinity with laissez-faire capitalism. Once the partnership of voracious industrial practice and economic theory was cemented in public policy, captains of industry enjoyed an unprecedented freedom to transform castles heretofore built in the air into thriving industrial plants. Standing alongside these essential elements for industrial development and corporate growth were the noble auxiliaries of industrial progress: transportation and communication.

The good old days of the canoe, the pony, the wagon, and stagecoach were mourned only briefly when men of the late nineteenth century marveled at what invention and technology had wrought. First, and perhaps most consequential, the railroad bound the nation together and at last gave it a geographic unity; rail conquered geography as track laced together East and West, North and South: from 1860, with thirty thousand miles of track in place, railroad construction virtually exploded to two hundred thousand miles by 1900.[40] Freight, mail, and passengers traveled from coast to coast with relative expedition and ease. And what the railroad left undone for communication was accomplished for the most part by a postal system and networks of telephone and telegraph.

Invention, a loyal and constant friend of the industrial corporation, affected the farm too. Young adults in 1890 remembered the crudities of agriculture from which machinery now spared them. Farming practice and habit followed for centuries were dispensed within a decade: plows, drills, binders, and threshers appeared to revolutionize farm life, labor, and production. Old men could remember how land drained of fertility from overuse lay fallow when virgin soil was plentiful for cultivation; and now, while no one foresaw a land shortage, hundreds of thousands of acres of new land were tilled alongside old land revived by innovative technique introduced by agronomy: crop rotation, intensive farming, improvement in variety of seed, and fertilization.

It was no idle boast, historians say, when Pennsylvania at the time of the Revolution was alleged capable of feeding all the colonies; neither was it mere hyperbole now to portray America's farms as being capable of filling the granaries of the Western world. Still, among these evidences of agricultural ingenuity and success stood an element of tragic irony, for, although American farms could produce enough to feed both America and Europe, farmers began to lose their independence, relative economic stability, and prosperity. Production stimulated by invention brought overproduction in its wake and a consequent decline in the price of agricultural commodities. Economic insecurity eroded the self-confidence of rural society and the always somewhat precarious hold rural America had on the tiller of political and social life experienced a further weakening.

The historic seesawing of urban and rural values in a contest for pre-eminence in shaping political and economic policy came to an abrupt halt with the loss of rural economic weight and a diminution of political influence. And now the scene shifts away from the farms to the factories for the performance of economic drama and from rural areas to urban centers for the approval of political policy. While it would be exaggeration to aver the total and complete exclusion of rural interests in the formulation of public policy, America, nevertheless, crossed the threshold of the age of the city. It was in the city, in the industrial strength, in the financial power concentrated there, and in the political power it was capable of wielding that the future of America was dictated.[41]

If urban centers held the key to the future, they were, nevertheless, plagued with serious problems of their own. In winning the battle with their rural counterparts, urban areas were left with all manner of critical issues which had either to be managed or redressed. Among these issues was one introduced by an important (some say, the most essential) factor of production: labor. Machinery and technological progress put working-men in jeopardy, for the laborer stood alone helpless before the strength of industrial giants. Seeking for a solution to their helplessness, they found it in labor organization. In factory and mine the labor movement had its start. The National Labor Union, the Knights of Labor, the American Federation of Labor, and various railroad brotherhoods engaged in legal, and sometimes illegal, means to produce a common bond among workingmen and employ strength against strength in collective bargaining. Sometimes successful, as often failing, these labor unions worked against high odds, first, to gain recognition as legal entities authorized to represent their members, and then against the power of corporations, on one hand, and public opinion, on the other, both determined to bring them to heel. The history of the labor movement in America is indeed checkered, and often a litany of excess, of arrogance, and illegality can be recited as illustrative of the nineteenth-century actions of both labor and industry.

Yet one important point should be remembered as industry and labor began an inevitable tug of war: power was on industry's side, with its immense financial resources and its ability to manipulate public policy, and on too many occasions to purchase the votes of politicians and the decisions of judges, and labor was destined to the losing side. Always ambitious and frequently arrogant, corporations saw the good of the nation through their own eyes, and considering the national temperament and its attitude toward manifest destiny this philosophy of industry was credible.

Industrial managers and corporation executives—the robber barons made notorious in the literature of courageous muckrakers—were convinced that what benefited them was also best for America. This twisted conception of economic and social policy, almost totally bereft of any fundamental altruism (or equity), made for exceptional material progress, and this was the kind of progress the age esteemed. But for all its material reward, this progress proved in the long run a serious impediment to the development of a balanced and humane society. Rugged individualism became an American ideal and achieved a status about equal to patriotism. In the last analysis, rugged individualism was the ideology progressivism set out to contradict.

The face of the nation was changing and its most characteristic illustration was growth: cities sprawled, farms enlarged, and production expanded; both in number and size industrial corporations outpaced every other example of growth; and while all this occurred the population of the country increased by leaps and bounds. Rural values regularly recommended large families and religious prescription gave its blessing to economic reality, so in the natural course of events the population rolls multiplied. But there was another side to population growth in America: immigration. We know from even a cursory reading of history how few Americans could lay claim to legitimate nativism. Forebears crossed the Atlantic from England, Ireland, Germany, Scandinavia, or from other parts of northern Europe and, arriving in this country, were in the habit, except for the Irish, of moving to rural areas in the West to sink roots and become intimately associated with what appeared to be the American way of life. To the extent they existed at all, problems of assimilation were ephemeral and left social equilibrium in balance.

These happy circumstances surrounding immigration were altered sharply in the decades after 1880. In the first place, due to bad political and economic conditions in Europe, immigration increased and, second, southern and eastern Europe rather than northern accounted for the bulk of it. In the decade, 1850-1860, 2.5 million persons arrived on America's shores; in the years 1900 to 1910, almost 9 million immigrants, most of southern and eastern European stock, landed.[42]

Numbers alone might not have made a great deal of difference, for the country was in a better position to accommodate this European rush to a land of greater promise, but the old immigration—before 1880—had brought people ready to become part of society and in many ways well qualified to make a rapid adjustment. The new immigration was strikingly different. Those who came, usually single men rather than families, stopped almost where they landed to further swell the population of urban centers, and with relatively little skill, but a great need of work to support themselves, engaged in unfair competition for existing jobs. Forced by circumstance to work for almost any compensation, they lowered the wage standard and the quality of craftsmanship established through years of determined effort.[43] And they showed, moreover, no inclination toward amalgamation but stayed by themselves in their own national ghettos where comfort was found in familiar custom and native language.

Custom acquired by habit and language learned at mother's knee were unsatisfactory skills for climbing social and economic ladders in a country now beginning to become jealous of its own standards and traditions. These persons were regarded as outsiders and so they remained—and some of course wanted to preserve their identity by remaining apart from the mainstream of American life; but to make matters worse, too many of these immigrants could not have been successful in their native country. Poorly educated, illiterate, or half-literate, their achievement of passable mastery of English—a prescriptive tongue in the United States—included linguistic elements clearly revealing them to be of foreign origin. If their dress, their manner, and their social standing did not confess to an immigrant status, their speech did and kept them at some disadvantage.

If all this were not enough to increase social problems in a country trying in largely unsystematic ways to absorb a flood of new people, troublesome religious issues arose: a majority of southern European immigrants were Roman Catholics and, in a country putting a high premium on fundamental Protestantism coupled with a traditional fear of the power of the Roman Church, this was enough to incite many Americans to fanatic action. The American Protective Association was organized in 1887 to immunize native Americans from contagion, keep immigrants in their place and repudiate the power of their Church. Ardent religionists were active in their opposition, on one hand, to anything threatening their creed and, on the other, in their attempt to control the influence of foreigners settled in their land; and labor unions, with a more rational case to argue, looked for ways to protect their interests against an erosion by cheap labor and unskilled workmen. In the end, public pressure was sufficient to assure the enactment of legislation controlling and shaping immigration policy. By 1917, although the good sense of some enactments could be debated, America had policies intended to regulate the stream of immigrants adding to her population.

But before this happened, and to some extent even after statutes were passed, conditions betrayed social difficulty; and among the most important of social issues facing the American nation as it sought for solutions was education. No country in the history of the modern world was asked to adopt so many new citizens and make them full partners in society. Not all by any means, but nevertheless many of the problems facing education as we enter the twentieth century had their source in social diversity, especially in the cities where a disproportionate share of immigrants found their homes.

Subjected to a variety of social, economic, and political phenomena which were new and different almost inevitably resulted in the development of an introspective attitude where the people reassessed national objective and purpose, on one hand, and international relations, on the other. The outcome of this reassessment domestically was an intense nationalism and an urgent drive for Americanization. Europe may have been a good ancestor whose cultural bequests were undeniable and, moreover, supplied this country with millions of new citizens, but the United States was now aware of national personality and power. More than anything else this new awareness was generated by American experience in war: the Spanish-American and World War I. But this experience, sucessful militarily as it turned out, introduced the United States to the world community for the first time as a dominant leader and world power. The American people came to have a new perception of themselves and they demanded of their schools a promotion of patriotism consistent with this perception. They began to show special concern for subjects in the curriculum which would foster patriotism, closely inspected the loyalty of teachers, and even paid special allegiance to the English language which, it was supposed, would produce social and political bonds.[44]

The question of social and political unity seemed less important generations before, when the country had various pockets in regional isolation. Now, however, immigration swelled the cities with diverse language, habit, and custom, and industry, with its ability to offer profitable employment, kept these people close to urban areas. Advances in transportation and communication, along with economic dependence among different sections of the country, helped make the nation whole and tended to justify the ideal of national personality. Looking across oceans, the spirit of nationalism was alive and strong and the spirit of manifest destiny was nourished, but within the nation's borders not even a cult of nationalism could conceal urgent issues which even the most prescient observer could not have predicted two or three decades before.

Urbanization was accompanied by slum, poverty, disease, vice, and crime: These social aberrations attracted the attention of a new brand of humanitarian who, having first tried to alleviate them by private initiative, finally turned to government for help, and sometimes out of frustration when help was not forthcoming preached social and political revolution. Europe had been a hotbed of radical political and social ideas, and these ideas began to infect the American social conscience. Socialism, heralded by tub-thumping politicians, was organized as a political party by Eugene V. Debs. In the general election of 1920, its presidential candidate won more than a million votes. Socialism promised reform; more extreme political talk incited anarchy.[45]

A new and striking corpus of social literature matured and began to find a large audience. On one side this literature promoted social and political utopia, illustrated in Edward Bellamy's *Looking Backward, 2000–1887* and Henry George's *Progress and Poverty;* another side to this literary outpouring was exhibited in muckraking journalism and social novels.[46] *McClure's Magazine* published articles by Ida Tarbell, Ray Standard Baker, and Lincoln Steffens; and Upton Sinclair published *The Jungle,* a literary exposé of monopolistic practice in the meat-packing industry. American literature, in addition to didactic journalism and literary documentary, adopted an urgent and profound naturalism in the works of Stephen Crane, Jack London, and Frank Norris. The probing eye of the journalist and the sharp pen of the novelist made the often lurid reality of American life parade in public view.

While criticism was rampant and reform slow in coming on a broad scale, there were, nevertheless, some optimistic signs that a sensitive American conscience had been pricked. Women's suffrage, an innovation promoted for a half-century and more, was finally adopted by constitutional amendment in 1919; another amendment removed the election of United States senators from a privileged sanctuary in state legislatures and gave it to the people. Before the Fourteenth Amendment was ten years old, the Civil Rights Act of 1875 made explicit the guarantees it implied, but left loopholes through which many states were quick to crawl. The federal statute made constitutional guarantees subject to conditions and limitations of state law. And when the constitutionality of state law was tested in federal courts, those parts of the federal statute incompatible with state law were struck down. A series of celebrated cases (the Benjamin Roberts case in Boston was prominent) sustained local practice relative to "separate but equal treatment" of citizens. Local practice, and precedent, was translated into legal doctrine in the 1896 United States Supreme Court decision in *Plessy* v. *Ferguson.*[47] The gain promised in the Fourteenth Amendment and the succeeding Civil Rights Act went largely unrealized and the social issues contaminated by legally protected inequality were allowed to fester.

For a long time politics had been conventional, and not since the age of Jackson had any real effort been made to promote the vision of political democracy implicit in the nation's charter. Political philosophy, dominated by laissez-faire theory, was more influential in keeping intact the status quo than in creating a climate wherein common men could prosper. Vast national resources were in the custody of private interest and monumental fortunes were reaped from the rape of these resources. Government stood by and in some instances encouraged these ravishments. But new political winds were blowing and brought the clean scent of a government whose function was to protect the people's interest and guarantee equality.

On the state level dozens of progressive politicians gained support, and slowly but surely state government began to take progressive political steps. With the election of Woodrow Wilson to the presidency, progressive political theory had an eloquent spokesman capable of translating the ideals of theory to political policy and of shaping far-reaching legislative reform. Monopoly was challenged by the power of the federal government and giant trusts and cartels were dismantled; the world of finance was reorganized and the Federal Reserve Banking system was introduced; and railroads, for long the most dominant of political and economic influences, were brought under control through the regulation of interstate commerce in 1887.[48]

While President Wilson's failure to get membership for the United States in the League of Nations is best remembered, his real legacy was political progressivism, henceforth a trademark of American political life. This political progressivism disclosed itself principally in government's relationship to economics, and here the benign policy of government was reversed. Progressivism wrote a new creed: government was to establish conditions conducive to private enterprise, protect private property, enforce contracts, and ensure the integrity of currency; to use the force of public policy and law to maintain competition in industry and to regulate commerce in those industries where competition was either unlikely or unfeasible and, finally, to supply services to the people when they could not be supplied by private initiative.

Progressive politics took an active role in social and economic life and adopted policies which, for the most part, have not been repealed. Politically, economically, and socially the twentieth-century face of America was altered, and the dominant personality husbanding this regeneration was Woodrow Wilson.

INTELLECTUAL QUICKENING

Shortly after the Treaty of Paris was signed, Benjamin Franklin, responding to someone who referred to the War of Independence, said: "Say, rather, the War of Revolution. The War for Independence is yet to be fought." Such patriots as Alexander Hamilton, Thomas Jefferson, Andrew Jackson, and Abraham Lincoln did their best to inspire the people to think of themselves, politically and culturally, as Americans but, although a good deal of progress was made it was mixed with vacillation. The "War for Independence" was fought during those long years separating the Revolution from Reconstruction, and many cultural battles were won, but the war itself was difficult to bring to a successful conclusion.

Nowhere were cultural ties with Britain closer than in language itself. In the first years of the Republic bravado counseled a jettisoning of English altogether and replacing it as an American vernacular with Hebrew or some other language. But cultural currents ran too deep and it was impossible to find a plausible alternative to British English capable of carrying the commerce of American thought. Predictably, English survived as a foundation for the American language. The American language evolved, depending heavily on English, Spanish, French, and Dutch as it matured, and retained a genius of its own to become remarkably distinctive in style, vocabulary, and usage from British English.

This linguistic and grammatical development was erratic and careful studies are still investigating it, but one point is evident: the literary apparatus employed in the United States, although on frequent occasions displaying a remarkable self-confidence, stayed under the literary wing of the British and failed for a long time to produce a native literature which could stand as a beacon for vernacular speech and writing. Americans proclaimed a literary independence from England, and sometimes blazed new linguistic trails, but when they paused to get their bearings they were without indigenous guidelines and had, in the end, to look to foreign lexicographers. Even then help was modest. For several decades the American reading public—literature being the usual source for language rule and regulation—depended mainly on the Bible, for even the best of English literature tended to escape their notice. If, for example, the words of Shakespeare were coming quickly to enrich speech and thought in England, they had no such effect in the United States. Only a handful of persons on this side of the Atlantic in 1800 had ever heard of Shakespeare and fewer still read him.[49]

The nineteenth century evidenced literary independence and more ground was gained during this century than in all the years before. Literary men appeared in greater number to practice their profession of words, and on the level of the common man, where language is most fully alive, the American language was further enriched by linguistic invention, by adopting English, Spanish, French, German, and other words and giving them a meaning suitable to the American ear and tongue, and by allowing imagination to affect vocabulary and syntax. The result was often unacceptable to the purist, but the purist's standards, under the circumstances, were almost entirely his own and had little effect on how people employed words in everyday speech. But this great surge for linguistic identity had a negative side too: many old words were purged from the American vocabulary and signs that American was a poor first cousin of British English receded.[50]

When we reach the last decades of the nineteenth century, the years of pugnacious linguistic self-assertion are pretty well over. America was ready for cultural independence; political hegemony had been assured; the time was ripe for intellectual quickening, for language—the vehicle to guide and maintain an American mental climate—reached the apex in its quest for independence.

The nineteenth-century spirit of progressive thought, we know, had infected theology. While fundamentalism in religion still clung bravely to a variety of creeds, liberalism, a far less austere interpretation of man's relationship to his Maker, bounded forward to capture the religious imagination of thousands. Religion in America was still taken seriously, for there was nothing in the code of liberal theology to amend a penetrating attachment to theism, but its character was altered. It became more optimistic and more humane; it talked of opportunity to live and be happy in the world God had made rather than of the duty to follow prescriptive religious codes.

This challenge of liberal theology to fundamentalism showed signs of sweeping across the religious terrain of America, and might have done so had it not been for the great influx of Roman Catholics who abhorred religious experiment and refused to stray on the reservation of liberal theologians. The Catholic Church turned out to be the principal bulwark against religious liberalism and with the resources at its disposal undertook to protect the citadel of fundamental faith.

But even the considerable power and persuasiveness of the Catholic Church could not stem the tide of the intellectual movement introduced by Charles Darwin in 1859. While no one would take Darwin's *Origin of Species* for a theological tract, it entered the arena of ideas to question the traditional and biblical accounts of the world's creation and the origin and nature of man.

Some evolutionary hypotheses were capable of accommodation to religious faith, although all but the most liberal theologians quaked at the thought of reinterpreting traditional accounts of creation. The central issue, where neither accommodation nor compromise was possible, was man's nature. If simply a product of evolutionary processes, man was only an animal without spiritual essence or human proclivity. To take evolution at face value meant to metamorphose all of society, to enlist in a human and social revolution without equal in the history of culture.[51]

First and foremost in the parade of evolutionists is Charles Darwin, but to be complete we should note how his work was forwarded by predecessors—Linnaeus, La Place, Lyell, Lamarck—and popularized by Thomas Huxley, Herbert Spencer, Edward Youmans, John Fiske, Chauncey Wright, John Draper, Robert Ingersoll, and Andrew D. White. The influence of the theory of evolution on the minds of Americans was impressive as was the work of its converts and popularizers. The result of this activity put conventional theology on the defensive by asking it for empirical proof of man's origin and nature. Proof it could not make. The keys to unlock the secrets of the universe had been for too long in the custody of theologians and philosophers, and they had failed; now it was the turn of the scientists who boasted proudly that they could teach men about the world and themselves.

Faced with the most pervasive threat since the advent of Christianity, religionists in America—fundamentalists, liberals, and idealists alike— showed a common face, rejected the doctrine of evolution and appealed to Humanism and spirituality. They refused to acknowledge any rupture in man's relationship to God. Where religionists and philosophers, who took seriously their allegiance to faith, made common cause, the followers of evolutionary theory split their forces between advocates, on one hand, of a naturalistic philosophy defining man as a complex biological organism with all the principles of natural science and the processes of empirical knowledge applied to him and, on the other, empiricists who looked for man's nature in his physical organism and the society nurturing him.[52]

Evolutionary force was apparent in man's biological constitution but it worked, too, on his social formation. Man, a product of society and culture as well as of biology, raised social science to a new level of significance. This conception of man, following the general track of evolution, produced the American philosophy, Pragmatism, the one regularly appealed to by exponents of Progressive education. And it was this conception of man, along with the progress demonstrated by the employment of scientific method in the natural and physical sciences, which led scholars to make their studies of man in society scientific by employing the method of proven worth in another field. The old study— moral philosophy—surrendered to social science: history, political science, economics, sociology, and anthropology. Social Darwinism, adopting the charter of Herbert Spencer, called attention to change, evolution, and genetics in society.[53]

PEDAGOGIC PIONEERS

In 1852 when Massachusetts enacted the first compulsory school attendance law, a progressive attitude toward learning was on exhibition. One after another the states followed Massachusetts. Yet these statutes never enjoyed universal support. Opposition lingered to compelling school attendance, and some of it was based on the belief that personal freedom would be impaired by such laws. Our interest now, however, is not in the adoption of compulsory attendance as an educational way of life, but to see it as a contributing factor to what was about to happen in American education. If sending children to school for necessary instruction was progressive, then accommodating instruction to children's needs and interests was even more so.

With limited social, political, and economic horizons, the majority of people in the decades immediately following the Civil War were content with scholastic practice and the results obtained therefrom. But, as we have seen, life in the United States was altered dramatically and radically in the last years of the century. Old educational ways, some said, were insufficient: they were unequal to the promise of the land. Unquestionably monumental accomplishments had occurred in schools; they had scholastic merit despite brutal indictments from contemporary critics.[54] Still, schools favored traditional ways and were comfortable with conventional pedagogy.

Large school populations and a pressing need for a higher degree of literacy in a society rapidly becoming more complex and interdependent called attention to schools, where in earlier days the public might have been indifferent. Yet if schools were deficient the general public seldom said so. Their principal critics were men of dedication and good intention who had enlisted in Progressive education.

In the vanguard of a long list of progressive educators, the one responsible for stimulating Progressive education was Francis W. Parker. A schoolmaster, an army officer in the Civil War, and a perceptive observer in travel through Europe, Parker became superintendent of the Quincy, Massachusetts schools in 1873.[55] His appointment was intended to introduce instructional reform because, as a result of an examination of the town's schools, the board of education found that standards in reading, writing, and spelling were low. Parker was to remedy this.

First, he abandoned old ways of teaching. According to Charles Francis Adams, a school-board member in Quincy at the time, grammar books filled with rubrics and old stories for developing reading skill and spelling, and copybooks for orthography and arithmetic were replaced. Schoolchildren were given magazines and newspapers for reading, practiced writing and speaking by reporting the usual occurrences of their lives, were exposed to real problems of practical arithmetic, and studied geography in their local surroundings.[56]

Perhaps new life breathed into the schools and an arousal of teachers to the importance of their work by the magnetic and optimistic spirit of Parker himself had as much to do with the success of the experiment in Quincy as anything else. In any case, Parker's plan, called a success, was imitated. He introduced reality to learning—what children studied made a difference to them—but demurred from making extravagant claims for the methods employed. Yet behind this modest reform which proved so fruitful lurked the disposition to downgrade the content of learning and emphasize its use. The curriculum idealized utility, offending adherents to decent learning, and the methods of the schools catered to the child-centered doctrine.

As often happens with educational innovation, controversy erupted. Parker left Quincy and, after a brief stop as a school supervisor in Boston, settled in Chicago and became principal of the Cook County Normal School.[57] There, until his death in 1902, Parker promoted the methods he used in Quincy.

When Parker was reforming pedagogy in Quincy and Chicago, John Dewey pursued philosophy, first as a student at the Johns Hopkins University, and then as a teacher of philosophy at the Universities of Michigan and Minnesota. In 1894 Dewey was appointed professor in the University of Chicago, an institution only recently organized but so well-endowed that it soon became an ornament to American higher education.

Almost at once, in connection with his duties as professor of philosophy, psychology, and pedagogy, Dewey established the Laboratory School. In this school Dewey expected to test philosophic principle but first wanted students to have an excellent elementary education. To this end there was a rich environment for learning, and with a talented staff of teachers to help students engage in discovery, they were allowed almost unlimited freedom to follow their curiosity.

Testimony on the effectiveness of this freedom abounded with praise, and the performance of students, on leaving school, tended to support it. But, one should remember, the children in the Laboratory School were few in number and exceptionally talented. Dewey knew what others forget: an educational program suited to genius may be useless for ordinary students.

Still, as Progressivism spread, the model—Dewey's school—was sanctified. And while Progressive practitioners were anxious to adopt Dewey as their mentor and guide, he demurred from acknowledging them as his disciples. In the end Dewey lost faith in Progressivism, not because it lacked promise, but because its promise went unrealized. Its proponents spent their time and talent excoriating conventional practice and when their exertions created a vacuum nothing was ready to replace what had been destroyed. In 1938 Dewey called Progressive education a failure.[58]

Following generally in the footsteps of Parker and Dewey and introducing innovation to schooling, Junius Meriam opened a Progressive experimental school in the University of Missouri, and Marietta Johnson, later associated with the Manketo (Minnesota) Normal School, founded and conducted a school in Fairhope, Alabama. Mrs. Johnson's school followed child-centered doctrine to an extreme and was described, and criticized, for its outright adoption of the educational principles of Jean Jacques Rousseau.[59]

Progressive education made its impact in elementary schools where, its promoters said, it could be most beneficial; or where, its detractors said, it could be most harmful. On a somewhat more modest scale secondary education was affected by Progressive thought. One could argue that the Report of the Committee of Ten pointed it in this direction. Yet the illustrations of Progressivism in secondary schools are hard to find. The clearest by far is the Gary (Indiana) Plan, one husbanded by William Wirt, a student of Dewey's, where Progressive practice was introduced by appealing to utility and capitalizing the interest and ability of students toward the objective of curricular reconstruction.[60] The dominating theme was personal reward from learning; the principal technique was to allow students to adopt their own educational gait.

In the colleges and universities of the country, the character Progressive education assumed in elementary and secondary schools was largely unknown. Progressive educators, of course, had aspirations for changing the whole of education, from the first to the last rungs of the American educational ladder, but for the most part higher schools were immune to the contagion of bold and vigorous Progressive thought. Elementary education, we think now, was most susceptible to the influence of Progressive doctrine, because its public foundation was newer and still somewhat unsteady. If not unsteady, it had not, at least, had time to sink its roots deeply in the traditional soil of American schooling. This was not so in the case of colleges. The higher learning, we know, had been promoted from early colonial times.

There are evidences of a kind of Progressivism in higher education, and we should not neglect them, but they are part of such things as Charles Eliot's electivism (which, it must be said, showed a greater affinity to the later Progressive education than anything else), the quick and general spread of land-grant (agricultural) colleges, the rise of genuine universities capable of rivaling the best centers of scholarship in Europe, and the definition of state universities as schools for public service.[61]

Charles Van Hise assumed the presidency of the University of Wisconsin in 1904 and almost at once announced a progressive policy of public service for the university of a progressive state. The university was to continue a proper and essential function, one of transmitting and extending the boundaries of knowledge but, in addition, it was to produce expert public officers who could contribute to the common good. It was, moreover, to extend its teaching office all across the state. The people, too, although they might not be enrolled as conventional students, were to benefit from various university-sponsored programs. This innovation at the University of Wisconsin, and its imitation elsewhere, has been heralded as the sign that Progressive education had found its way to higher schools. Yet, while this movement in state universities may be taken as a sign of change, and a good omen for a higher learning that involves itself directly with the public good, it cannot, in the last analysis, be certified as authentic Progressive education.

The curriculum of higher schools was expanded, there is no doubt of that, but this was an outcome from electivism. The old staples in the college course, those that paved the only road to the degree of bachelor of arts, were fast losing face, but this was due to the pressure from society for professional and practical collegiate study and not to any Progressive doctrine infiltrating the philosophy of higher education. And the doors of the colleges were opened to a class of students which heretofore never entertained the thought of attending college. This, too, while it appears to be progressive, had its stimulant, not in theory, but in the practical considerations of American life in the early twentieth century. Higher learning had not yet moved over the threshold of popularity, but its worth was noticed and appreciated. This worth served to whet the aspirations of clever and intelligent youth who saw a college degree as an economic and social lever. As it turned out, they were right. Still, to see the influence of Progressive education in any of these important occurrences, or to find its consequences in land-grant colleges, where utility was always paid its share of heed, is to stretch the evidence too far. Analysis of early twentieth-century movements in American higher education, confirms our earlier conclusion: colleges and universities were largely spared both the practice and theory of Progressive education, except, of course, in teacher education. There Progressive education made decided inroads.

Having looked at the accomplishments of an energetic cadre of educators, those men and women whom Cremin calls "pedagogic pioneers,"[62] we must turn to Progressive education itself to see how it was elaborated in the early years of the twentieth century.

CHAPTER ELEVEN

Progressive Education: Promise and Realization

Behind the idealism of pedagogic pioneers whose names we know, and reenforcing the optimism of educational scientists who tried to make school practice as clear and exact as laboratory experiment, lay a single and simple definition of progress: realization of a better world. Their decent humanitarian impulses, however, were only, some recent historians of progressivism say, the outward signs of a far more profound, and possibly insidious, social philosophy. Looking at the work of progressive educators in the schools, we see them trying to erect paradigms of school experience for the good of children; and we hear them talking with undisguised idealism about all the good that could come from properly conceived educational programs. Yet, so the recent interpretations of Progressive education go, this was a camouflage. They were mainly, or merely, the practitioners of an art whose ultimate purpose they neither knew nor understood. We shall see more of this later as we assess the meaning of Progressive education. But for now, we believe, the conviction of progressive men and women making education their life's work was that more than anything else a revitalization of schooling was the key to society's success. This quick recitation of definition, however, conceals all kinds of complexities. Scholars may have to study for years before the definitive story of Progressive education can be told.

Until that is done, the following interpretation of Progressive education is plausible and reasonably well documented. With uninhibited faith in the power of education, something inherited from their humanitarian ancestors, the progressives' missionary zeal motivated them to evangelize the schools.[1] Unquestionably the temper of America was receptive to progress, both politics and economics were nourished by its prospect and, to some extent, we are told, dominated by its social philosophy, so progressive experiments with education were given, at the outset, the benefit of every doubt. Then with the end of World War I, captivated by the idealism of Woodrow Wilson and the varying dreams of social philosophers, and even the expectations of common men, a social energy was mustered to drive forward this grand experiment with education. The question that intrigues revisionist historians is this: what was the ultimate source of this social energy? For a long time, elaborators of Progressive education found this source in social altruism and basic humanitarianism; revisionist historians tend to find conventional opinion unsatisfactory. The source, they think, is to be found in a doctrine of social control. The final verdict of history is yet to be made. In any case, the record we have tells us the years from 1918 to 1941—an interlude between two great wars which had engaged the attention, the manpower, the resources, the energy, and the will of the United States—were at the disposal of progressive educators, and for a long time they had their way. We want to see how they managed and controlled the schools.

Any social movement, especially one closely related to the dreams and aspirations of the people, is bound to suffer from being too long in the limelight. Besides Progressive education was excessively optimistic about its possibilities for reforming society. When the balance sheet of accomplishment was inspected by persons whose affinity to Progressive education was either fleeting or altogether absent, it showed Progressive education promising too much and accomplishing too little. Accomplishment, at least, fell below expectation.

Before signs of weakness surfaced in the progressive movement, its assumptions on the nature of learning, the preservation of culture, and the nature of society were pondered by intelligent outsiders. When, the critics began to ask, do schools with attention riveted on the entirely subjective desires of pupils handle a common core of basic knowledge essential to life in society? Thus—in opposition to Progressive education—Essentialism had its origin.[2]

While Essentialism harried the forward march of progressive pedagogues, philosophers now giving attention to educational theory plumbed the affirmations of Progressive education on such central points as the nature of man, of reality, of knowledge, of value, and educational objectives. For the most part, as John Dewey complained, Progressive education was a method without a theory, and so it remained; not a philosophy of education but only a process for achieving goals vaguely conceived, and habitually unable to depend on illumination from theory. Without any ideological commitment to Progressive education, although sharing and practicing a good deal of its pedagogy, John Dewey systematized a distinctive American philosophy—Pragmatism—which on many points gave progressive practice theoretic support.[3] But Pragmatism should not for this reason be judged synonymous with Progressive education.

With Pragmatism in the capable hands of Dewey, it was important for other educational theories to awaken and clarify their positions. So in the wake of Pragmatism we find more explicit formulations of Realism and Humanism. For the most part, these philosophies refused to ratify Pragmatism or approve the practices of Progressive education.

It is hard to be certain why Progressive education declined and all but disappeared after World War II. Although critics printed allegations of failure, failure is hard to prove; possibly, as with many social movements, it ran its course and drained a reservoir of idealism that for thirty years had kept it intact. Yet progressive educators tended to be exclusive and cultivated their creed among the initiated. Not reaching outside the ranks of professional educators for support, progressives too often formed a cult neither understood nor supported by the lay public who, in the last analysis, controlled the schools and set their priorities. But the corruptive and disruptive experience of World War II may have been the most significant factor of all: meeting and suppressing tyranny in war, the war's end brought America face to face with a world in disarray and in need of reconstruction, so Progressive education was abandoned by its adherents who, seeing a greater world to conquer, shifted their attention to larger social and political issues and from the United States to the world at large.

PROGRESSIVE EDUCATION

If the much-publicized educational reforms of Francis Parker, John Dewey, and Marietta Johnson, for example, do not form the core of Progressive education, they nevertheless seem to have inspired like-minded educators with faith in the power of education to remake persons and reshape society to enlist in the cause. Without actually achieving their goal, as a group they undertook to infuse American education with a new philosophy of schooling. And at this point we must be aware of the distinction between a philosophy of schooling and a philosophy of education. The latter, broad and comprehensive, probes issues with their roots in philosophy—the science of reason. A philosophy of schooling, content to stay within the school's boundaries, concentrates attention on the improvement and significance of instruction.

It is this side of Progressive education, the side always staying close to instruction and its various theories, that has its fullest, possibly its definitive, elaboration in Lawrence Cremin's *The Transformation of the School.* Later work may supersede what has been so well done, although it will not be easy. Since Cremin published his scholarly book, other hypotheses have been advanced to lend credence to the belief that Progressive education had other sides.

Both Michael Katz and David Tyack argue for an interpretation of Progressive education taking into account a history that Cremin either treats lightly or neglects altogether.[4] Following their hypotheses we are brought face to face with important conclusions of social philosophy. Determined to shape American society along lines compatible with the position and conviction of persons in charge of American economic institutions, education was commissioned to take the route of progressivism; and this route naturally enough led to places outside the classroom. Classroom method associated with progressive practice was only the most visible side of Progressive education. Other sides may have been more important. They are also extremely difficult to document, so these interpretations of Progressive education suffer from an abundance of speculation. The speculation may be plausible but, for the most part, it remains speculation.

In the first place, the kind of social control envisioned by this oligarchy in America needed help from education. Nurture was primary in the formation of citizens and the schools were the best places—at least, the most likely places—where nurture could be controlled. But controlling what went on inside the schoolhouse depended, as a first step, on a general political control of education. Starting with municipal reform and stripping school control from incumbent city politicians represented, so Katz says, "a class effort . . . as much a thrust for power by this group as it did a moral crusade for good government. . . . [And] an anti-immigrant and anti-working-class attitude underlay much of municipal reform."[5] In consequence of this political realignment, the schools were freed from their former masters and ended up under the thumb of "old-stock first citizens." In the same vein, Tyack aligns what he calls "administrative progressivism" with this struggle for political control of the schools and characterizes it as "a political-educational movement with an elitist philosophy and constituency."[6] If we adopt this thesis, we see Progressive education as part of a political movement to capture school control and, in the end, one intent on subverting the common good in the name of political reform and social uplift.

In this connection the name of George S. Counts fairly leaps to the page. Counts was a social reconstructionist. He asked whether the schools dared to build a new social order. He seems to have counseled teachers and other lower-echelon school personnel to become politically active. Yet counseling political activity is one thing; assessing motive for doing so is another. We cannot help recalling a meeting held during the past decade. George Counts, then active in university circles, was in an audience where the topic of his social reconstruction and his role with *The Social Frontier* were discussed and analyzed by young scholars. When their presentations were finished, Counts himself took the floor to complain that while much of the data revealed was accurate, their interpretations failed to assess his motives properly. Where the paper-readers concluded he was involved in a huge enterprise of social control—a kind of educational power-brokering—Counts himself maintained that his motives had nothing whatever to do with a comprehensive plan for social control. His investment, he said, was in the freedom of teachers to function fully as citizens and to give them, as professional persons, some voice in the policies of education. Thus, we see, the attribution of motive has its weak spots.

Tyack calls our attention to "administrative progressivism." It was illustrated, he says, in the adoption of the scientific method for school administration and the professional training of school executives.[7] Still, neither a science of school administration nor, for that matter, professional training for its practitioners would seem to have other than an accidental relationship to Progressive education. We need not doubt the progressive schoolmen's desire to have schools run efficiently, and they, too, must have been captivated by that American assignation with management. On the other hand, school administrators, in many cases converts to progressive ideology, were frequently sympathetic with the general direction taken by progressive schools. In the absence of better evidence, it is hard to accept the theory that school administration had any integral relationship to Progressive education. Yet Katz, following somewhat the same line, is convinced of this wedding of administration and progressivism and finds it less than praiseworthy. The men, he writes, who directed educational change espoused attitudes underlining "the essentially conservative nature of progressivism."[8] Besides being economically, socially, and racially biased, they embraced the doctrine that education was a means of social control. It could perform this role better in the dependable hands of efficient school administrators. Rather than being a radical movement, one prepared to put the destiny of society in the hands of the people, Progressive education is pictured as a movement which seldom had the fundamental good of the people at heart. This hypothesis runs almost directly counter to conventional views of Progressive education.

Similarly, to assign a principal motive of progressivism to various innovative practices is hazardous. It is easy to find an abundance of progressive educators promoting vocational and industrial education, but one looks in vain for any solid authentification of either in progressive creed. In the same way, the kindergarten, the junior high school, life-adjustment education, and the guidance movement had their adherents in progressive ranks, and there is a general sense in which all of these were evidences of educational progress. Convincing testimony making all these intrinsic elements in Progressive education has yet to be given.

The case for scientific pedagogy is easier to make. Both Katz and Tyack make it well.[9] Progressive education, we are led to believe, was more a method than anything else. As a method it should be clearly informed by those sciences capable of illuminating the nature of learning. So Progressive education, naturally enough, turned to scientific pedagogy and tried to improve it. Taking their basic naturalism into account, we are not surprised when progressive educators invested a good deal of confidence in physiological bases to learning. And whether scientific pedagogy is, indeed, a separate branch of educational progressivism has yet to be adequately demonstrated.

Progressive Education Theory

Without dismissing these sides to Progressive education, we turn here to follow the theory of Progressive education. When we do, our best guide is Lawrence Cremin's *The Transformation of the School.* He tells us how progressive thought found its way to teachers colleges where it converted a cadre of new teachers, and where it promoted school practices reinforced by the now thriving science of pedagogy.

As students passed through professional preparation, they were schooled in the creed of progressivism and, like their forebears, adopted education as a faith. But progressivism was more than faith: in the first place, the progressives took as their battle cry the perfectly sensible notion that education is more than book learning. Engaging pedagogic polemic they indicted schools as harbors of social and cultural myopia; life, they concluded in peroration, is too complex to be accounted for in the books. They wanted up-to-date educational practice employing all the techniques of scientific instruction. Teaching, long considered an art, now belonged to technicians, competent and skillful craftsmen capable of superintending instruction.

Besides, they embraced the child-centered school, using such overworked clichés as "we teach children not subjects," and, without becoming authentic disciples of Rousseau, nevertheless abandoned the conventional curriculum to allow students to follow an educational course of their own choosing. Knowledge appearing to have relevance to the student's life was praised by progressive teachers. The various elements of progressivism were held together by an almost frantic optimism that the good life—if only education measured up to its potential—is within the reach of all.

This progressive creed, hardly out of step with the generally progressive attitude of the people, and dressed up in ornamental language, was appealing. But idealism alone neither conducts schools nor teaches children, as progressive educators soon learned, so the more ambitious and able among them began to work along more serious academic lines.

Harold Rugg

Helped, no doubt, by the impression created in World War I that scientific method and psychological technique solve human problems, Harold Rugg (1886–1960) enlisted in progressive ranks and shortly became a leading figure. With a degree in civil engineering, Rugg turned abruptly to education and sociology and earned the Ph.D. degree from the University of Illinois in 1915. His mentor, later a leading Essentialist, was William C. Bagley.[10] In his early work in education, he demonstrated in books on educational statistics the worth of clear and demonstrable data for defining educational status and need. One side of progressivism, highly idealistic, was complemented, on the other, by an urgent positivism. But Rugg, who long occupied an important position in the progressive movement, went beyond tools of educational research and statistics: he addressed the urgent issue of child-centered schools. In a book by that name, written in 1928 with Ann Shumaker, he tried to put the child-centered school on a solid theoretical basis. This book, Peter Carbone says, in addition to emphasizing creative self-expression, defined the school's task "as one of drawing out the creative power which lay latent within every child."[11] Teachers were to be artists. Then he turned to another issue, one progressives wanted to capitalize: the reconstruction of society along lines making progress inevitable and guaranteeing human happiness and success was deployed as a doctrine of social engineering in his book *Culture and Education in America,* written in 1931. "It is now axiomatic," he wrote two years later, "that the production and distribution of goods can no longer be left to the vagaries of chance—specifically to the unbridled competitions of self-aggrandizing human nature."[12] This approach to social reconstruction, Carbone concludes, was too limited to be effective.[13] Leaving out social and political factors, he concentrated only on economic ones. In any case, Rugg recommended a social reconstruction based on design (a grand plan), consent (of the people), and technical skill in implementation. At every step education had a part to play.

This is but a glimpse of Rugg's work in connection with Progressive education. He wrote several books meant to shore up the foundations of the movement, to invest it with theory, and his social science textbooks were intended to awaken children to the realities of social life and inspire ideals of social reconstruction and regeneration.[14] He alone among the social reconstructionists succeeded in getting his books into the elementary and junior high schools throughout the country.[15] These books, however, put Rugg's reputation in some jeopardy. Always praised by his confreres, his critics saw a subversive element in his social science writing and called for the suppression of his books in the schools and his dethronement as a spokesman for American education.

Carbone is persuasive when he argues that these charges of subversive doctrine in Rugg's junior high-school textbooks (*Man and His Changing Society*) were groundless. He admits that Rugg praised Joseph Stalin and the social system of Soviet Russia, all the while missing the implications of its totalitarianism. Yet he thinks these books were purged from the schools (five million copies were sold in 1940, but sales dropped to twenty-one thousand by 1944) because of their criticism of American business practice and their habit of introducing controversial issues to the classroom rather than for a documented affinity to communism or socialism.[16]

While Rugg's excesses in promoting social engineering did not swamp him personally or professionally (for until the end of his life he was well-regarded among professional educators), they had the effect of discrediting Progressive education among large bodies of the lay public whose common sense said society was not subject to the laws conjured up by social scientists.

Resistance to social engineering, although slowing the scientific movement in education, did not stop it. When Edward L. Thorndike made his famous pronouncement that whatever "exists exists in some amount . . . [and that] to know something thoroughly means to know its quantity as well as its quality,"[17] he gave credence to a proposition which, while widely circulated, offended common sense and was often judged intellectually subversive. Most men knew some of life's realities could neither be weighed nor measured. We remember the controversy surrounding the Army tests administered during World War I and know of extravagant claims for measuring intellectual ability countered by arguments that nothing of the sort was possible. Still, progressive educators were supremely confident of the worth of measuring instruments produced by the sciences of psychology and education and were determined to use them to classify students according to ability, interest, and achievement.

Measurement brewed another problem, although one only tangential to school practice. In the debate over mental measurement, assertions were sometimes made by proponents of measurement on the meaning of mental age. They even talked about average mental age. This somewhat technical terminology, with useful but limited meaning, caused friction and misunderstanding when used indiscriminately. In the last analysis, to make and defend generalizations about the average mental age for Americans being fourteen, called into question the validity of mental measurement and the good sense of those who referred to an average American mentality. If these assertions were taken at face value, as was sometimes the case, it meant that many students in high schools and colleges lacked mental acumen to attend them. In another vein, the argument was made that schools, for all their extravagant claims, were unable to prepare persons for the serious business of life. For most students, these derisive critics said, schooling was waste for legitimate learning and could only be regarded as propaganda for maintaining the status quo.[18]

Curriculum Theories

Controversy raged: no sooner had critics tired of indicting schools than Progressive educators went to work showing how schools could speak directly to the issues of life. Too much in the curriculum, they alleged, was of little or no value; it should be purged and replaced with the minimum essentials necessary for living a good and decent life in American society.

The list of curriculum theorists is long, and its recitation unnecessary, but Franklin Bobbitt stood out. In 1924 Bobbitt published *How to Make a Curriculum.* He likened the builder of curricula to a "great engineer," and assumed social engineers were able, through analysis, to find the skills and competencies of life and then put them in the curriculum where students could master them.[19] Surprisingly enough, this job-analysis formula had a good deal of support among Progressive educators who believed, mistakenly as it turned out, that such formulas could improve the quality of curricula and enhance the character of life. As constant critics of the status quo, they should have known that this formula, even had it been possible to manage an analysis of life, would have rendered social change unlikely or impossible. They were, moreover, unwilling to define what they meant by "the good and happy life."

Curriculum building—an immensely important part of educational work—was simply unamenable to the pretensions of Bobbitt and the social engineers; but curriculum alone could hardly be expected to reconstruct society. Never actually pronounced a failure, the minimum essential approach to curriculum nevertheless failed, and Progressive education eventually discarded it altogether, but the idea itself proved durable enough to be revived later.[20] Success of an idea is convincing; failure seldom.

The Play School

Among the many trial-and-error features associated with Progressive education, some conspired to give the movement a bad name; none, however, was better at this than the play school. Accepting totally the child-centered doctrine, play-school promoters—the most illustrious was Caroline Pratt—wanted to give schoolchildren a variety of direct experience and render traditional schoolrooms obsolete. Instruction began with trips to parks, zoos, all manner of public places, and children returning to school were given various play materials—blocks, paints, toys, and clay—to portray what they had seen. Imaginative and creative capacity was put to work and while it was exploited, so play school advocates said, the usual outcomes of elementary teaching were recorded: reading, writing, arithmetic, history, geography, the arts, and physical education were all accounted for, but in an entirely unstructured and unpatterned way. A day in school was a day at play.[21]

Caroline Pratt said the schoolchild was an artist engrossed in making a personal interpretation of reality and, she wrote, "he is dominated by a desire to clarify this idea for *himself*. It is incidental to his purpose to clarify it for others."[22] Expressionism had partisans outside education, for in these years cadres of idealistic Americans, believing culture to be on the verge of a renaissance, cultivated and patronized literature, painting, music, and architecture to the end of overcoming the bleakness and aridity which, they said, characterized American life. With enthusiastic support from various quarters, the play school made its mark, but, as it turned out, the mark was on a branch, not on the trunk of American education. "The creative impulse is within the child himself," Rugg wrote in *The Child-Centered School*,[23] and proponents of the play school predicted that this discovery assured the efficacy of schooling. Among the innovations in centuries of educational history, they appeared convinced, this one, the play school, wherein the creative capacity of children was released, was the most consequential of all. Nothing, they boasted, could match it.

When progressive educators embraced the play school, they knew of its success in special schools with talented children, so it would be wrong to write off claims for the play school as hyperbole. But plucking a school practice from an especially conducive setting and using it in an ordinary schoolroom was a disaster. What in ideal circumstances produced artistry and unleashed creativity, under conventional school conditions elicited, Lawrence Cremin says, "every manner of shoddiness and self-deception. . . . In too many classrooms license began to pass for liberty, planlessness for spontaneity, recalcitrance for individuality, obfuscation for art, and chaos for education."[24] And the vocabulary of progressive educators justified this under the rubric of expressionism.

Such school practices were hard to conceal, and too many progressive educators, captivated by their pedagogic invention, rejected critical evaluation. In the eyes of the public this was not creative learning but nonsense, and the most articulate critics of progressivism were given ammunition to bombard its citadel for generations. Play schools generated a barbed humor insufficient to conceal a tragic irony: the lost time and weak skills of children in the hands of inartistic play-school teachers could seldom be recovered.

Yet if play schools were perversions of the child-centered doctrine, or extreme and unjustified exploitations of it, there was another side. It bore better fruit. At about the time the child-centered school captivated Progressive education, Sigmund Freud's interpretations of human nature and behavior were introduced to America. In 1909, for example, Freud lectured at Clark University, appearing under the sponsorship of its president, G. Stanley Hall. Within the next two decades Freud's psychological theories were translated to pedagogy and hundreds of teachers were educated according to the precepts of Freudian pedagogy.

Freud was represented as downgrading the teacher's function as a communicator of information and a hearer of lessons. Teaching should abound in opportunity for children to sublimate anti-social behavior.[25] A few schools were organized along these lines—the best known was Children's School, founded by Margaret Naumburg in 1915[26]—but neither Freudian theory nor its implied pedagogic practice had a profound effect on American schools. And their followers were regarded as having missed the mainstream of progressivism. Freud's theory had an effect, however, and a lasting one, on child-study, a movement with progressive partisans but one whose appeal ranged far beyond Progressive education.

Problem Solving

Flirting briefly with job-analysis curricula, progressive educators soon perceived the inherent obstacles to social reform, so they searched for something more representative of their hope for a better world. The function of education, they now proclaimed, was invested less in the realization of specific skill and more in problem-solving ability. Schools should teach children how to think. William Heard Kilpatrick was the herald for problem solving.

Kilpatrick, briefly encountering John Dewey in 1898 at the University of Chicago, appears to have neglected Dewey's philosophy and educational theory. Nine years later, however, Kilpatrick enrolled as a graduate student at Teachers College, Columbia University, and after graduation distinguished himself as a progressive educator. Early scholarly work led to publication on Dutch schools in colonial New York, Montessorian methods, and the kindergarten theories of Froebel, but he abandoned historical scholarship to enlist in the progressive crusade.[27]

Always faithful to progressivism, his special goal was to develop a method wherein Thorndike's Connectionism, which he endorsed, would complement Dewey's social objectives, which he approved. Kilpatrick's reconciliation of the law of effect with social purpose became the celebrated project method. His best remembered book, *Foundations of Method* (1925), was a thorough elaboration of project method teaching; a method henceforth indelibly stamped on Progressive education.

From Dewey Kilpatrick borrowed the notion that schools with superior social environments would enable children to learn what they lived, and went on to criticize methods of traditional education which, Kilpatrick thought, stunted moral and social formation. "As I see it," he wrote, "our schools have in the past chosen from the whole of life certain intellectualistic tools (skills and knowledges), have arranged these under the heads of reading, arithmetic, geography, and so on, and have taught these separately as if they would, when once acquired, recombine into the worthy life. This now seems to me to be very far from sufficient. Not only do these things not make up the whole of life, but we have so fixed attention upon the separate teaching of these as at times to starve the weightier matters of life and character. The only way to learn to live well is to practice living well."[28] To practice living well meant the adoption of the project method.

Translated to school practice the project was a series of problems originating in the student's own experience; and it was up to him to solve them. Teachers neither supplied nor formulated problems, although they were ready to help students whenever asked. The project method, deployed by Kilpatrick, involved four steps: identifying a problem with the intention of solving it, and intention was lodged in personal need; formulating a plan for solution; putting the plan into practice; and, finally, evaluating the solution. It was essential for teachers to remain aloof from the various steps of the project. Its principal value, popularizers said, was a non-directive chance to learn to think.

Problem-solving technique had merit, and we think few teachers were disposed to ignore it, but many educators, as it turned out, were reluctant to put the entire weight of learning on this method. Kilpatrick could appeal to Dewey for an endorsement of problem solving, for Dewey had employed it in the Laboratory School and praised it in books as a way to facilitate thinking. But Dewey recommended problem solving in a curriculum stripped of archaic features, revitalized by issues of contemporary social life and subjected to structure and design. Dewey, critical of conventional curricula, advocated reorganization rather than abandonment of subject matter. In experimental schools and books he promoted curricular reform. Kilpatrick, and Progressive education generally, refused to follow Dewey's prudent course. Unable to acknowledge the worth of fixed subject matter, Kilpatrick and progressive teachers invested confidence in problems arising in personal experience. Planning, executing, and judging as students wrestled with problems was the progressive definition of superior learning; and the curriculum, if the word is right, was characterized as emerging.[29]

Kilpatrick's progressive influence was immense: a popular writer, he was read eagerly by thousands of teachers and, as the senior philosophy of education professor at Teachers College, he taught hundreds of students who, in turn, became professors in other teachers colleges. A twenty-year professorship gave Kilpatrick a platform for popularizing Progressive education, and during this time its principal themes were infused with his interpretation and disposition. Kilpatrick's version of Progressive education was considered authentic by the rank and file. Still, in his custody educational theory withered. Concentrating on teaching technique, basic questions relative to human nature and educational objectives were slighted. Method had pride of place but this imbalance left Progressive education on uncertain ground, for it lacked the subsistence of theory, as Dewey charged.

Unquestionably Kilpatrick, wanting to follow Dewey, tried to translate Dewey's theories on social reconstruction and reorganization of experience into day-to-day teaching. In Kilpatrick's hands, however, Dewey's theories were sometimes hard to recognize. But Dewey, otherwise engaged, was indisposed to correct Kilpatrick; besides, he had already dismissed progressivism as education's savior. Still, Progressive education had sympathetic critics who, perceiving its promise, were disappointed at its lack of coherence and theoretic instability. The most prominent was Boyd H. Bode.[30]

Bode

Handicapped somewhat by location, Bode, with a good academic forum at Ohio State University, nevertheless began a theoretic excursion into Progressive education with the perfectly sensible assumption that teachers must not let students flounder without help. He praised the idealism of Progressive education and allied himself with educators wanting to build a better society; but he was critical of the faddism in Progressive education, especially the job-analysis approach to curriculum, and was skeptical of Kilpatrick's project method. Accepting Dewey's thesis that thinking is essentially problem solving, Bode acknowledged promising possibilities in a properly-managed project method technique. Yet the progressive willingness to relinquish learning to the felt needs of students troubled him. Education must have purpose, he maintained, and it cannot be found by manipulating statistics or gathering opinion: it comes from solid philosophic thought. The educational process needs direction, and direction is philosophy's business—a point, he thought, along with Dewey, where Progressive educators, and Kilpatrick chief among them, were weak or ambiguous. "Unless we know where we are going," he wrote in *Fundamentals of Education,* "there is not much comfort in being assured that we are on the way and traveling fast. . . . If education is to discharge its rightful function of leadership, it must clarify its guiding ideals."[31]

Guiding ideals, Bode said in *Modern Educational Theories,* were too often absent from progressive pedagogy; fault, he thought, rested heavily on the project method. Progressive education was attractive when it abandoned mechanical, perfunctory, and meaningless school practice, but in substituting projects for curricula "the emphasis on initiative and purposeful activity frequently suggests a mystic faith in a process of 'inner development' which requires nothing from the environment except to be let alone."[32] Instead of depending on students to dredge problems from limited experience, Bode commissioned schools to invest in the development and cultivation of intelligence so students would be able to meet the issues of the world. And the best preparation for this was schooling thoroughly infused with culture, for culture, he wrote, "means the capacity for constantly expanding in range and accuracy one's perception of meanings." Culture is essential to the realization of an ideal democracy.[33]

How schools could discharge this commission was an unanswered question, Bode's critics said. He was committed to a child-centered pedagogy, we know, and encouraged thinking. He wanted students equipped to live in the real world, but he rejected Kilpatrick's project method as just another formula. Bode recommended a wide range of techniques, to be adopted according to the learning situation, and demurred from anointing any one method. His attitude toward Progressive education, although temperate and friendly, encouraged some defection from progressive ranks, but did little to alter its course marked out mainly by Kilpatrick. Bode, however, revealed a weakness in Progressive education, already becoming doctrinaire and sometimes stridently committed to a preconception of authentic progressivism: a failure to concede that reform itself might be amended.[34]

Progressive education made its reputation trying to reform the conditions of learning, and for several years this appeared to be its charter. But in the late 1920s new perspective was added and now recommendation for educational change came from George S. Counts. Starting his career with a burning interest in scientific education, but seeing an overabundance of educational scientists and sensing the priority basic issues had over technique and science, he specialized in educational sociology and philosophy. Soon Counts had the reputation of a perceptive, eloquent social critic advocating that schools function as reforming agents in society.

Social criticism preceded Counts in America, so while hardly a pioneer in this enigmatic field, he, more than his predecessors, concentrated attention on schools. Famous muckrakers had exposed flagrant political and economic abuse and their work produced some good results; and Thorstein Veblen,[35] Upton Sinclair,[36] John Kirkpatrick,[37] and Harold Stearns,[38] in reviewing schools and colleges had been critical of their domination by industry and business. In the end, they concluded, the possibility of using schools and colleges to initiate social reform was remote so long as their control was vested in special interests. Why, they argued, use energy and talent to reform schools—making them better places for learning—when success was all but foreclosed by the strong hand of economic authority and power?

Concurring, Counts took this analysis as his point of departure and throughout a long and frequently controversial career attempted to wrestle educational control from special interests. Adopting the progressive creed of social reconstruction to achieve an ideal democratic society, Counts put the schools in the vanguard of social reform. In an audacious, popular book, *Dare the School Build a New Social Order?*, Counts defined the school's role as social transformation and commissioned the curriculum, especially of high schools, to concern itself forthrightly with issues whose resolution could ensure more effective democracy. And educators themselves should wade in the political stream, thus jettisoning the old assumption that teachers serve learning best by eschewing political alliances. Educational activism originated with Counts' crusade for social reform.

The Progressive education Counts ratified in various books, and especially as editor of the periodical *Social Frontier,* refused to curtail attention to pure pedagogy, heretofore its trademark. Counts and his cadre of followers were interested in better teaching, in fresh and imaginative schools. Ready to endorse any method whose effectiveness could be demonstrated, their preoccupation was with learning's social goals.[39]

So Progressive education, with broader dimensions and clearer, sometimes radical, social commitments, began to stray from the classroom. This lost some early converts who were afraid Progressive education was being unfaithful to its charge, but defection on this score was minor compared to another allegation. Radical change, Counts asserted, was essential to democracy's vitality, and preaching radical change left progressive educators vulnerable to the charge of subversion. Aspersions of un-Americanism were cast and strident critics tried to prove an affinity of Progressive education to a Communist plot to destroy the American republic.[40]

With its many sides Progressive education had a variety of spokesmen, so there was imprecision and confusion about what it stood for and its dominating theme. Even the publications on purpose and conviction by the Progressive Education Association (1918–1955) were unrepresentative of progressivism as a whole. Yet, with caution, they can be taken as generally illustrative of an idealism shared by all progressives. The Association's aim was to reform the schools of the United States, but in 1955, when the Association disbanded, its staunchest admirers admitted that this aim went largely unrealized. Progressive education certainly altered the character of elementary and secondary education, although the durability of its alteration can be debated. Colleges and universities were almost totally immune to it. Naturally Teachers College was affected, for the oasis for progressive thought was there, and signs of progressivism were evident in Bennington College of Vermont and the General College of the University of Minnesota.[41] But apart from a few examples, progressive experiments in higher learning were limited and usually inconsequential.

With eloquent support, novelty, and, most important of all, a generally progressive attitude in American society, why did Progressive education, after a short period of promise and prosperity, atrophy in American schools? Lawrence Cremin has an explanation.[42]

Evidencing some surprise that a sturdy movement of earlier years declined rapidly during and after World War II, Cremin nevertheless detects signs of decay in Progressive education itself. We have noticed the various offshoots of the progressive movement and are uncertain about the direction of the main crusade. Rugg's curricular disposition took one direction; Kilpatrick's projects another; and Counts chose to give special attention to a side of progressivism whose pedagogic affinities were obscure. Besides, variety, faction, and emphasis had their own clientele. Internal warring drained some of Progressive education's reforming zeal, but this was by no means the whole story or even its most important chapter: early progressives had set a fairly positive course, although their descendants were tempted to criticize traditional schools and saturate the literature with slogans. Parker, for example, demonstrated in Quincy what progressive teaching could accomplish; too many progressives in the following decades condemned old-fashioned schools without demonstrating how their own methods were superior. Fanatic but imprudent converts thought clichés and slogans convincing, but the public, demanding better evidence, remained largely unpersuaded.

At its best Progressive education was capable of conducting extraordinarily efficient schools. But such schools usually had talented teachers and students; too many teachers who embraced progressive practice lacked ingenuity and art, and too many students were indisposed to manage their own learning. In the hands of good teachers progressive pedagogy was an ornament to learning; in the custody of average teachers it was a lackluster educational experience. Some objective observers indicted run-of-the-mill progressive schools as being worse than traditional schools. Perhaps, in the end, Progressive education was swamped by excessive ambition.

Progressive educators were so aggressive they continued the charge after the battle was won. Some progressive practice was too infectious for alert teachers to miss, so they adopted it but refused enlistment in progressive ranks. Thus, when progressives excoriated schools for being unprogressive, their denunciations either fell on deaf ears or were ridiculed for their ignorance of educational reality.

Progressivism in America, we know, was an ideology not fully accounted for in its educational activity. Progressive education was fed in part by a strong progressive spirit in the country, and so long as that spirit remained intact Progressive education benefited. But with the end of World War II progressive spirit atrophied in an almost inevitable shift toward conservativism. Progressive education felt this shift too, although it could have been spared had it been more than a cult: now we hear a word with a strange ring, educationist. Only educationists were awarded full credentials in the cult, so as outsiders, the lay public, with final authority over the destiny of education, refused to leap to Progressive education's defense when it was jeopardized.

All these factors, Cremin alleges, speeded the descent of Progressive education from heights reached in the years prior to World War II, but as important as any of the preceding reasons was an American society changing too fast for Progressive education's pace; society, Cremin says, outgrew, and dated, Progressive education.[43] The interpretation is plausible, but another reason conspired to put Progressive education in a bad light. It had been infused, by Counts and others, with reforming zeal and, as we have seen, social reform was frequently suspiciously regarded as being either itself subversive or a tool of conspirators. Communism, unquestionably antithetical to American ideals, became a serious menace; if Progressive education, or any of its promoters, were in league with Communism, suppression was the best remedy. Neither the loyalty nor patriotism of any progressive educator need now be questioned, but the apparition of radical social reformers controlling schools was a cause for alarm and Progressive education was an inevitable and innocent victim.

All together these reasons spelled out the decline of Progressive education in the decade after World War II.

ESSENTIALISM

Progressive education's decline, due to a variety of factors, not the least of which was an excessive ambition to leave nothing undone, can be ascribed in part to internal decay, but a vigorous and vehement opposition should be alluded to as well. Labeled early as the epitome of soft pedagogy, Progressive education was never entirely able to change its image from a kind of learning depending solely on the interests of children and with a fundamental disrespect for the validity and stability of knowledge. Critics noted these points and capitalized them in an assault on progressive schooling: these were the Essentialists. Progressive education, they charged, stressed interest, individualism, and freedom (all, when properly balanced, meritorious), but forgot discipline, authority, truth, and tradition.

Traditional schools, Essentialists agreed, had lost their way and could stand improvement. But their perception of improvement was not discarding from the curriculum a common core to basic culture. Teachers should be better educated, not more highly trained as technicians; schools should be stripped of their dour demeanor and become pleasant places where children would take seriously the hard work of learning; and technique could embrace some elements of the project and activity methods in order to revitalize teaching. These reforms would embrace the school's principal mission of transmitting culture and intellectual refinement which, Essentialists alleged, progressive schools conspired to neglect.

William C. Bagley, of Teachers College, Columbia University, surrounded by Progressive education's most enthusiastic promoters, became, in the 1930s, its leading critic and a principal spokesman for Essentialism. *School and Society*, a respectable educational journal founded and edited by Bagley, was commissioned to hobble progressivism. And while this commission was too great to fulfill, the journal's pages carried regular reminders of weaknesses and shortcomings in progressive practice. Essentialism's posture was partly negative and its motivation sprang from an abhorrence of progressivism, but Essentialists were for something too: they wanted schools to teach the fundamentals—reading, writing, arithmetic, history, and English in an atmosphere where discipline and obedience could be cultivated.[44]

Regular promotion without regard to academic achievement was lamented by Nicholas Murray Butler, and he used various illustrations of learning's neglect to deplore the general and abrupt decline in academic standard. Bagley himself went beyond allegations of academic disappointment and accused progressive schools of contributing to a general decline in national morality. The jails, he said, were filled with examples of discipline neglected in schools, and the appalling record of crime could be attributed to the feebleness and vacuity of teaching infected by progressivism. Essentialistically oriented journals conducted surveys of academic accomplishment and published their dismay: the history of the republic was sorely neglected, knowledge of geography was deficient, and the basic facts of science and the fundamental operations of mathematics were absent from the repertoire of students from progressive schools. Indictments were severe and alarming; if only a few were true, the schools needed repair. The best and most economical repair, Essentialists argued, was a return to the essentials of learning.

While progressive advocates countered allegations, hard evidence of ineptitude could neither be concealed nor argued away. Parents, teachers, and professors (the latter were often eloquent) exhibited anxiety, naturally they were solicitous of the kind and quality of education for succeeding generations and could not have been silent. Still, the case for or against Progressive education was indecisive: more evidence was sought.

In 1938, J. W. Wrightstone published an *Appraisal of Newer Elementary School Practices*,[45] the account of a study comparing progressive with traditional school practice. Progressive schools appeared to have a slightly better record in teaching reading, but traditional schools were judged superior in spelling and arithmetic. If a general conclusion were to be drawn from this study, it would be that neither progressive nor traditional schools were clearly superior; so after all the debate, the financial expenditure, the reorganization of curricula, and realignment of method, one school, it seemed, was about as good as another. This judgment, if disappointing to progressives, discouraged Essentialists also. In the same year, however, another study published results applauding progressivism.

Beginning in 1930, the Eight-Year Study, involving thirty secondary schools and three hundred colleges, was mounted. Its purpose, apart from proving the efficacy of Progressive education, was to promote progressive practice in high schools; published reports were sympathetic to the work of progressive schools and sometimes went out of the way to praise them. Graduates of the thirty participating high schools were compared in their college work with graduates of conventional high schools and the study's conclusions were favorable to progressive schools.[46] Still, the case for Progressive education on the high-school level was unconvincing, for no sooner had the reports of the study appeared than Essentialists criticized both the design of the study and its objectivity.[47] In the end, and based only on evidence produced from studies comparing academic performance, the historian declares the issue debatable.

But Essentialism's assertions with respect to educational quality were independent of studies and research reports: they were rooted in the conviction that healthy societies require intellectually alert and decently educated citizens capable of settling into the traditions of Western culture; and to this end a mastery of the essentials of basic culture is vital.

America's entry into World War II had the effect of distracting both professional educators and the public from battles waged over Progressive education in preceding decades, and so for a while the educational issues begetting such ferment hibernated. With the war's end, however, progressive spirit was rekindled and a new direction for Progressive education was established. In the earlier years of the progressive movement, elementary education had attracted most attention and school practice was shaped along lines applicable to the first years of schooling. Now, however, an emphasis was put on secondary schools, and in 1946 five regional meetings were convened under the auspices of the United States Commissioner of Education, John W. Studebaker, to ponder the place of vocational education in the years ahead. Attendance at these regional meetings was by invitation, although it was expected that participants would represent a variety of educational interest. Yet no professors from arts and sciences colleges and universities were invited. The regional meetings recommended a broadening of vocational education into what was called "life adjustment education" and the appointment of a commission on Life Adjustment Education for Youth.[48]

In the following year a commission was appointed and from this commission Progressive education received a new charter: to promote life adjustment, a kind of education designed to equip "all American youth to live democratically with satisfaction to themselves and profit to society as home members, workers, and citizens."[49] The commission itself recommended an education for life adjustment emphasizing "active and creative achievements as well as an adjustment to existing conditions; it places a high premium upon learning to make wise choices, since the very concept of American democracy demands the appropriate revising of aims and the means of attaining them."[50] The commission was active for the next half-dozen years and prepared reports whose effect on the character of secondary schools was considerable. In general acceptance, life adjustment education may have been Progressive education's most effective thrust; it was also its last.

Almost silent during the war, Essentialists now renewed their attack on what was considered to be the worst side of progressivism: life adjustment. And Essentialist arguments were strengthened by changing conditions in American society: during the war a moratorium had been declared on school construction, but now, if the public were to make a huge investment in schools, educational direction should be clear; communism was threatening democratic values in the nation, so schools should be chastened of any semblance of subversive ideology, and life adjustment was somehow suspect; and, finally, talking about life adjustment seemed to make poor educational sense when society needed skillful people to conduct the business of American life. An attack on Progressive education was renewed, more thorough, vigorous, and insistent than before.[51]

Criticisms leveled at Progressive education, coming mainly from the Essentialist camp, make good reading even today; their authors, skillful and persuasive writers, had, they thought, a good case and wanted to make the most of it. The list of books and articles condemning progressive and life adjustment education is long, too long to exhibit any but the most prominent: Bernard Iddings Bell, in *Crisis in Education,* chastised the schools for their complicity in failing to promote sound learning and coddling American youth. It added up, he alleged, to a huge, costly educational program capable of producing nothing but mediocrity. The schools, in grasping for functions belonging properly to parents, churches, and other social agencies, were swamped in an overabundance of responsibility and neglected most the one thing they should have cultivated first: decent learning. The public, Bell wrote, should regain control of schools and set them right.

Along somewhat the same lines, Mortimer Smith, in *And Madly Teach,* indicted the whole establishment of educationists, charging them with intellectual and moral myopia, on one hand, and an adherence to an insidious party line, on the other. According to Smith, ". . . if anyone will take the trouble to investigate, it will be found that those who make up the staffs of the schools and colleges of education, and the administrators and teachers whom they train to run the system, have a truly amazing uniformity of opinion regarding the aims, the content, and the methods of education. They constitute a cohesive body of believers with a clearly formulated set of dogmas and doctrines, and they are perpetuating the faith by seeing to it, through state laws and rules of state departments of education, that only those teachers and administrators are certified who have been trained in correct dogma."[52] Smith recommended throwing out the "educationist" rascals and replacing them with persons who respected and understood education's historic role as an intellectual and moral teacher.

Bell and Smith published their books in 1949; four years later Albert Lynd's *Quakery in the Public Schools,* Arthur Bestor's *Educational Wastelands,* Robert Hutchins' *The Conflict in Education,* and Paul Woodring's *Let's Talk Sense About Our Schools* appeared; and the year following, Mortimer Smith's *The Diminished Mind,* and, in 1955, Arthur Bestor's *The Restoration of Learning.* While a brief, competent summary of these books would be difficult, their general thesis may be fairly stated as: returning to the schools their legitimate intellectual purpose by stressing once again the academic disciplines; assigning to public schools the function of providing all citizens with a basic education; reintroducing scholarship to schooling and educating teachers not in pedagogy but in the arts and sciences; and finally, returning control of schools to parents, withdrawing it from the hands of professional educators, and rewriting certification requirements for teachers in order to promote scholarship and educational decency and demote pedagogy and teacher training. If Hyman Rickover, in *Education and Freedom,* assessed the American attitude toward schools correctly, then Progressive education was about ready to surrender to Essentialism and good sense would again prevail in the schools: "Parents are no longer satisfied with life-adjustment schools. Parental objectives no longer coincide with those professed by the professional educationists."[53]

PHILOSOPHY OF EDUCATION

Neither Progressive education nor Essentialism was a philosophy of education: both were preoccupied with questions of curriculum and method without integration in established and systematic philosophy. Yet both cultivated a revival of interest in educational philosophy, for in the last analysis it was philosophy—fundamental educational theory—educators would have to consult to illuminate their plan for the education of the nation's youth. So while battles were waged in public print and elsewhere over the merits and demerits of Progressive and Essential education, educational philosophers, in their studies and classrooms, began to sharpen their philosophic tools.

We have followed American education long enough to know of its interest in educational philosophy; long before the progressive period philosophy influenced the definition of schooling. But in earlier days educational philosophy, wedded to general philosophy, appeared as a paragraph or a footnote in broad philosophical discourse; now it was studied as an independent discipline with authentic academic credentials. And much was expected from it, for the American public sensed that education was in trouble and called on philosophers for help to set a steady course for education to follow.

Philosophy, we know, had played this role before; throughout most of its history American education was infused with the spirit of Idealist philosophy, and the progressive reform was unquestionably a reaction to educational Idealism. There is, indeed, a disposition to believe that Essentialism was nothing more than an expression of the Idealist creed and, as such, an effort to regain control over education lost at the end of the nineteenth century. While Idealists may have infiltrated Essentialism, it would be extremely difficult to prove where Essentialism had either a special affinity for or an indebtedness to Idealism. Even the most prominent of Idealist educational philosophers, Herman H. Horne, who in his book *The Democratic Philosophy of Education* followed Dewey's *Democracy and Education* almost page by page giving an idealist interpretation to basic issues in educational theory, and sounded Essentialistic in many of his pronouncements, chose to retain his independence from Essentialism.[54] Yet Horne's extraordinary scholarship, his cogent and persuasive writing could neither revive Idealism nor restore it to a position of influence in American education.

The main reason for Idealism's loss of influence was the temper of America and a decline in devotion to religion, for Idealism, even without denominational allegiance, was intensely spiritual and regarded man, on whom any educational theory would have to concentrate, as an extension of an absolute or divine spirit. Idealism, moreover, departed from a common-sense explanation of metaphysics when it described reality as being spiritual rather than material. In twentieth-century America, when materialism came close to being a way of life, it was hard to be convincing about spiritual reality. But the metaphysics of Idealism while an important obstacle to its acceptance among teachers and educational theorists, was not the only deterrent: Idealists doubted the possibility of securing valid knowledge through the usual channels of sensory experience, for knowledge had an intuitive and cultural component immunizing it from the ordinary processes of discursive learning.

But these more esoteric philosophical considerations may not have bothered the educational public as much as the Idealist's definition of objectives and his deployment of the educational process. In an age when everyone was acutely aware of his body and when an abundance of psychological literature reminded teachers and students alike of the significance of mind/body relationships, the Idealists talked only about the development of the mind and seemed not to care whether students brought their bodies to school with them. Refinement of the intellect alone counted and to achieve it the educational process should be hard and rigorous, the curriculum should depend almost entirely on an accumulated wisdom contained in the books, and the methods devised through years of attention to a physiology of learning were ignored.[55] The American experience with schools conducted according to Idealist prescript had not been good, and memories of nineteenth-century educational practice dominated by Idealism were still too fresh to justify turning back the educational calendar. So, except for a historic interest in its pronouncements concerning ends and means of education, Idealism was jettisoned from its position of influence. Concurrently with its demise, other educational philosophies competed for places as theoretic directors of American schools: Pragmatism, Realism, and Humanism. The future of educational theory, and to some extent the future of American education, was in their hands.

PRAGMATISM

As a systematic philosophy, Pragmatism had strong American ties, for here it was rescued from philosophic oblivion and elevated to an organized and orderly system of thought about the world and its operations. Centuries before Pragmatism was cultivated on this side of the Atlantic by Charles Sanders Peirce, William James, and John Dewey, it had exerted some influence as a tributary of philosophy. Beginning with the question of the dependability of knowledge, ancient philosophers (the pre-Socratics and Heraclitus, we are told) expressed reasonable doubt about arriving at truth in a world whose most persistent reality was change. Even the ancient Sophists, who pretended to an ability to teach anyone anything, endorsed a fundamental skepticism, and one, it would appear, enabling them to make good their arrogant claim of being masters of all knowledge. The point was, of course, that if truth were unattainable, then opinion alone existed; and on the level of opinion, one is as good as another. Assuming a stance of rectitude, they extolled rhetoric, whose claim to fame was augmented in the absence of truth, because without truth the opinion to be followed should be the one supported by the best argument. In addition to skepticism, however, which always had some affinity to modern Pragmatism, these ancient Pragmatists refused to wed themselves to any principle or practice simply because it was reasonable: their test was result. Thus, almost from the outset, philosophy was given a Pragmatic hue and we should not be surprised to discover that it had enough durability to enter the modern world.

As philosophy matured, passing through its Christian and Medieval stages, it concurred in the logical paradigms of Aristotle, who had refined deductive methods of arriving at knowledge. Deduction, it must be admitted, took philosophy a long way and contributed some of the great ornaments of philosophical thought, but deduction was challenged in the seventeenth century by Francis Bacon (1561–1626) in his *Novum Organum,* and thereafter had to share a place with induction as a method of arriving at dependable knowledge. At this point Pragmatism again infected philosophy and became an important intellectual force as men pondered their existence and its meaning. Then two intellectual movements were mounted giving Pragmatism new vigor and strengthening it for an assault on the future: *Positive Philosophy,* by August Comte (1789–1857), accounted for one, wherein the meaning of reality was subject to the conditions and possibilities of the scientific method; the other was *Origin of Species,* by Charles Darwin (1809–1882), a disturbing challenge to the conventional theistic definition of man's nature.

American Pragmatism built on this foundation, and its first builders, apart from a general pragmatic disposition almost indigenous to America, were Charles Sanders Peirce (1839–1914), William James (1842–1910), and John Dewey (1859–1952). Whether or not Peirce was an authentic Pragmatist, as Pragmatism evolved in final form, is debated, but in any event his purpose was to bridge the gap which he believed existed between the subjectivism of modern philosophy and the objectivity of knowledge revealed by scientific method. Accomplishing this to his own satisfaction, he pronounced the Pragmatic criterion: the meaning of an idea is determined by putting it to use in the real world; whatever its consequences, they are its meaning.[56]

William James, one of America's most famous psychologists, found Pragmatism useful, although he did not endorse all its principles of knowledge and reality, and was instrumental in popularizing it, thus breaking ground for the systematic work of John Dewey. In 1896 James published a small book entitled *Pragmatism,* setting the stage for its general acceptance and further development.

John Dewey's philosophic itinerary is both long and complex: beginning as a Realist, he turned briefly to Idealism, and finally found himself in the role of Pragmatism's most important and erudite spokesman. In the last analysis, it was Dewey who shaped Pragmatism as a philosophic creed.

Dewey's brand of Pragmatism began by taking seriously two positions: the evolutionary hypothesis and the conviction that educational philosophy is the ultimate product of philosophic thinking and that schools are its testing ground.[57] Embracing evolution had the effect of putting Pragmatism outside the conventional boundaries of philosophies of man; inside these boundaries man was regarded distinctly from other forms of matter. But this was not all. Any doctrine making man a product of the evolutionary process was explicitly antagonistic to traditional religious attitudes regarding man's origin, nature, and destiny. Pragmatists were prepared to take man as they found him, and they found him an organism more highly developed than any other form of matter, but not different in kind: man was one with nature. Not now a creature of God or even a distinct species composed of mind and matter, man was subject to all the forces of nature which combine to make him what he is. Pragmatism's philosophy of man represented his evolution in three stages, beginning with the biological, running through the psychological, and ending at the final and highest stage, the sociological. The genius of education, Pragmatists were quick to say, was making men active agents in the world, promoting them from private and subjective experience to sensitivity in social relations and schooling them for useful and responsible membership in the community.[58]

In addition to blazing new trails in the philosophy of man, Dewey adopted the doctrine that change is the only fundamental reality: everything is in a constant state of flux, nothing remains the same. Under these circumstances room for conventional metaphysics and time for talk about reality in general were lacking, for in a world without stability it was pointless to identify ultimates, substances, and essences. In this world, as described by Pragmatist writers, the possibility of arriving at truth is foreclosed, but this did not leave men helpless, for they had tested hypotheses to depend on. In any case, there was nothing else. But this, the Pragmatist said, was better than it sounded: tested hypotheses are forged by methods of science and these methods should be employed with all human problems. While this approach offended traditional conceptions of truth, it nevertheless enabled men to deal directly with day-to-day reality. Action will not be hobbled by myth of truth. And, finally, Dewey's viewpoint embraced the criterion advanced earlier by Peirce: in order to determine the meaning of an idea, it must be put to practice; the consequences constitute its meaning.[59]

What, one may inquire, has this philosophy of Pragmatism to do with education? First, Dewey meant Pragmatic philosophy to be an expression of his pedagogic creed. Pragmatism described man, knowledge, reality; it was up to schools to make their instructional programs conform to this description; it was their responsibility to confront human and material reality as it is and not according to some antiquated, mystical interpretation of the nature of man and the world. Following Pragmatic doctrine faithfully, it is hard, or impossible, to state precise educational objectives or to construct a curriculum. Knowledge is not education's goal; a valid and effective experience is: from good school experiences and, too, from learning how to experience effectively, students will be better prepared for the indeterminate world. Only in the most general way are they being prepared for life in society, because, if the doctrine of change is taken

seriously, who can predict the future needs of life?[60] All this, according
to Dewey, leads to social efficiency, and education for social efficiency,
it was averred, is the finest objective of all.

On the level of school practice Pragmatism and Progressive education
had something in common, for much of the pedagogy invented in progressive schools was compatible with intimations of Pragmatic school
practice. The experimental method, Dewey said, is the method of learning,
and applies to all avenues of intellectual and moral human endeavor;
children's interests must be capitalized, for interest stimulates a reorganization of experience.[61] And, as in Progressive education, the child-centered
school was adopted without reservation. Facts and subject matter are
incidental to the process of experiencing, but here, as we have said, Dewey
parted company with progressive educators who were indifferent to the
content of experience. While Dewey agreed that subject matter lacked
inherent value, it was, nevertheless, a way of having worthwhile formative
and developmental experiences and, in Dewey's view, some experiences
were more formative and developmental than others.[62] Where progressive
educators trusted student interest entirely, Dewey wanted students guided
toward socially useful experience. But in the process of experiencing,
the principal technique was problem solving. According to Dewey, the
best education would produce persons capable of effective thinking, and
thinking was, he said, essentially a matter of problem solving.[63] The
school, Dewey maintained, and often he sounded authentically progressive, was responsible for giving children experience with the best kind
of living possible on their level of maturity, for in the last analysis, all
pragmatists agree, education is life itself.

Pragmatism's appeal to education, to teachers, and sometimes to students should not be discounted. It matured along with Progressive education to become a dominant force in American education, but unlike
progressivism it continued to thrive as an American philosophy after
Progressive education declined.

REALISM

The philosophic roots of Realism are as deep in the history of thought
as those of Pragmatism and, over the centuries, were cultivated a good
deal more energetically. Pragmatism flourished, as we have said, but
always on the fringe of accepted and authoritative philosophic doctrine
until almost the twentieth century; Realism, on the other hand, stabilized
by a conviction that a real and knowable world exists independently of
the knower, was always close enough to common sense to become a
philosophy of a majority of men. For centuries the contending philosophical traditions had been associated with Plato, an Idealist, and Aristotle,

a Realist, and the verdict of history, it can be said, went to Aristotle and Realism.

Still, we know, American education was much influenced by Idealism during the nineteenth century, and with the advent of the twentieth century it was Pragmatism that led the fight to reform educational philosophy. Had Pragmatism been compatible with the basic principles of Realism, then Realism would have lain dormant as an American philosophy, but Pragmatism represented interpretations of reality and knowledge unacceptable both to Realist and Idealist philosophers. Thus in a rupture with Idealism, Realism parted company also with a revitalized and systematized Pragmatism just appearing on the twentieth-century scene. More precisely, Idealism was rejected in the first decade of the century by the New Realism; Pragmatism was challenged by Critical Realists who came a few years later.[64] Comfortable, too, with the general theses of Realist philosophy, and properly speaking extensions of it, were systems of philosophic thought designated either as logical positivism or logical empiricism. But it was left to Critical Realism to formulate both a general and effective philosophy of education, and the conclusion reached must have given a good deal of comfort to Essentialists, whose position we already know.

Educational philosophers adopting Realism hastened to apply its theses to schooling. So Henry C. Morrison, Frederick S. Breed, William C. Bagley, Ross L. Finney, and Harry S. Broudy, in writing and teaching, became Realist spokesmen, and they meant to reject the propositions of Pragmatism and especially to denounce its assignation with soft pedagogy.[65] Beginning with a decent respect for the stubborn facts of science, Realists stressed the worth of knowledge and asserted its stability: without a knowledge of the functioning of the natural world it would, they averred, be impossible for men to adjust to reality. While Realism was as naturalistic as Pragmatism, Realists found structure in the world: laws of nature exist and men can discover them. Some laws are permanent, others relative, but none is subject to constant change. Knowledge of natural law as it functions in the physical universe and society is man's best chance to live a full, happy, and decent life.[66]

Beginning, as all philosophy of education must, with a philosophy of man, Realism affirmed the existence of both matter and spirit but rejected supernaturalism; thus, the man to be educated was to all intents and purposes a natural man and Realists refused to talk about any divinity in origin and destiny. Man is defined by what he is capable of doing, so from observation and research Realists concluded that he is capable of rational thought and responsible action. These were the capacities needing education's cultivation. So Realist educational philosophy had a conservative tendency: it found truth through the employment of scientific method and concluded that schooling must be committed to the transmission of intellectual and moral truth.[67]

Influenced by the writing of prominent Realist philosophers—some of whom spent little time on educational philosophy, such as Alfred North Whitehead[68] and Bertrand Russell[69] —Realist educational theory acknowledged the importance of setting educational objectives along lines compatible with the realities of life. It was possible, they maintained, to discover what men needed to know to live in society by conducting a careful scientific investigation of both physical and social reality. Schools should take the knowledge derived from research seriously, for it forms the basic culture of learning, and they should construct curricula and develop teaching methods to assure the perpetuation and assimilation of this knowledge. This meant the educational process should be conducted by teachers in possession of truth and value with a commitment to communicating them; what should be taught does not, Realists said, depend on what children want, but on what they need in order to live successful lives. To this end, school practice should encourage training, instruction, and discipline. The Realist, quite capable of employing the most advanced techniques of teaching to sustain and encourage learning, demanded a mastery of content, and deplored the pedagogy of Progressive education and Pragmatism which seemed both pointless and profitless. Knowledge, once obtained, should be taught with zeal and devotion to oncoming generations, and achievement from students should be demanded. Life is simply too short, Realists asserted, to unleash students to follow the uncertain, unmarked route of unaided discovery.[70]

HUMANISM

In the great debate between progressives and essentialists over educational purpose, Humanists rallied to the support of the latter, expecting that essential education would allow for the cultivation of distinctive human abilities. Although among the Humanists themselves some sharp differences existed in connection with the nature of man, truth, and culture, several common bonds enabled them to mount an assault on the "new education."

Humanism, it is fair to say, was organized roughly into three contingents: Literary Humanism, cultivated by such scholars as Nicholas Murray Butler, Mark Van Doren, and Norman Foerster, tended toward elitism and stressed a perpetuation of human culture by concentrating on the literary tradition; Rational Humanism, represented most eloquently by Robert Maynard Hutchins and Mortimer Adler, centered attention on intellectual education and the trained reason; and Christian Humanism, whose principal spokesmen were Thomas E. Sheilds, William F. Cunningham, and Jacques Maritain, was prepared to endorse both education for culture and reason and take into account, besides, the truths of revelation which demonstrated man's supernaturalism and his relationship to God.

Opposition to Naturalism in education frequently made for strange philosophic bedfellows and, considering its many sides, Humanism was no exception. Still, Humanists, although seldom in complete agreement philosophically, were close enough to speak almost with one voice about the purposes and means of education. They differed somewhat in their philosophy of man—and this always caused trouble—because neither Literary nor Rational Humanists were prepared to adopt revelation as a source of knowledge about man's origin, nature, and destiny; but they could agree to a wide range of metaphysical propositions and they found hardly anything in a theory of knowledge to separate them. Metaphysically and epistemologically Humanists were dualists—matter and spirit were real and distinct as were the knower and the thing known—and in the end philosophic realists.

Education was a way to cultivate human abilities—thought and expression—and while Humanists sometimes differed on the question of what should be taught to obtain this goal, they had no difficulty whatever in agreeing to the goal itself. And they refused, moreover, to treat children in schools as persons incapable of reasoning and abstraction; in a word, they were distressed by educational techniques geared to nothing more than a physiology of learning.[71]

On one hand, Humanists asserted the existence of truth and the possibility of achieving it; this formed the most important dimension of schooling. On the other, they saw the authenticity of moral value, of a standard of conduct for social life, and were determined to inculcate value as part of the scholastic experience of youth. They understood the need to live well, and were generous in support of an orderly society, but they were prepared, too, to talk about the life of the mind and the virtue of culture. All Humanists aligned themselves with the educational objective of civilizing mankind.

Literary, Rational, and Christian Humanists marched in cadence through all the natural and human virtues, but where the two former stopped Christian Humanists continued, to embrace revealed truth and the spiritual dignity of man. Christian Humanism was supernaturalistic; formally the other Humanisms were not, although some of their adherents had religious dispositions. In the end, however important this difference was in philosophic and religious principle, its educational consequences came to rest mainly on the curriculum. Christian Humanists, in acknowledging revelation as a custodian of truth, were convinced of the need to teach a positive religious creed as a basis for moral formation and character education. The curriculum of the Christian Humanist school was thus impregnated with elements of the religious heritage and permeated with religious perspective.[72]

Educational Humanism had priorities and proceeded to impose them on educational objectives and curricula; these priorities demonstrated a fundamental conviction that the formation of man's intellect and will is the principal business of education. But attention was not paid exclusively to liberal studies in any Humanist educational philosophy, and it would be wrong to think of Humanists as archaic schoolmasters conspiring to turn back the pages of the calendar to the classical age. They, as much as their naturalistic tormentors, were anxious to educate men to live in the contemporary world; such education, however, was built on the bedrock of established truth and solid moral value. In addition, they understood society to be demanding and rigorous of its members, rather than fluid and permissive, so they prescribed an educational program wherein mental discipline could be cultivated. They could abandon harsh educational regimens for a pleasant and happy school, but it was a school where excellence was prized in the realization of human talent, for discipline, they argued, is essential to any degree of excellence, and it mattered not whether excellence was sought in the liberal, the fine, or the practical arts. Humanism nailed learning to its educational mast, for only as a result of decent learning could men achieve their full potential as human beings.[73]

SCHOOLS AND SOCIETY

In the first three or four decades of the twentieth century attention was riveted on educational theory and method, and this entirely reasonable preoccupation was justified by events. But educational development had other sides at this time and we should pay them some heed, realizing that they embellished the mosaic of education without having been its determining theme.

Reorganization of Schools

Toward the end of the nineteenth century, American schools were organized into a single-ladder system: elementary, secondary, and higher education formed a single track and students moved from one level to another without interruption. However, as we have seen, the historical evolution of these levels had been somewhat discrete, so although the system had unity, doubt about its educational efficiency persisted. For one thing, the common school, the first rung of the educational ladder, had made its mark as a terminal school, the only school most children ever attended. In this tradition, it became a seven- eight- or nine-year school, depending on regional preference; but when it formed part of a system whose normal anticipation was for increasing numbers of students to attend high schools, the time spent in elementary schools seemed inordinately long. Questions raised about the length of elementary education were answered in the context of current psychological assumption relative to child development: were eight-year elementary schools and four-year high schools conducive to the most economical and effective learning?

This issue was first raised in 1888 by Charles W. Eliot, whom we have met so many times on these pages, before a session of the Department of Superintendence of the National Education Association, where it was phrased "Can School Programs Be Shortened and Enriched?"[74]

Various committees and commissions, most under the auspices of the National Education Association, examined the various sides to elementary and secondary school relationships and often produced conflicting proposals for school organization. Finally, however, preference for the eight-year elementary school weakened and a consensus was won for an abbreviated elementary school course. By 1905 the National Education Association adopted a six-year elementary school followed by a six-year high school as its official policy on school organization. Within the next four or five years the first reorganized school plan was implemented, either in Columbus, Ohio or Berkeley, California, by creating a junior high-school course from the seventh and eighth grades of the traditional elementary school and adding to it the first year of the conventional high school. Thus elementary education was set at six years, junior high-school instruction at three, and three years were allotted to the senior high-school course of study.

The trend to reorganize schools gained momentum slowly, but before a decade had passed junior high schools were familiar sights the country over. By 1946, in cities with comprehensive systems of elementary and secondary education, the most popular organizational plan, 6-3-3, was adopted by 35 percent of the cities; the 8-4 plan was followed in 23 percent of the city systems; 6-6 in 16 percent; 6-2-4 in 12 percent; and 6-3-3-2 in 4 percent. The last plan added the junior college to the local school system. The late 1940s represented the high-water mark for school reorganization, but even then, although reorganized schools were frequent, the traditional plan (8-4) was followed in a majority of school districts in the United States. After an initial surge, incentive for reorganization tapered off and in the 1950s and 1960s, instead of trying to reorganize schools, educators turned attention to a downward extension of the elementary school to include kindergartens, nursery schools, and child-care centers. The latter, especially, became a preoccupation of educational and social reformers in the decade between 1965 and 1975.

Private Schools

With the advent of the common school the days of private elementary schools were numbered, and soon a majority of children received their elementary schooling in public grade schools. Later, the same trend affected secondary education, although private preparatory schools, located principally in the Eastern United States, lingered on as important and valuable educational institutions. But without any question whatever, when secondary education increased in popularity, public high schools were the beneficiaries of the surge in enrollment. Public higher education, however, captured the fancy of the people less quickly, and not until the midpoint of the twentieth century did public college enrollment equal, and later surpass, enrollment in private colleges. Even so, the number of private colleges in the United States continued to exceed their public counterparts.

The rapid expansion of public education in the nineteenth and twentieth centuries is a fact of history, but it left unimpaired America's traditional affinity to private education. Public schools were available and so were educational alternatives. During this period the most visible and efficient alternative was a private school system conducted under the general auspices, although usually without the direct financial support, of the Roman Catholic Church.

During the country's earlier years, as we know, religion was held to be an imperative element of education; few schoolmasters thought it possible to conduct a respectable course of instruction without including denominational teaching. But the common school, with sectarian controversy surrounding it, redefined the essentials of public education and discarded sectarian religion from the curriculum. The Bible, we know, remained in school, but its reading was unaccompanied by comment or interpretation. This change in educational perspective was viewed with misgivings by many Americans, yet for the most part neither their own personal convictions nor the determination of their churches led to a plan for solution. While pockets of resistance to what was called the Godless public schools obtained, and some educational alternatives were provided, nothing amounting to a private school system was created. Not, at least, until a Roman Catholic Church policy with respect to education was formalized.

Immigration in the middle years of the nineteenth century had brought hundreds of thousands of Catholics—mostly Irish—to the United States, and their priests and bishops, Irish too, lived in constant dread of the anti-Catholic and irreligious sentiments associated with public education. In a sincere effort to protect religious faith from erosion in public schools, the Church, in the Third Plenary Council of 1884, legislated the erection of a parochial school system and decreed the attendance of all Catholic children in Catholic schools. Parents were obliged to protect their children from the evil lurking in public schools.[75]

Beginning slowly, Catholic parochial schools eventually blanketed the country and, while the Church policy was never so effective as to have every Catholic child in a Catholic school, offered an effective educational alternative to public education. Always educationally adequate, Catholic parochial schools prospered from the beginning of the twentieth century to about 1960. By then the need which had brought these schools into existence in the first place no longer seemed so apparent or imperative, so Catholic allegiance to parochial education weakened; besides, changes in the Church introduced elements of ecumenism which affected educational judgment; but most important of all was the increased financial burden of supporting parochial schools. One after another parish elementary schools were closed, until in 1975 the largest and most impressive private school system in the world became only a faint shadow of what it had been only two decades before.

The Great Depression

It has never been easy to measure the effect of the economic collapse of 1929 on American education. Schools were open, and we know that during these years of great poverty and destitution debates over educational philosophy continued unabated. Still, it is hard to know whether poverty and economic dislocation were allies or enemies of Progressive education. This much is certain, the progressive spirit in America, a reality for generations, began to atrophy, and optimism surrendered to despair. Despair bred a kind of radicalism, sometimes attributed to promoters of Progressive education; and radical pronouncements on social and economic theory motivated thoughtful citizens to become more conservative. This conservative revival took its toll on a variety of progressive social plans, including education.

A return to more orthodox social policy led schools to rescind their character as reforming agencies; they were recruited to perform the more humble task of helping a nation in distress. Economic burden was great; poverty was rampant; jobs were few. Schools encouraged students to remain in studies thus relieving further strain on an already precarious job market. As a matter of policy, labor organizations began to support various educational programs which would keep children in school longer —in some states compulsory attendance ages were revised upward—and they included both vocational programs connected with local high schools and a further development of junior colleges. Up to this time labor organizations were generally indifferent to educational policy; now they became intensely active. Part of their purpose was to enlighten labor

union membership, but the goal with longer range was to ensure an elevation of intellect and skill for the American people. This reflected a new
social consciousness for labor.

As it turned out, both labor and the population generally needed a
tender social conscience to meet the burdens of depression life. Government policy, which from the days of Woodrow Wilson had drifted toward
progressivism and inducted government as an active partner with citizens
in the affairs of life, under the conservative guidance of Herbert Hoover
returned to laissez-faire. The problems of economic life seemed insurmountable and government policy was sterile. If it is unfair, as partisan
politicians of recent generations frequently refuse to acknowledge, to
indict President Hoover for having precipitated depression, it is hard to
avoid the conclusion that his administration did little to arrest it.

Revitalized ideas of progress were introduced with Franklin D. Roose-
velt's election as president in 1932, and with his inauguration in 1933
the New Deal was born. The economic policies of the New Deal have
long been the subject of bitter debate and whether or not they were
responsible for restoring the nation's economic and social equilibrium
may be a moot point; but in any case, the action of government through
a variety of social programs ameliorated the economic deficiencies which
for so long had deprived millions of Americans of the necessities of life.
Educational policy, however, is hard to locate in the New Deal and
historians may always be uncertain if there was one. Still, government
did take some action along educational lines with the introduction of
such programs as the Civilian Conservation Corps and the National Youth
Administration. Both provided youth with means to continue their education either formally or informally, but neither had much effect on
public or private education, and both were terminated in the early 1940s.
The Public Works Administration made funds available for school building,
thus helping local communities, and the Works Project Administration
sponsored educational activity in nursery schools, adult education programs, vocational training, and the education of immigrants. With the
immersion of the nation in World War II, these assistance programs were
either downgraded or terminated, for the economic activity associated
with war changed the industrial face of the nation.

Post-War Idealism

The war proved but a brief interruption, as had the depression, in America's commitment to educational progress. Much had been accomplished,
of course, but idealistic persons perceived greater goals to master. As a
first step toward greater educational adequacy, the federal government
initiated an amazingly farsighted and successful educational program for

war veterans: the Serviceman's Readjustment Act of 1944. This act, among a number of other provisions of benefit to servicemen, offered tuition, subsistence, books and supplies, equipment, and counseling services for veterans to continue their education in school or college. Colleges were attended by 2,350,000 veterans, schools by 3,400,000, and on-the-job training had 2,390,000 veterans. This exceptionally generous and beneficial legislation proved to be an important factor in the nation's economic adjustment to peace. This legislative precedent was followed, although somewhat less generously, after the wars in Korea and Viet Nam; yet even with less generous features its social and educational consequences were noteworthy.

A good deal of idealism was reflected in the acts mentioned, but even more was evidenced in the educational policies of the Fair Deal, President Harry Truman's modernized version of the New Deal. By the late 1940s and early 1950s the nation could survey its elementary and secondary schools with pride and self-satisfaction. Undoubtedly important issues of educational policy were yet to be resolved, but the schools were there and students attended them. Higher education, however, was still beyond the reach of millions of American youth and now as a matter of national policy a program of higher education for democracy was adopted.

For the first time, and on a grand scale, the federal government undertook to popularize higher learning and thus make available to the nation's youth the benefit of college study. The underlying principle driving forward this optimistic endeavor was a conviction that every high-school graduate should have an opportunity, without personal cost, for at least two years of college education. Most of this higher learning would have been obtained, according to the plan, by creating a huge system of junior colleges, most attached to local school systems. But regular four-year public and private colleges were involved too. So the federal government introduced striking programs of aid to higher education intended to encourage its expansion. At the same time the public appetite for higher learning was whetted by national policy. The national security and welfare justified federal aid to higher learning, especially in scientific study and research, but also in technological, agricultural, medical, and engineering education. Millions of dollars were made available from public sources, and higher education in America enjoyed a period of unique prosperity. Colleges, used to living in poverty, now had the new experience of financial plenty. But public financial largess was only one side of this bright picture; the other side was painted by private benefaction which increased tremendously. Philanthropy had a long and close association with private colleges, so this alone was not new. The colleges had, toward the close of the nineteenth century, received huge benefactions from rich men who wanted to leave a living legacy in a college or university; now, however, although private gifts continued, the source of philanthropy was principally from foundations, of which the Carnegie, Rockefeller, and Ford were the richest and most prominent.

The old idealism of the nineteenth century recited the virtues of the common school and praised its capacity to revitalize American society; the new idealism of the 1950s and early 1960s was nurtured in the halls of colleges and universities: the greatness of America had yet to be fully demonstrated and higher education was to play a vital part.

Post-War Anxiety

Post-war America, as we have indicated, reflected a renewed faith in the power of education and its ability to act as a social panacea; but it reflected also a growing anxiety over a loss of faith in traditional American values. The years before the war had been hard and social discontent accompanied the economic depression. Communism, socialism, even anarchy, were preached during the 1930s and men, grasping for straws of survival, listened. During the war these cries for reform, and even for radical surgery on the American way of life, were little heard and after the war, because life was so much better, there was no great need to revive them. But what in the depression years could have been indicted as internal subversion was replaced, in a new international balance of power with the Soviet Union, by a fear of imported revolution. Among other persons and institutions, schools and colleges fell under the pall of suspicion and efforts were made, in a strange wedding of zeal and devotion, to purge them of an un-American character.

America's membership in the United Nations, while supported by a majority of citizens, was vigorously opposed by an outspoken minority. Schools and teachers, on any level, who supported a one-world philosophy appeared subversive to this cadre of American patriots. The loyalty of teachers and professors had to be tested and recorded, and this was done in many states with the statutory introduction of teachers' loyalty oaths. Besides, in the colleges and universities professors whose unorthodox social and political philosophies conflicted (or were thought to conflict) with a fundamental American patriotic creed were examined and re-examined, sometimes by investigating committees of Congress and sometimes by sensitive boards of trustees. An entirely commendable devotion to American ideals, for under any definition of academic freedom it would be impossible to countenance outright subversion, put even a prudent interpretation of academic freedom in some jeopardy. So along with prosperity in its post-war years, American education, especially higher education, labored under a burden of heavy suspicion about its loyalty and patriotism. The era of American educational progressivism ended on a sour note.

CHAPTER TWELVE
_____

Educational Policy
in a Period
of Social Ferment

During the middle years of the nineteenth century, when the common school was established as an essential correlate to political democracy, humanitarian spokesmen were quick to recite the school's social function. But even with the immense zeal and good will reflected in their social policy, humanitarians were riders, never drivers, on the reforming bandwagon. American social thought tended mainly to be conservative and schools, while championed, were never commissioned to reconstruct society. Conservatism was reinforced by conditions of American life and the schools, rather than being agents to metamorphose society, were delegated to perpetuate the status quo. That is until Progressive education gathered enough momentum to reintroduce the old humanitarian appeal: education is a principal instrument for initiating broad economic and social reform. Now under new auspices and generally better organized, a brand of progressive humanitarianism tried to do what before was left undone. The means to cultivate reform were better too, for the social sciences had matured to a point where social engineering was at least respectable even when it lacked universal appeal. But in the end, for reasons we already know, the great expectations of progressive educators went largely unrealized, and society proceeded along familiar paths unconvinced by the propositions of social philosophers.

After the Second World War, however, principles of democracy were interpreted literally and made a deeper impression on the social conscience. America's experience with totalitarian government, first in war and then in peace, served in some ways to mirror the flaws of her own democracy. Heretofore progressive social philosophers and educators had encouraged a full cultivation of equality in American life, but their idealism was little heeded. And no one should have been surprised, for neither philosophers nor educators alone wield an influence capable of redirecting the flow of social action. This is a role for politicians, and now the issue of equality attracted their attention. For the first time in her history the United States took seriously the ranging implications of equity in the land's fundamental law: the Constitution.

Some elements of equality, opportunity and education, had their origin in the earlier years of the twentieth century, and we have to return to pre-war periods to find their genesis, but equality was the central issue of the late 1950s and 1960s and by turning our attention to it we shall have in perspective the changing character of American education.

EQUALITY OF OPPORTUNITY

The immigrant on entering the United States in the late nineteenth and early twentieth century found more than myth in the assertion that America was a land of opportunity. But if more than myth, it was sometimes, and for some, less than truth. Hard work and good fortune had enabled millions of native and naturalized Americans to climb the ladder of economic and social success. Yet many found the door of opportunity closed and were right to inquire whether or not the constitutional guarantees of liberty and equality were genuine. One rung of the ladder of opportunity, most persons readily agreed, was schooling, and evidence was ample of how persons had used trained intelligence to overcome obstacles in their path. But the point was, as perceptive observers could easily illustrate, traditional school policy too often deprived thousands of Americans from finding a sturdy first rung on the educational ladder. Put bluntly, American society was frequently in violation of the principle of equality of opportunity.

The case has been proved too many times to reargue here, but in the 1940s and 1950s huge segments of society were indifferent or hostile to the issue of equality. The principle of equality of opportunity was stated in clear and concise prose, and adopted as a matter of national policy, in the first volume of the President's Commission on Higher Education in 1947: *Higher Education for American Democracy.* Although one is surprised to find a social manifesto so succinctly stated in a document pertaining to higher learning, the authors of the report were explicit: "If education is to make the attainment of a more perfect democracy one of its major goals, it is imperative that it extend its benefits to all on equal terms."[1] This principle dominated the educational policy of the years following its articulation.

With roots running to New Deal ideology, the Fair Deal doctrine of the Truman administration aspired to a reversal of old, government-sanctioned policies that as a matter of convention had accepted discrimination on the basis of race, religion, and national origin. These policies had been woven into the fabric of law—in the separate but equal doctrine expressed by the United States Supreme Court in *Plessy* v. *Ferguson* (1896)[2] —and social policy, and it was incumbent on post-war politics to redress these policies to ensure civil rights on an equitable basis to all citizens. Ensuring civil rights meant calling on the constitutional protection afforded citizens in the Bill of Rights and the Fourteenth Amendment and applying it especially to law enforcement, to the personal security of citizens regardless of station, to full rights of citizenship relative to voting and holding office, and to equality of opportunity for employment, housing, and all public services. The various states and the federal government began to enact laws proscribing discrimination, on one hand, and encouraging equality of opportunity, on the other.

The rupture with standard policy in its application to education began in the courts, and now the federal judiciary spearheaded assurances that all citizens be afforded equal protection of the law. Still, the separate but equal doctrine persisted without serious challenge: in *Sweatt* v. *Painter* (1950) the United States Supreme Court unanimously enjoined the University of Texas from conducting a separate (and newly instituted) law school for a Negro student and rejected the claim of its academic equivalence with the regular law school of the university.[3] Implicitly, however, the court validated the precedent set in the Gaines decision (1938), where the state of Missouri, while not required to admit a Negro student to the law school of the University of Missouri, was directed to provide equal legal education for him.[4] The separate but equal doctrine died hard, but it died finally in the monumental decision of the Supreme Court in *Brown* v. *The Board of Education of Topeka* in 1954. Nullifying the separate but equal doctrine, the court, moreover, declared separate schools inherently unequal and a separation of the races for schooling detrimental to students excluded from the educational mainstream. In addition, a year later, the court directed school jurisdictions to proceed "with all deliberate speed" to desegregate the public schools.[5] On a purely legal basis, equality of educational opportunity was secure; as a practical social and school matter, however, desegregation of American education had a long way to go.

With constitutional priorities ratified, the schools were delegated to help the poor and underprivileged achieve full participation in American life. Lacking some of the fervor of an earlier and more authentic progressivism, the schools, nevertheless, began a long crusade to cultivate equality of social and economic opportunity for all classes of citizens. Schooling, it was believed and asserted, could obtain justice for the poor and serve as an antidote to the poverty cycle. Equality of educational opportunity, now apparently assured by the verdict of the court, was a condition for the attainment of civil, social, and economic justice under the Constitution, so educators enlisted in the ranks and, it must be said, did their best to upgrade the quality of American life by changing the character of education.

At best, however, the crusade produced mixed results. On one side were members of the education fraternity, who saw no limit to the power of education, and the Negro community generally, which for generations encouraged education as a means for Negro advancement; but on the other side were confirmed segregationists, both North and South, who opposed all educational and social programs for the advancement of minorities, especially for Negroes, and tried their best to impede enforcement of the *Brown* decision.[6] And a neutral, but always highly effective, obstacle was present too: the best education took time to work its miracles. A commitment to education as a means for upgrading the quality of American life for disadvantaged persons was no doubt good, but this remedy was slow. Some citizens, overburdened in economic and social plight, were unwilling to wait.

A good case can be made for the effort spent in schools where, soon, it was taken for granted that education could alter the culture of poverty. Schools could engage in teaching the fundamental skills, making minority groups more versatile and able, and curricula could be infused with an abundance of marketable skills enabling economically deprived persons to compete more favorably for lucrative jobs and positions in the economic world. But more than this was needed if the attitudes of minorities were to be changed, from those of economic poverty and social abuse, to ones of optimism and aspiration relative to the conventional values of American life. Extending to all classes of citizens the opportunities of education would eliminate social and economic barriers, and the traditional minorities would thus be absorbed into a full partnership in American democracy. The social theory to be tested was characteristic of an idealism nourished by educators who for so long had an implicit faith in the power of education.[7]

But the educators, always at the forefront of this movement, were not alone in endorsing education as a means for social and economic amelioration. The Negro community, too, was ready to adopt the thesis that education was the means to social and economic advancement.[8] Acknowledging this thesis was, for the most part, a continuation of a policy toward education embraced by the Negro community shortly after the Civil War. Booker T. Washington, assuming the role of spokesman for his race, held up before it the vision of success obtained by a demonstration of ability, and what better way to realize ability than with a competent education? America's faith in education was shared by Negro leaders and by the rank and file too. Despite almost inordinately high odds this faith persisted and flourished from one generation to the next, and in the years surrounding the famous *Brown* decision it was reflected most explicitly in the activity of the National Association for the Advancement of Colored People. The untiring effort of this Association to keep before the courts and the public generally the issue of educational discrimination is in itself testimony to the Negro belief that a principal means to betterment is equal opportunity for schooling.

This faith in the power of education though, so much attested in the public record of educators and Negro leaders, was severely tried by deep-seated prejudice in many communities, where school and other integration was regularly retarded, and the impatience of large numbers in the Negro community to wait until the effect of better education could be realized became evident.

Entrenched social practice is tenacious, so the dual schools of the South were slow to respond to court orders to proceed with deliberate speed in the erection of a unitary school system. State and local school officers employed delaying tactics to impede the application of the *Brown* decision; in some counties public schools were dismantled in a tactic to circumvent the court's decision.[9] Where public policy refused to heed the decision of the federal court, as in the cases of schools in Little Rock, Arkansas, the University of Mississippi, and the University of Alabama, federal troops and troops of a federalized National Guard were used to ensure the safe attendance of Negro children in the schools. Overt Southern opposition to public-school desegregation was suppressed, although violence and its threat and some public discord accompanied its erosion.

While attention focused on the South, where, according to common opinion, most segregation existed, the cities of the North (where minority population was increasing) followed an insidious policy of perpetuating segregation while appearing to comply fully with the legal policies governing the conduct of public schools. The schools themselves may not have been directly culpable in violating law, but housing patterns made it almost inevitable that in the larger cities the urban poor and Negroes would be isolated in ghetto schools. Segregation in the North, not a matter of statute as for decades in the South, became segregation in fact with both persistent and detrimental effect.[10] But this problem was left untouched by the *Brown* decision and it remained for the courts in the 1970s to modify and eliminate the educational inequities resulting therefrom.

The Road to Integration

The Negro community's investment in education as a means for upward mobility, long a tradition among Negro leaders and associations, was managed more deliberately in the two decades after 1950. But it and the commitment of professional educators to employ scholastic means to achieve justice and equality for the poor and for minorities, despite good intention and the expenditure of immense sums of money, paid disappointing dividends. Desegregation could be eliminated in schools and communities; the force of law and public policy could eradicate obvious elements of civil inequality, but integration was another thing. And now the lesson so hard to learn was finally mastered: integration could not be purchased by reorganizing educational method and revamping curricula. For all its nobility of purpose, the movement was scarred by failure. Schooling alone was incapable of integrating society or eliminating the culture of poverty; something else had to be done.

The assessment that schools had not produced the desired effect of reducing poverty and relative ignorance, thus being a central force in assuring an integrated society, was authenticated and dramatized by racial disturbance and violence in Harlem, in 1964, in Watts, in 1965, and in Detroit, in 1967. In these communities the resources of society had been spent with generosity to improve schools; still, the Negro community felt deprived and in an intemperate moment resorted to mob action and violence to right the social wrongs so long inflicted on it. Urgency of conflict called for urgent remedy, but quick remedies are hard to find in complex societies. Yet these eruptions did lead to a reasonable conclusion that if educational programs so far conducted had not accomplished what was expected of them, then something should be done to redesign schools and school programs to make them contribute directly to solving the problem of social integration and economic equality. Educators, willing to admit temporary impasse, refused to abandon their faith in education as a means for social reform.

The Johnson Administration mounted a war on poverty and enacted the Civil Rights Act of 1964. Therein, education's role in the business of integration was reviewed. The principal item in this review was the Coleman Report, *Equality of Educational Opportunity,* of 1966, eventually widely circulated and generally believed because it appeared to be the dependable result of positive sociological research.[11] The old assumption that schools for Negro children were inferior and, moreover, that school learning by itself could banish the culture of poverty, was challenged. The Coleman Report recommended a new approach. Rather than spending money to redress school programs, the Report called for a reconstitution of school populations. Children of disadvantaged social classes would profit more from schooling, the Report concluded, by attending schools with middle- and upper-class children. Curriculum and methods of teaching were not the great emancipators; lessons learned from scholastic peer groups were. Differential rates in educational progress and achievement were accounted for, Coleman argued, by the sociological composition of schools. And sociological composition was a social and economic, not a pedagogic, issue. Children attended schools designated for their community, so a mixture of social classes in schools was hard to obtain.[12] Looking for an easier solution than the one in the Report, and blind to its findings, educators were determined to try again. They searched for new educational mechanisms to assure equality of educational result. And here the record of accomplishment is mixed: some produced good results; others were soon forgotten. Without going into detail on these "new" plans for securing integration, the more prominent ones can be presented generally.

Compensatory education, introduced in 1965, was intended to remedy the shortcomings of earlier nurture. This plan tried to stimulate and improve the academic performance of children from culturally and economically deprived homes by giving them experiences their homes and neighborhoods were helpless to provide. The point was that the early years of life are critical to learning, not only because basic skills are mastered but also because motives for learning are instilled. If children are surrounded by a culturally inadequate environment, it is unlikely they will find the necessary urge to seek for success; but if somehow personal motive should be present, even then the experience open to them in such cultural settings is bound to be defective. To redress the bleakness of deprived environment, educators invented a variety of compensatory programs, including Head Start, Higher Horizons and Upward Bound. At the outset these programs appeared to offer disadvantaged youth a solid educational foundation on which later schooling could stand, and a great deal of favorable publicity, as well as large sums of federal money, accompanied them, but in the end the consequences of compensatory education were, at best, inconclusive. Their initial effect, while good, tended to wear away as children from deprived homes and neighborhoods returned to their normal cultural setting. The school could not, despite zealous and generous effort, immunize these cultural deficiencies; and sympathetic critics of compensatory education were disposed to inquire whether the learning environment of the school can ever neutralize social forces in competition with the school. In any case, it became clear, the school has little control over the learning situations in society at large.

In addition, unsympathetic critics began to challenge the assumption basic to compensatory education. Some black spokesmen voiced the doubt that black children needed the company of white children in order to learn well. Other persons spoke disparagingly of educational standards which had their origin in a middle-class culture, or went beyond this bold assertion to an even bolder one: standards of educational decency could not be set at all. Differences in cultural background, they maintained, are no warrant for conclusions of inferiority. Any cultural or scholastic standard when translated to a minimum level of school achievement is artificial and fundamentally meaningless. A unitary educational system inherited from nineteenth-century social policy, and perpetuating academic standards reflecting what David Tyack calls "the one best system," was sometimes said to be inconsistent with twentieth-century social and educational requirements.[13]

One branch of the educational fraternity embraced the sociological theory that a conventional curriculum comes from middle-class life experience. Books, skills, even language itself, are distilled from an experience which is foreign to children from disadvantaged and minority homes. This curriculum, the new technicians argued, is mainly irrelevant. The assumption that basic American culture is exhumed from native and natural experience and has nothing much to do with civilization—that heritage long held precious by Western people—enabled schoolmasters to introduce English as a second language, while giving first place to black English or, in some schools, Spanish. It enabled them, moreover, to jettison traditional grammar and replace it with the speech and language habits children brought to school; and it authorized them to engage in a huge experiment of "black studies." History, civics, arithmetic, and literature, as well as other subjects in the curriculum, in a dramatic appeal to relevance, became black history, civics, arithmetic, and literature.

In a frantic search for relevance educators abandoned Shakespeare to make room for an ephemeral literature whose dominant themes were found in contemporary society. What qualified on the level of relevance, despite the hazards of certification, did not always pass muster as literature. Educators addicted to relevance did not mean, however, to exclude from academic consideration the tested, traditional culture; they meant to use "relevant" studies to introduce a multi-cultural curriculum wherefrom children would value their own and other cultural backgrounds. With an improved self-image and necessary skill developed from study of relevant subjects, children, heretofore culturally deprived and unable to compete in American society, would, the schoolmasters said, be better able to achieve equally with other children. It is an interesting item in the educational history of this frantic period that the rage for relevance could not be restricted to Negro children from underdeveloped communities—where some justification was possible—but spread also to schools with concentrations of Chicano, Puerto Rican, and American Indian children. But it did not stop there either, and invaded conventional middle-class schools and colleges where the flag of relevance was nailed to the students' banner of protest.[14]

Getting a good educational beginning and having studies with meaning were two ways of confronting the aggravated scholastic issue in the United States in the 1960s; organizing a new cadre of teachers for minority children was another. In 1968, for example, the Office of Education sponsored the Triple T Project. Its purpose was "to train teachers of teachers" in the educational problems common to inner-city children. But this was only one among many programs to reeducate teachers responsible for conducting the schooling of minority children. Following the sensible principle that, in order to be effective, teachers must be able to communicate with their students, these programs of teacher education had implicit promise, and are still cultivated, although not with the same enthusiasm of their inauguration.

Finally, in a determined effort to accelerate social integration by using schools as principal means, the techniques of community control of schools and the busing of children in urban areas were introduced. Community control, it was argued, would decentralize urban school districts and allow for the formulation of educational judgment in the community, by community leaders, parents, and students familiar with local educational needs and issues.[15] The other technique—busing—recommended first in the Coleman Report, was required by some federal district courts as a way of assuring greater academic achievement, thus equality of educational opportunity, for minority children. Taken from their own community and schooled with children from middle-class families, minority children would be more highly motivated to learn and better able to concentrate on study. Busing was both praised and condemned by those affected; and educational and political leaders took different sides on this highly volatile issue.[16] The theory justifying busing predicted social integration through schools, but if schools were to impose their good offices, community patterns of school attendance needed realignment. In the last analysis, many educators and political leaders saw education as a missionary effort to eliminate social disadvantage and economic deprivation, and to achieve social integration. It is still too early for historical perspective to appraise the efficacy of techniques which have generated vigorous emotional and political outburst.

THE NATURE/NURTURE DEBATE REVIVED

The war on poverty and the war to achieve equality of educational opportunity were waged fortified by the confident assumption that environment is the critical factor in the formation of human beings. Explicit allegiance to environmental determinism was absent in the pronouncements of educators and social theorists, but the assumption was there nevertheless: children are shaped by experience. If opportunity for rich experience is good, they become able and productive citizens; if opportunity for experience is defective, they suffer a life-long disadvantage. The educational programs generated in the 1960s and 1970s were grounded on the conviction that in a contest between heredity and environment, environment always wins. So long as this dogmatic assumption persisted, the educational community was enthusiastic and optimistic about the promise of good schooling to guarantee social and economic reform and to assure a fully integrated, democratic society. But the assumption was challenged.

In the 1960s, the old debate of the 1920s over the respective weight of heredity and environment was almost forgotten when Arthur Jensen published an article, "How Much Can We Boost I.Q. and Scholastic Achievement?" in the winter (1969) issue of the *Harvard Educational Review*.[17] Money and effort spent on the "compensatory" education of Negro children, Jensen alleged, was probably wasted, because their lack was not variety and richness in educational experience but talent. And talent's source is heredity not environment. Intelligence test scores for black children, Jensen found, average about fifteen points below those for white children. This deficiency would impede their progress in cognitive learning but would have a less limiting effect in rote and motor-skill learning. By concentrating on the latter, schools could prepare such persons for appropriate roles in American society.

Jensen's article struck an immensely sensitive nerve among some educators. They branded his conclusions rude and ungenerous and, on that score, rejected them. The reaction of Jensen's opponents and critics was no more praiseworthy than the enthusiasm of segregationists who believed they had at last the proof needed to authenticate the native inferiority of the Negro race. Katz wrote that Jensen's thesis was "eagerly seized upon by a variety of strange bedfellows, from Southern white supremacists to big-city school people anxious to excuse their own ineptitude."[18]

One must be cautious about Jensen's heredity theory, for his evidence is inconclusive, but environmentalists, who for so long supported economic, social, and educational programs to ameliorate the disadvantages of certain minorities, should pause long enough to examine their assumptions too.

The nature/nurture issue challenged one fundamental assumption with respect to the social reward from schooling. Another was challenged by Christopher Jencks in *Inequality: A Reassessment of the Effect of Family and Schooling in America.* Along with his collaborators he argued that the correlation between educational opportunity and social success is neither high nor certain. Luck and merit, they maintained, are more important in determining a person's place in the economic structure than academic success. The conclusion was clear and precise—although several critics have pointed to the study's serious flaws—education plays only a marginal role in determining patterns of equality, opportunity, and social mobility. Thus, it can do little to change them. America's faith in education, they appear to conclude, has been misplaced.[19]

Debate about heredity and environment, on one hand, and the ability of education to change society, on the other, has centered a great deal of attention on the schools. In consequence, some citizens have lost faith in education as a social force; others, however, ask the schools to ignore their critics and continue to invest society's resources to upgrade the quality of education for minorities and other underprivileged persons.

EDUCATIONAL CONTROL

Reflecting on the origins of schooling in America, we notice at once a tension which from the outset obtained between two assumptions on educational control and support. One, following for the most part the scholastic tradition of Great Britain, stressed the primacy of individual effort and forthrightly maintained the principle of "each man according to his own means." The other, steeped in the experience of colonial life and somewhat uneasy about putting total trust in private means to assure opportunity for schooling, acknowledged a collective responsibility for the achievement of social objectives and urged the utilization of public resources for education. Private schools, of which America's first centuries had plenty, were naturally enough nurtured in the first assumption; public schools were indebted to the second. But since public education, especially as the twentieth century recognizes it, was tardy of realization—being mainly a social phenomenon of the later nineteenth century—private schools had time to bury deep roots in the educational soil of the country.

One clear characteristic of American education can be described as public-private dualism, a partnership of public and private schools with a charter to assume the important responsibility of educating the nation's youth, but this charter was put in jeopardy in the 1950s and 1960s when social and educational theorists charged private schools with a separatism detrimental to the democratic sentiments education was committed to cultivate. To understand the full implications of this allegation, we should look more closely at the legal status of private education in the first years of the twentieth century.

The Foundations of Public-Private Dualism

Accepting the ancient tradition that private persons could engage in founding and conducting schools was not hard for America, but it was quite another thing to invest the state with authority to establish and maintain schools, and this turned out to be a difficult policy to embrace. But even admitting state authority in education, which was done eventually, did not solve the whole issue. Could children be compelled to attend schools?

To review here the details of compulsory attendance precedents is unnecessary. First instituted in Massachusetts in 1852, compulsory attendance legislation spread to all the forty-eight states by 1914, accompanied almost always by some political conflict and legal reservation. Allowing states to establish and support schools was hardly an unequivocal acknowledgement of the state's power to require children to attend them. Although compulsory attendance was never a federal constitutional question, the right of a state to compel school attendance was thought to contravene state constitutions and was litigated several times in state courts. In the end, both the police power of the state and the general welfare of society were convincing legal principles, so the statutes requiring school attendance of children between certain ages stood intact. But how much farther did the state's power over education extend?

By the middle 1900s the state's authority in education was illustrated in a number of ways, the most significant—supposedly because of its direct impact on families—was compulsory attendance. For the next fifty years the states were busy affirming this authority in the courts, and by the end of the century it was possible to detect a fairly clear picture of the state's place in education. Limited, one thinks, only by the Fourteenth Amendment, the state, not the local community, held the reins of educational control, a control demonstrated in the following legal principles. First, *state legislatures have the power to control public schools except as they are limited by federal and state constitutional provisions.* For a long time state constitutions had been in the habit of assigning to state legislatures a wide range of authority over schools, so state constitutional language seldom appeared as an impediment to state authority. Second, *both constitutional declaration and statute made it plain that authority over education was in no way inherent in local government.* A great deal of local activity in education for the establishment of schools, the employment of teachers and the support of instruction had made local school districts appear more powerful in the state than they were. Besides, the history of local activity in educational matters lent credence to the assumption that local school districts enjoyed autonomy. In a number of instances the courts corrected this assumption. Third, *in the organization of various educational units, school districts may be distinct from other branches of local government.* This principle authorized state legislatures to create school districts without legal allegiance to town, city, or county government, although in the historical development of public schools these government units had been deeply involved, and it was not always easy for them to disassociate themselves from the conduct of schools within their jurisdictions. Fourth, *state legislatures, in an exercise of their educational function, were not precluded from trying a variety of means for organizing, administering, and maintaining schools.* Legislatures were free to authorize a variety of ways for handling education in local communities. And finally, the principle was distilled through various judicial proceedings *that even when a state did not exercise its* authority over education by creating a state system of school administration, authority over education remained with the state. Thus, even in disuse this state authority was not eroded. These legal principles clearly assigned responsibility and authority for education to the state; yet the power of the state over educational affairs within its borders—although clearly great—was not absolute.

The fundamental law limiting state educational authority may be the state or federal constitution. If the former, such limitation applies to legislative enactment or administrative regulation, but if the latter, state activity is restrained by law more powerful than the state constitution. Federal constitutional restraint on state educational activity may be illustrated by two famous cases.

Between 1917 and 1921 several states enacted statutes requiring English as the language for all school instruction. Such a law, prohibiting the teaching of foreign language to pupils in private, parochial, and public elementary schools, was passed in Nebraska in 1919. Subsequent to the enactment of the law, Meyer, a teacher in a Lutheran parochial school, taught the German language to elementary-school students. He was arrested, tried, and convicted under the Nebraska statute. On appeal to the Supreme Court of Nebraska the law was upheld as a reasonable exercise of the state's police power, and the court called attention to conditions prevalent during the First World War. Thousands of men, the court wrote, from foreign-language-speaking homes and schools were "unable to read, write, or speak the language of their country, or understand words of command given in English." It was clear, too, the court reasoned, that anti-American and alien sentiments were fostered in schools where English was not used as a medium of instruction. This law, the court concluded, was neither an unreasonable interference with individual liberty nor an infringement of the liberty protection of the Fourteenth Amendment, the constitutional question at stake in the case.[20]

In 1921 the Supreme Courts of Iowa and Ohio, dealing with issues raised in connection with laws similar to Nebraska's, endorsed the precedent established by the Nebraska court, holding constitutional the state's "right to adopt a general policy of its own respecting the health, social welfare, and education of its citizens."[21] There was, the court wrote, no inherent right to teach German to children, especially when its teaching might prove inimical to the best interests of the state. The constitutionality of acts proscribing foreign-language teaching, the Ohio court added, depended on whether the general welfare required such legislation and in the court's opinion the legislature was the best judge of what the general welfare demanded.

State courts had spoken, and in every instance found the states exercising their police power properly without jeopardizing the constitutional protection afforded in the Fourteenth Amendment. Finally, the United

States Supreme Court was called on to give a definitive legal reply to the petition of Meyer on appeal from the Nebraska court's decision. The Supreme Court was asked to decide whether or not the Nebraska act deprived a person of liberty or property without due process of law. In *Meyer* v. *Nebraska* (1923) the Supreme Court declared the Nebraska law unconstitutional because it was an infringement of a person's liberty to pursue a lawful occupation, and by judicial interpretation this decision protected parents in their right to determine the course of instruction for their children.[22]

In 1922 the state of Oregon adopted a compulsory attendance law requiring, with certain exceptions, attendance in public schools of all normal children between the ages of eight and sixteen. Children who went to private schools or utilized the services of private teachers needed the permission of, and had to be examined by, the county superintendent of schools. Anticipating the enforcement of this law would demoralize or destroy private education in Oregon, the Society of Sisters, a Roman Catholic religious community, and the Hill Military Academy challenged its constitutionality. The challenge to the Oregon law was based on its conflict "with the right of parents to choose schools where their children will receive appropriate mental and religious training, the right of the child to influence the parents' choice of a school, the right of schools and teachers therein to engage in a useful business or profession . . . And, further, that unless the enforcement of the measure is enjoined the corporation's business and property will suffer irreparable injury."[23]

Defending the reasonableness of the law, its proponents recalled how the common-school system inaugurated in the nineteenth century had been applauded as a principal bulwark of democracy. Citizenship, they asserted, required the state to maintain a system of schools wherein youth could be trained in its civic responsibilities; juvenile delinquency, they alleged, became more widespread as attendance in non-public schools increased; and religious hostility and prejudice, they argued, were neutralized by attendance in public schools. Instruction in the details of the American form of government and its institutions, especially for immigrant children, moreover, could best be accomplished when children from all social classes met together in public schools. But the principal appeal was to patriotism, which, it was said, could be inculcated best in public schools. Without the law, the justifiers of the Oregon act maintained, the state would be deprived of means for prohibiting the teaching of subversive doctrine by bolshevists, syndicalists, and communists in private schools.

In its decision the Supreme Court reaffirmed the state's right to regulate schools and compel attendance in the name of public good, but it overruled the state's action to require all children to attend public schools, and thereby destroy the property of private schools and infringe the rights of parents to guide the education of their children. No question, the court wrote, "is raised concerning the power of the State reasonably to regulate all schools, to inspect, supervise and examine them, their teachers and pupils; to require that all children of proper age attend some school, that teachers be of good moral character and patriotic disposition, that certain studies plainly essential to good citizenship be taught, and that nothing be taught which is manifestly inimical to the public welfare. . . . These parties are engaged in a kind of undertaking, not inherently harmful, but long regarded as useful and meritorious."[24]

In asserting the right of parents over the education of their children, the Oregon and Nebraska decisions were important landmarks, but there was an even greater significance, especially in the Oregon decision. Until 1925, when the decision was rendered, private education in the United States, operating with the justification of tradition, lacked a precise legal charter. The Oregon decision gave it a charter, a legal basis, and guarantee for survival. And until the end of World War II neither the right of private schools to exist nor their value to American education was questioned. But after the war such questions were raised and the place of private education was put in some jeopardy.

Renewed Threat to Private Education

For several years many private schoolmen, especially those representing Roman Catholic schools, had appealed for public financial support. Put quickly, they maintained education was a citizen's right, to be exercised without respect to the type of school attended; and in withholding public funds from private schools, public policy was discriminating against children who, on a matter of religious conscience, found public schools unacceptable. Parents sending their children to private schools, because they were uncertain of the moral and religious values inculcated in public schools or because they rejected them, were subjected, so the argument ran, to double taxation: their taxes helped support public schools unused by their children and, in addition, they paid tuition to private schools their children attended. While the persuasiveness of this appeal to the public mind in the decade after World War II would be hard to measure, the appeal was nevertheless made with considerable vigor and it antagonized spokesmen for public education. On one hand, they feared any public financial support for private, and especially religious, schools would erode the principle of separation of church and state and eventually undermine American democracy; on the other, they saw in public education the best chance for achieving unity in American society. Private schools, they alleged, whatever educational value claimed for them, were, in the end, socially divisive institutions which, if they could not be eliminated from the American scene, should not, at least, be helped by public resources.[25]

Appealing to social unity and strength, an attack on private education was mounted and the virtues of public education were extolled. The public school alone, according to this version of educational policy, was capable of serving the interests of American democracy. In taking this bold stand in opposition to private and religious schools, the friends of a public education monopoly—principally John L. Childs,[26] Hollis L. Caswell,[27] and James B. Conant[28]—rejected the traditional proposition on which public-private dualism had stood for a century or more, and in addition overlooked a long history of social and educational contribution made by private education.

The proposition, regularly reinforced by practice, which American society had accepted to justify policies of public-private dualism can be stated quickly and directly. In the first place, it was recognized that American society was a pluralistic society wherein individuals and responsible groups had a right to maintain schools outside the public system. A free society without the freedom to conduct private schools would be a farce. Yet, enjoying this freedom to mount and maintain private schools, the fundamentals of American democracy's way of life would be accepted and taught and the academic standard imposed would be equal to the standard of public institutions. Finally, parents had the right to choose the kind of education they wanted for their children and to have it available either in public or private schools. Public education monopolists were prepared to abandon this proposition and, at the same time, blind themselves to history's record.

Normally enjoying more flexibility than public schools, private education had experimented more readily in curriculum and method and had developed scholastic programs and techniques which otherwise would have come tardily. There is more than hyperbole in the assertion that private education was frequently in the vanguard of pedagogic innovation: normal schools, progressive education, education of handicapped children, the kindergarten, junior colleges, and various practices related to remedial instruction are illustrative of private educational leadership. Yet, neither the theory supporting private education nor its record of accomplishment was entirely convincing in the years following World War II. The dogmatic assumption was advanced that democracy must have one school system; public schools alone contribute to the realization of democratic society. Spokesmen who stood against the private school argued, moreover, that anything other than a monolithic school system would rot away the foundation of democracy. Private schools, called undemocratic, were charged with fostering undemocratic values and sentiments by keeping children of various races, national backgrounds, religious faiths, and economic circumstances apart. Because children were apart in schools, it was said, they would be ignorant of human difference and similarity. A bond of social solidarity was held supreme and private education, these spokesmen said, should surrender to it.

During this period—1950 to 1970—private education withstood the assault mounted from bastions of theory. The American public, on the basis of arguments heard, was unready to jettison private schools. Yet, during this time private education began to wither. In the early 1950s religious schools showed considerable gain in number and enrollment, but after two decades the financial burden of maintaining private schools became too great and many were forced to close. In the final analysis, irrespective of the virtues of public-private dualism, public schools came to dominate the American educational picture. In the 1970s rather than arguing about the deficiencies of private education and its threat to social unity, sensitive Americans wondered if the disappearance of private schools would not, in the end, be detrimental to a democratic society. Swinging one way in the early years of the century, the pendulum of public opinion questioning the efficacy of private schools—only to have them saved by the monumental decision in the Oregon case—was swinging the other way in the 1970s, and effort was encouraged to preserve the democratic character of public-private dualism in American education.

SEPARATION OF CHURCH AND STATE

In the formative years of the nation, religion and education forged a close and effective working relationship; the ordinary colonial school, we know, was religious in content and purpose. Colonial schools, some scholars maintain, were conducted only to advance the objectives of institution-alized religion, but others, while adverting to the historical position wedding religion and education, interpret the partnership along broader lines. Religion, they say, was believed essential to a sound education, but schools were not mere handmaidens to the church. In any case, during the colonial and national periods few people thought seriously about divorcing religion from education, although there was a perceptible, if slow, trend away from the establishment of Bible commonwealths and an ecclesiastical social order securely buttressed by civil authority and a class-structured society. Yet, in the seventeenth century every colony in New England, save Rhode Island, had an established church and in the other colonies the situation was about the same. But colonial people, comfortable in this circumstance, discouraged change.

As the years wore on, however, the character of the country shifted, religious allegiances were altered, and the influence of the church over civil affairs was reduced. Then, suddenly, proponents of a new theory of government voiced opposition both to establishments of religion and

intrusions of the church into secular and civil affairs. Thomas Jefferson
and Benjamin Franklin, prominent and effective spokesmen who opposed
religious establishment, extended their demurrals to include religious and
denominational teaching in the schools. Franklin displayed only modest
interest in religion and banned it from the curriculum of his Philadelphia
Academy,[29] although schools for which Franklin's school served as a
prototype often embraced religious education. Jefferson, a constant
friend of wide and generous distribution of education to the children
of the country, consistently opposed religious instruction in schools
and colleges. Democracy, he argued, was impossible when citizens were
coerced religiously; and for Jefferson establishment of religion, inevitably
leading to some suppression of religious freedom, and religious instruction
in schools were forms of coercion.[30] Jefferson, the author of the Virginia
Act for Establishing Religious Freedom, passed in 1779, expressed a
minority view in the colonies, as did the act, for Jefferson's brand of
democracy was feared and despised in many parts of the country.

It could be argued, despite the undoubted influence exerted on later
times by Franklin and Jefferson, that neither was responsible for instituting a tradition wherein both the church and religious education were
sharply separated from the state. Their pronouncements in opposition
to official sectarian creeds and to religious education as limitations on
freedom were regularly countered by the statements of dozens of public
men, not always great historical figures but nevertheless influential at the
time, who defended the intimate relationship between religion and education and sometimes had friendly things to say about official religious
creeds.

Regardless of the arguments pro and con, public opinion adopted a
stance in the years prior to the ratification of the Constitution later
translated into the First Amendment: "Congress shall make no law
respecting an establishment of religion or prohibiting the free exercise
thereof; or abridging the freedom of speech or of the press; or the right
of the people peaceably to assemble, and to petition the government
for a redress of grievances." Yet, one should notice, this amendment
limited the action of Congress and the federal government, not the states,
and, moreover, skirted the issue of religion in education. One doubts,
therefore, that the First Amendment was the culmination of a tradition
erecting a wall of separation between religion and public education.

The protection afforded citizens in the First Amendment, indeed, the
whole Bill of Rights, seemed clear enough, although it applied, until 1868,
to congressional action. In 1868, the Fourteenth Amendment made the
Bill of Rights applicable to the states. Section I of the amendment reads:
"All persons born or naturalized in the United States and subject to the
jurisdiction thereof, are citizens of the United States and of the State
where they reside. No State shall abridge the privileges or immunities

of citizens of the United States; nor shall any State deprive any person of life, liberty, or property, without due process of law; nor deny to any person within its jurisdiction the equal protection of the laws."

Without the Fourteenth Amendment, it is doubtful that between 1950 and 1970 the federal government could have become involved in those educational issues relating to ensuring equality of educational opportunity; yet the Fourteenth Amendment alone gives us little insight into a constitutional stance relative to the place of religion in public education.

Decline in Support for Private and Religious Education

Despite an intimate association between organized religion and formal education during the early colonial years, the compact between the two began to erode about 1750, and denominational control over education suffered decline. Academies became more popular as they emphasized practical studies; higher education gave, because it had to, more attention to science and secular programs and less to divinity courses. Still, during these years evidence of public education was slim, and various civil jurisdictions awarded financial and other support to private and church schools.

Although only select private and religious schools were the beneficiaries of public money, the practice of school support between 1635 and 1870 established a precedent for using public funds for private education. Institutions ranging from denominational Latin grammar schools to private and (in their origin) nonsectarian academies were permitted to share in public funds and land grants. Even after laws were passed prohibiting sectarian teaching in public or common schools, private schools continued to receive, although less regularly, support from public sources. In some cases where schools were excluded from sharing in public resource, it was not because they were denominational or private. In Massachusetts, for example, a law prohibited academies from obtaining public land grants if other schools existed nearby; and the famous Massachusetts Law of 1827 forbade the teaching of sectarian doctrine in the common schools of the state, not the use of public money for church-related schools.

While the First Amendment is now interpreted to mean that public funds may not be used for denominational purposes in private schools, this meaning was by no means clear to President Grant, who twice urged the adoption of an amendment to the Constitution prohibiting the use of public money for church-related schools. This proposed amendment failed of adoption, yet it served to call attention to a practice long employed of using public money to aid private and religious schools, and shortly thereafter the states began to enact laws or adopt constitutional provisions limiting the use of public money to clear and specific public purposes. In some states the language of statute or constitutional prohibition specified religious institutions. The legal precedent restricting the use of public resources and excluding religious institutions and schools is not as ancient as alleged; the policy was ratified about 1880, but its origin can hardly be attributed to the first years of the nation's birth.[31]

Religious Teaching in Public Education

In parts of the country populated by persons of similar religious faith, schools traditionally incorporated sectarian instruction in their curricula. In most American colonies the degree of religious uniformity was sufficient to recommend both public support for schools and instruction for children in the creed of the principal religious sect practiced there. Yet this procedure, so long in force in this country, was thwarted by the introduction of denominational pluralism in the early years of the nineteenth century. Religious affiliation and outlook began to change and the adherence people paid to orthodox sects shifted—often in a dramatic fashion—to a variety of liberal creeds. At this point the relationship of schools to religious denominations became critical, for sectarian feeling was deep enough, indeed, often bitter enough, to challenge the control over instruction approved by tradition or custom. Effort by orthodox creeds to retain control of schools was inconsistent with the spirit of the time and with the tenor of the current democratic political philosophy. Persons of liberal religious tendency were in accord when the question of religious instruction in the schools was raised: orthodox control over social and political institutions had to be broken.

This spirit of religious liberalism became strong enough that by 1820 the old religious denominations—whose colonial affiliations dated to the first years of settlement—were forced to relinquish influence and control. Their surrender was reluctant and never without a fight. But even an eroded orthodoxy left the issue unsettled, because various liberal sects tried to take the place of orthodox creeds. Liberal religionists wanted sectarian teaching in the schools and sought after it as eagerly as their orthodox brethren. But differences among liberal sects were profound and they refused to allow any sect to dominate education after the fashion of orthodoxy. Possibly the only reasonable solution was the one finally adopted: sectarian teaching was proscribed in public schools. For most of the nineteenth century this policy was interpreted as an affirmation of religious education and effort was apparent to fortify education with religious worth, but it was nonsectarian religion.

The purpose of sectarian instruction in the schools was obvious: children should be schooled in, and persuaded of, the reasonableness and rectitude of sectarian doctrine. Nonsectarianism abandoned doctrine to invest in morality and asserted that morality could be inculcated best by beginning with a foundation of religious belief. The instrument thought most suitable to this purpose was the Bible, for it eschewed sect and spoke in direct language about divine moral imperative.

When a Massachusetts act, in 1827, declared common schools legally nonsectarian, particular reference was made to the employment of the Bible in school instruction, although without interpretation or commentary. So with this start the practice became usual in some states to require Bible reading without explanation as part of regular instructional exercises; in other states, where the issue of establishing a religious foundation for morality seemed less urgent, Bible reading was merely permitted; but in still other states the Bible appeared to contain elements of sectarianism, so its use in schools was prohibited. This, in general, was the situation until 1952. At first, some denominations, principally Roman Catholics, had opposed the use of the Bible in public education because the version commonly used in schools was inconsistent with Catholic Biblical scholarship,[32] but for the most part Bible reading in schools was not seen as a burning educational issue of the day. And the public schools, despite the possibility of introducing some religious instruction by using the Bible, were more and more characterized as secular agencies.

In 1952, however, where a New Jersey statute provided for the reading, without comment, of five verses from the Old Testament at the opening of each public school day, the constitutionality of Bible-reading statutes was challenged. For long dormant as an educational issue, people were awakened from indifference when the United States Supreme Court, on technical legal grounds, refused to take jurisdiction in a litigation involving the New Jersey law, and a lower-court decision which found no fault with New Jersey's statute was allowed to stand.[33]

At about the same time other issues related to religion in public education were raised, so the New Jersey case, though abortive, focused attention on a point of educational practice heretofore usually unnoticed. The hiatus was about to end. In June, 1963, the United States Supreme Court declared Bible reading and the recitation of the Lord's Prayer in public schools a violation of the "establishment clause" of the First Amendment. To this time the states had a variety of laws and regulations concerning Bible reading: in 1963, thirteen states required daily Bible reading; twenty-five states permitted it, but always without comment or explanation; eight states, labeling the Bible sectarian, prohibited it from public schools; and four states were silent.

The 1963 decision (*School District of Abington Township* v. *Schempp*) adjudicated two cases involving Bible reading: a Pennsylvania law required "at least ten verses from the Holy Bible shall be read, without comment, at the opening of each public school on each school day. Any child shall be excused from such Bible reading, or attending such Bible reading, upon the written request of his parent or guardian;" and a regulation of the Board of School Commissioners of Baltimore prescribing opening exercises consisting primarily of the "reading, without comment, of a chapter of the Holy Bible and/or the use of the Lord's Prayer."[34]

According to the court, schools following the Pennsylvania law and the regulation of Baltimore were imposing exercises under the requirements of compulsory attendance, and these exercises were in school buildings under the direct supervision of teachers. Further, the court wrote, these opening exercises were, and were intended to be, religious ceremonies. The Bible is an instrument with a definite religious, even sectarian character, so the court concluded, the law and the regulation required religious exercises conducted in direct violation of the rights of the initiators of the suits. These required exercises were, in the court's opinion, unmitigated when students could absent themselves on parental request, for in itself this could furnish no defense to a claim of unconstitutionality under the establishment clause of the First Amendment.

When the court struck down the practice of Bible reading in public education, it intentionally left untouched biblical study. The Bible, the court wrote, is worthy of study for its literary and historical qualities, and the decision was not intended to alter school programs including biblical and religious study when presented objectively in a secular curriculum. Rather than excluding biblical and religious studies from the schools, the court commended them and called attention to an academic incompleteness when comparative religion and the history of religion are excluded from the syllabus of civilization.[35] The court, however, was at pains to put these studies in a secular, not merely a nonsectarian, context, and the decision sparked a new approach to study about religion in public schools, an approach criticized by friends of Bible reading and religious study as being unsatisfactory. Since 1963 efforts have been made to amend the Constitution to permit what the Supreme Court prohibited: Bible reading in public schools. This proposed amendment, however, without widespread support, has little chance of adoption.

At about the time Bible reading in public education was revived and contested another religious practice—prayer—was introduced, or reintroduced, to the schools. Early American schools, we know, having a close relationship with organized Christianity, followed the practice of opening and closing the school day with prayer. Much of education's content in early schools was moral and religious, and in the nineteenth century especially the schools and their students gained a great deal of moral inspiration from the famous *McGuffey Readers*. Yet with the imposition of a nonsectarian code on public education in the nineteenth century, most states regarded public-school prayer a violation of law. Thereafter, prayer was an uncommon pedagogic practice. But in the 1950s, with the whetting of religious appetites, some states began to experiment with nonsectarian prayers. In 1951, for example, the New York State Board of Regents proposed the recitation of a nonsectarian prayer in the public schools of the state. Although the recommendation was spared public hostility, only about ten percent of the school districts chose to follow it. The prayer was brief and simple: "Almighty God, we acknowledge our dependence upon Thee, and we beg Thy blessings upon us, our parents, our teachers, and our country."

The constitutionality of an officially adopted prayer was challenged and, in 1962, in *Engel* v. *Vitale,* the United States Supreme Court declared the New York school prayer unconstitutional, because it constituted an establishment of religion by government, impermissible under the First Amendment. At first the court's decision was optimistically interpreted to mean that prayer in school was unconstitutional when composed by a government agency or whenever the state invaded the neutral ground of religious conscience. Later, however, the import of the decision was clear: *Engel* v. *Vitale* outlawed government-authored prayers and all other prayers as well. Irrespective of composition, prayer in public schools violated the First Amendment.[36]

Bible reading and prayer in public education were settled in the 1960s, so we can consider their record complete. But a decade before these decisions were rendered, when the tactic to return religion to public education was different, the outcome was similar. Perhaps the revival of Bible reading and prayer as academic exercises was in some way related to the failure of released-time programs experimented with in various places until their legality was rejected by the courts.

In the 1940s two school districts in Illinois instituted a novel program for teaching religion in the schools. During the regular school day, persons representing various denominations came to schools to teach the elements of their sect. Students could elect to attend the classes. Teachers were not paid with public funds, although the facilities of schools were used for religious classes. This was the situation leading to the *McCollum* v. *Board of Education* decision in 1948.

State courts found the practice legal; the United States Supreme Court declared it a violation of the First Amendment and articulated a principle which has since been followed: "To hold that a state cannot consistently with the First and Fourteenth Amendments utilize its public school system to aid any or all religious faiths or sects in the dissemination of their doctrines and ideals does not, as counsel urge, manifest a governmental hostility to religion or religious teachings. A manifestation of such hostility would be at war with our national tradition as embodied in the First Amendment's guaranty of the free exercise of religion. For the First Amendment rests upon the premise that both religion and government can best work to achieve their lofty aims if each is left free from the other within its respective sphere. Or, as we said in the *Everson* case, the First

Amendment has erected a wall between Church and State which must be kept high and impregnable."[37]

The decision adverted to tax-supported public-school buildings used for the dissemination of religious doctrines and concluded that the state was affording sectarian groups an invaluable aid in providing pupils for the religious classes through the use of the state's compulsory attendance laws. This, the court ruled, was not separation of church and state.

Still, another side to the issue was revealed in the released-time case in 1952 (*Zorach* v. *Clauson*). A New York law permitted public schools to release students from school, on the written request of their parents, to attend religious classes or participate in devotional exercises. Neither public funds nor buildings were involved, although students who chose to attend the classes in religion were under the jurisdiction of the school and subject to the compulsory attendance statute. In the wake of the *McCollum* decision which, as we have seen, raised a wall of separation between church and state, the New York practice showed signs of vulnerability, so a constitutional test was inevitable. The charge against released-time was clear and direct: it was an establishment of religion and public resources were used for religious and sectarian purposes. The United States Supreme Court demurred and held released-time permissible under the First Amendment doctrine because it neither prohibited the free exercise of religion nor made a law respecting an establishment of religion.

The court's opinion, moreover did not repeat the "wall of separation" metaphor employed in the *McCollum* decision. It explained instead that the separation of the state from religion should be cultivated without hostility, suspicion, and unfriendliness; church and state, the court averred, must maintain a symbiotic association, one wherein two dissimilar organisms learn to conduct their affairs without intrusion. In any case, the accent of the *Zorach* decision was different from the tone of the *McCollum* opinion. Justice William O. Douglas, writing for the majority, expressed the court's respect for religion and religious institutions: "When the state encourages religious instruction . . . it follows the best of our traditions"; although while the state may encourage religion, it cannot aid it. Government, however, should "sponsor an attitude that lets each religious group flourish."[38]

The effect of the Supreme Court decisions reviewed here was to insulate public schools from direct religious and sectarian influence: neither in prayer, Bible reading nor religious teaching could public resources be employed. If religion were to maintain a place in education other alternatives had to be found. One alternative, of course, was the private school, now secure under the protection of the *Oregon* decision, but the private school even at the most flourishing point of its American experience was unable to fulfill the educational demand of the country or satisfy large segments of the school population who sought for an instructional integration of religion, morality, and learning. Another alternative tested briefly, with some evidence of success, was shared-time. In shared-time programs, apparently permitted by most state laws and as yet untested on constitutional merit, students from private and religious schools used certain instructional facilities of public schools regularly. This brand of scholastic cooperation implemented public-private dualism on an operational level and made the partnership of public and private schools—so often idealized in theory—extend to the curriculum: students in private and religious schools were instructed therein in religion, literature, history, social studies—all those subjects assumed to have value orientation—but took other courses, in mathematics, science, art, mechanical and industrial art, and home economics, in public schools.[39]

This novel plan, practiced first in the early 1960s, showed considerable promise and is still followed in some localities, but after a brave beginning its popularity has receded. Whether shared-time will endure appears doubtful, for the schools standing to benefit most from such an arrangement, private and religious schools, have found it difficult or impossible, even with the financial relief implicit in shared-time, to remain solvent. And public-school educators, once enthusiastic about the academic possibilities of shared-time, have cooled to its prospects.

Education and the Child-Welfare Doctrine

So far, in looking at the relationship between religion and public education, we have seen a steady drift from conventions recommended and permitted in earlier years. Over the past three decades at least, the courts have required public education to be steadfastly nonsectarian and, some say, secular. Still, students attending private and religious schools are citizens and the benefits intended for citizens extend to them irrespective of the school they attend. This legal principle has a clear affirmation from the United States Supreme Court, although legal controversy and academic discord have accompanied its application.

Asserting a child's right as a citizen entitled to benefits offered by the public was the burden of the 1930 Supreme Court decision in *Cochran* v. *The Board of Education of Louisiana*. A Louisiana law permitted the state to supply textbooks to children attending private religious schools in the same way that books were supplied public-school children. The law was challenged on the ground that it either aided or advanced sectarian religion, but the court held it constitutional because it achieved a public purpose even though in doing so a private end was incidentally promoted.[40] And in *Everson* v. *The Board of Education* (1947) the legal principle cited in *Cochran* was ratified.[41]

The *Everson* case involved a New Jersey statute authorizing school districts to pay transportation costs for children attending private non-profit schools. In responding to the constitutional challenge, the court wrote that the wall of separation between church and state was not breached by such benefits, because children received them as citizens, not as students in one or another school. The state, the court said, is obliged to ignore the child's creed but not his need, and this New Jersey law, in contributing to the safe and expeditious transport of children to and from school, fulfilled a public purpose even when private schools obviously, but indirectly, benefited. The court's decision made auxiliary educational services available to all children without regard to the school they attend, and in the years following the decision a variety of auxiliary services have been awarded children in private and religious schools.

Supplying clear precedent for litigation respecting public educational benefits, the court, in the *Everson* case, declared against legal and official hostility to religion and religious schools: "Such is obviously not the purpose of the First Amendment. That Amendment requires the state to be neutral in its relations with groups of religious believers and non-believers; it does not require the state to be their adversary. State power is no more to be used so as to handicap religions than it is to favor them. . . . The First Amendment has erected a wall between church and state. That wall must be kept high and impregnable. We could not approve the slightest breach. New Jersey has not breached it here."[42]

EDUCATIONAL PURPOSE AND STANDARD

Control and support of schools and the place of religion in public education were sensitive issues accounting for ferment in American education following World War II, but they were not alone in generating controversy. Society was changing; its values were altered in a variety of important ways; and the nostalgic affinity to more settled years was shaken time and again. Social and educational questions were raised and almost inevitably their answers involved the conduct of schools.

Perhaps the date, more than any other, marking a new beginning was 1957, when the Soviet Union successfully launched a space vehicle, the famous Sputnik. This monumental scientific and engineering achievement by a cold war antagonist appeared as a bad omen and a decided threat to American world power and influence. Its aftermath introduced an intensive reexamination of American society, and foremost among those elements in society subject to scrutiny was education. Sound education, one heard now, was a principal means for obtaining and maintaining supremacy in international, military, economic, scientific, and political affairs, and American education, it was alleged, had in some respects betrayed the country by its ineptitude and, moreover, had allowed a foreign power to achieve both scientific success and international notoriety in the race for world loyalties. So after 1958 educators undertook to realign the objectives of schools, to make them more academic, intellectual, and above all more scientific. The federal government, too, involved itself in this upgrading and through a variety of agencies, including the Department of Defense, and programs supported scientific instruction in schools and colleges.

With all this attention, encouragement, and money, the schools retreated from progressive ideologies to which they had regularly showed some attachment, even when shying from their methods, and for a brief interlude embraced sturdy academic objectives. Schools began to emphasize science and mathematics and high praise was given schools and students excelling in these subjects. Other subjects in school curricula were put in some jeopardy through lack of attention and cultivation. Humanists and social scientists were hard pressed to defend their studies in competition with the superior claim of science and technology. But this interlude, wherein science was paid such extraordinary heed, was only temporary; soon this intense academic commitment was doubted and debated. The apex of scientific interest was reached and decline began.

Traditional versus Modern School Programs

Traditional education, although often caricatured, tended to stand on the premise that schools were intended to instruct children in those things enabling them to take productive places in society. Formal education was principally a preparation for life; and this preparation could and should include, depending on the capacity and motivation of students, a wide range of authentic academic programs. Schools were places where learning was prized above all other activities, and when traditional educators talked about learning they meant to emphasize literary and linguistic achievement. As we have said, the resurgence of academic objectives after 1958 was a good omen for the traditional school but, as we have said also, this resurgence was only temporary. Modern school programs, often reminding us of the progressive surge of earlier years, had their inception, or reincarnation, around 1960; disdaining an emphasis heretofore put on academic achievement, and in some instances rejecting academic achievement as a sensible school objective, these programs adopted the dogmatic assumption that schools were conducted uneconomically and unscientifically. In the wake of this assumption two new philosophies of schooling—humanism and behaviorism—made an appearance on the American educational scene.

Humanism

Captivated by the promise of novelty, humanist spokesmen began by indicting American schools for their failure to individualize. Schools, they
said, had adopted too literally the doctrine that education's purpose is to
ensure social solidarity and, moreover, students were taught in inartistic
and impersonal ways. The academic lock step, humanists charged, had
dulled education's soul. But this was not all—although alone, if accurate,
it was a serious charge: schools, humanists went on, were filled with
petty and oppressive rules; using fear of failure as a motivating force
they cultivated distrust of society and disrespect for persons and thus,
whatever their social objective may have been, were certain to fail in
its realization. The gulf between school life and real life was too great,
humanist writers alleged, and students ended up with an abundance either
of meaningless or irrelevant knowledge or, equally bad, learned nothing
at all from their time invested in schooling. From this point on the word
most often used in connection with modernized educational programs
was relevance, and it mattered not whether the word was carefully defined
or left simply to the personal interpretation of the student. Finally,
among all these criticisms leveled at the schools by romantic reformers,
were charges that the schools were incapable of promoting the one thing
they should have prized most: thought. In addition, they neglected affective learning. In the end, humanists maintained, the schools were hardly
more than custodial agencies and were in urgent need of radical reform.

To redress these shortcomings and, at the same time, to insulate education from objectives set by conservative schoolmen—good citizenship
and a mastery of basic knowledge—humanists proposed their own theory
of schooling, a theory sometimes suffering from the triteness of novelty.

Beginning with the assumption that human nature is good and that
traditional standards are artificial and meaningless, humanists eschewed
a comprehensive philosophy of education to deal directly with the moral
and intellectual appetite of students. More than anything else, save relevance, they praised the child-centered school (often pretending it to be
their invention), wherein students pursued courses of study which had
an appeal of suitability and satisfaction. The model most often displayed
for imitation was Summerhill, a British school founded by A. S. Neill
in the 1920s. Freedom was Summerhill's watchword: requirements were
abandoned and students did what they wanted. Educational facilities, instructional materials, and teachers were all there, but students used them
as they pleased or not at all. There were no examinations, no standards of
achievement had to be met, and no system of values was recommended
for emulation.[43] This was one way of breaking the academic lock step,
the worst of educational evils, humanists said, but, as it turned out, while
Summerhill could be used as a model for writers who wanted to infect

schools in America with what they liked to call educational excitement, schools following the Summerhill model rarely found much support in the United States. Other plans, variations of the Summerhill model, were substituted.

One popular plan, with some affinity to the British school, was the open classroom. Appearance was its most obvious departure from schools familiar to most Americans: no desks or chairs were arranged in neat rows in rooms, if indeed there were classrooms at all; children were not assigned places in school nor were they scheduled for prearranged courses of study. They were free to find a station and there engage in a kind of study personally interesting and satisfying. Students worked alone or in groups as they saw fit. While the best open classrooms had talented teachers and an abundance of instructional materials, they stood as resources to be utilized when the need arose. In open classrooms students were mainly independent to direct the course of their learning and to determine its pace. Teachers were ready to help, but they avoided intruding on the privacy of learning.

Other plans, such as the free school, were tried, but for the most part they were variations of the open classroom and shared its central character: all were student-centered and stressed activity in the same way old progressive schools idealized it.[44]

Always praising learning, discovery and personal meaning were promoted, for, according to humanists, the one law of learning with explicit validity was the law of effect. But in addition to learning what is satisfying and avoiding or ignoring the unpleasant and unrewarding, students in these schools were to be shaped by their social environment. Their motivation, arising from personal experience, was intrinsic and any motivation or instructional objective supplied by teachers was either rejected or discouraged. Teachers and pedagogic method were to facilitate the kind of learning students judged best for them.

Humanistic schooling was silent about standards of achievement and no body of knowledge was considered essential for all students. Students should learn to be themselves, to find their capacities and capitalize them, and schools should allow them ample opportunity to realize whatever talent they have. Obviously talent and interest differ greatly from one to another student—humanists are never blind to individual differences—so there is no talk about a uniform curriculum. In addition to learning what one wants to know, however, there is a point made in humanist schools about the development of self-concept and the cultivation of mental health. Education's objective is to provide students with means for obtaining personal happiness and it matters not where these means are found or what they are. In any case, they are bound to vary from one to another student. Still, humanists recognize that when students leave school they must live, and earn their living, in a complex and demanding society where standards of achievement, conduct, and morality are enforced. But the best way, they aver, for students to recognize what society expects is by discovering it on the anvil of personal experience. Codes pertaining to achievement, morality, and conduct should not be forced; they should arise naturally in the society of the school.[45]

These views of education are embraced by most humanists who see the schools (drastically reorganized in content and method) as principal means for their adoption, but other humanists functioning outside the main current of humanist thought are ready to dispense with schools altogether and dismantle compulsory attendance statutes now enforced by the states. Persons, they say, can be educated in many ways and places, and some think the schools the worst of all places. If schools are abandoned, education can still proceed, for there are in every community various alternatives to formal schooling which might, these innovators claim, be superior to the schools which only give the appearance of satisfaction. Carried to an extreme, humanist philosophy of schooling recommends a jettisoning of schools.[46]

Behaviorism

But if schooling, in the humanist conception, too often misses the mark, behaviorism is prepared to advance and justify a theory wherein schooling, if properly managed, is the only possible solution to the problems of human society. So behaviorist-inspired education has risen to challenge the de-schooling and anti-instructional assertions of humanists. Neither good people nor good societies just happen, behaviorists say; they are produced. And good people and good societies are the objectives of educational behaviorism.

While behaviorism as a psychological theory dates from the nineteenth century, its influence on education, except as it affected the work of Edward L. Thorndike, was modest. The bold assertion of the behaviorist that a controlled environment is capable of molding persons irrespective of individual characteristics and capacities was generally too arrogant and mechanistic for rank-and-file educators to accept; they preferred to regard personal formation along more conventional lines and to take into account the talent, the native motivation and the free will of persons being educated. Environment was one factor in human formation, but only one.

Whether behaviorist claims are more generally acknowledged in educational circles now than before is doubtful, but in 1971, after having carried out for a decade or more extensive laboratory research on conditioning, B. F. Skinner published *Beyond Freedom and Dignity,* wherein he argued, at times convincingly, that persons are the products of environmental conditioning. They are what their environment makes them: nothing more nor less.[47] As a result of Skinner's work and the notoriety won for his book, behaviorist influence on school learning increased tremendously.

In popularizing behavioral engineering Skinner, we know, was hardly inventing a new approach to human learning, for this had been tried before in the early years of the progressive period, but contemporary behaviorism was supported by experimental research giving it a validity and a respectability almost totally lacking in the older projection to conduct schools according to principles of human engineering. Armed with often convincing evidence, the pedagogic followers of Skinner argued that humanism was too vague in its approach to learning and left too much to chance. Besides, behaviorists said, humanism simply ignored the facts of life when it allowed children to follow their own desires. and motives, because they were not, in the final analysis, following them at all but merely drifting in the direction a chaotic environment urged on them.

Where humanists argued for a hands-off policy in school learning, believing somehow the genius of personality would thrive in consequence, behaviorists maintained that intervention in education was not only desirable but essential: the fault, behaviorists asserted with considerable zeal, was not with too much intervention but with the wrong kind. Teachers should be expected to teach, so much was taken for granted, but teaching should aim at producing the right kind of behavior. Behavior, they said, sometimes sounding ominous—although it would be hard to conceive of any learning indifferent to behavioral change—was capable of modification and the school should invest its best talent and its highest capital to do so. Education, it was asserted, is mainly a matter of creating the right kind of environment to improve behavior. Thus, it becomes the school's function and the teacher's role, first of all, to discover what desirable behavior is and then conduct the school's learning activities in such a way that this behavior will be adopted by all students.[48]

When teachers are clear about their objectives, and when they acknowledge their instructional role, operant conditioning (an application of the law of effect) and reinforcing stimuli can result in producing the kind of learning judged most beneficial, and this learning must not be stated in general terms but must be brought down to the level of specific competencies. What specific skill, as an instructional outcome, is the student now capable of using? The curriculum itself is filled with lists of competencies for which both teachers and students are responsible.

In an earlier educational period, we know, progressive educators had stressed the significance of student-centered education and for decades its praises were sung. In the late 1960s and the 1970s humanistic education heaped praise on individuality in instruction and modernized the progressive version of the child-centered school. Behaviorism, having none of this, refused to follow the same line. Schoolchildren were not to be mistreated nor was discipline expected to be cruel and harsh, but schools were places wherein certain behavioral skills were to be mastered and it was the teacher's responsibility, assuming a position at the center of the learning situation, to conduct and supervise this kind of learning. The teacher's duty is instruction and it matters little whether children are fond of their teacher: achievement counts. What have students learned? Have they realized the objectives set out in the first place? If they have, the teacher is judged effective; if not, the teacher's evaluation is adverse. This principle, if indeed it can be called a principle, forms the basis for what in recent years is called accountability. Teachers are accountable—responsible—for the achievement of their students, and if students fail to achieve the standards specified the fault must be either in the teacher's knowledge or skill.

This behavioral thrust in contemporary American education has introduced and approved the practice of framing behavioral objectives, and teachers have spent countless hours dissecting the curriculum searching for them. It has, in addition, enhanced the status of programmed instruction and teaching machines where the effect of conditioning can be seen quickly and clearly.[49] The schools, following this educational prescription, assume the character of a workshop and, their critics say, lose the human and cultural qualities conventionally associated with learning. But the intention of educational behaviorism is not to dehumanize learning, for, it is alleged, such features to learning can be produced better according to this plan than by following the haphazard methodology of humanistic and traditional education. Furthermore, they say there are better opportunities for individualizing instruction and communicating skills to students with a special need for them. Students can learn what they need to know and an assessment of their learning can be made directly and precisely.

Many familiar signs remain in behaviorist education, but these signs can be misleading, for learning is approached as an exercise in conditioning and in no other way. Still, conventional adherence to classroom management is there and all reminders of soft pedagogy are stripped away; punishment is employed as part of the conditioning process and is used with a specific purpose. Affective education, in which humanistic education indulges and which, they say, behaviorism neglects, is obtained by following methods common to all behaviorist learning. Finally, teaching for thinking, which most educators are quick to agree is the ultimate outcome of the educational process, is handled in the same precise, mechanical way as any other kind of learning. The realization of high educational effectiveness is the promise of behaviorism and, according to its most eloquent spokesmen, what is to be accomplished is defined with precision and exactness.

Thus, as education works its way through the eighth decade of this century, issues concerning purpose and method are unsettled. In earlier years debate raged over educational philosophy, school support and control, and religion in the schools—and to some extent these issues still linger on the fringe of scholastic consciousness. But more recently educational method has become a central issue, for the differences between humanistic and behavioristic education are not found principally in a philosophy of education but in a philosophy of schooling. Humanism and behaviorism, although differing considerably in method and emphasis, form a corps in modern education, and ranged against them are the traditional methodologies. Like so many other problems in American education, only time, experience and prudence will sort out and retain worthwhile and effective pedagogic practice and discard what is unproductive and dehumanizing.

War and Protest

What had come to be regarded as a self-evident proposition in American society was subjected to rude reappraisal as the United States became more deeply involved in the war in Viet Nam. What had for so long been taken for granted was the willingness of schools and colleges, along with their students, to support patriotically the nation at war. This had been demonstrated time and again in two world wars and there were no obvious signs of defection during the Korean War. But now the case was different, or more accurately, the authenticity of national purpose was perceived in divergent ways. At the outset student petition and demonstration had supported the initial action of the Kennedy Administration to introduce democracy to the countries of Southeast Asia, but as the country became more deeply involved in conflict so far from home, and as the reasons for the involvement of the United States appeared less certain and convincing, school and student support began to evaporate. Eventually student protest became so obtrusive in some colleges—lower schools were always less directly affected—that regular academic activities were interrupted or halted. Student strike, protest, and demonstration first took students away from regular studies as they declaimed against an involvement of the country in a war so far away and so uncertain in its ultimate purpose, and then they began to subject their courses of instruction to careful and critical, although not always responsible, analysis. One thing led to another until the schools and colleges were no longer in the custody of their boards of trustees, school committees, and administrators but were controlled by the pressure and counter-pressure of students. Academic buildings and administrators' offices were occupied and held as fortresses by student protesters as they bargained for what they liked to call their academic rights. The world of American education (except for elementary schools) was in turmoil and educational leaders, unused to what faced them now, were unable to find solutions satisfactory to students and compatible with the integrity of the educational process.[50]

Historically literate persons knew that student activism was invented before the twentieth century; they had seen it before in earlier generations or other places or had read about it, but historical perspective was helpless to still the ferment of activism and protest.

Schools and colleges were encouraged by their students to withhold all kinds of support from the military activity of the United States. Reserve officer training programs, common for decades in hundreds of American colleges and almost universal in land-grant institutions, were abandoned as colleges capitulated to student demand; curricular metamorphosis was introduced with surprising speed and without much attention to academic quality as students obtained direct and indirect control over the course of studies and made relevance their article of academic faith; courses which a decade earlier would not have been certified for academic credit and which at their best lacked scholastic standard became common features in the curricula of most schools. The management of schools, traditionally the province of persons responsible for their support, was expanded to include students: school boards and committees, boards of trustees, curriculum committees, personnel boards, tenure and promotion committees—in short, all those agencies in the schools responsible for orderly academic government and policy—were rendered almost totally ineffectual without student representatives. Administrators felt powerless to act, and were sometimes afraid to act, without student support or consent. The conviction that persons in the process of learning should not be charged with determining either the purpose or method of their education was assaulted, and the thought that education was too serious a matter to be left to student judgment alone was rejected by student activists with anger and sometimes with violence. In other eras the world of learning had accommodated to a new face, but nothing quite so grim as was witnessed now.

Historians may assert that this period of protest and student activism provided a needed catharsis for American education, and such assertions contain elements of truth, but they can argue also that irruptions were too penetrating and so lacking in common prudence and infested with political motive that the progress of schools and colleges in their search for better and more realistic educational standards was retarded and the quality of learning to which a generation of students was exposed was downgraded. The contemporary allegation making students the best and only judge of educational content and standard demeans learning to the level of merchandising, where consumer right is justified, and misplaces responsibility to the point where student interest, demand, and whim become impediments to decent learning. Still, during this interlude in the 1960s, in a determination to maintain peace in the schools, educators and school administrators regularly, and sometimes enthusiastically, capitulated before student pressure and in the end came close to surrendering their educational and moral authority.

Toward the termination of the Viet Nam War in 1974, however, the nation's economy no longer supported the luxuries afforded in more prosperous times. And student attitudes, earlier often characterized by an indifference to solid learning and academic accomplishment, began to change and a more traditional respect for learning started to return. Students in schools and colleges, who for a decade or more were careless of personal appearance, dress, and cleanliness, began to assume more conventional habits. This shift in attitude led some observers to take seriously a close correlation between economic conditions and scholastic motives.

In conducting a review of this period in American education, often frantic and frequently violent, the historian should remember that among sounds of protest and amid signs of negativism in classroom and on campus an idealism of purpose flourished. And this idealism was too often hidden behind unconventional dress and manner. Students in American schools, perhaps more able than their parents to afford idealism, and always with fewer obligations, were fully supportive of the general civil rights movement and of equality of educational opportunity; as a result of this consistent support many schools and colleges offered an educational chance to talented minority youth which otherwise might have been slow to come. And employing atypical arithmetic, women were counted with minorities. So schools and colleges, in addition to all the other problems heaped on them, were faced with the task of making special provision, and sometimes concession, to women students. The most obvious, although by no means the most important sign of this was the demise of the old-time male college. Schools that in some cases had for more than a hundred years set their educational sights on the education of men were put under extreme pressure to become coeducational. Tossing tradition aside, many of them did.

CHAPTER THIRTEEN

Culture and Education in Contemporary Society

The history of Western education reveals an almost constant debate over the means schooling should employ to inculcate each succeeding generation with values embraced by a society. Among the disputed educational issues Western man has wrestled with, the one most distinctly troublesome concerned what should be taught. Other issues, it is true, have been contested with extraordinary vigor, but the curricular question of what schools should teach stands first on the list. It should not surprise us, then, to learn that the principal educational debate, affecting all school levels, centers now on the content of teaching. When societies are self-confident, when they trust their fundamental instincts and values, they find it easier to set their educational compass, to define the work of schools and to elaborate their aspiration relative to the outcome of formal schooling. But in years of social stress and turmoil, when self-confidence declines and values are uncertainly held, educational expectation is blurred by conflicting loyalties and the mission of schooling becomes clouded and obscure. The course of American education so far seen attests the validity of this generalization.

The country's first schools settled on their curriculum giving hardly any thought to what they were doing. The syllabus of instruction for pupils assembled on benches before the teacher contained what most decently educated persons thought worth knowing. Educational goals were modest; the common branches, it was generally agreed, were enough, and few people had any doubt about what they were. Learning was to be useful, both temporally and eternally, so the schools undertook to teach their students how to use skills in connection with a decent life and to live in such a way as to ensure an eternal reward from a benevolent but always vigilant God.

377

Religious perspective braced by fundamental value tended to hold the syllabus steady, and for a long time schools were conducted without any thought that education could ever become a topic for serious social disagreement or national debate. But when religious perspective atrophied, a common consensus was impaired and schoolmasters lost confidence that they were teaching what all educated men believed to be true. With shifts in social and personal philosophy the goals of education were affected and inevitably the content of schooling was directly influenced. Yet religion was not the only theme capable of unifying a society, and with the dispersion of its influence a new ideal arose to take its place: democracy. Old-time schools, we have said, were always operated in a religious context, but with the idealization of democracy and the fragmentation of religious conviction, citizenship rather than religious rectitude became the common bond of schooling. And for a long time this worked remarkably well. The schools, accepting as their mission the inculcation of civic knowledge and virtue, produced generations of American citizens whose affinity to social and political purpose is amply evidenced on the pages of United States history.

Compared to what was yet to come in American education, these early years were easy ones. The idea that education had as its primary purpose the preparation of future citizens who could fulfill the requirements imposed by a democratic society, while never entirely abandoned, was altered somewhat. Ancient tensions between social purpose and individual development were given new life as American education matured, and what could have been accepted uncritically as the proper work for a school in the 1890s was rejected in the 1960s. But even here the issue could not stand still, for however much individual development might be prized, educators could not forget the possibilities residing in schools for social change, and education began to assume the character of a social tool. Schools adopted the function of catalysts and were called agents for change. The lexicon of the educator made change its most important word and schools were conducted along lines making traditional values hard to find. According to David Tyack in *The One Best System,* and Lawrence Cremin in his 1978 Hunt Lecture before the American Association of Colleges for Teacher Education, these years so illustrative of educational ferment resemble the common school movement of the mid-nineteenth century, and predict an educational reform whose consequences could dwarf those of that crusade. These prophecies may contain elements of hyperbole, yet they reveal signs of a basic uneasiness about contemporary education.

SCHOOLING AS CULTURAL TRANSMISSION

If we take a long view of the history of education, going back as far as the Golden Age of Greece, we find the function of schools narrowly defined, although, at the same time, we find the purpose of education broad and comprehensive.[1] In a small and cohesive society, such as Athens was, it was unnecessary for the schools to concern themselves with cultural transmission, for this was something to be done in the life of the city itself. And citizens of Athens took culture seriously, prized it highly and made every effort to see that oncoming generations could walk the cultural paths of their ancestors. Athens was one great school, but there were agents and agencies designated for the more humble tasks of instruction: to teach skill and basic information enabling young people to take advantage of the more fundamental educational opportunity offered in the life of the city. However important the work of instruction may have been, and no prospective citizen ignored the classes of schoolmasters, it was always clear that schoolmasters were there for the purpose of cultivating basic learning and not for the purpose of transmitting culture.[2] In addition, the whole business of teaching or inculcating value was outside the scope of their responsibility: this was too important to be left to teachers. There was a rich and abundant culture eagerly sought after but it could be communicated in the daily intercourse of life, in the theater, in the public assembly, in the gymnasium—even on the battlefield, or whenever two citizens met on the streets of the town of Athens. No school or teacher was charged with responsibility for its transmission.

If life in society had not changed, the modest expectations for schools might have persisted. But life in society did change and the comfortable cultural existence of the Athenian city state could not be duplicated as civilization spread thoughout the West. With remarkable and fundamental changes in the nature of civic societies, along with a reverence for the cultural monuments erected by earlier generations, the old-fashioned approach to cultural transmission was altered and schools were commissioned to communicate a literary and cultural inheritance. What they taught was what was considered most important for the conduct of a decent life, not necessarily what was needed to make a living. Schools began by eschewing utility, not because they misunderstood or denigrated it, but because they thought it less important than culture itself.[3] To trace in detail the course of school purpose is not the burden of this book, but schools, we know, began with a modest purpose of providing instruction in the tools of learning and then, with the development of society, to the higher purpose of transmitting culture. And they adhered to this ancient purpose for a long time.

Eventually, however, with the appearance of Christianity, a constant combat was joined between cultural and religious values: the classics represented the former; Christian wisdom shaped the latter. In the first years of Christianity in the West the assumption was common that culture and religion, the classics and faith, were incompatible; and determined effort was made by Christian scholars to erect an educational citadel wherein classical culture could not penetrate. In the end this Christian effort failed, but it had the effect of setting the stage for an essential compromise between classical knowledge and Christian belief which the schools shortly adopted as a way of educational life.[4] At certain times in some places culture or religion was given precedence in the school's course of instruction, but whichever had pride of place on a hierarchy of instructional objective both were heeded and neither was abandoned for reasons of utility.

School purpose had matured about so far when we first meet American educators in their colonial garb. They adopted the proposition that formal education should serve two masters: religion and culture; but they were always prepared to admit that religion was of greater value.[5]

Yet, even this definition of formal education's purpose could not last, for American society was too fluid, too erratic, too energetic and progressive for anything, even education, to stand still. Passing from colonial to national status the country began to expect something different from its schools; so taking a page from the book of European countries where a consciousness of national existence and personality was being kindled, American schoolmen defined the schools' purpose as civic rather than religious or cultural and established citizenship as the superior objective of formal education. This was done as a matter of public policy as schools turned away more and more from their private character to become agencies of government.

It would be inaccurate, of course, to assert that schools dismissed both religion and culture from the syllabus when they adopted citizenship as a principal objective, but by adopting a new principal objective the character of education was changed and some of the traditional educational values were, if not now sold at discount, at least diminished in their importance. And it is at this point where we see the first signs of the liberal and conservative debate concerning the purpose of formal education.

These two terms—liberal and conservative—have a vagueness allowing for their use in a variety of contexts. We are more familiar with their employment in identifying political stances, although even then they may conceal about as much as they reveal, and are often tempted to apply them in their political sense to education. While there may be some justification for doing so, the political implications of liberal and conservative distort somewhat educational meaning and end up by disguising their real significance.

Restricted to education, the conservative position embraces the proposition that the function of formal education is to teach what can be taught, that is, to transmit to students a cultural inheritance whose principal function is to help perfect the human abilities of thought and expression. Highly significant to this purpose, always aiding in its attainment, are skill, information, and discipline. With this banner nailed to his educational mast the conservative educator is ready to acknowledge the reality of change in society. He knows the calendar does not stand still and, moreover, that it cannot be turned back. So it would be wrong to think of the conservative as a person who refuses to allow anything new or different to find its way into the school, nor does he misunderstand the nature of human nature to suppose that students are only minds who when they come to school leave their bodies, their feeling, and their emotions behind. While allowing for all these elements of human nature some play in the work of the school, he nevertheless insists on prescribing the work of the school as first and foremost a transmission of the cultural inheritance to the end that human ability may be shaped.[6]

Liberalism in education is a sharp departure from the conservative creed. Instead of stressing an educational program directed toward the development of the human abilities, liberal educators center attention on education as a means for accommodating youth to the exigencies of social life. Instead of cultural content in the curriculum, the work of learning should be directed toward the possibility of having a variety of experiences which, it is hoped, will enable young persons to grow and develop into mature members of society. Something is to be learned in the liberally-oriented school, one should not doubt that, and the content of learning is given a respectable hearing, but both the act of learning and its content are superseded by the need to immerse students in the actual issues of social living and thus to learn, not from books or persons and not to be inundated by literary culture, but by doing. Although often lacking rational justification for their position, liberal educators take seriously (even before John Dewey did), the proposition that education is life and life is education. Liberally-based education can be just as serious, and in some ways just as demanding, as conservative schooling, but as we see, its perspective is different.[7]

And difference in perspective has to do mainly with attitudes relative to permanence and change. Conservative educators maintain that both principles of permanence and change must be taken into account in the management of sound learning. There are, they say, features in the nature of men and elements in the nature of society which remain the same and education in any age should be directed at them; besides, there are plenty of indications that man has evolved in history and that he lives, works, and plays now in ways different from before. Schooling and learning should accommodate to these changes, for change is real. Yet in the schooling of human beings the principle of permanence must be dominant. The liberal creed follows a different course with respect to change and permanence.

Man and society, it reads, are the harvest of evolution, so it is pointless to allow principles of permanence either for men or societies to direct the course of education, because there are none.

For most of the twentieth century American education has danced to the tune of conservatives and liberals. At times one or another doctrine gained the ascendancy and its voice was heard in the schools. But neither liberalism nor conservativism in the past seventy-five years had sufficient strength or stability to impress its theoretic mold on the character of American education for more than a short time. In the 1970s, after perhaps two decades of liberal domination, the picture of American education is taking on a more conservative hue. Possibly tired of the cost and confusion in schools conducted along liberal lines, the American public is heeding once again the call for a "back-to-the-basics movement," and any movement such as this is bound to have close affinity to the conservative creed.[8]

EDUCATIONAL ISSUES IN CONTEMPORARY SOCIETY

Difference in philosophic perspective must by no means be ignored as a contemporary educational issue, for in the last analysis it may be the most important issue of all. But in addition to philosophy, whose fundamental character we acknowledge, other important points remain in dispute in American education and we should pay them some heed.

The Dilemma of Democratic Education

Neither schools of the colonial period nor those of the early national era were asked to be democratic: they taught the children who enrolled and in the ordinary course of events this meant their students were from homes representing some cultural background and supported by sufficient resources to afford the leisure of schooling. Although this designation was not strictly accurate, children attending the schools were thought to belong to an elite. They came from a class in society that was expected to be educated.

In colonies where religious convictions were strong a theory of general education was sometimes proposed and public policy promoted the opening of schoolhouse doors on a more liberal basis, allowing all the children of the town to attend. We see signs of this most apparently in the early (1642) Massachusetts Bay Colony legislation requiring all inhabitants of the colony to be literate. However strong the appeal may have been to popular education in the New England colonies following the example of Massachusetts, the historical reality is that this determination for general education atrophied and in the end the opportunity for education settled back to more conventional ways. The children from the better homes attended schools, sometimes all the way through the colonial college, and the children of common men learned their letters if time and circumstance allowed but were not offered the opportunity later associated with public education when common schools were open to all the children of all the people.

Toward the end of the first quarter of the nineteenth century, however, the public attitude toward education changed, due largely to campaigns waged by public men and public-spirited citizens who adopted education as the theme for their social creed. As a result of this effort public policy was modified from the old-fashioned notion that children should be educated if their station in life recommended and if their economic resources allowed, to the stance that in the interest of a healthy political society and in order for democracy to flourish all children should have an opportunity for basic education. To promote political democracy and to ensure social solidarity the common school, later the public elementary school, was erected, and its doors were open to all. For a long time this policy and the educational practice it sustained fitted comfortably into American social theory, without any talk about popular education being inimical to the realization of talent and the production of leaders for American institutions. Absence of doubt about the efficacy of this policy in public education was due mainly to the fact that the common school as it made its first appearance on the American scene was strictly limited to elementary schooling without any expectation that public education would extend into the secondary school.[9] We know from our study so far, however, that the doctrine of public education was eventually applied to the high school as a result mainly of the Kalamazoo decision and the Report of the Committee of Ten, and thereafter the high school was no longer an institution reserved for the education of society's leaders, for those who were college bound, but became a school whose principal objective was preparation for life. Under the circumstances, with both elementary and secondary education concerned with preparing citizens for life in society, for social solidarity, the task of educating leaders for society was left forfeit. And as more and more students began to attend public institutions, especially the high schools which began now to dominate secondary education, the dilemma of democratic education disclosed itself.

Taken out of historical context, the dilemma of democratic education can be stated as follows: as a popular movement education is directed at the schooling of persons for social solidarity, for the welding of a society capable of working toward common ends. But in doing so, in directing attention and public resource toward an entirely worthy goal, the scholastic cultivation of talented persons for leadership in society is missed. One horn of the dilemma is the need for a solid and cohesive society which can be obtained, at least in part, by utilizing public education; the other horn is the development of individual talent which in the nature of things must be cultivated apart from the mainstream of educational effort. In striving for social solidarity, public education has pretty much abandoned its commitment to the preparation of leaders; but public schools in concentrating attention and effort on the preparation of leaders run the risk of forsaking social solidarity.

The debate of this issue over the past twenty-five years has not always concentrated on resolving the dilemma—of finding a compromise where both goods, social solidarity and individual development, can be cultivated —but instead has centered on eliminating one or the other. Along these lines the case for social solidarity, for an equal educational treatment of all schoolchildren, has been most publicized and most generally accepted. But this outcome has been based largely on an interpretation of equality of opportunity, the mainspring of democratic education, wherein the argument is made that everyone must be given the same opportunity, no more and no less; and to offer some students special programs or extraordinary learning opportunities because of their superior talent is a violation of the democratic principle of equal opportunity.[10]

To adopt a misinterpretation of equality, other spokesmen allege, is to assure a common level of mediocrity among Americans, for in conducting programs of public education for all children it becomes imperative that the level of teaching and the standard of achievement be geared to average capacity. This leaves two large classes in the school population without the kind of opportunity they are entitled to: the slow learner is unable to maintain the pace of average performance and thus falling behind misses an opportunity to develop his talent; the superior student is capable of achieving beyond the level of average performance and his talent is left unrealized. This lack of realization of ability has a dual effect. On one side of the picture are superior students whose capacity to achieve is allowed to lie fallow in an educational field where intensive cultivation is employed on a large middle group of so-called average students. This superior person, it is argued with some conviction, is being deprived of opportunity. On the other side of the picture, not taking directly into account the element of personal loss, is a society standing to benefit from persons who are exceptionally capable. They form a natural aristocracy equipped to make returns to society commensurate with their talent. But in schools where talent is ignored in deference to a faulty interpretation of democratic equality, the social benefits to be derived from such persons are missed.

To make special provision for persons of talent in public education, so a popular argument runs, is to cater to an elite and to promote elitism in American society. But elitism is often pictured as anathema to democracy.

Still, despite the deep feelings on both sides of this issue and democracy's profound aversion to an artificial elitism—one based on something other than talent—this dilemma of democratic education now stands in critical need of resolution. Yet signs that resolution is imminent are not promising, for in the 1960s and early 1970s the direction of public education in the high schools and colleges was more and more to promote equality—implying that equality means never to leave anyone out—and thus tended to compound rather than resolve the dilemma. The most convincing evidence that solidarity rather than talent was given priority can be found in the record of both public and private colleges, where admission requirements and policies were designed to comply with a theory of higher education making everyone eligible to try his hand at college or university study. Admitting students to institutions of higher learning by adopting the thesis that they are popular and democratic has, most observers agree, placed some burden on these schools to accommodate their programs of study and their standards to a new clientele. This accommodation of standard, it is alleged, is nothing more than a matter of discounting and diluting the quality of higher studies. Persons ready to justify the popularization of higher education, however, maintain that the new American college is not inferior to its ancestor, but only different. Still, even by encouraging persons in American society to pursue more and more education, without at the same time changing its character in such a way that students of superior capacity will profit from it, does not resolve the dilemma we have described: it only seeks to avoid it.[11]

While the past two decades have not been noted for their attention to the dilemma, preferring instead to adopt uniformity as the proper meaning of equality, this dilemma was noticed in the early years of the twentieth century and some educators in some school programs undertook to do something about it. Without any recorded place of origin and anonymous in prescription the first, and probably the most often used, scholastic plan for the resolution of the dilemma of democratic education was acceleration. Exceptionally able students on any educational level were simply allowed to proceed at their own pace and thus complete their studies more quickly. One notices, of course, that in adopting acceleration as a means of handling gifted children nothing more is added to the curricular experience: the same educational program is completed faster. In rare instances, following the technique of extra-promotion, students speed through their elementary and secondary schools and appear at college gates before their social and moral maturity is ready for the complexities of college life. Although the weaknesses of acceleration are apparent, there are advantages. The program is informal and is easily administered; it places no extra burden on the school. Besides, since the gifted student is not offered anything more from public instructional resources, acceleration escapes the indictment of being undemocratic and discriminatory. In consequence, acceleration is a little-publicized but commonly-used technique for resolving the dilemma.

If one advances the thesis, however, that a faster rate of learning is an insufficient response to the educational need of superior students, and over the years this thesis has been advanced, then something besides acceleration should be introduced. Many schools have tried to enrich the instruction of superior students and thus prepare them for leadership in society. Early admission programs for college-bound students have appeared as combinations of acceleration and enrichment, as have advanced placement programs, but more directly aimed at enrichment and not hurrying students through school faster are such plans as independent study and honors programs. In these programs schools make provision on a curricular level for superior students and give them educational opportunity for which they are qualified. This segregation of talented students and a concomitant employment of public resources for their development has led to a criticism of these programs as being undemocratic. One may be surprised to learn that this argument, an appeal to uniformity, carries a good deal of weight. As a matter of fact, most enrichment programs mounted in the schools over the past several decades have had to contend with this charge and in few instances have they been successful in nullifying it.

The key to successful enrichment programs has been flexibility in curricular organization and the assignment of students to curricular levels appropriate to their abilities and interests. This characteristic of flexibility was introduced first in Batavia, New York (thereafter called the Batavia Plan) where elementary-school students were grouped into two categories: students making normal academic progress were in one category and those making less than normal progress were in another. Batavia's use of flexibility was shortly adopted in Cambridge, Massachusetts, but according to the Cambridge Plan, as it came to be called, the elementary-school course was divided into two parallel courses—one of six and the other of eight years. The six-year course was intended for bright students; the eight-year course was for others. These two plans, with multiple variations, were tested in hundreds of schools across the United States.[12]

A few schools, like those in Pueblo, Colorado, as early as 1888, allowed for even greater flexibility and permitted each child in the elementary school to proceed at his own rate without regard for age or grade. But this freedom was so great as to become an impediment to expeditious school administration and it has not been followed or encouraged in many places. Still, the principle of flexibility was attractive and other enrichment models tried to retain it. In 1919, in Winnetka, Illinois, the elementary school was divided into two parts. One part consisted of achievement units; the other of self-expression and socializing activities. Children were encouraged to progress according to their ability in achievement units, but in other parts of the program all children were offered the same educational experience and kept a common instructional pace. Another plan aimed at cultivating ability and breaking the academic lock step in elementary education was developed in Dalton, Massachusetts. In the Dalton Plan students contracted with their teachers for a specified amount of work. The plan envisioned all students covering the regular curriculum, but with a contract each student proceeded at his own rate and gained as much enrichment as his motivation and ability recommended.[13]

More recently ideas and techniques for capitalizing on the principle of flexibility have been given some attention, but they have almost always taken second place to the doctrine of equality, and school systems have developed basic primary- or elementary-school units wherein the principle of flexibility is employed. Besides, suggestions have been made to apply this principle to all school levels. Such a proposal was made by Paul Woodring in his book, *A Fourth of a Nation.* Woodring called for the abandonment of the age-grade relationship to allow more mature and able students to proceed at their own pace; less mature and less able students could move as rapidly as their talent allowed.[14]

Despite the number and variety of plans appearing on the record of American educational history, the dilemma of democratic education stands almost undisturbed, and with the present penchant for misinterpreting the meaning of equality in democratic education one can hardly be optimistic about its prompt final and full resolution.

Cost and Control

Over the years the American public has become excited over issues in education relating to purpose, content, and method, and the pages of this book frequently evidence this, but however important these issues may be in the formulation of public policy they are paled by another: the cost of maintaining schools. While it is unnecessary to conduct a detailed historical tour now, we are aware how, almost from the beginning of colonial collective activity in schooling, the ugly apparition of cost heaved into view. When common schools were first proposed the record of frugality vis-à-vis education was already solid and protests were raised about the cost of a general elementary-school system conducted at public expense which, it was alleged, would surely lead to national bankruptcy. There are, then, paradoxes in the American character and a principal one is the great faith Americans have historically exhibited in education, on one hand, and their reluctance to support it with anything like generosity, on the other. When the high school made its first appearance as a public institution its growth was stunted by the contention that secondary education was too costly for the public to support and, in any case, secondary education was really a private not a public responsibility. The colleges, too, were exposed to the same exercise in penuriousness, and we know that public colleges founded before the enactment of the Land-Grant College law (1862) barely managed to exist in their state of near poverty, undernourished by public resource, uncultivated, and unloved. But the federal support afforded in the Land-Grant act shifted the burden of public support somewhat, at least changed its appearance, and thereafter state colleges began to make greater progress. It has been remarked, and the remark contains elements of truth, that most of the problems in American education would vanish in the face of greater financial support.

This thesis has not been tested often and never on a general scale. When it has been tested, and these tests may not have been entirely fair, infusions of money left scholastic issues mainly intact. That money alone may not be the answer to all educational questions was most clearly demonstrated in those programs and schools which in novel and expensive ways tried to improve the achievement of disadvantaged youth.

In the 1960s, in an era of prosperity, schools on all levels profited from the nation's high level of affluence. Sometimes habits of school finance were formed that in leaner years turned out to be extravagances. In the 1970s, along with most other things in the economy, school costs mounted and in a nation depending heavily on revenue from taxes on real property to support the schools, reaction to this increase was both quick and negative. Throughout the country school boards were admonished by their constituents to eliminate the frills and otherwise reduce the cost of education. But in spite of their best effort to do so, most school systems found saving hard and the cost of education continued to increase.

Assistance to local school districts from the state began to shrink in the 1970s, for the states, too, were faced with increased expenditures and declining revenue and this had the consequence of putting an even greater burden on local communities to maintain their schools. And as the financial base for public education came to be more directly local, another issue was raised. Is equal treatment before the law and equal access to public service—a constitutional principle of unequivocal standing—violated when in depending mainly on local revenue for the support of schools one school system is better able to support its schools than others? In California and a few other states this issue was raised in the courts, and the California Supreme Court held the financing of schools by means of the local property tax to be unconstitutional.[15] The base of support, the court held, should be state wide, for only then could the public be assured of equality of educational opportunity. The decision of the California court, however, was blunted when the United States Supreme Court refused to endorse it.[16]

When local school districts have been unable to raise money to support their schools fully, they have commonly turned to the state for assistance.

And over the years states have employed state equalization funds to maintain a minimum level of educational standard. But, as we have said, in the past decade state funds have not been readily available. In the absence of sufficient state resources it was only natural for the people to look to the federal government for help. And the federal aid issue, we know, has had a long and hectic history. Fearing federal control, local communities began by opposing federal aid, and the issue was compounded further when private and religious schools argued for some of the benefits of federal aid. Although long delayed, federal aid finally became a reality as a result of various congressional enactments and in the 1970s the federal government distributed several billion dollars annually for the support of education on all levels. These federal funds, however, are often restricted to certain educational programs, and while they have unquestionably relieved local communities and states of some financial burden, they have not succeeded in eliminating issues surrounding educational finance. In any case, irrespective of the source of funds, they come from revenue excised from the people. Federal aid has neither reduced the cost of public education nor has it silenced critics who maintain that public education in the United States is too expensive.

There is another side to this issue of school finance: control. He who pays the piper calls the tune if he has any musical preference. For a long time the legal principle has been clear: the state, not the local school district, has final jurisdiction over education. And since the clarification of this principle in several court decisions, tensions between local communities and the state have been reduced to a point where they are not an impediment to the management of schools. While being firm in an exercise of their authority, states have learned not to be heavily intrusive and the wedding of state and local educational authority has generally been a happy one.

At first, it was supposed, a relationship between the federal government, on one hand, and states and local communities, on the other, could imitate the state and local harmony and that friction, contests over authority, and debate concerning education's priorities would be rare. But as the federal government has administered its various programs through the Department of Health, Education, and Welfare, signs become clearer that state and local control is being siphoned away. Control lost by local and state jurisdictions ends up being exercised by agencies of the federal government, who allocate funds, supervise their use, set standards for educational practice and undertake an evaluation of the supported programs. In addition, while legally authorized to do so, federal agencies publish guidelines and these guidelines, with the force of law, become insidious elements of regulation and control of education on local levels.[17]

Some level of control, reasonable people generally agree, can legitimately accompany support; yet federal regulation may have stepped over the fine line separating respective jurisdictional authority to alter the character of American education in a fundamental way. Sometimes federal regulation appears to be both inane and ridiculous: in 1976, for example, following a guideline proscribing sex discrimination in the schools, the Department of Health, Education, and Welfare banned school functions, such as father-and-son and mother-and-daughter dinners, which separated the sexes. And along the same line, directives issued under Title IX from the same department threaten to change the character of interscholastic and intercollegiate sport by prohibiting school teams from restricting participation to boys. Hasty and ill-conceived federal educational guidelines, intended no doubt to ensure equity, have often violated canons of common sense and, moreover, have tried to enforce positions lacking public support.

In the nature of things federal aid is inevitably accompanied by some element of control, and it seems unlikely that this stark principle will ever be amended. So the problem for the American public and its educators is to find a way to shape federal control toward reasonable and useful ends, all the while recognizing the inevitability of tensions among various educational jurisdictions and striving to reduce them without at the same time eliminating the jurisdiction from which they come. American educational tradition rejects national control of education as being alien to democracy, but the financial plight of American education in the late 1970s has conspired to bring national control more nearly to reality in the United States.

Teachers and Their Status

While it may not be entirely accurate to include the American teacher in a category called contemporary issues, for teachers can hardly be educational issues in any conventional sense, yet the preparation of teachers for American schools, the academic conditions of their work, and their public image have an impact on the educational process. Besides, the living presence of the teacher converts the curriculum, the materials of instruction, and all the facilities of the school into an educational process. Although, clearly, the principal agent in the educational process is the student, the teacher is an important, perhaps essential, auxiliary, and the American public, conscious of this fact, is prepared to assess the performance of the teaching profession with a critical eye.

Throughout the greater part of American educational history, teachers were denied the status of professional persons. Not ranking on the same level with physicians, lawyers, and engineers, they had rather the status of public employees from whom not too much could be expected. When teachers were mainly hearers of lessons, and when this was all the public wanted them to be, there was little chance for an upward revision of their status. But schooling underwent considerable metamorphosis in the later years of the nineteenth century and was subject to even more rapid and radical change in the twentieth, so the old-fashioned teacher, only modestly educated and temporarily employed (most were young women who looked forward to marriage and life in the home as wife and mother), soon went out of date. Qualifications for teachers were raised and a public once content with teachers who had some instruction in a normal school now began to believe that teachers, whatever other qualifications they should have as directors of the learning process, should at least have a college education. Step by step the teaching profession raised itself, largely by the dint of its own labor, to a position of greater respect in the American community.[18] Yet authentic professionalism is still more an internal than an external characterization of American teachers, and they also labor under the disadvantage of a public perception of teaching as an occupation rather than a profession.

This debate over the professional status of teachers is endless, so it may be pointless for us to pursue it further here. Other sides to teaching are more important. The law of supply and demand is enforced on teachers: their ranks swell and shrink according to the need communities have for them. And present employment opportunities, as prospective teachers hardly need be told, are far from attractive. In addition, since the financing of American education has become more critical in the 1970s, school districts who otherwise might have appointed teachers for special programs, to reduce the size of classes, or to enrich the curriculum now refuse to do so.

At this point demographic projections make discouraging reading for aspiring teachers: declining birthrates for the past several years have affected elementary-school enrollment throughout the country and in a few years secondary schools and colleges will see their classes shrink. An oversupply of teachers may prove to be a boon to the school districts appointing them; it poses gloomy prospects for prospective teachers.

Despite the hazard one faces in looking to a career in teaching, the coin has another side. We have seen enough of the evolution of education in the United States to know that teachers were usually underpaid; their tenure was temporary; their work (with few aids to instruction) was hard; and they were without any or many benefits which, with the success of the American labor movement, had become almost commonplace for the worker in industry. Most of this has changed. Contemporary teachers, with the possibility of tenure, can look forward to stability in employment; salary schedules impose a certain regularity on economic security; and a variety of benefits (which are called fringe, although they are much more than that) remove many uncertainties and hardships from a teacher's domestic life.

Yet teachers continue to labor under the disadvantage of dealing with an intangible: the mind and character of a child in a formative stage. What is accomplished in aiding the child's development is hard to measure and even the best measures leave something to be desired. When a person goes to his dentist to have a painful tooth extracted, he knows exactly what has been done and is prepared to pay for relief from pain. At the same time he recognizes the special professional skill of the dentist. An ill person pays a visit to his physician, has the illness diagnosed and follows the therapy prescribed by the doctor. This special skill is seen and felt and doctors are accorded a high place on a professional hierarchy; people are always willing to pay for relief from pain and suffering. Similarly, the lawyer, representing his client, does technical work carrying toward a definite objective. The client knows what has been done or he knows how he has benefited. These practitioners of a professional art have produced tangible results; but can one see what teachers accomplish with equal clarity? The general effect of education may be apparent, although it is extremely hard to attribute this outcome to any one teacher or even to teaching itself, for, it may be argued, the child can learn from discovery and the artistry of a teacher may not figure at all.

The complexities of teaching and learning, the work of the teacher as a cooperative artist assisting nature, make precision of assessment unusually hard, yet teachers have felt a need to represent themselves as productive members of a profession. This need has led in recent years to the rise of pedagogic accountability: a way of determining precisely what has been taught and how the behavior of the child has been changed as a result of instruction. One should not be surprised to learn that accountability has stimulated considerable interest among school boards and the public generally; both want to know what returns come from the salaries being paid teachers. And some educators have regarded accountability as a panacea to the economic tensions existing between teachers and the communities they serve. While accountability was embraced with enthusiasm in the 1970s, it is important for the student of education to weigh it carefully and to see whether it is, in fact, a useful and praiseworthy instrument for the improvement of teaching and learning or whether it is only another example of educational humbug.[19]

Whether contemporary teachers are better educated than their predecessors is probably a moot point, although as a body they have more schooling than any previous generation of teachers. And one of the current issues surrounding teacher preparation is the design of this schooling, a philosophy of teacher education. Should the education of teachers be mainly liberal, stressing a commitment to culture, to an elevation of the mind and spirit, or should it be strictly professional and technical, totally preoccupied with the skills teachers must have in order to conduct the process involved in the education of youth?

For a great part of its history, we know, teacher education was accounted for in the liberal arts; and the generous assumption was made that a person in command of his subject was equipped to teach. Then pedagogy was elevated to the respectable status of a science, and it became conventional in teacher-education programs to blend a decent mastery of liberal learning with technical pedagogical competence.[20] In the 1970s a new prescription for teacher education has been written, one wherein performance or competency-based curricular experiences alone are cultivated. Only the very brave person would oppose acceptable pedagogic performance or competence, so the current apprach to the education of teachers begins with the benefit of the doubt. But a more thorough examination of what is involved has led various educators and college and university faculties to raise their voices in protest. The drive for competency-based curricula is fueled by a conviction that what passes for a decent education is composed of various skills and that these skills can be taken, one by one, and mastered. In possession of these skills teachers can enter their classrooms and communicate them to students. Every subject, it is said, can be reduced to components of competence, so precision and exactness introduced to instruction in this way make teachers accountable for their commission to instruct students. Skills and competencies are susceptible of measurement: students either have or have not mastered them. But before teachers can communicate them to students, before the work of instruction begins, they themselves must have mastered these skills. Gaining possession of skill along with the pedagogic performance or competence, so the current approach to the of competency-based instruction, is the principal task of teacher education.[21] This is the road, they say, to high-quality learning.

Once carefully husbanded by each state, teacher certification—unquestionably instrumental in elevating the standard of American education—has undergone some liberalization in the 1970s. In earlier years teachers were restricted in their mobility by special certification requirements imposed from state to state. While it was always possible for teachers to meet various state requirements and thus move from one place to another, respective state certification codes did not encourage mobility. Now, however, several states have entered reciprocal compacts, so a teaching certificate from one state is valid in any state participating in the reciprocal plan. The benefits of reciprocity may take some time to assess, for contemporary employment conditions tend to keep teachers where they are. On its face, however, reciprocity in certification should help strengthen and broaden the character of American schools.

For a long time dependent entirely on individual bargaining, the American teacher is now helped by professional teacher organizations in coming to agreement with school districts on such things as salary, working conditions and benefits. And in the tradition of labor organizations, teachers have in recent years resorted to strikes in order to gain leverage in collective bargaining. It is also worth noticing that strikes have been called despite state laws prohibiting teachers and other public employees from withholding their services as an economic weapon. Still, economic protection is only one benefit afforded by professional organizations and it may be fair to predict that the gains teachers make toward achieving full professional recognition will depend in large measure on the determination their organizations show toward establishing and maintaining professional standards for their members. Traditional professions did not have professional status conferred on them but won it by careful attention to details of excellence and by internal growth; teachers, it would seem, must adopt the same prescription.

Educational Equality

Although educational equality has attracted our attention before, even the risk of repetition warrants our returning to it as the most volatile issue in contemporary American education. The famous *Brown* decision of 1954, we know, outlawed segregation in public education and declared equal access to public schools for all citizens.[22] No child could be deprived of attendance in a unitary public-school system because of race, creed, or color. Following the command of the court, desegregation occurred, sometimes willingly but often with reluctance and resistance. By the mid-1970s, most observers would admit, desegregation was both a policy and practice in American public education: one system of schools was legally open to all children.

As a result of the Civil Rights legislation of the 1960s, and to some extent due to experience with desegregation, the first years of the 1970s could be characterized as an era for the promotion of integration. Policies of desegregation removed discriminatory practice from public schools; policies of integration sought, by using educational means, to balance attendance in public schools and thus to bring about a closer relationship between the races. The schools were used as instruments of social integration. In connection with policies of integration, usually under the direction of a federal court,[23] busing of children from one part of a school district to another, usually in urban or metropolitan areas, became a principal instrument. This relocation of children, not the fact of busing itself, interrupted the normal allegiance many people had to a local school, and on these grounds opposition was generated. But as many incidents attest, in Boston, in Louisville and elsewhere, a substantial part of the objection to school integration and its instrument, busing, was lodged in racial bias. The extent to which the schools are capable of dealing with such fundamental social issues is by no means clear; nor is it clear how schools can be used to solve social problems without having the character and standard of education affected.

Opponents of contemporary educational practice to promote integration argue down the sociological theory maintaining that black and white children must be educated together, if equality of opportunity is to be assured, as weak and unsound. The constitution and learning, they contend, are colorblind and, moreover, there is no assurance whatever of superior learning taking place by having the races educated together. They agree that an artificial separation of the races for purposes of schooling is undemocratic, but they oppose artificial integration through quotas of school enrollment in order to achieve an elusive equality of opportunity. The proposition that equality of opportunity begins in the composition of school classes is denied by opponents of integration; good education, they say instead, is produced by having superior teachers and superior facilities for directing learning activities.

However, superior instructional facilities for one group of students may not turn out to be equally beneficial for another group. Because of various inequities in educational and cultural opportunity in past generations, many members of minority groups have not been able to achieve a cultural level where either normal or superior instruction is conducive to effective learning. Too often they are not able to compete in a normal classroom and quite frequently this is due to an inability to read. In addition, there are cultural discrepancies which often make the world of conventional learning appear to be strange and forbidding, or irrelevant, to minorities. A popular corrective measure adopted by proponents of integration is to allow the social processes of the school to close this cultural gap. By deploying enrollment artfully minority children are made part of the conventional cultural stream, and it is expected that time will eliminate their cultural deficiency. Another recommendation is compensatory education.

Advocates of compensatory education aver that minority youth, being unable to compete in the average classroom, should be given special instruction which will raise them to average achievement levels for their grade. Simply mingling disadvantaged youth with children who have had greater cultural advantage, they say, will either take too long or will not produce the best results. The issue of educational disadvantage must be met directly; and this means giving such students instruction in those areas where they lack skill and ability.[24] While compensatory education has logic to recommend it, spokesmen for minorities often reject it as degrading and humiliating to those exposed to it. Such practice, they allege, centers attention on the shortcomings of minority children and further isolates them from the mainstream of American life and culture. Where compensatory education has been given a fair trial, there have been good results, but it tends to revive illusions of separation among persons in the disadvantaged category and its chances for having a fair trial are becoming rarer. Still, spokesmen for minorities sometimes take a position out of step with the rank and file to assert, on one hand, that in order to compete favorably in American society minorities need the skills and abilities of conventional culture, and they should obtain them by utilizing compensatory schooling if necessary; and, on the other hand, to reject the assertion that unless disadvantaged and minority children, usually black children, are educated with white children they are being deprived of equal educational opportunity. What evidence, they inquire, shows that only by being instructed with white children can black children learn effectively and meet the standards of achievement for success in American society?

The historical record is almost swamped by the issues surrounding the education of culturally and economically disadvantaged children, but other issues of educational equality, while receiving less attention, are nevertheless real. Thousands of handicapped children—blind, deaf, mentally retarded, and physically deformed—are enrolled in the schools. Until a decade or so ago conventional practice separated these children into special classes or special schools. More recently, and especially in the 1970s, this old practice has been revised and handicapped children are, so far as possible, assigned to regular classrooms where they receive most of their instruction, going outside the regular classrooms only for special needs.

This practice—called mainstreaming—appears beneficial to handicapped children, but it has the effect of altering conventional instructional procedures. A pertinent question, moreover, needs to be asked: does mainstreaming diminish educational opportunity for normal children? In addition, the inclusion of students with special needs in the regular classroom has altered considerably the kind of preparation an elementary-school teacher must have. A decent respect for the instruction afforded handicapped children—which need not be disputed—has at least made the work of the elementary teacher far more complex and demanding; besides, the doubt lingers in the minds of many educators that mainstreaming has enabled elementary schools to maintain their conventional standards for normal children. If, as we saw, the dilemma of democratic education impinges on the character and quality of American schools and somehow undermines the opportunity for talented children to realize their abilities, will mainstreaming have the effect of compounding the difficulty schools have in providing superior educational opportunity for persons of superior capacity?

While hardly any account of equality of educational opportunity is ever complete, the issue of affirmative action should not be missed. Except for the employment of teachers, elementary schools are little affected by directives and orders governing affirmative action, but on the higher educational levels both faculties and student bodies are expected, according to affirmative action codes, to mirror the composition of the general population. Thus, minorities and women should be found in the schools, both as teachers and students, in the same proportion as they are found to exist in the general population. Access to employment and schooling has been confused with the establishment of quotas, and in order to be in good standing, especially to be eligible for federal funds, schools and colleges have been asked to demonstrate how their students and faculties are composed and, moreover, what is being done to recruit minorities and women for places in the schools. The ideal of equality of opportunity, which has ample constitutional standing and the endorsement of persons of reason and good will, is in danger of being reduced to a facsimile of equality by subtle pressure from government agencies requiring schools and colleges to adopt affirmative action in admitting students and appointing faculty members. Sometimes, experience suggests but does not prove, that natural superiority is sacrificed to an appearance of equality.[25]

Allegations pointing to the unfairness of affirmative action have been circulating for a decade; with equal zeal advocates of affirmative action have made a convincing case. Both sides waited, anticipating that the verdict of the United States Supreme Court in *Regents of the University of California* v. *Bakke* (rendered in June, 1978) would ratify their stand. The apparent narrowness of the decision, which affirmed the verdict of the state court and directed Bakke's admission to medical school, may insulate affirmative action programs in housing and employment from similar assault. In education, however, its long-range consequences are somewhat unclear.

Allan Bakke, an engineer in his thirties, was refused admission to the University of California Medical School at Davis. He sued the university, alleging reverse discrimination: his medical aptitude test scores were higher than those of sixteen minority students admitted under a special admissions arrangement. The California Supreme Court ruled in favor of Bakke, and the university appealed to the United States Supreme Court. In a five to four decision, the court ruled that any reservation of places in schools by using quotas violates Title VI of the 1964 Civil Rights Act, which prohibits discrimination on the basis of race or color, and is illegal. The court added, however, that taking race or minority status into account in rating student application for college is permissible.[26] While short of being a ringing declaration for affirmative action in higher education, the decision, nevertheless, can be taken as favorable to it. Predictably, both the decision's narrow legal purview and its thin court majority have led to debate over its stability and its meaning for the future of equal educational opportunity.

Such litigation—testing the authority schools and colleges may exercise, for example, in admitting and assigning students, designing curricula for their study, and assessing their achievement—is illustrative of the role the judiciary plays in defining equality of educational opportunity. It has prompted a reappraisal of the civil rights implications in the Fourteenth Amendment, on the one hand, and a review of the proper role of courts, especially federal courts, as they legislate by judicial decree, on the other. Since its adoption in 1868, the Fourteenth Amendment has allowed the courts to interfere with state powers over legislative apportionment, abortion, pornography, crime, and so on. Many constitutional authorities are of the opinion that without the Fourteenth Amendment the federal courts could not intervene in educational matters on the state level. Some, however, especially Raoul Berger, in *Government by Judiciary: The Transformation of the Fourteenth Amendment,* published in 1978, argue that the Supreme Court was in error in *Brown* v. *Board of Education* (1954) when it invalidated laws forbidding black and white children to attend the same schools.

Berger's analysis takes exception not only to the *Brown* decision, but to that entire network of constitutional decisions underlying the nation's legal commitment to racial equality and opportunity. Berger maintains that neither the history nor the text of the Amendment supports those prohibitions outlawed by the Civil Rights Act. Yet, a majority of constitutional authorities, both scholars and judges, do not agree with Berger's premise that in the interpretation of the Constitution, judges must find the intent of those who framed it and its amendments. Instead, they maintain, whatever the intention of the authors of the amendment, constitutional guarantees require the courts to discern values that are embraced in contemporary society. Such values, although rooted in tradition and belief, are subject to the force of social evolution. So the ultimate touchstone for this theory of constitutional interpretation is the consent of the living rather than the intent of the dead. If a court makes a mistake in assessing the values of the people in any historical period, the remedy to the court's mistake is found in constitutional amendment and statute. If, therefore, there is a tendency toward government by judiciary, it can be halted or changed in a continuing social dialogue between the courts and other political institutions. Such a view endorses the idea of law as a living and changing social instrument rather than a fixed and arbitrary code imposed on society. Despite the sensible justification for judicial interpretation keeping abreast of the times, the theory persists with considerable appeal that the Constitution must be submitted for literal interpretation: it means what it says and no more.

Alternative Education

Dominated by a thesis of revision and reform, some educators have argued that American schools, especially public schools, do not provide a kind of educational opportunity relevant to life in society. Abandoning hope that public schools can be changed, these educators have posed several alternatives which, they say, will introduce reality and effectiveness to education. First, of course, is the private school which, operating outside the boundaries of public support, is capable of altering and adjusting its curriculum to capitalize the interests and needs of youth. But private schools, for all their potential for flexibility, have rarely followed the prospect recommended to them, although some private schools have, in various ways, proved to be an alternative, and a prized one, to public schools.

Alternative education, whether tested in the schools or only recommended by avant-garde educators, implies a non-academic kind of schooling. Its promoters argue that life is many things besides language, literature, and science, and, in any case, they allege, these subjects have little to do with the realities of life. What is needed instead is a kind of education putting students directly in contact with the art of living and if this learning can be put in the curriculum, or otherwise be managed by the school, students will be better off.

In the nature of things, however, the curriculum does not easily lend itself, nor does the atmosphere of the school, to education centered on life and experience. Recognizing this, reformers have tried to erect out-of-school programs by using community resources with which students can have experience. But this tactic has tempted the public to wonder why schools should be built and faculties assembled and why education should cost so much if students are simply going to learn from the general community where they live? Still, zeal is tenacious and ardent reformers refuse to give up: many of them go on to recommend the abolition of compulsory-attendance legislation, if not at all levels, at least in high schools. Even if this kind of alternative education can be dressed attractively, it suffers from a lack of structure and is always subject to the criticism that such education is anything students want to make it. And while one should not begin by supposing that all out-of-school learning is inconsequential, it is at least so unconventional as to raise questions about its fundamental quality.

Another dimension to alternative education is forged in those movements which, on one hand, encourage federal tax credits for parents who pay tuition for their children in private schools and, on the other, recommend a voucher system whereby parents may select schools for their children and use vouchers issued from a public treasury to pay the full tuition. Either approach reflects a disposition toward voluntarism in education—in some ways an alternative form of schooling—and, to some extent, a dissolution of the near-monopoly public schools have over education in the United States. Where the tax credit plan will lead is far from clear, burdened as it is with political and fiscal considerations.

The principal justification for voluntarism in education, its advocates say, is to be found apart from any enmity toward public education. Public schools would remain intact and parents could spend their vouchers in them; but private schools of all kinds, both religiously-related and independent, would be better positioned to offer meaningful competition with them. The beneficiaries of voluntarism, it is said, would be children in schools. In such a system schools would be forced to improve to the point where they could attract a clientele. The chances for a voucher system being adopted in any state are not good. Apart from a theoretical objection to any diminution of public education's influence, the following troubling considerations arise: a voucher system would have to be accompanied by safeguards capable of defining and maintaining the quality of schools eligible for voucher payments; and this could be a hazardous undertaking. In any case, it could lead to an inflation of an already inflated school bureaucracy and, even then, one could hardly be confident of the efficient regulation of such a plan.

The assertion is made, moreover, that parents are not usually in a position to make a judgment about the quality of schools their children should attend. Such evaluations must be left to experts able to see past the veneer of academic publicity and propaganda. If parents lack the ability to make the choice, then the voluntarism—the freedom—proclaimed for the system would indeed have a hollow sound. Lacking ability to choose, yet making the choice nevertheless, would have the effect of introducing Gresham's law to education. Poor, low-quality schools would crop up everywhere and parents, not knowing the difference, would patronize them. These poor schools, in an authentic application of Gresham's law, would drive out the good ones. In addition, despite innocent-sounding demurrals from voucher-system adherents,[27] conventional public education would be put in a position of serious jeopardy. One might go so far as to predict the destruction of public education, as it is known now, if voucher-type education were to become a commonplace.

Then, too, the constitutional status of a voucher program is by no means clear. Could religiously-related schools participate in such a plan with legal impunity? Practices similar to the voucher plan can be illustrated—the educational provisions of various GI Bills apply to religious as well as other schools, and government funds are used to support patients in religiously-owned nursing homes and hospitals—but the question remains concerning constitutionality, where religious schools would be included on a large scale, and the answer, at this point, is obscure. Finally, of course, even if the foregoing doubts were removed entirely, the problem of successful regulation of such a system would remain. Could it be managed? Many perceptive observers think not.

Innovation and the Standard of Learning

After decades of relative stability in 'objectives, curricula, and method, American education became enamored of the idea of change, and innovation, in the past twenty years has become a pedagogic watchword. Conventional study and scholastic stability went out of fashion and innovation became the only respectable stance for education and the educator. This shift, or drift, toward doing something different has not escaped criticism, for teachers and educators who are not certain that change inevitably bespeaks progress have called attention to the character of innovation in contemporary education. Their voice should give pause to people who are serious about educational quality. Whenever innovation is introduced to the educational process, it has almost always been at the expense of higher educational standard. And attentive schoolmen have been tempted to inquire why educational change should be accompanied by less demanding academic performance?

Responsible educators have refused to counsel immobility in the educational process, and they have not rejected the possibility of improving the character and quality of the schools; but both teachers and the public have criticized the schools for adopting change for the sake of change and for not being solicitous of scholastic standard and academic quality. It would be imprudent and inaccurate to claim that innovation in American education has always been accompanied by decline in standard; but in recent years the tendency has been to promote a kind of innovation that has, in fact, pared away scholastic sinew from American schools.

THE AMERICAN SCHOLASTIC LADDER

We have seen some of the issues confronting contemporary school practice and realize that their resolution may neither be full nor quick. In looking at these issues, we have, for the most part, been looking to the past, albeit the recent past, and now we should look to the future to see, if we can, what the major educational issues may be in the decade ahead.

Elementary Education

The most ominous factor promising to affect the character of elementary education is related to declining enrollment. These schools, their facilities and their faculties, have been organized over the years to handle an enrollment that will probably be reduced by half in the next decade. At the same time, especially with the acceptance of mainstreaming, a new type of elementary teacher is recommended: one capable of handling a variety of instructional problems with classes of increasing variation both in academic capacity and disposition toward learning. But, while the education fraternity is promoting the need for a new type of teacher to handle the multiple issues of a diversified class, or classes in an ungraded elementary school, the public is calling for a kind of elementary education which will once again give pride of place to basic education: reading, writing, and arithmetic.

If these conflicting tendencies are not enough to plague both educators and the public, then such things as the downward extension of elementary education, from the kindergarten through the nursery school to day-care centers for very young children, should complete the job. Social pressure coming from such political movements as women's liberation has pushed schools into a position of being custodial agencies.

The prospects for elementary education have yet another side: for most of its history, beginning surely with the advent of the common school, elementary education in the United States sought to introduce social solidarity to society and promote the inculcation of common civic virtue or citizenship. If the past is prelude to the future, this conventional purpose will be altered. And the alteration will take place mainly on the level of language. Once the bastion of basic American English instruction for all classes of the population, the elementary school, which prized a common culture, may turn instead toward multicultural and bilingual, or even multilingual, instruction. And American English, a common language melding citizens to national purpose and value, will be pushed aside to accommodate the perceived advantage of ethnic, cultural, and linguistic difference. Although good common sense would not recommend a return to the period in American history when linguistic and cultural difference were conceived to be weakness, and when only English had legal standing in the schools of some states, social and political philosophers wonder whether abdicating the place of common language has social, economic, and cultural implications that will not in the end weaken rather than strengthen American society. It is possible, they can argue, that multicultural and multilingual elementary education may end up by destroying the values it is expected to promote.

One of these values, so the record suggests, stands in particular need of cultivation—reading. Although evaluations of literacy, or the extent of functional illiteracy, must be stated with some caution, careful analysts allege that fifteen million American adults cannot read well enough to understand a newspaper. They say, too, that about seven million students of elementary and secondary schools have severe reading problems. In some urban school systems, the claim is made, almost half the students suffer from underachievement in reading.

Some good excuses can be advanced for the present state of reading skill, and some are fairly convincing. But the fact remains that for whatever reason or however good the excuse, an ability to read is imperative in contemporary society. Illiteracy stands as an immovable obstacle to success in any avenue of American life. In recognition of this, a national program, with various sponsorship, has set its sights on eliminating these stark deficiencies in reading ability. This program focuses on school and community recognition of the need for action, the assembling of financial resources from local, state, and federal jurisdictions to initiate effective reading and remedial reading programs for schoolchildren and for adults, a concentration on the preparation of teachers qualified to teach reading in all school subjects, and the development of materials of instruction—handbooks, kits, readers, and multimedia packages—for improving the teaching of reading.

Under these auspices, the right to read is promoted as a right basic to all the others one enjoys as an American citizen. Although unwritten, it may be the most important of all. At this time in our educational history, we must not neglect it.

Secondary Education

The future of American secondary education may be pondered by asking the question: what does graduation from high school represent? To have posed this question in the late nineteenth century, after high schools had been on the scene for about eighty years, would have produced an answer along the following lines, and this answer would not have stimulated much dissent. A high school education represented a fairly high level of academic competence. Students schooled in both English and a foreign language, probably Latin, would have been able to express themselves with fluency and accuracy. Conversant with history and mathematics, literature and language, they would also have had some knowledge of science. Of course, they would have had college admission requirements in mind as they pursued their studies, for secondary education was geared for college preparation. In addition to knowledge and skill, high-school graduates would have been disciplined by their academic experience: they would have demonstrated an ability to tackle new issues logically and precisely, and even in the absence of further education in college classrooms would have represented what most persons acknowledged to be a decent education.

In the early years of the twentieth century this same question would have elicited a response that high schools should concern themselves more with a preparation for life than for college. But even then high schools followed curricular practices making ample room for academic subjects, for it was maintained that even if college attendance was not in prospect for most high-school students, secondary study should be preoccupied with the development of thought and expression. So even with a change in general purpose, instructional priorities for the high schools did not change much, and one could have been fairly confident of a high-school graduate being able to handle the English language with accuracy and clarity, if not with elegance, and with being able to communicate his thought.

American high schools followed this route for a long time, committed to a literary education and determined to graduate students capable of expressing themselves. Then, in the 1950s, when the world was afflicted with international tension and anxiety, secondary education in the United States turned briefly to a concentration on science and mathematics. The race for world leadership, or only for national security, recommended high scientific and technological achievement and high schools undertook to do their part. But as it turned out, science could not dominate secondary education, and the scientists' rendezvous with destiny proved unattainable. After this interlude, where science was a curricular kingpin, high schools returned to their old academic habits; but once having abandoned their literary commitment it was difficult to return to it. And to make matters worse, the cultural hypothesis becoming popular told the American public that most of the old academic values were artificial and unimportant anyway. It was pointless to cling to them and make high-school students pursue largely or wholly irrelevant studies.

The rage for relevancy infected high schools most, but in the last analysis relevancy became so personalized as to put curricular responsibility in jeopardy. And to make matters worse, what solid academic subject was capable of demonstrating worth to a clientele which had been conditioned to doubt the relevance of anything academic?

In the absence of clear affirmation of purpose and positive corrective measures, high schools of the succeeding decades will stand as scholastic nomads, drifting from one innovative program to another but always steering away from conventional curricula, stored in the archives unused and untested. And a drift with the ephemeral interests of immature students will liberalize high-school curricula to the point of chaos. Almost any conceivable subject will qualify for a place in the curriculum and it will matter little whether it has disciplinary credentials. And intellectual habits of precision, perseverance, logical analysis, and effective expression —all provided for in the syllabus of traditional secondary education—will be abandoned to academic whim.

Evidence that high schools are becoming more liberal, that they have lost academic mooring, that conventional abilities of common learning are lacking, is mounting almost daily. Standardized tests, used regularly in one genre to appraise students for college entrance, may not tell the whole story of educational decline, but they point clearly enough to the fact that persons with high-school diplomas lack many of the educational skills and cultural appurtenances common to their precedessors of a decade or two ago.

Although testing is frequently held in disrepute, and test results are often discounted as being both unreliable and invalid, one finds some need to explain, or justify, the decline in secondary-school standards. The colleges, for so long used to relying on the results of Scholastic Aptitude Tests as a criterion for admission, now complain, almost in unison, about the precipitous decline in these scores on their applications for admission. Perhaps only two dozen high schools in the country have graduates whose test scores demonstrate an improvement rather than a decline in academic performance. Such evidences of declining standard have added momentum to drives in several states to establish by law certain minimum requirements of academic performance. Unless these minimum essentials can be demonstrated, a student would be denied a high-school diploma. Predictably, such drives are being resisted. One source of resistance is in a cadre of liberal, humanistic educators who, as a matter of principle, reject the old standards of academic decency as artificial and dehumanizing. They refuse to waste time mourning their passing. Another source of resistance is found among the advocates of educational relevancy. They argue that any establishment of minimum requirements for high-school graduation is bound to undermine the relevancy of school studies introduced to satisfy the needs of minority and other disadvantaged students. So at this moment the success or failure of the minimum-standard movement cannot be forecast. What can be forecast, however, is this: in the years ahead, secondary education in the United States will have one great commission to fulfill—the articulation of and adherence to a substantial and responsible philosophy.

The New American College

Any review of American education must take some time to reflect on the changing face of higher learning. We know what colleges and universities have been; we know what and how their students were taught and we have some grasp of the academic standard they tried to maintain. Throughout most of its American history, higher education was intended for an intellectual elite, and not many academic forecasters could have predicted the time when college and university attendance would be justified as a birthright. Since World War II, however, each succeeding decade has seen higher education become more popular. First, in the creation of junior and community colleges, and then in the democratization of the four-year college itself; and, finally, with the liberalization of graduate schools in universities.

The character of American higher education has changed, any perceptive observer admits so much, and many scholars are highly critical of these changes. They point to the modest requirements for admission, the undemanding and often non-academic courses in the college curriculum, to the inflated evaluations of student achievement, to the apparent inability of college graduates to perform on levels equal to those of high-school graduates a generation or two ago, and to the surrender of colleges and universities themselves to the exigencies of the marketplace.

The direction of junior colleges appears to be toward more and more non-academic studies leading to terminal degrees or certificates. Coming over the threshold of adulthood, young people in American society who lack the skill earlier schools should have taught them will turn to the junior college for what may amount to remedial education but, in addition, they will also be seeking saleable skill and this will take junior colleges into the arena of industrial, technical and vocational education. Only a few junior colleges will cling to the purpose of the first junior colleges of preparing students to attend a four-year college.

Four-year colleges, once citadels protecting the integrity of liberal learning, will further abandon a commitment to what was once their academic charter to become more and more professional and vocational in scope and objective. They will see themselves as places to train students to make a living and will forget about educating them to live well. This they will do partly because they will be reflecting the values of American society and partly because, for them, it will be a road to survival. And as this course of action is followed, the cultural level of the American higher learning will suffer a sharp decline.

The graduate school, once the true ornament of American higher education, will be populated by students who, unable to obtain what they need or think they need from the lower schools, are striving to complete their education. But these graduate schools, in former years concerned with advancing knowledge by pushing back its frontiers and with the education of scholars, will be preoccupied with the communication of skill and with the certification of their students to occupy positions in the economic community. The standard of education in America, especially in the higher schools, faces a future where it will be in almost constant jeopardy. Only traditional professional schools will essay to preserve their quality and their integrity, but surrounded by declining standards, even they may be fighting a losing battle.

If the battle is lost, some part of the blame may be laid at the door of an open admissions policy practiced now in a number of colleges and universities. At the outset, open admissions was thought to be an entirely appropriate policy for junior colleges, for it would allow them almost total freedom to reach those minority groups for whom the traditional college had few places. But then several universities began to follow suit: the University of Alaska, the University of the District of Columbia, the University of Arkansas, and the City University of New York took the lead in opening their doors to any student who wanted to come. Other schools followed in their wake, although not always with the same unbridled allegiance to the open admissions creed: opportunity for higher education must be extended to all.

A case history of open admissions is illustrated in the experience of the City University of New York by Theodore Gross in "How to Kill a College: The Private Papers of a Campus Dean."[28] With exceptional skill and insight, he parades before our eyes the record of a school that began its assignation with open admissions out of genuine concern for the minorities and the underprivileged who could not have met the former, fairly strict, standards of admission to the university. But this policy—to remain silent here about what the higher learning should be—led the school to the verge of financial collapse. In order to offer something for everyone, requirements and prerequisites were all but abolished and elective courses were introduced to make what is called a "cafeteria curriculum." Students followed the pleasure principle of course selection or took the courses they thought they wanted. The curriculum had courses "ranging from Shakespeare to Eldridge Cleaver, from Beethoven to Ellington, from Confucius to Martin Buber, from Basic Writing 1 for the poorly prepared to creative writing taught by the most sophisticated American novelists."[29]

This praiseworthy hunger for higher education was so great a temptation that students without credentials to succeed flocked to what had been one of the country's finest colleges. This invasion altered the personality of the school and changed the aspirations of its professors. This experience with open admissions, Gross concludes, demonstrates "most dramatically, that adequate preparation is essential to success" in college.[30] And that element of preparation most obviously lacking among a majority of the students who came as a result of the new policy was in a mastery of the English language itself. Yet this was a point few people in the college wanted to confront, or admit; in any case, they may have been powerless to do much about it, for a university can hardly be expected to return to the level of an elementary school and perform those humble tasks of teaching basic reading and writing. Should a college want to do so, it is unlikely that it could succeed, for neither its teachers nor its students appear willing to challenge the notion that students have a right to their own language and should not be cajoled into mastering a standard English. Without it, though, their destiny is almost certainly failure. Language ability, in any discipline, is a gateway to knowledge. "Knowledge is certainly not enough. It should lead to wisdom, which carries vision in its meaning. But without knowledge, wisdom is hard bought."[31]

City University's experiment with open admissions ended, but the reason for its termination was found not in its lack of academic soundness but because New York City ran out of funds to support so generous a policy. One wonders what educational solace can be found in this fact.

Yet, while the experiment with open admissions was coming to an abrupt halt at City University, an urgent reform was being readied at Harvard. The most ancient university in the land had made its indelible mark on the higher learning before: first, in the "Laws" of Henry Dunster, then in the bold elective thrusts of Charles Eliot and, again, in the widely-known and frequently followed recommendations in the 1945 Report of the Harvard Faculty: *General Education in a Free Society.*

General Education in a Free Society contained the charter for many of the erosions in the college curriculum over the past thirty years. It could be interpreted as authenticating departures from tested curricular traditions, and one by one the colleges across the country followed Harvard in exploiting these departures. At Harvard, for example, in his quest to join the company of educated men and women, a student is faced with the bewildering array of 2,600 courses from which to choose. Year after year he makes his choices; at the end of four years he is supposed to have acquired the foundations of the higher learning. He is an educated person. But there is nothing common about these foundations and, though Harvard apologists would likely deny it, some of the courses through which students pass do not contain much intellectual nourishment. What is true at Harvard is truer in other colleges of lesser stature. The basic question of what knowledge is of most worth is neither asked nor answered.

In a praiseworthy effort to wrestle this question at Harvard College, Dean Henry Rosovsky, in 1977, began what is called a "quiet revolution" to return a common core to the College's curriculum. Acknowledging the educational good sense of a core curriculum is not at stake among Harvard College faculty. Defining the core is the conundrum. If that is done, the next step, choosing courses for the core curriculum, "may seem the easiest and most obvious task in the process of mapping out a new educational course, but it is in fact the most precarious. People who agree on principles often cannot agree on particulars."[32] One must watch the progress of the Harvard endeavor to return structure to the college curriculum, for should the principle of core be adopted there, one can be fairly confident that it will be adopted in colleges the country over. Harvard has been an educational beacon too long for its light to dim much now. And American colleges have over the years demonstrated their precocity as students of a good master.

By any standard one would have to assess the progress of American education, on all levels, as a monumental achievement. From almost nothing, a vast and various school system was erected and this was done by accelerating the pace of history. But as we look past the decade of the 1970s, much of that great achievement is in danger of being wasted, and future generations, suffering from this waste, will be indisposed to heap praise on their immediate forebears.

NOTES

CHAPTER ONE

1. Edward Eggleston, *The Transit of Civilization: From England to America in the Seventeenth Century* (New York: D. Appleton & Co., 1900), p. 5.
2. Ralph Barton Perry, *Puritanism and Democracy* (New York: The Vanguard Press, 1944), pp. 62–81.
3. This is done by Puritanism's foremost authority, Perry Miller, *The New England Mind* (New York: The Macmillan Company, 1939); and by Lawrence A. Cremin, *American Education: The Colonial Experience 1607-1783* (New York: Harper & Row, Publishers, 1970).
4. Cremin, *American Education*, p. 24.
5. Miller, *The New England Mind*, pp. 64–88.
6. R. R. Bolgar, *The Classical Heritage and Its Beneficiaries* (New York: Cambridge University Press, 1954), pp. 333-335.
7. Miller, *The New England Mind*, pp. 100-101.
8. Owen C. Watkins, *The Puritan Experience* (London: Routledge & Kegan Paul, 1972), p. 7.
9. Miller, *The New England Mind*, p. 21.
10. Ibid., pp. 7-9; John Rogers, *The Doctrine of Faith* (London, 1629), pp. 361-365; and Cremin, *American Education*, pp. 31-57.
11. Samuel Eliot Morison, *The Puritan Pronaos* (New York: New York University Press, 1936), pp. 39-40; and Miller, *The New England Mind*, p. 35.
12. Carl R. Becker, *Beginnings of the American People* (Boston: Houghton Mifflin Company, 1915), p. 94; and Samuel Eliot Morison, *The Founding of Harvard College* (Cambridge: Harvard University Press, 1935), p. 361.
13. Miller, *The New England Mind*, p. 36.
14. Ibid.
15. Ibid., p. 37.
16. Cremin, *American Education*, p. 150.

411

17. Lyon G. Tyler, ed., *Narratives of Early Virginia, 1606–1625* (New York: Charles Scribner's Sons, 1907), p. 271.
18. Williston Walker, ed., *The Creeds and Platforms of Congregationalism* (New York: Charles Scribner's Sons, 1893), pp. 100–108, 116.
19. Cremin, *American Education*, pp. 163–164.
20. Ibid., p. 153.
21. Thomas Jefferson Wertenbaker, *The Founding of American Civilization: The Middle Colonies* (New York: Charles Scribner's Sons, 1938), pp. 71–76.
22. Thomas Jefferson Wertenbaker, *The Founding of American Civilization: The Old South* (New York: Charles Scribner's Sons, 1942), pp. 51–55.
23. Bolgar, *The Classical Heritage*, pp. 249–250.
24. Ibid., p. 248.
25. Ibid., p. 346.
26. Edward J. Power, *Evolution of Educational Doctrine* (New York: Appleton-Century-Crofts, 1969), pp. 205–218.
27. Morison, *The Puritan Pronaos*, p. 14.
28. Fritz Caspari, *Humanism and the Social Order in Tudor England* (Chicago: University of Chicago Press, 1954), pp. 35–38.
29. Morison, *The Puritan Pronaos*, p. 14.
30. Ibid., p. 15.
31. Ibid., pp. 39–46.
32. Miller, *The New England Mind*, p. 100.
33. Ibid., p. 101.
34. Perry Miller and Thomas H. Johnson, *The Puritans* (New York: The Macmillan Company, 1938), pp. 829–831.
35. Miller, *The New England Mind*, p. 5.
36. Herbert W. Schneider, *The Puritan Mind* (London: Constable & Co., Ltd., 1931), p. 215.
37. Miller, *The New England Mind*, p. 11.
38. Ibid., p. 21.
39. Edmund S. Morgan, *Visible Saints: The History of a Puritan Idea* (New York: New York University Press, 1963), p. 116.
40. Ibid.
41. Watkins, *The Puritan Experience*, pp. 63–67.
42. Miller, *The New England Mind*, p. 280.
43. Ibid., p. 97.
44. Morison, *The Puritan Pronaos*, p. 53.
45. Dixon Ryan Fox, *Ideas in Motion* (New York: D. Appleton-Century Company, 1935), pp. 3–36.
46. Perry, *Puritanism and Democracy*, pp. 286–290.
47. Ibid., p. 192; and Cremin, *American Education*, pp. 40–41.
48. Vernon L. Parrington, *The Colonial Mind, 1620–1800. Main Currents in American Thought: An Interpretation of American Literature from the Beginnings to 1920* (New York: Harcourt, Brace & World, 1927), I, 21–47.
49. Miller, *The New England Mind*, p. 111.
50. James Truslow Adams, *The Founding of New England* (Boston: The Atlantic Monthly Press, 1921), pp. 357–361; and Miller, *The New England Mind*, p. 66.
51. Ibid., pp. 66–67.
52. Ibid., p. 69.
53. Arthur O. Norton, "Harvard Text-Books and Reference Books of the Seventeenth Century," *Publications of the Colonial Society of Massachusetts*, XXVIII, 412–414; and Walter H. Small, *Early New England Schools* (Boston: Ginn & Co., 1914), pp. 190–191.

54. Morison, *The Puritan Pronaos,* p. 30; and Cremin, *American Education,* pp. 219-220.
55. Miller, *The New England Mind,* p. 70.
56. Ibid., p. 71.
57. William W. Sweet, *Religion in Colonial America* (New York: Charles Scribner's Sons, 1942), pp. 265-270.

CHAPTER TWO

1. Lawrence A. Cremin, *American Education: The Colonial Experience, 1607-1783* (New York: Harper & Row, Publishers, 1970), pp. 243-248.
2. Louis B. Wright, *The Cultural Life of the American Colonies, 1607-1763* (New York: Harper & Row, Publishers, 1957), p. 1.
3. Ibid.
4. Ibid.
5. Thomas Jefferson Wertenbaker, *The Planters of Colonial Virginia* (Princeton: Princeton University Press, 1922), pp. 52-53.
6. Cremin, *American Education,* p. 239.
7. Wright, *Cultural Life,* p. 10.
8. Cremin, *American Education,* p. 257.
9. Newton Edwards and Herman G. Richey, *The School in the American Social Order* (Boston: Houghton Mifflin Company, 1947), pp. 184-186.
10. Wright, *Cultural Life,* p. 23.
11. Cremin, *American Education,* pp. 9-10.
12. Wright, *Cultural Life,* p. 23.
13. Ibid., p. 24.
14. Cremin, *American Education,* pp. 374-375.
15. Wright, *Cultural Life,* p. 24.
16. Thomas Jefferson Wertenbaker, *The Puritan Oligarchy: The Founding of American Civilization* (New York: Charles Scribner's Sons, 1947), pp. 163-165.
17. Curtis P. Nettles, *The Roots of American Civilization: A History of Colonial Life* (New York: F. S. Crofts & Co., 1938), p. 497.
18. Perry Miller, *The New England Mind* (New York: The Macmillan Company, 1939), p. 21.
19. Bernard Farber, *Guardians of Virtue: Salem Families in 1800* (New York: Basic Books, 1972), p. 51; and Wertenbaker, *The Puritan Oligarchy,* p. 68, makes the same point.
20. H. L. Mencken, *The American Language: An Inquiry into the Development of English in the United States* (New York: Alfred A. Knopf, 1960), p. 104. Although this influence is clear enough, the colonists, especially those of New England Puritan disposition, preferred to stay away from Indians, who were commonly thought to be emissaries of the Devil. The smallpox, they concluded, was only one evidence of Indian evil. See Charles M. Segal and David C. Stineback, *Puritans, Indians and Manifest Destiny* (New York: G. P. Putnam's Sons, 1978).
21. Wright, *Cultural Life,* p. 45.
22. Carl L. Becker, *Beginnings of the American People* (Boston: Houghton Mifflin Company, 1915), p. 94.
23. Wesley Frank Craven, *The Colonies in Transition: 1660-1713* (New York: Harper & Row, Publishers, 1968), p. 3.
24. Becker, *Beginnings of the American People,* p. 88.

25. Maude W. Goodwin, *Dutch and English on the Hudson* (New Haven: Yale University Press, 1920), p. 47.
26. Cremin, *American Education,* pp. 242-243.
27. Edwards and Richey, *The School,* p. 134; and Wright, *Cultural Life,* p. 47.
28. Ellis H. Roberts, *New York: The Planting and Growth of the Empire State* (Boston: Houghton Mifflin Company, 1887), I, 80.
29. Wright, *Cultural Life,* pp. 48-49.
30. Mencken, *The American Language,* pp. 108-109.
31. Abbot E. Smith, *Colonists in Bondage: White Servitude and Convict Labor in America, 1607-1776* (Chapel Hill: University of North Carolina Press, 1947), pp. 16-17.
32. James Truslow Adams, *The Founding of New England* (Boston: The Atlantic Monthly Press, 1921), p. 434.
33. Cremin, *American Education,* p. 153.
34. Edmund S. Morgan, *Roger Williams: The Church and the State* (New York: Harcourt, Brace & World, Inc., 1967), p. 21.
35. Miller, *The New England Mind,* p. 491.
36. Clifford K. Shipton, "A Plea for Puritanism," *American Historical Review* XL (April, 1935): 464.
37. Quoted in Vernon L. Parrington, *Main Currents in American Thought: The Colonial Mind, 1620-1800* (New York: Harcourt, Brace & World, Inc., 1927), p. 31.
38. Wertenbaker, *The Puritan Oligarchy,* p. 65.
39. Shipton, "Plea for Puritanism," p. 467.
40. Morgan, *Roger Williams,* p. 24.
41. Edmund S. Morgan, *Visible Saints: The History of a Puritan Idea* (New York: New York University Press, 1963), p. 109.
42. Craven, *Colonies in Transition,* pp. 186-187.
43. Marcus W. Jernegan, *The American Colonies, 1492-1750* (New York: Longmans, Green & Co., 1929), p. 233.
44. Wertenbaker, *The Puritan Oligarchy,* p. 139.
45. Wright, *Cultural Life,* p. 99.
46. Jernegan, *The American Colonies,* pp. 179-180, quotes these legal prescriptions from the 1651 Act of the Massachusetts General Court.
47. Merle Curti, *The Social Ideas of American Educators* (New York: Charles Scribner's Sons, 1935), pp. 4-5.
48. Marcus W. Jernegan, *Laboring and Dependent Classes in Colonial America* (Chicago: University of Chicago Press, 1931), p. 82.
49. Samuel Eliot Morison, *The Puritan Pronaos: Studies in the Intellectual Life of New England in the Seventeenth Century* (New York: New York University Press, 1936), p. 69.
50. Edgar W. Knight, *Education in the United States* (Boston: Ginn & Co., 1951), p. 105, reprints the Law of 1647.
51. Ibid.
52. Edwards and Richey, *The School,* p. 65.
53. Ibid., p. 66.
54. William Heard Kilpatrick, *The Dutch Schools of New Netherland and Colonial New York* (Washington, D. C.: Government Printing Office, 1912), p. 38; for a recent and readable account of the colony, see Henri and Barbara Van der Zee, *A Sweet and Alien Land: The Story of Dutch New York* (New York: The Viking Press, 1978).
55. Edwards and Richey, *The School,* p. 137.
56. Kilpatrick, *Dutch Schools,* p. 124.

57. Quoted in James P. Wickersham, *A History of Education in Pennsylvania* (Lancaster, Pa.: 1885), p. 34.
58. Ibid., p. 40.
59. Wright, *Cultural Life*, p. 108.
60. Quoted in Elmer Ellsworth Brown, *The Making of Our Middle Schools* (New York: Longmans, Green & Co., 1918), p. 50.
61. Morison, *The Puritan Pronaos*, p. 18.
62. Beverly McAnear, "College Founding in the American Colonies, 1745-1775," *The Mississippi Valley Historical Review*, XLII (June, 1955): 24-34; and George Paul Schmidt, "Colleges in Ferment," *American Historical Review*, LIX (October, 1953): 19-42.
63. Morison, *The Puritan Pronaos*, p. 136. Colonists were given advice about reading, too. For examples, see Henry Peachman, *The Compleat Gentleman*, edited by Virgil B. Heltzel (Ithaca, N.Y.: Cornell University Press, 1962).
64. Morison, *The Puritan Pronaos*, pp. 106-109.
65. Wright, *Cultural Life*, pp. 129-132.
66. Cremin, *American Education*, p. 49.
67. Ibid., pp. 29 and 398.
68. Carl R. Fish, *The Rise of the Common Man, 1830-1850* (New York: The Macmillan Company, 1927), pp. 207-208.
69. Morison, *The Puritan Pronaos*, p. 125.
70. Wright, *Cultural Life*, p. 152.
71. Milton Ellis, Louise Pound, and George W. Spohn, eds., *American Literature* (New York: American Book Company, 1939), p. 1.
72. Ibid.
73. Morison, *The Puritan Pronaos*, p. 209.
74. Ibid., p. 191.
75. Ellis, *American Literature*, p. 2.
76. Ibid., p. 31.
77. Ibid., p. 38.
78. Ibid., p. 2.
79. Morgan, *Visible Saints*, pp. 151-152; and Herbert W. Schneider, *The Puritan Mind* (London: Constable & Co., Ltd., 1931), p. 118.
80. Melvin H. Buxbaum, *Benjamin Franklin and the Zealous Presbyterians* (University Park, Pa.: Pennsylvania State University Press, 1975), p. 77.
81. Ellis, *American Literature*, p. 50.
82. Cremin, *American Education*, p. 391.
83. Ibid., p. 447.
84. For an excellent review of the principal newspapers, see Wright, *Cultural Life*, pp. 242-246; and Frederic Hudson, *Journalism in the United States, From 1690-1872* (New York: Harper & Row, Publishers, 1873), pp. 53-60.
85. David Ramsay, *History of the American Revolution* (Philadelphia, 1789), I, 61-62, and quoted in Cremin, *American Education*, p. 448.
86. H. G. Good, *A History of American Education* (New York: The Macmillan Company, 1956), p. 27.
87. Ibid.
88. Wright, *Cultural Life*, p. 241.
89. Ibid., p. 251.

CHAPTER THREE

1. Bernard Bailyn, *Education in the Forming of American Society* (Chapel Hill: University of North Carolina Press, 1960), p. 15; and John Demos, *A Little Commonwealth: Family Life in Plymouth Colony* (New York: Oxford University Press, 1970), pp. 142-144.

2. Edward Eggleston, *The Transit of Civilization: From England to America in the Seventeenth Century* (New York: D. Appleton & Co., 1901), pp. 207-255; and John Calam, *Parsons and Pedagogues: The S. P. G. Adventure in American Education* (New York: Columbia University Press, 1971), p. 96.

3. Bernard Farber, *Guardians of Virtue: Salem Families in 1800* (New York: Basic Books, 1972), pp. 261-282.

4. Lawrence A. Cremin, *American Education: The Colonial Experience, 1607-1783* (New York: Harper & Row, Publishers, 1970), pp. 130-132.

5. William H. Woodward, *Studies in Education During the Age of the Renaissance, 1400-1600* (New York: Teachers College Press, 1967), pp. 48-64, summarizes Alberti's book.

6. Ibid., p. 58.

7. Arthur W. Calhoun, *A Social History of the American Family from Colonial Times to the Present* (New York: Barnes & Noble, Inc., 1945), I, 212; and, although the focus is French rather than British, Philip Ariés, *Centuries of Childhood: A Social History of Family Life* (New York: Alfred A. Knopf, 1962).

8. Fritz Caspari, *Humanism and the Social Order in Tudor England* (Chicago: University of Chicago Press, 1954), pp. 62-65.

9. Cremin, *American Education*, p. 118; Demos, *A Little Commonwealth*, p. 71; Farber, *Guardians of Virtue*, p. 160; and Ariés, *Centuries of Childhood*, p. 379.

10. Cremin, *American Education*, pp. 120-122.

11. Ibid., p. 122; and Farber, *Guardians of Virtue*, p. 4.

12. Robert F. Seybolt, *Apprenticeship and Apprenticeship Legislation in Colonial New England and New York* (New York: Teachers College Press, 1917), p. 13.

13. Cremin, *American Education*, p. 121.

14. Ibid., p. 122.

15. Kenneth A. Lockridge, *Literacy in Colonial New England: An Enquiry into the Social Context of Literacy in the Early Modern West* (New York: Norton, 1974), p. 77.

16. Edmund S. Morgan, *The Puritan Family: Religion and Domestic Relations in Seventeenth-Century New England* (New York: Harper & Row, Publishers, 1966), pp. 65-66.

17. According to Farber, *Guardians of Virtue*, p. 4, children were usually left free to play until they were about six.

18. One must be careful about inflating the place of games, for they were merely tolerated. Their excessive practice could be judged criminal (Ariés, *Centuries of Childhood*, p. 88).

19. Morgan, *The Puritan Family*, p. 66; and Thomas Jefferson Wertenbaker, *The Puritan Oligarchy: The Founding of American Civilization* (New York: Charles Scribner's Sons, 1947), pp. 165-166.

20. Wertenbaker, *The Puritan Oligarchy*, p. 177.

21. Demos, *A Little Commonwealth*, pp. 146-147.

22. *Boston Sermons* (1679), quoted in Morgan, *The Puritan Family*, p. 72.

23. Ibid., pp. 77-78; Demos, *A Little Commonwealth*, p. 71; and Farber, *Guardians of Virtue*, p. 163.

24. Philip J. Greven, *Four Generations: Population, Land, and Family in Colonial Andover, Massachusetts* (Ithaca: Cornell University Press, 1970), p. 77; and Demos, *A Little Commonwealth*, p. 104.

25. Morgan, *The Puritan Family*, pp. 78–86.

26. Cotton Mather, *Cares About the Nurseries* (Boston: 1702), p. 34, quoted in Morgan, *The Puritan Family*, p. 89.

27. Morgan, *The Puritan Family*, p. 92.

28. Perry Miller, *The New England Mind* (New York: The Macmillan Company, 1939), p. 280.

29. Marcus W. Jernegan, *Laboring and Dependent Classes in Colonial America, 1607-1783* (Chicago: University of Chicago Press, 1931), pp. 147-148.

30. Ibid.

31. Samuel Eliot Morison, *The Puritan Pronaos* (New York: New York University Press, 1936), p. 163.

32. Morgan, *The Puritan Family*, p. 102.

33. Ibid., pp. 15, 20.

34. Paul L. Ford, *The New-England Primer* (New York: Teachers College Press, 1962).

35. Ibid., "Introduction," pp. 23-24.

36. Ibid.

37. Ibid.

38. Ibid., "Introduction," p. 19.

39. Ibid., p. 53.

40. Eggleston, *Transit of Civilization*, p. 214.

41. Cremin, *American Education*, pp. 123-128.

42. Demos, *A Little Commonwealth*, pp. 12-13.

43. For other books, see Cremin, *American Education*, pp. 129-132.

44. Ariés, *Centuries of Childhood*, pp. 298-299, describes the book in some detail.

45. Ford, *The New-England Primer*, p. 43.

46. Cremin, *American Education*, p. 130.

47. Alice M. Earle, *Home Life in Colonial Days* (New York: The Macmillan Company, 1946), pp. 79-80.

48. Walter H. Small, *Early New England Schools* (Boston: Ginn & Co., 1914), pp. 141-147.

49. Cremin, *American Education*, pp. 132-133; and Demos, *A Little Commonwealth*, pp. 146-147.

50. Eggleston, *The Transit of Civilization*, pp. 242-244.

51. Morison, *The Puritan Pronaos*, p. 22.

52. Some caution is necessary here, for in some New England towns strangers were ordered to leave at once (Farber, *Guardians of Virtue*, p. 54). And see, Wertenbaker, *The Puritan Oligarchy*, p. 68.

53. Miller, *The New England Mind*, p. 67.

54. Edmund S. Morgan, *Visible Saints: The History of a Puritan Idea* (New York: New York University Press, 1963), p. 66.

55. Wertenbaker, *The Puritan Oligarchy*, p. 63.

56. Miller, *The New England Mind*, p. 298.

57. Morgan, *Visible Saints*, pp. 123-124.

CHAPTER FOUR

1. R. Freeman Butts, *The American Tradition in Religion and Education* (Boston: The Beacon Press, 1950), pp. 11-38. For a sharply different interpretation of the historical relationship between religion and education, see James M. O'Neill, *Religion and Education under the Constitution* (New York: Harper & Row, Publishers, 1949), pp. 23-42.
2. Cassiodorus, *An Introduction to Divine and Human Readings,* translated by Leslie Webber Jones (New York: Columbia University Press, 1946).
3. Edward J. Power, *Evolution of Educational Doctrine* (New York: Appleton-Century-Crofts, 1969), pp. 152-153.
4. H. E. Butler, *Quintilian* (Cambridge: Harvard University Press, 1922).
5. R. R. Bolgar, *The Classical Heritage and its Beneficiaries* (Cambridge: Cambridge University Press, 1954), pp. 239-264.
6. Vernon L. Parrington, *The Colonial Mind, 1620-1800* (New York: Harcourt, Brace & Co., 1927), p. 21.
7. This may account for the scholarly debates on the subject led by such prominent historical analysts as: Samuel Eliot Morison, *The Puritan Pronaos* (New York: New York University Press, 1936), pp. 15-16; Charles A. and Mary R. Beard, *The Rise of American Civilization* (New York: The Macmillan Company, 1927), II, 52; and Merle Curti, *The Social Ideas of American Educators* (New York: Charles Scribner's Sons, 1935), pp. 4-5.
8. Motives for founding colleges must have varied, yet most scholars agree that religion was a primary motive for colonial colleges. See Donald Tewksbury, *The Founding of American Colleges and Universities Before the Civil War* (New York: Teachers College Press, 1932), pp. 80-85. Although Tewksbury's work has not been superseded, Natalie A. Naylor has amended it somewhat in "The Ante-Bellum College Movement: A Reappraisal of Tewksbury's Founding of American Colleges and Universities," *History of Education Quarterly*, XIII, 3 (1973): 261-274.
9. William E. Dodd, *The Old South: Struggles for Democracy* (New York: The Macmillan Company, 1937), pp. 83-91.
10. Francis Bacon, *The Advancement of Learning,* ed. Joseph Devey, (New York: American Home Library Company, 1902), p. 11.
11. Ibid., p. 71.
12. Ibid.
13. Ibid., p. 93.
14. Ibid., p. 87.
15. Ibid.
16. Ibid., pp. 88-89.
17. Ibid., pp. 171-199.
18. Ibid., p. 211.
19. Ibid., p. 237.
20. Ibid., p. 243.
21. Ibid., p. 236.
22. Ibid., p. 245.
23. Ibid., p. 244.
24. Ibid., p. 250.
25. Ibid., p. 269.
26. Ibid.
27. Ibid., p. 302.
28. Ibid.

29. Ibid.
30. Ibid., p. 303.
31. Ibid.
32. Marcus W. Jernegan, *The American Colonies, 1492-1750: A Study of Their Political, Economic and Social Development* (New York: Longmans, Green & Co., 1929), pp. 290-303.
33. R. H. Tawney, *Religion and the Rise of Capitalism: A Historical Study* (New York: Harcourt, Brace & Co., 1926), pp. 316-317; and Frank Tracy Carlton, *Economic Influences Upon Educational Progress in the United States, 1820-1850* (New York: Teachers College Press, 1965), pp. 4-15.
34. Ralph Barton Perry, *Puritanism and Democracy* (New York: The Vanguard Press, 1944), pp. 82-116.
35. See Harvey Wish, *Society and Thought in Early America* (New York: Longmans, Green & Co., 1950), pp. 295-298.
36. William H. Woodward, *Vittorino da Feltre and Other Humanist Educators* (New York: Teachers College Press, 1963), pp. 184-186.
37. Lawrence A. Cremin, *The American Common School* (New York: Teachers College Press, 1951), pp. 55-62.
38. Elsie W. Clews, *Educational Legislation and Administration of the Colonial Governments* (New York: The Macmillan Company, 1899), pp. 90-95.
39. Edgar W. Knight, *Public Education in the South* (Boston: Ginn & Co., 1922), pp. 24-27.
40. Marcus W. Jernegan, *Laboring and Dependent Classes in Colonial America, 1607-1783* (Chicago: University of Chicago Press, 1931), pp. 175-179; and Morison, *The Puritan Pronaos,* pp. 60-65.
41. Clews, *Educational Legislation,* pp. 97-99.
42. Cloyer Meriwether, *Our Colonial Curriculum, 1607-1776* (Washington, D.C.: Capital Publishing Company, 1907), pp. 281-287; and Robert F. Seybolt, *Apprenticeship and Apprenticeship Legislation in Colonial New England and New York* (New York: Teachers College Press, 1916), pp. 35-39.
43. Sanford H. Cobb, *The Rise of Religious Liberty in America* (New York: The Macmillan Company, 1902), pp. 303-305.
44. It may be argued, however, that such laws were not kept in force because the tradition of compulsory education was so strong as to make them unnecessary. Without further evidence, so far unearthed, this argument lacks persuasion. See Newton Edwards and Herman G. Richey, *The School in the American Social Order* (New York: Houghton Mifflin Company, 1947), p. 100.
45. Edgar W. Knight, *Education in the United States* (Boston: Ginn & Co., 1934), p. 85; and Curti, *Social Ideas of American Educators,* pp. 4-5.
46. Clews, *Educational Legislation,* pp. 95-96.
47. Walter H. Small, *Early New England Schools* (Boston: Ginn & Co., 1914), pp. 33, 42-45.
48. Sadie Bell, *The Church, the State, and Education in Virginia* (New York: Science Press, 1930), pp. 117-121.
49. Guy F. Wells, *Parish Education in Colonial Virginia* (New York: Teachers College Press, 1923), pp. 37-41.

CHAPTER FIVE

1. Lawrence A. Cremin, *American Education: The Colonial Experience, 1607-1783* (New York: Harper & Row, Publishers, 1970), p. 453, quotes one clear declaration of this authority from Charles Chauncy, *Civil Magistrates Must Be Just, Ruling in the Fear of God* (Boston: 1747), pp. 33-34.
2. Elsie W. Clews, *Educational Legislation and Administration of the Colonial Governments* (New York: The Macmillan Company, 1899), p. 79.
3. John F. Sly, *Town Government in Massachusetts, 1620-1930* (Cambridge: Harvard University Press, 1930), pp. 75-76.
4. Edward McCrady, Jr., "Education in South Carolina Prior to and during the Revolution," *South Carolina Historical Collections,* IV (1887): 7-15.
5. Walter H. Small, *Early New England Schools* (Boston: Ginn & Co., 1914), p. 188.
6. Carl Bridenbaugh, "The New England Town: A Way of Life," *Proceedings of the American Antiquarian Society,* new series, LVI (1946): 19-48.
7. Robert F. Seybolt, *Source Studies in American Colonial Education: The Private School* (Urbana: University of Illinois Press, 1925), pp. 100-102.
8. Harlan Updegraff, *The Origin of the Moving School in Massachusetts* (New York: Teachers College Press, 1907), pp. 136-149.
9. Small, *Early New England Schools,* pp. 14, 162.
10. Cremin, *American Education,* p. 174.
11. Edward Eggleston, *Transit of Civilization: From England to America in the Seventeenth Century* (New York: D. Appleton & Co., 1901), p. 244; and Seybolt, *The Private School,* pp. 69-82.
12. Robert F. Seybolt, *The Private Schools of Colonial Boston* (Cambridge: Harvard University Press, 1935), p. 12.
13. Robert F. Seybolt, *The Public Schools of Colonial Boston, 1635-1775* (Cambridge: Harvard University Press, 1935), pp. 21-27.
14. Updegraff, *Origin of the Moving School,* p. 172.
15. William Heard Kilpatrick, *The Dutch Schools of New Netherland and Colonial New York* (Washington, D. C.: Government Printing Office, 1912), pp. 43-47.
16. Paul L. Ford, ed., *The New-England Primer* (New York: Teachers College Press, 1962), "Introduction," pp. 12-13.
17. Cremin, *American Education,* p. 185, says Edward Cocker's *The Tutor to Writing and Arithmetic,* published in London in 1664, was available in the colonies. It appears not to have been used extensively.
18. Cremin, *American Education,* pp. 154-155; 187-189.
19. Ibid., p. 188; and see Small, *Early New England Schools,* pp. 180-191.
20. Samuel E. Weber, *The Charity School Movement in Colonial Pennsylvania* (Philadelphia: George F. Lasher Press, 1905), pp. 33-51; and John Calam, *Parsons and Pedagogues: The S. P. G. Adventure in American Education* (New York: Columbia University Press, 1971).
21. M. G. Brumbaugh, *The Life and Works of Christopher Dock* (Philadelphia: J. B. Lippincott Company, 1908), pp. 95-100.
22. Robert Middlekauff, *Ancients and Axioms: Secondary Education in Eighteenth-Century New England* (New Haven: Yale University Press, 1963), pp. 54-58.
23. We are indebted for our knowledge of Cheever to Cotton Mather's *Corderius Americanus: An Essay upon the Good Education of Children* (Boston: John Allen, 1708). The only biography of Cheever is Elizabeth Porter Gould's *Ezekiel Cheever: Schoolmaster* (Boston: The Palmer Company, 1904).
24. Samuel Eliot Morison, *The Puritan Pronaos* (New York: New York University Press, 1936), pp. 101-103.

25. Ibid.
26. Literature on the early colleges is extensive and good. For a brief, solid description, see ibid., pp. 25-53; and Cremin, *American Education*, pp. 206-224.
27. Donald Tewksbury, *The Founding of American Colleges and Universities Before the Civil War* (New York: Teachers College Press, 1932), pp. 142-154.
28. Perry Miller, *The New England Mind* (New York: The Macmillan Company, 1939), p. 73.
29. Tewksbury, *Founding of American Colleges*, pp. 74-78.
30. Samuel Eliot Morison, *Harvard College in the Seventeenth Century* (Cambridge: Harvard University Press, 1936), II, 12-15.

CHAPTER SIX

1. The "Proposals" are quoted in various books on Franklin: Thomas Woody, *Educational Veiws of Benjamin Franklin* (New York: McGraw-Hill Book Company, 1931); John H. Best, *Benjamin Franklin on Education* (New York: Teachers College Press, 1962). The extract here is from *The Papers of Benjamin Franklin*, Leonard W. Labaree and Whitfield J. Bell, Jr., eds., (New Haven: Yale University Press, 1959), III, 397-421.
2. Noah Webster, "Dangers of a Foreign Education," *The American Magazine* (May, 1788): pp. 307-373.
3. Noah Webster, *Dissertations on the English Language* (Boston: 1789), pp. 20-23.
4. On the drift toward revolution, see Arthur M. Schlesinger, Jr., *Prelude to Independence* (New York: Alfred A. Knopf, 1958), pp. 234-255; and Bernard Bailyn, *The Ideological Origins of the American Revolution* (Cambridge: Harvard University Press, 1967), pp. 161-162.
5. An excellent synthesis of Enlightenment thought is made by Peter Gay, *The Enlightenment: An Interpretation* (New York: Alfred A. Knopf, 1966-1969), II, 319-368.
6. *Sir Isaac Newton's Mathematical Princples of Natural Philosophy and His System of the World*, trans. Andrew Motte (Berkeley: University of California Press, 1960), pp. 1-28.
7. In 1616, William Harvey, an English physician, discovered the circulation of the blood.
8. Sir Robert Boyle formulated a famous law of gases.
9. Jack Rochford Vrooman, *René Descartes: A Biography* (New York: G. P. Putnam's Sons, 1970), chapter 3.
10. Paolo Rossi, *Francis Bacon: From Magic to Science*, trans. Sacha Rabinovitch (Chicago: University of Chicago Press, 1968), pp. 189-192.
11. Charles A. and Mary R. Beard, *The Rise of American Civilization* (New York: The Macmillan Company, 1927), I, 443.
12. Newton Edwards and Herman G. Richey, *The School in the American Social Order* (New York: Houghton Mifflin Company, 1947), p. 209.
13. Brooke Hindle, *The Pursuit of Science in Revolutionary America, 1735-1789* (Chapel Hill: University of North Carolina Press, 1956), pp. 133-145.
14. Edwards and Richey, *The School*, p. 211.
15. John Dunn, *The Political Thought of John Locke* (Cambridge: Cambridge University Press, 1969), pp. 43-57.
16. John Locke, *An Essay Concerning Human Understanding*, 28th ed. (London: T. Tegg and Son, 1838), I, ii, 4; I, iv, 4; I, iv, 3-4; II, i, 3-4; II, vii-ix; and II, ix, 5-6.

17. John W. Yolton, ed., *John Locke: Problems and Perspectives* (Cambridge: Cambridge University Press, 1969), pp. 99-136.
18. Roy J. Honeywell, *The Educational Work of Thomas Jefferson* (Cambridge: Harvard University Press, 1931), pp. 10-12.
19. Merle Curti, *The Growth of American Thought,* 3rd ed. (New York: Harper & Row, Publishers, 1964), p. 168.
20. Jean Jacques Rousseau, *Émile,* trans. Barbara Foxley (New York: E. P. Dutton, 1911).
21. Bernard Bailyn, "Political Experience and Enlightenment Ideas in Eighteenth-Century America," *American Historical Review,* LXVII (January, 1962): 339-351.
22. Herbert M. Morais, *Deism in Eighteenth Century America* (New York: Columbia University Press, 1934), pp. 13-28.
23. Earl M. Wilbur, *A History of Unitarianism* (Cambridge: Harvard University Press, 1952), II, 451-452.
24. Perry Miller, *The Transcendentalists* (Cambridge: Harvard University Press, 1950). This anthology contains the expressions of a variety of Transcendental spokesmen on various fundamental social issues.
25. Alice Felt Tyler, *Freedom's Ferment* (Minneapolis: University of Minnesota Press, 1944), pp. 25-29.
26. Alan Heimert, *Religion and the American Mind from the Great Awakening to the Revolution* (Cambridge: Harvard University Press, 1966), pp. 59-66.
27. Benjamin Franklin to Joseph Priestly, June 7, 1782, in Jared Sparks, ed., *The Works of Benjamin Franklin* (Boston: 1840), IX, 226-227.
28. Allen O. Hansen, *Liberalism and American Education in the Eighteenth Century* (New York: The Macmillan Company, 1926), pp. 48-63.
29. Bernard Smith, *The Democratic Spirit* (New York: Alfred A. Knopf, 1941), pp. 122-124.
30. R. Freeman Butts, *The American Tradition in Religion and Education* (Boston: Beacon Press, 1950), pp. 68-110, argues that religion and education were separated by public policy at this time.
31. Louis M. Hacker, *The Triumph of American Capitalism* (New York: Simon & Schuster, 1940), pp. 178-195.
32. Thomas C. Cochran and William Miller, *The Age of Enterprise* (New York: The Macmillan Company, 1942), pp. 30-43.
33. For further amplification here, see Dumas Malone, "The Relevance of Mr. Jefferson," *Virginia Quarterly Review,* XXXVI (Summer, 1961): 332-349; and Cecelia M. Kenyon, "Alexander Hamilton: Rousseau of the Right," *Political Science Quarterly,* LXXIII, No. 2 (June, 1958): 161-178.
34. Saul K. Padover, *The Mind of Alexander Hamilton* (New York: Harper & Row, Publishers, 1958), p. 13.
35. Quoted from *The Federalist* (No. 35) in Padover, *The Mind of Alexander Hamilton,* p. 16.
36. Padover, *The Mind of Alexander Hamilton,* p. 13.
37. Vernon L. Parrington, *The Colonial Mind, 1620-1800* (New York: Harcourt, Brace & Co., 1922), I, 316-317.
38. Ibid., pp. 355-356.
39. "Original Papers in Relation to a Course of Liberal Education," *The American Journal of Science and Arts,* XV (January, 1829): 297-351.
40. In John H. Best, ed., *Benjamin Franklin on Education* (New York: Teachers College Press, 1962), pp. 165-171.
41. Carl Van Doren, *Benjamin Franklin* (New York: The Viking Press, 1938), pp. 260-268.

42. In Labaree and Bell, *op. cit.,* III, 397–421.

43. Lawrence A. Cremin, *American Education: The Colonial Experience, 1607–1783* (New York: Harper & Row, Publishers, 1970), p. 377.

44. Merrill D. Peterson, *Thomas Jefferson and the New Nation* (New York: Oxford University Press, 1970).

45. "A Bill for the More General Diffusion of Knowledge," in *The Papers of Thomas Jefferson,* ed. Julian P. Boyd, et al. (Princeton: Princeton University Press, 1950 et. seq.), II, 526-533.

46. Thomas Jefferson, *Notes on the State of Virginia, with an Appendix* (Boston: David Carlisle, 1801), 8th edition, Query XIV, pp. 216-217.

47. Ibid.

48. Ibid.

49. In Benjamin Rush, *A Plan for the Establishment of Public Schools and the Diffusion of Knowledge in Pennsylvania* (Philadelphia: 1786), pp. 13–36.

50. Ibid., p. 28.

51. Ibid., pp. 3-12.

52. Ibid., p. 5. For an interesting general view of Benjamin Rush, see Richard M. Gummere, *Seven Wise Men of Colonial America* (Cambridge: Harvard University Press, 1967), pp. 64-80.

CHAPTER SEVEN

1. Benjamin P. Poore, *The Federal and State Constitutions, Colonial Charters, and Other Organic Laws of the United States,* 2 vols. (Washington, D. C.: Government Printing Office, 1878), Article III of the Ordinance of 1787 is reprinted in I: 431.

2. John C. Fitzpatrick, ed., *Writings of George Washington, 1745–1799* (Washington, D. C.: Government Printing Office, 1939), XXX, 493-494; XXXV, 316-317. Washington and others were interested in a national university. See Edgar B. Wesley, *Proposed: The University of the United States* (Minneapolis: University of Minnesota Press, 1936).

3. Allen O. Hansen, *Liberalism and American Education in the Eighteenth Century* (New York: The Macmillan Company, 1926), p. 110.

4. Quoted in ibid., pp. 63-78.

5. Quoted in Newton Edwards and Herman G. Richey, *The School in the American Social Order* (New York: Houghton Mifflin Company, 1947), p. 243.

6. Edgar W. Knight, *Education in the United States* (New York: Ginn & Co., 1951), pp. 285, 288.

7. Edwards and Richey, *The School,* p. 245.

8. "The Trustees of Dartmouth College v. Woodward," in *Reports of Cases Argued and Decided in the Supreme Court of the United States* (Newark, N. J.: 1882), IV, 625-654. For an appraisal of the consequences of the decision, see Gordon R. Clapp, "The College Charter," *Journal of Higher Education,* V (February, 1934): 79-87.

9. Donald Tewksbury, *The Founding of American Colleges and Universities Before the Civil War* (New York: Teachers College Press, 1932), pp. 150-151. He argued, with some persuasiveness, that the Dartmouth College decision checked the state university development for a half-century. John S. Brubacher and Willis Rudy, *Higher Education in Transition* (New York: Harper & Row, Publishers, 1958), p. 59, are of the opinion that the decision encouraged the multiplication of public and private colleges. See also, George Paul Schmidt, "Colleges in Ferment,"

American Historical Review, LIX (October, 1953): 19-42; and Frederick S. Rudolph, *The American College and University: A History* (New York: Alfred A. Knopf, 1962), pp. 207-220.

10. Carl F. Kaestle, ed., *Joseph Lancaster and the Monitorial School Movement: A Documentary History* (New York: Teachers College Press, 1973), pp. 43-49.

11. Adolphe E. Meyer, *An Educational History of the American People* (New York: McGraw-Hill Book Company, 1957), p. 128.

12. Knight, *Education,* p. 167.

13. Michael B. Katz, *Class, Bureaucracy, and Schools* (New York: Praeger Publishers, 1971), pp. 7-13. For the story of this controversy, see Vincent P. Lannie, *Public Money and Parochial Education* (Cleveland: Press of Case Western Reserve University, 1968).

14. Neil G. McCluskey, ed., *Catholic Education in America: A Documentary History* (New York: Teachers College Press, 1964), pp. 13-14. Pp. 65-77 reprint the "Petition of the Catholics of New York for a Portion of the Common-School Fund (1840)."

15. Oscar Browning, ed., *Milton's Tractate on Education* (Cambridge: 1883), pp. 3-4.

16. Theodore R. Sizer, ed., *The Age of the Academies* (New York: Teachers College Press, 1964), p. 11.

17. *American Journal of Education,* I (1855): 368.

18. Alexander Inglis, *The Rise of the High School in Massachusetts* (New York: The Macmillan Company, 1911), pp. 8, 57.

19. Walter J. Gifford, *Historical Development of the New York State High School System* (Harrisonburg, Va.: the author, 1922), pp. 187-188.

20. Sizer, *Age of the Academies,* p. 21.

21. Ibid., p. 36.

22. "Original Papers in Relation to a Course of Liberal Education," *The American Journal of Science and the Arts,* XV (1829): 318-319.

23. George Paul Schmidt, "Intellectual Crosscurrents in American Colleges," *American Historical Review,* XLII (October, 1936): 46-67; and Rudolph, *The American College,* p. 47.

24. Lawrence A. Cremin, *The American Common School* (New York: Teachers College Press, 1951), pp. 219-221.

25. Merle Curti, *The Social Ideas of American Educators* (New York: Charles Scribner's Sons, 1935), p. 85.

26. *American Annals of Education,* I (March, 1831): 125.

27. Josiah Holbrook, "The American Lyceum, or Society for Improvement of Schools and Diffusion of Useful Knowledge," *American Journal of Education,* III (1828): 715-721; Albert Mock, *The Mid-western Academy Movement* (Indianapolis: the author, 1949), pp. 24-29; Edgar W. Knight, *The Academy Movement in the South* (Chapel Hill: University of North Carolina Press, 1920), p. 24; George F. Miller, *The Academy System of the State of New York* (New York: Arno Press, 1969), p. 76; and Carl Bode, *The American Lyceum: Town Meeting of the Mind* (New York: Oxford University Press, 1956), p. 16.

28. For the others both mentioned and discussed, see Edwards and Richey, *The School,* pp. 352-356; Knight, *Education in the United States,* pp. 221-236; and Meyer, *An Educational History,* pp. 156-159.

29. Jonathan Messerli, *Horace Mann: A Biography* (New York: Alfred A. Knopf, 1972); Lawrence A. Cremin, ed., *The Republic and the School: Horace Mann on the Education of Free Men* (New York: Teachers College Press, 1957); Raymond B. Culver, *Horace Mann and Religion in the Massachusetts Public Schools* (New Haven: Yale University Press, 1929); Burke A. Hinsdale, *Horace Mann and the*

Common School Revival in the United States (New York: Charles Scribner's Sons, 1898); and E. F. F. Williams, *Horace Mann, Educational Statesman* (New York: The Macmillan Company, 1937).

30. *Essays upon Popular Education* (Boston: 1826); and Jonathan Messerli, "James Carter's Liabilities as a Common School Reformer," *History of Education Quarterly*, V (March, 1965): 14-25.

31. John S. Brubacher, *Henry Barnard on Education* (New York: Russell and Russell, 1965), pp. 3-20; and Henry Barnard, ed., *American Journal of Education* (Syracuse, N. Y.: reprinted by C. W. Bardeen, 1902).

32. Knight, *Education in the United States*, pp. 221-227.

33. J. F. Tuttle, "Caleb Mills and the Indiana Common Schools," *American Journal of Education*, XXXI (1902): 135-144.

34. Culver, *Horace Mann and Religion*, pp. 65-81.

35. Herman G. Richey, "Reappraisal of the State School System of the Pre-Civil-War Period," *Elementary School Journal*, XLI (October, 1940): 122-123.

36. Knight, *Education in the United States*, p. 427.

37. David B. Tyack, *Turning Points in American Educational History* (Waltham, Mass.: Blaisdell Publishing Company, 1967), pp. 194-213.

38. William Holmes McGuffey, "The Third Eclectic Reader," *The Eclectic Reader; consisting of Progressive Lessons in Reading and Spelling* (Cincinnati: Truman & Smith, 1853), p. 58.

39. Richard D. Mosier, *Making the American Mind: Social and Moral Ideas in the McGuffey Readers* (New York: King's Crown Press, 1947), p. 98; and Alice McGuffey Ruggles, *The Story of the McGuffeys* (New York: American Book Company, 1950).

40. I. L. Kandel, *History of Secondary Education* (New York: Houghton Mifflin Company, 1930), pp. 425-428.

41. *Annual Report of Women's Educational and Industrial Union for the Year Ending May 6, 1879* (Boston: 1879), p. 9.

42. Joseph White, National Education Association, *Addresses and Proceedings, 1873*, p. 43; and Alexander J. Inglis, *The Rise of the High School in Massachusetts* (New York: 1911), p. 46.

43. Samuel Eliot Morison, *Development of Harvard University Since the Inauguration of President Eliot, 1869-1929* (Cambridge: Harvard University Press, 1930), pp. xlii-xliii; and Richard Hofstadter and C. DeWitt Hardy, *Development and Scope of Higher Education in the United States* (New York: Columbia University Press, 1952), p. 51.

44. Ibid., pp. 88-94.

45. Robert S. Fletcher, *History of Oberlin College* (Oberlin, Ohio: Oberlin College, 1943), I, chapter 16; II, 718; and Robert S. Fletcher, "The First Coeds," *American Scholar*, 7 (Winter, 1938): 76-86.

46. Charles A. Harper, *A Century of Public Teacher Education* (Washington: National Education Association, 1939), pp. 35-36; and Merle L. Borrowman, ed., *Teacher Education in America: A Documentary History* (New York: Teachers College Press, 1965), pp. 1-52.

47. Knight, *Education in the United States*, p. 167.

48. J. P. Gordy, *The Rise and Growth of the Normal-School Idea in the United States* (Washington: 1891), pp. 135-142; and Arthur O. Norton, *The First State Normal School in America* (Cambridge: Harvard University Press, 1926), pp. xlii-xlvi.

CHAPTER EIGHT

1. Louis B. Wright, "Franklin's Legacy to the Gilded Age," *The Virginia Quarterly Review,* XXII (1946): 268-279.
2. Richard D. Mosier, *Making the American Mind* (New York: King's Crown Press, 1947), pp. 98-102.
3. Perry Miller, *The New England Mind* (New York: The Macmillan Company, 1939), p. 111.
4. Alice Felt Tyler, *Freedom's Ferment* (Minneapolis: University of Minnesota Press, 1944), p. 224.
5. Perry Miller, *The Transcendentalists* (Cambridge: Harvard University Press, 1950), pp. 6-15.
6. Howard Mumford Jones, ed., *Emerson on Education: Selections* (New York: Teachers College Press, 1966), p. 20.
7. Ibid., pp. 58-59.
8. Herbert W. Schneider, *A History of American Philosophy* (New York: Columbia University Press, 1946), pp. 280-286.
9. R. R. Bolgar, *The Classical Heritage and Its Beneficiaries* (Cambridge: Cambridge University Press, 1954), p. 175, is very likely correct when he says: "Any philosopher who sought to advance from the Augustinian position by drawing more heavily on ancient sources was bound in practice to end up as a Neoplatonist."
10. Harvey G. Townsend, *Philosophical Ideas in the United States* (New York: American Book Company, 1968), pp. 116-130.
11. Merle Curti, *The Social Ideas of American Educators* (New York: Charles Scribner's Sons, 1935), pp. 310-336; and Kurt F. Leidecker, *Yankee Teacher: The Life of William Torrey Harris* (New York: Philosophical Library, 1946), pp. 83-84.
12. Oscar Cargill, *Intellectual America: Ideas on the March* (New York: The Macmillan Company, 1941), pp. 44-47.
13. Miller, *The New England Mind,* pp. 100-101.
14. George H. Mead, *Movements of Thought in the Nineteenth Century* (Chicago: University of Chicago Press, 1962), pp. 342-343; and Vernon L. Parrington, *Main Currents in American Thought: The Beginnings of Critical Realism in America, 1860-1920* (New York: Harcourt, Brace & Co., 1930), III, 202-203.
15. James McCosh, *The Religious Aspect of Evolution* (1888).
16. A Tennessee law prohibiting the teaching of evolution in the schools was violated by John Scopes. For the account of this famous trial, see Ray Ginger, *Six Days or Forever? Tennessee v. John Scopes* (Boston: Beacon Press, 1958); and Lawrence W. Levine, *Defender of the Faith, William Jennings Bryan: The Last Decade, 1915-1925* (New York: Oxford University Press, 1965), pp. 254, 270.
17. John Higham, *Strangers in the Land: Patterns of American Nativism, 1860-1925* (New Brunswick, N. J.: Rutgers University Press, 1975), pp. 49-50, 71-72. For illustrations ranging beyond nativism, see Gustavus Myers, *History of Bigotry in the United States* (New York: Random House, 1943); and for the place of immigrant children in the schools—especially Italians and Russian Jews—consult Michael R. Olneck and Marvin Lazerson, "The School Achievement of Immigrant Children: 1900-1930," *History of Education Quarterly,* XIV (Winter, 1974): 453-477.
18. Timothy Smith, "Immigrant Social Aspirations and American Education: 1880-1930," *American Quarterly,* 21 (Fall, 1969): 523-543.
19. Colin Greer, *The Great School Legend* (New York: Basic Books, Inc., 1972), pp. 59-60.
20. Israel Zangwill, *The Melting-Pot* (New York: The Macmillan Company, 1909), p. 37.

21. Ellwood P. Cubberley, *Changing Conceptions of Education* (Boston: Houghton Mifflin Co., 1909), pp. 15-16.
22. William T. Harris, "The Pedagogical Creed of William T. Harris," in O. H. Lang, ed., *Educational Creeds of the Nineteenth Century* (New York: Arno Press, 1971), p. 43.
23. An old but valuable work to examine in this connection is J. S. Roberts, *William T. Harris: A Critical Study of His Educational and Related Philosophical Views* (Washington, D. C.: Government Printing Office, 1924).
24. O. B. Frothingham, *Transcendentalism in New England* (New York: G. P. Putnam's Sons, 1876), pp. 257-258.
25. Lawrence A. Cremin, *The Transformation of the School* (New York: Alfred A. Knopf, 1961), p. 14.
26. William T. Harris, *Psychologic Foundations of Education* (New York: D. Appleton & Co., 1898), p. 323.
27. Ibid., p. 227.
28. William T. Harris, "The Separation of the Church from the Tax-Supported School," *Educational Review*, XXVI (October, 1903): 224.
29. Neil G. McCluskey, *Public Schools and Moral Education* (New York: Columbia University Press, 1958), p. 117.
30. Forest C. Ensign, *Compulsory School Attendance and Child Labor* (New York: Arno Press, 1969), pp. 256-258.
31. Louise B. Swiniarski, "A Comparative Study of Elizabeth Palmer Peabody and Susan Elizabeth Blow" (Chestnut Hill, Mass.: Doctoral Dissertation, Boston College, microfilm, 1976), pp. 50, 54.
32. Ibid., pp. 115-117.
33. Neil G. McCluskey, *Catholic Education in America: A Documentary History* (New York: Teachers College Press, 1964), p. 25.
34. Earle D. Ross, *Democracy's College: The Land-Grant College Movement in the Formative State* (Ames: Iowa State College Press, 1942), p. 22.
35. Edward A. Krug, *The Shaping of the American High School* (New York: Harper & Row, Publishers, 1964), I, 5-8.
36. 30 *Michigan Reports* 69 (1874-1875).
37. H. G. Lull, *Inherited Tendencies of Secondary Instruction in the United States* (Berkeley: University of California Press, 1913), p. 252.
38. National Education Association, *Report of the Committee of Ten on Secondary School Studies: With the Reports of the Conferences Arranged by the Committee* (New York: published for the National Education Association by the American Book Company, 1894).
39. Ibid., p. 51.
40. Theodore R. Sizer, *Secondary Schools at the Turn of the Century* (New Haven: Yale University Press, 1964), pp. 199-207.
41. These issues are discussed in some detail by Charles W. Eliot, *Educational Reform* (New York: Century Company, 1898), pp. 149-176; and Edward Krug, ed., *Charles W. Eliot and Popular Education* (New York: Teachers College Press, 1961), pp. 147-166.
42. S. R. Logan, "The Junior High School and Its Relations," *Progressive Education*, VI (1929): 17-22.
43. George Paul Schmidt, *The Liberal Arts College: A Chapter in American Cultural History* (New Brunswick, N. J.: Rutgers University Press, 1957), pp. 155-161.
44. Edward D. Eddy, *Colleges for Our Land and Time: The Land-Grant Idea in American Education* (New York: Harper & Row, Publishers, 1957), pp. 82-86.
45. Lawrence Veysey, *The Emergence of the American University* (Chicago: University of Chicago Press, 1965), pp. 264-268.

46. John C. French, *History of the University Founded by Johns Hopkins* (Baltimore: Johns Hopkins University Press, 1946), p. 109.

47. John S. Brubacher and Willis D. Rudy, *Higher Education in Transition* (New York: Harper & Row, Publishers, 1958), pp. 139-170.

48. Eliot, *Educational Reform,* p. 1.

49. William Tucker, *My Generation* (Boston: Houghton Mifflin Company, 1919), pp. 337-338; Abraham Flexner, *Universities, American, English, German* (New York: Oxford University Press, 1930), pp. 55-56, 72, 140-144, 151-152; and David Starr Jordan, "University Tendencies in America," *Popular Science Monthly,* 63 (June, 1903): 145.

50. William R. Harper, *The Trend in Higher Education* (Chicago: University of Chicago Press, 1905), p. 382.

51. Cremin, *Transformation of the School,* pp. 168-176.

CHAPTER NINE

1. Clarence J. Karier, *Shaping the American Educational State* (New York: The Free Press, 1975), p. 129, draws the quick conclusion that all this was due to Enlightenment influence.

2. Lester Ward, *Dynamic Sociology* (New York: D. Appleton & Co., 1883), 2 vols.

3. Ralph Gabriel, *The Course of American Democratic Thought* (New York: The Ronald Press Company, 1956), p. 215, calls Ward the Father of the "American concept of the planned society."

4. Ward, *Dynamic Sociology,* II, 589.

5. Lester Ward, "Education," an unpublished ms., excerpted in Karier, *Shaping the American Educational State,* pp. 145-159. For Ward's view, see pp. 145-146.

6. Lawrence A. Cremin, *The Transformation of the School* (New York: Alfred A. Knopf, 1961), pp. 23-24.

7. Calvin M. Woodward, *The Manual Training School* (Boston: 1887), pp. 243-245.

8. Cremin, *Transformation of the School,* p. 29.

9. Nicholas Murray Butler, *The Argument for Manual Training* (New York: 1888), p. 390.

10. John Amos Comenius, *The Great Didactic,* trans. M. W. Keatinge (London: 1896).

11. Gerald L. Gutek, *Pestalozzi and Education* (New York: Random House, 1968), pp. 30-45.

12. Johann F. Herbart, *The Science of Education: Its General Principles Deduced from Its Aim, and The Aesthetic Revelation of the World,* trans. H. M. and E. Felkin (Boston: D. C. Heath & Co., 1908).

13. Harold B. Dunkel, *Herbart and Herbartianism: An Educational Ghost Story* (Chicago: University of Chicago Press, 1970).

14. Herbart, *Science of Education,* p. 108.

15. Dunkel, *Herbart and Herbartianism,* p. 28.

16. Charles W. Eliot, *Educational Reform* (New York: Century Company, 1898), p. 1.

17. National Education Association, *Report of the Committee of Ten on Secondary School Studies* (New York: published for the National Education Association by the American Book Company, 1894), pp. 51-53.

18. Dunkel, *Herbart and Herbartianism,* p. 75.

19. Ibid., p. iii.

20. Henry C. Morrison, *The Practice of Teaching in the Secondary School* (Chicago: University of Chicago Press, 1931), p. 424.

21. Edward L. Thorndike, "The Evolution of Human Intellect," *Popular Science Monthly,* LX (November, 1901): 65.
22. Herbert Spencer's most famous essay was "What Knowledge is of Most Worth?" His answer: scientific knowledge. This essay is reproduced in Herbert Spencer, *Education: Intellectual, Moral, Physical* (New York: 1860).
23. Geraldine M. Joncich, ed., *Psychology and the Science of Eduation: Selected Writings of Edward L. Thorndike* (New York: Teachers College Press, 1962), p. 3.
24. Walter B. Kolesnik, *Mental Discipline and Modern Education* (Madison: University of Wisconsin Press, 1958), pp. 65-68.
25. Edward L. Thorndike, *Educational Psychology: The Psychology of Learning* (New York: Teachers College, Columbia University, 1914), II, 4.
26. *Cardinal Principles of Secondary Education,* United States Bureau of Education Bulletin no. 35 (Washington, D. C., 1918), p. 2.
27. See Robert S. Woodworth, *Contemporary Schools of Psychology* (New York: The Ronald Press Company, 1931), p. 101.
28. P. T. Orata, *The Theory of Identical Elements* (Columbus: Ohio State University Press, 1928), p. 41; Charles H. Judd, *Education as Cultivation of the Higher Mental Processes* (New York: The Macmillan Company, 1936), p. 198; and Kolesnik, *Mental Discipline,* p. 29.
29. Cremin, *Transformation of the School,* pp. 7-8, summarizes Joseph M. Rice, "The Futility of the Spelling Grind," *The Forum,* XXIII (1897): 163-172.
30. Quoted in Joncich, *Science of Education,* p. 148.
31. Frank Freeman, *Mental Tests: Their History, Principles and Application* (Boston: Houghton Mifflin Company, 1939).
32. Walter Lippmann's and Lewis M. Terman's articles appeared in *The New Republic,* XXXII and XXXIII, and are excerpted in Karier, *Shaping the American Educational State,* pp. 283-316.
33. Ibid., p. 287.
34. Ibid., p. 291.
35. Ibid., p. 283.
36. Ibid., p. 305.
37. Ibid.
38. H. L. Caswell, *City School Surveys* (New York: Teachers College Press, 1929), pp. 16-25.
39. Charles E. Strickland and Charles Burgess, eds., *Health, Growth, and Heredity: G. Stanley Hall on Natural Education* (New York: Teachers College Press, 1965), p. 13.
40. Ibid., p. 16; and Dorothy Ross, *G. Stanley Hall: The Psychologist as Prophet* (Chicago: University of Chicago Press, 1972), pp. 282-284.
41. Merle L. Borrowman, ed., *Teacher Education in America: A Documentary History* (New York: Teachers College Press, 1965), pp. 19-26.
42. Norman Foerster, *The American State University* (Chapel Hill: University of North Carolina Press, 1937), pp. 272-274.
43. Borrowman, *Teacher Education,* pp. 29-39.
44. W. R. Burgess, *Trends of School Costs* (New York: Russell Sage Foundation, 1920), pp. 32-33. This study is reported in R. Freeman Butts and Lawrence A. Cremin, *A History of Education in American Culture* (New York: Henry Holt & Co., 1953), p. 454.
45. Richard Hofstadter and Walter P. Metzger, *The Development of Academic Freedom in the United States* (New York: Columbia University Press, 1955), pp. 363-366.
46. American Association of University Professors, *Report of the Committee on Academic Freedom and Tenure* (December, 1915), pp. 6-29.

47. Quoted in Karier, *Shaping the American Educational State*, p. 151.
48. Edward A. Ross, *Social Control* (New York: The Macmillan Company, 1906), p. 168. Quoted in Karier, *Shaping the American Educational State*, p. 129.
49. Ibid., p. 151.
50. Edward G. Hartmann, *The Movement to Americanize the Immigrant* (New York: Columbia University Press, 1948), pp. 121-128; and Robert A. Carlson, *The Quest for Conformity: Americanization Through Education* (New York: John Wiley & Sons, 1975), pp. 90-93.
51. Daniel P. O'Reilly, *The School Controversy: 1891-1893* (Washington: The Catholic University of America Press, 1943), p. 107.
52. *Meyer v. Nebraska*, 262 U.S. 390.
53. *Pierce v. Society of Sisters*, 268, U.S. 510.
54. *Congressional Globe*, 41:2, p. 478.
55. George S. Counts, *Dare the School Build a New Social Order?* (New York: John Day, 1932), p. 56.

CHAPTER TEN

1. Mark Van Doren, *Liberal Education* (New York: Henry Holt & Co., 1943), p. 67.
2. W. H. Heck, *Mental Discipline and Educational Values* (New York: John Lane, 1911), p. 28.
3. William H. Payne, *Contributions to the Science of Education* (New York: American Book Company, 1886), p. 50.
4. William C. Bagley, *Determinism in Education* (Baltimore: Warwick & York, 1928), pp. 86-87.
5. George H. Mead, *Movements of Thought in the Nineteenth Century* (Chicago: University of Chicago Press, 1962), pp. 405-417.
6. Paul Shorey, *The Assault on Humanism* (Boston: The Atlantic Monthly Press, 1917), pp. 38-65.
7. Richard T. Ely, *Ground Under Our Feet* (New York: The Macmillan Company, 1938), p. 185.
8. Sidney L. Jackson, *America's Struggle for Free Schools* (Washington, D. C.: American Council on Public Affairs, 1941), pp. 172-173; and Frank Tracy Carlton, *Economic Influences upon Educational Progress in the United States, 1820-1850* (New York: Teachers College Press, 1965), pp. 49-82. This book was first published in 1908.
9. Lawrence A. Cremin, *The American Common School* (New York: Teachers College Press, 1951), pp. 219-221.
10. Roger DeGuimps, *Pestalozzi, His Life and Works* (New York: D. Appleton, 1890), p. 246.
11. Henry Barnard, *Pestalozzi and His Educational System* (Syracuse, N.Y.: C. W. Bardeen, 1854), pp. 74-75.
12. Samuel C. Parker, *A Textbook in the History of Modern Elementary Education* (Boston: Ginn & Co., 1912), p. 339.
13. Walter B. Kolesnik, *Mental Discipline and Modern Education* (Madison: University of Wisconsin Press, 1958), pp. 25-26.
14. Newton Edwards and Herman G. Richey, *The School in the American Social Order* (Boston: Houghton Mifflin Company, 1947), p. 727.
15. Adolphe E. Meyer, *An Educational History of the American People* (New York: McGraw-Hill Book Company, 1957), pp. 303-304.
16. Charles W. Eliot, *Educational Reform* (New York: Century Company, 1909), p. 185.

17. Meyer, *Education History,* p. 237.
18. Lawrence A. Cremin, *The Transformation of the School* (New York: Alfred A. Knopf, 1961), pp. 19-20.
19. Ibid., p. 150.
20. Theodore R. Sizer, *The Age of the Academies* (New York: Teachers College Press, 1964), pp. 10-11.
21. I. L. Kandel, *History of Secondary Education: A Study in the Development of Liberal Education* (Boston: Houghton Mifflin Company, 1930), pp. 448-449.
22. Edward A. Krug, *The Shaping of the American High School, 1920-1941* (Madison: University of Wisconsin Press, 1972), II, 65.
23. Philip R. V. Curoe, *Educational Attitudes and Policies of Organized Labor in the United States* (New York: Teachers College Press, 1926), p. 191; and United States Department of Agriculture, Office of Experimental Stations, *Circular No. 60* (1904).
24. Willis Rudy, *Schools in an Age of Mass Culture* (Englewood Cliffs, N. J.: Prentice-Hall, Inc., 1965), p. 18.
25. National Education Association, *Report of the Committee of Ten on Secondary School Studies* (New York: published for the National Education Association by the American Book Company, 1894), p. 17.
26. "Report of the Committee on College Entrance Requirements," in National Education Association, *Journal of Proceedings and Addresses of the Thirty-Eighth Annual Meeting* (Chicago, 1899), p. 672.
27. For a good discussion of this point, see Robert L. Church and Michael W. Sedlak, *Education in the United States: An Interpretive History* (New York: The Free Press, 1976), pp. 296-297.
28. Carnegie Foundation for the Advancement of Teaching, *Annual Report, 1906,* p. 38.
29. "Original Papers in Relation to a Course of Liberal Education," *American Journal of Science and Arts,* 15 (1829): 297-351. A more convenient source for the Report of the Yale Faculty is Richard Hofstadter and Wilson Smith, eds., *American Higher Education: A Documentary History* (Chicago: University of Chicago Press, 1961), I, 275-297.
30. Richard Hofstadter and C. DeWitt Hardy, *The Development and Scope of Higher Education in the United States* (New York: Columbia University Press, 1952), pp. 48-56.
31. Allan Nevins, *The State Universities and Democracy* (Urbana: University of Illinois Press, 1962), p. vi.
32. John S. Brubacher and Willis D. Rudy, *Higher Education in Transition* (New York: Harper & Row, Publishers, 1958), pp. 96-115.
33. David B. Tyack, *The One Best System: A History of American Urban Education* (Cambridge: Harvard University Press, 1974); and Michael B. Katz, *Class, Bureaucracy, and Schools: The Illusion of Educational Change in America* (New York: Praeger Publishers, 1971).
34. Katz, *Class, Bureaucracy, and Schools,* p. 7.
35. Tyack, *The One Best System,* p. 11.
36. Ibid., p. 144.
37. Ibid., p. 140.
38. Ibid., p. 135.
39. Ibid.
40. Louis M. Hacker, *The Triumph of American Capitalism* (New York: Simon and Schuster, 1940), pp. 403-405.
41. Arthur M. Schlesinger, *The Rise of the City, 1878-1898* (New York: The Macmillan Company, 1933), pp. 67-68.

42. Marcus L. Hansen, *The Immigrant in American History* (Cambridge: Harvard University Press, 1938).

43. Herbert Harris, *American Labor* (New Haven: Yale University Press, 1938), pp. 204-207.

44. Howard K. Beale, *Are American Teachers Free?* (New York: Charles Scribner's Sons, 1936), p. 115; and Robert S. and Helen M. Lynd, *Middletown: A Study in Modern American Culture* (New York: Harcourt, Brace & Co., 1929), pp. 198-199.

45. William Preston, Jr., *Aliens and Dissenters: Federal Suppression of Radicals, 1903-1933* (Cambridge: Harvard University Press, 1963), chapters 7 and 8.

46. Herbert Shapiro, ed., *The Muckrakers and American Society* (Boston: D. C. Heath and Company, 1968), pp. 21-23; the history of muckraking is told with skill and perspicuity by Louis Filler, *Crusaders for American Liberalism* (Yellow Springs, Ohio: Antioch College Press, 1950).

47. *Plessy* v. *Ferguson,* 163 U.S. 537.

48. *The Interstate Commerce Act,* 24 Stat. 379; and see I. L. Sharfman, *The Interstate Commerce Commission* (New York: The Commonwealth Fund, 1931), pp. 11-19.

49. Bliss Perry, *The American Spirit in Literature* (New Haven: Yale University Press, 1918), p. 61.

50. H. L. Mencken, *The American Language: An Inquiry into the Development of English in the United States* (New York: Alfred A. Knopf, 1960), pp. 90-92.

51. Richard Hofstadter, *Social Darwinism in American Thought* (Boston: Beacon Press, 1955), pp. 24-30.

52. Merle Curti, *The Growth of American Thought* (New York: Harper & Row, Publishers, 1964), chapter 22.

53. Philip P. Wiener, *Evolution and the Founders of Pragmatism* (Cambridge: Harvard University Press, 1949), pp. 141-148; and Stow Persons, ed., *Evolutionary Thought in America* (New Haven: Yale University Press, 1950).

54. John Dewey's, *School and Society* (Chicago: University of Chicago Press, 1899), pp. 23-24, illustrates the most perceptive of these indictments.

55. Cremin, *Transformation of the School,* p. 129.

56. Ibid., pp. 129-130; see also Charles F. Adams, Jr., *The New Departure in the Common Schools of Quincy and Other Papers on Educational Topics* (Boston: 1879), pp. 33-35, 43.

57. Cremin, *Transformation of the School,* p. 131.

58. John Dewey, *Experience and Education* (New York: The Macmillan Company, 1938), pp. vi-vii.

59. Marietta Johnson, *Thirty Years With an Idea* (University, Ala.: University of Alabama Press, 1974), pp. 17-33; and Cremin, *Transformation of the School,* pp. 147-151, 153.

60. Cremin, *Transformation of the School,* p. 154.

61. See Frederick S. Rudolph, *Curriculum: A History of the American Undergraduate Course of Study Since 1636* (San Francisco: Jossey-Bass, 1977).

62. Cremin, *Transformation of the School,* pp. 127-176, gives a clear and accurate picture of them.

CHAPTER ELEVEN

1. Illustrations of this faith in education are plentiful in Henry J. Perkinson, *The Imperfect Panacea: American Faith in Education, 1865-1976* (New York: Random House, 1977).

2. William C. Bagley, "The Significance of the Essential Movement in Educational Theory," *Classical Journal,* 22 (1940): 334.
3. J. Donald Butler, *Four Philosophies: And Their Practice in Education and Religion* (New York: Harper & Row, Publishers, 1957), p. 493.
4. Michael B. Katz, *Class, Bureaucracy, and Schools* (New York: Praeger Publishers, 1971; and David B. Tyack, *The One Best System: A History of American Urban Education* (Cambridge: Harvard University Press, 1974).
5. Katz, *Class, Bureaucracy, and Schools,* p. 115.
6. Tyack, *The One Best System,* p. 196.
7. Ibid., p. 182.
8. Katz, *Class, Bureaucracy, and Schools,* p. 123.
9. Ibid., p. 120; and Tyack, *The One Best System,* p. 182.
10. Peter F. Carbone, Jr., *The Social and Educational Thought of Harold Rugg* (Durham: Duke University Press, 1977), p. 9.
11. Ibid., p. 21.
12. Harold R. Rugg, *The Great Technology: Social Chaos and the Public Mind* (New York: John Day Company, 1933), p. 172.
13. Carbone, *Harold Rugg,* p. 60.
14. Rugg's social studies textbooks were published under the title *Man and His Changing Society* (Boston: Ginn & Co., 1931-1937).
15. Carbone, *Harold Rugg,* p. 24.
16. Ibid., p. 26.
17. Quoted in Geraldine M. Joncich, ed., *Psychology and the Science of Education: Selected Writings of Edward L. Thorndike* (New York: Teachers College Press, 1962), p. 151.
18. For an exposition of the two sides, see Max McConn, *College or Kindergarten?* (New York: New Republic, Inc., 1928), pp. 45-77; and Harold E. Stearns, ed., *Civilization in the United States* (New York: Harcourt, Brace and Co., 1922), pp. 88-89.
19. Lawrence A. Cremin, *The Transformation of the School* (New York: Alfred A. Knopf, 1961), p. 199.
20. Stanley M. Elam, *Performance-Based Teacher Education: What is the State of the Art?* (Washington, D. C.: American Association of Colleges for Teacher Education, 1972), pp. 16-31.
21. Cremin, *Transformation of the School,* p. 203.
22. Caroline Pratt and Jessie Stanton, *Before Books* (New York: Adelphi Company, 1926), pp. 2-3; quoted in Cremin, *Transformation of the School,* p. 205.
23. Harold Rugg and Ann Shumaker, *The Child-Centered School* (Yonkers, N. Y.: The World Book Company, 1928), p. 228; and quoted in Carbone, *Harold Rugg,* p. 21.
24. Cremin, *Transformation of the School,* p. 207.
25. Ibid., pp. 209-210.
26. Ibid., pp. 211-212; and Robert H. Beck, "Progressive Education and American Progressivism: Margaret Naumburg," *Teachers College Record,* LX (1958-1959): 198-208.
27. William Heard Kilpatrick, *The Dutch Schools of New Netherland and Colonial New York* (Washington, D. C.: Government Printing Office, 1912); *The Montessori System Examined* (Boston: Houghton Mifflin Company, 1914); and *Froebel's Kindergarten Principles Critically Examined* (New York: The Macmillan Company, 1916).
28. William Heard Kilpatrick, *Foundations of Method* (New York: The Macmillan Company, 1925), pp. 108-109; quoted in Cremin, *Transformation of the School,* pp. 217-218.

29. Kilpatrick, *Foundations of Method,* pp. 266-267.
30. Cremin, *Transformation of the School,* pp. 220-224; discusses Bode.
31. Boyd H. Bode, *Fundamentals of Education* (New York: The Macmillan Company, 1921), pp. 241-242.
32. Boyd H. Bode, *Modern Educational Theories* (New York: The Macmillan Company, 1927), p. 163; quoted in Cremin, *Transformation of the School,* p. 224.
33. Quoted in Cremin, *Transformation of the School,* p. 223.
34. Boyd H. Bode, *Progressive Education at the Crossroads* (New York: Newsome & Co., 1938), pp. 43-44.
35. Thorstein Veblen, *The Higher Learning in America* (New York: Viking Press, 1918).
36. Upton Sinclair, *The Goose-Step* (Pasadena, Calif.: the author, 1923) and *The Goslings* (Pasadena, Calif.: the author, 1924).
37. John E. Kirkpatrick, *The American College and Its Rulers* (New York: New Republic, Inc., 1926).
38. Harold E. Stearns, ed., *Civilization in the United States* (New York: Harcourt, Brace & Co., 1922).
39. *The Social Frontier,* I (1934-1935): 4-5. In 1939 the name of the journal was changed to *Frontiers of Democracy.* See Cremin, *Transformation of the School,* pp. 232-233.
40. Cremin, *Transformation of the School,* pp. 233-234.
41. Ibid., p. 311 and p. 314. See Barbara Jones, *Bennington College* (New York: Harper & Row, Publishers, 1946), pp. 3-8; and Malcolm S. MacLean, "The General College: The University of Minnesota," in William S. Gray, *General Education: Its Nature, Scope, and Essential Elements* (Chicago: University of Chicago Press, 1934), pp. 119-127.
42. Cremin, *Transformation of the School,* pp. 348-351.
43. Ibid., pp. 350-351.
44. William C. Bagley, "An Essentialist's Platform for the Advancement of American Education," *Educational Administration and Supervision,* 24 (April, 1938): 241-256.
45. J. W. Wrightstone, *Appraisal of Newer Elementary School Practices* (New York: Teachers College Press, 1938).
46. This high school-college experiment is discussed in five volumes: *Adventures in American Education.* A one-volume summary is by William M. Aikin, *The Story of the Eight-Year Study* (New York: McGraw-Hill Book Company, 1942).
47. A good example is W. H. Lancelot, "A Close-up of the Eight-Year Study," *School and Society,* 42 (1939): 141-144.
48. This is discussed in Cremin, *Transformation of the School,* pp. 334-336.
49. United States Office of Education, *Vitalizing Secondary Education: Report of the First Commission on Life Adjustment Education for Youth* (Washington, D. C.: 1951), p. 1; and quoted in Cremin, *Transformation of the School,* p. 336.
50. United States Office of Education, *Vitalizing Secondary Education,* p. 1; and quoted in Cremin, *Transformation of the School,* p. 336.
51. All are discussed in Cremin, *Transformation of the School,* pp. 338-347.
52. Mortimer Smith, *And Madly Teach* (Chicago: H. Regnery Company, 1949), p. 7; and quoted in Cremin, *Transformation of the School,* p. 340.
53. Hyman Rickover, *Education and Freedom* (New York: E. P. Dutton & Co., 1959), p. 189; and quoted in Cremin, *Transformation of the School,* p. 347.
54. Herman H. Horne, *The Democratic Philosophy of Education* (New York: The Macmillan Company, 1932).
55. Herman H. Horne, *The Philosophy of Education* (New York: The Macmillan Company, 1930), p. 199.

56. Butler, *Four Philosophies*, p. 433.
57. John Dewey, *Democracy and Education* (New York: The Macmillan Company, 1916), pp. 383, 392-395.
58. John Dewey, *Experience and Education* (New York: The Macmillan Company, 1938), pp. 99-103.
59. Butler, *Four Philosophies*, p. 443.
60. Dewey, *Experience and Education*, p. 35.
61. Ibid., pp. 96-97.
62. Ibid., p. 11.
63. John Dewey, *Logic, The Theory of Inquiry* (New York: Henry Holt & Co., 1938), p. 105.
64. William Pepperell Montague, "The Story of American Realism," in Walter G. Muelder and Lawrence Sears, *The Development of American Philosophy* (Boston: Houghton Mifflin Company, 1940), p. 421.
65. John Wild, "Education and Human Society: A Realist View," in *Modern Philosophies and Education*, The Fifty-fourth Yearbook of the National Society for the Study of Education, Part I (Chicago: University of Chicago Press, 1955), p. 32, expresses a conventional Realist position when he writes: "The realist cannot agree with Dewey's lifelong polemic against classical philosophy and his instrumentalist attempt to degrade reason from its natural guiding position to a subservient one."
66. Ibid., pp. 40-42.
67. Harry S. Broudy, *Building a Philosophy of Education* (Englewood Cliffs, N. J.: Prentice-Hall, Inc., 1961), p. 146.
68. Alfred North Whitehead, *The Aims of Education* (New York: The Macmillan Company, 1929).
69. Bertrand Russell, *Education and the Good Life* (New York: Boni & Liveright, 1926).
70. Wild, "A Realist View," pp. 34-36.
71. William F. Cunningham, *The Pivotal Problems of Education* (New York: The Macmillan Company, 1940), pp. 291-298; and Jacques Maritain, "Thomist Views on Education," in *Modern Philosophies and Education*, The Fifty-fourth Yearbook of the National Society for the Study of Education, Part I (Chicago: University of Chicago Press, 1955), p. 69.
72. Maritain, "Thomist Views on Education," in *Modern Philosophies and Education*, pp. 85-88.
73. Robert M. Hutchins, *Education for Freedom* (Baton Rouge, La.: Louisiana State University Press, 1943), p. 59.
74. Charles W. Eliot, *Educational Reform* (New York: Century Company, 1898), pp. 51-76.
75. Neil G. McCluskey, *Catholic Education in America: A Documentary History* (New York: Teachers College Press, 1964), p. 25.

CHAPTER TWELVE

1. *Higher Education for American Democracy: A Report of the President's Commission on Higher Education* (New York: Harper & Row, Publishers, 1947), I, 38; excerpted in Richard Hofstadter and Wilson Smith, *American Higher Education: A Documentary History* (Chicago: University of Chicago Press, 1961), II, 970-1002.
2. *Plessy* v. *Ferguson*, 163 U.S. 537.

Robert M. Hutchins, *Education for Freedom* (Baton Rouge, La.: Louisiana State

3. *Sweatt* v. *Painter*, 339 U.S. 629.
4. *Missouri ex rel. Gaines* v. *Canada*, 305 U.S. 337.
5. *Brown* v. *Board of Education of Topeka*, 347 U.S. 483.
6. These impediments brought the federal judiciary into the operation of some local school systems. On the issue of government by judiciary, see Raoul Berger, *Government By Judiciary: The Transformation of the Fourteenth Amendment* (Cambridge: Harvard University Press, 1978).
7. Charles A. Valentine, *Culture and Poverty: Critiques and Counter-Proposals* (Chicago: University of Chicago Press, 1968), pp. 127-140.
8. Timothy Smith, "Native Blacks and Foreign Whites: Varying Responses to Educational Opportunity in America, 1880-1950," *Perspectives in American History*, VI (1972): 309-337.
9. Robert C. Smith, *They Closed Their Schools* (Chapel Hill: University of North Carolina Press, 1965), pp. 185-207.
10. Robert L. Crain, *The Politics of School Desegregation* (Chicago: Aldine Publishing Company, 1968), pp. 350-355.
11. James S. Coleman et al., *Equality of Educational Opportunity* (Washington, D. C.: Government Printing Office, 1966). Daniel P. Moynihan, "Sources of Resistance to the Coleman Report," *Harvard Educational Review*, XXXVIII (Winter, 1968): 23-36, suspected that public officers tried to restrict circulation of the report. Other analysis of Coleman's work may be found in the same issue.
12. Coleman, *Equality of Educational Opportunity*, pp. 469-470; and James S. Coleman, "The Concept of Equality of Educational Opportunity," *Harvard Educational Review*, XXXVIII (Winter, 1968): 7-22.
13. David B. Tyack, *The One Best System: A History of American Urban Education* (Cambridge: Harvard University Press, 1974), p. 281; and Marvin Lazerson, "Social Reform and Early Childhood Education: Some Historical Perspectives," *Urban Education*, II (April, 1970): 84-102.
14. Jerome S. Bruner, "The Skill of Relevance or the Relevance of Skills," *Saturday Review*, (April 18, 1970): pp. 66-68, 78-79.
15. Leonard Fein, *The Ecology of the Public Schools: An Inquiry into Community Control* (New York: Pegasus, 1971), pp. 74-76.
16. Lillian B. Rubin, *Busing and Backlash: White Against White in a California School District* (Berkeley: University of California Press, 1972), pp. 24-31; and Carolyn Ralston, "Desegregation in Berkeley, California," in Francis A. J. Ianni, ed., *Conflict and Change in Education* (Glenview, Ill.: Scott, Foresman & Co., 1975).
17. Arthur Jensen, "How Much Can We Boost I. Q. and Scholastic Achievement?" *Harvard Educational Review*, XXXIX (Winter, 1969): 1-123.
18. Michael B. Katz, *Class, Bureaucracy, and Schools* (New York: Praeger Publishers, 1971), p. 111; see also Alan Gartner, Colin Greer, and Frank Riessman, eds., *The New Assault on Equality: I. Q. and Social Stratification* (New York: Harper & Row, Publishers, 1974), pp. 7-84.
19. Christopher Jencks et al., *Inequality: A Reassessment of the Effect of Family and Schooling in America* (New York: Basic Books, 1972), pp. 14-18.
20. *Nebraska Dist. of Evangelical Lutheran Synod* v. *McKelvie*, 104 Neb. 93, 175 N. W. 531, 7 A. L. R. 1688.
21. *Iowa* v. *Bartels*, 191 Iowa 1060, 181 N. W. 508.
22. *Meyer* v. *Nebraska*, 262 U.S. 390.
23. *Pierce* v. *Society of Sisters and Hill Military Academy*, 268 U.S. 510.
24. Ibid.
25. John S. Brubacher, *Modern Philosophies of Education* (New York: McGraw-Hill Book Company, 1950), p. 142.

26. John L. Childs, "American Democracy and the Common School System," *Jewish Education*, 21 (1949): 32-37.

27. Hollis L. Caswell, "The Great Reappraisal of Public Education," *Teachers College Record*, 54 (1952): 12-22.

28. R. Freeman Butts and Lawrence A. Cremin, *A History of Education in American Culture* (New York: Henry Holt & Co., 1953), p. 527.

29. Although Franklin spoke of the "Excellency of the Christian Religion above all others ancient or modern," in "Proposals Relating to the Education of Youth in Pensilvania," *The Papers of Benjamin Franklin* (New Haven: Yale University Press, 1961), ed. Leonard W. Labaree et al., III, 397-419, he makes no provision for religious instruction either in the "Proposals" or in the "Idea of the English School" (ibid., IV, 102-108).

30. *The Papers of Thomas Jefferson* (Princeton, N. J.: Princeton University Press, 1950), ed. Julian P. Boyd, II, 545-547.

31. Raymond McLaughlin, *A History of State Legislation Affecting Private Elementary and Secondary Schools in the United States, 1870-1945* (Washington, D. C.: The Catholic University of America Press, 1946), pp. 54-59.

32. Neil G. McCluskey, *Catholic Education in America: A Documentary History* (New York: Teachers College Press, 1964), p. 13.

33. *Doremus v. Board of Education*, 342 U.S. 429.

34. *School District of Abington Township v. Schempp*, 347 U.S. 203.

35. Ibid.

36. *Engel v. Vitale*, 370 U.S. 421.

37. *McCollum v. Board of Education*, 333 U.S. 203.

38. *Zorach v. Clauson*, 343 U.S. 306.

39. Joseph P. Locigno, *Education: To Whom Does It Belong?* (New York: Desclée Company Inc., 1968), pp. 33-64.

40. *Cochran v. Board of Education*, 281 U.S. 370.

41. *Everson v. Board of Education*, 330 U.S. 1.

42. Ibid.,

43. A. S. Neill, *Summerhill: A Radical Approach to Child Rearing* (New York: Hart Company, Inc., 1960).

44. Jonathan Kozol, *Free Schools* (New York: Houghton Mifflin Company, 1972), pp. 7-12.

45. The most optimistic expression of this scholastic idealism is George Leonard's *Education and Ecstasy* (New York: Dell, 1968).

46. Ivan D. Illich, *Celebration of Awareness: A Call for Institutional Revolution* (New York: Doubleday, 1970), p. 123.

47. B. F. Skinner, *Beyond Freedom and Dignity* (New York: Alfred A. Knopf, 1971), pp. 184-215.

48. B. F. Skinner, *The Technology of Teaching* (New York: Appleton-Century-Crofts, 1968), pp. 185-198.

49. B. F. Skinner, "Teaching Machines," *Scientific American*, 205 (November, 1961): 97.

50. Harold L. Hodgkinson, *Institutions in Transition: A Profile of Change in Higher Education* (New York: McGraw-Hill Book Company, 1971), chapter 7; Leon D. Epstein, *Governing the University: The Campus and the Public Interest* (Jossey-Bass, 1974), chapter 9; and Alain Touraine, *The Academic System in American Society* (New York: McGraw-Hill Book Company, 1974), chapter 5.

CHAPTER THIRTEEN

1. Edward J. Power, "Equilibrium: An Ideal of Classical Education," *Paideia*, I (1972): 1-8.
2. Frederick A. G. Beck, *Greek Education: 450-350 B.C.* (New York: Barnes & Noble, Inc., 1964), pp. 97-141.
3. H. I. Marrou, *A History of Education in Antiquity* (New York: Sheed & Ward, 1956), pp. 100-101.
4. R. R. Bolgar, *The Classical Heritage and Its Beneficiaries* (Cambridge: Cambridge University Press, 1954), pp. 45-58.
5. Louis B. Wright, *The Cultural Life of the American Colonies, 1607-1763* (New York: Harper & Row, Publishers, 1957), pp. 98-99.
6. For competent illustrations of this position, see Robert M. Hutchins, *The Higher Learning in America* (New Haven: Yale University Press, 1936), pp. 110-119; I. L. Kandel, *The Cult of Uncertainty* (New York: The Macmillan Company, 1943), pp. 96-129; Jacques Maritain, *Education at the Crossroads* (New Haven: Yale University Press, 1943), pp. 88-103; and Arthur E. Bestor, *The Restoration of Learning* (New York: Alfred A. Knopf, 1955), pp. 40-57.
7. For illustrations of the liberal attitude, see Theodore Brameld, *Education for the Emerging Age* (New York: Harper & Row, Publishers, 1961); George S. Counts, *Dare the School Build a New Social Order?* (New York: The John Day Co., 1932); and Sidney Hook, *Education for Modern Man* (New York: Alfred A. Knopf, 1963).
8. James D. Koerner, ed., *The Case for Basic Education* (Boston: Little, Brown & Co., 1959), p. 32.
9. Lawrence A. Cremin, *The American Common School* (New York: Teachers College Press, 1951), pp. 47-49.
10. John Rawls, *A Theory of Justice* (Cambridge: Harvard University Press, 1971), p. 3; and Donald M. Levine and Mary Jo Bane, eds., *The "Inequality" Controversy: Schooling and Distributive Justice* (New York: Basic Books, 1975), pp. 66-71.
11. Carnegie Commission on Higher Education, *The Purposes and the Performance of Higher Education in the United States* (New York: McGraw-Hill Book Company, 1973), pp. 81-94; K. Patricia Cross, *Beyond the Open Door: New Students to Higher Education* (San Francisco: Jossey-Bass, 1974), pp. 163-167; and Richard I. Ferrin, *A Decade of Change in Free-Access Higher Education* (New York: College Entrance Examination Board, 1971), pp. 33-39.
12. Edward J. Power, *Education for American Democracy* (New York: McGraw-Hill Book Company, 1965), pp. 401-402.
13. Ibid., p. 402.
14. Paul Woodring, *A Fourth of a Nation* (New York: McGraw-Hill Book Company, 1957), pp. 143-158.
15. *Serrano v. Priest*, 96 *California Reporter* 601-626 (1971).
16. *San Antonio Independent School District v. Rodriquez*, 36 Law. Ed. 2d 16 (1973).
17. The American Association of School Administrators, *The Federal Government and Public Schools* (Washington, D. C.: 1965), pp. 58-68.
18. Willard S. Elsbree, *The American Teacher* (New York: American Book Company, 1939), pp. 499-533.
19. Henry S. Dyer, "Toward Objective Criteria of Professional Accountability in the Schools," *Phi Delta Kappan*, 52 (1970): 206-211.
20. *The Improvement of Teacher Education: A Final Report by the Commission on Teacher Education* (Washington, D. C.: American Council on Education, 1946), pp. 82-102.

21. Benjamin Rosner, *The Power of Competency-Based Teacher Education* (Boston: Allyn and Bacon, 1972), pp. 8-14; and Benjamin Rosner and Patricia Kay, "Will the Promise of C/PBTE Be Fulfilled?", *Phi Delta Kappan,* 56 (January, 1974); 290-295.

22. *Brown* v. *Board of Education of Topeka,* 347 U.S. 483.

23. In *Swann* v. *Charlotte-Mecklenburg Board of Education,* 402 U.S. 1 (1971), the United States Supreme Court declared a mandatory racial mixing of school-children constitutional.

24. Edmund W. Gordon and Doxey A. Wilkerson, *Compensatory Education for the Disadvantaged—Preschool through College* (New York: College Entrance Examination Board, 1966), pp. 76-81.

25. Richard A. Lester, *Antibias Regulations of Universities* (New York: McGraw-Hill Book Company, 1974), pp. 48-49; and Daniel Seligman, "How 'Equal Opportunity' Turned into Employment Quotas," *Fortune* (March, 1973): pp. 160-168.

26. U. S. 46 *Law Week* (June 28, 1978), p. 4896.

27. *Education Vouchers: A Report on Financing Education by Payments to Parents* (Cambridge, Mass.: Center for the Study of Public Policy, December 1970).

28. Theodore L. Gross, "How to Kill a College: The Private Papers of a Campus Dean," *Saturday Review* (February 4, 1978): pp. 13-20.

29. Ibid., p. 13.

30. Ibid., p. 16.

31. Ibid., p. 20.

32. Susan Schiefelbein, "Confusion at Harvard: What Makes an 'Educated Man' "? *Saturday Review* (April 1, 1978): p. 16.

BIBLIOGRAPHY

Adams, James Truslow. *The Founding of New England.* Boston: The Atlantic Monthly Press, 1921.

Aikin, William M. *The Story of the Eight-Year Study.* New York: McGraw-Hill Book Company, 1942.

Ariès, Philippe. *Centuries of Childhood: A Social History of Family Life.* Translated by Robert Baldick. New York, Alfred A. Knopf, 1962.

Arrowood, Charles F. *Thomas Jefferson and Education in a Republic.* New York: McGraw-Hill Book Company, 1930.

Bagley, William C. *Determinism in Education.* Baltimore: Warwick & York, 1928.

Bailyn, Bernard. *Education in the Forming of American Society.* Chapel Hill: University of North Carolina Press, 1960.

Barnard, Henry. *Normal Schools and Other Institutions, Agencies, and Means Designed for the Professional Education of Teachers.* Hartford: 1851.

Barnard, Henry. *Pestalozzi and His Educational System.* Syracuse, N. Y.: 1854.

Beard, Charles A., and Mary R. Beard. *The Rise of American Civilization.* 2 vols. New York: The Macmillan Company, 1927.

Bell, Sadie. *The Church, the State, and Education in Virginia.* Philadelphia: Science Press, 1930.

Berger, Raoul. *Government By Judiciary: The Transformation of the Fourteenth Amendment.* Cambridge, Mass.: Harvard University Press, 1978.

Best, John H., ed. *Benjamin Franklin on Education.* New York: Teachers College Press, 1962.

Bestor, Arthur E. *Backwoods Utopias.* Philadelphia: University of Pennsylvania Press, 1950.

Bestor, Arthur E. *Educational Wastelands.* Urbana, Ill.: University of Illinois Press, 1953.

Bestor, Arthur E. *The Restoration of Learning.* New York: Alfred A. Knopf, 1955.

Binder, Frederick M. *The Age of the Common School, 1830-1865.* New York: John Wiley and Sons, Inc., 1974.

Boas, Louise. *Women's Education Begins.* Newton, Mass.: Wheaton College Press, 1935.

Bode, Boyd H. *Fundamentals of Education.* New York: The Macmillan Company, 1921.

Bode, Boyd H. *Modern Educational Theories.* New York: The Macmillan Company, 1927.

Bode, Boyd H. *Progressive Education at the Crossroads.* New York: Newsome & Company, 1938.

Bolger, R. R. *The Classical Heritage and Its Beneficiaries.* Cambridge: Cambridge University Press, 1954.

Bond, Horace Mann. *The Education of the Negro in the American Social Order.* Englewood Cliffs, N. J.: Prentice-Hall, Inc., 1934.

Boorstin, Daniel. *The Americans: The National Experience.* New York: Random House, 1965.

Borrowman, Merle. *The Liberal and Technical in Teacher Education: A Historical Survey of American Thought.* New York: Teachers College Press, 1956.

Borrowman, Merle, ed. *Teacher Education in America: A Documentary History.* New York: Teachers College Press, 1965.

Bowers, Claude A. *The Progressive Educator and the Depression: The Radical Years.* New York: Random House, 1969.

Bowes, Frederick. *The Culture of Early Charleston.* Chapel Hill: University of North Carolina Press, 1942.

Brameld, Theodore. *Education for the Emerging Age.* New York: Harper & Row, Publishers, 1961.

Breed, Frederick S. *Education and the New Realism.* New York: The Macmillan Company, 1939.

Bremer, Ann, and John Bremer. *Open Education: A Beginning.* New York: Holt, Rinehart & Winston, 1972.

Bridenbaugh, Carl. *Cities in the Wilderness: The First Century of Urban Life in America, 1625-1742.* New York: Ronald Press, 1938.

Brigham, Charles. *History and Bibliography of American Newspapers, 1690-1820* Worcester, Mass.: American Antiquarian Society, 1961.

Broudy, Harry S. *Building a Philosophy of Education.* Englewood Cliffs, N. J.: Prentice-Hall, Inc., 1961.

Broudy, Harry S., et al. *Democracy and Excellence in American Secondary Education.* Chicago: Rand McNally, 1964.

Brown, Elmer E. *The Making of Our Middle Schools: An Account of the Development of Secondary Education in the United States.* New York: Longmans, Green & Co., 1903.

Brubacher, John S. *Henry Barnard on Education.* New York: Russell & Russell, 1965.

Brubacher, John S. *Modern Philosophies of Education.* New York: McGraw-Hill Book Company, 1950.

Brubacher, John S., and Willis Rudy. *Higher Education in Transition.* New York: Harper & Row, Publishers, 1958.

Bullard, Asa. *Fifty Years with the Sabbath Schools.* Boston: Lockwood, Brooks & Co., 1876.

Butler, J. Donald. *Four Philosophies: And Their Practice in Education and Religion.* New York: Harper & Row, Publishers, 1957.

Butler, J. Donald. *Idealism in Education.* New York: Harper & Row, Publishers, 1966.

Butler, Nicholas Murray. *The Argument for Manual Training.* New York: 1888.

Butts, R. Freeman. *The American Tradition in Religion and Education.* Boston: The Beacon Press, 1950.

Butts, R. Freeman. *The College Charts Its Course: Historical Conceptions and Current Proposals.* New York: McGraw-Hill Book Company, 1939.

Calam, John. *Parsons and Pedagogues: The S. P. G. Adventure in American Education.* New York: Columbia University Press, 1971.

Calhoun, Arthur W. *A Social History of the American Family from Colonial Times to the Present.* 3 vols. New York: Barnes & Noble, Inc., 1945.

Carbone, Peter F., Jr. *The Social and Educational Thought of Harold Rugg.* Durham, N. C.: Duke University Press, 1977.

Cargill, Oscar. *Intellectual America: Ideas on the March.* New York: The Macmillan Company, 1941.

Carlson, Robert A. *The Quest for Conformity: Americanization Through Education.* New York: John Wiley and Sons, Inc., 1975.

Carlton, Frank Tracy. *Economic Influences Upon Educational Progress in the United States, 1820–1850.* New York: Teachers College Press, 1965.

Carnegie Commission on Higher Education. *New Students and New Places.* New York: McGraw-Hill Book Company, 1971.

Carpenter, Charles. *History of American Schoolbooks.* Philadelphia: University of Pennsylvania Press, 1963.

Carter, James G. *Essays upon Popular Education, Containing a Particular Examination of the Schools of Massachusetts and the Outline of an Institution for the Education of Teachers.* Boston: Bowles & Dearborn, 1826.

Childs, John L. *American Pragmatism and Education.* New York: Henry Holt & Co., 1956.

Clews, Elsie W. *Educational Legislation and Administration of the Colonial Governments.* New York: The Macmillan Company, 1899.

Clifford, Geraldine Joncich. *The Shape of American Education.* Englewood Cliffs, N. J.: Prentice-Hall, Inc., 1975.

Cobb, Sanford H. *The Rise of Religious Liberty In America.* New York: The Macmillan Company, 1902.

Cochran, Thomas C., and William Miller. *The Age of Enterprise.* New York: The Macmillan Company, 1942.

Coleman, James S., et al. *Equality of Educational Opportunity.* Washington, D. C.: Government Printing Office, 1966.

Comenius, John Amos. *The Great Didactic.* Translated by M. W. Keatinge. London: Adam & Charles Black, Ltd., 1923.

Commons, John R., et al. *History of Labor in the United States.* New York: The Macmillan Company, 1926.

Conant, James B. *The American High School Today.* New York: McGraw-Hill Book Company, 1959.

Counts, George S. *Dare the School Build a New Social Order?* New York: The John Day Company, 1932.

Counts, George S. *Prospects for American Democracy.* New York: The John Day Company, 1938.

Counts, George S. *Secondary Education and Industrialism.* Cambridge: Harvard University Press, 1929.

Crain, Robert L. *The Politics of School Desegregation.* Chicago: Aldine Publishing Company, 1969.

Craven, Wesley Frank. *The Colonies in Transition: 1660-1713.* New York: Harper & Row, Publishers, 1968.

Cremin, Lawrence A. *The American Common School.* New York: Teachers College Press, 1951.

Cremin, Lawrence A. *American Education: The Colonial Experience, 1607-1783.* New York: Harper & Row, Publishers, 1970.

Cremin, Lawrence A., ed. *The Republic and the School: Horace Mann on the Education of Free Men.* New York: Teachers College Press, 1957.

Cremin, Lawrence A. *The Transformation of the School: Progressivism in American Education, 1876-1957.* New York: Alfred A. Knopf, 1961.

Cross, K. Patricia. *Beyond the Open Door: New Students to Higher Education.* San Francisco: Jossey-Bass, Inc., 1971.

Cubberley, Ellwood P. *Changing Conceptions of Education.* Boston: Houghton Mifflin Company, 1909.

Culver, Raymond B. *Horace Mann and Religion in the Massachusetts Public Schools.* New Haven: Yale University Press, 1929.

Cunningham, William F. *The Pivotal Problems of Education.* New York: The Macmillan Company, 1940.

Curoe, Philip R. V. *Educational Attitudes and Policies of Organized Labor in the United States.* New York: Teachers College Press, 1926.

Curti, Merle. *The Growth of American Thought.* New York: Harper & Row, Publishers, 1964.

Curti, Merle. *The Social Ideas of American Educators.* New York: Charles Scribner's Sons, 1935.

Curti, Merle, and Robert Bremner. *Philanthropy in the Shaping of American Higher Education.* New Brunswick, N. J.: Rutgers University Press, 1965.

Davis, Sheldon E. *Educational Periodicals During the Nineteenth Century.* Washington, D. C.: Government Printing Office, 1919.

De Guimps, Roger. *Pestalozzi, His Life and Works.* New York: D. Appleton Company, 1890.

De Mause, Lloyd, ed. *The History of Childhood.* New York: Psychohistory Press, 1974.

Demos, John. *A Little Commonwealth.* New York: Oxford University Press, 1970.

Dewey, John. *Democracy and Education.* New York: The Macmillan Company, 1916.

Dewey, John. *Experience and Education.* New York: The Macmillan Company, 1938.

Dewey, John. *My Pedagogic Creed.* New York: E. L. Kellog & Co., 1897.

Dewey, John. *School and Society.* Chicago: University of Chicago Press, 1915.

Dorfman, Joseph. *The Economic Mind in American Civilization, 1606-1865.* 2 vols. New York: The Viking Press, 1946.

Dow, George F. *Every Day Life in the Massachusetts Bay Colony.* Boston: Society for the Preservation of New England, 1935.

Dunkel, Harold B. *Herbart and Education.* New York: Random House, 1969.

Dunkel, Harold B. *Herbart and Herbartianism: An Educational Ghost Story.* Chicago: University of Chicago Press, 1970.

Dunn, John. *The Political Thought of John Locke.* Cambridge: Cambridge University Press, 1969.

Dupuis, Adrian. *Philosophy of Education in Historical Perspective.* Chicago: Rand McNally College Publishing Company, 1966.

Earle, Alice M. *Child Life in Colonial Days.* New York: The Macmillan Company, 1946.

Earle, Alice M. *Home Life in Colonial Days.* New York: The Macmillan Company, 1946.

Eddy, Edward D. *Colleges for Our Land and Time: The Land-Grant Idea in American Education.* New York: Harper & Row, Publishers, 1957.

Eggleston, Edward. *The Transit of Civilization: From England to America in the Seventeeth Century.* New York: D. Appleton Company, 1900.

Eliot, Charles W. *Educational Reform: Essays and Addresses.* New York: Century Company, 1909.

Elkind, David. *Children and Adolescents: Interpretive Essays on Jean Piaget.* New York: Oxford University Press, 1970.

Elsbree, Willard S. *The American Teacher.* New York: American Book Company, 1939.

Elson, Ruth M. *Guardians of Tradition: American Schoolbooks of the Nineteenth Century.* Lincoln, Neb.: University of Nebraska Press, 1964.

Ely, Richard T. *Ground Under Our Feet.* New York: The Macmillan Company, 1938.

Ensign, Forest C. *Compulsory School Attendance and Child Labor.* New York: Arno Press, 1969.

Epstein, Leon D. *Governing the University: The Campus and the Public Interest.* San Francisco: Jossey-Bass, Inc., 1974.

Farber, Bernard. *Guardians of Virtue.* New York: Basic Books, 1972.

Fein, Leonard. *The Ecology of the Public Schools: An Inquiry into Community Control.* New York: Pegasus, 1971.

Fellman, David, ed. *The Supreme Court and Education.* New York: Teachers College Press, 1969.

Ferrin, Richard I. *A Decade of Change in Free-Access Higher Education.* New York: College Entrance Examination Board, 1971.

Filler, Louis. *Crusaders for American Liberalism.* Yellow Springs, Ohio: Antioch College Press, 1950.

Fish, Carl R. *The Rise of the Common Man, 1830–1860.* New York: The Macmillan Company, 1927.

Fisher, Berenice. *Industrial Education: American Ideals and Institutions.* Madison: University of Wisconsin Press, 1967.

Fleming, Stanford. *Children and Puritanism: The Place of Children in the Life and Thought of the New England Churches.* New Haven: Yale University Press, 1933.

Flexner, Abraham. *Universities, American, English, German.* New York: Oxford University Press, 1930.

Foerster, Norman. *The American State University.* Chapel Hill: University of North Carolina Press, 1937.

Ford, Paul Leicester, ed. *The New England Primer.* New York: Teachers College Press, 1962.

Fox, Dixon Ryan. *Ideas in Motion.* New York: D. Appleton-Century Company, 1935.

Freeman, Frank. *Mental Tests: Their History, Principles and Application.* Boston: Houghton Mifflin Company, 1939.

Gabriel, Ralph. *The Course of American Democratic Thought: An Intellectual History since 1815.* New York: Ronald Press, 1956.

Gardner, John. *Excellence: Can We Be Equal and Excellent Too?* New York: Harper & Row, Publishers, 1961.

Gartner, Alan; Colin Greer; and Frank Riessman. *The New Assault on Equality: I. Q. and Social Stratification.* New York: Harper & Row, Publishers, 1974.

Gay, Peter. *The Enlightenment: An Interpretation.* 2 vols. New York: Alfred A. Knopf, 1966-1969.

Geiger, George R. *John Dewey: In Perspective.* New York: Oxford University Press, 1958.

Gordon, Edmund W., and Doxey A. Wilkerson. *Compensatory Education for the Disadvantaged—Preschool through College.* New York: College Entrance Examination Board, 1966.

Gordy, J. P. *The Rise and Growth of the Normal-School Idea in the United States.* Washington, D. C.: Government Printing Office, 1891.

Graham, Frank D. *Social Goals and Economic Institutions.* Princeton, N. J.: Princeton University Press, 1942.

Greene, Evarts B. *The Revolutionary Generation, 1763-1790.* New York: The Macmillan Company, 1943.

Greer, Colin. *The Great School Legend: A Revisionist Interpretation of American Public Education.* New York: Basic Books, 1972.

Greven, Philip J. *Four Generations: Population, Land, and Family in Colonial Andover, Massachusetts.* Ithaca, N. Y.: Cornell University Press, 1970.

Grizzell, Emit D. *The Origin and Development of the High School in New England Before 1865.* New York: The Macmillan Company, 1923.

Gutek, Gerald L. *The Educational Theory of George S. Counts.* Columbus, Ohio: Ohio State University Press, 1970.

Gutek, Gerald L. *Pestalozzi and Education.* New York: Random House, 1968.

Hacker, Louis M. *The Triumph of American Capitalism.* New York: Simon & Schuster, 1940.

Handlin, Oscar. *John Dewey's Challenge to Education: Historical Perspectives on the Cultural Context.* New York: Harper & Row, Publishers, 1950.

Handlin, Oscar. *The Uprooted.* Boston: Little, Brown & Co., 1951.

Handlin, Oscar, and Mary Handlin. *The American College and American Culture: Socialization as a Function of Higher Education.* New York: McGraw-Hill Book Company, 1970.

Hansen, Allen O. *Liberalism and American Education in the Eighteenth Century.* New York: The Macmillan Company, 1926.

Hansen, Marcus L. *The Atlantic Migration: 1607-1860.* Cambridge: Harvard University Press, 1940.

Hansen, Marcus L. *The Immigrant in American History.* New York: Harper & Row, Publishers, 1964.

Harper, Charles A. *A Century of Public Teacher Education.* Washington, D. C.: National Education Association, 1939.

Harper, William R. *The Trend in Higher Education.* Chicago: University of Chicago Press, 1905.

Harris, Herbert. *American Labor.* New Haven: Yale University Press, 1945.

Harris, William T. *Psychologic Foundations of Education.* New York: D. Appleton Company, 1898.

Hartmann, Edward G. *The Movement to Americanize the Immigrant.* New York: Columbia University Press, 1948.

Haskins, George L. *Law and Authority in Early Massachusetts.* New York: The Macmillan Company, 1960.

Hawkins, Hugh. *Between Harvard and America: The Educational Leadership of Charles W. Eliot.* New York: Oxford University Press, 1972.

Hayes, Cecil B. *The American Lyceum: Its History and Contribution to Education.* Washington, D. C.: Government Printing Office, 1932.

Healey, Robert M. *Jefferson on Religion in Public Education.* New Haven: Yale University Press, 1962.

Heatwole, Cornelius J. *A History of Education in Virginia.* New York: The Macmillan Company, 1916.

Heimert, Alan. *Religion and the American Mind from the Great Awakening to the Revolution.* Cambridge: Harvard University Press, 1966.

Herbart, Johann F. *The Science of Education: Its General Principles Deduced from Its Aim, and The Aesthetic Revelation of the World.* Translated by H. M. and E. Felkin. Boston: D. C. Heath & Co., 1908.

Herbst, Jurgen. *The German Historical School in American Scholarship: A Study in the Transfer of Culture.* Ithaca, N. Y.: Cornell University Press, 1965.

Heslep, Robert D. *Thomas Jefferson and Education.* New York: Random House, 1969.

Higham, John. *Strangers in the Land: Patterns of American Nativism, 1860-1925.* New Brunswick, N. J.: Rutgers University Press, 1975.

Hindle, Brooke. *The Pursuit of Science in Revolutionary America, 1735-1789.* Chapel Hill: University of North Carolina Press, 1956.

Hinsdale, Burke A. *Horace Mann and the Common School Revival in the United States.* New York: Charles Scribner's Sons, 1898.

Hodgkinson, Harold L. *Institutions in Transition: A Profile of Change in Higher Education.* New York: McGraw-Hill Book Company, 1971.

Hofstadter, Richard. *The Age of Reform: From Bryan to F.D.R.* New York: Alfred A. Knopf, 1955.

Hofstadter, Richard. *The American Political Tradition.* New York: Random House, 1961.

Hofstadter, Richard. *Anti-Intellectualism in American Life.* New York: Alfred A. Knopf, 1963.

Hofstadter, Richard. *Social Darwinism in American Thought.* Boston: The Beacon Press, 1955.

Hofstadter, Richard, and C. DeWitt Hardy. *The Development and Scope of Higher Education in the United States.* New York: Columbia University Press, 1952.

Hofstadter, Richard, and Walter P. Metzger. *The Development of Academic Freedom in the United States.* New York: Columbia University Press, 1955.

Hofstadter, Richard, and Wilson Smith. *American Higher Education: A Documentary History.* 2 vols. Chicago: University of Chicago Press, 1961.

Holbrook, Stewart H. *The Age of the Moguls.* New York: Doubleday & Co., 1953.

Hollis, Andrew P. *The Contributions of the Oswego Normal School to Educational Progress in the United States.* Boston: D. C. Heath Company, 1898.

Honeywell, Roy J. *The Educational Work of Thomas Jefferson.* Cambridge: Harvard University Press, 1931.

Hook, Sidney. *Education for Modern Man.* New York: Alfred A. Knopf, 1963.

Horne, Herman H. *The Philosophy of Education.* New York: The Macmillan Company, 1930.

Hudson, Frederic. *Journalism in the United States, From 1690-1872.* New York: Harper & Row, Publishers, 1873.

Hunt, David. *Parents and Children in History.* New York: Basic Books, 1970.

Hutchins, Robert M. *The Conflict in Education in a Democratic Society.* New York: Harper & Row, Publishers, 1953.

Hutchins, Robert M. *Education for Freedom.* Baton Rouge, La.: Louisiana State University Press, 1943.

Hutchins, Robert M. *The Higher Learning in America.* New Haven: Yale University Press, 1936.

Ianni, Francis A. J., ed. *Conflict and Change in Education.* Glenview, Ill.: Scott, Foresman & Co., 1975.

Illich, Ivan D. *Celebration of Awareness: A Call for Institutional Revolution.* New York: Doubleday & Co., 1970.

Inglis, Alexander J. *The Rise of the High School in Massachusetts.* New York: The Macmillan Company, 1911.

Jackson, George L. *The Development of School Support in Colonial Massachusetts.* New York: Teachers College Press, 1909.

Jackson, Sideny L. *America's Struggle for Free Schools: Social Tension and Education in New England and New York.* Washington, D. C.: American Council on Public Affairs, 1941.

Jencks, Christopher, et al. *Inequality: A Reassessment of the Effect of Family and Schooling in America.* New York: Basic Books, 1972.

Jernegan, Marcus W. *The American Colonies, 1492-1750: A Study of Their Political, Economic and Social Development.* New York: Longmans, Green & Co., 1929.

Jernegan, Marcus W. *Laboring and Dependent Classes in Colonial America, 1607-1783.* Chicago: University of Chicago Press, 1931.

Johnson, Clifton. *Old-Time Schools and Schoolbooks.* New York: The Macmillan Company, 1904.

Johnson, Marietta. *Thirty Years With an Idea.* University, Ala.: University of Alabama Press, 1974.

Johnson, Marietta. *Youth in a World of Men.* New York: The John Day Company, 1929.

Joncich, Geraldine M., ed. *Psychology and the Science of Education: Selected Writings of Edward L. Thorndike.* New York: Teachers College Press, 1962.

Jones, Howard Mumford, ed. *Emerson on Education: Selections.* New York: Teachers College Press, 1966.

Jones, Maldwyn. *American Immigration.* Chicago: University of Chicago Press, 1960.

Josephson, Matthew. *The Robber Barons.* New York: Harcourt, Brace & Co., 1934.

Judd, Charles H. *Education as Cultivation of the Higher Mental Processes.* New York: The Macmillan Company, 1936.

Kaestle, Carl F., ed. *Joseph Lancaster and the Monitorial School Movement.* New York: Teachers College Press, 1973.

Kandel, I. L. *The Cult of Uncertainty.* New York: The Macmillan Company, 1943.

Kandel, I. L. *History of Secondary Education.* Boston: Houghton Mifflin Company, 1930.

Karier, Clarence, et al. *Roots of Crisis: American Education in the Twentieth Century.* Chicago: Rand McNally, 1973.

Karier, Clarence. *Shaping the American Educational State.* New York: The Free Press, 1975.

Katz, Michael B. *Class, Bureaucracy, and Schools: The Illusion of Educational Change in America.* New York: Praeger Publishers, Inc., 1971.

Katz, Michael B. *The Irony of Early School Reform.* Cambridge: Harvard University Press, 1968.

Katz, Michael B., ed. *School Reform: Past and Present.* Boston: Little, Brown & Co., 1971.

Kilpatrick, William Heard. *The Dutch Schools of New Netherland and Colonial New York.* Washington, D. C.: Government Printing Office, 1912.

Kilpatrick, William Heard. *Foundations of Method.* New York: The Macmillan Company, 1925.

Kirkpatrick, John E. *The American College and Its Rulers.* New York: The New Republic, 1926.

Knight, Edgar W. *Public Education in the South.* Boston: Ginn & Co., 1922.

Koerner, James D., ed. *The Case for Basic Education.* Boston: Little, Brown & Co., 1959.

Koerner, James D. *The Miseducation of American Teachers.* Boston: Houghton Mifflin Company, 1963.

Kolesnik, Walter B. *Humanism and/or Behaviorism in Education.* Boston: Allyn and Bacon, 1975.

Kolesnik, Walter B. *Mental Discipline and Modern Education.* Madison: University of Wisconsin Press, 1958.

Kozol, Jonathan. *Free Schools.* Boston: Houghton Mifflin Company, 1972.

Krug, Edward A., ed. *Charles W. Eliot and Popular Education.* New York: Teachers College Press, 1961.

Krug, Edward A. *The Shaping of the American High School.* New York: Harper & Row, Publishers, 1964.

Krug, Edward A. *The Shaping of the American High School, 1920-1941.* Madison: University of Wisconsin Press, 1972.

Lannie, Vincent P., ed. *Henry Barnard: American Educator.* New York: Teachers College Press, 1974.

Lannie, Vincent P. *Public Money and Parochial Education: Bishop Hughes, Governor Seward, and the New York School Controversy.* Cleveland: Press of Case Western Reserve University, 1968.

Lazerson, Marvin, and W. Norton Grubb, eds. *American Education and Vocationalism: A Documentary History.* New York: Teachers College Press, 1974.

Lee, Gordon C., ed. *Crusade Against Ignorance: Thomas Jefferson on Education.* New York: Teachers College Press, 1961.

Leidecker, Kurt F. *Yankee Teacher: The Life of William Torrey Harris.* New York: Philosophical Library, 1946.

Leonard, George. *Education and Ecstasy.* New York: Dell, 1968.

Lester, Richard A. *Antibias Regulation of Universities.* New York: McGraw-Hill Book Company, 1974.

Leuchtenburg, William E. *A Troubled Feast: American Society Since 1945.* Boston: Allyn and Bacon, 1973.

Lippmann, Walter. *The Public Philosophy.* Boston: Little, Brown & Co., 1955.

Locigno, Joseph P. *Education: To Whom Does It Belong.* New York: Desclée Company, Inc., 1968.

Locke, John. *An Essay Concerning Human Understanding.* 28th ed. London: T. Tegg and Son, 1838.

Lockridge, Kenneth A. *Literacy in Colonial New England.* New York: Norton, 1974.

Lockridge, Kenneth A. *A New England Town.* New York: Norton, 1970.

Lynd, Albert. *Quackery in the Public Schools.* Boston: Little, Brown & Co., 1953.

McCarthy, Charles. *The Wisconsin Idea.* New York: The Macmillan Company, 1912.

McCluskey, Neil G., ed. *Catholic Education in America: A Documentary History.* New York: Teachers College Press, 1964.

McCluskey, Neil G. *Public Schools and Moral Education.* New York: Columbia University Press, 1958.

McConn, Max. *College or Kindergarten?* New York: The New Republic, 1928.

Maddox, William A. *The Free School Idea in Virginia before the Civil War: A Phase of Political and Social Evolution.* New York: Teachers College Press, 1918.

Main, Jackson Turner. *The Social Structure of Revolutionary America.* Princeton, N. J.: Princeton University Press, 1965.

Mangum, Vernon L. *The American Normal School, Its Rise and Development in Massachusetts.* Baltimore: Warwick & York, 1928.

Maritain, Jacques. *Education at the Crossroads.* New Haven: Yale University Press, 1943.

Martin, William O. *Realism in Education.* New York: Harper & Row, Publishers, 1969.

Mead, George H. *Movements of Thought in the Nineteenth Century.* Chicago: University of Chicago Press, 1962.

Mencken, H. L. *The American Language: An Inquiry into the Development of English in the United States.* New York: Alfred A. Knopf, 1960.

Meriwether, Cloyer. *Our Colonial Curriculum, 1607–1776.* Washington, D. C.: Capital Publishing Company, 1907.

Messerli, Jonathan. *Horace Mann: A Biography.* New York: Alfred A. Knopf, 1972.

Middlekauff, Robert. *Ancients and Axioms: Secondary Education in Eighteenth Century New England.* New Haven: Yale University Press, 1963.

Miller, Perry. *The New England Mind: From Colony to Province.* Cambridge: Harvard University Press, 1953.

Miller, Perry. *The New England Mind: The Seventeenth Century.* New York: The Macmillan Company, 1939.

Miller, Perry. *Orthodoxy in Massachusetts, 1630–1650.* Cambridge: Harvard University Press, 1933.

Miller, Perry. *The Transcendentalists.* Cambridge: Harvard University Press, 1950.

Mills, Nicolaus, ed. *The Great School Bus Controversy.* New York: Teachers College Press, 1973.

Moore, Ernest Carroll. *Fifty Years of American Education: A Sketch of the Progress of Education in the United States for 1867–1917.* Boston: Ginn & Co., 1917.

Morais, Herbert M. *Deism in Eighteenth Century America.* New York: Columbia University Press, 1934.

Morgan, Edmund S. *The Puritan Family: Religion and Domestic Relations in Seventeenth-Century New England.* New York: Harper & Row, Publishers, 1966.

Morgan, Edmund S. *Visible Saints: The History of a Puritan Idea.* New York: New York University Press, 1963.

Morgan, Howard W., ed. *The Gilded Age: A Reappraisal.* Syracuse, N. Y.: Syracuse University Press, 1970.

Morison, Samuel Eliot. *Builders of the Bay Colony.* Boston: Houghton Mifflin Company, 1930.

Morison, Samuel Eliot. *The Founding of Harvard College.* Cambridge: Harvard University Press, 1935.

Morison, Samuel Eliot. *The Puritan Pronaos: Studies in the Intellectual Life of New England in the Seventeenth Century.* New York: New York University Press, 1936.

Morris, Richard B. *Government and Labor in Early America.* New York: Columbia University Press, 1946.

Mosier, Richard D. *Making the American Mind: Social and Moral Ideas in the McGuffey Readers.* New York: King's Crown Press, 1947.

Mosteller, Frederick, and Daniel P. Moynihan, eds. *On Equality of Educational Opportunity.* New York: Random House, 1972.

Moynihan, Daniel P. *Maximum Feasible Misunderstanding: Community Action in the War on Poverty.* New York: The Free Press, 1969.

Muelder, Walter G., and Lawrence Sears. *The Development of American Philosophy.* Boston: Houghton Mifflin Company, 1940.

Myers, Gustavus. *History of Bigotry in the United States.* New York: Random House, 1943.

National Education Association. *Report of the Committee of Ten on Secondary School Studies.* New York: American Book Company, 1894.

Neill, A. S. *Summerhill: A Radical Approach to Child Rearing.* New York: Hart Company, Inc., 1960.

Nevins, Allan. *The State Universities and Democracy.* Urbana, Ill.: University of Illinois Press, 1962.

Norton, Arthur O. *The First State Normal School in America.* Cambridge: Harvard University Press, 1926.

Oettinger, Anthony G. *Run, Computer Run: The Mythology of Educational Innovation* Cambridge: Harvard University Press, 1969.

O'Neill, James M. *Religion and Education under the Constitution.* New York: Harper & Row, Publishers, 1949.

O'Neill, William. *The Progressive Years: America Comes of Age.* New York: Dodd, Mead & Co., 1975.

Orata, Pedro T. *The Theory of Identical Elements.* Columbus: Ohio State University Press, 1928.

O'Reilly, Daniel P. *The School Controversy (1891-1893)*. Washington, D. C.: The Catholic University of America Press, 1943.

Pangburn, Jessie M. *The Evolution of the American Teachers College*. New York: Teachers College Press, 1932.

Parrington, Vernon L. *Main Currents in American Thought: An Interpretation of American Literature from the Beginnings to 1920. The Colonial Mind, 1620-1800*. New York: Harcourt, Brace & Co., 1927.

Parrington, Vernon L. *Main Currents in American Thought: The Beginnings of Critical Realism in America, 1860-1920*. New York: Harcourt, Brace & Co., 1930.

Pease, Otis, ed. *The Progressive Years: The Spirit and Achievement of American Reform*. New York: George Braziller, 1962.

Pelling, Henry. *American Labor*. Chicago: University of Chicago Press, 1961.

Perkins, James A. *The University in Transition*. Princeton, N. J.: Princeton University Press, 1966.

Perkinson, Henry J. *The Imperfect Panacea: American Faith in Education, 1865-1976*. New York: Random House, 1977.

Perkinson, Henry J. *Two Hundred Years of American Educational Thought*. New York: David McKay Company, 1976.

Perry, Bliss. *The American Spirit in Literature*. New Haven: Yale University Press, 1918.

Perry, Ralph Barton. *Puritanism and Democracy*. New York: The Vanguard Press, 1944.

Persons, Stow, ed. *Evolutionary Thought in America*. New Haven: Yale University Press, 1950.

Pessen, Edward. *Riches, Class and Power before the Civil War*. Lexington, Mass.: D. C. Heath Company, 1973.

Peterson, George E. *The New England Colleges in the Age of the University*. Amherst, Mass.: Amherst College Press, 1964.

Peterson, LeRoy J., et al. *The Law and Public School Operation*. New York: Harper & Row, Publishers, 1969.

Peterson, Merrill D. *Thomas Jefferson and the New Nation*. New York: Oxford University Press, 1970.

Power, Edward J. *Catholic Higher Learning in America: A History*. New York: Appleton-Century-Crofts, 1972.

Power, Edward J. *Education for American Democracy*. New York: McGraw Hill Book Company, 1965.

Power, Edward J. *Evolution of Educational Doctrine*. New York: Appleton-Century-Crofts, 1969.

President and Fellows of Harvard College. *General Education in a Free Society: Report of the Harvard Committee*. Cambridge: Harvard University Press, 1945.

Preston, William, Jr. *Aliens and Dissenters: Federal Suppression of Radicals, 1903-1933*. Cambridge: Harvard University Press, 1963.

Ravitch, Diane. *A Critique of the Radical Attack on the Schools*. New York: Basic Books, 1978.

Rawls, John. *A Theory of Justice*. Cambridge: Harvard University Press, 1971.

Reisner, Edward H. *The Evolution of the Common School*. New York: The Macmillan Company, 1930.

Rickover, Hyman G. *Education and Freedom.* New York: E. P. Dutton & Co., 1959.

Rodgers, Daniel T. *The Work Ethic in Industrial America, 1850-1920.* Chicago: University of Chicago Press, 1978.

Rosner, Benjamin. *The Power of Competency-Based Teacher Education.* Boston: Allyn and Bacon, 1972.

Ross, Dorothy. *G. Stanley Hall: The Psychologist as Prophet.* Chicago: University of Chicago Press, 1972.

Ross, Earle D. *Democracy's College: The Land-Grant Movement in the Formative Stage.* Ames: Iowa State College Press, 1942.

Ross, Edward A. *Social Control.* New York: The Macmillan Company, 1906.

Rossi, Paolo. *Francis Bacon: From Magic to Science.* Translated by Sacha Rabinovitch. Chicago: University of Chicago Press, 1968.

Rousseau, Jean Jacques. *Émile.* Translated by Barbara Foxley. New York: E. P. Dutton & Co., 1911.

Rudolph, Frederick S. *The American College and University: A History.* New York: Alfred A. Knopf, 1962.

Rudolph, Frederick S. *Curriculum: A History of the American Undergraduate Course of Study Since 1636.* San Francisco: Jossey-Bass, 1977.

Rudolph, Frederick S. *Essays on Education in the Early Republic.* Cambridge: Harvard University Press, 1965.

Rudy, Willis. *Schools in an Age of Mass Culture.* Englewood Cliffs, N. J.: Prentice-Hall, Inc., 1965.

Rugg, Harold. *Culture and Education in America.* New York: Harcourt, Brace & Co., 1931.

Rugg, Harold, and Ann Shumaker. *The Child-Centered School.* New York: The World Book Company, 1928.

Ruggles, Alice McGuffey. *The Story of the McGuffeys.* New York: American Book Company, 1950.

Schlesinger, Arthur M. *The Rise of the City, 1878-1898.* New York: The Macmillan Company, 1933.

Schlesinger, Arthur M., Jr. *Prelude to Independence.* New York: Alfred A. Knopf, 1958.

Schmidt, George Paul. *The Liberal Arts College: A Chapter in American Cultural History.* New Brunswick, N. J.: Rutgers University Press, 1957.

Schneider, Herbert W. *A History of American Philosophy.* New York: Columbia University Press, 1946.

Schneider, Herbert W. *The Puritan Mind.* London: Constable & Co., Ltd., 1931.

Segal, Charles M., and David C. Stineback. *Puritans, Indians and Manifest Destiny.* New York: G. P. Putnam's Sons, 1978.

Seybolt, Robert F. *Apprenticeship and Apprenticeship Legislation in Colonial New England and New York.* New York: Teachers College Press, 1916.

Seybolt, Robert F. *Source Studies in American Colonial Educaton: The Private School.* Urbana, Ill.: University of Illinois Press, 1925.

Seybolt, Robert F. *Source Studies in American Colonial Education: The Public Schools of Colonial Boston, 1635-1775.* Cambridge: Harvard University Press, 1935.

Shapiro, Herbert, ed. *The Muckrakers and American Society.* Boston: D. C. Heath Company, 1968.

Shorey, Paul. *The Assault on Humanism.* Boston: Atlantic Monthly Press, 1917.

Silberman, Charles. *Crisis in Black and White.* New York: Random House, 1964.

Silberman, Charles. *Crisis in the Classroom: The Remaking of American Education.* New York: Random House, 1970.

Sizer, Theodore R., ed. *The Age of the Academies.* New York: Teachers College Press, 1964.

Sizer, Theodore R., ed. *Religion and Public Education.* Boston: Houghton Mifflin Company, 1967.

Sizer, Theodore R. *Secondary Schools at the Turn of the Century.* New Haven: Yale University Press, 1964.

Skinner, B. F. *Beyond Freedom and Dignity.* New York: Alfred A. Knopf, 1971.

Skinner, B. F. *The Technology of Teaching.* New York: Appleton-Century-Crofts, 1968.

Sly, John F. *Town Government in Massachusetts, 1620-1930.* Cambridge: Harvard University Press, 1930.

Small, Walter H. *Early New England Schools.* Boston: Ginn & Co., 1914.

Smelser, Marshall. *The Democratic Republic, 1801-1815.* New York: Harper & Row, Publishers, 1968.

Smith, Abbot E. *Colonists in Bondage: White Servitude and Convict Labor in America: 1607-1776.* Chapel Hill: University of North Carolina Press, 1947.

Smith, Mortimer. *And Madly Teach.* Chicago: H. Regnery Company, 1949.

Smith, Mortimer. *The Diminished Mind: A Study of Planned Mediocrity in Our Public Schools.* Chicago: H. Regnery Company, 1954.

Smith, Wilson, ed. *Theories of Education in Early America: 1655-1819.* New York: The Bobbs-Merrill Company, Inc., 1973.

Spencer, Herbert. *Education: Intellectual, Moral, Physical.* New York: D. Appleton Company, 1860.

Standing, E. M. *Maria Montessori: Her Life and Work.* New York: The American Library, 1962.

Stowe, Calvin E. *Common Schools and Teachers' Seminaries.* Boston: Marsh, Capen, Lyon & Webb, 1839.

Strickland, Charles E., and Charles Burgess, eds. *Health, Growth, and Heredity: G. Stanley Hall on Natural Education.* New York: Teachers College Press, 1965.

Sullivan, Mark. *Our Times; the United States, 1900-1925.* 6 vols. New York: Charles Scribner's Sons, 1926-1935.

Sweet, William W. *Religion in Colonial America.* New York: Charles Scribner's Sons, 1942.

Taft, Philip. *Organized Labor in American History.* New York: Harper & Row, Publishers, 1964.

Tawney, R. H. *Religion and the Rise of Capitalism: A Historical Study.* New York: Harcourt, Brace & Co., 1926.

Tennenbaum, Samuel. *William Heard Kilpatrick: Trail Blazer in Education.* New York: Harper & Row, Publishers, 1951.

Tewksbury, Donald. *The Founding of American Colleges and Universities Before the Civil War.* New York: Teachers College Press, 1932.

Thorndike, Edward L. *Educational Psychology: The Psychology of Learning.* New York: Teachers College Press, 1914.

Touraine, Alain. *The Academic System in American Society.* New York: McGraw-Hill Book Company, 1974.

Townsend, Harvey G. *Philosophical Ideas in the United States.* New York: American Book Company, 1968.

Tyack, David B. *The One Best System: A History of American Urban Education.* Cambridge: Harvard University Press, 1974.

Tyack, David B. *Turning Points in American Educational History.* Waltham, Mass.: Blaisdell Publishing Company, 1967.

Tyler, Alice Felt. *Freedom's Ferment: Phases of American Social History to 1860.* Minneapolis: University of Minnesota Press, 1944.

Updegraff, Harlan. *The Origin of the Moving School in Massachusetts.* New York: Teachers College Press, 1907.

Valentine, Charles A. *Culture and Poverty: Critiques and Counter-Proposals.* Chicago: University of Chicago Press, 1968.

Van der Zee, Henri and Barbara. *A Sweet and Alien Land: The Story of Dutch New York.* New York: The Viking Press, 1978.

Van Doren, Carl. *Benjamin Franklin.* New York: The Viking Press, 1938.

Van Doren, Mark. *Liberal Education.* New York: Henry Holt & Co., 1943.

Veblen, Thorstein. *The Higher Learning in America.* New York: B. W. Huebsch, 1918.

Veysey, Lawrence. *The Emergence of the American University.* Chicago: University of Chicago Press, 1965.

Violas, Paul C. *The Training of the Urban Working Class: A History of Twentieth Century American Education.* Chicago: Rand McNally College Publishing Company, 1978.

Ward, Lester Frank. *Dynamic Sociology.* 2 vols. New York: D. Appleton Company, 1883.

Weber, Evelyn. *The Kindergarten: Its Encounter with Educational Thought in America.* New York: Teachers College Press, 1969.

Weber, Samuel E. *The Charity School Movement in Colonial Pennsylvania.* Philadelphia: George F. Lasher, 1905.

Wells, Guy F. *Parish Education in Virginia.* New York: Teachers College Press, 1923.

Wertenbaker, Thomas Jefferson. *The Founding of American Civilization: The Middle Colonies.* New York: Charles Scribner's Sons, 1938.

Wertenbaker, Thomas Jefferson. *The Founding of American Civilization: The Old South.* New York: Charles Scribner's Sons, 1942.

Wertenbaker, Thomas Jefferson. *The Puritan Oligarchy: The Founding of American Civilization.* New York: Charles Scribner's Sons, 1947.

Wesley, Edgar B. *N E A: The First Hundred Years; The Building of the Teaching Profession.* New York: Harper & Row, Publishers, 1957.

Wesley, Edgar B. *Proposed: The University of the United States.* Minneapolis: University of Minnesota Press, 1936.

White, Morton. *The Origins of Dewey's Instrumentalism.* New York: Columbia University Press, 1943.

Whitehead, Alfred North. *The Aims of Education.* New York: The Macmillan Company, 1929.

Wiener, Philip P. *Evolution and the Founders of Pragmatism.* Cambridge: Harvard University Press, 1949.

Wilbur, Earl M. *A History of Unitarianism.* 2 vols. Cambridge: Harvard University Press, 1952.

Williams, E. I. F. *Horace Mann: Educational Statesman.* New York: The Macmillan Company, 1937.

Wise, Arthur E. *Rich Schools, Poor Schools: The Promise of Equal Educational Opportunity.* Chicago: University of Chicago Press, 1968.

Wish, Harvey. *Society and Thought in Early America.* New York: Longmans, Green & Co., 1950.

Woefel, Norman. *Molders of the American Mind.* New York: Columbia University Press, 1933.

Woodring, Paul. *A Fourth of a Nation.* New York: McGraw-Hill Book Company, 1957.

Woodward, Calvin. *Educational Value of Manual Training.* Boston: D. C. Heath Company, 1890.

Woodworth, Robert S. *Contemporary Schools of Psychology.* New York: Ronald Press, 1931.

Woytanowitz, George M. *University Extension: The Early Years in the United States, 1885-1915.* Iowa City: National University Extension Association and The American College Testing Program, 1974.

Wright, Louis B. *The Cultural Life of the American Colonies, 1607-1763.* New York: Harper & Row, Publishers, 1957.

Wright, Thomas G. *Literary Culture in New England, 1620-1730.* New Haven: Yale University Press, 1920.

Yolton, John W. *John Locke and the Way of Ideas.* Oxford: Clarendon Press, 1956.

Zangwill, Israel. *The Melting-Pot, Drama in Four Acts.* New York: The Macmillan Company, 1909.

Ziff, Larzer. *Puritanism in America.* New York: The Viking Press, 1973.

A Time Line of Educational Events

HISTORICAL EVENTS

1492-1493: Christopher Columbus (1451?-1506)

On the first of four voyages, he sailed to the Bahamas and Cuba, thinking he had discovered the Indies.

1517: Martin Luther (1483-1546)

An Augustinian monk and professor at the University of Wittenberg, Luther nailed 95 theses of protest to the court church door.

1519-1522: Ferdinand Magellan (1480-1521)

Although he was killed enroute, one of his vessels completed the circumnavagation of the world.

1541: John Calvin (1509-1564)

Introduced religious reformation to Geneva and adopted the doctrine of predestination.

1584: Sir Walter Raleigh (1552?-1618)

His expedition landed on Roanoke Island and he named the country Virginia.

1607: Founding of Jamestown Colony

At the mouth of the James River a colony was established and held together by Captain John Smith.

1620: Plymouth Colony

The Pilgrims left England on the *Mayflower* and reached Cape Cod. Drawing up the Mayflower Compact, they resettled at Plymouth.

1630: Massachusetts Bay Colony

Seventeen ships brought about 1,000 persons to the colony under the governorship of John Winthrop.

1630–1642: The Great Migration to Massachusetts Bay

During these years some 16,000 settlers arrived from England.

1664: Surrender of New Amsterdam

English took control from the Dutch and changed the colony's name to New York.

1733: Founding of Georgia

The last of the thirteen English colonies on the continent.

1755–1763: The French and Indian War

With British victory, Canada passed to English hands.

1765: Stamp Act

American colonists resisted a law requiring stamps on documents, newspapers, playing cards, and dice.

1775–1783: War for Independence

Beginning with the battles at Lexington and Concord, the war ended when Cornwallis surrendered at Yorktown.

1776: Declaration of Independence

Written by Thomas Jefferson, the declaration was adopted by the Continental Congress.

1777: Articles of Confederation

The Articles provided for a confederacy to be known as the United States of America.

1783: Treaty of Paris

Great Britain and the United States signed a treaty recognizing the independence of the latter country.

1803: The Louisiana Purchase

French territory was purchased by the United States doubling the size of the country.

1812–1814: War of 1812

The Treaty of Ghent brought the war to a close and all captured territory was returned.

1823: The Monroe Doctrine

President Monroe declared that European intervention in this hemisphere would not be tolerated.

1825: Completion of the Erie Canal

The canal connected the Hudson River with Lake Erie.

1828: The Baltimore and Ohio Railroad

Work began on the first American public railroad.

1861–1865: The Civil War

Beginning at Fort Sumter in Charleston Harbor, the war ended with Lee's capitulation at Appomattox.

1879: Thomas A. Edison (1847–1931)

Perfected the incandescent electric lamp.

1883: Northern Pacific railroad completed

The second transcontinental railroad; by 1893 five were finished.

1887: Interstate Commerce Act

Created the Interstate Commerce Commission to regulate railway rates.

1890: Sherman Anti-Trust Act

Declared restraint of trade illegal.

1913: Federal Reserve Bank Act

The country was divided into 12 districts, each with a federal reserve bank.

1914–1918: World War I

On April 6, 1917, the United States declared war on Germany.

1919: The Treaty of Versailles	The treaty was signed June 28, 1919. The United States refused to ratify it.
1920: Transcontinental air mail service	Service established between New York and San Francisco.
1927: The flight of Charles A. Lindbergh (1902–1974) —New York to Paris	Crossed the Atlantic in 33 hours and 39 minutes.
1929: Stock Market crash	A prolonged economic depression began.
1941–1945: World War II	Attack on Pearl Harbor, December 7, 1941, brought war to the United States.
1957: Sputnik	The age of space exploration begins with Russia's Sputnik in orbit.
1969: Moon landing	On July 20th, Apollo 11 landed and for the first time men walked on the moon.

AMERICAN SCHOOLS

	Origin	Purpose
Preelementary		
Infant school	Originated with Robert Owen in New Lanark, Scotland. First infant school in America opened in Boston, 1818.	Town schools admitted only children able to read. These schools taught reading.
Nursery school	Proposed by Comenius in 17th century. First public nursery school opened in New York City, 1919.	For personal growth and social adjustment; and to care for children not cared for at home.

| Kindergarten | Founded by Froebel for Germany in 1816. First English-speaking kindergarten opened in Boston, 1860; first public kindergarten, St. Louis, 1873. | To prepare children to enter first grade; and to offer chance for self-development education. |

Elementary

| Dame school | First elementary school in English America; kept in a woman teacher's home where the kitchen was the classroom. | Rudiments for boys; cooking and sewing for girls. |

| Petty school | Southern counterpart of dame school; conducted by masters. | Reading and writing taught; girls seldom attended. |

| Town school | Established in Massachusetts, and elsewhere in New England, as a result of the law of 1647. | To produce a literate body of citizens for church and state. |

| Sunday school | Invented by Robert Raikes in England. Sunday schools were opened in Charleston, S.C. (1787), New York (1793), Pittsburgh (1809), and several other cities. | Instruction confined to reading—from the Bible—and writing. |

| Monitorial school | Developed by Andrew Bell, in India, and Joseph Lancaster, in Scotland, in the late 18th century. Introduced to the United States in 1806. | Hailed as the greatest educational discovery since the alphabet, this plan of mutual instruction was used in elementary, and sometimes secondary schools. |

Common school	Grew from colonial town school. Began to flourish from 1830 to 1850. First eight-grade common school in Quincy, Massachusetts, 1848.	To build a base for common citizenship for all children: citizenship replaced religion as the scholastic objective.
Public elementary school	Evolved from common school to become the first rung on the American educational ladder.	To offer fundamental literary, social, and civic instruction: education for citizenship.

Secondary

Latin grammar school	Imitation of European secondary education. Boston Latin School, in 1635, was first. The only American secondary school for a century.	A classical curriculum to prepare young gentlemen for college.
Academy	Benjamin Franklin founded the Philadelphia Academy in 1749.	Offered classical curriculum in English. Stressed useful rather than ornamental studies.
High school	The first American high school opened in Boston in 1821.	To prepare boys and girls for life rather than for college.
Junior high school	Conducted first in Berkeley, California, and Columbus, Ohio, around 1910.	To abbreviate elementary schooling and to smooth the transition from elementary to high-school study.

Higher

Private college	Harvard, in 1636, started a long procession of church-related colleges.	Initially, the education of clergymen; later, liberal learning in art and science for secular students.

State college	Georgia, chartered in 1785, was first.	Liberal learning wherein religious perspective was heeded.
Normal school	First public normal school opened at Lexington, Massachusetts, in 1839.	Without a college curriculum, gave instruction in pedagogy.
Private university	The age of the American university was ushered in at Johns Hopkins, founded in 1876.	Graduate instruction with an emphasis on research and scholarship.
Public university	State colleges were upgraded to university status following the Land-Grant College Act of 1862.	Professional education, scholarship, and public service.
Teachers college	Teachers College, Columbia University, in 1887, was first. Thereafter both public and private teachers colleges multiplied.	Melding professional and liberal curricula, these colleges educated a majority of America's elementary and secondary teachers.
Junior/ community college	First public junior college opened at Joliet, Illinois, 1902.	Both public and private junior/community colleges offer preparatory and terminal curricula.

NOTABLE INDIVIDUALS

Francis Bacon (1561–1626)	His *Advancement of Learning* confirmed American colonists in their educational convictions.
John Harvard (1607–1638)	His gift to infant Harvard College laid the foundation for its growth.
Henry Dunster (1609?–1659)	As Harvard's second president, he gave American higher education its administrative character.

Ezekiel Cheever (1615–1708)	A famous colonial schoolmaster and author of the first American textbook.
James Blair (1655–1743)	First president of the College of William and Mary.
Christopher Dock (1698–1771)	An innovative colonial teacher.
Benjamin Franklin (1706–1790)	The Academy's founder and a promoter of an English curriculum in secondary schools.
Thomas Jefferson (1743–1826)	The author of a plan for public education in Virginia.
Adam Smith (1723–1790)	The author of *Wealth of Nations.*
Alexander Hamilton (1757–1804)	Through public and private action, he tried to maintain aristocratic interests.
Benjamin Rush (1745?–1813)	Popularized public education and proposed a national university.
James Madison (1751–1836)	Recommended tax support for schools.
DeWitt Clinton (1769–1828)	Promoted philanthropy in education.
Daniel Webster (1782–1852)	Defended the college in the Dartmouth College case.
Gideon Hawley (1785–1870)	Appointed New York State's first superintendent of schools in 1812.
Emma Willard (1787–1870)	Pioneered for women's higher education.
James G. Carter (1795–1849)	Inspired the first public normal school and wrote the 1827 Massachusetts High School Act.

Samuel R. Hall (1795–1877)	Founded the first private normal school in Concord, Vermont, in 1823.
Noah Webster (1758–1843)	Wrote dictionaries, spellers, and textbooks, and advocated the development of American English.
August Comte (1798–1857)	The founder of Positivism, a type of social physics describing the natural law governing society.
Horace Mann (1796–1859)	The most prominent and influential of 19th-century educational reformers.
Ralph Waldo Emerson (1803–1882)	In "The American Scholar" address declared America's intellectual independence from Europe.
Charles Darwin (1809–1882)	The *Origin of Species,* the most important work of modern biology.
Henry Barnard (1811–1900)	Scholar, educator, and first United States Commissioner of Education.
Francis W. Parker (1807–1902)	Reduced formalism and expanded the scope of elementary education. Sometimes credited with inventing Progressive education.
Herbert Spencer (1820–1903)	The founder of sociology and a leading exponent of the theory of evolution.
Edward A. Sheldon (1823–1897)	Introduced Pestalozzian methods to America.
Charles W. Eliot (1834–1926)	President of Harvard for 40 years and an effective American educational leader.
Wilhelm Wundt (1832–1920)	His *Principles of Physiological Psychology* created modern experimental psychology.

William T. Harris (1835–1909)	An educational philosopher and administrator; and the fourth United States Commissioner of Education.
Charles Sanders Peirce (1839–1914)	His work set the foundation for American Pragmatism and experimentalism in education.
Daniel Coit Gilman (1831–1908)	As the Johns Hopkins University's first president, he promoted university ideals.
William Rainey Harper (1856–1906)	The University of Chicago's first president.
John Dewey (1859–1952)	America's foremost educational philosopher.
Alfred North Whitehead (1861–1947)	His Realist philosophy offered an alternative to Pragmatism.
Nicholas Murray Butler (1862–1947)	A classical humanist and promoter of Essentialistic education.
William Heard Kilpatrick (1871–1965)	An experimentalist who popularized the project method.
Charles H. Judd (1873–1946)	Improved the credentials of scientific education.
Edward L. Thorndike (1874–1949)	Systematized educational psychology with the laws of learning and introduced measurement to pedagogy.
William C. Bagley (1874–1946)	Led the essentialistic crusade against Progressive education.
Frederick S. Breed (1876–1952)	A Reasist philosopher who opposed soft pedagogy.
Boyd H. Bode (1873–1953)	A careful and friendly critic of Progressive education.

Lewis M. Terman (1877–1956)	Developed the American version of standardized intelligence tests.
Walter Lippmann (1889–1974)	Perceptive social philosopher and journalist, who resisted the mental testing movement.
Robert M. Hutchins (1899–1977)	An eloquent educational spokesman who stressed learning's intellectual objectives.

LEGAL ACTION

1563: Statute of Artificers	English law requiring masters to give apprentices literary instruction.
1601: English Poor Law	Poor people were to be trained in useful occupations.
1636: Massachusetts Bay Colony College Act	Provided for a college—later Harvard—to prepare ministers.
1642: Massachusetts Compulsory Education Law	Required that every inhabitant of the colony be literate.
1647: Massachusetts Compulsory School Law	Prescribed a reading school for towns with 50 families and a grammar school for towns with 100 families.
1692: Massachusetts Law for Teachers	Teachers declared exempt from taxes, military duty, and the watch.
1758: New Jersey Licensing Law	Teachers were required to have a license from the Bishop of London.
1776: Massachusetts Teachers' Oath	Loyalty oath demanded of teachers.
1779: Jefferson's Education Bill	Proposed law to erect a system of public education for Virginia rejected.

1785: University of Georgia
        chartered

Legislative action creating the first
state college.

1785–1787: Northwest Ordinances

Sections of the national domain
reserved for education.

1795: Connecticut School Aid Law

Permanent state school fund
authorized.

1802: Pennsylvania Pauper
        School Law

Provision made for public support
to educate the poor.

1812: New York State
        Education Law

Office of state superintendent for
education established.

1817: Michigan College Act

University of Michigan chartered by
the legislature.

1819: Dartmouth College decision

United States Supreme Court
declared charters inviolable; private
character of college preserved.

1827: Dedham Act

Sectarian instruction prohibited in
Massachusetts common schools.

1827: James Carter High
        School Act

Massachusetts law required towns
with 500 families to open a high
school.

1837: State Board of
        Education Law

Massachusetts created a state board
of education with Horace Mann as
its first secretary.

1852: Compulsory Attendance Law

Children in Massachusetts between
ages 9 and 14 were required to
attend school.

1862: Morrill Act
        (Land-Grant College Act)

Congress granted land for the
establishment of agricultural
colleges.

1867: Federal Education Act

Congress authorized the United
States Department of Education.

1867: Rate-Bills abolished	New York State outlawed rate-bills and authorized public funds for teachers' salaries.
1868: Fourteenth Amendment	No person shall be deprived "of life, liberty, or property, without due process of law."
1870: Fifteenth Amendment	The right to vote shall not be abridged because of "race, color, or previous condition of servitude."
1874: Kalamazoo decision	Michigan Supreme Court found public high schools constitutional.
1875: Civil Rights Act	Federal law requiring equal protection of law for all citizens; declared unconstitutional in 1883.
1890: Second Morrill Act	Authorized federal appropriations for land-grant colleges.
1896: *Plessy* v. *Ferguson*	United States Supreme Court pronounced the "separate but equal" doctrine.
1908: *Berea College* v. *Kentucky*	Kentucky's law prohibiting coeducation of whites and Negroes was upheld by the United States Supreme Court.
1917: Smith-Hughes Act	Congress authorized federal aid for vocational education.
1920: Nineteenth Amendment	Woman suffrage adopted.
1921: Immigration Act	Limited immigration to 3 percent of the foreign-born persons residing in the United States as of the 1890 Census.
1923: *Meyer* v. *Nebraska*	Nebraska's law prohibiting teaching German in the schools declared void.

1925: *Pierce* v. *Society of Sisters*	Oregon's law requiring attendance of all children in public schools ruled invalid.
1930: *Cochran* v. *Board of Education*	Louisiana's law authorizing public funds for textbooks in private schools upheld.
1931: California Teachers' Oath	Certification code required teachers to swear allegiance to state and federal law.
1944: G I Bill	Educational benefits for World War II veterans.
1946: Fulbright Act	Congress authorized funds for scholarships in foreign countries.
1947: *Everson* v. *Board of Education*	New Jersey law allocating public funds for the transportation of private school students upheld.
1948: *McCollum* v. *Board of Education*	Religious instruction in public schools declared illegal.
1952: *Zorach* v. *Clauson*	Religious instruction during school day but away from public school ruled legal.
1954: *Brown* v. *Board of Education of Topeka*	Segregation in public education declared unconstitutional.
1958: National Defense Education Act	Federal aid allocated to schools with defense-related programs.
1962: *Engel* v. *Vitale*	Prayer in public schools declared unconstitutional.
1963: *Abington Township* v. *Schempp*	Bible reading in public schools ruled unconstitutional.
1964: Higher Education Facilities Act	Federal funds appropriated for college classrooms and other instructional resources.

1964: Civil Rights Act

All citizens guaranteed the full privileges of citizenship.

1978: *Regents of the University of California* v. *Bakke*

Reservation of places in schools by racial quotas ruled illegal.

INDEX